Also by John Calvin Batchelor

THE FURTHER ADVENTURES
OF HALLEY'S COMET

THE BIRTH OF THE PEOPLE'S
REPUBLIC OF ANTARCTICA

AMERICAN FALLS

AMERICAN FALLS

A NOVEL

JOHN CALVIN BATCHELOR

W·W·Norton & Company · New York · London

*The text of this book is composed in Bembo, with
display type set in Typositor Willow. Composition and
manufacturing by The Haddon Craftsmen, Inc.
Book design by Antonina Krass.*

First Edition

Library of Congress Cataloging in Publication Data
Batchelor, John Calvin.
American falls.
I. Title.
PS3552.A8268A8   1985   813'.54   85–3094

ISBN 0-393-02211-0

W. W. Norton & Company, Inc., 500 Fifth Avenue, New York, N. Y. 10110
W. W. Norton & Company Ltd., 37 Great Russell Street, London WC1B 3NU
1 2 3 4 5 6 7 8 9 0

CONTENTS

PART TWO | THE ORDEAL OF JOHN OLIPHANT
April 1855 and November 9–19, 1864

PART THREE | THE ATTACK ON NEW-YORK
November 19–30, 1864

EPILOGUE | THE PEACE OF AMAZIAH BUTTER
December 1864–June and July 1865

THE WAR BETWEEN
THE SECRET SERVICES

1861–1864

WASHINGTON CITY, DISTRICT OF COLUMBIA

The United States Secret Service

The United States Secret Service was rudimentarily organized in the summer and fall of 1861 by Secretary of State William H. Seward. Seward recruited agents to ferret out Confederate conspirators as near as the Capitol building and as far away as Canada and Europe. Seward's spontaneous genius, however, was to hire Lafayette C. Baker, then 35, a former San Francisco Vigilante who had already distinguished himself as a special Army agent behind enemy lines.

In early 1862, Seward decided that it was expedient to separate his foreign counterespionage operation from the domestic one. He assigned Lafayette Baker to the control of the newly appointed secretary of war, Edwin M. Stanton. It was this alliance that marked the definitive birth of the United States Secret Service.

With Stanton's ready funds, Lafayette Baker was able to establish a headquarters in Washington City, to enlist a coterie of detectives, to gather a legion of informers, and to sponsor an elite cavalry unit that was called Baker's Rangers. The Secret Service proceeded in its manifold tasks of pursuing Confederate agents, entrapping corrupt government officials and contractors, closing saloons and gambling houses in Washington, and arresting disloyal soldiers and citizens. Also, in 1863, Baker's Rangers was expanded into a first-rate volunteer regiment, the First District of Columbia Cavalry, in order to combat the Confederate guerrilla chieftain, John Singleton Mosby, whose irregular battalion routinely raided the District of Columbia out of Virginia.

By 1864, the United States Secret Service had evolved into a tight, efficient cadre of detectives. It was nominally under the command of the provost-marshal-general of the War Department, but it was actually free to operate independently of all but War Secretary Stanton's direction. Lafayette Baker, now a colonel in the U.S. Volunteers, remained the Secret Service's supreme head. He was uniformly regarded as ruthless. The newspapers often referred to the military jail in Washington City not as Old Capitol Prison but rather as Baker's Bastille.

In the summer of 1864, a new crisis challenged the counterespionage forces of both the State and War Departments. The slaughter of the war, the hated Draft, the forthcoming Presidential Election, and the military stalemate on the battlefields had all made the Union cause increasingly vulnerable to civilian dissent, and had also strengthened the hand of the Confederate conspirators. In the fall, the War Department ordered the United States Secret Service to turn away from its anti-corruption and internal security chores. Instead, it was ordered to confront the threat of the saboteurs and provocateurs of the Confederate States Secret Service based in Canada.

The Confederate States Secret Service

The Confederate States Secret Service was hydra-headed, and therefore never enjoyed a single focus. In 1861, Confederate president Jefferson Davis dispatched several major agents abroad, to Canada and Europe. The Confederate War Department controlled spies of various caliber in Washington City. By 1862, Confederate secretary of state Judah P. Benjamin supervised two major missions in Europe, and employed his emissaries there—James Mason in London and John Slidell in Paris—as the dual heads of the Secret Service in Europe.

The chief task for Mason and Slidell and their agents was to persuade the British and French governments to recognize the Confederacy as an independent republic. Also important was the supervision of the gun-running and cotton-trading that maintained the Confederate war effort. In 1863, the Confederate Secret Service in Europe expanded its operation in order to purchase and build gunboats for the Confederate Navy.

The battlefield defeats of 1863 staggered the Confederacy. The Army no longer expected military victory. The Secret Service in Europe no longer expected diplomatic recognition. In Richmond, the Confederate government embarked on a new course that was intended to draw out the military stalemate in order to maneuver for armistice.

In the spring of 1864, Jefferson Davis, looking to weaken the Union war effort, approved a master plan to provoke dissent in the United States. Jefferson Davis recruited his longtime friend, former U.S. Cabinet officer Jacob P. Thompson, to head a Secret Service mission to Canada. Jacob

Thompson, under the guise of being the Confederate commissioner to Canada, established his headquarters in Toronto. He proceeded to gather about him a small army of Confederate soldiers, many of whom had fled across the border from Union prison camps. Jacob Thompson's Secret Service associates, Clement Clay, James Holcombe, George Sanders, and Beverley Tucker, established an adjunct post in Montreal. Their combined efforts through the summer of 1864 included peace overtures to President Lincoln while at the same time they funded the anti-Lincoln parties in the Union whose members were called Copperheads—for the poisonous snake.

In the fall of 1864, the Confederate States Secret Service in Canada moved beyond intrigue to terror and sabotage. There was a naval raid on Lake Erie in September. There was a cavalry raid on St. Albans, Vermont, in October. And by November, there was a new master plan for sabotage against the North's major cities by cadres of Confederate volunteers who aimed to revenge the South.

Principal Characters

The United States of America

CABINET: William H. Seward, *Secretary of State;* Edwin M. Stanton, *Secretary of War*

SECRET SERVICE: Col. Lafayette C. Baker, *Chief;* Usher Skelton, *Chief Clerk;* Mrs. Bridey Lamont, *Recording Clerk;* Milo Baker, Calvin Baker, Edgar Quillermouth, Bob Dailey, John Odell, *Detectives;* Capt. Amaziah Butter, *First D.C. Cavalry;* Gouverneur Nevers, Wild Jack Goodenough, Joshua Rue, *Department of the East Detectives, on detached service*

THE BUTTERS OF BANGOR, MAINE: Chisholm "Chip" Butter and Mrs. Louise Butter; Capt. Amaziah Butter, *First D.C. Cavalry and Secret Service,* and Mrs. Desire Drummond Butter; Capt. Augustus Butter, *17th Maine Infantry;* Lt. Calvin Butter, *First Mounted Regiment, Sixth Maine Battery;* Lt. Thomas Butter, *20th Maine Infantry*

THE LAMONTS OF WASHINGTON, D.C.: W. D. Lamont (d. 1861); Maj. David Lamont (d. 1862); Mrs. Bridey Lamont; Miss Vera Lamont; David and Maude Lamont

The Confederate States of America

SECRET SERVICE, IN EUROPE: John Cross Oliphant, Mrs. Narcissa Royall Winwood, *Agents*

15

SECRET SERVICE, IN CANADA: Jacob P. "Jake" Thompson, *Commissioner to Canada at Toronto and Chief;* Clement C. Clay, James Holcombe, *Commissioners to Canada at Montreal;* Capt. Thomas B. Hines, Beverley Tucker, George N. Sanders, *Agents;* Lt.-Col. Robert Martin, Capt. Robert Cobb Kennedy, Lt. John Headley, Lt. John Ashbrook, Lt. James Harrington, Lt. James Chenault, Lt. John Price, Lt. Timothy Cook, Lt. Leslie Dennis, *Special Service Agents*

SECRET SERVICE, IN NEW-YORK: Capt. W. A. Longuemare, *Agent,* and Mrs. Dorothea Longuemare

THE ROYALLS OF BEAUFORT, SOUTH CAROLINA: J. Granby Royall (d. 1864) and Mrs. Mary Talbird Royall (d. 1840) and Mrs. Pamela Tempest Royall; Mrs. Narcissa Royall Winwood and Brig.-Gen. Venable Hawkes Winwood (d. 1864); Col. Johnny Royall (d. 1864) and Mrs. Elizabeth De Treville Royall; Capt. Talbird Royall (d. 1862) and Mrs. Sally Peniclair Royall; Mrs. Camellia Royall Oliphant and John Cross Oliphant; Mrs. Laura Royall Rogers and Capt. Lucas Rogers (d. 1864); Sophy and Mary Winwood; Ensign Harry Royall (d. 1864) and Phillip Royall (d. 1862); Alice, Mary, and Faith Oliphant; Rosemary, Noah, Michael, Jimmie, Jinna, Cato, and Nell, *Slaves*

NONPARTISANS: Edmund Homes; Sir Henry Blondel; Isaac Keats, *British Secret Service;* Capt. Maximillian Millerand, Capt. Paul Fresque, *French Secret Service;* Franny Wooster

(For complete list of characters, see page 562)

PART ONE

THE CONFEDERATE
CONSPIRACY AGAINST
THE UNION

October 31–November 9, 1864

NEW-YORK, NEW YORK

CHAPTER 1

John Oliphant
at Niagara Falls, New York

MONDAY AFTERNOON, OCTOBER 31

It was All Hallow's Eve, 1864, and the afternoon train out of Toronto and limited to the border was running late as it rolled slowly out onto the Suspension Bridge that joined the United Province of Canada to the United States of America. There was a spontaneous frenzy in the four passenger cars as the veteran travelers conversed generously with those for whom this was their first venture onto John A. Roebling's grand and expensive bridge, an iron-built cobweb stretched eight hundred feet tower to tower across the gray shale chasm cut by the Niagara River.

"God bless us!" cried one pilgrim, throwing open a car window. And it was not only the man-made creation of the bridge that excited the others to reply with a heartfelt "Amen!" For there was also the privileged opportunity to view some of nature's finest handiwork. Two hundred and fifty feet below the rails, white water rapids poured over boulders as big as elephants as the current ripped northward to the legendary Niagara Whirlpool, that dark vortex that marked the elbow in the river as it fell toward Lake Ontario. And then, as Engine No. 30 of the Great Western Railroad eased across the midpoint of the bridge, penetrating the imaginary but profound frontier, the passengers gained the proper vantage to peer around the chasm's bluffs and two miles to the south.

There, like a panorama of heaven, they could behold the three-sided canyon of the Niagara Gorge and its world-famous twin cataracts: the bright concave cascade of the Horseshoe Falls at the far end; the thick white curtain of the American Falls to the left—each of these immense phenomena sending spray like gossamer out into the blue gorge. And there again, exactly as promised in the circular advertisements for tourists, and also in the ponderous sermons by preachers in their pulpits straining to portray the miracle of Noah's triumph over the flood, stood the beginnings of a beauteous rainbow. The autumn was too late, the sun too low in the turquoise sky to the west, for there to have been a complete prismatic arc across the gorge, but what light there was shot through the spray to create the foot of an illusion, neatly fixed pillars of red, yellow, and blue anchored in the rockfall below the inmost edge of the American Falls.

"There, can you see to the right?" spoke up John Oliphant, a dark and darkly complected man seated at the rear of the first-class coach. "On the Canadian side? That's the Horseshoe Falls, for the shape. And to the left, that sheer wall of water, on the American side? That's called the American Falls."

"Yes, yes! And do you see the rainbow in between?" replied the sturdy and fair young man seated at Oliphant's side, Robert Cobb Kennedy. Kennedy pointed, "An omen, a handsome omen of success, don't you agree, Mr. Oliphant?"

"It is lovely, Mr. Kennedy, certainly it is lovely," said Oliphant. At 38, Oliphant was older than Kennedy by more than a decade, and spoke with the easy authority of his experience as a long-voyager. Oliphant had seen the wonders of the world, and thought the twin falls the most splendid of all. Still, he did not embrace Kennedy's mystical imagery of success, because Oliphant was a cautious, acute, and superstitious man, and he did not want to invite bad luck with optimism. The simple fact was that Oliphant was once again inside the territory of the United States, and thus in plain jeopardy.

Kennedy leaned toward the window, and pointed at the Falls, "I do favor those soft colors, don't you?"

Oliphant smiled, and nodded. Though both men were exceedingly well dressed as gentlemen of the most fortunate American class, Oliphant thought Kennedy's appetite for bright clothes almost overmuch, especially his striped scarlet waistcoat. Oliphant's taste was for quiet severity; his shirt of Sea Island cotton shimmered white against his charcoal morning coat.

Oliphant continued, wanting to show more sympathy for Kennedy's fascination. "There are regiments of rainbows on summer days. So many it can look as if they're fighting for space, and stealing each other's colors. What I mean to say, is that they tumble about each other like children."

"Oh, sir!" said Kennedy. "Can you get among them? Have you been that close?"

Oliphant laughed, and said, "I have, yes. It was foolish of me, but I was told that Mr. Dickens went down among them when he was visiting here. And so I didn't feel that obvious. Last summer, I remember—" Oliphant stopped abruptly for another kind of memory of Niagara Falls the July before, a dreary and unhappy one, that had included Abraham Lincoln's emissaries on one side, and Jefferson Davis's emissaries on the other, and that had turned upon mean-spirited intrigue and the futility of a contrived Peace Conference at Niagara Falls's International Hotel. The truth was that Oliphant's previous visit to the Falls had not been as a tourist but rather as a secret agent, and that he had departed feeling ill-used and tainted by friend and foe. The truth was also that Oliphant was the most veteran of the surviving Confederate agents based in Europe, and that this fact alone made him sad and regretful for all the failed schemes of the Confederate Secret Service that he had been ordered to attend.

Oliphant sighed. He had lost the joy of the rainbows, and repeated emptily, "Last summer."

Kennedy waited a moment for Oliphant's distraction to pass, and then pressed, "What's that island there, between the two falls? Can you reach it? Such a river! It must sound like the Gulf in storm! And I know rivers— at least, I know the Mississippi."

Oliphant looked through the window. Kennedy was referring to the small island that hung above the Niagara Gorge to the left, dividing the twin falls with a quarter-mile-wide strip of trees. Oliphant said, "That's called Goat Island." The view was closing as the train crept ahead, so Oliphant continued hurriedly, trying to regain his enthusiasm, "There's a little suspension bridge to Goat Island from the village, for carriages and those on foot. The island is about seventy acres, and very damp and windy, but also restful. I was told that a hermit once lived there. He was found one day in the whirlpool down river, where the river sends all its victims. The story was that he tried to cross the gorge by walking on a rainbow."

Kennedy sat up straight. "That's wonderful, Mr. Oliphant, on a rainbow!"

Oliphant smiled, "I thought you'd like that. They buried him on Goat

Island. In what they call a pleasure garden. A lot of linden and birches actually, though beautiful."

Kennedy touched the glass of the window. "Why did he try to walk across on the rainbow?"

Oliphant nodded. "A good question. Goat Island is a peculiar place. It makes you think of things like that. When I was there, I was thinking of, well— It is an ominous place, Mr. Kennedy. Omens and omens at every turn. A place for prophecy. And for peace."

"Tell me more, please."

The vantage had closed now, but Oliphant's gaze and reference remained southward. "About prophecy? That's not for me to say. You should visit Goat Island for yourself, and ask yourself what you—see. I saw a beautiful and mysterious place, for stories, and for lovers."

Oliphant was enjoying himself again, and continued, "What I liked best about the island is that you can actually get down to the foot of the Falls. By a staircase at the head of Goat Island. Turn left for the Horseshoe Falls, and turn right for the American Falls, along a rocky escarpment. And when you get just up to the edge of the American Falls, with the water roaring above you, why there's a cave underneath the Falls that you can reach by climbing some steps up and passing along a ledge and through the spray. It's a cavern, really, about a hundred feet high. It's spectacularly windy inside, which is why they call it the Cave of the Winds. You get soaked by the spray, but that's all right. Inside, you can look back through the falling water. And the sound! Like a hurricane, like a sea breaking over the bow, like— force, pure force. Perhaps there is no metaphor other than that the Falls sound like the Falls. My guide told me that whenever he felt put-upon, or world-weary, he got himself down to the Cave of the Winds, and found peaceful-ness. I felt peace there too." Oliphant laughed. "I was also terrified. You're right underneath the torrent!"

Kennedy was rapturous and gripped Oliphant's sleeve. "How—what— how? Oh, wonderful! The way you tell it, I feel that I've been there! Am there now! Truly! I read at school once about the Falls. A long time back. I wish I could remember—I do remember that it said this whole canyon was formed when some ancient deluge swept from out of the Northwest, and broke down the natural barriers between the Great Lakes, between Lake Erie and Lake Ontario. Does that sound right? A great flood? Do you think?"

Oliphant took out his briar pipe and fiddled with it while he considered

Kennedy's question. Oliphant liked Kennedy. And he was delighted by Kennedy's incessant curiosity. Yet he had only known the man for a little more than twenty-four hours, since their chance introduction at luncheon the day before in Toronto. And in that time Kennedy had bombarded him with questions. And when Kennedy had not been asking for information or opinion, he had been flattering Oliphant for his wit or experience, or for the vault of general knowledge that one acquired inadvertently when one had crossed as many seas and countries as Oliphant had. Kennedy was overwhelmingly fraternal, and Oliphant, without a brother, was shy of this sort of conduct. Still again, it was not without its pleasure—Kennedy could make him laugh about rainbows!—and so Oliphant, while side-stepping Kennedy's momentum, did so with the gentleness of an older brother. Oliphant replied, "A flood, perhaps. I've read enough of geology, Mr. Kennedy, to know that I don't know very much about how the world was put together."

Oliphant used his dull-gold lighter and blew smoke every which way, adding, "Yet if it's any help to you, I think of what my father would have said. He was a circumspect and diligent pastor, you see, and he would have said to me, 'John, those are the Lord Almighty's secrets, and in the tight keep of the angels, and Amen!' " At this, they both laughed.

The train had passed off the Suspension Bridge now, and it jerked forward the short distance to the southbound depot. The view from the passenger windows became the soft brown and gold canopy of fading autumn as the forest thereabout blanketed the earth with leaves in anticipation of the heavy snows coming on. To the south, the treeline was parted by a broad avenue, the Whirlpool Road, that led from the Suspension Bridge and the southbound depot down two miles to the village of Niagara Falls. That road was frantic now, because of the approach of the train, with wagons and carriages rushing along, with horsemen and pedestrians turning their attention eagerly, and with enterprising hack drivers crowding up to the depot's drive.

This was only a passing interruption, however, in the steady traffic that bypassed the train station for the carriage and pedestrian roadway that swung like a ribbon twenty feet beneath the railway level of the Suspension Bridge. For this was a major border crossing, vital to the commerce of two young countries, and haste was the rule for Americans and Canadians on their busy, profitable rounds.

And then the view from the passenger cars was blocked by the dark bulk of another train on a siding, its mammoth engine immaculately kept and prepared—the New York Central's connecting express to Albany and points southward.

There was deliberate and military confusion on the southbound depot platform. The detraining passengers were confronted by a line of blue-coated soldiers, pillar to post, who were distinctive for their grave bearing and their color. This was a company of Negro volunteers, understrength because it had been collected overquickly by the Department of the East from several shattered commands in a United States colored division. The company was now on detached service in order to bolster the Union defenses along the border, where there were rumors of invasion by Confederates from Canada.

The crisis on the frontier, constant since the previous Christmas, had been exacerbated two weeks before by the Confederate guerrilla raid on St. Albans, Vermont, a farming village near Lake Champlain. The raiders had ridden out of Canada to rob, kill, and burn, promising, "We will treat you as the people of Atlanta were treated!" and "We're coming back again, and will burn every town in Vermont!" And then the guerrillas had ridden back into Canada, where, after their capture by pursuing Americans and British soldiers, they now rested in jail with the de jure protection of Canada's governor-general.

One result of the St. Albans' raid was that Canada and the United States were tangled once again in a diplomatic tar patch. Another result was that the Americans along the frontier were in a panicky fury, demanding that all border crossings remain on constant alert. Also, civil disorder and hanging vigilantism were in the cool fall air, for every day the newspapers along the frontier reported letters from anonymous friends in Canada that warned of impending attacks by the hordes of Confederate guerrillas lurking in Montreal and Toronto.

A hogshead-sized first sergeant, with a very black skin color and an unavoidable basso-profundo voice, was addressing the disembarking passengers with a short request repeated in several versions, "Step to de left, ladies and gent'men, if ya please, to de left!"

It was unsaid but obvious that the officers and adjutants waiting nearby were there to inspect the newcomers. The officers were white men, all in the sky-blue uniform of the United States Invalid Corps. The four queues, one from each car, formed up slowly to wend past lieutenants showing their ill health with bad pallor and crankiness. The first-class passengers were provided with special consideration—the attention of the captain of the command, a gray-skinned young man leaning too heavily on a cane.

There were hard words from the civilians as they endured the challenge and interrogation. "Damn Yankees in Toronto afore Christmas, mark me!" and "Damn guv'ner-gin'ral mus' do somethin', and soon!" and "Damn Lincoln'll have us each in a cell or grave soon!"

This last remark, spoken openly by a plump, angry-faced drummer, in a surrounding that was already made anxious by the banging of the trainmen preparing the limited for the yards, was readily heard and agreed to by the majority of the bystanders. This was a Canadian crowd; and it was generally understood that Canadians had no love for the United States, and had not since at least the bloody battles along the border in the War of 1812–15. More bluntly, the recent civil war in America had provided Canada's three million with a grasping hope for the breakup of the brutally self-righteous American Republic of thirty-one million.

And the already bleak mood on the platform eroded still further when one old woman started to reprimand a lieutenant with "Good Christian wives should not be ogled by King Lincoln's musket-bearing darkies!"

A beauty in the first-class line, who was chaperoned by a red-nosed matron, attempted to separate herself from the surliness of the Canadians by sparkling before the Invalid Corps captain. There was no reason for him to speak to her—she was hardly suspect as a guerrilla—but he did anyway. He said that his name was Christian Ferry, and doffed his hat.

She responded with a curtsey and said that her name was Miss Margaret Cappawhite of Brooklyn, New York. Captain Ferry appeared captivated, and asked more of her affairs. Miss Cappawhite blushed for the flirtation and said that she was returning home after a long visit with her cousins in Toronto.

Ferry dipped his head and smiled. "I should have thought a lady, such as yourself, would have too many suitors to busy herself with travel so late in the year."

Miss Cappawhite did not respond. Instead, her chaperone spoke. "Thank'ee very much, sir, but her *feeantsee,* brave Dick Duffy, was kilt in the Wilderness battle this May past."

Ferry startled. "I was there, too, and certainly did not intend to compromise a memory." He spoke delicately and straightened himself to show his respect, a well-proportioned young man with bushy eyebrows and a red beard. As he arranged himself, however, he also had to reposition his cane for balance, raising the hem of his left trouser leg.

There was no proper foot there, rather a black leather wrapping with laces where there should have been an ankle. It looked like a hoof.

Miss Cappawhite dropped her gaze and stared. She also made a strange sound, a small swallowing like gagging. Her chaperone reached for her.

Ferry pulled back his mangled foot and reached for Miss Cappawhite too. "Please, please, forgive me. I did not mean—"

"Hail Columbia," started Miss Cappawhite. "Hail Columbia—Hail Columbia! Hail! Columbia! Hail! Columbia!"

Miss Cappawhite's outburst stunned and silenced the crowd. Tentatively, some few moved to comfort the hysterical woman. Some others moved to give sympathy to the chagrined Captain Ferry. Most recovered from their surprise quickly in order to shield themselves in any way they could from more of the inconsolable sorrow that they daily observed or, for the American bystanders, suffered—wearing black armbands, consoling bereaved neighbors, or enduring sad reminiscences of a lost son, husband, or father.

Meanwhile, with a swift, deft courtliness, Kennedy, the young rainbow enthusiast, had come forward to help the chaperone comfort Miss Cappawhite, and to get her through the cordon of troops to a platform bench. Once Miss Cappawhite's wild grief had ebbed, and the scene had returned to a more normal hubbub, Kennedy returned to the side of his traveling companion, Oliphant.

Presently, as the queue moved along, Oliphant and Kennedy walked before Captain Ferry and his adjutant. Ferry, who had carefully watched Kennedy's rescue of Miss Cappawhite, spoke sharply and ordered Kennedy to identify himself.

Kennedy grinned at the officiousness, and said, "Say what you want to me, just leave the ladies alone."

"What's that?" asked Ferry.

Kennedy pretended to ignore Ferry's counter. "My name is Kennedy, R. C. Kennedy, of Missouri. I'm traveling to New-York on holiday. And, and, to cast my vote for General McClellan, and against Lincoln!"

Ferry scowled, "What is it you say, mister?"

Kennedy replied, "I say I know to mind my own, and not to frighten womenfolk."

Ferry's face showed his anger. But then he seemed to make a decision not to compound his recent embarrassment. He told his adjutant to record Kennedy's information. He paused to recover his calm, and might then have asked more penetrating questions if not for Oliphant's interruption.

Oliphant said, "This is an unusual procedure here, isn't it, Captain?"

Ferry nodded. "We've had trouble, sir, at the Suspension Bridge this morning—are you two gentlemen together?"

"I'm John Oliphant, of Philadelphia, a financial representative. Mr. Kennedy is a recent acquaintance. Would you like proof of my identity? I'm happy to oblige."

Ferry looked to be persuaded by Oliphant's gravity. "No, sir, that won't be necessary. I'm sure—that is, thank you, sir."

"This is a hard duty for you, Captain," continued Oliphant. He meant to disarm further Ferry's temper and curiosity. He also felt sympathetic to Ferry's wound. "That leg couldn't be up to this standing about."

Ferry tapped his prosthetic boot with his cane. "It's as good as it'll ever be, sir, and better than most after those Napoleon guns have done. They knocked me down like a ten-pin. It could've been worse. I guess I'm lucky."

Oliphant grimaced. "I guess you are."

Ferry seemed discomfitted by the attention, and changed the subject abruptly. "The Rebs made a try at the Suspension Bridge this morning, sir. Escaped Reb prisoners, four of 'em, and crazed on the run—"

"Escaped from where?" interjected Kennedy.

"Nothing to do with us, I'm sure," said Oliphant quickly. He stepped forward to screen Kennedy off from Ferry, and asked, "But what could there be to fear from tourists and the like?"

"I can't say, sir," said Ferry. "Orders from General Dix in New-York, though. We're to interview all suspicious persons coming across the border. Down in Buffalo, it's worse—they're building redoubts on the harbor, and arming the tugs. Everyone's scared bad because of St. Albans, and then this had to happen. The Rebs killed a man at the bridge—a riverman. And you can be sure I've had a day already keeping the sheriff from taking the Rebs for rope justice."

Ferry looked at Oliphant. "I'm sorry to pester you with my worry, sir, and I didn't mean to imply—by talking with you—that you're suspicious or—"

"I understand, Captain," said Oliphant. "You've not offended in the slightest—not anyone. But please, get off that leg soon."

Oliphant looked over to Kennedy, and then moved off slowly toward the stone-built depot.

Kennedy stayed close behind Oliphant. Once the two were in privacy beneath the eaves, Kennedy started, "Are you unhappy with me, Mr. Oliphant? I apologize. I forgot myself. I shouldn't have. It was just— Have I made trouble for you?"

"No, I think not," said Oliphant. "No. But in future, Mr. Kennedy, it might be best for you to remember where you are before you start what you cannot possibly finish."

"I am sorry, sir. I didn't mean it to go so far. When he spoke about those poor boys, I just had to know where they were from. I—this isn't the same as soldiering, is it?"

"I wouldn't know about soldiering." Oliphant could see that Kennedy's contrition was complete, and eased up. He added, "I suppose that St. Albans has shaken everyone. What could they have been thinking of in Montreal to send those men on a raid like that?" Oliphant mumbled to himself, "Oh, I know, it was—well, I know who ordered it, but still—"

"I thought it a great show," said Kennedy. "All the boys in Toronto did."

"It was a disaster, and contemptible, and ruinous to both sides," said Oliphant.

Kennedy looked struck. "Sir?"

Oliphant waved away the debate, and tried to speak lightly, "Missouri is it now, Mr. Kennedy? Yesterday it was Louisiana."

"It is Louisiana, sir. I was thinking Missouri was better than the bottom truth."

Oliphant nodded. He really did not feel witty after all; in fact, he was feeling anxious, and distracted. He added in an afterthought, "I've always found that there is nothing better than the bottom truth."

Kennedy nodded gravely. "Yes, sir."

Oliphant turned abruptly away and stepped through the depot door into the waiting room. The high-beamed chamber was warm and crowded with weekend hosts come to say farewell to their guests or to fetch late season patrons. The room seemed especially frantic, because the southbound passengers were hurrying their ticket-buying or baggage-checking in order to gain enough time to dine at the adjacent Centre House before the scheduled departure of the New York Central Express.

Oliphant checked his pocket watch. It was near 4 P.M., and he had a lot to do in less than an hour. Kennedy was showing no inclination to part, and yet Oliphant knew that Kennedy had a crucial rendezvous with others.

Oliphant turned back to Kennedy and frowned. Kennedy beamed, and glanced about the room as if looking over a ball.

Oliphant argued with himself. This must be the end of his association with Kennedy. They must go their separate ways. He had done Kennedy a favor to travel with him this far, and he was under no obligation to— Oliphant sighed and pulled back. He did like Kennedy. And, judging by the incident with Captain Ferry, Kennedy probably did need some help in dealing with his immediate future. But Oliphant could not tarry. Kennedy had his own assignment, and it was beyond Oliphant to affect it. Oliphant thought, Let him go, don't interfere, stay clear.

A burly woman pushed by with a large wicker basket. Oliphant was forced closer to Kennedy. He started to speak, and then choked his words. What could he say? "Be careful?" Of course not. He must do this respectfully. He must not patronize. Yet he must get away! Kennedy was involved with the most reckless kind of— Oliphant stopped himself again. He did not even want to think any more about what he had learned the day before in Toronto, at the Queen's Hotel Bar, the well-known roost of the Confederate Secret Service in Canada.

Oliphant started again, "Mr. Kennedy, I suppose that this is where we must part."

Kennedy smiled, and said, "You have been very good to me, sir, and I very much appreciate your advice."

Oliphant offered his hand. "Yes, yes."

Kennedy took Oliphant's hand. "I wish that I could return the favor."

Oliphant repeated, "Yes, yes." There must be something more he could say; he felt that at the least he should warn him. But how does one warn a soldier?

Gratitude and the hearts of the young relieved Oliphant of his dilemma. The crowd parted to reveal Miss Cappawhite and her chaperone standing on line to go into dinner. They looked kindly toward Kennedy and Oliphant, and Kennedy, looking past Oliphant's shoulder, lifted his hat. Kennedy was a pretty fellow—euphoric eyes, a fancy blond moustache, and long, graceful limbs. He also possessed a young man's need to please young women.

Oliphant relaxed. And he did say, "Be careful," when Robert Cobb Kennedy of West Felicia Parish, Louisiana, a descendant of the Georgia Cobbs, a graduate of the United States Military Academy at West Point, a captain in the First Louisiana Infantry, C.S.A., and as of late one of the newest recruits in the Confederate Secret Service in Canada, excused himself for Miss Cappawhite's sad smile.

What Oliphant learned inadvertently—as he rushed through his tasks of telegraphing his banker in New-York, and dining alone, and collecting his thoughts—was that the prisoners who had been captured that morning at the Suspension Bridge were actually Confederate officers who had escaped two weeks before from the prisoner-of-war camp on Johnson's Island, at the western end of Lake Erie, above Sandusky. They had clung to a raft of driftwood to slip off the island, and then had been picked up by a paid accomplice, a fisherman, who had transported them to Kelley's Island, where they had purchased passage on a coal steamer bound eventually for Port Maitland, Ontario.

At the Cleveland stopover, however, one of the group had accidentally revealed himself to a ship's officer. Four of the fugitives had fled again, on another steamer for Buffalo. There, they had concealed themselves from increasingly heated pursuit (Buffalo was garrisoned by a makeshift colored regiment and a battalion of the Invalid Corps) by lodging with a landlady whose Southern sympathies were for hire. When their money had finished, they had struck out on foot along the Niagara River. Bad luck had crippled one with a recurrence of the grippe. Finally, they had dared a try at the Suspension Bridge by overpowering a teamster for his wagon and then masquerading as day laborers going across to Canada.

It had been a pathetic ruse. They had not known about the border passes that had been required since 1862 on the carriage roadway of the bridge (though not on the passenger trains). The ensuing combat with the border guards had left one fugitive cut about the face. Worse, an elderly riverman, Lonesome Hyde, had chanced upon the fray and been brained. He had died at noon. The four captured fugitives had been hurried to the garrison's encampment down the line from the depot, where they had been chained together to await transport back to Buffalo.

Near train time, Oliphant had strolled to the extreme end of the south-bound platform. He had been told that the prisoners were in the stable a quarter-mile in the distance, and he idly stared at the temporary jail. He thought, They are doomed men.

Oliphant had come out for exercise, for a smoke, and also to try to soothe a toothache. The tooth had flamed up when, famished after a rough Atlantic crossing from Liverpool that had kept him from even subsistence rations, he had overeagerly bitten into a chop in a Halifax restaurant. The tooth had settled down during his brief stopovers at Montreal and Toronto, but it was now aching again because of another too-quick bite of a hard roll in the Centre House dining room.

Oliphant rocked on his cane and felt his jaw. There were claws of shadowy pain. And the possibility of a complete eruption frightened him. At the same time, he felt that he might make some use of the upset. He knew that the tooth was easily treatable once he reached a good dentist in New-York. And he could strike a deal: No toothache, dear Lord, and I shall continue without complaint. He also discovered that by holding his briar pipe in his mouth in a special way, and by keeping his head still, the tooth stayed quiet. As further precaution, he surveyed the platform for some distractions.

The Albany Express was pulled up to the southbound depot now, like an iron volcano billowing smoke into the darkening sky. Trainmen and passengers surrounded the cars like pagan supplicants, on-loading baggage, bargaining for snacks and better compartments, dancing steps made urgent by the potency of the steam engine. On the center track, a long freight train rolled steadily toward the Suspension Bridge, Canada, and the Hamilton mills. The pervasive sound, above the hiss of the steam boiler, was that of the percussive click-clacking of heavily laden cars as they passed over switches and misaligned ties.

Oliphant turned toward the freight. He was especially engaged by the legends on the sides of the cars, because they suggested to him the stock prices he had absorbed from the Saturday copy of the *New-York Tribune* in his lettercase. Hudson Railway at 122½, up from 120½; New York Central at 121, up from 117½; New York and Erie at 97¼, up from 96½.

Oliphant was enjoying himself. It was impossible to witness such a display of competitive industry anywhere else in the world, and standing there, working his memory through the progress of the New-York Stock Exchange the previous week, he experienced the thrill—and it was an optimistic thrill—that he always felt whenever he returned to America again from abroad.

For only America seemed to understand the possibility of the railroad, and the future it portended. In 1848, when he had first gone abroad to complete his studies, there had been fewer than ten thousand miles of railroad bed in

North America—more than in Great Britain, but merely a "prime of the capital pump" in Oliphant's youthfully arrogant opinion. He had proclaimed as much to his mentors at the University of Edinburgh, and had been returned condescending mutters. Now, there were some fifty thousand miles of road on the continent, twisting like restless serpents from Bangor to St. Joseph, and each week added to the number as much as it added to the profit of the railroad men. Oliphant presumed that there was no limit to the rails, and no limit to the wealth that they could gather for those shrewd enough to envision and invest. Upon his return from Europe in 1850, Oliphant had seen to it that he and his two sisters' husbands in Philadelphia had become acute participants in the burgeoning splendor of the railroads. And from South Carolina, after 1855, Oliphant had continued to reach out through the stock exchanges, diversifying his stock purchases from the North into the South and into the booming Northwest from Ohio to Wisconsin.

He had been right to do so; he had been proud of his foresight; he had been rewarded with a fortune. But for the war, he might have had his own railroad, the Savannah, Albany & Gulf, a sizable portion of which he had purchased despite the genteel derision of his Southern in-laws for his practice of converting land and crop profits into stock shares. Oliphant had endured their disbelief as he had foreborn the disapproving gaze of his own father, the now deceased Reverend J. D. Oliphant, a man who, regardless of the fact that he had been born into landed wealth in Pennsylvania, and had married into more, had never missed an opportunity to warn his son of the sin of avarice—only slightly less heinous a vice, in the Reverend Oliphant's opinion, than the sin of pride.

Certainly, Oliphant had known all the while what fashionable opinion had called him in mockery, and he also had known and accepted the truth of it. John Cross Oliphant, originally of Philadelphia, Pennsylvania, and then of Beaufort, South Carolina, and now of no particular address, was a modern, accomplished, forward-looking, and unapologetic capitalist. Oliphant opined that, borrowing jocularly from Mr. Adam Smith's image, capitalism was the invisible hand that led his life. Capitalism had made him lordly without need of bloodlines, ancestral homes, or any title other than *American*.

Oliphant believed, accordingly, in God the Father Almighty, Maker of Heaven and Earth, and in His Only Son, Jesus Christ, and also in the virtues of probity, industry, and loyalty, and in one more thing, though it lacked a mellifluous, classically rooted word: the aggrandizing of self by making money with money, and the arguably corresponding benefit such a pursuit bestowed upon society. Some said, "Greed!" Oliphant said, "Tomorrow."

But for the war, he would have been ten times as prosperous as his Philadelphia brothers-in-law. But for the war, he would have done his best to be one of the men who was to build, at long last, the Pacific Railroad. But for the war— He stopped the thought. But then it came back at him in the click-clacking rhythm of the freight cars rolling by—"But-for-the-war! But-for-the-war! But-for-the-war!"

And so he sighed and let the melancholy get at him. But for the war, he would not have been alone on a platform at Niagara Falls, watching a reminder of his former destiny slip past, and disinclined to look too carefully toward his future, where there might be no destiny at all.

The freight train ended, and there was a discovery for Oliphant down the tracks. A detail of soldiers had collected the four captured fugitives, and was leading them up toward the waiting Express. The contingent was directed by the same large first sergeant who had addressed the passengers on the platform. His profound voice sounded over the sixty yards to Oliphant, "Keep up der! Sma'tlee! Private Gooze, he'p 'em der! Eyes front! Eyes on Papa Pinkey! Give way!"

This flurry was directed specifically at the rear of the parade, where one prisoner had fallen, and where a gangly young soldier—Private Gooze— moved dexterously to sling his musket and to give the invalid prisoner his strength.

Oliphant started to turn his head to the spectacle, but was restrained by a small stab beneath his eye. He compromised with his tooth by rearranging his whole body in order to witness the irony of it. For here were trim, kempt black men, in the uniform of the United States, escorting under arms four tattered, emaciated Confederate soldiers, the rear of the detail brought up by a two-toned, two-headed, four-legged animal walking as much as dragging in the gravel.

Another audience stood by, and threateningly. There were trainmen, teamsters, and idlers arranged in clusters of twos and threes at the freight platform of the northbound depot, catercorner across the tracks from Oliphant. And like a pack collecting about the prey, they shook their fists and tested their belligerence with vulgarities that bayed a theme and a refrain, "God damn Reb trash!" "Throw'd 'em in de river!" "Give 'em what dey gave po' Lonesome!" "Here's rope!" "Damn Reb trash!"

The first sergeant studied the threat and the terrain. There was another freight train half a mile down the line, its engine spitting black clouds as it churned up onto the plateau. The first sergeant must have seen that he could use the oncoming train as a screen, because with a crackling series of commands, he turned his detail left from the inmost of the tracks to the outermost roadbed, the one that ran below Oliphant. It was a wearying expedition for the prisoners, who staggered with their chains up and down the small ravines between the parallel roads. And precisely as Private Gooze and the invalid reached the last rail, they collapsed headlong between the ties.

This triggered the worst in the younger hecklers, boys still too young for the Union Draft but old enough to have been tainted by the hatred of the war. It also gave them a target. One boy lobbed a stone in a high trajectory that ricocheted near the first sergeant. More stones followed, and the crashing and pinging of the rocks became part of the growling chorus against the Confederate prisoners.

As the stones fell about him, the first sergeant loped up and down the length of his detail to reconsider the field: the oncoming freight that would soon protect his men; the age of the stone-throwers; the travelers up on the southbound platform who were just then discovering the trouble because of the teamster who was banging a crowbar on an iron railing, clang! clang! clang! The first sergeant could have blown his whistle to signal for assistance from the depot; he could have ordered his men to make a run to scatter the boys; he could even have retreated to let the passion cool. In truth, however, the stone-throwing was futile—the range too long and the arms too poor for more than nuisance. The first sergeant threw his hands up, and thundered to his men to keep on, "Move it der! Look ta me! Look ta Papa Pinkey! Der none else t'here boys! Close up, sma'tlee!"

The detail approached Oliphant's position. The stone-throwing was somewhat more effective as the range closed. Oliphant could estimate that it would be another half-minute before the freight train would intervene. This obvious fact aroused the mob. The older men cheered the youths to throw harder, and cursed the first sergeant nakedly, "A dime for de gray woolyhead! Go down, nigger!"

The first sergeant only glanced up at Oliphant as he marched past. He jumped outside of the roadbed and paused purposefully to stare at the mob. His strategy seemed to be to make himself a target for the stone-throwers, to draw off the fire from the troops and prisoners.

But his ruse worked too well. The first sergeant had continued past Oliphant only a dozen yards when a stone ricocheted off a rail and caught him across the back of the neck. It was a wild, improbable shot, but it did damage. The first sergeant went down on one knee, one hand at the blood on his neck, the other gnarled in the gravel to hold him up. The stone-throwers howled for their score, and redirected all their fire. Rocks clattered all about, missing the first sergeant, striking him, drenching him.

At this, Oliphant acted, and did so in a manner he knew, given his present vulnerability in the United States, was indiscreet. This was not, truth be told, his fight to win or lose. And yet it felt as if he were being directed by some invisible hand. Then again, Oliphant knew that what he intended was not splendid heroism. Simply, he dropped his walking cane and lettercase, reached into his breast pocket, pulled out his handkerchief, and proceeded to wave it vigorously up and down, while looking into the center of the mob. He meant to distract them, perhaps even to draw off some of the fire, as the first sergeant had done.

There was no certain result. But the fusillade did seem to ebb. And Oliphant kept waving his handkerchief as hard as he could right up until the locomotive and the freight rumbled heavily past, filling the scene with a sooty fog, and dividing the attackers and the victims.

The guard detail continued along the roadbed in good order. Their discipline was absolute as they passed Oliphant's position, and then the first sergeant's. The first sergeant had arighted himself now, and stood with his back to Oliphant, watching his men move along.

Oliphant pulled in his handkerchief and balled it in his hand. It occurred to him that perhaps the first sergeant had not seen what he had done, and perhaps that no one had seen it. Oliphant slipped the handkerchief into his capecoat pocket and thought, Just as well—no harm done.

Suddenly, the first sergeant spoke out, without turning, but very clearly and loudly above the click-clacking sound of the freight, and obviously directing his remark to Oliphant. He said, "No sir, thank'ee! No, sir! No surrender fer Pinkey dis day!" And then the first sergeant marched off.

Oliphant picked up his cane and lettercase. He had not let go of his briar, but the contents had spilled in the excitement, so he had to fetch his tobacco pouch from the folds of his Inverness. He realized that his hand was actually shaking, just as they said it would with the delayed shock of a battle, no matter how large or small the jeopardy had been. Oliphant used his lighter and then cradled it in his palm—a dull-gold prize, with his raised initials beneath an engraved image of a ten-point buck's head. He puffed harder to calm himself, and put his weight back on his heels. He had ground his teeth in his fear, and his attention was again for his tooth.

What remained of his thoughts turned upon what he had done, why he had done it, and how little it appeared to signify. Within moments of what he saw as yet another miserable demonstration of the irreparable dissolution of the Republic, and decency with it, there was no indication that anyone cared about the incident.

Perhaps, he thought, there was no outrage left. Perhaps it was enough to keep on, as the first sergeant had done, as certain Liberal members of Parliament had pontificated to Oliphant in London earlier that month, "The North must muddle through, and the South must fall." Perhaps, too, as Oliphant's father had written to him in 1860 when, on his deathbed, he had looked at the collapse of the Buchanan Administration after Lincoln's election and been remorseful of his own Abolitionist fervor of the previous decade, "When murder is the work, the left hand must never know what the right hand does." Perhaps so much, indeed, that Oliphant thought it best to reject all but the most present circumstances. The onrushing commerce of the railroad was at the American door, and soul-searching sentiment was an aged, long overstayed guest in the American house.

"Mr. Oliphant?" came a voice from behind.

Oliphant spun around to find that he was doubly flanked by four young men in a group pose that was both vigilant and military. They had come up behind him so quietly that Oliphant was momentarily speechless. Yet he did know their faces—from Toronto's Queen's Hotel Bar the day before. They were so-called special agents in the Confederate Secret Service in Canada.

Oliphant knew two of them still better, by reputation and introduction. The speaker was Lieutenant-Colonel Martin, of Kentucky, a sandy-haired six-footer with a bend in his lean frame, from a wound, it was said. At Martin's right was his adjutant, Headley, also of Kentucky, cherubic-faced and powerfully built, with mud-brown teeth from tobacco chewing. Both Martin and Headley, and probably the others, were renowned as cavalry officers who had ridden with the celebrated and now dead guerrilla general, John Hunt Morgan. These were veterans of Morgan's Raiders.

Oliphant had recovered himself now, but he still did not want to speak. He did not want to have anything to do with them. For he knew one more profound detail about the quartet. They were in Niagara Falls en route to a special assignment for Jake Thompson, the de facto chief of the Secret Service in Canada. Their mission was some sort of sabotage in New-York.

Martin waited also, but when it was clear that Oliphant was not going to respond, he continued in a pleading tone, "It's about Captain Kennedy, sir—"

Oliphant was angry. "Mr. Martin, please!"

Martin shook his head as if Oliphant did not understand. "Sir, I know we shouldn't come to you. We wouldn't if we weren't at wit's end. I know Mr. Thompson said— I apologize, sir."

Oliphant waved an interruption. "Our meeting yesterday was accidental. Surely you remember that Mr. Thompson said that you were not to approach me again once we crossed the border. There can be no thought to us cooperating. This isn't a battlefield, Mr. Martin, and I am not your superior, or your comrade. Think!"

Headley tried, "He's askin' for you, sir, Captain Kennedy, sir. He's raving, and is askin' for you."

"No!" snapped Oliphant. "This is— I said I'd travel to the border with him. It was only a favor to Mr. Thompson. Because he's the odd man in your—company. I can't be involved anymore. Mr. Kennedy is your responsibility now. He's your problem. No!" Oliphant exhaled, "Do you realize what you are asking?"

"Sir, sir, we do," said Martin. "But he's new to us, too. He just joined our expedition last week, and we don't know how to figure him. We've been waitin' for him all day. And now he's got this plan—about the boys they took at the bridge?—and I can't control him. The prisoners the Yankees got, sir. Captain Kennedy wants to rescue 'em. You've got to help us, sir. We can't make him understand it's crazy. He says he'll listen to you."

"What? What?" Oliphant turned half away.

"Please, Mr. Oliphant," said Martin. "If Captain Kennedy keeps on like this, he's gonna get us all caught. He's actin' crazy, sir. Mr. Thompson said you were the wisest—he said—he said that you can do what whole corps can't do, sir. Please?"

Oliphant turned back to Martin and his men. It was probably true that they could not handle Kennedy. They were experienced guerrillas, true, but they were also Kentucky farmboys, and Kennedy was a Louisiana gentleman —a planter's son—of a life and temperament most alien to them. Oliphant sighed. Their need overcame his own. He relented curtly, "Lead the way." And he fell in with them without anything like resolve.

Oliphant argued with himself as he walked along. Why was he so wary of Martin and his men, and so angry with them? He must be fair-minded.

All told, these were soldiers with courageous records. They had survived the western campaigns of the Ohio, Cumberland, and Tennessee river valleys for which there had been no match in bloodthirstiness until the recent Wilderness campaign in Virginia. And they were here today as extraordinary volunteers in the service of the same men who commanded Oliphant—the Confederate Cabinet in Richmond. Granted, they were not the most effective men in the Secret Service's control. But they were dangerous enough. They and their kind—like the St. Albans guerrillas—were great shots, indefatigable horsemen, rugged woodsmen, without balanced thoughts for property or politics or their own futures, as close to fearless as was humanly understandable.

And this was too close for Oliphant. It was the well of his jeopardy and disapproval. Oliphant was an agent of the Secret Service too, but he was not what these men had become—what these men had been ordered to become by the Secret Service in Canada.

For Martin and his men were not just special agents on a mission, they were also adventurers, daredevils, fantasists. In the first passion of the war, they had been the most romantic of cavaliers, rewarded for their storybook ferocity with promotions and decorations. But now, in late 1864, after the massacres in Virginia, with Sherman's army holding Atlanta, with Sheridan's army slashing through the Shenandoah Valley, with Grant's armies surrounding Lee's starving remnant at Richmond and Petersburg, with all this and the North still drafting and recruiting hundreds of thousands of men to pound the South the more come the spring of 1865, all the bold, sad, desperate men like Martin and the rest were used up, lost, without a country or a home, in shock for their survival, with little to offer but murderous skills that no longer signified.

For what use was a brave man who, given a horse, a carbine, and a head start, would actually try to outfox a company of Federal soldiers? What use was a singular gray-coated hero when there were armies of blue-coated heroes to hunt him to death?

The answer, Oliphant knew, was none. Examples of this nothingness walked alongside him on the platform. The answer also made Oliphant feel cold and heavy. Martin and the rest were bloodily, dauntlessly obedient, and they were prepared to follow their orders regardless of their meaninglessness. Martin and his men would try against any odds, and would try the most impossible of escapades, because they had no limits and recognized no limits. Like the Spartans, they did not know how to quit. Like the Athenians, their pride would not let them quit. They kept on with the war because they believed in themselves and in their commanders and in a dream of Southern liberty and independence that was gone forever in the defeats of 1863.

What was left in the fall of 1864, Oliphant believed, was to make a deal. What was important, Oliphant believed, was for reasonable men to negotiate for a conditional surrender, or was at least for shrewd men to acquire the provisions that could keep the Confederacy alive long enough to oblige the United States into an armistice that was not a total defeat for the Confederate states. That conditional surrender or armistice was Oliphant's main hope and task. And a Byzantine negotiation that might make possible some sort of deal was why Oliphant had crossed the Atlantic once again, and was en route to New-York. It was certainly a grim hope, and it would be a grimmer task. Yet Oliphant believed it was a rational hope, and that it was a job that he could try to do.

Neither Oliphant's ambition nor his mission had a place for men like these. Oliphant did not know the full details of their assignment—he did not want to know!—but he knew it was closer to revenge than it was to hope. Yet because war was a madness that made rational men speak of peace even as they launched regiments into suicidal assaults, Oliphant acknowledged that Martin and his men served the same South as he.

They had reached the passengers on the platform now. Martin ushered Oliphant to the left. The five of them descended a staircase down the side of the depot building, to a small yard off the station drive. They picked their way around a trash heap of wagon wheels and smashed crates and descended into a muddy ravine. Here, up against a wind-split chestnut, four more of Martin's men were guarding Kennedy closely.

Kennedy looked trapped and very agitated. But he controlled himself enough to wave hello to Oliphant.

Martin leaned closer to Oliphant, and began softly, "Speak sense to him, Mr. Oliphant. He's had a rough time in the Yankee prison camp, and only escaped a month ago. He's spooked, you know, like they get in prison. We've tried. It's this plan of his—you'll hear."

Oliphant stepped toward Kennedy, and the guards parted. Oliphant tried a half smile, and poked away a broken bottle with his cane tip. "Mr. Kennedy," he began, "Mr. Martin says you asked for me. How can I help you?"

Kennedy waited while Martin flung his arms like a commander on the march, directing his men to keep watch in all directions. Kennedy smiled and then sagged. "I told them, Mr. Oliphant, that you'd understand. That you'd see that I wasn't crazy like they think. I used my greenbacks to get a wagon and team over there." Kennedy pointed into the distance, to a brightly painted barn that was identified with a sign, Raven's Tours. Kennedy continued, "I can do it! I can try! You know I'm not crazy. Tell Colonel Martin. He doesn't know me well enough to see that I wouldn't try unless I could succeed. The Yankees can't outride me. And these field hands haven't even got good rifles, I've checked!"

Oliphant sighed. "They're better soldiers than that."

"What if they are! I've got surprise!" Kennedy talked faster, recounting what he had learned of the course that had delivered those four fugitives to the baggage car of the Albany Express. What he proposed was a single-handed rescue. He began to repeat himself. He mentioned some wild incident at West Point when he had rescued fellow cadets from a county jail. He waved his hands, and exclaimed, "I can do it! I can get them off lickety-split, and across the bridge before the Yankees get off a shot! There's a chance! I can make it!"

"Mr. Kennedy," started Oliphant again. Kennedy kept talking. Oliphant interrupted firmly. "Mr. Kennedy, you must get on, and look to yourself. Mr. Martin is your leader, and he has told me that he needs your support."

"No, sir, no!" said Kennedy. "What's the purpose of this special service, of anything we're doing, if we let four brother officers swing? Please, Mr. Oliphant, I know you understand me. As a gentleman, you must!"

Kennedy pulled himself to attention and then did something Oliphant thought most bizarre, and yet did it without self-conscious vanity. He opened his arms like an actor might and sang out as if he were on stage, "Oh, never, never, will a true Confederate soldier forsake his friends or fear his foes! For while Our Lord's Cross floats defiance, I don't give a damn how the wind blows!"

Oliphant looked back to Martin and Headley for help. They stood blank-faced. Oliphant turned back to Kennedy and nodded as if in sympathy. He thought, Be delicate, John. He said, "Mr. Kennedy, it's not for me to comment on your proposed tactics, but—if my amateur's advice means anything to you—hear me now—I'd say that your plan is ill-conceived. You don't know this neighborhood. And you would be risking the prisoners' lives as well as your own trying to get across the most heavily guarded bridge in the North. And believe me, you can't cross that river unless on the bridge. No matter how hard you swim or—" Oliphant finished softly, and smiled trying to be convincing, "Not even on a rainbow."

Martin spoke up, "Listen to him, Captain."

"It can't be done!" said Headley, kicking woodchips.

Headley's angry tone seemed to reignite Kennedy. He appealed, "Colonel Martin, I was there like them! At Johnson's Island! For more than a year! I just got out in September—with my hands, my hands! You have to crawl, dig with your hands, and get over that wall, and swim for it. Floating and swimming until you can't anymore, and praying! I know! I know what they'll do to them! Put them in cages for hogs and half underwater in the dark, till they come for them—"

"Stop it, stop it!" cried Martin. "Mr. Oliphant, make him stop! We have a mission. We can't! He'll get us all caught!"

Martin's plea seemed to penetrate Kennedy's illusion. Kennedy recovered something of his sense of proportion then and put his hands out as if praying. "All right. I see. I see that I'm not alone here, and can't ask you all— All right. But let me go to them, just that. I shall only talk to them if I can get close. I see, I do, I see that it wouldn't work with all of you here. I won't give us away. The Yankees don't know me. I can give those poor boys some comfort. And take what messages I can to their kin. It's the least thing to do."

"It isn't much to ask," said Martin to Headley.

Headley replied, "If he promises no more outbursts."

Oliphant frowned and shook his head. He tried to resist his inclination to interfere further, but he could not. These might be veteran horse soldiers; they were also young men who did not appreciate the dangers of passion.

Oliphant started, "I recommend against any sort of contact, Mr. Martin. I urge you gentlemen to quit this debate and to get on that train now."

Kennedy stabbed out his hands in protest, but Oliphant caught them with his cane and shoved them aside. Oliphant said, "Mr. Kennedy, you must understand my reasons. You can't be permitted even to see those men. I have seen them, and I know. I have all your welfares in mind. You can't see those men precisely because you might know them. And you are not strong enough for that burden. Not here. Not now. We are in the United States."

"Oh, no, no," cried Kennedy. But he sounded defeated, and he lowered his head.

Oliphant stepped forward in sympathy. Kennedy began weeping in chokes. Oliphant understood a little more of Robert Cobb Kennedy now. This was Kennedy's first venture outside of the companionship of his brother officers since he had escaped from Johnson's Island in September. Part of him still felt as if he were inside that prison camp, seeing things as those four prisoners must. Kennedy was a man who had not yet remembered how to be free, or how to protect himself in the world.

Kennedy was shaking with his tears and staggered back. Oliphant took pity. For the tears, at least, he could offer his handkerchief, and did.

Martin and Headley backed away in embarrassment. Martin's men watched for a moment and then too turned away. Oliphant reached out awkwardly and found himself standing beneath a tree with a frightened, sensitive young man weeping against his breast.

Oliphant got Kennedy moving slowly, up out of the ravine, back into the yard, and up onto the stairway. Kennedy was sluggish, like a drunken man. Now Oliphant needed help, yet Martin and his men had gone on ahead, back into the crowd, two by two, as prescribed for their kind of work. Oliphant took Kennedy's weight and eased him up the stairs, onto the platform. Oliphant paused for his breath. Prepared or not, he was going to have to care for Kennedy a little longer.

Oliphant reached into his morning coat for his billfold. He waved a greenback at a porter and made a request. The porter ran to the train, while Oliphant tried to soothe Kennedy. "It'll be fine now, just a moment more and we'll be fine."

There was an anxious delay for Oliphant—the stationmaster calling out, "All aboard! All aboard for Buffalo, Rochester, Syracuse, Utica, Amsterdam, Schenectady, and Albany!"—and then Miss Margaret Cappawhite appeared, coatless and bright with curiosity, in the coach stairwell.

Oliphant beckoned, and she descended the stairs and skipped across the platform. Oliphant started to introduce himself. Yet she said that she knew his name, because Kennedy had spoken of him to her. She reached for Kennedy's arm. He was still weeping, but quietly now, like a mourner.

Oliphant said, "Thank you, Miss Cappawhite, he's in need of some kindness—"

Miss Cappawhite said, "You can tell me. It's an old wound that's weakened him, isn't it? Aye, and I'm sure I don't care how he got it, or why, Mr. Oliphant, or where either. You can trust me with him. We were about to dine together, and he heard these men talking of something, and he made his excuses and dashed. I don't know why. Do you?"

Oliphant did not reply. He passed Kennedy to Miss Cappawhite's careful embrace. She whispered to Kennedy, and her touch did seem to strengthen him. Kennedy looked up to Oliphant and managed to speak before parting. "Thank you, sir. I'm sorry. I can't seem to stop crying. I'm not myself. I'm sorry."

Oliphant stood fast while Miss Cappawhite helped Kennedy to the car. Oliphant delayed getting up in order to collect himself. He tightened his top hat, flapped out his Inverness, and got out his briar and tobacco. He was thinking of the topsy-turvy passions of the war—Miss Cappawhite, the stone-throwers, Kennedy—that found him as if guided by an invisible hand. He laughed. No, John, you can do better. That found me because America's fate was out of control, and mine might be too. That found me because, as America was a nation divided against itself, I am a man divided against myself.

The bottom truth! He had told poor Kennedy, there was no better than the bottom truth! And so confess it, John!

The bottom truth was that for three years he had gone along with a war against the country he loved. The bottom truth was that for more than two years he had been an agent for a cause he had never truly believed in. The bottom truth was that he had committed himself to rebellion and calamity because he was in love with a woman who could never be his. That war, that cause, and that woman were ahead of him in New-York.

Oliphant relaxed. He smiled without true pleasure. Did the truth set him free? Perhaps. It was the wrong time and place to argue with himself further. He too must get on. Whatever else, New-York was ahead. And fate, like a train, was not long-patient. He placed his briar in his mouth, carefully avoiding the sore tooth, and then he went forward. The fire in his mouth was passed for the moment, and that gave him some peace.

CHAPTER 2

Amaziah Butter at
Washington City, District of Columbia

TUESDAY AFTERNOON, NOVEMBER 1

At dusk on All Saints' Day, the United States steamer *Washington's Crossing* pushed hard against the astonishing southward current of the Potomac River. From the vantage of her hurricane deck, Washington City lay mottled and damp just up ahead in the soggy basin of a river bend as an evening rainstorm settled across the mile-wide wash of the river to subdue what little light remained of the day. Captain Amaziah Butter, the full-bearded, burly, and bespectacled cavalry officer leaning against the railing of that hurricane deck, threw out his hand at the angry clouds and turned to his companion to say, "They're sucking mud with their porridge at camp tonight."

First Lieutenant Thad Bell, a shorter version of Butter's blockiness, responded, "You mean the boys at the Petersburg works?"

Butter grunted; he pictured the trenches becoming creek beds, and the rain blowing through the tent flaps. He added, "Everywhere out there. Everyone."

"That's why I'd like your kind of duty—nice dry room in Washington,

I'll bet," said Bell. "You provost-marshal men have this war right. After three months at home, my bones still ain't ready for camp life. That damp gets inside you, and—"

"The boys'll be building winter quarters soon," interrupted Butter. "You'll get yourself a good roof and a wood floor."

"You'd get it for us if you was still my tentmate, Amaziah," said Bell. "I do wish you was coming out with me. It wasn't the same after you left. All summer, I was sharing with whoever was left over. I guess you ain't coming back?"

Butter sighed. Going back to the siege at Petersburg? Not hardly. And yet he could almost wish that he was. Butter said, "My wife cursed me at the door. Desire, she cursed me, and wouldn't let me back into my own house. She said I was going back to the Jerusalem Turnpike at Petersburg, and that this provost-marshal work was just a deception. I tried to tell her. She wouldn't hear me out."

Bell squinted, and spoke conspiratorily, "It's Secret Service work you're on, isn't it, Amaziah? That's what you're doing here? That's what you couldn't tell her?"

Butter looked down at the ship's wake. "I don't think I should say, Thad."

"I know it's none of my affair, and if you can't say, you can't. But we're old comrades now. And I've been waiting to ask for four days. And now that we're here, and aren't likely to see each other— It is Secret Service— I'm right?"

"I'm not going to say you're wrong," replied Butter. He tightened his muscles at this. Thad Bell was one of the two best friends he had made in the Army in three years. They had shared a tent for eight months the fall, winter, and spring before. Their four days sailing together from Portland had been a pleasant reunion for them. And yet something about the Secret Service made him wary to tell the truth. What was the truth? That Butter was a twice-invalided cavalry officer who had by good luck become an acting-assistant-provost-marshal (enforcing the Draft in Bangor, Maine) and then had, by bad luck, become a special agent for the Secret Service. Butter sighed again, and tried to be more candid. "I'm a babe in this business, Thad, and I'd appreciate if—I think it best if you wouldn't ask me more, and we could carry on like we have been. Old tentmates headed in different directions for now."

"Is it bad," asked Bell, "what you're doing?"

"It isn't as bad as Petersburg," said Butter.

Bell snorted, "Hell ain't even gonna be that bad."

Washington's Crossing was built for speed, a converted Confederate block-ade runner that had been captured off Cape Hatteras the previous year, with two masts, paddle wheel amidships, empty gunmounts for 32-pounders aft. She vibrated with her oversized engines and sounded her horns as she passed the marker buoy to starboard off the fortification near the Cavalry Depot at Geesborough Point on the Maryland shore. She was making for the Eastern Branch of the river and the Navy Yards. To port, the Virginia shoreline was low-wooded and rolling, with a break made by Arlington's shabby wharfs and the storage depots strung along the riverbank to the Long Bridge—that mile-long, makeshift conduit that connected Washington to Virginia. To starboard, the Maryland shore was similarly wooded—poplars and scrub pines like loblolly and yellow—save for the massive masonry and earthen mounds that marked the river defenses of the Cavalry Depot. All appeared quiet here, a stormy fall afternoon sweeping and slickening the forest. The informed opinion would add, however, that at least a half-dozen of Washington's forty-odd forts could direct their artillery fire at anything at this juncture of the river.

This theoretical cross-fire was the subject of excited exchanges between a veteran naval officer and two young artillery officers who shared the hurricane deck with Captain Butter and Lieutenant Bell. The young officers were new to the lexicon of the war, because they belonged to the newly formed Massachusetts artillery regiment that filled the holds and berths of the ship. They were listening attentively to the naval officer as he held forth on the power of the Rodman smoothbore 15-inchers that were the major weapons in Washington's defenses. The naval officer illustrated his report with anecdotes of naval battles off Port Royal Sound, South Carolina, in 1861; off Fort Fisher, North Carolina, in 1863; and off Mobile, Alabama, the previous August. He even quoted Admiral Farragut's remarks after Farragut's fleet had captured Fort Gaines and Fort Powell off Mobile Bay: Farragut had said, "Give me wooden ships with hearts of iron, and guns that throw tons of fire!" The naval officer added, "I've seen men killed just by the concussion of those guns' shells. Not a mark on them. Dead like sleep, but dead."

"Like this here?" asked an artilleryman; he produced an oilskin folder and pulled out a carefully wrapped and mounted photograph. "Look here, sir, me and my friend had this made in Boston Harbor."

The naval officer took the photograph and held it up to a swinging lantern. "Why that's you lying there!"

"Yes, that's me. They make photographs like these at Gettysburg now," explained the artilleryman. "For souvenirs. You just lay down in the rocks at Little Round Top and play dead, and they photograph you. All the boys who go there have them. I saw one, and we had this made before we left home."

"Good God," said the naval officer. "I—" He turned to Butter and Bell. "Have you gentlemen ever seen anything like this?"

Bell moved over to look, and said, "Dead men look deader."

"They don't!" protested the artilleryman. "Not till they puff up and get black. Right after, they look like this."

Bell, who was the same age as the two artillerymen, about 23, and pugnacious, said, "A corpse is crushed into the ground. Look at your arms! And your eyes are shut! Men die looking! It's a surprise!"

The naval officer tried to arbitrate. "You were at Gettysburg, were you, Lieutenant?"

"No, sir," said Bell. "Petersburg, and Petersburg again, and again till I got hit in August. But he was, Captain Butter was, with the First Maine and the Cavalry Corps."

The naval officer pointed at the photograph. "What do you make of this play-acting then, Captain?"

Butter did not want to participate, but he could not stop himself from glancing at the photograph of two bodies crumpled atop each other in a rockfall like awkward lovers; Butter said, "I've no good opinion."

The second artilleryman asked, "Haven't you ever been curious, sir, what you'd look like dead? It's what you can never see."

Butter said, "Would you believe me if I told you that, sometimes, you see that too?"

The two artillerymen looked at each other for reactions, and shrugged, and then the first man turned to Butter. "Sir, how, sir?"

"Oh hell, Amaziah," said Bell, "he'll find out."

Butter turned back to the river, and concluded, "I've no good opinion, none at all."

The naval officer spoke slowly to Butter and Bell, "Good evening to you, gentlemen."

Washington's Crossing gave way passing the U.S. Arsenal at Greenleaf's Point on the District's riverbank to a gunboat that was escorting two following frigates out of the quays. Their goods off-loaded, the frigates were now covered with troops huddling under tarpaulins; they were likely bound for City Point or Bermuda Hundred in Virginia to reinforce the Army of the Potomac and the Army of the James. Washington City was not only the capital and seat of government; it was also the terminal point for the northern railroads delivering recruits, draftees, and returned invalids like Bell, so that they could be enshipped or entrained into Virginia to swell the combined might of the Federal armies that were encamped in those celebrated hundred thousand campfires besieging Richmond and Petersburg.

Lieutenant-General Ulysses S. Grant, bivouacked at the bluff of City Point on the James River near Petersburg as general-in-chief of all the Union armies, had positioned Major-General George Meade's Army of the Potomac and Major-General Benjamin F. Butler's Army of the James in order to enclose Confederate Major-General Robert E. Lee's Army of Northern Virginia like a great gripping hand—the fingertips at Richmond and the heel of the palm at Petersburg. The hand would close eventually, and squeeze the life out of the Confederacy. But when? when? The military stalemate in Virginia wore down the Union cause like continually worse and worse weather. There had been nearly a hundred and fifty thousand Federal battle casualties in Virginia in Grant's campaign from the Wilderness in May to Petersburg in September and October, and there was no victory yet. Lee, outgunned, outnumbered, and trapped, had held out against all reason, for his heart was very strong, and the hearts of his men were hardened against the notion of capitulation. The Confederate works at Petersburg—the weak flank in Lee's defensive perimeter—were still deep and fierce, as Captain Butter and Lieutenant Bell knew too well, since each of them, in their day, had tried at them and fallen in the dust. Only the week before, on October 27 and 28, Grant had tried to extend his siege lines at Lee's northern and southern flanks at Fair Oaks and Hatcher's Run, and the demonstrations had cost the Union another thirty-three hundred casualties.

The men on the two frigates passing *Washington's Crossing* to port were called up to fill the new empty places in the Union lines, and also the places abandoned by regiments that were rushing home after their service had expired. The lights of the tents of thousands of more replacements were visible from the hurricane deck along the Virginia and Maryland shore, especially at the ramshackle Uniontown just ahead. Those men were cooking their suppers in the mud and awaiting rumors to tell them when it would be their turn to go to Virginia. Tonight, though, there was some peace. The pandemic rumor was for the unannounced but obvious ceasefire in Virginia, or Georgia, Tennessee, Alabama, Mississippi—everywhere the Federals and Confederates were locked in opposition, preparing themselves for the hard winter the farmers said was coming on, and looking to Washington City as the United States went about the vulnerable business of electing a president and Congress during wartime.

Off Polar Point, *Washington's Crossing* backed her engines to come about for the Navy Yard looming to port with its great barnlike buildings and craneneck towers. The maneuver had to be sharp to skirt a twin-turreted ironclad lying by a repair barge in the channel. The paddle wheels in reverse shook the ship until the bolts seemed to rattle, so much so that Captain Butter had to back away from the railing. The rain had begun slowly, a misty gusting off the river, and it had cleared the hurricane deck of all but the two cavalry officers. Butter was smoking a cigar as best he could in the shelter of his broad-brimmed hat and turned-up collar. Bell had declined a smoke, and stood by nervously fastening and unfastening the bone buttons on his greatcoat.

Butter watched Bell and wanted to give comfort; he tried by repeating the obvious. "You're trying for a ship out tonight?"

"I was thinkin' I might," said Bell. "I don't know anybody in Washington but you, and I guess you'll be on your way tonight?"

Butter said, "I don't know where I'll be, Thad. I guess we'll have to wait this war out for a night in Washington together."

Bell pointed toward Virginia. "I best get on, then. The boys are sure to need me if they were in the fight at Hatcher's Run Thursday."

Butter shoved a cigar at Bell again. This time, Bell took it, and bent forward to accept a light from Butter. Butter puffed harder and harder to make a large black cloud. Bell was so anxious at their imminent separation that he struggled to keep his smoke lit. Butter felt bad for him. The newspapers had said that Hatcher's Run had been another slaughter—as many as four regiments' worth of casualties. Thad Bell was going back to a living graveyard. Butter wanted to ease Bell's as well as his own fear of Petersburg and also to speak as optimistically as possible. He said, "You can be sure the First Maine was there. The First Maine always rides to the sound of guns. Old Smithie, before they gave him that star and the brigade, he gave us a motto. After Gettysburg. A Frenchie motto, '*A Fin.*' It means, 'To the end.' "

Bell laughed, and Butter did not. Butter had not meant it as a jest. Butter and Bell were both Maine men who had individually and together seen a lot of the war in Virginia. Butter had served in the First Maine Cavalry before transferring into the First District of Columbia Cavalry—a regiment primarily raised in Maine in the fall of 1863—where he had befriended Bell. Butter had been badly wounded at Petersburg the previous June, and after a month's stay in hospital, had been shipped home to Bangor as an invalid, where, after his recovery in September, he had become an acting-assistant-provost-marshal. Thad Bell had fought on with the First D.C. through the summer, right up until he had been badly wounded in the August catastrophe at Sycamore Church, near Petersburg, when the regiment, guarding a herd of beef cattle, had been surrounded and massacred by a Confederate raiding party. After that, the First D.C. had ceased to exist—half of it in captivity in Richmond, most of the other half dead or invalided like Bell—and the War Department had merged its survivors with the also much reduced First Maine Cavalry. Thad Bell was returning to the remnant of two remnants; but he was also joining a unit that had become one of those veteran regiments that had refused to disband after its three years of volunteer service had expired. The First Maine was generally known as proud, battle-weary, and resolute. It was also bivouacked near the same spot on the Jerusalem Turnpike where Butter had fallen and lain and agonized for three days nearly six months before.

Bell's voice was fragile after his laughter. "You say you do know my new colonel, this Jon Cilley?"

"He's a fair man, and smart, Thad," said Butter; he had already reviewed this information for Bell, but was willing to do it again to pass the time, and to calm Bell. "He captained B Company in '61 when I went into D Company as a second lieutenant. He was hurt before Gettysburg, and volunteered back into the saddle. You say hello for me like I said. Maybe he'll give you a company of the First D.C. men."

"I don't want that," said Bell, "just a dry tent before Christmas." He turned. "You have any messages for the boys?"

"I would if I knew who wasn't gone or in Libby Prison," said Butter. "You just tell 'em that Maine's right with the war—and there isn't anybody posing dead for photographs."

Bell asked, "God Almighty, Amaziah, when're those Rebs quitting?"

Butter blew a cloud into the mist, and said, "It's going to end when it ends. So keep that tent dry."

"You expect you'll need a bunk 'fore winter's done?"

"Maybe. I hope not. But maybe. After what I've learned this fall, anything's likely in this war—anything at all."

Bell leaned closer. Butter sensed that Bell was trying to restrain himself from running on. Bell started then stopped; he cleared his throat, took the cigar out of his mouth, and smiled peculiarly. "It is Secret Service work, isn't it? What you've been doing all fall? Why you were up to Canada? You're working for Colonel Baker, aren't you?"

Butter was prepared, and replied easily, "Don't fret yourself, Thad, and remember to vote for Mr. Lincoln."

Below them, at the waist of the ship on the boiler deck, there was a rush of exuberant soldiers assembling for off-loading. Four days before, Butter and Bell had met by chance on the train from Bangor to Portland, and had hurriedly decided to board *Washington's Crossing* in Portland Harbor to continue their trip, not realizing that it would lay over a night in Boston Harbor to take on this fresh regiment. Most of the troops on the boiler deck were teenaged boys with a considerable portion of their bounty money left in their pockets, and so they fell in laughing and hooting in anticipation of an opportunity at Washington City's notorious pleasure palaces. At the least, they wanted a solid meal on land.

The first sergeants did their best to contain the adolescent enthusiasm. However, the jubilation seemed to be matched by the sharp whistles, grinding machines, and general chaos of the Navy Yard. The steam dynamo was like a bandleader, and the workmen of the yard scurried with ropes and pulleys like instruments. Even the hissing rainfall and the animal sounds from the hauling oxen and horses contributed to the impression of an enormous musical competition. It was the easiest solution for the sergeants then to organize their men by urging them to sing out in boisterous voice a boast that had been, in the first years of the war, that most popular of war cries, *"Yes, we'll rally round the flag, boys, we'll rally once again, shouting the Battle-Cry of Freedom! We will rally from the hill-side, we will rally from the plain, shouting the Battle-Cry of Freedom!"*

And, tired as he was, and sea-woozy, Captain Amaziah Butter of Bangor, Maine, a stubborn, un-ironical, and semi-invalid patriot at 27, was tempted to whisper along as the 4th Massachusetts Heavy Artillery Regiment, U.S. Volunteers, launched into the chorus, *"The Union forever! Hurrah, boys, hurrah! Down with the traitors, up with the stars! While we rally round the flag, rally once again! Shouting the Battle-Cry of Freedom!"*

Pennsylvania Avenue bisected Washington City with a line that extended from the village of Georgetown, on the heights northwest of Capitol Hill, down to the Eastern Branch of the Potomac, southwest of Capitol Hill. The northwestern course of Pennsylvania Avenue, facing the rear facade of the Capitol building, had grown from the first as the main Federal thoroughfare, tree-lined and well-kempt, passing amid the hotel district, the newspaper and theater district, the embassy district, and the secret dens of gamblers and prostitutes, to the vast soggy quadrangle between West Fifteenth and West Seventeenth streets that contained most of the executive branch at the mouth of the Tiber Creek. The center of this Federal quadrangle was the President's House, a symmetrically rambling thirty-one-room mansion fashioned upon the designs of an English duke's manor. And surrounding the White House, like outbuildings, were the ducal departments of War, Navy, Interior, and that vast and new neo-classical edifice of Treasury.

The southeastern trail of Pennsylvania Avenue had fared less happily, however, a result of poor planning on a mad king's scale. Once off Capitol Hill, it was apparent that all of the District of Columbia was a marshy lowland suspect of yellow fever and malaria each hot season, when the joke was that the dust clouds meant that Washington was three feet in the air. In the wet months, the jest was turned so that the capital was said to be three feet beneath the Potomac. The open evidence was that Washington City was an Enlightenment dreamer's imperial fantasy; the secret fact was that it was an inauthentic Southern town—called the national village—that had been propped up in a swamp. Strangely, the Capitol building itself faced east, and Europe, as if it were guarding the city and country expanding behind it. Accordingly, east of the Capitol building, outside the magical redoubt of democracy, along the mile and a half of Pennsylvania Avenue to the Eastern Branch of the Potomac, there was no spirit of growth, only played-out and deserted fields that, in a storm, became muddy pools large enough to drown an ox.

Captain Butter skated around one of those mudholes as he emerged from his climb up from the Navy Yard at East Fifth Street and onto a large, rut-marked square where North Carolina Avenue intersected with Pennsylvania Avenue. The right and left of the square ahead showed the lights of clapboard farmhouses that had been converted to inns and boardinghouses for government and military men. Beyond the treeline, there were layered shadows thrown by regimental campfires. The gaslights on Pennsylvania Avenue created circles of yellow illumination in the gloom, and up ahead, Butter could see a caravan of Quartermaster Corps wagons drag across Pennsylvania Avenue to plunge again into the dark. Butter tossed his shoulders and struck out in the direction of the Capitol building.

Butter actually preferred this part of Washington, because it was barely civilized, much more akin to the American frontier than the northwestern part of the city. Butter regarded himself as a frontiersman, out of the deep, rich Maine woods, and he was naturally suspicious of hotels, shops, and other trappings of wealth. The truth was, though, that he was the eldest son of a newly prosperous timberman of Bangor, and had enjoyed a childhood, education, and marriage that identified him as an exemplary and blessed member of New-England's middle class. Nevertheless, Butter held fast to his dreams of himself as a woodsman, and splashed up the trail hefting his kit on his shoulder like a log, humming a nameless tune, and chewing on an unlit cigar.

After two more blocks of sagging buildings, Butter paused to collect himself. Here was his destination, an unpainted, two-story, wood-built structure at 217 Pennsylvania Avenue. It was squeezed between other undistinguished two- and three-story houses that were more commercial than residential, because this neighborhood, dreary as it was, was only a short walk to the Capitol building and catered to the poorer members of Congress who could not afford the hotel district or Georgetown. There was nothing commercial about 217 Pennsylvania Avenue, however, because it was an anonymous government building. Its flagpole was empty; its front stoop was guarded by a single sentry. The only signs of anything extraordinary were the half-dozen mounts and two excellent carriages arranged before this, the headquarters of the United States Secret Service.

The sentry passed Butter without challenge. Inside, the first floor was divided by a center hall off of which were the doors to guard rooms, storage rooms, the telegraph key, the kitchen, and the large duty room to the left. The duty room was an ill-lit mess of hardback benches, desks shoved together to form islands, and gunracks; its chief distinction was the effect of the beautifully mounted portraits of Washington, Jefferson, Lafayette, and other heroes of the Revolution that were hung along the far wall, representing the booty of a civil war that could appropriate the homes and furnishings of rebellious Marylanders and Virginians and call them war reparations.

The last time Butter had been in the duty room, the January before, it had been crowded with ruffians, informers, and dispatch carriers. Tonight, with the dinner hour, there were only a few figures playing cards at the rear, and a noncommissioned duty officer at the desk by the front window.

Also, there was an older woman in a ragged coat standing heavily before the duty desk. She appeared to be very upset and either about to weep or trying to control her tears. The sergeant, a rosy, hairless man, was trying to quiet and console her.

Butter held himself back by the doorjamb. He had hoped that he would know the duty sergeant, so that he could ask after the fate of his comrades in the now obliterated First D.C.—for the First D.C. had been raised to serve the Secret Service exclusively, and it had, until Grant's spring campaign had sent it against Petersburg.

The sergeant was a stranger to Butter, however; Butter assumed that he was one of a single detached unit that the War Department had left the Secret Service. Butter knew that it would not be like the Secret Service to go without some troopers to give it the appearance of a military command. Butter also knew that the real strength of the Secret Service was the dozen men of its detective force who undertook the busy tasks of chasing enemy agents, arresting the corrupt and the disloyal, and procuring counterintelligence from a spider's web of informers and agents from Washington to Canada.

Butter stopped himself. He could no longer opine so disapprovingly of the detectives. In truth, he had now become one of the Secret Service's agents, even if he still wore the uniform of the U.S. Volunteers. The blue tunic was a thin armor, though, from the fact that he was now actually, as he had been only nominally while commanding Company G of the First D.C., in the control of Colonel Lafayette Baker.

For at the center of the Secret Service was its one and only chief, the tireless, hard-minded, and censorious Lafayette C. Baker. While Butter and the First D.C. had chased Confederate guerrillas like John Singleton Mosby the fall before, and while the First D.C. had ridden into Virginia with the Army of the Potomac the spring before, the detectives of the Secret Service had continued their duties of enforcing the orders of Colonel Baker.

The intuitions and fantasies and prejudices of Colonel Baker, thought Butter. For it was also a fact that Butter did not like or trust the man. He regarded Lafayette Baker as an American freebooter who, by some twist, had become necessary, some said indispensable, to the Union cause. Butter had seen Baker turn from a patriot to a bully to a ferret to a popinjay in as many winks of an eye. Lafayette Baker did actually wear a gold badge that read, "Death To Traitors." Butter winced. The Secret Service had always made Butter—a man naturally dyspeptic—outright gaseous and cramp-ridden. So now he shrank against the duty room wall and pressed his hand on his abdomen, because he was back in the keep of Lafayette Baker's secret police.

The duty sergeant barked at the old woman out of frustration. He also stood and stepped past the woman to address Butter. "How can I help you, Captain?"

"Help me!" cried the woman. "You must help me! I tol' ye an' tol' ye! Miz Lincoln, she says you must help me!"

The sergeant would not look at her, but he remarked, "Mrs. Mallon, don't lie to me now about seein' Mrs. Lincoln. We've tried to help you. You know."

"I ain't lyin'! And you've done naught but tell me you ain't the man for the job!" She turned to follow the sergeant's gaze, and discovered Butter. She was middle-aged, her skin like horsehide, and she was wrapped in an old blue coat belted with a rope. She held out hands like red flames, "Are ye *Kare-nell* Baker?"

"No, ma'am, I'm not, my name is Butter."

"Butter!" shouted the sergeant. "Where in hell—guard, guard!" The duty room door opened, and a private ducked in. The sergeant cried, "Fetch Mr. Skelton, fast! Captain Butter's here!"

"No! No!" screamed Mrs. Mallon. She seized the sergeant's blouse, and, catching him off-balance, tumbled him back over his chair. She bellowed, "Don't ye know? He's out there! My baby's out there!" She was weeping again, more desperate than hysterical. She addressed the whole room, and especially Butter. "Please, boys, May Mallon ain't meanin' to devil ye. Ye can fin' him, sure, he's my baby. He don't know'd his name. So ye got to take me wit'cha. He's simple, and they snatched him from my yard. Aye, take me out there. To Gin'ral Grant. I can fin' my baby. Whyn't ye min' me? Mary and Joseph, he's only 12 years old!"

Butter watched the sergeant as he got up and knew from the man's expression that Mrs. Mallon's story was probably true. She was talking about the so-called bounty men—scoundrels who had snatched her son and sold him to a recruiting station for the several hundred dollars the Federal, State, and Municipal governments now were obliged to offer to get men to enlist. From Mrs. Mallon's remarks, her son must be simple-minded, and therefore had been unable to resist the scheme. It was a crime on everyone's part, not the least the provost-marshal men who had cooperated in the deal. Butter also knew that it was not extraordinary these days, with the half-million man call-up of July still not met by the September Draft. The fear of the Draft had made many men very wicked, and the fear of the war had made their wickedness appear somehow clever. Nevertheless, the district quotas had to be filled, and whether by volunteers, hirelings, substitutes, draftees, felons, or the kidnapped, they would be.

Mrs. Mallon controlled her wailing. "I had a visitation, in the chapel at St. Matthew's down the road. I can tell ye, and if'n yer not of the faith— Sweet Mary Mother of God had him by the hand and were leadin' him through hundreds of white tents. So white, blazin' white! I called to him, 'Kevin, darlin', Kevin, here's Mommy.' "

"Mrs. Mallon," said the sergeant, "please, there's nothing we can do."

"He's only 12 years old!" she screamed, and then she had a knife from the fold of her coat, and held it high, calling, "My baby! My baby!"

The duty room door opened again, and a short, bulbous man entered quickly; he was Lafayette Baker's chief clerk, Usher Skelton. Behind Usher Skelton was a young, dark-haired woman in a blue shawl. The young woman swept past Butter to Mrs. Mallon.

"Please don't hurt yourself," said the woman to Mrs. Mallon.

"Oh, dear, don't ye know what's happened?"

The woman said, "Give me that thing, and we can find out."

Mrs. Mallon dropped her arm. Butter saw his chance and reached past the dark-haired woman to get ahold of the hilt of the knife, so that when Mrs. Mallon jerked again Butter grabbed the knife away.

"Fine, fine," observed Usher Skelton impatiently. "Get her upstairs, will you, Mrs. Lamont? Sergeant Spinner, help her into my office, and get someone for her—a priest, Father Mark perhaps, someone." Usher Skelton wore his whiskers like a goat's, and bobbed his head when he spoke; he turned toward Butter, bobbing. "You're Butter, yes? Where've you been? We've expected you for two days."

Butter grunted; he rotated the knife in his hand and, once Mrs. Mallon had been taken from the room, he put it on the desk.

Usher Skelton continued, "It's no matter. Let me gather my things, and send after the colonel. And then we're away. The colonel'll split peas for missing you! Why couldn't you have gotten here an hour sooner? Boy! Boy!"

An aged Negro appeared from the rear of the room. Butter knew him as the office servant, Job "White-Pine" Mills. Usher Skelton told him to fetch the carriage driver and to ready the harness, and then Usher Skelton darted for the telegraph key.

Butter said, "Hello, White-Pine, you remember me?"

"Certain, suh, ye one of Mastuh Tory's boys."

"I hear Major Wetherbee's got out of Richmond, that right?"

"Yassuh, Mastuh Tory's got out of prison and gone mean, suh. At da War Wagon, wid dat hound of his. Dog's gone mean too."

"Rufus isn't a mean dog, just ornery, like Major Wetherbee." Butter smiled. "Major Wetherbee's less ornery when he's not drinking."

"Well, he's drinkin' and orneryin' all de time now, suh."

Three men came up behind White-Pine, and seeing them, White-Pine left. Butter knew them too. They were three of the Secret Service's best and most veteran detectives: Edgar Quillermouth, Bob Dailey, and Milo Baker. Milo Baker was one of two of Lafayette Baker's brothers in the Secret Service; pale and slim, he was the opposite of the exaggerated and robust and plain arrogant Lafayette Baker. Indeed, Lafayette Baker had not only brought his brothers into the Secret Service; he had also tried to influence the First District of Columbia Cavalry by placing his first cousin, Joseph Stannard "Stan" Baker, as a major commanding one of the regiment's two battalions, and yet another cousin, Byron Baker, as the quartermaster of the regiment. Major Stan Baker had always greatly irritated Butter's mentor in the regiment, Major Tory Wetherbee. Majors Baker and Wetherbee had served together since 1862 in what had been known as Baker's Rangers until it had become the core of the First D.C. Now, Major Stan Baker was a prisoner of war in Richmond at Libby Prison, and Major Tory Wetherbee, who had somehow escaped from Libby, was derelict in a Washington saloon. Of consequence, Butter presumed that what had attracted the trio of detectives had been their overhearing his inquiry after Tory Wetherbee.

"Bless me, it is true, you've come back," began Edgar Quillermouth, an ex-medical student whom Butter had worked with the year before, capturing and transporting some of Mosby's guerrillas; Butter thought him a cynical, tricky man, who dressed in brown to look like a scholar. Quillermouth continued, "You've gained weight, Captain. The hearthfire! The marriage bed! How're the bowels?"

Butter said, "I was asking after Major Wetherbee's health."

Milo Baker grinned. "Your hero crawled out of Richmond and fell into a barrel of whiskey."

"Did more," said Quillermouth, grinning too and winking at Milo Baker. "It seems Wetherbee's sworn he'll have his revenge for Sycamore Church. Seems he thinks your regiment was sold out to the Rebs by Colonel Baker's enemies at City Point."

Butter would not take the bait. He stood still. It might be true, but probably was not. When Butter had last seen Wetherbee, the June before, Wetherbee had despised Lafayette Baker only slightly less than he hated Ulysses S. Grant and the Union high command at City Point, Virginia. Wetherbee's antipathy had not only been because of Baker's bullying excesses against Secessionists and pro-Southern men along the Potomac, or because of Grant's wasting of whole corps at the Wilderness and Petersburg. It had also been a matter of Wetherbee's history and sense of honor. Major Torrance Wetherbee was a Marylander and a West Point man, class of 1854, who had served before the war with brother officers who had now become the Confederate general staff. More, the elite cavalry unit that had become Baker's Rangers had once been known as the Second U.S. Dragoons, commanded by Colonel Robert E. Lee. Worse for Wetherbee, all of his kin were either with Lee at Richmond and Petersburg or with Jubal Early and the Confederate cavalry in the Shenandoah Valley.

"What'cha come back here for, Captain Butter?" asked Bob Dailey, the youngest detective, a so-called Indian fighter from Kansas, pimply faced and a dead shot. "You was out of it, wasn't you? Maybe you're still thinkin' of chasin' Mosby. That ain't a sport no more. Ain't you heard Sheridan's got Mosby backed up in the Valley with Early?"

Milo Baker grinned. "Mosby's runnin' and Phil Sheridan's hangin' what he catches."

Butter meant to stop their teasing. He had chased Mosby and his 43rd Battalion of Irregulars enough in his time, but he had never hanged Mosby's men to stop their raids, and did not like the implication. Butter mumbled, "You can't hang hate."

Quillermouth asked, "Petersburg teach you that? We heard that, after you went down, you crawled to the Jerusalem Plank Road. Them Reb corpses talked to you, did they? Tell you that you can't hang a hating corpse?"

Butter was annoyed. "Mr. Quillermouth, I'd take it kindly if you didn't go on about Petersburg. Those that've been there, don't need to talk about it, and those that haven't, don't know anything about it."

Milo Baker laughed. "Smart men don't talk to corpses, Edgar."

"Smart men stay at home when they're at home," remarked Quillermouth, gesturing toward Butter. "Ain't that right? Only *heroes* volunteer from a marriage bed. Does that make you a *hero,* Captain Butter?"

Butter rubbed his abdomen and turned toward a new disturbance. Usher Skelton reappeared from the hall carrying a lettercase. Behind Usher Skelton again was the dark-haired woman, Mrs. Lamont, who was now dressed for the storm outside in a maroon paletot with a long scarf twirled around her head. She was carrying a large pile of folders and a letterbook.

Usher Skelton squealed at Butter. "We must hurry, Captain!" But then Usher Skelton jumped as if surprised by the portrait of the Marquis de Lafayette on the near wall, and he charged off to the telegraph key at the rear.

Butter meant to give his back to the detectives. He edged toward Mrs. Lamont, and said, "That was brave of you, ma'am, with the knife. What do you make of that lady, Mrs. Mallon?"

"What do I think, Captain?" replied Mrs. Lamont; she frowned then shook her head. "I think that the war is cruel and sad and that they stole her son and sold him to my country because my country is buying boys like sheep and that I don't know, I don't know— I have to pray harder and harder to understand and forgive—"

Butter gasped. Mrs. Lamont frowned again, this time at the eavesdropping of the three detectives, and she backed off. Butter watched her closely and was decidedly persuaded by her manner. She was plain to see at first, with shadows around her eyes; however, she had a wonderfully oval face and a vanilla complexion. Butter wanted to continue their conversation. Instead, Quillermouth came up rudely and pulled Butter aside. Bob Dailey and Milo Baker bent close to listen.

"What do you know, Captain?" started Quillermouth. "Why are you here?"

Butter spoke flatly. "I was ordered here."

"You can do better," said Quillermouth. "It's been bad since Early's raid, but—the colonel's gone wild! The colonel's off every night for some muscular conversation at Old Capitol. He's there tonight." Quillermouth made a fist; he meant torture of the captured Confederate spies, agents, and couriers at the nearby military jail called Old Capitol Prison. Quillermouth continued, "And he was off with Mr. Dana all day. They was shoutin' at each other, yes sir, about something in New-York. It all doesn't figure, unless— and this is a confidence between old comrades." Quillermouth spat across and hit the mark in a cuspidor; this made him smile, and then he continued, "The colonel and John Odell were up to the Canadian border last weekend. There's been bee-buzzin' ever since. So we figure the colonel's after Jake Thompson and George Sanders and them, right? Is that why you're here? Have you been up to Canada too? That would figure, you bein' from Maine.

What is it? Has the colonel got a trap set for the Reb Secret Service?"

Milo Baker interrupted, "Or is it a parley between Ol' Abe and Ol' Jeff? Are they talking about peace?"

Butter looked at Milo Baker. So it was true that Lafayette Baker shared his secrets with no one but War Secretary Stanton, and maybe not even with him. Butter certainly did not know what Colonel Baker was up to—either with Assistant War Secretary Charles Dana in New-York, or with his own bodyguard John Odell in Canada. And Butter did not want to know what Lafayette Baker was torturing men for at Old Capitol—though he could guess about that sad business, and that it related to Butter's own recent work for the Secret Service.

Butter looked away for a moment and reconsidered his assumption about these detectives. At least he now understood what it was that these three wanted from him—not gossip about Wetherbee, but intrigue.

"It ain't peace, is it, Captain?" continued Quillermouth. "It's the Rebs, and the Copperheads? The colonel's got some surprise planned, and you're part of it? It's the conspiracy they've been talking about. There's more to it than electioneering? The Rebs really are planning to strike? And the colonel's got a trap? Go ahead, give us a hint, and we can do the rest. We're going to know soon anyway. We're all on the same side."

Butter was in control of his thoughts now and found a slight enjoyment in pretending, for a moment, that he was going to tell them something important. All the dissenting, anti-war, or pro-peace people in the Union were grouped with the genuinely disloyal or pro-Southern people, and the mix was collectively called Copperheads. But Butter thought these three men truly reptilian, and venomous. Also, in the Secret Service, information was a powerful weapon. It therefore pleased Butter no little to smile defiantly at Quillermouth and say, "I was ordered here by Colonel Baker and General Holt and Secretary Stanton. I am generally uninformed. A man out of a bed, as you say."

Usher Skelton was back, grabbing at Butter and Mrs. Lamont. They went directly out into the rain and down to Colonel Baker's empty carriage. Usher Skelton helped Mrs. Lamont inside, but he pushed Butter as he got in, so that Butter fell against Mrs. Lamont. The files fell from her lap and scattered on the carriage floor. Butter cursed and apologized for cursing. Mrs. Lamont just bent to the task of cleaning up.

Usher Skelton got halfway in himself, but then he removed his top hat to search its lining for small notepapers. He exclaimed, "Damn! Damn!

What have I forgotten?" He then hopped down from the cabin to turn completely around, as if searching the neighborhood, while he grumbled to himself, "Where are you, oh, where are you, Colonel?" Finally, Usher Skelton groaned and dove back inside the carriage, pounding on the cabin side, and yelling to the driver, "War Department, and fly!"

TUESDAY EVENING, NOVEMBER 1

Off West Seventeenth Street, at the edge of the Federal Quadrangle, and not two stones' throw from the White House, the twin dank barracks of the old War Department and the present Navy Department were known to burn gaslight day and night, and Sundays too, because of the gloominess of the buildings and because none of the occupants was ever known to leave. In the farthermost of the barracks, Gideon "Father" Welles, the white-bearded secretary of the Navy, was most disliked for his haughtiness; and since he was a former newspaper editor from Connecticut, the newspaper-men were dutifully mischievous, making him out a forgotten Jonah in the belly of the enormous Union warfleet. Welles was said to amuse himself by avoiding decisions and disputes, and to have rendered his greatest service to the nation by simply not interfering with the acuity of his assistant secretary, Gustavus V. Fox, the true schemer in the department.

Next door to the Navy Department was the barracks of the old War Department, which was now given over to the Army and the Army chief-of-staff Major-General Henry W. Halleck, Lincoln's so-called White House General. Here, even the scheming was secondary to the continuous incoming barrage that was known to break more general officers at their desks than it ever had in their tents in the field. The source of this barrage was the new, brick-built War Department building directly across West Seventeenth Street. The War Department building was a three-story fortress that was said to be lit by demons, and from which—the joke continued—no occupant or visitor was ever known to leave.

The War Department was ruled by War Secretary Edwin McMasters Stanton, who was called the little black terrier. He was squat and black-bearded, at 50, without a moustache but with a silver streak in his thinning hair and shaped beard that made it look as if lightning had struck twice. He peered over egg-shaped spectacles, and furiously. Stanton barked and Stanton bit and Stanton hung on his prey. He was a wealthy man, a Pittsburgh attorney and constitutional expert, who was said to enjoy his pleasures and his snobbish wife; however, for the term of his office since January 1862, he had not been seen to laugh, and he had camped like a Mongol emperor in his office.

Stanton had moved to Washington in 1858 to become famous for arguing cases at the Supreme Court, or wherever else he could attack his opponents. Stanton had insinuated himself in the bickering counsels of the Buchanan Cabinet and had served as attorney general in the treacherous closing weeks of the Buchanan Administration, after South Carolina's secession. Along with three other Cabinet officers, Jeremiah Black, Joseph P. Holt, and John A. Dix, and in close concert with the redoubtable New York Republican senator William H. Seward, Stanton had helped to form the clique that had been called the "firemen" of the Union, as first the Southern "Fire-eater" members of the Cabinet had fallen away—Cobb of Georgia from Treasury, Floyd of Virginia from War, and the shrewd Jacob P. Thompson of Mississippi from Interior—and then the states of the lower South had followed South Carolina into rebellion like a forest swept by fire.

At that time, and certainly since replacing the corrupt Pennsylvanian Simon Cameron at the War Department, Stanton had been infamous for his bitter, merciless tongue. He condemned everyone at first meeting—including Lincoln, whom he had called an ape—and only afterward did Stanton reconsider his meanspiritedness. More troublesome, he was always quick to accuse men of being traitors and to punish them without decent attention to the protection of the laws he was sworn to uphold. He was not known to have a warm friend, or to care for his adversaries more than a horsefly. In sum, Stanton was a vitriolic, cruel-minded, and unforgiving patriot; an Episcopalian who did not go to church; an anti-slavery Democrat who, by 1864, had found it useful to have a hand in every clique, especially those of the Radical "Black" Republicans in Congress.

Consequently, Stanton was one of the most reviled men in America. The newspapermen cursed him privately and thought him a mad Abolitionist. He was not simply that—too stern, high-handed, and angry to settle for merely enforcing the Emancipation Proclamation. Stanton was for the Union and for victory, or perhaps only for victory, in all directions. Some said he was hated second only to Jefferson Davis, but then, Davis was not also hated by Europe and especially Great Britain for the repeated boasts Stanton made about a war with those who had coddled the Confederacy once the Union was safe and the Secessionists hanged. Stanton threatened and Stanton assaulted and Stanton remembered where those he called traitors hid their money. Everyone, including Lincoln, gave way to him eventually, and also assumed that he would die of internal explosion—but not before Stanton had won out, and the Union was restored, and revenge was had.

Captain Butter did not think himself overimaginative, then, when, seated beside Mrs. Lamont in the corridor outside Stanton's offices at the War Department building, he sensed fear in the lady. He was afraid too, as he had been the half-dozen times he had been obliged to call here in consultation over the pursuit of the Virginia raider John Singleton Mosby.

Butter knew the routine business of these corridors was war-making, and that meant murder. Butter was not one of those in America who had become fascinated with death. He did not believe that his grave was imminent or necessary. He intended to remain a mortal sinner as long as his luck allowed. But now, tonight, here, he felt his luck pressed.

As his father had warned him, Butter was in among the "bloody thanes." Chisholm "Chip" Butter had traveled to the Republican Party Convention in Chicago in 1860 in order to nominate then New York senator William H. Seward for president; he had been one of those who had been persuaded to switch his vote to Abraham Lincoln of Illinois in exchange for the promise of having the Maine Abolitionist senator Hannibal Hamlin placed second on the ticket as vice-presidential nominee. Ever since that tricky episode, and particularly since Hannibal Hamlin had been displaced on the 1864 Republican ticket by the Tennessee military governor and suspiciously mild-tempered Andrew Johnson, Chip Butter had opined darkly about the men who surrounded Lincoln. Chip Butter thought them ambitious, envious, and ruthless conspirators, men who counted upon Lincoln's always obvious and now increasingly detached melancholia in order to advance their own power. Chip Butter had warned Butter the week before, when he had delivered the telegram that had fetched Butter back to Washington, "I ain't saying it's bad, Amaziah, you going among them, and I'm proud, proud, that they recognize your spirit. But your mother took me to this famous play once in Boston —about the bloody thanes of Old Scotland."

Butter smiled, and rocked back on the bench in the corridor, thinking of his father's roundaboutness: a man who, at 55, could bring down a hardwood tree with a double-bladed axe and a song on his lips, but who could not say what he really meant without a month's buildup. Butter used the memory of his father to dispel his fear of this place for a moment. He also thought to share his newfound good spirits with Mrs. Lamont.

"Excuse me, ma'am," he began, "Mr. Skelton didn't properly introduce us. I'm Amaziah Butter." She glanced at him cautiously, and Butter tried, "Have you been here before?"

"Yes, I have. My husband had an office just there," she said, pointing.

"He's best out of here, if he is."

"He's been missing in action since December of 1862," she replied. "He was delivering overcoats to the Army, before Fredericksburg, the battle."

"Yes, ma'am, forgive me." Butter nodded. "I was one of those who was glad to get those coats. It was cold."

"Is this it?" she asked, tapping Butter's greatcoat. She was not as morbid as Butter had assumed; she was mostly mysterious. There could not have been more than a dozen female clerk-copyists in government, and Butter had thought they were all at Treasury.

"No, ma'am, I lost that one," continued Butter. "My wife made me this one."

"You're a fortunate man, Captain Butter." She smiled. "I am Bridey Lamont. You were at Fredericksburg? Can you tell me, did you know—?"

Doors banged open all along the corridor, and Mrs. Lamont's question was overwhelmed by men pouring toward them from the left and right. There was a herd of red-faced Army officers and another herd of dripping clerks just in from the rain, and then there was a stampede into Stanton's offices.

Usher Skelton appeared from out of the office door and grabbed at Butter like a prize. They passed swiftly through the outer office, into the clerks' vestibule, and then through an archway into Stanton's private chamber.

The room was cavernous, badly lit, and thick with tobacco smoke, like a library with the fireplace flue clogged up. The walls were lined with law books and loose drawers of files piled high atop one another. At the room's center was a gigantic desk that was also partially a conference table, with chairs shoved up against it.

No sooner were Butter and Mrs. Lamont in the room than they were forced to the side by another arriving party of officers wearing wet ponchos. It looked to Butter as if an alarm had roused the whole general staff, but then again he observed that these were not field officers, rather they were War Department staffmen. The room filled with more than twenty men, until there was insufficient space for the civilian clerks to keep discreetly separate from the Army, or for the staff officers to remain properly behind their respective generals.

There was a distinct pause in the jostling when four more civilians entered the room. Yet these were well-dressed men, very different from the rumpled War Department clerks. They were also an advance guard, for with the slamming of a door like a cannon salute, a cigar-fuming, diminutive man with a turkey-like head swept in, followed by two obeisant aides bearing wet umbrellas.

Butter leaned closer to Mrs. Lamont, and asked, "Mr. Seward?" Mrs. Lamont nodded.

Butter also recognized the major-general who then stepped out from the pack of his staff officers to greet Secretary of State Seward. He was Joseph P. Holt, a tall, jowly, clean-shaven and oak-like Kentuckian who, as judge-advocate-general of the Army, was the chief of the Bureau of Military Justice, and therefore the master of all military intelligence.

Another major-general joined General Holt in welcoming Seward; he was Provost-Marshal-General James B. Fry, a cadaverous, mustachioed man. Fry was a regular Army officer who had been tainted from field command by his part in the defeat at the First Battle of Bull Run. As provost-marshal-general, Fry was overlord of the Draft and the state provost-marshal's offices enforcing it. This made Fry Butter's ostensible commander. However, in the confusion of command structures in the War Department, Butter, as an acting-assistant-provost-marshal at Bangor, could simultaneously serve as a special agent for Colonel Lafayette Baker. For Lafayette Baker himself, though chief of the very independent Secret Service, held his colonel's rank in the provost-marshal-general's office.

It was a briar-patch, Butter knew, and it was probably deliberate. For the only thing that was absolutely true was that all the War Department men in the room were firmly under the heel of War Secretary Stanton.

Butter searched the room for Mr. Stanton. Butter was so bumped about by the clerks as they competed for positions that it was not until Butter went up on his toes that he could examine the whole room. And there was Stanton, yet most extraordinarily. The war secretary was seated in a wheelchair in the far corner, by the heating stove; he was also tucked into a dark wool blanket, and dressed with several scarves and a pullover cap, looking very pale and weak.

General Holt began the meeting like a polished master of ceremonies. He was lavishly deferential to Seward who, as secretary of state, was the senior Cabinet officer, the so-called prime minister. But then again, Holt did demonstrate some intimacy with Seward when he called him "Governor" rather than "Mr. Secretary"; this was Seward's longtime personal preference because of his triumphant earlier years as New York's governor.

"And it is good of you, Governor," continued Holt, after a rambling declaration about the wretched weather, "to come over—"

Seward harrumphed; he had seated himself on a small leather couch across from Stanton's elephantine desk, so that he occupied the centerground between the military, the War Department clerks, and the State Department men bunched behind him. Seward slid onto the small of his back and put one leg up on a chair. He said, "Get on with it, General."

"Mr. Stanton wouldn't have asked you on such a night," said Holt, who seemed to be stalling, "if it wasn't that a crisis is hard upon us, and—"

Seward rolled his head toward Stanton in the far corner. Two officers stepped back to give Seward a clear line of vision. Seward said, "Why aren't you home in bed, Mr. Stanton?"

Stanton's voice was clearly cracked as he managed to reply, "Only—a— fever."

"At my age," said Seward, puffing on his cigar like a locomotive pushing uphill, "that's the hot breath of the Reaper."

Stanton coughed, and waved at Holt. "Get on with it, General."

Holt turned to look in the direction of the entranceway and the clerks' vestibule; he then looked over to Usher Skelton, Butter, and Mrs. Lamont, who were congregated by the largest bookshelf. Holt spread out his hands, and asked, "Where the devil is Colonel Baker?"

Usher Skelton sounded cowed. "I've sent everywhere for him, sir. He went out to supper with Mr. Dana, sir. We didn't know when Captain Butter would arrive, sir."

Holt said, "None of us knew!" Holt bowed to Seward. "Excuse me, Governor." And then he exhaled in frustration and pushed through the staff officers to Stanton. They whispered closely together.

Meanwhile, Seward asked one of his aides a question, and then pointed across the room at Butter and asked no one in particular, "Is this the officer from Maine? The one who's done all this investigating?"

Provost-Marshal-General Fry, seeing that Holt and Stanton were absorbed, walked over and pulled Butter into the best light on the carpeted area in front of Stanton's desk.

Fry began, "I'd like to introduce Captain Butter, sir, a fine officer. He was promoted to first lieutenant for his bravery at Middletown, and brevetted captain after Shepardstown where he was wounded, and—"

Butter was amazed that General Fry knew his record; he was also embarrassed to be on display in front of the staffmen and clerks.

Fry looked over at one of his staffmen. The adjutant had a sheet of paper in his hands, and whispered loudly, "First D.C."

"Yes," nodded Fry for the prompting; he continued, "After he recovered, he was appointed a captain in the First D.C. He was wounded again in Kautz's raid on Petersburg last June. He's now reenlisted for the duration. From Bangor, sir. From a fighting family. All the brothers are in the Army, and in Virginia."

Seward made a humming sound of approval. To Butter, Seward appeared a shadow behind a twirling lit cigar. Seward pointed again, "Do I know you, son, or someone?"

Butter nodded. "My father, sir, Chisholm Butter. He was one of your delegates at Chicago."

"Right," said Seward with satisfaction. "God bless, and give my regards to your dad."

Butter nodded. "Yes, sir, I shall, yes, sir."

General Holt strode back to the center of the room. He was holding the lapels of his tunic in the manner of a veteran prosecutor about to address a court. At the same time, he showed what Butter thought was obvious agitation and uncertainty, when he stumbled into Butter, bumping him slightly aside.

Holt began hesitantly, "Governor, Mr. Stanton feels that we'll just have to go ahead without Colonel Baker, and trust Colonel Baker arrives soon enough."

Seward was casual. "It's your party, General."

"Yes," said Holt, "and we do have much to cover." Holt raised his arm to the side. "My assistant Major Turner will start."

A heavily bearded, middle-aged man—an attorney rammed into a tailor-made uniform—came into the light; he was Major Levi Turner, the assistant-judge-advocate-general, and Holt's man in the field. Turner addressed Seward calmly, "You do know, sir, that Captain Butter is the man we enlisted to continue our investigation after I visited Maine in August? I explained in my report to you that Captain Butter—"

Seward interjected, "I have a library of reports, Major. You mean about the alleged raids? About that bank robbery in Maine? And your Sons of Liberty hocus-pocus?"

"It is the truth, sir," replied Major Turner evenly. "Captain Butter has

tracked down the truth of it, and more than that. He has discovered the trail
of a vast conspiracy against us by the Rebel Secret Service."

Seward rotated his cigar. "I'll be the judge of that, Major."

Holt stepped past Turner and bent toward Seward's couch. The State
Department clerks fluttered back like pigeons. Holt spoke huskily and defen-
sively. "We've asked you here to hear Captain Butter's report, sir. He's just
off his ship, and that's why this rush. We're hoping his report will persuade
you to our recommendation about arresting the Rebs and the Copperheads."

"I know why I'm asked here!" barked Seward. "And I've come here to
demonstrate that I'm not to be persuaded. Not tonight. Not tomorrow. And
not until after the Election!"

Holt pulled back and turned helplessly to Turner. Holt and Turner
stepped over to General Fry, and all three looked toward Stanton's corner.

Stanton flapped his hands, and croaked, "Castine—Castine—General. Tell
him—about the raid at Castine."

Holt spun around with new energy. Butter could see that he was expert
at public performances, and adept at appearing to speak intimately with a
judge despite a crowded courtroom. Seward was on the high bench here, and
Holt appealed, "Governor, you've seen the report from Maine today? It will
be in tomorrow's papers. The news from Governor Cony? About the Reb
raid on Castine last night? By their Secret Service? It means that it's begun,
their plot's begun. What we've been warning you about."

"Nothing them Maine men can't handle," said Seward. "Hardly a conspiracy, General, more a little hell-raising by drunken deserters. And Sam Cony
can protect his own, can't he, Captain Butter?"

Butter flinched, and nodded without sincerity. A Rebel raid on Castine
last night? He knew nothing about it. But then he had been at sea. Castine?
That was Penobscot Bay! That was the fort protecting the mouth of the
Penobscot River to Bangor!

Butter felt a pull at his back, and he turned. Mrs. Lamont stood right
behind him, with an opened folder at her waist. There was a telegram atop
the papers, and Butter read it quickly in the bad light: "Raid on water
battery at midnight. . . . A raiding party from landside . . . garrison rallied
and pursued. . . . Raiders took to boats and escaped." It was signed by Sam
Cony, the governor of Maine.

General Holt was repeating the details of the raid on Castine as if it was
the most heinous Confederate act since Fort Sumter, and then he recovered
his line of thought to keep on gruffly. "Last week, you asked for proof,

Governor, for proof of our claims. Well, now we offer Castine. All right, it was botched, but they were Rebs! And who is to say how many more there might be waiting to try again? And it fits our theory exactly. What more can we show you? Unless you need to see another St. Albans before you'll believe."

Seward was suddenly stern. "You let me take care of St. Albans." He sounded more irritated than angry. "That's between me and Her Majesty's Government, and I don't need your help. I don't want any of your men in Montreal poking into my affairs. And you tell that to Colonel Baker. The St. Albans raiders are mine to deal with."

Stanton was flapping his hands again, and displayed a temper not even illness could weaken. "Get on to Captain Butter!"

Holt was excited too, and raised his hand toward Butter. "We have Captain Butter now, Governor. This boy's been among them!" Holt turned toward Butter as toward a star witness, and spoke right at Butter's face, though his remarks were for Seward. "He predicted St. Albans. In his initial report in October, he said it was going to happen, and it did. He said who was going to do it—Morgan's men—and he was right!"

Seward replied easily, "Prophecy doesn't make policy. I make policy."

"But it's on!" insisted Holt. "We've definite intelligence now that Jake Thompson's launched his saboteurs. For Election Day! That's our guess! That is Captain Butter's guess!"

"Sir," interrupted Major Turner, stepping up to General Holt, and speaking to him in a supportive manner, "the intelligence report from Toronto, sir."

"Yes, yes!" said Holt, leaning back toward Seward. "There is definite intelligence, Governor. We have Captain Butter, and we also have a report from an informer in Toronto about the Reb plan. We know for certain that there is to be a coordinated raid on New-York, Boston, Buffalo, Cincinnati, Chicago. Every major city." Holt was speaking in short breaths. "It's on! For Election Day! It's on!"

Seward paused to roll his head around and confer with his aides. General Holt's staff and General Fry's staff also took the opportunity to mumble among themselves.

When Seward started again, he sounded paternal. "General, this is interesting news, but General Holt, please, you know what this business is. If I believed every informer who tracked mud into my office in the past month—" Seward hesitated, grinning like a man enjoying his own tall tale before delivering the punch line, and then he finished, "I'd have to believe that Lee was Jesus himself, and that Jeff Davis was having tea tonight with Queen Victoria."

The laughter in the room was sudden and spontaneous, and there was even applause from the State Department clerks.

Butter watched General Holt's reaction, however, and was astounded to see Holt scowl. For the first time, Butter realized that this conference was not like a courtroom at all. This was a battle! That was why the two generals and the two secretaries had surrounded themselves with their staffs. These were warriors of protocol. And they were expert at concealing their advances and retreats with diplomacy. But what Butter now saw, for just a flash, was Holt's fury.

The bloody thanes, thought Butter, the bloody, bloody thanes always stabbing at each other.

Seward was bolstered by the laughter and was not showing mercy. He waved his cigar at Holt. "And your turncoat, this Toronto informer. Did you pay him? How much did it cost the Treasury for your so-called definite intelligence? How much? Tell me."

Holt sagged, and looked to Major Turner. Turner spoke quietly, "He asked for a hundred thousand, but we haven't—"

"A hundred thousand?" said Seward. "You could buy Toronto for that."

The clerks smirked again, and Turner tried, "We didn't pay it yet—"

"This was your surprise, wasn't it, General?" Seward said to Holt. "It's the moment I was supposed to collapse to your demands?" Seward looked toward Stanton, and added, "The crucial moment, eh, Mr. Stanton? The great revelation! Well—I've heard too many recently."

Stanton strained to speak through a dry cough. "Let—the boy—talk."

Holt had quit etiquette; he was ignoring everything but his own temper. He barked at Seward, "They're legions of Copperheads in New-York and Chicago! Traitors everywhere! And the Sons of Liberty are armed! You know this! You know!"

Seward took out his pocket watch and dangled it before his eyes like a pendulum; he said, "You can have a quarter-hour more, General, to tell me what I need to know, and then I'll have done."

Holt said, "It only takes a quarter-minute to set a fire."

"Last night was Halloween," replied Seward. He hauled in his pocket watch and continued, "And there never was a goblin yet that could take away at night what law got for you in the day."

Seward waved his hand at the whole assembly. "We are the law, gentlemen. I understand you are worried about the Reb Secret Service, and what they might do. And so this is what I say. You can post troops along the border, you can dispatch regiments to the cities and companies to the firehouses, you can make whatever show you think necessary in New-York or Chicago or Boston. But—but, until after the Election, you can't arrest anyone, not a Reb spy, not a Reb agent, not a Copperhead madman. Not unless you catch them with a torch in a crib, and then I want you to rescue the baby in that crib and leave that arsonist be."

Seward made them wait while he blew smoke from his cigar. Butter could see that Seward commanded this congregation as a pastor controlled a wedding or a funeral. Seward was at least the second most powerful man in the country, and it was his to say what this meeting meant or did not mean. Seward began again with fatherly certitude, "I have discussed this with the attorney general and I have discussed this with the president. And— I say, Mr. Stanton, the attorney general might have been invited tonight, mightn't he? I say it again, Mr. Stanton, Mr. Bates might have been interested to hear your recommendation to arrest hundreds of our citizens in one sweep."

General Holt exhaled, a cry of rejection, "Ahhhh!"

Seward raised his voice. "There will be no roundups, no raids, no arrests. That is the verdict of this government, and that is my verdict. We've trouble enough in the Northwest without more show trials like in Indianapolis. And in the East, in New York, they're going for McClellan with a clear majority as of tonight. And I'll not have you destroying Mr. Weed's work to catch the president up. No, I'll certainly not have you frightening our greatest state into voting for Little Mac, Seymour, and the fool Democrats! And don't shake Jake Thompson and the Reb Secret Service at me again! I've sufficient bogeymen in town from Mexico and France!"

Seward changed his tone to that of a patriarch instructing his wayward children. "This is Tuesday. One week before the Election. The Election, General, the Election, Mr. Stanton. I know politics and I know elections. Do I truly have to remind you that one of the major charges against this Administration is arbitrary arrests? That Little Mac has been damning us for Fort Lafayette and Fort Warren and Old Capitol? Don't you gentlemen know that daily the Copperhead press reports the number of citizens you have put in jail? And have you also overlooked the newspapers owned by our so-called friends, where they joke about us turning Old Glory into the 'Bars and Bars'?"

One War Department clerk chuckled, but he was instantly silenced by the weighty grumble that emanated from the officers.

Seward waited out the disturbance, and then finished like a man closing a burial vault and walking away. "The Election, gentlemen, that is what we must care about. There will be time for all of our pet projects afterward. Right now, it is the Election that must pertain. And—this must be said— if you try anything so reckless as mass arrests one week before this Election it will be the last thing you try for this Administration. And I don't mean no arrests in the newspapers. I mean no arrests."

General Holt was in retreat to Stanton's side. The remarks about "fool Democrats" and "arbitrary arrests" and "Bars and Bars" had seemed to weaken him; the threat had broken him.

Butter watched the staffs redeploy about their commanders. The battle was not over; this was the pause between bombardments and assaults. And while he studied their tactics, Butter slowly came to understand that the underlying theme of this contest tonight was not security but politics.

Stanton and Holt did serve a Republican Administration, but they were actually veteran Democrats and, worse for them, they were Democrats who had served the failed Buchanan Administration ably but ultimately as failures too.

William H. Seward, on the other hand, was second only to Lincoln as a Republican party savior. More, Seward was not only the prime minister of the country, he was also the premier politician of his party.

Therefore, Seward confronted the War Department tonight as both patriot and partisan. Seward had met Stanton's and Holt's ploys with ploys of his own, and then he had countered with electioneering. For Seward, the rule seemed to be: Threaten my authority and I'll threaten back; but threaten my party, and I'll throttle you.

There was more grumbling from Stanton's corner, and Butter turned to watch a new sally; but this time it would be led by the rhetorically smooth Major Turner. For Major Turner then protected General Holt's reversal by stepping forward with an eloquent reintroduction of the purpose of the meeting, in which Turner repeatedly mentioned "Captain Butter's crucial report."

Meanwhile, Butter retreated several steps from the center of the arena. It was now clear to Butter that he would be the next soldier sent into the fight, and he instinctively sought shelter to prepare himself. At the same time, he was thinking of how right his father had been, and of how cozy the muddy trenches of Virginia seemed to him now, and of how he wished he could unlearn what he knew of the Rebel Secret Service and the Sons of Liberty and the conspiracy against the Union. At the very least, he wished he could forget what he knew of his father's premonition—about the perils of the thanes of *Macbeth*.

In his drift, Butter brushed Mrs. Lamont's hip. She ignored him, because she was seated sideways on the arm of a bench and writing faster in her letterbook than any of the other recording clerks in the room. No faction, especially that of the absent Colonel Baker's, trusted any other with the actual transcript of this engagement.

Butter gripped his own logbook and shrugged off his greatcoat. His blouse was sweated through already, even though the room was not overwarm. Worse, his bowels were rumbling, and he regretted the piece of undercooked chicken that he had grabbed at the Navy Yard. He used his trick from the battlefield and squeezed his rectal muscles while picturing a creek flowing uphill.

The room was noisy with anticipation. Butter heard his name called out. He moved forward and looked from one angry face to another. Butter was intimidated. The combined counterespionage authority of the United States government was about to scrutinize his performance. Nevertheless, he felt that if he could find the slightest sign of support or approval, he could get through this test. He remembered Mrs. Lamont, and looked around. She was not smiling, but then again, she was not unhappy, and she even looked curious.

Butter began his report off-balance. "Well, sirs, I've never done this before, but—"

July, August, and September 1864

Captain Butter's report began with the recounting of the betrayal of one brother by another. In early July 1864, J. Q. Howard, the American consul at the Canadian Bay of Fundy fishing port of St. John's, New Brunswick, was approached by a local Anglican clergyman, the Reverend J. D. Collins. The Reverend Collins said that his younger brother, William Collins, was back in St. John's after three years' service with the Confederate

Army. The Collins brothers were Ulstermen, who had emigrated to Canada as boys, and had since parted ways. What was most crucial was that the Reverend Collins believed that Captain William Collins was not done with the Confederacy, and that he intended some sort of guerrilla raid on Maine's border.

J. Q. Howard immediately telegraphed the State Department in Washington. He was returned instructions by Assistant Secretary of State F. W. Seward (Secretary of State Seward's son) to apprise Maine's governor Samuel Cony at Augusta. The younger Seward passed on the alert to Stanton at the War Department. Telegrams flew back and forth between St. John's, Augusta, and Washington, and then, as the Reverend Collins further updated his information, between Augusta and the Maine lumbertown of Calais, in Washington County, at the border on the St. Croix River.

About midday, on July 18, a trio dressed as rivermen walked up from the St. Croix and into Calais, a dusty boomtown of five thousand, its main street lined with large, well-built wood and brick structures. The trio's destination was the imposing three-story Calais Bank in the middle of North Street. One of the men—tall, red-bearded, and quick—walked up to the bank's cashier, J. J. Lee, and asked to exchange gold pieces for greenbacks. When Lee saw the man reach for a revolver, he gave the alarm. Maine State Guardsmen were in hiding throughout the town and around the building, because J. Q. Howard's telegram that morning had warned of a raiding party on the river headed for this bank. There was screaming, but no shots were fired. The State Guardsmen arrested the trio and dragged them to the municipal court next door. The trio's leader said that he was Captain William Collins of the Fifteenth Mississippi Infantry, C.S.A.; he was found to have on him a new Confederate flag. The second man was Kevin Phillips, a simpleton who was Collins's bodyguard. The third and youngest raider was Francis Jones, of St. Louis. Each man was indicted for attempted bank robbery, and held on twenty thousand dollars bail.

That night, Calais overflowed with lumbermen come to volunteer to patrol the border and also to demand these captured raiders be hanged immediately. The sheriff of Washington County, Henry Brown, arrived in time to engineer a surreptitious transfer of the three prisoners from Calais to his jail at the county seat, Machias, a fishing port fifty miles by road south on the Atlantic.

After a few days, the prisoner Francis Jones wrote his mother in St. Louis. Sheriff Brown routinely opened his prisoners' correspondence, and was stunned to find in the letter that Jones had told his mother that, though he was in jail for bank robbery, he was not a bandit. Rather, Jones wrote, he and his two comrades had been "acting under the express orders of President Davis."

Henry Brown consulted with his brother-in-law, the Machias town attorney, and then tried rudimentary counterespionage. He befriended Jones by playing chess with him. One night, in late July, Jones began weeping for his ruin and burst out his confession.

Francis Jones said that he had been a courier for the Confederate secretary of war James A. Seddon for over a year. He said that, for Seddon, he had contacted every important anti-Union provocateur in the North, many of whom were leaders in the underground army of Copperheads known as the Sons of Liberty.

Jones also said that he had been sent to Toronto the spring before in order to serve the recently posted Confederate commissioners to Canada, particularly Jacob P. Thompson, who was actually a chief of the Confederate Secret Service.

In May, Jones continued, he had learned the full extent of a Confederate conspiracy to fracture the Union, including guerrilla raids on Northern cities, the assassinations of officials, and the armed uprising of the Sons of Liberty.

Jones told Henry Brown that he had balked at the fiendishness of the conspiracy, because he was being bombarded by letters from his mother begging him to return to the Union cause. Jones said that he had even written War Secretary Stanton in Washington, asking to be permitted to take the oath of allegiance that meant a Confederate soldier would be forgiven his rebellion. In return, Jones had received a letter from Assistant War Secretary Charles Dana refusing his request.

By that time it was June, Jones said, and the Confederate Secret Service agents in Toronto had surmised his wavering. He was punished by being posted to St. John's. There, Jones had come under the command of Captain William Collins, who had been assigned as a leader in a wing of the conspiracy.

The master plan, Jones declared, included a component that called for Collins and a volunteer band of scouts from St. John's to rendezvous with as many as five thousand guerrillas who were to be transported to the coast of Maine by the Confederate warships C.S.S. *Tallahassee, Florida,* and *Alabama.* The guerrillas were then to have divided into three columns to scorch

Maine, supported by naval bombardments.

Henry Brown asked what part the bank robbery was to have played in the plot. Jones replied that the robbery had been Collins's idea, to finance his scouts and himself while they waited for the signal from Toronto that would mean the guerrilla attack was imminent.

Henry Brown asked for the date of the attack. Jones replied that the date had been set and reset so many times, no one knew for sure when it might be. Sooner rather than later, perhaps, said Jones, or maybe later now that Collins was captured.

Henry Brown was flabbergasted. He left Jones still crying, and scribbled down the confession as best he could remember. Brown then made sure that Jones was safe from reprisals by William Collins. Finally, Brown wrote Secretary of State Seward.

In mid-August, Assistant-Judge-Advocate-General Major Levi Turner arrived at Henry Brown's house in Machias. That night, Major Turner interviewed Francis Jones, and Jones reiterated his earlier confession. Turner, an experienced attorney, pressed Jones for more details. In response, Jones provided two more astonishing claims. Jones said that, in April, Confederate Navy Secretary Stephen Mallory had sent 150 seamen through the blockade to Halifax. The seamen had then traveled to Toronto to await their part in the raid on Maine, for they were to man the warships after the guerrillas were put ashore. Included in the Navy detachment, Jones said, had been several topographers, who had then been infiltrated into Maine to survey the seacoast for safe, hidden anchorages for the warships.

Major Turner was unimpressed; it all sounded too fanciful. Yet Jones's second claim jolted even Turner. Jones said that the naval raid on Maine was to be coordinated with another naval raid, this one on Lake Erie, where Confederate raiders were set to commandeer the only Union gunboat on the Great Lakes, the steam frigate U.S.S. *Michigan,* and to use it first to free the thousands of prisoners of war at Johnson's Island, and then to shell the major cities along the lake.

At the evening's end, however, Major Turner remained more suspicious than alarmed. After all, he knew that Jones was a self-condemned criminal, who needed mercy regardless of how many lies it took to purchase. Also, it was the middle of August, and no piece of this plot had surfaced.

But then again, Major Turner told Sheriff Brown after Jones had been led away, what if the boy was telling even half-truths?

Major Turner left Machias the next day by stagecoach to the railroad head at Bangor. Before he departed for Washington, he planned to call upon a young officer whose name he had been given by Colonel Lafayette Baker —Captain Amaziah Butter.

It so happened that Butter was not only the son of a prominent Maine Republican, but he was also the grandson of a legendary lawman and United States Marshal in Maine, A. A. "Black Bear" Butter. This latter fact, learned accidentally by Lafayette Baker (one night in the fall of 1863 when Butter had arrested a gang of horse thieves at the Cavalry Depot), had very much pleased Baker, a legendary member of the San Francisco Vigilantes in the 1850s.

Turner did not care about reputations; he needed an investigator who knew Maine and the Canadian frontier well enough to substantiate or disprove Jones's claims. Unfortunately, Butter was just home from hospital to convalesce, and he was unfit for anything more than getting out of bed. Regardless, Turner spent the evening with Captain Butter, and dined with Butter, his wife Desire, and Captain Butter's mother and father.

What Turner told the Butters went beyond Jones's confession, because Turner understood the political peril if there actually was such a Confederate conspiracy. Lincoln's reelection, Turner said, was in jeopardy. In June, Lincoln had been renominated at Baltimore as the Republican candidate, but he had suffered severe political setbacks ever since.

Most damaging was the criticism of three powerful New York Republicans who had helped elect Lincoln in 1860: Henry Raymond, the owner-editor of the *New-York Times;* Horace Greeley, the owner-editor of the *New-York Tribune,* and Thurlow Weed, the Republican party boss in New York and Secretary of State Seward's longtime confidant. Each of the three had proposed or attempted indelicate peace negotiations with the Confederate government over the summer out of a fear of Lincoln's defeat unless the war was stopped. These maneuvers had inadvertently contributed to the Cabinet's and the electorate's failing confidence in Lincoln.

Worse, the Democratic party—crippled since 1860 because of its associations with the Secessionists—had recovered much of its prestige by the patriotic endeavors of its largest faction, the so-called War Democracy. And now, in August, with Grant's armies sweltering at Richmond and Petersburg, with Sherman's army stalled outside of Atlanta, and with the Shenandoah Valley again become a launching zone for terrifying Confederate cavalry raids, the Democrats had hopes that they could regain the presidency by offering the citizens what they wanted: peace. After having failed to enlist

Ulysses S. Grant, the Democrats were set to meet in convention at Chicago the last week of August, when both factions of the party—War Democracy and Peace Democracy—intended to nominate a candidate of irreproachable loyalty who could promise to stop the slaughter, negotiate a peace, and rally all. Their candidate, Turner predicted firmly, would be 38-year-old Major-General George B. McClellan of New Jersey, twice dismissed by Lincoln from command of the Army of the Potomac for failing to carry the attack against Richmond.

In sum, Turner explained to the Butters, the Union was more politically fragile than ever before, and also more vulnerable to sabotage. A spark in Republican Maine could become a fire in ambivalent New York that could then become a conflagration in the Northwest, where the Copperheads had always been strong, and where Unionism was said to be made of tinder. It was not an exaggeration, said Turner, to worry that the fate of the Union was again, despite the North's overwhelming military might, in the balance. The Rebels could still gain a qualified victory, and Confederate independence, simply by not capitulating on the battlefield while Lincoln lost at the polls. Turner concluded with the confidence that Abraham Lincoln was said to be isolated and depressed at the White House.

Yet Lincoln could have been no grimmer than Major Turner as he left Bangor and entrained to Washington City to make his report and to display Francis Jones's twelve-page and completely unverified confession at the War Department, where, on August 22, a week before the Democratic Convention, the accepted opinion was that only a miracle—the direct intervention of Divine Providence—could save Lincoln and the Republican party and preserve the Union as it once had been.

Within the next month, not one but three miracles halted Lincoln's political collapse and buoyed the Republican party. And they were Napoleonic miracles, for, as Bonaparte had said, "Providence is always on the side of the heaviest battalions."

First, in mid-August, even as Major Turner had sat with the Butters, there was the beginning of a break in the continent-wide military stalemate. Horace Greeley's *New-York Tribune* announced, "GREAT NEWS FROM MOBILE —Details of Farragut's Victory—Capture of Rebel Ships and Forts—A Severe Blow to the Enemy." And there was a full-page map of the naval battle at the Confederate forts outside Mobile Bay, along with the report that Admiral David G. Farragut and his fleet pilot had lashed themselves high atop the mast of the flagship U.S.S. *Hartford* in order to direct *Hartford* to sail under enemy guns and trade shot and grape until the Confederates struck their colors and Mobile was out of the war as a Confederate supply port.

Then, on the first weekend in September, the nation was amazed as Horace Greeley's *Tribune* announced, "GLORIOUS NEWS—Capture of Atlanta—Our Troops Enter the Town on Friday Morning—Official Confirmation— Dispatches from Secretary Stanton—A Great Battle at Eastpoint—Rebel Army Cut in Two—Gen. Hardee Killed—Rebels Suffer Terrible Loss— Our 18th Corps Holds Atlanta." And there was the correcting official report from Major-General William T. Sherman, "Hood, at Atlanta, finding me on his road, the only one that could supply him, and between him and a considerable part of his army, blew up his magazines in Atlanta, and left in the nighttime, when the 20th Corps of Gen. Slocum took possession of the place. So Atlanta is ours, and fairly won."

The joy and relief in the North were unabated for two weeks. Lincoln hopefully proclaimed that on Sunday, September 11, "[T]hanksgiving be offered Him for His mercy in preserving our national existence against the insurgent rebels . . . and for blessing and comfort from the Father of Mercies to the sick, wounded, and prisoners, and the orphans and widows of those who have fallen in the service of their country, and that He will continue to uphold the Government of the United States against all the efforts of public enemies and secret foes."

And then, on the first day of fall, yet another triumph for Lincoln arrived from the Shenandoah Valley, as Horace Greeley's *Tribune* announced, "A GLORIOUS VICTORY—Sheridan Defeats Early—Fierce and Decisive Battle— Several Rebel Generals Killed—5000 Rebels Killed and Wounded—2500 Prisoners Captured—The Enemy Driven Beyond Winchester—They Leave All Their Dead Behind—Gallant Behavior of Our Troops—Rejoicing Over the Good News." Major-General Philip H. "Little Phil" Sheridan, commanding the Cavalry Corps of the Army of the Potomac, and Grant's right-hand man, dispatched his typically succinct appraisal, "I am tonight (11:30 P.M., Sept. 22) pushing down the Valley. The victory was very complete."

In the meantime, Major Turner's report on Francis Jones had become part of the War Department's larger but similarly sketchy intelligence about Confederate and Copperhead intrigues in the North. Stanton pounded his agents and provost-marshals to bring him better information, and for results.

In mid-September, there were several arrests of alleged traitors in the Northwest, particularly in Indiana, where large caches of arms were discovered along with a hint of a failed or delayed plot by the secret army of the Sons of Liberty to burn the statehouse.

Also in the Northwest, Federal agents gained rumors about a Confederate Secret Service plot to facilitate mass escapes from the prisoner-of-war camps in Ohio and Illinois in order to launch the prisoners on a pillage raid against Columbus and Chicago. More, in St. Louis there were incendiary attacks on transport riverboats by Confederate raiders; Federal agents pursued the saboteurs across the Northwest without catching them.

And most spectacularly—and most menacingly for Major Turner's report —on September 20 Federal agents accidentally and at the last moment thwarted a plot by Rebel raiders out of Canada to commandeer the only warship on the Great Lakes, the U.S.S. *Michigan* on Lake Erie.

In late September, then, Stanton paused to look more closely at Francis Jones's confession. Stanton had found no satisfaction so far in the haphazard and piecemeal Federal defenses against the Confederate and Copperhead schemes. He needed to develop an overall strategy, and for that he needed to be able to anticipate where the saboteurs, provocateurs, and traitors would strike next.

But how much of what Francis Jones had said was fantasy? How many of the secret plots, the acts of sabotage, and the rumors of impending raids that had emerged in September were just random dissent and treachery? And how many of them were part of this alleged Confederate Secret Service conspiracy organized in Canada?

Stanton called in his counterespionage chiefs—Major-General Holt, Major-General Fry, Colonel Baker—and demanded answers. Stanton fumed that no one had yet exploited Francis Jones, the single crack in the Rebel Secret Service. And he said that he could no longer ignore the fact that Maine's governor Sam Cony and Maine's provost-marshal-general were not competent to conduct counterintelligence in Maine, New Brunswick, and the Maritimes.

It was at this point that Lafayette Baker came forward to resubmit the name of Captain Amaziah Butter. Lafayette Baker said that Butter was the man for the job of investigating Francis Jones—because he was already familiar with the matter, because he knew the border, because he knew the Secret Service, and because he was as stubborn as the Union.

Stanton approved immediately. That evening, September 28, a lengthy telegram went out of 217 Pennsylvania Avenue from Lafayette Baker to Amaziah Butter in Bangor. Butter's assignment was to find the truth, and quickly.

October 1864

Amaziah Butter, on his feet again, had been assigned to the assistant-provost-marshal's office in Bangor, and therefore was in a position to know that the state provost-marshal-general's office in Augusta had been stumbling in its attempt to explore Francis Jones's confession.

On Friday morning, September 29, Butter boarded the stagecoach at Bangor for the hundred-mile trip to Calais on the trail called the Airline —because it was the as-the-crow-flies route through Maine's rolling forest to the Canadian frontier. Three days later, in Calais, Butter had completed his interviews with Sheriff Brown, and his interrogation of Francis Jones, who had been brought back to Calais to stand trial.

Butter immediately sailed for St. John's on a schooner provided by Governor Cony in order to visit with State Department Consul J. Q. Howard. At Howard's direction, Butter sailed again for Halifax, the major Atlantic port of Nova Scotia, where the European steamers called, and also where the Confederate blockade runners routinely traded their cargo and deposited their passengers.

Butter made a breakthrough at Halifax, aided by informants in State Department hire. Butter was able to locate a confectionery shop on the waterfront where, it was said, suspicious gentlemen had boarded in the spare room in July. The shopkeeper's daughter, Sally O'Hare, said that the July tenants had filled their room with maps. She showed Butter a charcoal portrait of herself that one of the boarders had drawn and presented to her upon his departure. On its reverse was a quick sketch of a shoreline that Butter instantly recognized as Maine's Penobscot Bay from Deer Isle to the mouth of the Penobscot River. The sketch also had depth markings.

Butter then began an arduous sailing expedition south along Maine's wind-whipped coast. He touched at Lubec and Jonesport in Washington County, at several points on Mt. Desert Island in Hancock County, and then all along Penobscot Bay from Stonington to Castine to Belfast and up to Bucksport, before returning up river to Bangor in mid-October.

Butter was exhausted, and there was numbness in his feet and hands, but he gathered himself to write his report to the War Department. He opened with a succinct response to Lafayette Baker. The truth of it was that there had been a Confederate Secret Service plot to invade Maine from the sea.

During May and June, Butter wrote, Maine fishermen had spied strangers walking along the seacoast. They were distinguished for carrying easels and other artist's paraphernalia. When challenged, they had said they were watercolorists. Butter opined that they were actually Confederate Navy topographers.

In mid-September, Butter wrote, fishermen out of Northeast Harbor on Mt. Desert Island had spotted a ship that they called ghost-like. It was painted gray, with its smokestacks tipped back to lower its profile. When questioned by Butter in October, one old salt had not hesitated to identify the sighting, *"Tallahassee,* boy, every soul knows. I seen her at Halifax too—*Tallahassee,* sure." Butter added that C.S.S. *Tallahassee* was the only one of the three warships named by Francis Jones that was not now captured or sunk by the U.S. Navy.

Butter's written report also included re-creations of his interrogation of Francis Jones at Calais. Butter's conversation with Jones had been difficult, for Jones had grown increasingly depressed since his August confession to Major Turner. Jones had been so intractable that he had not wanted to reconfirm many of the details he had already enumerated. Nevertheless, Butter had been able to push Jones into an important slip.

Butter had asked, "What sort of men would volunteer for a raid on Maine?"

Jones had replied, "They were to be well paid in plunder."

Butter had replied, "Well paid in rope, you mean—a raid without hope of resupply or escape?"

And Jones had boasted, "That wouldn't bother Mosby's or Morgan's buckos."

Francis Jones's mention of Mosby had connected for Butter with Sally O'Hare's statement in Halifax that her admirer had been a Virginian, who had wooed her with stories of moonlit rides along the Potomac River with a great cavalier on a gray charger. She could not name the cavalier. But Butter knew that horse, because he had chased it on too many moonlit nights —Lieutenant-Colonel John Mosby's stallion.

More tellingly still, Jones had bragged to Butter of the daring of the Confederate soldiers in Toronto. Jones had said that they were kept in high style by the enormous war chest of the Confederate Secret Service—over half a million dollars from the sale of a blockade runner's cotton at Halifax.

When encouraged by Butter, Jones had spoken adoringly of one particular

Confederate Secret Service agent, Captain Thomas B. Hines of Kentucky. Tom Hines had been one of John Hunt Morgan's greatest guerrilla fighters. Tom Hines had become a so-called master agent for the Secret Service chief in Canada, Jake Thompson. Jones had also said that he had rendezvoused with Tom Hines many times throughout Canada, the Northwest, and the East. Jones had described Tom Hines as aloof, soft-spoken, well educated, and deadly. And Jones had said that the reason Tom Hines was so openly worshipped was that the predominant company of men in Secret Service hire in Toronto were veterans of Morgan's Kentucky Raiders.

Butter had tried, "But John Morgan is dead. Why are they in Canada?"

Jones had replied, "Because they want to fight. Because they want revenge."

"Revenge for what?" Butter had asked.

And Jones had shrugged. "For Morgan bein' shot in the back, I suppose. And for the South, yes, for the South bein' back-shot, too."

And without further explanation, despite Butter's badgering, Jones had declared that Tom Hines was the mastermind of something called the "Northwest Conspiracy."

Butter closed his written report with speculative conclusions and recommendations. It was not his to set policy, he knew, but the logic of his investigation propelled him, and so did his pride of service.

Butter argued that even if the Confederate plot to invade Maine from the sea with Mosby's and Morgan's guerrillas, and to bombard Maine from warships, was now discouraged or delayed, the nucleus of the plotters remained in place in Canada.

Butter argued that the planned raid against Maine was only part of a greater plot against several parts of the North, in particular against the Northwest, and that the Confederate failure in Maine did not mean that the master plan was not proceeding.

And Butter argued that neither Maine nor the Union would be truly secure from attack from Canada until master agents like Tom Hines were captured.

Butter ended his written report with his most far-reaching speculation, "The most inviting date for a coordinated attack by Rebel agents from Canada was August 29–31, during the Democratic Convention at Chicago. That was called off for unknown reasons. Tom Hines and his men—Morgan's—could now be looking to launch their attack on Election Day, November 8."

With this, Butter regarded his work done, and he rose early on October

18 to ride down Bangor's State Street to post his report with the first train south. He was in such a good mood that he paused to pull it out and add a postscript. He was thinking of his comrade, Major Tory Wetherbee, who had always said while they were chasing Mosby in Virginia, "Remember, Zee, they are us, so think what you'd do with us chasin' you."

Butter therefore wrote below his signature, "The Rebs in Canada are not crazed. They are most dangerous. Because if I were them, I'd be dangerous too." And then he sealed his report and mailed it.

It was fate that the next day, October 19, four Confederate veterans of Morgan's Raiders brought their chargers in line at the north end of Main Street in St. Albans, Vermont, a flourishing town of three thousand located about fifteen miles from the Canadian border. Down the road, on the steps of the American House, Lieutenant Bennett Young unfurled a new Confederate flag and waved a pistol over the bystanders, booming, "This town is now in the possession of the Confederate States of America."

And so began the most sensational Confederate raid in New-England to date, resulting in a bank robbery of more than $150,000 in cash and gold, the murder of one man, the theft of a dozen horses, and the firing of the town center with the use of a chemical solution called "Greek Fire." The guerrillas were pursued by Vermonters into Canada, and were eventually arrested by the British military. By then, however, Vermont was hysterical, and Governor J. Gregory Smith (a St. Albans resident) and the whole state legislature was ready to recess to take to arms and sail Lake Champlain for the border.

The telegraph lines on the evening of the 19th, and the newspaper headlines for the next week, were heavy with the shock of the vulnerability of the United States to Canadian-based Rebels. There were renewed calls for Secretary Seward's old chestnut, the invasion and annexation of Canada; there were also renewed calls for Secretary Stanton's old acorn, a war with Great Britain. Both public outcries were exacerbated by the fact that the Montreal constabulary, who finally took the guerrillas into custody to stand trial, not only refused to give them over to Vermont, but also kept hold of the stolen money as evidence.

Within the same week, the War Department digested Captain Butter's written report. Stanton and his chiefs had heard the name Tom Hines before. And large amounts of bribe money had purchased inexact rumors of this so-called Northwest Conspiracy. Yet Butter's report provided alarming evidence and frightening suppositions. Butter was the first to make a persuasive case for a continent-wide conspiracy authored in Canada and executed by men like Morgan's Raiders, which could well mean that the incident in Maine was linked to the incidents in Indiana, St. Louis, Lake Erie, and St. Albans. The earlier episodes might have come to nothing much; St. Albans was a staggering civil and political catastrophe. And, from what Butter had uncovered, there was now reason to believe that St. Albans was only the beginning of what the Rebels in Canada might try. Stanton knew that he must penetrate and shatter the Confederate Secret Service at Toronto and Montreal. And that he must do it now.

In preparation, Stanton took three actions. He ordered the purchase of a Rebel turncoat in Toronto, someone with access to Jake Thompson, no matter the cost. He ordered the drawing up of a list of names for a mass arrest of Copperhead and Confederate agents inside and outside the country. And he ordered Lafayette Baker to fetch the prescient Captain Butter to Washington.

For his part, Butter went cold when he read of St. Albans in the newspaper. Morgan's Raiders were afield and aflame. And Butter was revealed as the spookily prophetic bearer of bad tidings. He had thought himself out of the war at least until the spring. Now, he could see the worst ahead again. He told his wife, Desire, that he was going up to his father's lumber camp for a rest. For her part, Desire Drummond Butter, black-haired and rangy —a horsewoman, a sailor, and a shot—the eldest daughter of a wealthy Bangor shipowner—was furious for Butter's endless volunteering. She had put him back together after his wounding at Shepardstown in the summer of 1863, only to have him turn to duty in the newly formed First D.C.; then she had put him back together again the summer before, after the First D.C. had proved even more reckless than the First Maine. Then she had reluctantly agreed to his remaining in the Army after his three-year service had expired in October, only because he had promised he would only serve as an acting-assistant-provost-marshal in Bangor.

Desire read Lafayette Baker's telegram ordering Butter to Washington, and then she burned it. The next day, she barred the door to an adjutant who had come to inquire why Butter had not reported in. That night, she met the Bangor assistant-provost-marshal with a shotgun, "Get away, devilish man, and know I'll speak with buckshot tomorrow! He's served his time in your hell, and I'll be damned if he goes again!"

Butter could not be shielded indefinitely. When he returned from the lumber camp the next day, Desire refused to let him in and cursed him from the window. "You liar! It's not Washington! You're going back to the Jerusalem Turnpike, and make me a widow and my babies fatherless!"

And the next day, October 29, Butter awakened in his father's home to find Chip Butter opening the window on a rainy day, and standing by with a new telegram from Lafayette Baker that had been sent via the governor for hand delivery to Amaziah Butter.

LATER TUESDAY EVENING, NOVEMBER 1

Captain Butter's report (excluding all the personal details) exhausted Secretary Seward's allotted quarter-hour, and three-quarters of an hour more as well. Butter closed his monologue as off-balance as he had begun, looking up from his logbook and mumbling, "I got here as soon as I could."

Butter stood like a watchtower in a room now so dense with smoke that it looked to him like the battle of Fredericksburg. The cigar fumes swept from Seward's side of the room and collided with the cigar fumes from Stanton's side of the room. Men were coughing and clearing their throats like the loading of muskets and cannons. There was also movement in the room as staffmen and clerks slapped their boots on the wood floor and shifted their bodies over creaking benches. Then there was an advance from the right, and Butter readied himself.

General Holt reached Butter's side and took hold of his arm; Holt said, "Fine, son, fine." Holt pulled Butter toward Stanton's corner. Holt asked Stanton, "Was there more the Captain hasn't covered?"

Stanton was bent forward in his wheelchair; he said, "The Election."

"Yes!" responded Holt, turning Butter toward Seward. "Election Day, Governor," continued Holt, "now you understand. We don't have a week to wait. They will strike Election Day, and we must strike first!"

Suddenly Seward was on his feet and moving toward Butter, holding his cigar before him like a saber. Seward was more than a head shorter than General Holt, who was himself not Butter's height or breadth. Seward stood before Butter without looking up, and gestured toward the logbook in Butter's hand. "The Northwest Conspiracy, that's what you call it?"

"Sir," said Butter, "it's what Francis Jones called it."

Holt contributed, "We think it's a major part of their plan, meant to provoke insurrection in Illinois, Indiana, and Ohio."

Seward held up his hand. "Morgan's men, eh, General? Rascally Kentuckians?"

Holt, the Kentuckian, gagged at Seward's implied insult.

Seward was smiling, and addressed Butter's logbook again. "And the what? The New-England Conspiracy or some such? That was the attack on Maine?"

"Sir, I believe so, sir," said Butter. "They meant to rob and burn from Bangor to Portland."

"It is incredible," said Seward. "Even for them, incredible."

Butter said, "I wouldn't have believed it if I hadn't found it, sir."

"And you say the overall conspiracy is still in motion?" asked Seward. "The Sons of Liberty uprisings in the cities, the breakouts at the prisoner-of-war camps, the incendiary attacks? That Jake Thompson still aims to do this?"

"I can't speak about him, sir," said Butter. "I do believe that this Captain Tom Hines, and guerrillas like him, that they're capable of almost anything, and coming on."

"The devil with Tom Hines and John Morgan!" flared Seward. Seward finally looked up into Butter's face, and he posed his next question deliberately, speaking as if for the recording clerks. "What I want to know—is it your opinion that Rebel guerrillas and Copperhead bushwhackers plan to attack New-York and Chicago and Boston on Election Day, like they did at St. Albans?"

Butter glanced at Holt, and at Major Turner standing behind his chief. They looked dejected. In the corner, Stanton had his head in his hands. Butter turned back to Seward and sighed. "Yes, sir."

Seward asked, "Why do you believe this?"

"Why?" Butter was confused. "Why do—?" Butter tried to recover, and to sound authoritative. "Because I know guerrillas and that they're dangerous. Because that's when we'll be the most vulnerable, and that's what I would try if I was as far down as them. Because I believe it, sir."

"Can you prove it?" asked Seward.

Butter saw the trap but went ahead anyway. "No, sir, but how could anyone until after the Rebs attack?"

"Can you prove it, Captain!" roared Seward.

Butter conceded, "No, sir."

Seward smiled. "It's a guess, a blizzard-coming-tonight guess?"

Butter was unsure of how to respond, and grunted.

"Governor," attempted Holt again, "this isn't electioneering, I swear. You know Jake Thompson's capable of this. You know Jeff Davis would burn the White House if he could. And we have a report tonight—from our source in Toronto—that a gang of saboteurs has crossed the border at Niagara Falls, heading for New-York."

Seward held up his hand again, and said, "More of your Kentuckians, I suppose?" Holt sputtered. Seward put his cigar in his mouth, and talked around it. "I've listened to the last of your surprises tonight. Niagara Falls, you say? Why not Detroit, or Rouse's Point too? Why not the Armada off Baltimore? For a hundred thousand dollars, I should think your turncoat in Toronto could use imagination."

General Holt sputtered the more. Major Turner folded up a sheet in his hand and put it away.

Seward stepped back and used an orator's grace to extend his arm toward Stanton. "I've given you my time and ear. Nothing I've heard from Captain Butter proves a thing, or alters my opinion. Your task is to protect the Union, not arrest it. Post your troops, alert your departments, deploy your agents, sleep under the beds of these Sons of Liberty if you like—but no arrests. I want you to carry on, like this boy here carried on, vigilantly and quietly against our public enemies and secret foes. Most of all, quietly."

"Damn it!" cried General Holt; but as soon as he began, he stopped, because he could see Stanton shaking his head.

Seward ignored the outburst and turned away slowly. An aide had Seward's coat ready, and the State Department clerks were ready to go. But Seward froze everyone for a moment when he leaned back, and said, "There is something I want different."

Seward nodded at Butter's bulk like a man picking out a fir tree. "The way to preserve this blessed Union is to put good Republican boys between us and the damned Rebs. So I want Captain Butter in New-York City."

Provost-Marshal-General Fry spoke up. "I expect Colonel Baker will make the assignments for New-York."

"You tell Colonel Baker, when you find him," said Seward, who was sure enough of his victory now to skip toward his coat, "that Captain Butter is too good an officer to do anything less than help protect our greatest city."

General Fry responded submissively, "Yes, sir, New-York, sir."

Butter was caught unaware, because he was still mulling over Seward's questions about why he believed the Rebs were coming on. And when he did realize what fate Seward had assigned him, it was too late to protest. And yet he must. But the time was not right. He would resist later. He would— Butter sighed. New-York? He turned to find Mrs. Lamont, and shrugged at her. He wanted to communicate how foolish it was to send a woodsman and horse soldier to New-York. He wanted her to smile in agreement. Instead, she looked at him as if he were a tree trunk on its way downriver. Then he knew—he was going to New-York.

CHAPTER 3

John Oliphant
at New-York, New York

FRIDAY MORNING, NOVEMBER 4

In the bedroom of a third-floor parlor suite of the Astor House, John Oliphant awoke from a confused dream to the smell of peaches and lemons, and something else very sweet. He felt a cool hand at his neck and thought, perfume. He opened his eyes to see dark-blond ringlets, a kind smile and large eyes, and also a tall-crowned hat with a white plume. He said, "Dorothea."

"Good morning, darling, are you happy to see me?" Mrs. Dorothea Longuemare leaned closer, rustling her crinolines; and just when she could have bitten him, she kissed him, and said, "You've been in town since Tuesday, I understand, but not a word to me."

Oliphant rolled away from her and reached for his pocket watch on the side table. It was 6:40 A.M., just past dawn. He pushed himself up and worked his jaw to check his injured tooth. There was no pain, the new gold filling firmly in place. He said, "I've been hard-pressed, Dorothea." Then, because he thought it was gentler, he added, "I've been too hard-pressed."

"John, John, when aren't you?" She stood back, her arms on her hips, to display herself. She was expensively dressed in several shades of turquoise, her paletot open wide to reveal the pinkish flower patterns on her dress. She said, "You're most unoccupied, now, and— Would you like some soothing companionship?"

Oliphant did not have a good answer. He pulled on his robe without disturbing the bedcovers and then eased out of bed on the opposite side from her. He walked to the window to part the drapes, slip the latch, and pry open the sash on an effervescently lucid morning, smelling of the onshore breeze and horses and the breakfast cooking fires in evidence by the twisted columns of ash from chimney pipes across the varied urban landscape to the east. Oliphant shook himself awake, and tried to orient himself with the view as a ship's captain might find his bearings by studying the distant profile of a landfall. Three stories below Oliphant was the frenzied panorama of the very heart of New-York, the triangular junction formed where Broadway met Park Row and Vesey and Ann streets, a grand crossroad that fit roughly at the apex of the much larger and sylvan triangle of City Hall Park, at the base of which was the ersatz Hôtel de Ville of City Hall, its clock tower peaked with a statue of Justice.

Dorothea came up beside him and shut the drapes. "Don't forget me, dear one. We can pretend we're just in from a daybreak drive after a night of ball-dancing, and we are in need of some fun before we sleep." She laughed. "You said you preferred the dawn, and I know I do with you."

Oliphant reopened the drapes partway. This was his choicest moment of the day, and this was one of his choicest spots to enjoy it from. He could hear the clatter of the carriages, the bellowing of the horsecar drivers, the cries of frantic pedestrians, the bells from the church towers at the quarter-hour, and the near distant sounds of the harbor with its ship's whistles and horns announcing arrival at or departure from the largest city in the New World and also, in Oliphant's opinion, the greatest city of the world's future. Oliphant felt suddenly better for the sensations of New-York. He worked his jaw again, cleared phlegm from his throat, and tried, "I've thought of you, Dorothea, I can't pretend that I haven't thought of you."

"Charmed," she said. "I thought I'd be cross with you, but now, how can I? The most charming Yankee. My Yankee." She placed the back of her hand on his cheek and leaned to kiss his neck. She whispered, "Make love to me, John, and make all that disappear."

Oliphant sighed. "I'm hardly awake." He relaxed a moment, and it was enough for her to insert herself in his embrace and tempt him to kiss her.

She was rough, and he responded. She tasted of peaches too, and her lips were extremely warm, and as moist as ripe fruit. When he attempted to break the embrace, she simultaneously began pulling at his gown with one hand and opening her collar buttons with the other to reveal her white, flushed neck. Oliphant backed away to recover, but she had his hand now, and put it against her breast. He felt her smooth skin and then snapped back his hand. He turned against the window frame and ducked his head outside as if nothing had happened. He asked, "Have you brought me the newspapers?"

He heard her make a small sound of irritation, and he started again, "I wonder what they're going on about today?" He nodded out, across the park wood to the wide clearing where Park Row met Nassau Street to form the so-called Newspaper Row on Publishing Square: five- and six-story brick and masonry fortresses of journalism among which were the buildings of the powerful *New-York Times* and *New-York Tribune*.

Dorothea finally spoke, but from well behind him; she said, "The news is that Dorothea is not to be resisted and that Grant is drinking and Lee is preparing for sainthood and Lincoln is constipated and Jeff Davis would be if he weren't made of wood and Dorothea is not to be teased or disappointed. No later direct news."

Oliphant turned around to find her at his bed. Her paletot was on the post and her dress was down to her ankles, with her crinolines and petticoat soon to follow. She was splendidly voluptuous, slim-shouldered, and long-waisted. She was also a Virginia beauty with a less than happy history. At 30, she had one dead husband, and two small children staying with her mother in Lynchburg; more, she had a new husband who adored her but whom she had married only to spite her widowhood and whom she tolerated only for his status. Mrs. Dorothea Longuemare was married to the major Confederate Secret Service agent in New-York.

Watching her undress, Oliphant felt outmaneuvered and yet blamed himself. This was his fault, for a weakness that had shown itself the previous Christmas when he had been alone in New-York and despairing for human company. Dorothea had been more than that, a genuinely forceful lover and, by turns, an inspired coquette. Oliphant knew it was unfair to criticize her. She was as undone by the war as everyone else; and if she could find pleasure anywhere, it was a victory to be possessed selfishly.

Oliphant also felt that, if he made love to Dorothea, he would despise himself. He stepped to the bed. She had paused at the removing of her petticoat in order to gain some acknowledgment from him that he wanted this, and her, too. He looked down at her, and said softly, "Dorothea, it isn't you. I can't. I'm not right."

Dorothea countered sharply, "Narcissa, Narcissa, Narcissa, that's your trouble, John! And she's over there in England and I'm here—that should be testimony enough!" She reached up, letting the petticoat slip down, and whispered, "Please?"

He said, "I can't. I must go."

She said, "We'll be quick. But not too quick."

He touched her hat. She laughed for forgetting to remove it, and then threw out her hands and left it. Her coo toppled him, and he let himself fall against her and then atop her. She was hotter than the Sea Islands in August, and also as salty, a thick liquid on her lips that arose from her desire and ruled him like a potion. She did soothe him with her cool hands. She did make him uncoil with shudders. She did hurt him when she bit. And she did have more power in her hips, legs, and arms than he might ever have again. Yet when she screamed at him, and demanded that he tell her she was wonderful, he could not, though he kept on, and pushed into her tender wetness and simple passion, pitying himself, pitying her, and feeling humiliated for the unadorned fact that this was wonderful, and terrible.

Within half an hour, Oliphant was finishing his dressing when there was a knock at the outside door. He paused at the wardrobe to consider Dorothea still buried under the bedcovers, and said, "It's the boy with my papers and coffee."

She peeked out, yawning, "Send him away and come back."

Oliphant finished his cuff links, pulled on his high-buttoned waistcoat, and grabbed his morning coat. "I'm away, Dorothea, it's after seven." He closed the bedroom door behind him. The suite consisted of a bedroom, a long parlor with elegant cherrywood furniture, and an entry vestibule. It was Oliphant's favorite suite in the Astor House, and he knew it like a home. He stopped at the small divan by the fireplace to put his left boot up and secure the laces. He was outfitted in his usual charcoal tweed on charcoal tweed, a fresh undyed cotton shirt with a stand-up collar, and a black tie in a bow. He shook himself out, walked over to the vestibule, felt Dorothea's bite on his clavicle, and, smiling, opened the door.

"Sir! Forgive me! Good morning! This is urgent business, and you must excuse my presumption!" It was Captain W. A. Longuemare, Dorothea's husband. Dorothea had once joked to Oliphant that Longuemare was a Missouri goose on stilts; he did have fine, goosefeathery white hair, and he was shaped in a bloated, top-heavy manner, with an overlong and unfortunate neck. In addition, his fussily cut and pointed beard did look like a duck's bill. This morning he was dressed in dark-green stripes like a sportsman. However, his foppish and foolish looks were not a fair measure of his prowess. Oliphant knew him as a hard-working man who was given to showy living and cunning. Longuemare was in New-York at Jefferson Davis's direction to help organize the pro-Southern elements here and to counsel the anti-Lincoln press. Longuemare was also a perceptive man, and he waited carefully as Oliphant hesitated at the door. Finally, Longuemare added, "I must come in, Mr. Oliphant. I know I'm not welcome, but I must."

"Yes, you're not welcome," said Oliphant weakly, but he stepped aside. Longuemare walked in muttering his gratitude. It was immediately clear that Longuemare did not know that Dorothea was here.

Longuemare said, "It is very good of you to overlook our past disagreements like this."

"I'm not overlooking anything," said Oliphant. "I let you in. I am in haste, however, for an appointment at eight."

Longuemare started again with apologies for his presumption. Though both were Secret Service agents, Oliphant was not connected to Longuemare, and disapproved of his activities in New-York. Longuemare knew this, and in the past they had agreed not to pretend to camaraderie, and certainly not to collaboration. Also, their differences were further complicated by the fact that the Confederate Cabinet was competitive and bickering. Longuemare reported to Secretary of War James Seddon, while Oliphant reported to Secretary of State Judah P. Benjamin, a man who usually regarded the military as futile, and who definitely regarded provocateurs and saboteurs as madmen. Oliphant agreed completely with his chief.

Longuemare was spinning around the fireplace now, near the bedroom door, and Oliphant caught up with him. Longuemare turned to declare, "I have shocking news!"

Oliphant looked at him and then at the bedroom. "Yes?"

"Ben Butler has arrived in the city from Fortress Monroe!" Longuemare spoke as portentously as one might announce a sentence of execution. "He's here at the head of ten regiments that are assigned to garrison New-York through the Election! Butler's at the Fifth Avenue Hotel right now!"

Oliphant got to the mantel; he hoped Dorothea had heard her husband's voice. Oliphant tried a dismissal. "I hardly think—that they'll want my rooms, Mr. Longuemare, and it's no concern of mine."

"No, I say Butler, Ben Butler, Beast Butler! He's taken over the city with ten regiments from the Army of the James! And my plan is upset and in peril!"

Longuemare then explained in bursts that Major-General Benjamin Franklin Butler, commanding the Army of the James at Fortress Monroe in Virginia, had suddenly arrived at New-York's brilliant Fifth Avenue Hotel the night before along with his staff and a headquarters company. General Butler was said to be on special assignment for War Secretary Stanton. He was also said to be in command of up to ten thousand troops, including cavalry and artillery, who were arriving by steamer from Virginia. The troops were said to be posted to New-York to augment the State Militia and the Metropolitan Police in order to ensure a peaceful Election Day.

"Lincoln is desperate," continued Longuemare, "and Stanton is thrashing about trying to prop him up. The Yankees have been unsound since the Wilderness massacre. Two months ago, Lincoln wanted to quit and let McClellan negotiate an armistice. We could've had anything we wanted short of New-England." Longuemare laughed. Oliphant did not. Longuemare saw this, and recovered. "We'd beaten them, Mr. Oliphant! By all rights, we'd won! Now—Abe's put back up by the newspapers. He's got the blood scent after Atlanta and the Valley. He's wild enough to try and reelect himself with bayonets at the polls. There's the tyrant for you."

"I'm not interested in political lectures," said Oliphant.

"Very well. Ben Butler's not here to talk. And he's no fool. Remember how he behaved in New Orleans. It will be the same all over. Informers are rushing to him now. There'll be mass arrests, and outrages against womenfolk, and confiscations, certain."

A knock at the door gave Oliphant some relief. This time it was the houseboy with a tray of coffee, fruit, rolls, and copies of the *Times, Tribune,* and James Gordon Bennett's Democratic-biased *New-York Herald.* Oliphant dismissed the boy with a quarter. He took up a cup of coffee quickly and turned through the papers. The headlines announced more advances by Sheridan in the Shenandoah Valley and electioneering in New-York. There would be a Republican parade and rally tonight, and there would be a Democratic parade and rally tomorrow night. Oliphant sampled an apple slice, and said, "There's nothing here about Ben Butler. So if you've come to warn me, thank you. I don't suspect I'm in danger. My work's nearly done, and I won't be compromised at all, if you leave me."

"Warn you? No, sir. I've come to inform you what it means. Ben Butler is secret so far, and aimed at us. Mr. Oliphant—I've come to ask your help for my plan, or what's left of it. My Northwest Conspiracy."

"I do not even want to hear about it." Oliphant crossed to the window nearest the bedroom door. He listened for Dorothea while pretending to take in the view. Across the canyon of Broadway, catercorner from the quietly elegant Astor House, sprawled the neighborhood's pièce de résistance, Phineas T. Barnum's garish, five-story American Museum—a world-famous house of fun and freaks, the most popular place in New-York after the bawdyhouses and saloons. Oliphant watched the attendants scramble about the American Museum's facade to hang the day's billboards. He tried to lose himself in the childishness of Barnum's, while Longuemare kept hammering at him with his warnings about Butler and his pleas for help.

Suddenly Oliphant heard loud thumps from his bedroom. What was Dorothea doing in there? It sounded like a collision.

Longuemare heard the thumps too and stopped talking. He asked, "You have company? Is it safe to talk here?"

"I'm not sure what you want of me. No. Nothing is safe."

"I agree," said Longuemare, moving closer, "so we must take risks everywhere. That is why I must have the Confederate gold you control."

Oliphant jerked about and took Longuemare by the arm to get him away from the bedroom. He walked Longuemare to the far end of the parlor, to the window overlooking Vesey Street, St. Paul's Church, and the brick-faced canyon of Broadway extending south toward Trinity Church's steeple.

Longuemare misunderstood, presuming that Oliphant's attention was acquiescence; he continued more forcefully, "I need your help, you see, Mr. Oliphant. You have heard of the Northwest Conspiracy?"

Oliphant nodded inattentively. He was worried that Dorothea was about to charge out. And do what? Scream for the fact that she could not seduce her men away from the war? Or just for her frustration with her fate?

Longuemare pressed, "It was my plan, originally. Did you know? It was meant to take the Northwest out of the war. They're most sympathetic to our cause, you know? President Davis approved it two years ago, but it wasn't until this past spring it was thought possible to go ahead. And to expand it. You know, don't you, why Mr. Thompson, Mr. Clay, and Mr. Holcombe were sent to Canada?"

Oliphant sighed. "Mr. Longuemare, I know most of everything."

Oliphant looked out toward Trinity Church. He wanted to be as far away as the clouds floating over the steeple. The Northwest Conspiracy? Oliphant knew that it was an outlandish plot. It was based upon the political theory that the strident anti-war dissent in the Northwest of the country (Ohio, Indiana, Illinois, Michigan, Wisconsin) could somehow be transformed into open secession from the United States. And this would create the so-called Northwest Confederacy. Jefferson Davis had grabbed at this desperate speculation in his own desperation; he had sent Jake Thompson and his group to Canada in April in order to fund and provoke rebellion in the Northwest. Jake Thompson and his colleagues aimed to fashion their uprising about the secret anti-war society known as the Sons of Liberty.

In Oliphant's opinion, Jake Thompson's work was wretched and hopeless, and if there were occasional spasms of an organized rebellion in the Northwest, that did not change the fact that the Northwest Conspiracy remained a dark, conceited fantasy.

Nevertheless, Longuemare, its original author, kept jabbering, "Well, sir, we're ready here, most ready. My plan has been greatly developed over the summer. This operation will not only be in the Northwest, but throughout the East. Mr. Thompson is the overall commander now, from Chicago to Boston. I'm in charge of the effort here in New-York. It's true that we've had several delays over the summer, but when you consider the number of men involved, and the aim— We're definitely set for Election Day, you see. Now do you understand? We can stop Lincoln's reelection the same way they're trying to maintain their tyranny—with guns and main force! We can bring down the Union from inside!"

Oliphant waved away the notion. "Lee's men are starving, and so is the South. Unless you can force the North to feed us too—or get New-York's food to Richmond—or—" Oliphant lost his thought.

Longuemare did not care, because he was not listening. He preached his vision. "There are thousands of men here in the city to take up our cause. I promise you! For Election Day! But now, Ben Butler's arrival has scared my boys. These Sons of Liberty got secret oaths and secret handshakes and they'll shake you to kingdom come. But now they're shaking, and losing their grip, yes, sir! I need men who can fight, not clerks and altar boys. And for a price, a very high price, there are men who will fight for me. They're rabble, and blackguards. But they'll fight. And this time, I've assured 'em the militia and police are promised to stay out of it. So there will only be Ben Butler's men, and they don't know the city!"

Oliphant finally understood what Longuemare was saying and looked around. Was Longuemare serious? He was talking about hiring the outlaw gangs of the Bowery and Five Points for this so-called operation on Election Day. Oliphant spoke firmly, "This is not my affair, and is not going to be."

"But Governor Seymour is with us! And Fernando Wood and Vallandigham and all the Peace Democracy! Seymour's been promised a seat in McClellan's Cabinet, at War, I hear, and so has Wood, at Treasury. So you see it is coming together. They want us to succeed. They want the war stopped. And once the shooting stops, we'll be—victory—a Southern Republic!"

Oliphant thought Longuemare crazed. "McClellan has a ghost's chance. Vallandigham and the Democrats are disgraced. Seymour is for himself, and Wood, he is odious. How can you deal with them? They're some of the worst men in the North. Opportunists and liars."

"They want the war stopped," protested Longuemare.

"How? With the gangs? You would actually hire them?"

"As a vanguard to hearten the Sons of Liberty. We have a battle plan."

Oliphant shouted, "You are insane!" He made two fists, and then modulated his voice. "The Sons of Liberty are a chimera. And the gangs are murderers, not soldiers. What they did in the Draft Riots was not human."

"I must have gold to hire them," said Longuemare quickly. "You have it, or can get it."

"I shall have nothing to do with this, and neither will Richmond. Please, go, leave me, go."

"You aren't so high, Mr. Oliphant. This isn't your Carolina society now. And the gold you control isn't all yours, and even what is yours shouldn't be kept back from our cause. I wouldn't ask you, knowing your general reluctance from risk, if not for the press of time. And Jake Thompson—"

"Mr. Thompson told you to approach me? I was with him at Toronto Sunday—and I don't believe it."

"Not yet, he hasn't," conceded Longuemare; then he pointed at Oliphant like an accuser. "But he will approve, and so will Richmond, once I explain my plan to them. Of course, by then, it might be too late for Election Day. I was hoping you would see as I do. That you might risk something for once. However, if you must have Richmond's approval, I shall get it, and then we can proceed. That is, if you still take orders."

Oliphant started to defend himself. "You are mistaken about my loyalty, if that is what you are challenging."

"Then you'll help me?"

Oliphant looked at the bedroom door. "I'm not so high, as you say, but no, I cannot agree."

"This is a war," said Longuemare, "and not a gentleman's adventure. Even if I don't have works and cannoneers, I still have a fight here. Do you think Colonel Martin and his men are tourists? They were sent here to ignite— yes, ignite!—my plan. You do know what they have volunteered to do? On Election Day, they—"

"Sir, enough," interrupted Oliphant. "And my association with those men was accidental, and is finished."

"They speak well of you for your help at the border," continued Longuemare, who was speaking seductively again, "and Captain Kennedy thinks you a prince. At dinner last night, he nearly stole Dorothea away to find out about you."

All of the pieces of the puzzle of the morning's events—how the two Longuemares had found him—were in place, and Oliphant felt compromised, and foolish. He said, "My regards to Mr. Kennedy," and then he took Longuemare by the arm again, "and now you must go."

They moved to the vestibule. But even with the door opened, Longuemare tried to exact half-promises; he asked, "You will think on what I have said? You will prepare yourself to act on an approval from Richmond?"

Oliphant said nothing and shut Longuemare out with a mumbled "Good-bye." He then crossed to the bedroom door and opened it to discover that the room had been ransacked, his clothes tossed on the floor and the bed, the pillows and blankets tossed on the bureau. Dorothea, however, was dressed neatly and seated on the chair by the bed. She had Oliphant's lettercase in her lap. She had pulled many of his papers out.

"So your Narcissa," she began, "your dear Narcissa is coming at last."

Oliphant nodded. "Your husband has gone."

"My husband is a blind fool, and they've got him putting on a hangman's noose for a collar, and now he wants you to join him on the gallows, and my lover is dead and buried six weeks, and there isn't anything you can say, so don't."

"Yes, Dorothea. Your lover?"

"You didn't know him. He was just another man who loved Virginia more than sense. And now he's dead by his own hand, like all you brave Rebels soon." She fussed with her dress and let the lettercase drop to the floor as she rose. She deliberately walked on the letters and his letterbook. She said,

"I know you can't love me—because of Narcissa. You can come away with me, though. You can. We could come back when it's over, and you could go back to your wife and children, and you would be alive for me to meet someday when we're old, here, for the memory."

She brushed her hair with her hand and ducked to the mirror to straighten her hat. Oliphant was impressed by the performance, a belle mourning the passing of her own youth at least twenty years too soon.

Dorothea continued, "Don't become one of them, John. Don't let Narcissa make you one. You don't have their hatred in you, so don't take on their peacock's tragedy."

Oliphant knelt to gather up his papers. He carefully arranged the letters from his wife in Savannah, Mrs. Camellia Royall Oliphant, and from his sister-in-law in London, Mrs. Narcissa Royall Winwood. When he looked up, Dorothea put her hand on his head.

"You're too grave by half, John. It doesn't become you."

LATER FRIDAY MORNING, NOVEMBER 4

When John Jacob Astor completed the Astor House in 1832, he intended it to be the most prestigious address in America; and by the time of his death, in 1848, thanks to his Midas fortune and his overarching influence, it was. Five and a half stories and stone finished, it was constructed with classical revival elements, with honeycombs of rooms about a central courtyard that made the whole like a Napoleonic infantry square on Broadway. Its collection of registries included the names of every important person, American or foreign, to call in New-York for three decades. More, the Astor House had come to be known as the American government house, where presidents, Cabinet secretaries, and congressmen stopped to do their private and public business.

After 1860, the Astor House was the beehive of the Republicans, and therefore the popularly recognized commercial palace serving the North's throne. It was here, en route from Springfield, that President-Elect Lincoln had stopped to receive and dine with the truly powerful before he entrained again to sneak into Washington City—stalked by rumors of assassins. It was also here, since the fall of Fort Sumter, that New York State's richest men (and thereby the Union's, since New York was the first state by far) had gathered to negotiate contracts for Connecticut guns and Pennsylvania butter and the more problematical arrangements for European credit to hold off the imminent threat of national bankruptcy.

Most tellingly of all—it explained the weight of the place in 1864—it was at the Astor House that Thurlow "The Dictator" Weed held court. Thurlow Weed, at 67, was the uncontested head of New York's Republican party, and much more: Weed was the author of William H. Seward's career, from Whig attorney to New York governor to Republican senator to Lincoln's secretary of state; Weed, before his retirement from the editorship of the *Albany Evening Journal,* had been the scribe of the so-called Albany Regency, that Whig-become-Republican cabal that had built the canals, railroads, bridges, and factories that had made New York an empire; and Weed, after Seward had been outfoxed in his pursuit of the presidential nomination by Lincoln's supporters at the Republican Convention at Chicago in 1860, had been co-author of Lincoln's Cabinet and the dozens of lesser political appointments that truly worked the Union. No one in the nation was more dazzling or effective as king-maker than Thurlow Weed. It was said that he understood American politics, because he understood that, in a democracy, politics was the plain-dressed and plain-spoken pursuit of money.

A squat bull of a man, with a poor farmboy's devotion to gold, and with an appreciation of self-congratulatory patriotism, Weed ruled politicians, ambitious soldiers, and envious merchants with iron-handed magnanimity. The joke might be that Lincoln had a cubbyhole in his desk marked W, for correspondence from both Weed and Weed's hated New-York Democratic rival, the ex-mayor and present congressman Fernando Wood; but the fact was that when Lincoln needed money for emergencies, and Congress would not give it to him, Lincoln was known to telegraph Weed at the Astor House, and Weed would then produce cash on the table in the White House within forty-eight hours, with a list of the contributors' names attached.

By 1864, then, Thurlow Weed shook hands for the Union. And he knew how to employ such a potency to secure elections. The New York Democratic Party, headed by Governor Horatio Seymour in the mansion at Albany, might have the affection of the majority of the voters in the state, but the Republicans had Weed. On November 4, with the Election four days hence, Thurlow Weed was ready, said the newspapermen, to use white and black magic to carry the polls. He would drink widow's tears and wrap his party in Old Glory, and he would make sure that the Democrats were embalmed with Dixie and shrouded in the Stars and Bars. He would win a majority for Lincoln in New York at all peril and at any cost—if not that of his own fortune. And the redoubt from which he would launch his final assaults was the Astor House. In November 1864, the Astor House *was* Weed, and it was daily filled with the servants of his ruthless suzerainty.

John Oliphant descended to the cool, pale, austere ground-floor corridor of the Astor House before eight o'clock. The public rooms of the Astor House were distributed along the encircling corridor; in the front were the main dining room, the Rotunda Bar, and the ballroom; around back were the dozen cozier rooms for private parties. The main entranceway was on Broadway, a seven-stepped portico with Greek columns and an understated entablature. There were also two unadorned side entrances, north from Barclay Street and south from Vesey Street.

This morning, the flow of gentlemen from all directions matched that of an early evening. There was even a line of march to and from the garden in the inner courtyard, for November was still mild, and it was a bright, promising day. The conversations in pairs or trios were always discreet, yet they united to a hubbub about the Election, more specifically, about to-night's Republican parade and rally at Union Square, and also about the intelligence that General McClellan was due in town today (his home was on East Thirty-fourth Street) in order to preside over a Democratic parade and rally at Madison Square on Saturday night.

The main desk was on the north side of the corridor, so Oliphant had to cross the front atrium, where packs of partisans were congregated for coffee and debate. The Astor House's management prided itself that this was not an overly sumptuous stopping place, like the newer hotels uptown. There were only hardbacked chairs and benches in the atrium, and if they had been removed, given the false columns and frieze decorating the plain walls, the atrium would have resembled exactly a modern agora. The sunlight through the front entrance cast a grid pattern of shadows on the marble floor, and made it appear to Oliphant that these were symmetrically arranged Republican Athenians.

The desk clerks were burdened by an arriving party off of a European steamer. Oliphant lined up behind two weary yet swivel-headed Nordic gentlemen. In hesitant English, they asked Oliphant for reassurance that this was indeed the Astor House, and he replied in French, which made them smile, because they could thank him in French. They were even more delighted when two arm-in-arm beauties, looking sleepy and naughty in their ball gowns from the night before, passed behind them.

The clerk handed Oliphant the contents of his mailbox, saying, "These all came within the past quarter-hour, sir." He meant three particular envelopes, and he continued, reading from a reminder note to himself, "And a gentleman, a Mr. Durant, he has left word that he is pleased to meet you in the dining room as early as you wish."

Oliphant sat down nearby. The first envelope was a hand-delivered note from Oliphant's banker, Edmund Homes, confirming their luncheon engagement today at Delmonico's.

The second envelope was a telegram from Montreal, and it was not in cipher, though it was signed with a *nom de guerre*. It was actually from the Confederate Secret Service agent Beverley Tucker. Oliphant had first made Beverley Tucker's acquaintance several years before in Liverpool, where Tucker had been serving as the United States Consul. It was Beverley Tucker who had beckoned Oliphant from Europe once again—Oliphant's third trip across this year—and it was because of Beverley Tucker that Oliphant was engaged in this present business.

In truth, Oliphant was participating not because he trusted Beverley Tucker—for Tucker was a Virginia planter and firebrand whose pretentious Anglophilia irked Oliphant. Oliphant was in New-York because his chief, Secretary of State Judah Benjamin, had also approved of the scheme, which Benjamin thought one of the very few that had been conceived by the agents in Canada that was not outright folly.

Oliphant's distrust of Beverley Tucker and his comrades stemmed from the July before, when the agents in Canada had involved him in a so-called Peace Conference at Niagara Falls. They had lured Horace Greeley and one of Lincoln's private secretaries, John Hay, to the border, where they twisted Greeley's naive ambitions as a peace-maker into propaganda against Lincoln. Oliphant had been present as Judah Benjamin's representative, and had been appalled—for the Confederate agents had never meant to negotiate sincerely. The deception had been primarily engineered not by Beverley Tucker but by his close associate, the Kentuckian George N. Sanders. Oliphant had long despised George Sanders as an opportunistic voluptuary who aggrandized himself as a Secret Service agent. And Oliphant knew that George Sanders had now become unbalanced by the death in September of his son, Reid Sanders, at Fort Warren, the prisoner-of-war camp in Boston harbor. George

Sanders believed that his son had been deliberately murdered by War Department agents. In revenge, George Sanders had sponsored and launched the St. Albans raid two weeks before. And Oliphant also knew from his stopover in Montreal the week before that George Sanders was hungry for worse than St. Albans. In all, Montreal and Toronto were full of men with wild and vengeful temperaments. They were of no profound concern to Oliphant except that he was now, at Judah Benjamin's direction, representing them to others who were even worse.

Beverley Tucker's telegram was to the point: No deal unless——. Oliphant wrote a terse reply, and made a copy with his letterbook: Received and understood, more later——. Oliphant attracted the clerk again, and said, "Immediate, please, for the Hotel St. Lawrence, Montreal."

Oliphant passed under the main dining room's archway at precisely 8 A.M. and gave his name to the majordomo. Oliphant spotted Durant, on the far side, beneath one of the satellite chandeliers, but did not return his wave. Oliphant waited overlong to show his dissatisfaction in general and also to open the third envelope again. It smelled of Dorothea, and read, "Dinner tomorrow? Sandwich Islands Sunday?"

Dorothea's peach and lemon scent was a fine antidote to the turbulent room reeking of bacon and tobacco. The majordomo led a weaving course through the diners; one table of military men had their chairs pushed so far back to make space for their dress swords that the majordomo and Oliphant were forced to detour a long way around.

Durant was standing when Oliphant reached him. He was a thin, awkward man, with eyeglasses over a sharp nose and heavy gray moustache that made him appear a competent rodent. This was their third breakfast in three days, and the man irritated Oliphant because he preferred to talk before dining. The waiter seated Oliphant, poured coffee, and uncovered the dishes. Durant had ordered excessively again. Oliphant chose the scrambled eggs mixed with salmon; he began with a bowl of cut fruit.

Durant opened, "I have a surprise for you."

"I don't want surprises," replied Oliphant.

"It is a tease. You shall judge." Durant took more bacon, and asked, "You have word from Montreal?"

Oliphant was annoyed and pushed away the fruit to try the eggs. The only hot thing was the coffee. After testing the rolls, Oliphant abandoned the meal for more fruit. He wanted a pan-broiled brook trout and tea, and also silence.

"My associates," continued Durant, "have told me that they are ready to proceed immediately after the Election. And that you are not to worry for Mr. Lincoln's success in the Election. It is arranged."

"Bad marriages, table settings, and funerals are arranged, Mr. Durant, not elections."

Durant shrugged and tapped a copy of the *Times* beside him. "Have you seen Mr. George Sanders' letter in here? He says the Election is a farce, and urges all Reb sympathizers in the North not to participate."

"Electioneering," said Oliphant, "is for sanguine men, and rascals."

Durant finally acknowledged Oliphant's temper and pointed to Oliphant's lettercase. "You have bad news, then? Mr. Tucker has second thoughts?"

Oliphant swallowed a fruit slice. "Mr. Tucker reiterates that he cannot be enticed across the border—moved to cross the border—without a signed document that guarantees his safety by your sponsors. And I do not mean signed by any other than Mr. Weed."

"We have the same impasse again. A matter of risk and gain. Please," Durant wagged his finger, "I've tried. Last night. You know. My associates would be lastingly vulnerable to such a document."

"Excuse me, Mr. Durant, but my associates are immediately vulnerable."

Durant asked, "And what would it be if such a document fell into Mr. Greeley's hands?"

Oliphant smiled as he got out his pipe and tobacco. Horace "Old White-Coat" Greeley hated Thurlow Weed more than he hated William H. Seward, but Greeley hated both more than perdition, for what he believed had been the theft of Seward's vacated Senate seat from him after Seward had joined the Cabinet. Oliphant was in Thurlow Weed's keep, and was dealing with a Weed lackey, and their subject was treasonous—trading with the enemy. It therefore amused Oliphant that Durant should see Thurlow Weed's risk only in terms of Horace Greeley, quite apart from the law. Oliphant said, "We must try to be practical men, Mr. Durant, to come to a practical arrangement."

Durant replied, "But the war will end soon, you can't deny it. And then the dogmatic men will root for paper weapons like pigs for truffles. And such a document would— No, sir, it can't be done."

Oliphant said, "I had been permitted to hope."

"I do have that surprise," said Durant; he rose abruptly. "Look there!" Durant waved in a cheering salute.

His reference across the room was to Thurlow Weed himself. Weed was just entering the dining room amid a swarm of acolytes and the full attention of the serving staff. Thurlow Weed's swollen breadth illustrated relaxed beneficence, that jowly white-haired lion's head, that shining gold waistcoat, that old-fashioned high top hat that he handed off to the servants. Weed gave the roomful of observers a slight wave, and stepped to a round table beneath the central chandelier. He remarked to many diners as he passed them; however, he sat alone at a table set for five. Two septuagenarians, one in an Invalid Corps brigadier's uniform, walked over to Weed, and were invited to sit. Weed then leaned sideways for a moment and, looking across to Durant, coiled his fingers in a subtle beckoning. Durant jumped to his master.

Oliphant smiled at the whole show and prepared the bowl of his pipe. He assumed that this demonstration was prearranged. After three days of negotiations, Oliphant was finally to be introduced to Thurlow Weed. Though if this was the surprise Durant had promised, Oliphant thought it hardly that, and also thought it most inadequate to settle the negotiations.

Oliphant and Durant were go-betweens in a contest of polar-opposite players. Durant represented the part of a group of Northern men, chief among whom were Thurlow Weed and three leading Republican party members—the New York Collector of Customs and Weed crony, Simeon Draper; and two close Lincoln political advisers in Washington City, Leonard Swett and Ward Lamon. Their desire was to make the war pay. The means to their end was a delicate piece of legislation that had been passed by Congress the July before in an attempt to control illicit interstate and international cotton trading. Congress had directed the Treasury Department to license factors to export cotton from captured Southern ports such as Norfolk, Virginia; Beaufort, South Carolina; and Pensacola and Fernandina, Florida. These licenses were to be issued only to loyal Union men by Assistant Secretary of the Treasury H. A. Risley. The Congress thereby hoped to revive the cotton trade that had long been suppressed by the war, to control the illicit trade raging across the battle lines, and to gain much-needed customs revenue for the government.

Soon enough, however, H. A. Risley had been drawn into a scheme proposed by Thurlow Weed and his ring. The plan was to withhold the factor licenses until Weed's ring had secured their own members, or surrogates, at each port. The effect would be that the cotton—both captured and privately held—would be exported exclusively by men who had never before factored a bale, or even visited the ports. And there would be no recourse for the planters: Either turn over your cotton and accept a percentage of its worth, or watch it rot on the wharf.

Weed's ring had then gone a step farther, and it was a Midas step. Durant, at Weed's direction, had contacted the Confederate Secret Service in Canada —Beverley Tucker and his colleagues. Durant proposed a business deal. Weed's ring would employ its factors as a front for trade with the Confederacy. Durant offered to exchange non-contraband goods from the North and Europe for the huge supply of cotton that was held by the Confederate government in warehouses throughout the South.

This ostensibly would only be the barter of non-contraband goods for non-contraband goods, since cotton was not on the list of proscribed merchandise, like guns and ammunition. But given that the Confederacy was financially strangled, that the only resource it had was cotton, and that with Mobile out of the war only the port of Wilmington, North Carolina, remained as a way for the Confederacy to send its cotton through the blockade to Europe, and then only haphazardly, the offer tempted Richmond to the extreme.

Oliphant represented the Confederate agents in Canada, who were speaking for the South. It had been particularly left to Beverley Tucker, an experienced cotton trader, to explore the possibilities of the barter. Richmond did not want money for its cotton, nor did it necessarily want armaments. Richmond wanted the non-contraband goods that could be brought into the South on ships that would not have to run the blockade, because they would be traveling under the protection of the U.S. Treasury —goods that could then be transferred surreptitiously to Confederate agents through the Union lines. Most of all, Richmond wanted food. War Secretary Seddon's estimate in September had been that there was only enough food in the Confederate territory to feed the armies for ninety days. But this was a bookkeeper's fantasy. How long could Lee's and the other armies really stand up? It was not just that the soldiers were hungry; every family in the South faced a winter of deprivation, and this daily increased the Army's desertion rate. Jefferson Davis's spoken-aloud estimate was that a majority of the South's possible soldiery was absent without leave.

The Confederacy was blind with hunger. And to bargain with the very men who advised the government that sought to starve it to death was a senseless try. It was also a chance. For what Richmond, and then Beverley Tucker, and now Oliphant sought to close was a transaction of humbling magnitude. There were in those warehouses a half-million bales of Confederate cotton worth as much as a quarter of a billion dollars in cotton-needful

Europe. If Oliphant could succeed, even in part, not only would Weed and the members of his ring each become millionaires several times over, but also the Union military stranglehold of the South would be loosened—for the moment. Bluntly, what Oliphant was negotiating was a means to extend the war by as much as a year. And all this with bacon less edible than that which curled in fat on Durant's plate.

Or so had been Oliphant's hope, and a very dim hope, upon leaving Canada. Now, after three days of Durant's teasing and wiggling, Oliphant lit his pipe and blew clouds with an unhappy opinion. Weed and his ring wanted, yet they wanted without risk. The South merely wanted, and, like the heavy loser who gambled on, the South had only risk.

An excitement began suddenly at the dining room's archway; there was a small applause and cries of "Hurrah!"

Oliphant could see a Negro family being ushered in by the Invalid Corps brigadier. The father was tall, clean shaven, in a captain's uniform and Wellington boots. The mother was round and glowing, outfitted in mauve layers like one of Queen Victoria's ladies in waiting, with a purple spoon bonnet. The four children were in short pants or frocks, the boys wearing tiny Zouave caps. The brigadier guided them to Weed's table. Weed bounced up to shake hands and kiss fingers.

Durant then emerged from behind Weed and encouraged Oliphant to come across. Durant flapped harder, so that Oliphant, annoyed, pushed up and walked toward the exit. Durant intercepted him, and begged, "Mr. Weed, sir, would appreciate a moment with you, sir."

Oliphant wanted to get out, but said, "Yes, yes."

Thurlow Weed was distributing coins to the children. Weed glanced at Oliphant and then spoke out to Durant and Oliphant, "These are my babies. Wouldn't you do anything for them? Their daddy so brave and their names so beautiful. Nothing'd be too much to ask to do for them. Ain't that right?"

Oliphant stood still and silent. Weed spread his arms and swept the children to the side, directing the brigadier to seat each child at the table. Weed looked back to Oliphant, and frowned, and smiled, revealing dark-brown teeth among several gold ones, and then he turned away, muttering to the waiters for sweet rolls. Oliphant turned about-face.

Durant caught up to Oliphant on the way out; Durant tried, "Mr. Weed has kindly offered us the use of his private rooms again, to continue our conference."

"Our conference is at an end," said Oliphant. "So I don't know why."

"My surprise, my surprise."

"Really, Mr. Durant, I can't call this suasion. Either there is to be a written contract or there is not to be."

Durant said, "You have said that you shall be judge. Come along then, and do so."

Thurlow Weed's sanctum sanctorum was the Astor House's Room Number 11. It was a spacious suite of rooms, garrisoned by portraits of every major Whig politician (most prominently Henry Clay and Daniel Webster) and decorated by landscape paintings of the Erie Canal. It was located one flight up from the ground floor on the Vesey Street side. It was known as a place to take off your boots, as the gargantuan Mexican hero and former general-in-chief of the Army, Winfield Scott, had often done, and to pad around delighting in Weed's cigars and loquacity. It was also where the New York Republican Party had come to terms with Abraham Lincoln's election in 1860, and had then set about to assure itself that even if Lincoln and his Illinois men had the White House, Thurlow Weed and his cronies would have the port of New-York and the factories of New York State's river valleys. Oliphant had met here with Durant on Wednesday afternoon, along with the horse-faced Simeon Draper and Lincoln's personal aide Leonard Swett. Subsequently, Oliphant had met with Durant and others elsewhere in further discussions of the cotton-trading scheme. And so Oliphant went along with Durant this morning curious as to why Durant had chosen just this moment to return to Number 11.

The anteroom was dark and crowded with damask-covered couches and low tables. Oliphant followed Durant in and was nearly through the room when he stopped in alarm. There was a chunky, very intimidating man seated by the door to the inner office. He wore a large hat pulled down so low that his ears stuck out.

Durant noticed Oliphant's reaction and paused to offer his assurances that there was no trouble. Durant then spoke to the doorkeeper. "Mr. Oliphant's unarmed. So am I." The doorkeeper did not respond. Durant sprang the door, and spoke straight ahead. "Good morning, sir. Mr. Oliphant is with me."

Oliphant glanced once more at the doorkeeper and stepped ahead to slide into the inner office behind Durant. The drapes were drawn, and the room was very dim. A lone man sat beside Thurlow Weed's black wood desk. He was thick-chested, heavily bearded, short-armed, and wore a long dark riding slicker over good worsted clothes. Oliphant could not see his face for the stiff-brimmed blue hat.

Durant continued in his supplicatory tone, "I've brought Mr. Oliphant, sir. He's still in need of our assurances." Durant turned back to Oliphant. "Mr. Oliphant, I would like to introduce you to Colonel Lafayette Baker, of the War Department."

Lafayette Baker rose, and spoke aggressively, "The United States Secret Service."

Durant commented, "Correct, please, correct, Colonel Lafayette Baker, chief of the Secret Service."

Oliphant could not react other than with gentility. He tucked his letter-case under his left arm and held out his right hand. Lafayette Baker held out his. They gripped each other. Lafayette Baker squeezed.

Oliphant took a seat opposite the desk. He had a better view of the man now as Durant pulled back a drape. Lafayette Baker had a high forehead, long nose, heavy eyelids, and he was not as old as the gray in his beard made him first appear. He wore two pistols under the riding slicker; they were Navy Colt six-shooters that hung from a cartridge belt with a gold buckle. Lafayette Baker also had his trouser legs tucked inside his boots like a cavalryman.

Durant began a chatty, ambiguous introduction to the meeting at hand. He repeated Oliphant's need for assurances, and he also remarked upon Colonel Baker's generous cooperation. Then Durant became even more obscure. He changed the subject to the seeming non sequitur of the gold market. He talked about the gossip in New-York that Confederate vice-president Alexander Stephens might be in Canada for peace negotiations. Durant was no longer making any sense to Oliphant.

Finally, Lafayette Baker cut Durant off by loudly addressing Oliphant. "You know who I am. And I know what you're about, Mr. Oliphant, if I don't know who you are, not nearly."

Oliphant said, "I am a financial representative."

Lafayette Baker squinted. "You're a Reb agent as sure as John Brown's molderin'."

Durant started, "Mr. Oliphant has come all the way from England to—"

"Oh, let me talk, Durant," snapped Lafayette Baker. "We'll miss the piss pot altogether for you worryin' us." Lafayette Baker threw his thumb out from himself toward Oliphant. "I've come today to settle this business. I'm the man who's to escort Mr. Beverley Tucker across the frontier. Durant says he needs Mr. Tucker in New-York for six hours, to make small talk, I suppose, and to sign some papers. And then I'm to take Mr. Tucker through the lines to Richmond. To Jeff Davis, I suppose."

Oliphant exhaled. "So, you're the surprise."

"I don't surprise you, no sir," said Lafayette Baker; he acted as barbed and confident as a golden eagle. He continued, "You're too back in the saddle for surprises. Still, you ain't sure 'bout what I'm proposin'. Colonel Baker, you say to yourself, he's the lawman who's filled Old Capitol Prison and Fort Lafayette with the blackguards who make war on the United States and keep people in chains. Colonel Baker, you say, he's caught more Reb spies than a stable has flies. Now why's he here sayin' how d'you do to a Reb agent? Ask him. And he'll tell you. For his share. That's why. And for his star his enemies in Congress have kept from him."

Oliphant could not hold back. "Star?"

"Brigadier's star," replied Lafayette Baker; he put his thumbs inside his gold belt buckle, and stretched his legs. "Tell me," he began again. "I was ripe to help your gang last week. At the Suspension Bridge at Niagara Falls. I was up there waitin' for Tucker. And he didn't show up. Must've been some mix-up, mmh?"

Oliphant nodded with understanding, but not for Lafayette Baker. Lafayette Baker was more of a surprise for Oliphant than he thought he was, but he was not, indeed, a complete revelation. Beverley Tucker and George Sanders had told Oliphant in Montreal that Weed's ring had hired a War Department agent to provide security for their scheme. Tucker and Sanders had also vaguely told Oliphant about a rendezvous at Niagara Falls the week before that they had backed out of at the last moment. They said they had preferred to await Oliphant's arrival.

The result of Tucker's and Sanders's plotting was that Oliphant had been dispatched to New-York as a go-between; but he had not reached New-York with the significant intelligence that the Weed hireling was the notorious chief of the United States Secret Service, a man whom the London press castigated as a brute the likes of the French Secret Police monster, Joseph Fouche. Tucker and Sanders had not lied to Oliphant—they had merely withheld. Oliphant, so far from blaming Tucker and Sanders for their intrigue, instead chastised himself for not anticipating that there would be turns upon turns in such a vortex.

Oliphant needed time to himself to reconsider this affair. He tried to put off Lafayette Baker. "I believe, Mr. Baker, that this offer of yours differs very little, if not at all, from the last." Oliphant looked at Durant. "Its inadequacy is why I require a contract with Mr. Weed's signature."

"So it's horse-tradin', is it?" said Lafayette Baker. "You want to watch the nag work the fields first? Here's proof, then, sir." Baker opened his arms. "You telegraph Mr. Tucker that I'm coming to Montreal. Right to his hotel. To sit down with him for a glass of whiskey. And George Sanders too, sure, we can have a laugh! And when they see I'm not afraid of them, then what's keepin' their bottle corked?"

Oliphant addressed Durant. "If this is in lieu of a contract, it is very meager."

Durant made a sound of protest. Lafayette Baker overcalled him. "What I want, Mr. Oliphant, is to know who you are. And what's this for you? I'm of the opinion that if you know what a man wants, you can learn to trust him—or not. You're no Southron. You're a Yankee, or were. Durant says you're from Philadelphia."

"Does he?" responded Oliphant; he felt himself on the defensive now, and concentrated. Lafayette Baker might be a brute, but he was clever.

"He says you married one of their ladies, a Sea Island belle, nice and fancy. But you must have blood kin in the Army—our Army?"

"I was born near Philadelphia, at a farm near Valley Forge."

"That don't make no account. My granddaddy, a real patriot, fought with Ethan Allen, and was one of them that captured Fort Ticonderoga. He was Remember Baker of the Green Mountain Boys." Lafayette Baker settled into his chair; he was about to tell a story, but then came alert. "You're a slave owner, ain'tcha?"

"My grandfather kept slaves at Valley Forge," said Oliphant.

"You think that's godly, that one man should own another?" asked Lafayette Baker. "I like to hear what you people make of your sin."

"No, I do not think of it as godly, Mr. Baker."

"Colonel. Colonel Baker. So why're you Jeff Davis's errand boy? What's your profit?"

Oliphant sighed. "I have had my reasons, one upon another."

"For profit!" exclaimed Lafayette Baker. "For profit is why, same as you keep slaves and wreck the Union and sneak—for profit. We understand each other. But look at you, all prim like Sir Scallywag. You think the war's not mannerly because it's not written down on a piece of paper to sign, nice and safe? Maybe you'll get more interested in this rude war if you remember that I could raise my voice a little and John Odell out there would have you at Fort Lafayette by noontime. And why don't I? Because there's no profit in it. You believe me?"

"Yes, I do," said Oliphant.

Lafayette Baker frowned, and asked, "What kind of man are you?"

"I am an American, like you, Mr. Baker."

Lafayette Baker rocked in place and stared at Oliphant.

Durant started again in the tense silence. Durant said that there was an additional service that Lafayette Baker could render while he was in Montreal, and that there was additional profit in it. Lafayette Baker grunted, but remained belligerently fixed on Oliphant. Durant talked faster: All Baker had to do, he said, was to ascertain whether or not Confederate vice-president Alexander Stephens had arrived in Montreal. It concerned a rumor of peace negotiations, explained Durant. It was such a small thing, said Durant, but could profoundly affect the Gold Exchange.

Lafayette Baker twisted about and slapped his open hand on the desk. "How much? How much is it worth to me?"

Durant said, "It could mean as much as seventy thousand."

Lafayette Baker hooted, "That's rich! For sayin' a rat's jumped ship? Whyn't ask Sir Scallywag here?"

"If you will excuse me," said Oliphant; he stood, and bowed casually. He hoped he could avoid Lafayette Baker's temper. He added, "Mr. Durant, you have your own business with Mr. Baker. Good morning to you."

Durant appealed, "You will pass on our offer—Colonel Baker's proposal —to Montreal?"

Oliphant nodded in assent, and decided not to comment further.

Lafayette Baker then hopped up to escort Oliphant to the door. He spoke confidentially. "Your fine manners there, they won't help you if we ever meet at the wrong time for you. Don't mistake me, this matter concluded—" Baker paused; his tone was that of a shopkeeper promising the delivery date of certain fine goods, "—I'm sworn to my duty. Here, you see, sir, you see what that says?" Lafayette Baker held back his slicker and frock coat to reveal a gold badge pinned on his vestcoat at the left breast; he continued, "It says, 'Death To Traitors.' President Lincoln likes me to show it to rats. He says it makes 'em roll on their backs."

Oliphant waited until he was certain that Baker was not going to assault him; he then said quietly, "I understand your special position."

Lafayette Baker stepped out of Oliphant's path and gestured toward the door. "I ain't a traitor, you remember, Mr. Oliphant. This is a business transaction, and I leave it at that. Don't let me see you in Washington City. I'm the law there, beginning and end."

FRIDAY AFTERNOON, NOVEMBER 4

Leaving the clubby quiet of Delmonico's restaurant, Oliphant was in a low mood. He faced the prospect of a weekend alone, and also the necessity of making difficult decisions about Weed's ring and Lafayette Baker by intuition, and by himself. He was thankful therefore for the present amiable company of his banker and young friend, Edmund Homes. He and Homes were chatting pleasantly of things in general, though Homes still clung to his thoughts on the gold market. Homes was an angular, pink-faced 25-year-old, the youngest son of English provincial gentry, from Norfolk. Homes was dressed even more conservatively than Oliphant, in a double-breasted cheviot morning coat and light gray trousers, a high collar, and even higher top hat. Overcoats were unnecessary on such a bright, warmish day. Oliphant and Homes tapped their walking canes in tandem and touched their brims to similar strollers as they ambled through the rift of Beaver Street in the financial district, and then veered toward the small park at Bowling Green.

At luncheon, Edmund Homes had revealed a wavering conservatism when he had questioned Oliphant about the war and gold: How much to unload? How long to wait? The week before, American gold coins, each supposedly worth one American dollar in currency (listed as 100), had closed at 220 on the New-York Gold Exchange. Today, the price was over 230; in fact, a runner had brought a report to Delmonico's just before 2 P.M. that it was 236½ and climbing again. A few diners had quit their coffee and sweets to dash off, making those left in the room even more anxious for the undeniable financial panic everywhere that was showing itself nakedly in gold speculation.

The Election was an earthen dam above the Union: Would it hold and Lincoln be returned and the war drag on? Would it break and McClellan sweep out the Radical "Black" Republicans and pronounce an armistice? And what would either of these possibilities mean for the gold market? The size and ferocity of this war made it impossible to find a comparable model. Such a three-year-long catastrophe (with estimates of over a half-million dead combatants, uncounted millions invalided, and the national debt exceeding 400 hundred million dollars) would have destroyed any other modern nation. How long could America continue? And what would it look like when America fell apart? Unless it had already fallen, and this gold fever was anarchy in money.

Edmund Homes, like many erudite Europeans, found the American civil war a lurid and awesome drama—a marriage scandal writ interminably, he said. At the lunch table, Homes had prodded Oliphant for bulletins. Homes would jot down Oliphant's instructions about his portfolio of stocks, and then he would ask Oliphant about Grant's alcoholized blunders, or Lee's pious doggedness, or Jefferson Davis's martinet intractability, or McClellan's hardening speeches about a military solution in his Administration, or Lincoln's rumored peace-feelers. Homes's most colorful line of inquiry, after the gold volatility, concerned Sherman and his army at Atlanta: Was Sherman cut off? What would happen if the Confederate Army counterattacked and Sherman was besieged? Could the North suffer Sherman's entrapment?

Oliphant had tried to put Homes off. "The gold I care about is in my mouth—modern dentistry is worth millions!" and, "Georgians I know would say that an Atlanta address isn't a panacea!"

At the same time, Oliphant had tried to answer Homes while maintaining the useful fiction that his opinions were those of a wealthy, displaced planter and speculator who had not bothered to choose between the North and the South. Homes had obliged Oliphant's masquerade as usual. They had not spoken directly of the reason for Oliphant's incessant travels in the two years of their commercial relationship. And if every now and again, when they met in New-York or London, or corresponded, there was a weighty ambiguity in one another's language about how much Oliphant actually knew, then both Homes and Oliphant were phlegmatic enough to let the moments pass unresolved. Homes, after all, was a deep-seated Tory and disliked Great Britain's octogenarian, inconstant, and militant prime minister Viscount (H. J. T.) Palmerston and his Liberal party government more openly than any Union or Confederate diplomat might show, not to start to speak of his distaste for French emperor Napoleon III's appetite for Mexico, or Austria's and Russia's ambitions in the Americas. And Oliphant throughout spoke as dishearteningly of Jefferson Davis, the two-room-cabin Kentucky-born melancholic, as he did of Abraham Lincoln, the one-room-cabin Kentucky-born melancholic.

Oliphant and Homes paused at Bowling Green, where the oval-shaped crossroad opened northward onto the beginning of the profound corridor of Broadway, New-York's metaphorically golden four and a half miles of commerce to Central Park. The carriage and wagon traffic was furious, hack drivers being mercurial and politic, private drivers imitating the ramming ability of the Roman trireme. The three-story townhouses hereabout were elegantly shuttered, and the sun from the southwest made the brick facades shine scarlet and the windows blaze bronze. It was a sublime, contemplative afternoon, and Oliphant did not want Homes to leave him.

Homes said, "Here, it's gone three, sir! Could you join me? General Ben Butler is invited to make an address at the New Custom House."

That was not the sort of company that Oliphant desired. "I thought Butler being in New-York was a secret?"

Homes looked playful. "It is. Mr. Simeon Draper's secret, and therefore, about the same as Bonaparte returned from Elba."

"Has he?" Oliphant teased. "You best to your horse, or regiment."

They continued through Bowling Green Park, with orangish yellow maples and brown grass, with traders gathered to chat and smoke on the benches. Homes threw his hand vaguely east. "I shall actually be home for the Christmas holyday, sir, and there's a campaign to have me at my sister's with her noisy brood. Might I expect to see you in London?"

"I would like that. Last Christmas, here, despite your kindness, it was Christmas without a family." Oliphant sensed something unsaid by Homes, and asked, "What's the occasion for your trip?"

"A delicate matter," said Homes. "Miss VanderHorst has accepted me, brave girl, and so have a few members of her family—her father notwithstanding."

"I didn't know! Wonderful, Edmund! Why haven't you told me?"

"I'm still accustoming myself to it myself."

"It gets easier. Though I understand. Have you a date?"

"Little Easter, can you imagine it?" Homes laughed. "April in New-York with all that blessed English-like rain? And me, a husband. Does it get easier? I suppose."

"She's a beautiful woman, Edmund. She'll make you."

"She'll bury me, or her relatives will. They think me a redcoat. All that remains to make a proper war of it is for my sisters to snub her as a fortune hunter. And her with her father's estate half the size of Surrey. I'm the one who feels the pretender."

"Marry well, and merry," said Oliphant. "That is Southern advice. The Royalls made me feel the same as you, and truly, I was a pretender. All we solemn young men are pretenders."

They crossed the cobblestones of State Street and gained the lightly wooded open area of the Battery, the largely man-made cornerpiece of Manhattan Island. From here, there was a wide and clear vantage of the harbor. Closer at hand, couples joined at the hip and governesses with children strolled the promenade, along with three old seamen who were wrapped similarly in long woolen scarves and leaning on canes of exotic South American lumber.

Oliphant touched Homes's arm. "Do you have to go on to that glum lecture? Can't you walk a while longer?"

Homes nodded; he also spoke more affectionately, as if he had sensed Oliphant's need. "I suppose it would be impossible for Mrs. Oliphant and your children to join you in London, if you can get over?"

"They are best and safest in Savannah," said Oliphant.

"Of course, the blockade—I suspect, though, it isn't as happy in Savannah as it was?"

"Yes, the blockade," began Oliphant. He wanted to avoid the dark topic of his family's isolation in Savannah. He wanted to return to the gaiety of the wedding plans. He tried, "Wouldn't it be grand, though, all of us with you and Miss VanderHorst at the Saville? A lovely goose liver Perigord pie on Boxing Day?"

"Please." Homes patted his abdomen. "I've overeaten."

They were at the foremost lip of the promenade, at the rail above the seawall of boulders. Oliphant was looking out on the most perfect natural harbor that he had ever visited—a God-given bottle shape. And there was also an endless blue sky decorated by fleet white clouds, and a vast green carpet of sea that sparkled so starkly that it hurt to stare too long at any one point, better to shift one's gaze to the coastal steamers pushing past the profile of Governor's Island toward the East River's wharfs, or to look to the broad inland sloops that used the Hudson River's current and the ebbing tide like engines. There were so many kinds of ships at cross angles to each other that it was difficult to follow one for long, full sails melting into coal black plumes, and dark bows rising and falling into the wash of small waves. Oliphant was attracted at last to one particularly long twin-stacked steamer just then clearing Bedloe's Island to the southwest and making hard up the Hudson River. Its company markings were indistinct. Oliphant pointed. "Can you make her out, Edmund?"

"I can guess, sir. *Pandora,* out of Nicaragua. She's due to dock about now."

"Loaded with passengers from California," said Oliphant. "What a find! Those 49er tales of soft nights, sudden fortunes, Spanish pleasures. Do you know the story of the Highlanders, before they left Scotland last century, getting together to celebrate, and calling it, 'Dancing America'? Well, I've heard of 'Dancing California'!"

"*Pandora*'s loaded with gold dust more than passengers."

"Oh, Edmund, not so serious. You're not wed yet. For the dreams out there! I've never been to California, nor farther—the Pacific, the Orient. Haven't you a yearning? The Sandwich Islands! The volcanoes on Hawaii Island and the beach where Captain Cook died?"

Homes moaned, "I must admit that I must prepare myself just for the Atlantic crossing. All we English do not savor the brine and deep. When the sky disappears behind the crest of a wave, I get to my cabin and hold my breath in the hope that I can increase the ship's buoyancy."

Oliphant smiled and rocked forward to study the events seaward and then, leaning back, turned toward the city. He was enjoying himself for the moment, allowing the aphrodisiacal salt air and the cool wind to clear out his worries—Durant's filthy deceptions, Lafayette Baker's vulgar threats, George Sanders's undersided intrigue, and Beverley Tucker's idolatrous worship of cotton as the cure for the South's mortal wounds. It was always the same tired tale with the cotton men—they and their so-called secret weapon, King Cotton—when the truth had been there for all to see at the secession, that cotton was neither king nor knave. It was only a natural resource, like gold, whose dearth or abundance could never dominate so diversified an international economy, or dictate international politics. Due to the pigheadedness of the planters who dominated the Confederate government, however, Oliphant had been directed to cross and recross the Atlantic for nearly three years in pursuit of the illusory promise of King Cotton. What the Confederacy had wanted was European recognition forced by the threat of a cotton famine. What the European governments had returned was a chatty ignorance of and an often rude indifference toward America—North and South.

And now, Oliphant wanted done with all of them—Confederate schemers, Union tyrants, European deceivers. He ached in his heart to be free of them all and to get on a ship bound for the half of the world that was covered with ocean and trimmed with reef-rimmed islands that were populated by bare-breasted Polynesian princesses. In truth, Oliphant knew he would settle for sailing anywhere away from here, excepting that he knew that he could not solve the worst of his troubles without a means of travel through time.

"Edmund," began Oliphant, "I've a confession for you. I've often thought, standing here, that I was at the bow of a gigantic earthen ship called *New-York*. Blunt prow, bloated amidships, tapered aft, with her steam up from the chimneys and stacks fed by the coal bin of the markets. And she was heading out. Not into the Atlantic. Into the future."

Homes responded happily, "Three-quarters of a million for a crew, and those captains of industry, that sort of thing?"

"You do please me, you do!" declared Oliphant. "We should cry, 'Up anchor!' and 'Make sail!' To sail as far as possible on such a democratic vessel. With you aboard, now, Edmund—to be wedded to an American, and so to be an American! A ship where anyone with spirit, and truly anyone with Lincoln's luck, can rise to the quarterdeck."

"She's a fine ship, sir," said Homes.

"Doesn't make you seasick?"

"Only when I think about the wedding-purchased passage."

They laughed, and then they turned along the promenade. Directly ahead was Castle Garden, the large, dilapidated circular building that sat overlooking the Hudson River, like an abandoned three-layered wedding cake, or an arrested Tower of Babel. Castle Garden was used as the very entry portal for all immigrants arriving in New-York, and just then there were two passenger barges docking at Castle Garden's wharf.

Oliphant pointed to the barges and tried to continue his fun. "Here's steerage coming aboard, Edmund. Where they shall be challenged, insulted, inspected, and released onto the foredeck of our ship *New-York.*"

Oliphant stopped to watch clumps of immigrant families climb out of the barges. There were four children for every female, old women with infants, old men with huge lumpy sacks on their shoulders, and young men in slop clothes carrying only their hats. Then a line of customs officers formed up, and the immigrants, visibly cowed, drew back. Presently, the immigrants deployed into queues that disappeared slowly into Castle Garden.

Oliphant said, "Perhaps I've gone too far, spoken too glibly, the poor folk."

"Irish, sir," said Homes. "They're heartier than they look."

"Lord Almighty, I hope so," said Oliphant; he walked forward to the edge of Castle Garden to peer through the broken window panes. The interior was divided by low partitions. He could see half-naked bodies in one section. In another, there was a Federal Army recruiting station, with a long line already established, men eager for the six-hundred-dollar bounty New-York offered for volunteers. Oliphant stepped back over a smashed-down fence and spoke to Homes. "They shouldn't do that. Do you see the recruiters? What do those boys know of the war? No sooner do they get here than they leave their families for Virginia."

"It is why many of them come over, sir," said Homes. "And you can be sure Lord Palmerston's men rejoice to be rid of them. The Union recruits openly at Dublin dockside, and at Queenstown."

"And so my country," started Oliphant, "my country, North and South, makes your merchant fleet supreme because of the raiding and blockading of our own, and we fill your munitions factories with work, and we help develop your woolen mills because of the shortage of cotton, and we even drain off the Irish poor. A practical, profitable war, for England."

"That is one way to look at it, sir."

Oliphant saw Homes's defensive wince and shook his head. "I apologize, Edmund. I've spoken wrongly. Really. I shouldn't have singled out England. I feel especially cruel for having joked about those poor people. God bless them, each and every one. Still, it isn't right, about the recruiters. It isn't decent."

"This war flatters no one," said Homes. "No less England."

They passed around Castle Garden at a distance because of the smell of a pile of garbage and discarded clothing. Outside the exit of the building, off Battery Place, entrepreneurs were arranged at booths beneath posters offering land, or work in mines, or a free passage to New Jersey in exchange for day labor. There was also a small, fenced-off area where untended children sat with their bundles. Each child had a sign hung over his or her head. The children looked up with expectation as Oliphant and Homes passed by. The signs generally identified the children by name and place of origin, "Goldie of Kerry," or "Brian Kelly of Sligo." Oliphant startled to find the mirror image of his middle daughter in the child labeled, "Anna of Rathnew."

Oliphant asked, "It would be disruptive, I suppose, to try to give them money, would it?"

Homes said, "They're to be met. And which one? And how much?"

"All of them!" cried Oliphant. "All of it! It shall all be theirs!"

"Mr. Oliphant, are you all right?" Homes took Oliphant by the arm and led him to the curb at Battery Place. Before them was the lengthy sweep of West Street, a broad avenue that stretched to the vanishing point up the west bank of the Hudson River. There was a vast forest of naked masts along the fifty piers. There was also a herd of wagons rattling a drumbeat as they fed and fed upon the ship's stores.

Oliphant was embarrassed for his outburst. He puzzled why he should have done such a thing. Was it Narcissa? Again, there were so many possible explanations that he shook his head. "I'm sorry, Edmund. I'm missing my daughters, you see, and they reminded me. It has been more than a year since I saw them. Not since the summer, a year ago."

"Yes," said Homes, "and here I have spoken of the blockade at Savannah. Can you forgive me my clumsiness?" Homes stepped in front of Oliphant and looked into his face. Homes continued, "I pray, I have always prayed, sir, for you and your family. Mrs. Winwood, when I was in London last spring, she shared some confidences with me. And, God, Mr. Oliphant, you are a valiant man, for what you are doing for your people."

Oliphant could not resist his gloom the longer. He gestured toward the river. "Mrs. Winwood is due next Tuesday, here." Oliphant straightened, and pointed more carefully out across the river, to Jersey City and the pier of the Cunard Company. "Aboard *Australasian*," he explained. "It isn't a happy arrival. You see, her husband, General Winwood, was lost in July in the Shenandoah Valley. Not that she—he was lost, he is missing. And her last brother, the eldest son, Johnny, was killed at Petersburg in August. The worst of it is that my father-in-law, Mr. Royall, passed away at the end of September. It has been three awful months upon three awful years."

Homes said, "Now I'm the one who didn't know— Good God! Please, please. I am very grieved for you. I didn't know General Winwood, of course, or the Royall brothers. But Mr. Royall! He was a lovely man, and very good to me."

Oliphant said, "The Royalls are down to the sisters and sisters-in-law, and the grandchildren. And me. Can you believe it?"

"What a thing! Mr. Oliphant, you take too much upon yourself. I have long wanted to do more for you."

Oliphant was now too grim to continue about the Royalls. "This is wrong talk, on such a day. Wrong, Edmund. You're to be married, and here I am tolling the dead." Oliphant tried a smile. "Could you dine with me tonight? I could make up to you for this display of temper and grief. We could forget with some Madeira."

"I wish that I could." Homes bounced his cane tip off his boot. "I'm already promised for the whole weekend. Those in-laws-to-be I mentioned."

"Certainly," said Oliphant. He wanted to conceal his disappointment. "You have quite an ordeal ahead of you. I remember when I first met the Royalls. It was—an ordeal." Oliphant laughed a little. "An ordeal."

"I could try to put them off for just tonight, sir."

"No, no, you must go." Oliphant could see Homes's concern for him, and felt wonderfully stronger for the man's compassion. Oliphant smiled broadly. "You can't put the VanderHorsts off! If they are like the Royalls, it can't be done. They are your destiny."

"Oh my," said Homes.

They laughed together again, though not as heartily as before, and then strolled a short way up West Street, to the Rector Street intersection opposite the Baltimore-bound screw propeller ships. Oliphant saw Homes glance through a window to a wall clock. Oliphant said, "You must get on, I've kept you too long."

"No, it's fine, sir, I was just—"

"I have to get on myself," said Oliphant.

Homes struggled to hail a hack as the traffic swelled at the end of the business day. Finally, he was successful and turned to say farewell.

"One last question," said Oliphant, holding the cabin door open. Oliphant's melancholy had ahold of him again, and he could not ignore some dark thoughts. "Could you, Edmund, if I were to ask, could you get up, say, ten thousand in gold in a night?"

Homes startled, "Gold? Ten thousand? Why, yes. Yes, sir. Thrice that. A single night? Yes, I could."

"From my own accounts, you understand, not from the trust funds."

Homes said, "Yes, sir, I understand. Are you sure, gold?"

Oliphant was thinking of Longuemare's threat. It felt sinister even to mention it; and yet he was, if an impotent agent, still a Confederate one. And Richmond was bloody-minded, and unpredictable. He said, "It would have to be in gold."

"Is there some difficulty, sir?"

Oliphant feinted, "What would it mean if Alexander Stephens was in Canada for peace negotiations? A rendezvous with Lincoln's men. In terms of gold prices?"

"Is he? Why—is he?"

"Not to my knowledge." Oliphant had his answer. It would mean a lightning bolt. So that was Durant's game within the game, and why Durant had tried to hire Lafayette Baker for that lordly bribe: Durant thought he could manipulate the gold exchange, or at least anticipate a panic. Oliphant sagged. Understanding the intrigues did not solve them. Nevertheless, he must act on his perceptions, and he must be cautious.

Oliphant spoke solemnly to Homes, "Thank you, Edmund, for your care. I want you to hear me now, and not to comment. If there was some difficulty, as you say, well— You do know my solicitor in London?"

"Mr. Abrams is well known to me, sir."

"Very well, then, good," said Olipahnt; he offered his hand, and they parted affectionately. Oliphant turned away and continued up West Street along the inmost walkway. From this vantage, Oliphant could read the notices on the wooden facades of the piers, announcing the passage and freight prices to Venezuela, Vera Cruz, San Francisco, Portland. The horse-cars worked slowly through the criss-crossing traffic, just as the departing ships and barges had to slide carefully out into the myriad fleet of steamers and sloops jamming the river.

The noise was extreme and had the effect of pushing Oliphant deeper into his thoughts. He hugged the building fronts and lost himself in the crowd. At Cortlandt Street, the pedestrian rush was impenetrable for a while, with the day workers pouring across West Street to the New Jersey ferry piers, and so Oliphant retreated to an alcove. He had a notion to continue up West Street to the California-via-Nicaragua pier to entertain himself by watching the off-loading of *Pandora*. When the traffic cleared he started to do just that. But then he stopped as if shot. Up ahead, he saw the same dwarfish old woman once again.

She was less than three feet tall. Her head was overlarge, and her hair was piled atop her head and held with a greasy turban. Her clothes were dark rags that did not conform to the shape of a human figure. And she walked with a tentative shuffle while looking down at her bare and swollen red feet.

None of this would ordinarily have distinguished her from the hundreds of similar wretches who wandered the city daily, vanishing with the night into the horrors of the infamous Fourth and Sixth Wards east of Broadway. Yet Oliphant was sure it was the same poor creature whom he had seen three times previously: at the Chambers Street railroad station the day he arrived; in front of the dentist's office on Tuesday; in City Hall Park the day before. Now here she was on West Street. And what made Oliphant most sure that it was the same woman was that she carried a grotesque and unforgettable version of a beggar's cup. It was a skull, gray with grime, one eye socket smashed out, its crown broken open to receive coins; and painted on the forehead was the word, REAP.

Oliphant recovered his bearings and fled east on Vesey Street. She seemed to be following him. He hurried on, since this route would take him back to the Astor House. He crossed Washington Street and then Greenwich Street quickly, and was in sight of St. Paul's steeple when he stopped. This was not worthy. What was there to be afraid of?

Oliphant paused at a shop to buy a copy of an evening paper. He glanced at the headlines, and was most unsurprised to see a report of Major-General Benjamin F. Butler's arrival in the city. So much for secrets—though there was not a specific mention of the ten regiments that Longuemare had reported had come with Butler.

Oliphant folded up the paper. What did he care about Butler? He chose some rich tobacco, paid, and went back on the sidewalk. By this time, he had set his mind.

He intended to get to the Astor House bar and enjoy a long smoke and some good wine. And then he would telegraph Beverley Tucker at Montreal to beware the approach of Lafayette Baker. And Oliphant would be blunt, because he was done with their stupid intrigues; he would telegraph, "The cotton deal is a failure."

Yet Oliphant would do none of this before he had conducted himself with proper charity. He studied the pedestrian flow. There she was, coming toward him, a tiny human being making her way as best she could through the threats of hurtling people and stomping horses. She halted at a curb, and drew back, apparently frightened by a dog that was feeding on the garbage in the gutter.

Oliphant walked toward her; by the time he arrived he had a roll of greenbacks in his hand. He did not want to scare her, and waited a moment before he reached down. Her odor made him gag, so he held his breath and released the money into the skull's opening. But the roll of bills opened up and did not go in properly. Oliphant tried again. She moved to help. Oliphant felt the touch of her hand, as dry and cold as stone.

FRIDAY EVENING, NOVEMBER 4

The Rotunda Bar at the Astor House was a cavern of dark wood held up by thick iron pillars. It was gaslit so brilliantly that the brass fixtures reflected a dull orange and the faces of the numerous patrons looked a sweaty yellow. The room was large enough to be divided into adjacent open areas about several bar counters that were fitted in the center, along the walls, and into the rear concave shape of the room beneath a bank of translucent windows onto the courtyard. At the bars themselves, the ornaments were subdued—none of those irksome mirrors or pornographic paintings—and subordinated to the beer taps and plates of treats. There was space for several hundred men overall. And on the right sort of evening, with the tobacco cloud as thick as fog, with the smell of men, beer, whiskey, and roasted meat, with the laughter like detonations amid the rumbling murmur, with all this and with the prospect of expeditions out to the theater, opera, or bawdy-house and then later to return back here for a last drink, the easy impression was that of gentlemanly gladiators massed in the arena.

And tonight, there was an imminent and extraordinary event to celebrate —the torchlight parade of Republicans up Broadway to the rally at Union Square. The Rotunda Bar had filled early and then shown itself protean, accepting more and more of the partisans until it became Republicanism itself, men singing, "Ain't You Glad You Joined the Republicans?" to the tapped beat of boots and the raised chime of toasts to Abraham Lincoln and Andrew Johnson and the holy Union cause. Soon there were so many stovepipe-hat conclaves that each seemed to vent tobacco smoke like factory stacks as the great industrial empire of New York State manufactured its dreams for the Election. Tonight, New-York! And next Tuesday, the Union forever! Who can stop us? The Democrats to the devil! Who is not with us? Jeff Davis to hell!

Despite the din, Oliphant was able to find pleasure. He had tucked himself onto a bench to the left of the main door, with a good view out onto the center of the room, while remaining protected from the surges of the crowd at the nearest bar counter. He had also supplied himself with more than a few glasses of champagne, and if he was not prepared to join the songfest, he was certainly aglow with the spectacle. They were Republicans, true, but also fathers, husbands, lovers, and sons, and their humor was restorative. Oliphant drained his glass.

"Mr. Oliphant, sir," called a voice from nearby. "Mr. Oliphant, it's me, Kennedy, sir!"

Oliphant looked up and smiled. "Yes, it is, yes." Kennedy was in bright new clothes, a beige morning coat and light blue pants, a waistcoat of cool navy stripes, and a pale blue tie. This time Kennedy's taste for colors pleased Oliphant, for he stood out among the brown and black clothing of the Republicans like a blossom in a muddy spring garden. As Narcissa would have said, he was "the handsomest man to see." Oliphant was genuinely delighted. He made room on the bench, and said, "Let me buy you a drink, Mr. Kennedy. Let me buy you dinner."

"Sir, oh, sir, I am ashamed," started Kennedy; he bowed his head. "And I am so relieved to have found you."

"Whatever is this?" asked Oliphant. "You're just in need of wine. Sit, sir. What a happy chance to have met like this."

"It isn't a chance, sir." Kennedy bent forward, his face inches from Oliphant's. "I'm here to apologize, sir, and to explain. The gentleman who called on you this morning, Captain Longuemare. Last night, at dinner, it was I who recommended that Captain Longuemare call on you. And I know now that I was wrong to have presumed upon you."

Oliphant thought for a moment and then smiled again. "Calm yourself, and sit by me." Oliphant flagged a bar boy and ordered two more glasses of champagne—the good enough and available Bininger's Mum. Kennedy settled in to Oliphant's right and started his plea again. Oliphant cut him off and would not let him talk until the wine arrived. Then, Oliphant started, speaking deliberately to penetrate the constant roar of the room, "Mr. Longuemare, and Mrs. Longuemare, and I have had a long acquaintanceship. There was no serious bother to me this morning. It is no matter."

"Sir, it is! I didn't know who you were before. I mean, I knew some of it, but not— Mrs. Longuemare told me. I know now! Of your importance to our cause!"

"Drink," said Oliphant. "Drink again. There. Now, whatever you have learned of me, I'm not half what you think. And even that will disappear in sight of the bottom of this glass. A toast then, indulge me." Oliphant waited just long enough for Kennedy to understand that he must obey Oliphant's whimsy. Oliphant continued, "To love! And love's month— April next year for a friend of mine. And all the other months for all my other friends." Kennedy drank the toast. Oliphant laughed, and said, "Thank you. So now we can talk of finer things. Some decent fish, for example. And you can tell me what you have done today. It was superb down at the Battery. Have you had a proper tour of the city? I've missed you. It wasn't right of me to abandon you at the station. But now I can show you the sights."

Kennedy seemed contained, and nodded. "I was at Barnum's while I waited for you."

"I've never been, sad snob that I am."

"Miss Cappawhite recommended that I go. You remember her? She's been most generous. I was over to Brooklyn yesterday. And she's asked me to come to church services Sunday. To the Reverend Beecher's! Isn't it the way? Meet a beautiful girl, and she's abolitionized!"

Oliphant stopped the bar boy and made him leave a half-empty magnum; he refilled Kennedy's glass and propped the bottle between his boots. Oliphant joked, "The like-minded of this world, Mr. Kennedy, they bore each other. It's better to spice the fish stew mercilessly. Oh, I am so hungry, and so happy that you are here!"

"They have a wonderful pet seal at Barnum's," said Kennedy. "As you mention fish. A rare fellow. They call him Ned the Learned Seal. He can count his own fish."

"You must take me to see him," said Oliphant. "We share an appetite for fish, Ned and I." Oliphant was almost convinced that he had persuaded Kennedy to his own state of mind; he also knew that he must keep Kennedy amused. Oliphant might have, except that several tipsy Republicans just then began singing nearby.

"We'll hang Jeff Davis on a sour apple tree! . . ."

When the song finished, Kennedy was dire-faced again. Kennedy mumbled at first, and then he tried, "I really did come here to ask for your forgiveness, Mr. Oliphant. I can't drink with you any more unless you hear my petition. And forgive me."

Oliphant could not wholly resist. Kennedy needed to do penance as much as he needed a political education. He was naive and abused. Longuemare and his crowd had duped him, and sent him to win Oliphant to their mad schemes. Oliphant leaned forward for more wine, and said, "There is nothing that you have done that requires forgiveness. But, I forgive you. There. Now you can dine with me."

"No, no, sir. Surely you know that we're pressed for time. You must come with me and see the particulars of the mission."

"You are new to these people and this city," said Oliphant. "Mission? It's always the same with them. Their secrets, their plots, their desperate decisions. I've heard them all before, and— Now, I've forgiven you for something that doesn't matter. Trust me, and forget their notions. This, what? Affair. It shall come to nothing because it is nothing. At most, a fantasy of idleness and bitterness."

"But Captain Longuemare is a veteran of this work!" protested Kennedy. "And Colonel Martin and his men are acting under orders. And there's a whole society. Thousands!" Kennedy lowered his eyes. "We can't talk here."

"Yes we can, Mr. Kennedy, that's part of the joke." Oliphant smiled to show his confidence. "You mean the Sons of Liberty, don't you? Copperhead password-givers? And Fernando Wood and Clement Vallandigham and Longuemare's fantastic Northwest Conspiracy? Look. Look at the room. See? I've said it, and no one cares. No one does care, except perhaps a few stupid detectives. You think these Republicans care? Overfed, over-stimulated, and nearly victorious. I know what I say, Mr. Kennedy, I know."

Kennedy tried, "Captain Longuemare says there are spies against us every-where."

"Will you trust me?" continued Oliphant. "And to call them spies flatters them. I've met the chief of their spies. The head of the United States Secret Service. Truly. I met him this morning. Upstairs here. He's an arrogant clerk, scuffling for gratuities. It's all a grim, grim joke."

"You're important and informed, sir," said Kennedy. "You must know this is a crucial time. I've lost the last year, in that prison. But now I am trying. I do believe that this Election will settle the war and the fate of our people, forever. I don't understand it all, but I believe that. This is a time that will not come again. You've seen the Yankee papers? And now, what about Butler? What about the fact that Beast Butler is here to use bayonets to make them vote for Lincoln?"

"Oh, electioneering!" cried Oliphant. He relaxed, and started again, "Butler is a crude show. Only that. And proof that Lincoln's men don't even trust their own people. The War Department—both War Departments—are like courtesans. They fancy each other's tricks, and they think the disgust and fear they cause is actually respect. They call vice a mandate, and—so, don't read the papers. Don't listen to the plotters. It is all a trite, degrading game. Whatever the point was, it is lost now."

Kennedy nodded as if he understood, but then he returned to his appeal with new fervor. Soon Kennedy was rambling on about politics. He used men's names like wine labels—McClellan, Seymour, and Davis, always Jefferson Davis. It was, for Oliphant, like listening to a drunken man who was trying to convince himself that the quality of his drink somehow justified his stupor.

Kennedy also said that he was much taken with the "cool manner" of the Kentucky guerrillas, Martin and Headley and the others, whom he had gotten to know a little better in the last four days. Kennedy again cursed Major-General Ben Butler, whom he often called "Beast Butler," an identity that Butler had won for his notorious suppression of resistance during his tenure as Union military commander of captured New Orleans in 1862. Kennedy spoke most fervently when he mentioned a young woman he had met recently who was a member of the Sons of Liberty, a Miss MacDonald.

Oliphant puffed on his pipe and let Kennedy talk. Oliphant's hope was that he could get enough champagne into Kennedy to undo his logic. But then Kennedy, struggling to make what he said sound as portentous as possible, used a word that angered Oliphant. Kennedy said, "Incendiarism."

Oliphant stomped his heel. "No!"

"Like Sheridan in the Valley," explained Kennedy. "Horace Greeley celebrates Sheridan for burning towns."

"You don't mean it!" barked Oliphant. "It's not worthy of you to talk like them. Greeley is a double-dealer. No! And don't prop yourself up by calling it some euphemism. Incendiarism! It's arson and murder, you mean, so say it. No! It makes us the same as the worst of them."

"But Mr. Oliphant, it is what they told me of their plan."

Oliphant was furious and shook both hands at Kennedy, spilling wine and crying, "How could you listen to them? You should have walked away! I should have too. I should have thrown Longuemare out! But no, here I am, playing along. Not much different than you. Well, stop it. I shall stop it! They want a fine fellow like you to ruin himself by doing their crimes for them. It's the worst, the worst!"

"I don't understand, sir. They told me that you knew all about it."

Oliphant stood up, wobbly but determined; he said, "I suppose I did know. Yes, and I did nothing, and that was wrong. Get up! Get up now. You've done your job after all. I shall go with you now, Mr. Kennedy. Let me see these outlaws. I shall show you what they are. Oh, don't soothe me. Get up!"

The City Hall clock tower showed past 8 P.M. as Oliphant and Kennedy burst out of the Astor House. They were immediately surrounded by a circus of Republicans who were battling for transportation to the parade. The assembly point for the parade was said to be at Madison Square, at 8:30; the route to be followed was reported to resemble an ampersand that was to finish at Union Square. It was all too sketchy and frantic for anyone but a sober man to figure. Most thereabout had long since admitted a drunken incomprehension, and were now begging for anything on wheels moving uptown.

Oliphant scowled at the chaos and demanded that Kennedy tell him their destination. Kennedy named an address off Washington Square, about a mile and a half north. Since this was the same general direction that the Republicans were following, Oliphant could see that they would have to fight for a hack. The crowd was riotous! One obese man masquerading as George Washington tried to pull Kennedy up onto a flatbed wagon as it rolled by. Boys ran by handing out Roman candles and volcanoes, keeping the firecrackers to themselves for mischief. There were two wagons overfilled with drunkards and wrapped in red, white, and blue bunting, pulled up before the Astor House. The first had a large poster board that announced, "Lincoln for President/Johnson for Vice-President/Fenton for Governor/Alvord for Lt. Governor." The second's poster board had a more provocative display, three familiar portraits surrounded by the announcement, "Grant, Sherman, Farragut—Our Peace Commissioners."

Oliphant was too angry to wait. He told Kennedy that they would walk. They pushed up Broadway through spontaneous singing and, at Chambers Street, a whole marching band. Farther on, Kennedy applauded a lone piper who strutted between the horsecar tracks bleating a war tune. Kennedy also lifted his hat to every attractive lady, and was otherwise so open-faced that he was soon festooned with "Lincoln & Johnson" buttons and carrying a bouquet of small United States flags.

More, Kennedy commented as they maneuvered through the stream of pedestrians: "Yankees like a high time, sir, and aren't only for prayer and money, true?" "There couldn't be another road like this Broadway—row upon row of great friendly buildings that each could hold everyone in any town in my parish!" "Their women aren't like ours, sweet as cane and gentle. Yet there's force to them, this look-at-youness!"

Kennedy's high spirits gradually calmed Oliphant. Oliphant decided that rather than being stern with Kennedy, he would try pedagogy. Oliphant began to instruct Kennedy about the Election and the plotters against it. Oliphant said that the paramount issue next Tuesday was "War or Peace?"

Kennedy interrupted to say that he thought it was "Slave or Free?"

That was 1860, explained Oliphant; in 1864, no one, not Lincoln and his moderate and radical Republicans, nor McClellan and his so-called War and Peace Democrats, made a serious pretense that the issue of slavery could any longer justify the slaughter of the war, and any spokesman who maintained that the war must continue in order to free the slaves was likely to be stoned. The Election of 1864 was about peace, said Oliphant: When? How? Who would bring it? And what would the peace look like?

Understanding this, the peace faction in the United States was concentrating its opposition to Lincoln in the least traditional and most disaffected section of the Union, the Northwest.

Early in the war, the leader of the peace faction had been a Democratic congressman from the Northwest, Clement L. Vallandigham, a dapper, delicate-featured, 40-year-old demagogue. Vallandigham had doggedly opposed the war as illegal and the Draft as tyranny. His position was understood as disguised support for the Secessionists. In the spring of 1863, the War Department had arrested Vallandigham for treason. The uproar in the Northwest had been such that, after Vallandigham's conviction by a military court, Lincoln had been obliged to commute the sentence from a prison term to exile. Vallandigham had removed to Canada. Subsequently, the hale and eloquent New York Democratic congressman Fernando Wood, an ex-New-York mayor with dyed black hair and a grandiose temper, had become the chief spokesman for peace in the North.

Meanwhile, the fiercest of Lincoln's opponents in the Northwest, and also in the East (including many of those opposed to the war as well as those disposed to the Confederacy), had coalesced around the old secret society called the Knights of the Golden Circle. Founded in the early 1850s as a filibustering club, the Knights of the Golden Circle had aimed to conquer and annex Central America, the Caribbean Islands, and South America in order to construct, with the South, a huge so-called golden circle for slavery. When war had come in 1861, the Knights of the Golden Circle had tacitly sided with the Confederacy.

By the spring of 1863, the Knights of the Golden Circle in the Northwest claimed to have up to 300,000 members arranged in small, secret clubs called castles. The leadership thereupon decided to change the organization's focus to one of open rebellion from the Union, and to arm. A new name was chosen to reflect the new paramilitary nature of the society. The Order of American Knights was born.

The O.A.K. was powerful and defiant. It promoted Vallandigham as the Democratic candidate for governor in Ohio, though he was still in exile. In Indiana, the O.A.K. was so intimidating that the governor could not call the legislature into session for fear of a vote of secession. And in southern Illinois, the part of the state called Egypt because its major city was Cairo, the O.A.K. held open-air assemblies and ignored the Draft.

The Union Army's successes at Vicksburg and Gettysburg in July 1863 set back the plans and undercut the strength of the O.A.K. By the winter of 1864, the O.A.K. was demoralized and in need of reawakening. In

February 1864, in New-York, a secret meeting chaired by Congressman Fernando Wood reorganized the O.A.K. into a stricter, more militant society. Again, the name was changed, this time to give the organization credence throughout the Union. Borrowing the aura of the Boston patriots in the Revolutionary War, the Sons of Liberty was born.

Soon after, Jefferson Davis dispatched a series of Secret Service agents to open relations with the Sons of Liberty, and to offer assistance in advancing plans for insurrection. That was why Jake Thompson and his fellow agents were in Canada. Through the spring and summer of 1864, huge sums of Confederate gold helped to purchase arms in New-York that were then given over to the Sons of Liberty in the East and Northwest. Also, the Confederate Secret Service agents offered the Sons of Liberty a master plot, long percolating, to take the Northwest out of the Union in one coordinated, seditious blow called the Northwest Conspiracy.

Clement Vallandigham had been named Supreme Commander of the Sons of Liberty in February 1864. In June 1864, Vallandigham returned from Canada in order to promote a peace plank for the upcoming Democratic convention platform. The Federal authorities knew Vallandigham was back, and that he had been in close concert with Jake Thompson and the Confederate Secret Service in Canada; but they were too unsure of the Union cause in the Northwest to arrest him again. Soon, Vallandigham was in control of the Peace Democracy, the minority aspect of the Democratic party that included Fernando Wood, New York governor Horatio Seymour, Connecticut governor Thomas Seymour, and also Ohio congressman George H. Pendleton, who would become the Democratic vice-presidential nominee. By August, at the convention in Chicago, Vallandigham was in a strong enough position to draft the crucial sections of the party platform. He made an armistice and peace negotiations primary, and he was deliberately ambiguous about whether or not the Democrats wanted to restore the Union as it once had been.

This single-minded drive for peace fractured the Democratic party. It also tainted the presidential nominee, Major-General George B. McClellan, who was the spokesman for the majority aspect of the party called the War Democracy. Worse, the Republicans were able to point to Vallandigham's reputation as a collaborationist as a way to smear the whole party as treasonous. And while, in August, Lincoln had looked vulnerable to McClellan's popularity and the Democratic strategy for a so-called honorable peace, the military victories of September and October had gradually restored Lincoln's prestige and reinforced the Republican party strategy for the continuation of the war until the Union was again whole and safe.

Oliphant spoke carefully to Kennedy. He paraphrased at length from McClellan's speeches to illustrate the popular opinion that if "Little Mac" had not been able to solve the split in his own party, how could he be trusted to solve the nation's division? And Oliphant made a special point about the Republican party: Unable to win or end the war, it was likely to win the Election merely by standing for patriotism and the status quo, while the Democrats hacked at each other about peace.

Oliphant stopped his monologue. He was about to relate his analysis of Lincoln. But then he realized that Kennedy was strolling alongside singing softly to himself.

"Mine eyes have seen the glory of the coming of the Lord," sang Kennedy, *"He is trampling out the vintage where the grapes of wrath are stored; He hath loosed the faithful lightning of His terrible swift sword; His truth is marching on."*

"Mr. Kennedy!" said Oliphant.

"Sir?" asked Kennedy. "Yes, it is a ponderous tune. I've just learned it. This Mrs. Howe is so pious. Battle isn't nearly so preacherly."

Oliphant sighed. "I suppose it isn't yours to master all these miserable politics. Or perhaps not to master more than political songs. Lord knows you've had a hard time of it."

Kennedy was somber. "Many've had it worse. I got out of that cage."

"You did, and you're here, and fine," replied Oliphant. "Why should you care? Or choose between waffling McClellan and empty, empty Lincoln? When it's laid out to see, it's mud. An Election to display that we are as frightened as wounded beasts."

Kennedy startled. "We, sir? How do you mean, *we* are frightened?"

"Because we are, all of us—all of us Americans."

"Yes." Kennedy sounded perplexed, and tried again, "Yes. Yes, sir. I do appreciate you helping me like this. I was never a bookish one. At West Point, my rooms were known for song and camaraderie. My mother says that I can't sit still. Back home, I was known as a fellow toward what's called a lady's fool."

"The very best sort of politics," laughed Oliphant; he took two flags from Kennedy's bouquet to hand them to two boys walking past them.

Oliphant and Kennedy then strode into Washington Square, a happy rectangle just west of Broadway with thirty-year-old trees and Chinese pagodas. In the center there was a granite-built fountain that served as a rendezvous for couples. The townhouses on the four sides of the park were alight with content home life. It was an excellent fall evening with a new moon, so it was star bright and smelled of the miniature mountain range of burning leaves at the top of the park at the foot of Fifth Avenue. In the distance was the sound of band music.

Oliphant was charmed. He regretted his earlier temper. Kennedy was neither a dupe nor an innocent; he was only a soldier far from home, and that was a very good reason to be patient with him, and forgiving.

"There's the shop!" called Kennedy. "The second house, with the trim, see?"

"Mr. Kennedy, if we must go in— Must we?" Oliphant paused, and studied their destination. It was a three-story house with the ground floor converted into a music shop. The sign over the shop door read,

MacDonald's Fine Instruments
Pianos—Strings—Repairs
Since 1850
A. W. MacDonald & Son

The shades were drawn in the house above, and the music shop itself showed only a dim gaslight. Oliphant started to point this out, when Kennedy jumped down the two steps from the sidewalk, to ring the shop bell. Oliphant shifted on the sidewalk, and called out, "No one's home, Mr. Kennedy. Come on now. Won't you dine with me?"

Kennedy said, "Katie's sure to be here, at least." Kennedy rang several times, and then waved at Oliphant. "I shall get around back and let you in."

Kennedy disappeared into the shrubbery before Oliphant could object. Oliphant tapped his cane and spun around. He felt foolish. This house of secret convocations was as ordinary as beer. The rest of the street appeared similarly innocuous, with several houses having jeweler's, chemist's, or haberdasher's shops on the ground floor. Oliphant turned back to the music store. He liked the flower boxes, and the still-bright marigolds. This house was certainly not Longuemare's usual sort of opera-going crowd. These were Irish shopkeepers—good Catholics, keen businessmen, large-fisted and quarrelsomely cliquish, with platter-faced women and vast families.

But then, thought Oliphant, it was true that the Sons of Liberty in New-York was heavy with Irish. It was not that difficult for a man to go from being anti-Protestant and anti-rich to being anti-Republican and anti-war. The Republican party was built upon several foundations, and one of them was the xenophobic and rabidly anti-Catholic Know-Nothing party of the 1840s and '50s. The Irish had suffered more than most from persecution in the North, and it was not far-fetched for them to see the war as hypocritical, and for them to believe that the only time America tolerated them was when it needed boys to fill the Draft. Oliphant imagined what he would meet inside: thick-necked, red-faced Ulstermen.

Soon enough, there was a noise from inside the shop, and then Kennedy popped open the shop door. He had an oil lamp; he called, "Sir, here we are. Katie's here, like I said. Come in!"

"Mr. Kennedy, must we? I mean—" Oliphant stepped down, and looked in the door. Kennedy tugged on Oliphant's arm, and Oliphant went along. They picked their way through display cases of instruments and two pianos wedged together along the wall. The shop looked cluttered, but very clean; it smelled of old paper and varnish. They paused at a curtain in the back.

"Upstairs now, sir," said Kennedy. "Katie's in the kitchen."

"Who is Katie?" asked Oliphant. But Kennedy was off again, up a narrow staircase and through a door into a dark hall. The dominant odor now was that of baking bread. Kennedy opened one more door to reveal a glowing kitchen.

Oliphant peeked. A solid, red-haired woman in a loose gray frock stood alone behind a table in the center of the room. Her hands were plunged in dough. There were bread loaves cooling on the windowsill, and the large oven radiated an orange fire. The woman had been working so hard that her face was dappled with sweat beads that covered a Milky Way of freckles.

Kennedy gestured to Oliphant at the doorjamb. "Mr. Oliphant, I'm pleased to introduce Miss Katherine MacDonald."

She did not look up, but she said, "Katie."

"A pleasure, Miss MacDonald," said Oliphant, stepping inside. She was even-featured, fine-figured, with muscular forearms. Oliphant guessed that she was about 20 years old. He added, "I apologize for our pushing in like this, at an inconvenient time."

She began, "The row Bobby sent up would've announced Cromwell a-marchin'." She was not smiling. "It'd be good of you to sit and keep your words soft. There's three babies asleep above us, and a small fellow dozed off through that door."

"We could try another time," said Oliphant.

"Bobby tells me you're a family man, and sure you know there's children either asleep or underfoot. The house is jammed up just now, with my sister in Washington to visit her husband in hospital and my brother's wife with her family in Philadelphia. We'll get on. Bobby, give the man a chair, and take one for yourself. Would you like tea and buttered rolls? I know you've not had your supper yet."

Oliphant sat reluctantly by the table while Kennedy helped pour the tea and arrange a plate of rolls. Oliphant commented, "I'm sorry to hear of your brother-in-law."

Katie MacDonald set down a butter plate. "He's improved since they got him up to the new Sanitation Commission place. It's a leg, we tell Louise, only a leg, but he's a horsecar driver, and not worth much unless it heals."

Kennedy tore the bread. "An Army wagon went over it."

"They'd've amputated it if Louise'd not stopped it," she said. "Those surgeons are quick with the knife on common soldiers. Never a thought they might as well cut his throat and make a widow rather than leave a one-legged fool who'll make his wife keep him in whiskey money while she's slaving away her youth."

Oliphant nodded. "It is very sad when you—"

"Not so sad that there's not choices to make and things to do," she interrupted. She flipped a mass of dough into a bowl, and began on another batch. She began again softly, "Wooleyhan, my dad's friend, Wooleyhan, he tells a story about the famine in Ireland. A man named Brann came home from the English cotton mills after six months, and he finds his family dead. The last two still watching for him at the door, but dead. He takes the money he's saved and goes out to the quarry to buy good gravestones. He takes the two at the door, and digs up the others from the yard. And he uses the rest of the money to send them off with a fine funeral, proper, with a priest. The last coppers he has, he uses to light candles for them in the church. Now, then. He made his choices. He acted. When others might have quit, he chose! Now, my sister-in-law Billie's in Philadelphia to help her ma bury her uncle, dead of the bad water at Army camp, and she took the money she'd had from lace-making to get her ma through it. So I declare, choose, and act. It's all sad, Mr. Oliphant, but that doesn't mean there aren't things to be done."

Oliphant was puzzled by her pique, and defended himself. "I spoke in sympathy, not disinterest, Miss MacDonald."

"It's good you're a sensitive man, though it's wasted on me. Bobby tells me what you've said of us. That we're idle and bitter."

Kennedy flinched. "No, Katie."

Katie MacDonald continued, "I take offense at your words, Mr. Oliphant. Not easily. Not for my own sake. It's a fact that there's among us those who'd drink up and rob Brooks Brothers again rather than make a stand against the war. My dad and my brother, Barney, tonight, they're at a grand meeting of the Sons of Liberty over at Jersey City, where there'll be that said. 'To the streets,' they'll cry, 'and this time no O'Brien son of 'em will stop us though they turn guns on women and babies!' Oh, aye, it'll be boasts against the Protestant landlords, and there'll be a prize nailed up for the man who first bites the buttons off Ol' Dix's blue coat. Right, then, and I wager you could find such foolishness among any lot who've been kept down and scared. But hasn't there always been big-talkin' and nastiness before you give the boot to the tyrants? In Charleston once, and in Boston ninety years back? And those patriots, their talk came to more than fantasy. And it wasn't idle. Not idle at all! You small, small man, not idle! Though I won't hide my bitterness!"

Kennedy stood and tried both to calm Katie MacDonald and to defend Oliphant. She scoffed, and used a husky, penetrating voice to quote what Kennedy had told her—before he had brought Oliphant in—of Oliphant's opinion of the Sons of Liberty.

Kennedy pleaded, "He didn't mean it that way."

She replied, "Oh? And how am I to hear, 'A fantasy of idleness and bitterness'? And who is it he thinks has been dying in Virginia for the Union Army? No, it's not the Protestant rich boys! It's the boys from the homes of this idle and bitter lot!"

Oliphant watched Kennedy tussle with Katie MacDonald; he was sympathetic to both. She was not as hot-headed as she might have been. Therefore, Oliphant thought her more alarming, and took her seriously.

She waved the flag of rebellion, and the threat of the Draft Riots, when tens of thousands in New-York—and Katie MacDonald might have been one of them—had taken over the city for four steamy days and nights in July 1863. It had been a spontaneous rage at the Conscription Act, the battle casualty rate, and everything Abraham Lincoln represented, especially his Emancipation Proclamation and his willingness to continue the war to free the slaves. The Draft Riots had been anarchy to an unthinkable extreme. Even as the Federal Army had been pursuing Lee's Army of Northern Virginia after the spectacular Union victory at Gettysburg, the mob in New-York had risen up like a forest fire. The rioters had murdered police and militia, had mutilated and hanged Negroes and Orientals from lamp posts, had pillaged shops from Madison Square to Fulton Street, and had set fire to whole city blocks, standing back to cheer as pillars of smoke roared into the sky. Eventually, the War Department had been forced to rush in twelve infantry regiments from the Gettysburg battlefield to quell the rampage. But even then the rioters had only been cowed by the artillery, not defeated, and they had retired to their homes to seethe against the Union cause. Since then, there had been a question that had haunted New-York: "What will we do if they come out again, and this time they are organized?"

Oliphant tasted his tea and waited for a break in the argument between Kennedy and Miss MacDonald. He wanted to speak carefully, because Katie MacDonald was the embodiment of the revolutionary organization that so worried New-York. Oliphant began, "Miss MacDonald, I apologize for my earlier remark. I was wrong to say you were idle. I would like now to speak to what I know to be true of the Sons of Liberty."

She slammed the dough down. "And I shall crown you if you do! My dad'll be home later tonight, and he's the one to charm with your ways. I've seen too many young widows come in the shop to sell us worthless fiddles to buy milk for their babies to debate the more. No, nay, none of that Rebel eloquence."

Oliphant said, "We have common concerns, Miss MacDonald. The war is wrong and crazed. I just do not believe your tactics will stop the fighting. Do you know that Longuemare wants to hire the gangs to do this work?"

"And what if he does? The gangs aren't devils. They're boys like Bobby, and where do you think the gangs've learned their ways with guns? They're ex-soldiers, or on the run from the Draft, and they've finished dying for other men's gain."

Oliphant slumped in his seat; he was melting with the heat of the oven and with her barrage. He tried, "I think I understand—"

"Devil you do! Sure, we're fighting the same enemy, but we're not on the same side, and don't you know it! Don't judge me, you pious man. I'm not my dad, and I'm not my Uncle Larry. I've no more use for your slaveholdin' Jeff Davis and his Protestant Rebels than I do for Father Abraham and that butcher shop. Don't whine to me about your tactics or your plots from Richmond and Toronto neither."

Oliphant sat up straight. She knew about Toronto, which probably meant that she knew about the whole Secret Service organization. This was not a simple partisan. Katie MacDonald was very well informed, and persuasive.

Katie MacDonald took several deep breaths, and pressed, "Now then, what Bobby has asked you, Mr. Oliphant, and what Captain Longuemare has asked you, and what I'm asking you, is will you help us do what we must with that gold of yours?"

Oliphant answered, "It is not mine to say whether I can or not."

"And I say that if you're not prepared to risk for your cause, then you're not the man Bobby says you are."

"Miss MacDonald," objected Oliphant, "I am just one man in a long chain of command."

"Chain is it? I know something of chains, like the chains they put the boys in to take them to Virginia after the Draft's got them." She pointed a flour-coated hand at him. "We're right to risk perishing for what we want, Mr. Oliphant. Because we're perishing for what we don't want anyway. And you! If you won't help us, with your chain of command, then you're just another glad gentleman who only fights this war at the Astor House bar."

With that, she waved her hand in emphasis, and accidentally knocked a small clay bowl from the table, which shattered on the floor.

Kennedy said, "Katie, this isn't right. Mr. Oliphant is telling you true." And then he stooped to clean up.

She said, "Don't cut yourself; leave it." She walked around to kneel beside Kennedy. She brushed her face, smearing flecks of flour on her eyebrows, and asked Kennedy, "What's he for, then, when he won't even hear our plan?"

"He didn't say he wouldn't hear us out," replied Kennedy; still kneeling, he turned to Oliphant. "You will hear us out, Mr. Oliphant, even if you can't promise—even if you need to follow procedures?"

Oliphant hesitated. He was weakening under the force of their passion. He said, "Perhaps I have been unfair."

Katie MacDonald stood again. "You Rebs are hollow talk." She stomped to the oven, and started again with her back to them. "Uncle Larry, he comes back from Toronto and tells me of the Rebel notions of liberty and the Rebel bank accounts. Uncle Larry's very taken with Mr. Jake Thompson and his high ways and his high talk. Well, I'm not. We haven't your Rebel tailors or horse artillery here. We have got beliefs."

She turned and jerked her head at Oliphant. "I was born in this country, and I will be damned—damned!—if I will stand by and watch my kin marched off like sheep to die in Virginia another year. I'm sad for the poor slaves, and I'm sad for all the dead boys like Bobby's brothers. But you tell me how keeping shut about this war and voting for McClellan is going to help the slaves or the dead. No! This war is useless killing and more grief than rocks in Ulster. I'm saying a simple thing—Stop the war now! And there's none of you, Rebs or Yankees or my own family, who'll mind me!"

Katie MacDonald turned away to pry open the oven door with a stick. She used a long-handled paddle to scoop out several loaves and shift them to the shelf beneath the windowsill.

Oliphant thought her motion was relaxed and lovely. He also thought her knowledgeable beyond his expectations. Apparently, her Uncle Larry was an intimate of Jake Thompson's. That would explain the genesis of the tactical operation in New-York. The MacDonalds were likely the contacts between the Secret Service in Canada and the Sons of Liberty in New-York. This meant that, despite Oliphant's efforts to stay clear of Longuemare and the whole Secret Service sabotage plot, he was now sitting in the kitchen of the headquarters of a possible New-York uprising. None of this seemed a fantasy. The Sons of Liberty were busy and enraged.

Oliphant decided to compromise. Rather than continue to argue with Katie MacDonald, he would let her lecture him. She seemed to know a great deal more than he did right now about a horrible prospect. And since there was the ugly possibility that he could be ordered to cooperate with the Sons of Liberty, he needed all the information he could get about their plot.

It made Oliphant feel despondent, but he said, "Miss MacDonald, Mr. Kennedy, I regret my dismissiveness. If you will be patient with me—I want to hear your proposal. But you must understand that I can only take it under advisement. And that I have no authority."

Katie MacDonald asked quickly, "But you can tell them in Richmond what you think of it?"

Oliphant nodded. "Yes, but with difficulty, and slowly."

Kennedy and Katie MacDonald were instantly transformed, the pleading and accusing replaced with the confidence of veteran agents. They cleared the table of bowls and pans. Katie then smoothed a thin layer of flour across the table top. She used her index finger to sketch a map of New-York, the harbor, Brooklyn, and the New Jersey shoreline. She divided the city of New-York into three so-called battle zones: from the Hudson River to Broadway; from Broadway to the East River; and from Fulton Street to the Battery. She marked the Federal and State armories with mounds of brown sugar, and she built a tower of flour paste to indicate the Metropolitan Police Headquarters at 300 Mulberry Street northeast of City Hall. Precinct houses were marked by lesser towers.

Then Katie MacDonald presented the plan of attack for Election Day. Fort Lafayette, the military prison on a rocky islet in the Verrazano Narrows, was to be stormed by men in rowboats from the Brooklyn shore; and to emphasize her point, Katie MacDonald flattened the sugar lump that represented the target. With that, she talked faster and faster. Kennedy stuck matches in the flour paste of the precinct houses, and lit them playfully.

Oliphant listened closely but was gradually overwhelmed. Katie Mac-Donald was coolly discussing the sacking of New-York. It was too incredible for him to judge it now. He just nodded along and concealed his surprise.

At some point in her monologue, Katie MacDonald had to pause because of the crying of a baby in the adjoining room. She fetched the child and propped it on her shoulder while she continued her presentation. She laughed when the baby cooed, and then pointed at a sugar lump that represented a Federal armory. "There're six Napoleons there, for the taking. We'll have artillery this time. You see, the guards are with us, and we have the key."

LATER FRIDAY EVENING, NOVEMBER 4

Oliphant and Kennedy left the MacDonald music shop past ten o'clock. Outside, Kennedy was immediately attracted by the noise and music of the Republican party rally at Union Square just uptown a few blocks. As they drifted in that direction, they could see down through the cross streets that there was a human-held river of fire moving steadily up Broadway. This was the tail end of the Republican parade, and it seemed to dance and throb with the pure yellow glow of the torches and the leaping orange flames from the Roman candles.

Oliphant followed Kennedy most reluctantly. He was exhausted by Katie MacDonald's power, by all the urgent demands made on him since dawn, and by the fact that he had drunk too much and eaten too little since his luncheon. Yet he could not manage to resist Kennedy's charioteer's momentum. Still, he could appeal to Kennedy, "Truly, I must have something to eat."

Kennedy bargained, "We can't miss it, Mr. Oliphant!"

"But wine and tea and bread and butter aren't enough."

"The Yankees in a war dance!" cried Kennedy.

"You must promise to get me to supper soon. I don't feel strong."

Oliphant complained a little longer, but was then stunned into silence by the spectacular scene at Union Square. The Republican crowd swelled up from Broadway and across the park that dominated the square. The park, a neatly landscaped oval with a central fountain, had been refashioned into a natural coliseum to welcome and accommodate the celebrants. There were bandstands at four sides. There was a speaker's stage decorated with Chinese lanterns and large portraits of the candidates and backed by a gigantic scaffolding. The east side of the park was lined with open wagons mounted with batteries of fireworks. And there were bonfires lit at strategic points about the park to create a five-pointed star.

The largest of the bonfires was at the south end of the park, where the marchers broke from the ranks of the parade and re-formed into their neighborhood political clubs in order to compete with each other in song, *"We are springing to the call, from the East and from the West, shouting the Battle-Cry of Freedom! And we'll hurl the Rebel crew from the land we love the best, shouting the Battle-Cry of Freedom!"*

The artificial box canyon of the surrounding brick buildings made for echo upon echo as the clubs bellowed the chorus, *"The Union forever! Hurrah, boys, hurrah! Down with the traitors, up with the stars! While we rally round the flag, rally once again! Shouting the Battle-Cry of Freedom!"*

At this, men would leap into the air in gymnastic contortions to the constant pounding of the kettle drums, and members of the various neighborhood Union War Eagle clubs or Lincoln & Johnson clubs would douse each other with beer and then try to drown out the band music with shouts of "Hurrah!"

Oliphant stood back from the performance and thought them all madmen. He was nakedly frightened by the mob spirit in these partisans, and felt he could see malevolence beneath their jubilation like timber rot below decks. Even worse, he was thinking of the ghastly ferocity that a mob could generate. If this was as many as ten thousand men, then it was only half the number that Katie MacDonald had claimed that the Sons of Liberty could marshal to attack New-York.

The enormity of their plan! She had promised a Babylonian rampage. They would raid the arsenals. They would besiege the precinct houses. They would dismantle Fort Lafayette stone by stone. They would rob the Sub-treasury gold vaults in the Old Custom House at Wall Street. They would capture City Hall. They would occupy all the polling places and destroy the ballots. They would command the telegraph offices, the landing slips, the railroad stations, and the bridges. And by sundown on Election Day they would announce to the United States that New-York was done with the war, the Election, and the Union.

It was not to be a singular revolt. Oliphant had told Longuemare that he knew most of everything, especially about the Northwest Conspiracy, but he had not known how far along Jake Thompson and the Secret Service in Canada had gone with their plans. Along with New-York, there were to be simultaneous attacks in Boston, Buffalo, Cincinnati, Chicago. Vallandigham himself was said to have approved of the plot. In New-York, Fernando Wood was said to have offered the *Daily News,* owned by his brother, as the means to announce the uprising on Election morning. More, Jake Thompson had dispatched Martin, Headley, Kennedy, and the other six as shock troops. Their task, in the first stages of the attack, was to set fires at strategic points throughout the city using Greek Fire, a phosphorous solution that was reported to burn hotter than ordinary flame and to be impossible to extinguish with water.

What did the conspirators want from Oliphant? Twenty-five thousand dollars in gold! It seemed that Ben Butler's sudden arrival in New-York had hit them hard. The Sons of Liberty were primarily shopkeepers and day laborers. They did not have confidence enough to confront infantry and artillery at the very first of the rebellion. The meeting that night in Jersey City was said to be in order to debate what could be done to save the plot. The New-York leadership of the Sons of Liberty was said to prefer delaying the attack until after Ben Butler and his men left the city, even if that meant waiting until after Election Day.

Longuemare's solution to the dilemma was ad hoc. He aimed to hire the gangs of the "Bloody Ould" Sixth Ward—the very same men who had led the Draft Riots—to lead the attack long enough to give heart to the Sons of Liberty. And the signal for the assault by the gangs was to be the incendiarism. Yet the gangs would not agree to the proposal unless they were paid in advance, and in gold. With Jake Thompson and his funds too far away, and the funds in New-York depleted, Longuemare had been forced to appeal to Oliphant.

What did Oliphant think of the plot? That it was mad. That it sickened him. That even to hear part of it made him feel guilty for all of it. Katie MacDonald had stood there with a baby on her shoulder and declared, "They'll negotiate with us, or they'll shovel the ashes of the city when we're done! Fernando Wood's to go to Lincoln at the White House to declare

New-York a free city! And whether we've burned it or freed it, we'll be rid of the bloody Union!"

Oliphant was also sickened by hunger, drink, talk, and his black, black doubts. Kennedy had him by the arm as they stood at the periphery of the park opposite University Place and Fourteenth Street. Gradually, they were pushed farther and farther into the park, and Kennedy's desire for a better view drew them closer and closer toward the center of the crowd.

Some fool had thrown wet wood on the bonfires, which made a black smoky cloud that whipped around in the wind and drove people into coughing fits. There were boys dangling from tree limbs and lobbing firecrackers into the night, which scattered doves and Republicans alike. A little order was reestablished when the bands ceased their competitive thumping to permit a Negro soloist to take center stage on the speaker's platform. The soloist was dressed in the costume of the Goddess of Liberty, and immediately sang out Francis Scott Key's "Star-Spangled Banner." When she reached the final stanza—*"Then conjure we must, when our cause is just, and this be our motto, 'In God We Trust.' And the star-spangled banner in triumph shall wave, o'er the land of the free and the home of the brave!"*—one of the wagons of fireworks let go with a salvo of red, white, and blue rockets.

Oliphant was now desperate with hunger and so faint he was hoarse. He begged, "Mr. Kennedy, please, get me out of here." There was no response. Oliphant tugged on Kennedy's arm, and there was still nothing. Oliphant was suddenly nauseous from the press of the crowd and the smell of vomit in the grass. He lunged at Kennedy, and cried, "Please!"

And then he realized that he had hold of the arm of a stranger. The man turned and grinned. Oliphant recoiled and plunged away into an opening in the surrounding shoulders. He found a tree trunk and clutched it to steady himself. The buildings around the park seemed to sway as the shadows cast by the bonfires danced across their facades like spectres. Oliphant stumbled onward until he was right up against a quartet of private soldiers carrying a banner before them, "We Strike Hard!"

A hand grabbed at Oliphant's hat. Another hand yanked away his cane. Oliphant felt someone reaching into his coat. He yelled, "No!" He gave in to his panic. He also surrendered to his shame, his disgust at humanity up close, and his fear of the mob. He ran helter-skelter, looking for a friendly face, or at least something human. Instead, he only saw the faces of beasts. There were lions growling, dogs snapping, snakes hissing. He crashed through the bushes and fell hard on the street pavement, scraping his knee.

He scrambled up, and hobbled across University Place to the entry portal of the Presbyterian church there. He had lost his hat, cane, pipe, billfold, and sense of balance.

A string of firecrackers exploded nearby. Oliphant covered his ears and prayed. He must gain control of himself. He tasted acid on his lips.

Across the square, the podium speaker thundered forth, "Peace is surrender!"

The assembly replied, "The Democrats are Peace Liars!"

The speaker on the podium cried, "On to Richmond!"

The assembly boomed, "Burn Richmond! Burn Richmond!"

Oliphant huddled against the stone wall. He thought he heard his name being called out. He opened his eyes, or thought he did. Why was he lying on the ground? He heard his name again. But he was afraid to look up. He thought that if he did, he would find himself confronted by the old woman with the skull. Why was she following him? What did she want from him? If only he could just lie here, she might go away. He gagged. He squeezed his eyes shut again. He pictured Katie MacDonald with the baby on her shoulder. He pictured the baby's face. It was the hag! He screamed, or thought he did. He heard his name again. It was Kennedy.

"Mr. Oliphant! Are you hurt?"

Oliphant rolled into the stone wall, and declared, "It is doom! I shall tell Richmond! The plan is doom! We shall all die!"

Kennedy had hold of Oliphant, and spoke soothingly, "I'm here, sir. I've got you. Can you stand?"

"Make her go away," said Oliphant.

"Please try to stand, Mr. Oliphant. I've got you now. I'll get you home."

As Oliphant relaxed into Kennedy's care, the rally trembled with cheers. The speaker was done, and there was a signal for the full ignition of the fireworks.

The bombardment began with a volley of rockets that was meant to be as awesome as that of Grant's at Richmond or Sherman's at Atlanta. All at once the gigantic scaffolding behind the speaker's stage exploded into life. Letter by letter, sculptures of fire lit up to spell out, "Lincoln—Johnson—Fenton—Alvord."

Then detonations pounded the park and the sky above crackled with stars that seemed to melt toward the earth. As Union Square was set alight, Oliphant began to recover himself. Kennedy was strong, and the fear was past. It was also apparent to Oliphant that the Republicans were now encircled by men, women, and children. These onlookers were not partisans, nor were they a mob. They were the American people, curious and delighted on a cool Friday evening. And they were moved to sing along with the Lincolnites, so that by the final stanza of the "Battle Hymn of the Republic" there were tens of thousands of voices lifted in unison:

"In the beauty of the lilies, Christ was born across the sea, with a glory in His bosom, that transfigures you and me! As He died to make men holy, let us die to make men free! While God is marching on!"

CHAPTER 4

Amaziah Butter
at New-York, New York

SUNDAY MORNING, NOVEMBER 6

An hour before first light, Captain Amaziah Butter slumped out of the Secret Service boardinghouse on William Street. He pulled his draped greatcoat close about him like a cape and slowly set out in search of something he could digest without exploding internally. His first stop, however, was to fix his bearings. He stood beneath a street lamp and studied the map they had drawn for him to make certain that he could at least get from William Street to City Hall Park. He located his position on the paper, turned northward, and carefully struck out toward a hot-corn-vendor's stand at what he presumed was the corner of Fulton Street. With every step, his bowels churned like bubbling soup. He also discovered that he could not squeeze his bare hands tight enough to make a fist.

Since Wednesday evening, Butter had been traveling this same twisting half-mile route, but always before either in the company of others or in daylight. Now, alone, hunger-worn but not hungry, and in the unquiet dimness of this perpetually restless place, he felt put-upon and intimidated and worse: He felt deserted by his lifelong excellent sense of direction. Butter the woodsman knew that he could find his way through a forest even if he lacked a compass or moonlight or shoes. But this New-York City was unique for him. It was the only place he had ever been that did not smell like America—the tanginess of the woods, the moldering of the fields, the rain-coming pregnancy of the air. New-York smelled like nothing but New-York. More difficult for him, this was only his fourth morning ever in New-York, and his opinion had hardly altered from the first moment. He had needed only a single look when he had stepped off the ferry from New Jersey on Wednesday afternoon to know that he distrusted everything and everyone, including his own footing, in this mysterious and sinister city.

Butter counted the change in his pocket and then paid the silent crone of a vendor for two ears of corn wrapped in newsprint. He had had to husband his expense allotment since Friday, and this was the way he had been dining. It was also the way he had been reading the news—upside down and a day old. He felt too overwhelmed by events to want or need more vital information than yesterday's headlines.

Butter strode up Fulton from lamp to lamp reading more of Major-General Butler's surprising arrival in the city. That is, surprising for everyone else; for Butter it followed logically from the War Department meeting. Also for Butter it was the one heartening aspect to his present assignment. At least he was not the only soldier the War Department had assigned to New-York. Butter re-read the Butler headlines, and then skipped over to the announcement from Major-General John Dix, the military commander of New-England and New York, that all was calm, and would remain so.

Butter sighed at General Dix's reported assurances. He ate more of his breakfast and proceeded more cautiously along Fulton Street, keeping to the outermost edge of the sidewalk because he was suspicious of the ceaseless size and unknown occupants of the buildings above him. He was forcing himself to walk rather than lope; he was forcing himself to observe rather than lower his eyes. Ahead of him, milk wagons, teamsters hauling huge crates, and lone riders asleep in the saddle made the intersection at Fulton and Broadway appear more congested at this hour than Bangor might ever be except at noontime. Also, there was the usual fleet of newspaper wagons rolling rapidly in all directions, carrying the morning's news. And most likely, Butter thought, it was bad news, for New-York seemed to favor dire reports and ominous events the way Bangor favored bright skies. Butter pushed aside his notion. When he wanted to frighten himself to alert, he thought of New-York as an island prison fortress—seventy times seventy Fort Lafayettes. But he had no patience for imaginings this morning.

He stumbled up Broadway hugging the St. Paul's side of the avenue.

Broadway was too vast and endless for Butter to contemplate. He did note that Barnum's American Museum was eerily still, and that Park Row, along Newspaper Row, was turbulent with men, horses, and wagons. Butter's attention was chiefly for the portentous bulk of the Astor House. It showed a few dim room lights above and the brightly lit colonnaded entrance below. Butter stopped at the corner of Vesey and counted up three floors of the Astor House to the windows where he knew John Oliphant's suite to be. It was dark, and the drapes were drawn.

Butter finished his meal as he reached the Astor House's main doors. He wiped his hand on the newsprint, tucked the wastepaper in his coat, and plunged inside. He hopped back immediately, because the atrium was being washed down by several Negroes, and there was a layer of water everywhere like a soapy sea. One of the gang looked up and grinned. "It's okay, mister." Butter smiled, and crossed the floor with giant steps that made little squeaking sounds. At last, he reached the hall and turned to the main desk. He rang once and a clerk appeared.

"The key for No. 12 Vesey, please," started Butter. "I'm Captain Butter. They were supposed to tell you—"

"Yes, sir," said the clerk. "I have it right here."

"And is there anything for me? From Colonel Baker? Telegrams, or a note?"

"Yes, sir, there is—two messages left for you." The clerk handed over the key and two envelopes, both addressed to Butter.

Butter decided not to open them here. He also decided to avoid the floorwashers by detouring through the central courtyard. But in the dimness, and in his haste, he almost ran over an embracing couple on the path through the chrysanthemums. She did something quickly with her dress. Butter was embarrassed and jumped by them as if leaping over a creek.

He reentered the hallway and tried to slow himself down. He used the key on a door just past the Vesey Street side entrance that was marked "No. 12/Private/No Exit." Down a dark flight of narrow stairs, he opened another door to enter the rear of one of the smaller of the shops that encircled the street level of the Astor House. No. 12 Vesey Street's display window was empty, however, and the front window's curtains were kept shut. For this was the secret New-York headquarters of the United States Secret Service.

The Negro detective seated on the first desk stood quickly and smiled, saying, "Cap' Butter, mornin'." There were three other desks in the long, low-beamed room. The rest was bare except for the well-stocked gunrack on the wall to the left and the banker's safe behind Lafayette Baker's overlarge and padlocked-shut desk. There was also a potbelly stove by the rear steps. The room needed paint, but was clean-swept and cozy, smelling of the green coffee on the stove.

The detective, Walter Daggett, a limber, chubby man, brushed his coat of cigar ash, and waited for Butter to acknowledge his greeting. Butter did grunt. Then Daggett continued, "Lo' Josh, he's fetchin' yer tea now, suh. And Mr. Nevers, he said he left a note for ya."

"Right, good, that's good. I should have some tea, and eat some more, good, Mr. Daggett. You say Mr. Nevers left a note?"

"Dat's it dere," said Daggett, pointing at the envelopes in Butter's hand.

"Right, right." Butter shed his greatcoat but left his hat on. He was trying to think of what he could say to appear that he was in charge and unflustered. He asked Daggett, "You say Mr. Nevers isn't here? Well, what is there on Oliphant that's new? I mean, since last night?"

"Nothin', suh. Louie Delta's up dere now. Mr. Oliphant's asleep and all. Mr. Nevers's gone out for a bit to get his breakfast and all. He says he's meetin' ya later on, and if ya want him afore, I can get a call to him. Mr. Nevers, he left a report for ya on de Rebs, from las' night. Did you want me to get a call to Mr. Nevers?"

"No, no, it's fine," said Butter. He hoped it really was. He needed to wake up more completely. He flopped down in the chair of the desk he had appropriated as his own.

Just then, Lo' Josh, the skeletally thin and very old Negro caretaker of No. 12 Vesey Street, popped up the trapdoor behind Butter. He was coming up from the underground passageway that connected to the Astor House kitchens; he was carrying a tray of hot rolls and cheese and a tea kettle. Butter nodded to Lo' Josh's cheery greeting, and waited until Lo' Josh had served him a mug of tea before turning to the messages.

The first envelope contained a telegram from Colonel Lafayette Baker. This was the first communication that Butter had had from Lafayette Baker since Baker had left Butter in charge of the headquarters on Friday morning. Butter could see immediately that the telegram was as cryptic and unhelpful as Baker had been on Friday. It read, "Maintain your surveillance. I shall return presently. Do not reply to this telegram. Await my instructions. If there is trouble, ask Nevers."

Butter read it twice more and sighed. This was more of the same confusion that Butter had felt from the first he had realized that he was going to New-York. Lafayette Baker had not concealed his dislike of the fact that Butter had been assigned to New-York by the secretary of state without his prior consultation. Yet Baker had accepted the situation soon enough, and had even seemed to sympathize with Butter's complaint that this was not his kind of work. Butter had thought that Baker would just let him tag along to New-York, sit in the corner, and watch.

The Secret Service had appeared to have the operation well in hand. The Rebel guerrillas, whose names had been purchased from an informer in Toronto, had been followed all the way from Canada to their New-York hotels. Since then, they had been kept under constant close watch. All had appeared routine, and the guerrillas had acted no more threateningly than other young gentlemen on the town.

On Friday morning, however, Lafayette Baker had stunned Butter by telling him that he was to be in temporary command of the surveillance of the guerrillas. Lafayette Baker had then vanished with the other detectives, without telling Butter where he was going or when he would return. Now Butter was informed by the telegraph wire that he was to continue to do exactly what he had been doing. Basically, that meant to sit still and fret for his ignorance. Lafayette Baker had told him nothing and had left him nothing to do but watch while the New-York detectives carried on the surveillance, and here Lafayette Baker was telling him more of nothing, and leaving him more of nothing to do, with the same advice as before, to ask Gouverneur Nevers.

Butter reconsidered. This telegram did tell him one thing new. Dated the night before, it was from Montreal. Now why was Lafayette Baker in Canada? And what did he mean that he would be back presently? Was that today? Tomorrow? And one more question: What would Lafayette Baker make of the unavoidable fact that Butter was under an unavoidable order to present himself to Major-General Butler at his hotel in two hours to report on the whole operation?

Butter slapped down Baker's telegram and opened the second envelope. It was from Gouverneur Nevers. Nevers was a New-York detective from the Department of the East. Lafayette Baker had told Butter on Wednesday that Gouverneur Nevers was General Dix's part of this operation. Walter Daggett and Louie Delta were just two of Nevers's apparently numberless and all-Negro company of detectives. Nevers called his people "bokes"— or spies in the slang vernacular of New-York's criminal element. Nevers further divided his people into "gagers," or eyes, who tended to be mobile and male, and "wattles," or ears, who tended to be older, stationary, and very often female or children. Yet these peculiar distinctions did not concern Butter. What did was that Gouverneur Nevers and his secret company were extremely competent and vigorous, and were the eyes and ears and foot soldiers of this present Secret Service assignment.

Also, and most crucially to Butter this morning, it had been Nevers's people who had discovered Friday evening what Butter considered to be a major break in this business. They had found the man Butter believed to be the master Confederate agent in charge of the threatened attack on New-York. His name was John C. Oliphant, and he was asleep three floors above Butter, with detective Louie Delta just outside his door.

Nevers's message was succinct despite its considerable detail. He recounted the night's activities of each of the nine Confederate guerrillas, who were spread in pairs in hotels on or off Broadway. Nevers also included the information that Oliphant, after a late supper with Kennedy and a Mrs. Longuemare, had retired to his rooms with Mrs. Longuemare, who had left in an apparent huff after 2 A.M.

Nevers closed his report with a postscript, "Madison Square at 8. Brooklyn at 10. All quiet along Broadway. G.N."

Butter slapped Nevers's note down on Baker's telegram, and got his logbook from out of his greatcoat. He found a sharpened pencil in the desk and began to record everything he had learned so far. Whether or not Lafayette Baker trusted him, whether or not he was there in New-York only as a sop to Seward, Butter did not intend to allow himself to be overwhelmed by events without keeping a record of his defeat. He asked Walter Daggett, "What time did Oliphant turn out his light?"

"An hour after you left, Cap'," said Daggett.

Butter asked, "Any telegrams for him this morning?"

"Nothin' comin' or goin' since he turned out," said Daggett.

Butter flipped to the special page he had reserved for John Oliphant. This was his pride—the way he intended to demonstrate that, even if his assignment to New-York was a mistake and a fluke, Butter was capable of responding like a good soldier. He had set this page aside the first moment one of Nevers's men had brought word of the discovery of a man whom Butter felt exactly fit his definition of a Rebel master agent—John C. Oliphant.

Since then Butter had covered this page with notations of Oliphant's manner, whereabouts, and associations. Most important, the page included a record of Oliphant's conduct from his rendezvous with the young Captain Kennedy (who had led Nevers's men to Oliphant) in the Astor House Bar on Friday night, to his trip later that night to the suspected Sons of Liberty house on Washington Square, to his still later attendance of the rally at Union Square, and then through Oliphant's leisurely activities all day Saturday in company with Kennedy and later Mrs. Longuemare.

Butter believed wholeheartedly that this page justified his theory that Oliphant was the ringleader and the banker for the guerrillas in New-York —that not only was John Oliphant as important a Rebel agent as Captain Tom Hines, but also that John Oliphant was the Tom Hines of New-York. Yet, as Gouverneur Nevers continued to insist, there was still no good evidence. The page was a trail. It was not proof.

Butter looked up at Daggett. "Were you able to overhear anything? He was in there with Mrs. Longuemare for over two hours."

"Two long hours, Cap'. Dere was some fierce yellin' and carryin' on by dat woman, surely was. I listened for a while. She was makin' herself plain 'bout Mr. Oliphant's wife an' his other kinfolk, specially dis lady named Narcissa."

"Who's that?" Oliphant wrote the name.

"I don't know. Dat lady, Miz Longuemare, kept yellin' Narcissa dis, and Narcissa dat, and to blazes wid Narcissa!"

Butter underlined the name. "What did Oliphant say?"

"He's smart." Walter Daggett smiled. "He kept shut."

Butter continued to write while stuffing bread and cheese in his mouth. He slurped his tea and checked the clock on the wall. He estimated how long he had slept and how long it was until Election Day; he marked down these calculations too. He kept his notes to the facts, and resisted the temptation to record anything that could be regarded by unsympathetic eyes as unsubstantiated opinion. He had so far avoided writing down that he thought Oliphant was a master agent.

It was not that Butter was not pleased with his work, because he certainly was, especially with his secret treasure of John Oliphant. And he looked forward to making his report to Lafayette Baker. But he also knew that at some point, given the usual sort of bonehead maneuvers in this war, this logbook could be his only defense in a court-martial, or in one of Lafayette Baker's drumhead courts, and he did not want it to reveal more than the mind of an obedient trooper. In addition, Butter knew that his caution was caused by more than the threat of some future discipline. He was acting the same way he had all those times in Virginia, when he had sat on horseback and calculated how many rounds of ammunition his company had remaining, and how long they could stay on the line at this rate of fire. It was Butter's way of fighting his fear of the unknown—with the very specific and immediate. The truth was that, here in New-York, Butter felt himself trapped inside a crisis that was worse than Virginia. There, his uniform had protected him from doubt. Here, he felt as out of place and vulnerable as a grinning pumpkin lantern sitting on a front porch—pleasing no one and threatening no one and really most useless.

Butter dotted his i's and crossed his t's and recorded the time before he closed the book. He pulled out a sheet of foolscap and began a letter to his wife, Desire, his fifth letter to her in six days. He was going to tell her how right she had been, how wrong he had been, and how homesick he felt. However, he also felt that his nerves might be better served with a double-bladed axe and a dozen whacks at his desk.

And then Butter experienced an odd sensation. As he wrote, he found his thoughts drifting to the kindness of Mrs. Bridey Lamont. She had told him, as they left the War Department Tuesday night, "Button up that overcoat, Captain Butter, and don't lose it this time."

LATER SUNDAY MORNING, NOVEMBER 6

Almost two hours later, in the full light of a breezy, cloudy morning, Captain Butter was touring the western periphery of Madison Square, the neatly wooded and landscaped expanse between Twenty-third and Twenty-sixth streets where Broadway veered past Fifth Avenue to form an asymmetrical X. Butter stayed close to the shrubbery that surrounded the oval-shaped park at the center of the square, because he did not want to worry himself the more by getting too close to Ben Butler's men. For there they were, fifty yards across Broadway at the entrance of the Hoffman House, making an undeniably grand display. There were black carriages, huge sentries, a picket line of courier mounts, and a clutch of aides-de-camp out for a smoke. There was also, on the hotel's flagstaff beneath Old Glory, a two-starred pennant signifying that this was the headquarters of Major-General Benjamin F. Butler.

The Hoffman House itself was no less impressive than the headquarters' company. Its bright green awnings and tall deep-set windows made it appear a jewel of a hotel. The scaffolding at its beige granite face indicated that it was a very new hotel, open for business less than a week. Butter had been told that the Hoffman House had been built upon the ruins of the stores burnt down in the Draft Riots, and he could see this morning that it was every-thing a phoenix should be, and a worthy neighbor to the larger and famously luxurious Fifth Avenue Hotel just south one block. Indeed, Madison Square was a man-made arena of elite addresses, like the St. James Hotel and the Holland House. Butter pulled his arms close about him as he rotated in place to study the square once more. He was surrounded by privilege, and this made him feel most insignificant. He instinctively retreated closer to the bushes. It was still very early on a Sunday morning. The bells were tolling Roman Catholic masses. The horsecars and wagons were delivering servants and goods to the hotels. And, thought Butter, the rich men who owned and lived on Madison Square were probably sleeping on, indifferent to—

Butter quit his philosophizing because he had become tangled with a hedge. Besides, what did it matter that people were wealthy? It was a stupid prejudice of his, and he was tired of it. He wanted to be rich himself someday. He spoke aloud his dear Great-aunt Mercy's adage, "The rich are always with us." It made him laugh a little. Even so, he retreated farther into the park.

The morning might be peaceful, but the park was littered with the leavings of anything but a calm Saturday night. Butter knew that the Democratic party clubs had gathered here in the tens of thousands to sing and dance for their candidates, and also to cheer Major-General George B. McClellan. McClellan had been in prominent attendance nearby at the Fifth Avenue Hotel. As the torchlight parade had filed by, McClellan had come out on the balcony over the colonnaded entrance of the hotel to wave his hat to his supporters and then to take a seat in a rocking chair to watch. He had steadfastly refused to speak, however, and this perhaps more than the prospect of victory on Election Day had stirred the Democrats into a frenzy of self-adulation by the light of fireworks.

Gouverneur Nevers had told Butter that the celebration had been three times as large as the Republican rally on Friday night. Butter could see it in the trash. He stepped through more rubbish than at a remount camp. He also felt, as he walked from discarded poster to poster, on the trees, in the bushes, on the pathways, that he was strolling into a political maze.

"How Are You Draft?" asked one poster.

"Washington Gave Us Liberties, McClellan Will Preserve Them!" declared another.

"George B. McClellan, Old Abe's Substitute Without the Bounty!" exclaimed a third.

And strung between two teetering and charred poles was Butter's favorite, one that he could actually agree with, "Fort Lafayette, We'll Laugh at You Yet!"

But then Butter spied one poster nailed to a tree that angered him enough to pull it down. It was a caricature of two bent-back Negro slaves carrying an open coffin between them; in the coffin was a caricature of Abraham Lincoln, rendered as half-man and half-ape. The caption below the drawing read, "Back to Africa to Bury De Massah!"

Butter held the poster at arm's length and scowled. He carefully ripped it into halves, quarters, and shreds, and tossed it down. He squinted to see the clock across Broadway. It was time to go. And he found that it was easier now to march toward his appointment at the Hoffman House.

Butter was interrupted almost immediately by a sudden excitement down Broadway. The clattering of horse hooves and grating of steel-rimmed wheels came first, and then wide around the corner from Twenty-third and onto Broadway there appeared a military escort and four-team coach, the two-star pennant of a major-general flapping above the uniformed driver and coachman. The two outriders bore down on Butter, and he backed off quickly. Across the way, Ben Butler's headquarters' company reacted with equal speed, aides tossing away cigars and sentries snapping to attention. The coach did not turn toward the Hoffman House. Rather, it rolled slowly to a stop near Butter's position. The coachman leaped down and opened a cabin door.

Butter nodded as a Negro gentleman ducked his head out of the coach and pointed toward him. He should have known right away that this had something to do with Gouverneur Nevers. Nevers beckoned again, and smiled beautifully. He was a mocha-colored, clean-shaven, medium-sized man, dressed this morning in a perfectly fitted gray morning coat and dark gray pants, with a low gray silk top hat. What made Gouverneur Nevers especially identifiable at a distance were those remarkable shoulders and those scarlet kid gloves.

Nevers leaned down as Butter neared. "Good morning, Cap'n."

"This is some rig, Mr. Nevers."

"It is that." Nevers looked most pleased. He tossed his head to indicate something behind him, and said, "Come on up, and meet my boss."

"But what about—"

"We got time, Cap'n, and I think they know we're here."

Butter climbed in and sat down on the couch seat across from Nevers and the man he knew to be Nevers's chief. Here was Major-General John A. Dix, a jowly, large-headed man, with wispy white hair and large earlobes. He was a grandfatherly figure who sat calmly with a black shawl over his undress uniform coat. He was also wearing black satin slippers. But John Dix's authority was more than paternal; he was the commander of the Department of the East's seven states (New York and all of New-England) in general, and New-York City in particular.

Butter waited for Nevers or General Dix to start, and when they did not, he said, "Sir, Captain Butter, sir, for the Secret Service temporary, sir."

Dix took an unlit cigar from his mouth, and began, "Mr. Nevers tells me you're a trustworthy soldier, Captain, and about as at home in this city as a blue jay."

Butter sighed, and wondered why hoary old generals had to be ironical. Dix expected some response, so Butter said, "Yes, sir."

Dix continued, "I also have it from Mr. Stanton that you're a Seward-pleaser. That Mr. Seward thinks you can save this city by yourself, or some such. That you're a Republican patriot."

Butter sighed again. "Sir?" This was not a good beginning: John Dix was an old Barnburner, or anti-slavery Democrat. During the last days of the Buchanan Administration, John Dix had served as treasury secretary, and had been celebrated as one of the staunchest friends of the Union. Now, Dix was thought too old for field command. He had been semi-retired during the reorganization of the general staff after Gettysburg. He had then been assigned outside of Washington City, like any number of politically trouble-some or militarily disgraced generals. This did not mean he was incompetent or without power. Butter could assume that it did mean that Dix was touchy about Republican challenges to his authority.

Butter started again hoping to avoid Dix's temper; he said, "I don't know about all that, sir. What I do know is that they told me I had to go to New-York, and that Colonel Baker's now left me in charge till he returns. I don't know why he did, sir."

"You can guess, Captain," said Dix. "You're the one's been on the Reb's trail since summer, eh? A regular bloodhound."

"I'm just an acting-assistant-provost-marshal," said Butter.

"Don't fence me, Captain. You were at that meeting that sent Ben Butler here. When Seward and Stanton jawed about how ol' John Dix just wouldn't do. You know more than you've been telling, and more than you're sayin' now. Temporary or gilded, you're Secret Service."

Butter decided not to speak to what he could not definitively refute. He replied, "I'm just following orders, sir. Colonel Baker told me to hold on. I'm holding on."

"Baker's in Canada," said Dix. "Do you know why?"

"No, sir, I don't, and that's the truth. I didn't even know he was in Canada until this morning. He sent me a wire telling me to await his orders, and to—"

Dix interrupted; he was smiling. "Maybe you don't know why. Maybe you're just what Mr. Nevers says you are. Maybe." Dix nodded to Nevers. "Tell him, Mr. Nevers."

Nevers spoke directly to Butter. "I said you were a horse soldier without a horse."

Dix continued, "Maybe, maybe—maybe I'm going to trust you, Captain Butter." Dix turned in his seat and parted the curtain to tap the glass toward the Hoffman House. "You are going over and tell Ben Butler what he wants to know. That's what I want you to do. Scare him with what you know. Tell him everything about the Rebs and the Sons of Liberty. Make him understand that it's not him rescuing me. That it'll be me who saves him if trouble comes. When it comes." Dix looked back at Butter. "Is it coming? I know what Mr. Nevers thinks. What do you think?"

"I can't say, sir." Butter deepened his tone. "We're watching these guerrillas from Canada. They're just like the men who attacked St. Albans. They're capable of real misery. And since we're not supposed to arrest them, well, it's worked out that they keep leading us to more and more of their friends. New-York's a Copperhead sink. And Friday, I think they led us to their ringleader, maybe."

"Who's that?" asked Dix.

"His name's John Oliphant, and he's—"

"Tell Ben Butler!" exclaimed Dix. "Don't tell me. I know. He doesn't. And tell him how we can't arrest a horse thief if he's a Copperhead without the newspapers hollering tyranny. You tell him what Seward's done—tied our hands and told us to bob for rascals. Damnation! And what do they give me for help, with the whole border pestilential with Rebs? Ben Butler!

They've got a hundred thousand dollars to buy the names of nine guerrillas, but they don't have a regiment to give me without sending Ben Butler!" Dix paused to chew on his cigar. He continued in short-breathed frustration. "I've got two battalions of invalids, a militia that's Copperhead to the quick, a half-sized police force of fat men, a beat-up colored regiment, five governors who want me retired to Hades, two governors, the Seymour brothers, who think I'm already in hell, a drummer for a mayor of New-York, and —and Mr. Nevers and his boys. That's what I have to protect twelve million citizens. What I want to know, Captain, is do I have you too? Or are you one of Colonel Baker's bully boys?"

Butter said, "I am that horse soldier, sir."

Dix snorted, "All right, I got you for this morning." He waved his hand toward the roof of the cabin. "It's your fight now, Captain, but once— Ben Butler! Ben Butler voted for Jeff Davis at the Charleston convention in '60, did you know that? And he was one of the bolters at Baltimore who nominated that Kentucky milquetoast Breckinridge and backed that ungodly slavery platform. I'm a Democrat, Captain, born and raised in the Democracy, God bless it. And they call Ben Butler a Democrat! After Chancellorsville, he was part of the cabal of generals that was going to take over the War Department and replace Hooker with McClellan again, and sell out the Union! And at Fort Monroe, he uses his relatives to trade with the damn slaveholding planters in North Carolina! Facts, Captain. On-a-Bible facts! Now they send him here to help Ol' Dix! John Pope lost a damned army at Second Bull Run, and he sits in Milwaukee with more Copperheads than virgins in his department, and they don't send *him* Ben Butler. And John Schofield in Ohio, and George Cadwallader in Pennsylvania—all of us shelved billygoats— And they send me Ben Butler! Don't they know me? Who do they think has held New-York together since the riots, through six call-ups and as many drafts? This is my city! I'm the shepherd! I've fought Fire-eaters and fool Democrats and Weed and Wood and the damn Know-Nothings and the damn Copperheads and Satan for it. I'm ready to fight the Republicans too. I'm ready, son. Only I can save it because only I know it!"

Dix folded himself back into the corner of the coach, fluffed out his shawl, and seethed. The three of them sat in silence. Butter was extremely impressed. Dix was as tough as Seward, perhaps tougher. Butter hoped that he would not have to choose between them, or be judged because he could not.

Gouverneur Nevers slipped his pocket watch from his waistcoat and showed its face to Butter. Nevers shifted to speak gently to Dix. "This is your Broadway, General. I don't help them to applesauce, 'less you say scoop."

Dix came alert and laughed. He put his hand on Nevers's sleeve and leaned toward Butter. "I want to give you advice, Captain, same as I gave the president once. Mr. Buchanan, not Abe—Abe don't listen— You listen. There's rascaldom that needs you, and there's rascaldom that you need. That's politics."

Butter nodded because he thought it was expected.

Dix grinned. "This gentleman of color here, Mr. Nevers. You need him till he puts you on the boat out of this city. And he ain't the rascal he pretends. But be sure—you need him, like I do. You don't believe it yet. You will. Meantime, you do right and—" Dix stopped smiling and spoke hotly, "Help God preserve the sweet Union!"

"Yes, sir," said Butter, relieved that the interview was ending with an order he could agree to sincerely. Nevers opened the cabin door toward the Hoffman House. Butter climbed down first and stepped back a little. Now that he was away from them, he realized he was deeply puzzled. He did not have the confidence in his political education to be able to judge a lordly bulldog like John Dix, or to interpret the meaning of most of what he said. His more immediate challenge was Gouverneur Nevers.

For four days now, Gouverneur Nevers had soared in and out of Butter's presence like a monarch butterfly of a dandy who might at the same time be an absolutely lawless poseur. Nevers had deliberately hinted at a background that sounded like the lives of a dozen men all sewn together. Either he was the bastard son of a mysterious foreigner who could have been anyone from a Spanish pirate to a Moroccan slavemaster, or he was some sort of gambler who had once won a large sum of gold in a single evening and now had several wives of several colors on several continents, or he was a freed slave who had joined the Army as a mule-handler and traveled with the Dragoons in Texas before the war and possibly with the Dragoons to Harper's Ferry, or he was a master thief of some unknown type who had worked for Lafayette Baker in Richmond and New Orleans earlier in the war.

On Thursday, Butter had looked upon Nevers as a bizarre creature of a strange city, perhaps employed by the provost-marshal's office of the Department of the East to monitor the Negro quarters. But then, Lafayette Baker had treated Nevers very seriously, even a little gingerly, and had introduced him to Butter as "my New-York comrade." And now! General Dix seemed peculiarly admiring of Nevers, and something more, something hidden and dependent.

Butter could just not make what he knew of Nevers and what he saw of Nevers fit together. Butter knew himself to be a patriot who was in need of an affirmation of his service, or at least needful of one commanding officer he could rely upon. The crucial question about Nevers was, Was he only a patriot? And who could he be working for? General Dix? Lafayette Baker?

Also, Nevers was different. Butter knew himself to be no better than the next man who had never experienced a daily relationship with a Negro. Butter was reluctant to admit, but could confess to himself, that Nevers could make him feel discomfitted and disoriented. For heaven's sake, Nevers was a Negro! And this was not some colored regiment commanded by white officers where there were rules and routines. This was New-York!

Nevers was down now and strolling toward Butter. They stood together to watch General Dix's escort and coach proceed north up Broadway. They then turned to move slowly toward the Hoffman House. The front of the hotel had become a wall of military preparedness and propriety, with two white-gloved, full dress aides-de-camp standing at the entrance.

Butter said, "They look mighty impatient."

Nevers said, "The general does go on when he goes on."

Butter spoke hesitantly, meaning to convey his confusion. "I don't understand, Mr. Nevers."

Nevers was casual. "Ask me, Cap'n."

"I'm asking. I don't understand any of this, or why we on the same side have to carry on like we're on different sides, or why Colonel Baker keeps telling me to ask you, or why General Dix now tells me to ask you, or— or any of it. I don't understand any of it!"

Nevers laughed. "You said that yesterday, Cap'n."

Butter grunted. "And the day before, and the day before that."

At the steps, Butter returned the salute of the aides, and identified himself. The aides were bland-faced duplicates of the diffident rich boys Butter had thought that he had left behind him at Bowdoin College. They ushered Butter and Nevers into a white marble lobby of heavy carpet, too much furniture, and purple drapery. Two parlors were still shut off for construction. There were a dozen giant sentinels distributed at every portal and at the main desk; the hotel clerks were huddled to one side; there were no civilian guests evident. Whatever else was true about Ben Butler, it was clear to Butter that he possessed a sharp, vigilant, and ostentatious outfit. Butter thought to brush some pieces of leaves from his coat.

The aides kept Butter and Nevers waiting at the main desk until two very well dressed staff officers—red sashes, gold epaulets, dress swords, cocked, plumed hats—approached from the right. At close distance, they were icier, slightly older versions of the cock-of-the-walk aides. The first man introduced himself as Major Haggerty, General Butler's senior A.D.C. and acting-judge-advocate-general, or chief of security. Haggerty was handsome, puckered-lipped, and neatly barbered; he looked to Butter to be a Beacon Hill Bostonian. Haggerty introduced the second man as Captain Puffer, his assistant. Puffer was taller than Haggerty, and even better looking. Both men were effortlessly arrogant and correct, like sons and grandsons of rich men. Butter listened to their polite opening remarks and girded himself. This was the political Army, and even more, this was the high-minded and unerring face of pure prestige. Their scabbards were made of gold.

Haggerty changed his tone when he said, "The General has been asking why General Dix did not come in?"

"Sir?" tried Butter.

Haggerty pressed. "General Dix, the man you were just talking with outside."

Butter nodded. "I can't say, Major. I don't know."

Haggerty smiled. Puffer stepped up to Butter and pointed at Nevers standing behind. Puffer asked, "Who is this character, Captain?"

Butter said, "Mr. Nevers is assisting me, at Colonel Baker's direction."

"Your name is Nevers, is that right?" asked Puffer.

"Yassuh, I's de guide. Cap'n here, he gets los' easy, suhs."

Butter turned to frown in puzzlement at Nevers. Nevers shrugged. Meanwhile, Haggerty and Puffer conferred briefly and then gave a signal. Immediately an escort of troopers and aides fell in beside Butter and Nevers. Haggerty and Puffer led the way. They climbed to the second floor, where there was still the smell of fresh paint and sawdust. The hall-runner was only half laid, and there were doors not yet set on their hinges. Otherwise, it looked to be a pleasure palace of a barracks, with sentries at every door and an aide and master sergeant at a desk before the double doors of a suite at the corridor's end. Haggerty told Butter to wait, and then he and Puffer went into the suite just as a Negro houseboy was rolling out a serving table.

Butter turned to Nevers and whispered, "You did that on purpose."

Nevers said, "General Dix offered me a ride. He aimed to see you."

"No, no, I mean downstairs—that talking, you know."

"Oh." Nevers smiled. "A whaling man told me a story once, from when he was on the slavers. He said the way you did it was to hit the woolies hard, just hit them hard for no reason, and remember to heave the sassy ones over. So I figure it like this. You get across your way, and I'll get across mine."

Butter thought a moment, and then showed his agitation more than he had wanted to. "You, Mr. Nevers, I don't understand you!"

Nevers smiled. "Keep askin', Cap'n. You're smart, for a sore-footed Bobalishunist."

The suite doors opened; yet another slick-haired blond aide appeared to invite them inside. The large parlor had been cleared of most of its furniture and established with dining tables that were covered with maps and boxes of files. The front drapes were half drawn; the view was straight out over Madison Square Park. Bookends of adjutants stood by the fireplace, and Haggerty and Puffer were off at the right by an archway onto a dining alcove. There, at the table, Major-General Benjamin Franklin Butler sat with his back to the room. He was still in his robe, and he was eating his breakfast and reading the Sunday papers.

Butter and Nevers remained as still and quiet as the rest until, after several minutes, Ben Butler arose. Immediately, his orderly was at his side to help him finish dressing, while a Negro houseboy cleared away the dishes.

Ben Butler was a pork belly of a man, hooknosed and meaty faced, with small eyes that were notoriously crossed, and only a few greased-down hairs on his bald head. Butter had not needed John Dix's opinion of the man to know his own. Ben Butler was the Union's most famous political general, and its most ambitious. In April 1861, he had been the first to raise a volunteer legion (in his home state of Massachusetts) to sail for Washington City to help secure its defenses. In the fall of 1862, he had assumed military command of New Orleans after its fall to Admiral Farragut, and he had organized a brutally efficient administration that had earned him two nicknames: "Silverspoon," for his alleged robbing of rich Secessionists of their buried household treasures; and "Beast," for his alleged harassing of the recalcitrant ladies of New Orleans by declaring that any one of them who was found disrespectful to a Union soldier would be treated as "a woman of the town, plying her trade." Not surprisingly, the more Ben Butler had been reviled by the Southern press, the more he had been celebrated in the North.

Most crucially for Butter, Ben Butler was the commander of the Army of the James. It had been under Butler's control that the First D.C. Cavalry had crossed the James River at Bermuda Hundred the June before and made its wild run at Petersburg in what had come to be called Kautz's Raid. Butter had lain on that field for three days because Ben Butler and his staff had withdrawn the infantry support for Kautz's Raid without properly informing the cavalry.

Butter stood by and studied Ben Butler most closely as he dressed. He had been long curious about what sort of man had let him nearly shake to death. Yet Butter was not necessarily condemnatory of a man who was also a Union legend. Butter did not have an easy cynicism toward the Union command like Tory Wetherbee. Butter had ordered men to their deaths as well. If Ben Butler had a troubled, paradoxical reputation, so did every man who had stayed too long at war.

At last, the orderly carried over the general's sword, a gleaming saber that was longer than Butler's legs. Ben Butler buckled it on, and turned toward the room. He had to lift the sword very high as he stepped across the parlor and then up before a tall front window. Ben Butler still had not spoken. He stood with his back to the room as he gazed down upon Madison Square. Butler's motion did seem to be a signal to the aides, however, for almost immediately the suite doors opened again, and a line of staff officers and aides-de-camp filed in to fill up the room with square and correct shoulders.

Finally, the doors were shut, and Ben Butler acknowledged the assembly for the first time by tapping on the window pane and speaking without turning around. He said, "Gentlemen, every meal could be my last."

Captain Puffer spoke to the room also. "The General will have your attention."

Butler continued, "I've had three notes, no, four notes—four, isn't it Peter?"

Major Haggerty replied, "Yes, sir, four."

"Four then," said Butler, still not turning around, "since Thursday. Four notes warning me of assassination. Three anonymous friends, and one newspaperman. Assassination! All right. There's worse deaths than that. My friends in Boston write me that they've heard that I'm to be shot down in the streets."

Haggerty spoke to the assembly like a caption writer. "The General is the only one who can scare Rebeldom without an army behind him."

Butler rapped hard on the window. "Last night, down there, there was a spectacle of treason I shall not forget. That was my party once. And now, it's Copperheadism and Seymourism and treachery. They—they shouted for my head!" Butler laughed, and finally turned around to face his audience. He looked rosy. He nodded several times, explaining, "The blessed thing is— You will appreciate this, gentlemen. They shouted for my head. But they thought I was still at the Fifth Avenue Hotel. What a mess that was. And so, while they cheered Little Mac, they cursed me. But I couldn't answer them, because I wasn't there. 'Beast!' they cried. 'Beast!' 'Beast!' I can't say that I'm not tempted to give them what they asked for."

The staff returned a chorus of approval. "At 'em, General!" and "No mercy, General!"

Puffer added, "They'll say it till they surrender, General."

Butler dragged his sword as he moved to stand before the next tall window. He spoke to the back wall now. "A week ago, I was winning this war, my share of it. Then, orders, gentlemen. Get up to New-York, and make a show, Mr. Stanton tells me. Collect brigades, get the steamers and guns, and get there, General Grant tells me. All right, we had twelve hours to put together the brigades and to assemble the transport. They told us to take ships bound for our poor boys from the prison camps at Savannah. I protested, but, no. So, it was done. And I congratulate you, gentlemen. There's not another staff in the Army that could do what you've done. To move five thousand men out of the lines in Virginia and onto ships with their equipment and horses and to get them five hundred miles to another port, and all within ninety-six hours. Not another staff in the world! General Grant says, 'Go!' and we go. Because we know how to go!"

Haggerty said, "You're the man for the job, General."

"Blessed right!" said Butler. "We're the men for the job! I know many of you have just arrived, and you've outrun your kits and your sweethearts and—"

Butler broke off and strolled back to the first window. He stopped to rock on his heels for a moment, nodding in thought. Then he beamed. He threw his right hand, thumb out, over his shoulder, toward the window and Madison Square. Butler spoke lightly, "Still, Old Dix fights me like a widow lady at a will-reading. Old Dix takes drives around like some grande dame and whines that I'm stepping on his skirts."

The staffmen laughed and applauded. Even Butter could smile; now he was able to comprehend this performance and also to understand why Major Haggerty had inquired after General Dix so suspiciously. Ben Butler must regard General Dix's sudden appearance and disappearance out front as an insult. There seemed some old, open rivalry between them. So Ben Butler, a natural showman, had set out to win back with rhetoric and drama any possible respect he might have lost among his staff.

Butter saw something else in this theater. Butter had heard the tales of Ben Butler's scandalous river parties on specially fitted seagoing tugs off Fortress Monroe, and of Ben Butler's ten-course dinners for politicians and ladies at mansions near the battlefront while the bombardments continued outside. Now Butter knew the stories were true. Ben Butler was that rare thing—an ugly fat man with a voice like a file over a sawblade who could carry on like a tenor at the opera playing a Napoleonic field marshal, or perhaps Bonaparte himself.

Butler waited upon the approbation. He began again, "It's four thousand seven hundred men I've got, and a crack staff to make them fight like forty thousand. It's me between the mob and President Lincoln, as ever. It's ours to man the works. For the Union, gentlemen, for the Election. It shouldn't be flapjack-making to elect a government during a war. And it won't be. Tuesday is a battle! It's a fight! The victory will be when the people go to the polls and go home again and do so in peace! Remember this, gentlemen, Abraham Lincoln is president as long as we're in the field. And New-York is loyal as long as we're in the field. Let Little Mac shame his uniform. Let gold go to 300. Let them try a riot. Let them shoot at me. We've been through worse, and shall again. And we will win this fight because we are loyal and because we are right!"

The applause was heavy and in earnest—no amusement this time. The staff officers looked grim and proud. As their clapping lessened, Butler began his own applause, intending it as a tribute to his staff.

When Butler stopped clapping, Major Haggerty and Captain Puffer cleared the room of staff officers and aides. Soon, only Butter and Nevers remained along with Haggerty and Puffer and a scholarly brigadier who came over to Butter to introduce himself as General Gordon, acting-chief-of-staff.

Butter thought General Gordon most polite. He could not relax, however, because something about this show seemed false. Butter's caution was reinforced when General Butler's mood noticeably changed as he took a seat in a high-backed chair that did not flatter him. General Gordon took a smaller chair next to Butler's, and lit up his pipe. Butler spoke quietly to Gordon, and then slapped his hand on the table before him. He looked up and across the room at Butter and scowled. "You're Baker's man, aren't you, Captain? Secret Service? Where's Baker?"

Major Haggerty stepped up from behind Butler and whispered into the General's ear while laying a folder down before him. Butler picked up a sheet, read it, and shook it at Butter. "Canada? Why's Baker in Canada with a Reb plot here? Well, come on, come on, Captain. I'm not a secret policeman. Stanton wires me to help Dix, but won't tell me how. Dana wires me to help Baker, but won't tell me how. And now Baker"—he shook the paper again—"wires me to help Butter. You're Butter." Butler slammed the paper down. "Step up, soldier, step up. And before I help you, I want you to help me."

Butter was intimidated; he crossed the room and saluted. "Sir?"

General Butler sifted through other folders on the table. Haggerty reached down and picked out one in particular. Butler opened it and ran his finger across the top page. He got his spectacles from his vest pocket, put them on carefully, and read. Then he looked up. "This is incredible, Captain. Do you know what this says? There's some Reb plot to sack the city on Election Day. Everybody and Jesus seems to believe it. Convince me, Captain. Who's doing what, and when, and how?"

"My best intelligence, sir," began Butter, "is that there is a Rebel plot to attack the city on Election Day. And that the plot is broad and very serious. It's being directed out of Canada by the Reb Secret Service there. Here in New-York the Rebs are in alliance with the Copperhead gang that calls itself the Sons of Liberty."

General Butler flinched and turned to Haggerty and Puffer. "George? Peter? What's going on here? You said this was rubbish."

"Not rubbish, sir," said Haggerty. "More like the War Department's hysteria."

Butler turned back to Butter. "Go on, Captain."

"The Reb Secret Service in Canada has been working on a plot against us for some time. The Lake Erie piracy might've been part of it. And the St. Albans raid. And last Monday's raid at Castine. I'm not saying it's a successful plot. But they've been raising all kinds of Cain, sir."

Butler nodded. "All right, Captain, what are you doing about it?"

Butter glanced back at Nevers. It was just now clear to Butter that he had been left the task of explaining something he was not necessarily meant to understand in its entirety. Butter sighed, and tried to satisfy more parties than he could count, and also to tell the truth. "My further best intelligence, sir, is that your presence in New-York has frightened the Copperheads badly. Mr. Nevers has told me that there was a big meeting of the Sons of Liberty in New Jersey Friday night. And that they are scared, and don't want to fight your troops. That they've probably decided to wait until you leave, and maybe even called it off altogether. They're mostly old men, sir, or boys, draft evaders, and shop clerks. Mr. Nevers says they don't want to fight. I tend to believe it." Butter paused, and then made what seemed like a good decision; he added, "I also believe that they don't want to fight you."

Butler tapped the folder. "It's most good of you to say that, Captain. Most good. Blowhards and rabble." Butler reached into the folder. "So what about this report from Dana and Baker that an informer in Toronto has sold us the names of guerrillas? That there are guerrillas here to burn the city? Are they backed off too? Is it true they're here or more loose talk?"

Butter again twisted to look at Nevers. He turned back and spoke forcefully. "The Reb plot is serious, sir. There are guerrillas here who've been followed from Toronto. They crossed the border last Monday. The suspicion is that they're here to assist the Sons of Liberty as an incendiary corps. They certainly fit the type like those in Vermont and Maine."

Butler said, "What are you talking about?"

"The guerrillas, sir," said Butter. He knew that he was doing this badly, that he was committing the shavetail mistake of telling a superior officer too much detail. He knew that he should have just mumbled that all was well and in hand and then answered only the questions put to him. But he felt tested, and threatened. More, he felt proud of what he had done and ill-used despite his service. Butter lowered his head and talked quickly. "They're cavalrymen, probably. From the West, very likely out of John Morgan's old command, and all officers. That's the same sort who raided St. Albans, and the sort the Reb Secret Service likes to use. They crossed the border in a group, but have been staying in pairs in the city. They have an abundance of money, room at the good houses, drink at the best bars, attend theater, lectures, and all the political events. Many of them were down in Madison Square last night. They've only been together once since Tuesday, and that was Thursday night, when they met at a house off Washington Square Park. A music shop, that Mr. Nevers says is owned by commanders of the Sons of Liberty."

General Gordon interrupted, "Excuse me, Captain, but how do you know all this?"

"Some of it's guesswork, sir. A lot is what Mr. Nevers calls leather-work.

I've been on this trail for a while now. I've gotten to recognizing the patterns."

"And you have been following these guerrillas?" asked Gordon.

"They've been followed all week, sir," replied Butter. "I didn't get sent here till Wednesday. Colonel Baker put me in charge of the detail on Friday, when he went off. Mr. Nevers has two of his men on each of them, so that's four for each pair. Mr. Nevers' opinion is that as long as we're on their tails, they're not likely to trouble us. Mr. Nevers has this theory that I like, sir. He says that there are four criteria for a successful crime. He calls them the magic M's. The Rebs have the men, that's one. They have the method—they're probably planning on using Greek Fire like at St. Albans—that's two M's. And they have the moment picked out, that'd be Election Day, and that's three M's. What they don't have yet is the fourth M—the magic. Mr. Nevers says they won't have it as long as we're on their backsides. And I agree."

General Gordon smiled. "The magic M's? That's fascinating, Captain. Could you tell us"—Gordon glanced at Butler—"who is this Mr. Nevers whom you speak for?"

Butter turned around again and motioned at Nevers. Nevers remained in place. Butter looked at General Gordon and shrugged. "That's Mr. Nevers, sir, he's—"

Butler slapped the top of the folder. "Captain Butter!"

Butter said, "Sir?"

Butler looked annoyed and impatient. "Why haven't you arrested the whole bunch? What are you trailing them for?"

"It's orders, sir," said Butter.

"Orders!" exclaimed Butler. "Are they guerrillas? Are they planning to set fires?"

"I believe so, sir. I can't prove it, but—"

"Arrest them, Captain!" cried Butler. "This morning! Now! I want them in Fort Lafayette this afternoon!"

Butter did not want to say what he now realized he had to say—that by Seward's order the guerrillas could not be arrested. He shuffled in place, looked down, and waited for Butler's blast.

It did not come. Instead, Major Haggerty leaned close to Butler's ear again and whispered at length. General Gordon leaned toward them to contribute some short remarks. Butler ended the conference with a sharp, "All right, all right!"

Butler then waved at Butter, and began, "So it's politics, is that right, Captain? Seward's game? And Stanton's? And maybe Old Dix's too? Answer me, Captain. Do you realize what they're asking? Do you know what this 'No Arrest' order means?"

Butter knew; he also knew that he must not be drawn into this debate. The truth might be, thought Butter, that he had been manipulated by Stanton and Seward and Dix. He was not now going to permit Ben Butler to turn him around also. He was going to try a subordinate's best recourse in such a predicament. He was going to stand silent.

Butler added dismissively, "Maybe you don't know," and tossed his hand in disgust.

There was a pause, and then Major Haggerty spoke up, "You there, Nevers, what is it you're doing here?"

Nevers replied, "Whut dey tell me, suh."

Butter sighed and risked Haggerty's ire. "Mr. Nevers is a detective for the Department of the East. He's assisting me. He's essential to my job. I've found him knowledgeable, resourceful, and tireless."

Haggerty said, "And loyal, Captain? These are confidential conversations."

Captain Puffer added, "Why's he fitted out like a piano player in a bordello? This isn't the place for gypsy talents."

Butter waited for Nevers to speak. When it was obvious that he was not going to defend himself, Butter tried to draw Haggerty's and Puffer's attention back to himself. He said, "Mr. Nevers is my assistant. I'm in charge of this detail until Colonel Baker's return."

General Butler started again, "It's Seward, isn't it Captain? You were at this famous conference at the War Department, weren't you? It's Seward who says no arrests until after the Election? It's Seward protecting Weed and the damn New York Republicans? It's Seward who's so cowed by the newspapers that he's afraid of one arrest!"

Butter bowed his head.

"Their bloody game!" said Butler. "You see it, Peter? Alf? They send me up here to protect New-York. But they give me kindling for a battlefield. And they won't let me do what's necessary. It's tidy, I'll grant that. If anything happens they can smear it on me. And if nothing happens, then the War Department gets the credit. When they know—Seward knows—that the safest way to hold this Election in New-York is to put half of the city in chains while the other half goes to the polls saying its 'Hail Mary's. The few good people in this city want me to do just that. They've already petitioned me to—" Butler dropped off. "What does it matter when the Administration won't take responsibility for its largest city?"

General Gordon spoke diplomatically. "We've surprised the Copperheads, Ben. The Captain said so. They don't want to fight you. And even if Seward won't let us arrest the Rebs, there aren't but a handful of them. The Captain seems to know everything about them except their shoe sizes, and he might know that too. I think we're in a strong position for the moment. The guerrillas don't know we're on to them, and the Captain and his men will know beforehand if they make a move. You will, won't you, Captain?"

"Yes, sir," said Butter. He felt good about liking General Gordon. The man was reasonable and was willing to make the best of the situation. Butter added, "The men we're watching aren't going to slip us. And Colonel Baker'll be back to take charge soon enough."

"I want more! There must be more!" Butler stood abruptly and leaned across the map of New-York on the table. He ducked his head, so that his jaw rested on a wake of flesh. He studied the map a moment, and made a claw with his right hand that he swept along the length of Manhattan Island. Butler looked up. "Come here, Captain, come up."

Butter took small steps forward. He looked down, mostly at the long black hairs on Butler's head. There was also the strong smell of Butler's eau de cologne.

General Butler continued, "You're a soldier, Captain, you know tactical problems, and you've seen traps before. Look at this. I've only got ten regiments up here so far, with artillery elements. I've had to send two regiments up to Buffalo to keep Old Dix from crying. And there's another company of horse artillery gone to Albany. And Seymour sent the arms in the Federal armories upriver, so we have to rely upon our own stores. What I've got left is made-up brigades. They aren't the western men General Grant said I could have. There are even some New York regiments, of questionable loyalty if it comes to a fight."

Butler pounded the map. "And I can't station them in the city! No! Stanton says I can't land them because there aren't sufficient bivouacs in the city, but that's nonsense. No, the reason I've got to keep over four thousand men packed atop each other in steamers is because of Seward again. He's afraid the sight of bluecoats would make these Copperheads vote for McClellan, which they're going to do anyway. And so my boys sit on steamers at slips on the East and Hudson rivers, and out here at Staten Island,

and—and, New-York is left to the mob!"

Butler reached up suddenly and tugged at Butter's tunic like a beggar; he also sounded as if he were pleading when he continued. "Look at this. Look! I've only got three gunboats to cover my landing points if I have to bring the troops onshore—here, at Wall Street and Cortlandt Street. There'll be a revenue cutter to guard the Hudson River cable, and another cutter to protect the High Bridge over the Harlem River and also the Croton Aqueduct. I'll have tugs for dispatch boats to New Jersey if they cut the telegraph wires. I do have a company of troopers hidden in the basement of the American Telegraph Company. But the Brooklyn Navy Yard only has a garrison of old men. And the Metropolitan Police claim they can protect the regimental armories and the gun shops. But how do I know they can? There's only a company at Fort Lafayette, and there's not enough on Governor's Island to man the batteries, and—"

Butler straightened up and fell more than sat back into his chair. He stared at Butter with crossed eyes that also looked swollen. He said, "It's not a defense, Captain, it's an honor guard for a funeral. And what if they have artillery! Twenty thousand troops couldn't guard this city from itself, and I have less than a quarter of that. This isn't like Washington. The enemy is inside the gates! At the first attack, the police'll pull back, like they did in the riots. I'll have to land troops at wharfs where there's no cover. And then you know what happens? Tell him, George."

General Gordon lit a match with his thumb and spoke as he puffed at his pipe, "The fires will start."

Butler said, "That's their weapon, their best and worst weapon. And I can't fight it! The fire department will be unprotected—they'll stone them from the rooftops. My troops will be pinned down at the landing points. I'll only have gunboats to defend a city that is filling with smoke."

Butler stood again, and gestured like an orator. "What sort of Election will that be? There will be no one at the polls! How will that look for Seward and Lincoln? Not one vote recorded in our largest city? The mob won't have to win to have achieved the worst. No Election in New-York! What will Richmond say? And Europe? How can this country watch its largest city burn and cower on Election Day and call itself a democracy? Captain, do you understand me? I am talking about the politics of this crisis now. War is politics. The mob will win if it stops the vote. We will lose if we don't stop them now!"

Butter kept his eyes on the map. He wished he could distinguish it from all the other charts he had studied before he had had to fight on the fields they represented. He also wished he knew how to answer. Butter tried, "Sir, it's bad-sounding, sir."

"And my orders don't put me in charge of this city, only troops," continued Butler. "Dix wants to ship me to Vermont. Stanton says I don't need territorial control. Don't need! Until the territory's on fire! Do you follow me, Captain? I need your help! I must have it! The fires, do you understand how dangerous those fires will be? And what it means to have Reb guerrillas out there who aim to set fires?"

Butter sighed. "Yes, sir, I do, sir."

"You will help me? You will arrest them now?"

Butter was trapped; he began weakly, "I can't speak for Colonel Baker, sir, and his orders were—"

"Forget Baker! Forget Stanton and Seward. Will you help me?"

Butter could not look at Butler; he could not answer either.

Butler sat in his chair again and waved at Major Haggerty. "Read the order to him, Peter, about terror."

Haggerty took a sheet from his coat and unfolded it. "The General's Order Number 1, to be published tomorrow, reminds the citizens of New-York that, 'The Armies of the United States are ministers of good and not of evil. They are safeguards of constitutional liberty, which is freedom to do right, not wrong. They can be a terror to evil-doers only, and those who fear them are accused by their own consciences'—"

General Butler interrupted; he was calmer. "Thank you, Peter. A 'terror to evil-doers only.' Do you hear, Captain?"

Butter resisted. "Terror isn't my ken, sir."

Butter tried once more directly. "You won't arrest them?"

"My orders are to supervise their surveillance, sir."

Something dark and furious passed across Ben Butler's face. Then he smiled, not happily, and turned to Major Haggerty; he said, "Peter?"

Butter was on alert. He suspected they would now try to extract with trickery what they had not achieved with force of will. Butter watched Major Haggerty move around the table and step very close to him, so that while Butter faced General Butler, Haggerty stood slightly behind him at his right.

Haggerty began smoothly, "Terror is a matter for the intellectuals, isn't it, Captain? You do your duty like a good soldier. How many Reb incendiaries are there, then?"

Butter replied, "Nine, sir, possibly ten."

Haggerty said, "We need exactness, Captain."

Butter said, "It was nine until Friday night, sir. When Mr. Nevers' men followed one of the guerrillas to the Astor House, where he had a rendezvous with a gentleman who might be the—"

Haggerty interrupted, "You say you have them all under surveillance. You have their addresses and know their whereabouts at all times?"

"Yes, sir."

"Could you tell us their names?"

This was too simple. Haggerty must think him a fool. Butter spoke flatly, "Yes, sir, I could."

General Gordon seemed to anticipate Butter's reaction, because he over-called Haggerty's next remark. "Excuse me, what about this gentleman at the Astor House?"

Butter replied quickly, "I think he's important, sir. He's been a frequent visitor there for years. He's most wealthy. In the past he's registered his home address as both Philadelphia and Beaufort, South Carolina. The desk clerks at the Astor House know him well, sir. He always stays in the same suite. It might be that he crossed the border with the guerrillas last Monday. I telegraphed the garrison at Niagara Falls to inquire, but the commander there has since died."

Gordon said, "What's important about this man?"

"Well, sir, I think he's the master agent. I can't prove it, yet, I know, but— It's my opinion that Reb Secret Service operations each have a master agent in command. Someone like him—older, shrewder, well traveled. Someone to handle the money and to maintain discipline. The Rebs in Toronto are said to favor a master agent named Captain Tom Hines, of Morgan's Raiders. I think this John Oliphant is—" Butter stopped, and sagged. His pride had caused him to do what no man could have done. He had given away his prize when he had given them John Oliphant's name.

Gordon took up a pencil and wrote on the top of a folder; simultaneously he carefully edged past Butter's error. "What does Colonel Baker make of John Oliphant?"

Butter recovered as evenly as possible. "He doesn't know about him yet, sir. You see, we found him Friday night, and Colonel Baker left Friday morning."

Butler waved his hand at Major Haggerty. "I'll wager he's the one manipulating the Gold Exchange, Peter. I'd like a long chat with Mr. John Oliphant."

Butter winced; he could neither stop this nor comment.

Butler looked at Butter. "But that would jeopardize your work, wouldn't it?"

Butter was worn down; he nodded. "I think so, sir."

Butler spoke quietly. "I hope I don't have to do that, Captain. And if you do your work properly, there won't be any need for Major Haggerty and Captain Puffer to intervene."

Butter no longer felt defiant; after all, he had lost. He said, "Yes, sir, I understand, sir."

Butler nodded toward the door. The interview was apparently done. Haggerty and Puffer were in motion to usher Butter and Nevers out. Butler added, "Very well, Captain. I appreciate your position, and your contribution. Remember this. I don't particularly care about your skulking around, or your theories and your master spies. What I do care about is that this city stays at peace and that I don't get shot in the meantime." Butler tossed his hand as a man might shoo a thought, and remarked, "Your Colonel Baker will hear from us. And you might, too."

"Yes, sir," said Butter, backing away. He felt some small release and turned to corral Nevers to make their escape. Haggerty and Puffer stood serenely before the doorway.

"Oh, Captain?" called out General Gordon; he paused to puff on his pipe, and then spoke casually, as if in afterthought, "I was wondering what John Oliphant's up to today? You are keeping a close watch on him yourself, of course, aren't you?"

Butter turned halfway around, and replied, "Very close, sir. He's said to be going to Henry Ward Beecher's church in Brooklyn with another of the Rebs. At least, that's what Mr. Nevers' men tell me."

Captain Puffer stepped up to Nevers. "Tell the General where Oliphant is going."

Nevers bowed, and looked playfully at Butter before he turned to speak. "Yassuh. Mastuh Oliphant and his'n is gwine to church service in Brooklyn. To hear de Reverend Beecher a'preachin' fer de Union and Fader Abraham and de po' niggers."

LATER SUNDAY MORNING, NOVEMBER 6

Henry Ward Beecher's Plymouth Congregational Church, world famous as the most profound Lincolnite pulpit in the United States, was
located a several minutes' leisurely walk up a gentle slope from Brooklyn's
Fulton Street ferry slip. At just past ten o'clock Sunday morning, an eager,
church-bound crowd streamed off a ferry and through the gates of the ferry
house. This was the last connection convenient to Beecher's ten-thirty service, and there was a slight rush. The well-to-do were obliged to jostle with
the more modest pilgrims while waiting for their carriages to roll off the
boat. The excitement was the more intense because this was not only Communion Sunday, but it would also be Beecher's Election sermon. The
newspapermen, the thrill-seekers, and the overdressed tourists were sure to
be plentiful, and the seats were sure to be scarce.

The majority of the worshippers knew the route well, and turned abruptly
from the rough alleys of Brooklyn's commercial quarter of Water and Front
streets to march in orderly files up Hicks and Henry streets. A few wandered
off to the right, however, gaining Columbia Street, where they could
combine their trek with a view of the deep panorama to the west. Below
were Brooklyn's wharfs and dockside warehouses. Out farther was the
wind-chopped and happily blue East River, which even on Sunday morning
showed all manner of barges and steamers. The most singular impression was
of the forest of ships' masts along New-York's Water Street across the river.
Behind the line of masts was the blockish red and black profile of the city,
highlighted by a dozen church steeples, from Trinity's to St. Paul's to the
tighter grouping of spires north of Houston Street. A careful eye could also
distinguish between the bell towers and the iron-built fire towers. The view
was all the more excellent because a strong wind from the west had cleared
the city of its chimney smoke, except for the sooty concentration in the Five
Points area. That breeze also pushed great, silver cloud banks from the west,
so that the sunlight flashed on and off the city to make its windows glimmer
like embers. And in the far distance, one could make out sailing ships pushing
into the Hudson River like easy swimmers before the rusty autumnal banks
of New Jersey.

Captain Butter was persuaded by the view. Here on Columbia Heights
he felt free of New-York for the moment. Yet he was not distracted
overlong from his quicksight of two figures ahead of him up the promenade.

There was the limber, brightly dressed Captain Kennedy gesturing at the landscape. And there was the steady, soberly suited John Oliphant tapping his cane and listening to Kennedy.

Beyond the pair, Butter could also see Gouverneur Nevers by a tree at an intersection. It was Nevers's opinion that the correct way to follow a subject was to place one detective in front and one behind, and to switch positions at regular intervals. Butter thought this tedious work, but he had accepted it as he had so many of Nevers's instructions. It was only one small aspect of Nevers's gambits. He had told Butter that he had made a study of Europe's most famous detectives, especially a Parisian master criminal turned detective named Vidocq. Vidocq was said to have been a genius at disguises, false dialects, and an ability to disappear-in-the-open, and Nevers none too modestly claimed to have improved upon many of his idol's tricks.

Butter saw Nevers dart into the treeline. After Oliphant and Kennedy made the same turn, Butter hurried up the incline. He emerged on Orange Street in a residential quarter—the brick roadway covered with straw to muffle wheels and horse hooves; the close-built, cozy houses overgrown with climbing ivy; and the rows of arching maples providing a golden canopy. Orange Street sloped down two brief blocks to what was now a small riot of horseflesh, carriages, and churchgoers sprawled curb to curb. For the Plymouth Congregational Church was just beyond on Orange, midway between Hicks and Henry.

Butter spied Oliphant and Kennedy at the edge of the crowd. They seemed to be looking for a path through the confusion. Then suddenly they reversed their course, sliding along the curb to the door of a half-open green barouche. They tipped their hats to several ladies in the carriage.

"That'd be Miss Margaret Cappawhite and her family. Two aunts, a sister, and her mother."

Butter looked around in surprise. "Mr. Nevers, please make a noise first when you do that."

"Do what, Cap'n? Oh." Nevers stepped in front of Butter, and continued, "Kennedy called at the Cappawhites' house on Thursday. My wattles have it that Margaret Cappawhite and Kennedy met at the Suspension Bridge last Monday. It's a large, old Irish family. They live just nearby here. The brother is a Navy lieutenant with Admiral Farragut in the Gulf. The father is dead. Miss Cappawhite's fiancé was killed, last May, in Virginia, with the 10th New York."

Butter did not think of questioning Nevers's information. Nevers's so-called ears—the secondary agents called "wattles"—seemed to have access to every kitchen in New-York, where family secrets were transformed into certain facts. Butter said, "The Cappawhites don't sound like Copperheads."

"Not likely. She's just sweet on Kennedy, and invited him here today. The Cappawhites are members of the congregation." Nevers shifted his position, glanced once over his shoulder, and looked back to Butter. "Look here, now, Cap'n. Here's a bulletin. Look right over my left ear. That yellow house. My bokes are there. In front. See?"

Butter glanced at a group of white men near a large rhododendron. Butter was looking for some of Nevers's detectives, but could not find them. Butter said, "Where?"

Nevers said, "You won't see my bokes, Cap'n. Look at the yellow house. The tall man is Lieutenant-Colonel Martin. The bulky one is Lieutenant Headley."

Butter jumped. "The Rebs are here! It's a rendezvous!"

"I can't say that it is. Oliphant and Kennedy are over there, and Martin and Headley are noticeably far away."

"It means something, Mr. Nevers. This is the first time we've seen them near Oliphant." Butter watched more carefully. Oliphant and Kennedy were helping the Cappawhites down from the barouche. They had not made a sign toward Martin and Headley. Butter said, "It must mean something."

"It might be that they're just here to hear Beecher, Cap'n."

"I certainly hope so." Butter squinted at Martin and Headley. They did not look dangerous. But they were Morgan's Raiders, and they were standing with their hands in their pockets across from Beecher's church. Butter felt his anxiety, and blurted, "But what if this is a rendezvous? Or worse! What if they're going to try something, like an abduction, or something?"

Nevers smiled. "You're a fretsome man, Cap'n. You scared those generals, all right. Now don't scare yourself."

"But General Butler said they were threatening him with assassination. What if they're going to try abduction instead? It's what Mosby liked to do, and Morgan made it an art. What if they're so frustrated by the Copperheads backing out that they aim to grab Beecher? Oh, Lordie, what if—"

Nevers shook his head in disagreement. "Easy now, easy. That don't follow from what we know. Oliphant isn't that kind of man, and these guerrillas just aren't right for that."

"Please, Mr. Nevers," begged Butter. "I told General Butler I had this under control. If they were to snatch Beecher, or shoot him! Oh, God, shoot him!"

Nevers spoke soberly. "Just what you see, Cap'n. I told you. In this work, it's just what you see that matters."

Butter was now panicked. "That Haggerty and Puffer will have me upside down in Fort Lafayette!"

Nevers glanced back toward the crowd; when he turned back he was abrupt. "What is it you want me to do, Cap'n?"

"What? Stay with them. And if they try— I suppose we'll have to— I don't know! If there was trouble, I was supposed to ask you! I'm asking. What can we do?"

Nevers nodded toward the church. "Fine. Oliphant and Kennedy are going in. And nothing bad is going to happen if you stay on their backsides. So get there."

Butter charged into the crowd. He needed to reach Oliphant quickly. And he had best get close, because, given the size of the crowd, there was the real possibility that he could be shut out of the church. The bell ringing made the atmosphere robust and the crowd anxious. Butter had to use his weight impolitely, but he did not hesitate to push back at the iron-hipped ladies. Finally, he reached the sidewalk just ten feet behind Oliphant, Kennedy, and the Cappawhites.

Butter stretched to get ahead. When one of the Cappawhite women slipped suddenly out of the way, Butter had to veer aside to keep from running up on Kennedy's heels. He was now slightly in front, and when he stopped to fall into line, he almost collided with John Oliphant.

Oliphant was shorter than Butter, and much narrower. He had a tight-skinned face, a prominent, thin nose, and tapered black eyebrows that looked to Butter like wings. In all, Butter thought Oliphant overdone. His motions were so controlled and unambiguous, his clothing was so well cut and fitted, and his bearing was so cultivated and restrained as to appear to be that of someone very contrived, or else someone most secretive. On another day, Butter would have dismissed Oliphant as a typically haughty Boston banker. Today, Butter had darker notions. He leaned close and heard Oliphant's voice.

Oliphant was speaking to Kennedy with a pleasant baritone. "A happier notion, to be sure—" Kennedy laughed.

Then Butter, not minding his step, was trapped between the waist-high iron fence in front of the church door and a surging queue of worshippers.

Oliphant, Kennedy, and the Cappawhites were in a parallel queue winding toward the center door. There was nothing Butter could do but follow along into the left-hand door.

The Plymouth Church was an unimposing brick barn of a building. It appeared more an assembly hall than a house of worship. It lacked a steeple; the tall upper windows were unadorned; the facade was plain, even bland. The single indication that this was indeed a church was a cut stone laid in the masonry some thirty feet above the street that was inscribed, "Plymouth Church 1849."

Inside, the simplicity continued. The foyer was attenuated, and painted white, with a pale stone floor. The wooden doors into the nave were guarded by pleasant ushers who were inspecting the faces of the worshippers. The pews on the ground floor were rented yearly by wealthier members of the congregation. Only those elect and their guests were permitted to pass through on a Sunday as well attended as this. The others were directed to the staircases on either side of the foyer for the climb to the second- and third-level galleries.

Butter was now trapped by the milling crowd. He could only watch as Oliphant and Kennedy walked through with the Cappawhites into the pews. Neither Martin nor Headley was in sight. And where was Nevers?

Butter tried to force his way. But the congregation compressed about him. Butter was a head over most, and twice the size of the ladies, but he could not resist. He was pushed away from the doors and drawn to the right. He decided that, if he could not get in with his quarry, he had best get to a vantage over them. He gave himself up to the wave that carried him up the stairs.

On the second level, he found he could not choose his course either. He was thrust forward along the aisle. At last he got ahead of the rush, and detoured into an as yet half-empty pew. An usher thrust a hymnal at him, scowling at Butter's presumption to find his own seat. A young couple squeezed by and tripped on his boots. Butter did not want to sit. He wanted to find Nevers. He wanted to locate Oliphant and Kennedy below. This was wrong!

But then Butter did sit. There was a sudden stab in his bowels like a mischievously shoved stick. Butter hugged the hymnal against his chest and bent forward, not in prayer but in regret for the tiny slab of bacon and small piece of fried bread he had eaten on the ferry crossing. Ben Butler's breakfast had made him feel hungry. Now, he repented as his bowels churned.

The organ voluntary began. The vast chamber was a coliseum of expectant faces; the united reference was to the small stage at the fore of the nave. In another church of this wealth and prestige, the sanctuary would have featured two flanking pulpits, or choir stalls, or large crosses. In Beecher's Plymouth Church, however, the walls were plain white plaster, the pews and paneling were plain dark wood, the windows were plain glass, and the sanctuary was a simple elevated platform. On the platform, there were a small basket of flowers, three small chairs, and a narrow lectern. A large Bible lay open on the lectern.

Butter raised his head higher. His curiosity was making him feel better, but he did not yet trust his innards to shift his position to search for Oliphant and Kennedy. Instead, he swept his eyes around the sanctuary. He noticed two odd exceptions to the church's austerity. The first was the bold modern clock on the front of the rear gallery. The second was the prodigiously large housing for the organ that was set above the sanctuary's stage. It was a most elaborate construction for a church organ. It looked like a Greek temple, at least thirty feet from floor to ceiling, with a facade of four Ionic columns on solid pedestals, a sophisticated entablature, and a peaked roof that was topped by carved wooden figures, the centermost of which was a cherub tooting a horn.

The organ voluntary closed. Of a sudden a stout, agile man in a Geneva robe appeared on the sanctuary stage. He had popped from a small door fitted like a secret panel in the base of the organ housing. Butter knew immediately that this was Henry Ward Beecher, at 51, making his renowned theatrical entrance like an aged lion springing from his lair.

As the last note of the organ faded, Beecher established his jaw out over the congregation. He paused momentously, and then began a brief invocation in a calm voice that required one's keen attention. The audience was his, and in profound confidence he fixed this service in holy time, the twentieth Sunday of Pentecost.

Beecher then held out both hands, and urged, "Let us worship God together."

The organ rose to full volume again, and the congregation stood to sing a decidedly celebratory hymn. The tune and words were unknown to Butter, despite his years of attendance in the Butter pew at Bangor's First Congregational Church. But that had been country Calvinism, and this was Beecher.

Butter opened the hymnal to the correct place and sang a stanza. It improved his mood. He edged forward to peer over the rail of the gallery.

He searched the pews systematically. There was Kennedy! There were two Cappawhites pressed against his sides, singing merrily. And just along in the left front pew was Oliphant, holding a hymnal up for the elderly mother and looking relaxed and pious.

Beecher took control again after the hymn. His legs seemed to grip the platform like a captain on his quarterdeck. He expanded his features and began a dramatic recitation of the acts of confession.

"Our Savior, lover of children," said Beecher, "we pray for one of the meekest among us, Sophie Armitage, 7 years old and terribly grieved. She has lost her brother, Parker. Parker is dead of his wounds at hospital in Washington. And Sophie is afraid. She cannot accept that Parker is gone. She is afraid. She has not eaten the past week, and is so reduced that we are afraid, too, dear Jesus. We are afraid . . ."

Butter opened his mouth in surprise. The woman next to him was weeping. Butter felt like crying too. What was this? Why should Parker and Sophie Armitage upset him? After all, he had seen so many Parkers taken away after a battle. Butter bent his head and tried to stop listening as Beecher moved into the afflictions of his congregation—death, paralysis, illness, penury. Somehow, the overwhelming burdensomeness of the list permitted Butter to recover himself. He took a breath and looked up. Perhaps it had been unwise to sit here in worship while he was on duty.

"Let us pray, as our Lord Jesus Christ has taught us," said Beecher. " 'Our Father, which art in heaven, hallowed be thy name' . . ."

As the whole assembly recited aloud with Beecher, Butter opened his eyes and stared down at Oliphant's head. Butter started a silent prayer, "Lord, I need help, too. I'm afraid, too. Let me do my duty and not disgrace myself. Don't let me hurt that man. Amen." Butter twisted in his seat. He thought of Parker Armitage. He glanced at the brass U.S. buttons on his coat, and registered an exception to his plea, "Unless I have to."

The hymn that followed was lively and again unfamiliar to Butter. The congregation sent up a brave noise. Butter stood shakily but did not sing. Mostly, he wanted to rest balled up in a corner and fight what gravity was doing to his insides.

Seated again, Butter felt slightly better as a preaching assistant took the podium for the scriptural lessons from the Prophets and from the Gospels. Meanwhile, Beecher had moved to Butter's side of the stage, so that Butter enjoyed a closer view. Beecher had an orator's mouth for those muscular jaws, and a Roman head like a marble bust. He looked stern, vain, commanding, and, despite the obvious strength, as exhausted as a veteran sergeant at Petersburg. Butter thought, He's fought this war too.

The preaching assistant finished the Old Testament lesson, and moved on to the Gospels. " 'And he began again to teach by the seaside,' " read the assistant, from the fourth chapter of Mark, " 'and there was gathered unto him a great multitude, so that he entered into a ship and sat in the sea; and the whole multitude was by the sea on the land. And he taught them many things by parable. And he said unto them, Is a candle brought to be put under a bushel, or under a bed? and not to be set on a candlestick? For there is nothing hid, which shall not be manifested; neither was anything kept secret, but that it should come abroad. If any man have ears to hear, let him hear.' "

A hand gripped Butter's shoulder. Before Butter could turn, he heard Nevers say, "Come with me, Cap'n."

Butter grabbed at Nevers's sleeve, but Nevers was instantly away, into the line of worshippers who were standing in the aisle behind the pews. Butter stepped through a gap in the boots, saying, "Excuse me, please, excuse me."

Butter looked around. Nevers was just ahead. But Butter was in trouble, and not the kind that Nevers could repair. The cramps had begun. The gas was spontaneous. He curled forward, tightened his sphincter muscles, and pursued Nevers. Yet why was Nevers going forward toward the front of the gallery? The exit was back the other way!

Nevers cleared the last of the worshippers in the aisle; he leaned down to fiddle with a panel on the side of the organ housing. Nevers pushed, and the panel opened on hinges. Nevers ducked down and disappeared. Butter followed quickly, and found himself inside the Greek temple.

"Mr. Nevers," began Butter, but he stopped at sight of the curved and vaulting organ, which dominated the space like the engine room of a fantastic steamer. The organist sat in the cockpit, his back to Butter and Nevers. The organist's assistant was a small Negro boy, perhaps 8 years old, who was dressed like a preacher, but in short pants; he sat below the keyboard holding a stack of music scores.

Nevers bowed to the organist and his assistant when they glanced about. Nevers put his finger to his lips, and said, "Sshh." The boy was transfixed in surprise. The organist frowned, but did not have time to react further, because he had to perform a hymn. He worked his feet and threw his hands across the keyboard as if they were dancing spiders. The chamber vibrated with a whooshing roar that burst into a mixture of whines and thunder. Butter was stunned by the noise and grabbed the back wall of the chamber.

Oddly, the music seemed to quiet his bowels.

When the hymn ended, the organist gathered up his music, dimmed the gas lamp over his seat, and turned to face Nevers; he whispered, "Yes? How can I help you?"

Nevers moved over and stretched up to speak into the organist's ear. The organist, a bony, solemn man, nodded in seeming approval. He climbed down from his perch and opened a trapdoor in the floor. He spoke to the boy, "Come now, Paul."

The boy Paul could not stop staring at Nevers. When Nevers leaned down to whisper to him, Paul smiled as brightly as gold and hopped over to descend into the trapdoor. The organist followed, pulling the door shut behind him.

Butter looked at Nevers. The keyboard above them glowed white because of the daylight pouring through the organ pipes. Nevers twirled his top hat in his hand, and moved from the ledge to the seat to climb up to sit cross-legged atop the organ's woodwork.

Butter whispered, "What are you doing?"

Nevers looked around. "Come on up, Cap'n, and listen about our sweet Lord Jesus."

Butter started up. "But is there trouble? What's that for!"

Nevers had pulled his revolver from his hidden holster; he laid it on his knee. He spoke calmly. "It's uncomfortable when I sit like this."

Butter was awkward for his size, and cautious for his intestinal chaos, but he did get up next to Nevers. He said, "Please don't frighten me. Tell me what we're doing."

Nevers pointed through the openings between the organ pipes and the four Ionic columns. Butter could see the back of Beecher's head, the long gray hair over his collar. Nevers whispered, "We're listening to the word of God."

Beecher began his sermon. "Time and again I have come before you upon the eve of a great battle." Beecher filled the church with an intimate tone. Butter was struck that Beecher was not speaking with force, like a general. He sounded more like the Army physicians who had once told Butter that he was a lucky man that the shell fragments had not lodged deeper. Beecher continued, "Time and again. Time and again. Upon the hour of another contest between the North and the South that has sent men—men! Not armies, not regiments, not blue or butternut lines. But men! Children of God, lambs of Our Savior Jesus, crashing against each other in murderous catastrophes that sear wounds that cannot ever be hidden or forgotten. Battles in which there are no victors and no vanquished. Battles in which everyone suffers in sadness, misery, fear.

"I come today before another battle, and one more fateful and profound than Bull Run or Antietam or Fredericksburg or Gettysburg or the Wilderness. More determinate of our futures than all the bloodletting that has gone before. The election of the president of the United States. Two days hence. The election of our new president."

Beecher paused. The congregation stirred with tried patience. Butter leaned forward. Was something wrong? Beecher's pause continued. The congregation could have heard the blood in its ears for the silence.

"No!" cried Beecher. Butter tightened.

"No! No! No!" cried Beecher. Butter eased back. This was style, not alarm.

Beecher breathed deeply, and spoke again. "I am not here, we are not here, today, to speak to that. No, my friends, we are not here for electioneering. And any man or woman who came today for that purpose should rise and go along, because you will not find it here. I say, rise and go along, for this is God's house, and we are here for peace, for release, and to share the Lord's supper."

Beecher paused again, and said, "I say once more, if any man or woman came today to politick, go now."

There were coughs, there were several babies whimpering, and there was a flutter of papers when one man dropped a pad, but there was not one person who dared to rise.

Beecher began again, friendly and cheery. "And he taught them many things by parable. And he said, 'If any man have ears to hear, let him hear.' A candle. A light. A light of hope. A light of forgiveness and virtue and of hope, of hope, of hope! And Jesus asked them. Does one bring a light to put it under a bushel or under a bed? No, of course not. A candle is for a candlestick, and a light is for a lamp. The light of Jesus, and the lamp of history. Light, hard-fought, dearly won, paid in blood. The light of our Lord Jesus. Our Lord's beautiful, golden, warm, loving, and blessed light. It is not hidden. For nothing is hidden that shall not be known. And there is no secret that shall not be known. So, my friends, know it, see it, feel it. Feel the warmth of Jesus. He is for you. Today. Not for the politicians. Not for others. For you. Let Jesus into your hearts, and feel his strength . . ."

Butter pulled back and shook himself. So this was Beecher. Butter had expected an exhorter, or a campaigner, or a propagandist. He had thought that Beecher would use this weighty occasion to preach for Lincoln, or to try to equate a vote for Lincoln with a vote for Christianity. After all, these two thousand worshippers were a pittance of the audience Beecher's sermon would reach once the newspaper accounts of it were published.

But no! The legendary partisan was missing. Butter knew Beecher by reputation and by result. This was the Abolitionist hero who had declared, during the Kansas-Nebraska debacle of 1855, that a Sharpe's rifle was better than a Bible when converting a slaver, so that afterward the Free Soilers in Kansas called the guns smuggled in to them "Beecher's Bibles." This was the man who had pronounced, during the Fugitive Slave Law debacle of 1858, that, "If I had a son who was a slave, and did not seek for liberty at every hazard and at every cost, I would write his name, 'Disowned!' " This was the man who had produced, at the Reverend J. P. Thompson's Broadway Tabernacle Church, during the Harper's Ferry debacle of 1859, the very chains that had bound John Brown on the scaffold, and had thrown them to the floor and stomped on them with his heel, and had cried, "The fate of the slaver states!" This was the man who had taunted pro-Confederate England during the Trent Affair debacle of 1861, crying, "That the best blood of England must flow for the outrage England has perpetrated on America!" but who had later plunged himself through a speaking tour in Great Britain in 1863 to face down tens of thousands in assembly halls in order to defend America and the Union cause. And this was the man for whom there had been few equals in moral power during the rhetorical warfare between North and South over the question of slavery, and for whom there had been no equal in moral authority during the military warfare between North and South over the fate of the Union.

This was Beecher! Yet the iron man was not present. The hero was not to be heard. For what was Beecher preaching two days before the Election that might very well fix the fate of all the slaves and all the states of America? He was preaching a personal Savior. He was preaching the power of Jesus, and that the light of Jesus would fill the hearts of anyone who was open to Him. Butter listened, and he was persuaded. Butter wore a uniform that could be said to be spun from the whole cloth of Beecher's genius, and yet here he was, sitting atop Plymouth Church's organ, and feeling naked for Beecher having stripped away all but the necessity of clothing himself with the love and hope of Jesus. Butter listened, and he was amazed.

Nevers jolted Butter when he touched him; Nevers said, "Cap'n? Can you see up to the third tier?"

"What? What is it?" He turned to where Nevers was pointing.

"The third tier, in the back. Count off four from the last row. See? Martin and Headley?"

Butter squinted and counted. "Yes, I think so."

"Here's news for you. Two more, Ashbrook and Harrington, are right below Martin and Headley. And in the same row, past the lady in the silver, all together four more, Chenault and Cook and Dennis and Price."

"They're all here!" Butter pulled at his beard. "Why? Do you think— Am I right? Is it abduction or—?"

Nevers held up a finger to quiet Butter. He waited for Beecher to conclude a long, sing-song sentence, and then added, "It ain't my notion. But you're the Cap'n, so my bokes're at the exits. And right on top of 'em. See?"

"Just a rendezvous, then? Maybe a meeting with Oliphant?"

"I ain't seen any of 'em move toward him, or him toward them. Maybe after." Nevers shrugged. "We're ready, but—"

"But what? Do you think I'm wrong? Tell me."

Nevers nodded. "You know your John Mosby and your John Morgan, but I don't figure Oliphant for troubling the Reverend Beecher. Just look at him. He could be troublesome, I'll grant that, and those other Rebs are like heavy guns, but not here, not today."

Butter peered down at Oliphant. He was statuesque, and serenely fixed on Beecher. Butter thought him like a secret, and wished that, as Jesus promised in the parable, he would come abroad. Butter began, "Maybe they are just here for the services. Maybe they—"

Butter twisted suddenly. Simultaneously with the increase of his tension, his body had betrayed him. What might be happening out in the church was worrisome, but what was happening inside him was perilous. Butter was in pain, and he had to get out. He gasped, "Mr. Nevers, I have to— Don't jump them unless they— "

"Are you all right?" asked Nevers.

Butter could not wait to answer. He crawled down off the organ. The only hope was an exit through the trapdoor. He raised the panel and descended into a dark, low, narrow passageway, which he thought would take him to the rear of the sanctuary. He moved toward the gray light at his left and came upon a four-foot-high door. In his bewilderment, he might have opened it if he had not at that moment heard Beecher's voice.

Beecher boomed, "Ask yourself. Ask long. Listen long." Beecher lowered his voice to a hush. "Jesus answers quietly, as the leaves fall."

This was the sanctuary door! He was in Beecher's lair, exactly opposite to where he wanted to be. Butter recoiled, and started back along the passageway. But the gas explosions overwhelmed him, and he lowered to his knees. He tried to crawl. The pain reached a peak. He must not quit. He balled his hands and waited for the spasm to pass.

Suddenly there was a light before his closed eyes. It was the organist's assistant, Paul, leaning over him with a candle, asking, "Is you shot?"

"Help me, please, get me to a privy."

"You ain't shot? You want a privy?" Paul gave Butter his hand, and pulled him forward. They passed the trapdoor, and proceeded slowly to the rear, which opened onto a hallway behind the sanctuary. Butter stepped out carefully, remaining bent over. To the right and left there were several dozen men dressed like seminarians. They were listening to Beecher through half-opened doors. They were surrounded by carts stacked with silver plates of bread pieces and trays holding small cups of wine for the eucharistic celebration.

Paul led Butter through the group to the left. The seminarians parted without comment. Paul stopped Butter at a niche in the hallway; there was a door that opened into a janitor's room. Here, Butter found a rudimentary privy, and delirious relief.

After a while, Butter untangled his trousers from his boots and sat up. His limbs felt limp, his skin was clammy, and there was an ache in his back, but he had control again. He could hear the organ booming out again, and the voices of thousands lifted in the offertory hymn. That meant that Beecher's sermon was done, and they were passing the collection plates. He knew they would soon be moving into the Communion service.

Butter sighed and relaxed. He began to think that he would survive this. He also dared to think that Oliphant and the Rebs had only come to hear Beecher. That his panic had come out of his doubts of his own competence, and out of his intestinal crisis.

There was a noise outside the privy door. The boy Paul had come back. He said, "You dere, mister?"

"Yes, I'm here. Thank you, really, thank you."

"You want da king?" asked Paul.

"Who?" said Butter. "I'm fine now."

Paul left Butter again, and it was some time before he returned. He walked up close to the privy door and lowered a silver tray underneath the bottom of the half-door. It was a Communion tray, and it contained a piece of bread and a cup of wine. Paul said, "Dat king, mister, he say you need Jesus's help."

Butter could not imagine what Paul meant, but he ate the bread and drank the wine without trying to solve the mystery. The sacrament did make him feel better. Paul was waiting for the tray. When Butter slipped it back to him, he asked, "Who's the king?"

Paul slipped away without answering. Above, the organ roared to full pitch, and Butter heard a hymn that he knew as sure as he knew the Penobscot River. It was Charles Wesley's "Jesus, Lover of My Soul." Butter hummed along, and sang briefly, *"Leave ah! leave me not alone! Still support and comfort me! All my trust on thee is stayed! All my help from thee I bring!"*

The singing made Butter relax still more. He smiled. Here, hunched over the privy, he saw the tiny miracle of his rescue by the little boy with the candle. He also saw that it was going to be a routinely safe and righteous day at Henry Ward Beecher's Plymouth Congregational Church. Beecher might be worn down like the nation, but he was rugged and confident, because he had placed his fate in Jesus's care, and because he believed in fair-mindedness and forgiveness. Butter saw that he should follow the example. He must find confidence in his faith, and give God Almighty a little help by trusting in his own sense of proportion.

There would be no abduction or assassination. That had been a phantom out of Butter's confusion. For today, Butter had met the enemy, and they had worshipped together and shared Communion. He might not have any better understanding of the secrets of John Oliphant and the guerrillas than before, but he could grant that they were not devils.

The battle would continue after church. For now, Butter could light up his cigar stub and laugh. He could also take pleasure in the solution to one tiny mystery. He knew this "king." Above in the church, Gouverneur Nevers, of the fabled land of a child's imagination, ruled vigilantly and regally inside a Greek temple, inside a Christian one.

MONDAY, NOVEMBER 7

The telegrams began raining down upon Secret Service Headquarters from past midnight Monday morning onward. They came from all points of the compass, so that by the time Butter had returned to his desk, past 2 A.M., there was a pool of paper to soak him in gloom.

What did he have to cheer him anyway? After a day and a night of trailing

John Oliphant continuously, Butter was obliged to acknowledge to himself that Oliphant had behaved as unthreateningly as a mourning dove. Oliphant, with Kennedy, had proceeded from Beecher's church to the Cappawhites' home for lunch and an afternoon-long visit; Oliphant and Kennedy had afterward returned to Beecher's evening service, and had then gone on to a late-night supper at the Astor House before retiring. At no time had Oliphant attempted to meet with the other guerrillas, or even to pause in his busy, courtly attendance of the Cappawhites, Beecher, or Captain Kennedy. And what was equally puzzling to Butter was that Martin, Headley, and the other guerrillas had acted as peacefully as a flight of those same doves overindulging in a park. Nevers's men had followed them from Beecher's to a carriage drive with lady companions out to a place called Coney Island, and then back to New-York for Sunday evening entertainment at various expensive hotel bars. Not once had they done anything inconsistent with boyish celebration.

But now the telegrams! Butter sat at his desk and faced evidence that all around New-York and its apparent tranquility was a shapeless and impending peril. Butter's immediate worry was Lafayette Baker. Baker had wired that he was returning to New-York, but that he would be delayed for an indeterminate time at Rouse's Point (on Lake Champlain at the New York–Canadian frontier). Baker also communicated that, while Butter was to continue his supervision of the operation, not only was he not to do anything assertive, but also he was not to cooperate further with either General Dix or General Butler.

Butter was irked enough that Lafayette Baker was not returning with some haste. However, the clear implication that Baker had been in communication with Generals Dix and Butler made Butter feel both unfairly judged and inconsequential. And Lafayette Baker repeated this aggravating message throughout the night in two more pointed telegrams, both including the line, "You are not to meet again with Dix or Butler, or any other superior officer or governmental official."

The worries that kept Butter sleepless, however, were the telegrams from Chicago and Washington. At first, the news was vague and suggestive. Butter learned that the Secret Service detective Bob Dailey was in Chicago to supervise the same sort of surveillance operation as Butter's: A gang of guerrillas had been trailed from Toronto, and were being closely watched by a combined Secret Service and provost-marshal team.

Late Saturday night, Bob Dailey had initially telegraphed Lafayette Baker care of Butter that there was trouble. Then late Sunday night the information became more detailed, and names were mentioned. Apparently, throughout Sunday, military commanders had made mass arrests of suspected guerrillas and Copperhead leaders. The telegrams from the War Department to the attention of both Baker and Butter helped to clarify the situation. The news was that military commanders in Chicago had intervened in the Secret Service operation. The news was also that Captain Tom Hines and several agents of the Confederate Secret Service had been arrested by a combination of Invalid Corps troops and Chicago police.

By 9 A.M. Monday, Butter was vacant-eyed at his desk. He was struggling to put together all the telegrams as one might try to reassemble a broken jar. He felt that all the pieces that he needed to determine how the Chicago arrests affected his own responsibility were here, but that he lacked the intelligence to make them hold a recognizable, or useful, shape.

Butter's dilemma got worse. Gouverneur Nevers returned to No. 12 Vesey through the trapdoor entrance he preferred to the door from the Astor House. Butter barely greeted him because he was disappointed that it was not Lo' Josh with more tea.

Nevers sat beside Butter's desk. "All quiet on Broadway, if you're asking."

"I'm not."

Nevers produced a telegram from his coat. "I expect you'll want to see this right away. It's from General Cook, at Springfield, Illinois, to General Dix."

Butter smoothed out the page and read carefully. It was marked as received not one hour before. It said, "For your information. The Rebel agent Th. H. Hines, earlier reported captured, remains at large. The search continues. A description of Hines will follow. He is known to be using the alias Dr. Hunter. You are advised that Hines may be coming your way. You should regard him as extremely dangerous."

Butter read it again, and could not stop himself from saying, "Oh, God, oh, God, oh, God."

"Tell me about Tom Hines," said Nevers.

"This is the worst!" shouted Butter, shaking the wire. "Do you know what this means? They launched this crazy raid in Chicago! And they missed the ringleader! They've done exactly what Mr. Seward said they couldn't do. Look at this!" Butter pounded the pile of telegrams. "They started their raids last night! Ten men arrested so far. And you know what I'd bet my boots on? Do you?"

Nevers nodded. "That they're all Morgan's men."

"Damn right! The commandant of the prison camp in Chicago—what's his name?" Butter pulled out a wire that had arrived earlier from Assistant War Secretary Dana to Butter as one of a number of "For Your Information" communications. Butter continued, "Here—Sweet, Colonel Sweet, he must've panicked when he found out the Reb plot included a breakout at his camp, since at his camp—this Camp Douglas—there are hundreds of Morgan's Raiders there. The boneheads, the boneheads, why'd they tell him about the guerrillas? What's he do, then? He calls in the Chicago police and starts making arrests!"

Nevers said, "Maybe that's what they wanted him to do."

"You mean make the arrests? But Mr. Seward said they couldn't. I was there. He told Mr. Stanton that they couldn't arrest anyone."

"Maybe he meant only New-York," said Nevers.

"No, he meant—" Butter paused. "You mean they made the arrests in Chicago because Seward's from New York, and— Lordie, what do I care about their damn politics!" Butter slapped the telegram again. "They missed Tom Hines! If they're so God Almighty smart, how'd they miss him?"

Nevers smiled. "Tell me about him, Cap'n."

"Oh, what do I know!" Butter exhaled, and started again, "What I do know, from my work in Maine and the Maritimes in October, is that there's been this plot by the Reb Secret Service in Canada. Did you know about this? They called it the Northwest Conspiracy at one point. It's probably called Burn Yankeedom now. It was to be one coordinated strike against all our cities. But along the way, the Rebs have kept paring the plan down. They didn't attack in July, the original date of the Democratic Convention. Then they didn't attack in August during the actual Democratic Convention. Now, the assumption is that— You know, Election Day. Well, Tom Hines is one of the Rebs' master agents. The agent of agents. I heard about him first in Maine. He's traveled everywhere setting up the plan. He's been in New-York too. He's helped buy guns for the Sons of Liberty here. And, if all these wires are right, he certainly would have been the master agent for Chicago. And—"

"What's he look like?"

"Hines? I've never seen him. He's said to like disguises. He was a literature teacher at the Masonic College in Oldham, Kentucky. He rode with Morgan from the first. He helped Morgan break out of Ohio State Prison last year. Morgan's men are said to worship him."

Nevers tapped his lips in thought. He said, "A dodger."

"What?" Butter was too aggravated to sit. He stood to pace behind the desk and to warm his hands at the stove. "It's what I told them would happen. And I don't say that feeling good about it. I told them to get Hines. How could they have missed him? He's the one that really matters. He's—he's like John Oliphant, you see. The brain. The cool, deadly one."

"Maybe," said Nevers.

"What does that mean!" Butter turned his back to Nevers and spoke to Lafayette Baker's empty desk. "And where's Colonel Baker when we need him? And why's he after me for talking with Generals Dix and Butler? What am I supposed to do when they order me around like an Army mule? And for pity's sake what's it mean that Tom Hines might be coming here?"

Nevers stood beside Butter and said, "Do you think you can sleep? We can have Lo' Josh set up a cot here for you. It would be better if you could sleep some and get your strength up. You'll need it sooner than later."

"No, no! I'm alone here. How can I sleep again with—and what about Hines? And Oliphant? And what if Colonel Baker—"

"All quiet on Broadway, Cap'n," said Nevers, gesturing to Lo' Josh in the front of the room. "And I'll be close by."

A single jolt in the side awakened Butter. He sat forward on the cot and looked around. Nevers was standing beside him. The clock showed past 5 P.M. He had slept for over seven hours yet did not feel that much better for it. He had covered his head with his hat, had tied his bandana around his eyes and ears to block out the light and the noise, sleeping like a trooper on the march—without dreams. Now he had to suffer the world coming back at him all at once. The dampness and his swollen joints told him that it must be raining outside. His back hurt from the softness of the cot, and his left wrist tingled because he had lain atop it.

Nevers said, "Trouble comin' on, Cap'n."

Butter yanked his overcoat close about him and turned to sit on the edge of the cot delicately, so that it would not collapse. He was hungry, and his bladder ached. He mumbled, "Tell me. Oliphant? Hines? Baker?"

Nevers showed two fingers. "General Butler's twins, Haggerty and Puffer."

Butter jumped up. "Where?"

"You've got time. They're just leaving the Hoffman House."

"You've had them watched?" Butter worked his limbs. "Of course you have. Right. What do they want?"

"I'm guessing they'll want heads." Nevers backed up to Butter's desk and tapped the stack of telegrams. "There's more from Chicago. They still ain't got Tom Hines. But they've got vigilantes in the streets and're arresting Copperheads like drunks. The Copperheads are crying foul and are charging President Lincoln with everything but murderin' Little Nell."

Butter appreciated the jest but did not smile. He threw himself to his desk to pick up the top telegrams—from the War Department. He did not have the patience to read them. He waved them and said, "It's what Mr. Seward said would happen."

Nevers shook his head. "Did Mr. Seward say what we're to do about Tom Hines?"

Butter grunted. "We've got other problems." He then searched the pile. "Where's Colonel Baker now?"

Nevers indicated the papers to the left. "He's comin' like flyin'."

Butter took up the stack of new telegrams from the War Department about Chicago, as well as the stack from Lafayette Baker; then he descended through the trapdoor to the privy. By the time he returned, he felt up-to-date about the mess out west, and he had also been able to follow Lafayette Baker's paper tracks from Rouse's Point south along the Rutland & Burlington railway to the connecting Hudson River Railroad line at Troy. Baker seemed to be sending a wire from each new station. The last message was much the same as the first: "You are to hold firm. You are not to cooperate with General Butler. Ask Nevers."

Lo' Josh had a tray for Butter of bread and slices of cold ham, along with a pot of tea. Butter ate quickly while getting out his logbook to record what seemed necessary. "What does Colonel Baker want me to keep asking you? Am I missing something?"

Nevers smiled. "Here's a wire from Bob Dailey."

Bob Dailey was still en route from Chicago; he had been traveling since Sunday. Butter assumed that he was coming to report to Baker as to how he had failed in Chicago. Butter did not want to have to face a similar circumstance. Butter asked, "How's Broadway, Mr. Nevers?"

Nevers did not answer because of the noise outside the front window. There were horses, carriages, and men arriving in a rush. Nevers put up his hand to delay Lo' Josh from unlocking the front door. Nevers looked at Butter. "That'll be trouble in white gloves, Cap'n."

Butter recorded the time of the event in his logbook just in case this was the last thing he might be able to write. He did feel strong again, and he was not shy to face Haggerty and Puffer, but still, they were not coming for tea. Butter also thought to stash away the collection of telegrams in the bottom drawer of his desk. He wished that he could lock them in Lafayette Baker's safe, or perhaps had time to destroy them. As Butter finished, he thought to make a show of bravado with Nevers. "You didn't tell me about Broadway."

Nevers smiled, turned down the oil lamp on Butter's desk, used his foot to get a chair into the shadows to the side, and sat like a cat might, suddenly and compactly. He said, "Wet and quiet."

Someone was trying the front door. The pounding began. Butter finished the buttons on his coat and found his hat under the desk. He drained the teacup. He thought, What've I forgotten? He said, "Is Oliphant upstairs?"

Nevers said, "He's dressing for dinner. He's dining with Captain Kennedy and Miss Katie MacDonald."

The pounding was furious. There were shouts. Butter said, "What do you really think they want?"

"It don't matter 'less you give it to 'em," replied Nevers.

Butter agreed. He pulled his greatcoat close like armor, and spoke to Lo' Josh. "All right, let them in, and stoke the stove, please?"

Lo' Josh opened the door and had to jump clear as four large troopers carrying carbines poured inside. They marched in double file, past Butter and Nevers to the back of the room, leaving a dark water stain from their dripping ponchos. They returned to the front door, their inspection complete.

Two aides held up umbrellas just outside the doorway to form an awning. One small lieutenant slipped in carrying two lettercases. Finally, Major Peter Haggerty and Captain Alfred Puffer stepped down from their carriage and slowly strolled into the room. They did not look at Butter as they drifted forward to his desk. The two aides came inside to take Haggerty's and Puffer's rain capes. Butter looked at Nevers when the aides helped Haggerty and Puffer change from their dark gloves to white ones. Nevers, however, seemed to be watching the clock.

Haggerty straightened his dress tunic and began softly, "Good afternoon, Captain. We seem to need your assistance once again. And I assured the General that you would be eager to help. Oh—" Haggerty threw his hand at the troopers. "I apologize for this unannounced call. You prefer it, I'm sure, to coming out to visit us."

Captain Puffer stood behind Haggerty; he extended his long neck, turned his head from Nevers to Butter to Lo' Josh, and asked, "Is this your whole business?"

Butter chose to answer Puffer's insinuation rather than Haggerty's implied demand. He said, "Yes, sir, this is headquarters. You've met Mr. Nevers. And that's Lo' Josh, the custodian here. Colonel Baker and his detective force are expected momentarily. With many, many detectives. General Dix's detective force remains on station, and—"

Puffer snapped, "How many detectives is that, and what sort of detectives does General Dix employ?" Puffer pointed at Nevers. "More like him?"

Haggerty waved off Puffer and spoke to Butter. "What we need to know, Captain Butter, is the status of the suspects. The General has been most concerned that the Rebel saboteurs might strike on their own, quite apart from the Sons of Liberty as you theorized. Your assurance about the Copperheads continues?"

"Yes, sir, General Butler has backed them off, sir."

"I'm not as sanguine about this as the General, Captain," said Haggerty. "And why is it that we haven't had a report from you today on your investigations?"

Butter shrugged. "I've been busy here, sir."

Haggerty looked pleased. "Why don't we take this opportunity to review the report you meant to send us?"

"Sir!" said Butter. "The guerrillas are in their hotels or nearabouts. Mr. Nevers' men are close atop all of them. I have personally supervised the surveillance of their leader since yesterday. All is— It's quiet, sir."

Puffer stepped up. "Where's John Oliphant now?"

Butter said, "Under close surveillance, sir."

Haggerty smiled. "Well and good, Captain. But can't you provide us with more detail? It would please the General."

Butter stared straight ahead.

Major Haggerty continued, "You have kept yourself informed of the events in Chicago, haven't you? It would seem to confirm your suspicion of a widespread Rebel conspiracy. The General is very pleased with your report yesterday. Your mention of Captain Tom Hines was most impressive. The General feels that the events in Chicago provide an excellent example of how we should continue here. Don't you agree, Captain?"

Butter waited. He glanced at Nevers, and then at the clock. Now he understood why Nevers was watching the time. Haggerty and Puffer were here for results. Only Lafayette Baker was powerful enough to fend off Ben Butler's hand. And Baker's last telegram had placed him at Croton-on-Hudson. Butter was not sure exactly where that was, but he hoped it was close, and he hoped Lafayette Baker really could fly.

Captain Puffer stepped in front of Major Haggerty. Puffer began sharply, "Perhaps you don't understand Major Haggerty, Captain. The situation has deteriorated badly since yesterday. The reports from Chicago might very well trigger the guerrillas here to act in desperation. We believe that the best solution is to act first. The solution to our problem, and yours, is the detention of all the suspects. Immediately."

Butter tried an explanation. "I can't do that, sir. My orders are to await Colonel Baker."

Puffer scoffed, "Colonel Baker will be informed when, and if, he arrives."

Major Haggerty spoke more evenly. "I sympathize with your concern, Captain. Put yourself at ease. All you need do is provide us with the names and addresses of the suspects. We are prepared to provide our own security. And I'm sure your colonel will agree with our decision. The political situation can be contained. Our actions tonight would be timed so that even if there were reports, they would be too late to be published until after the balloting is well under way tomorrow, and probably not until Wednesday."

Butter lowered his head. "Sir, I cannot."

Haggerty added, "We can cut your orders, Captain, right now."

Butter turned slightly toward Nevers and sighed.

Puffer lifted his foot and stomped once. "We can arrest you to start the show, Captain. Major Haggerty has appealed to you. I have appealed to you. We do have John Oliphant's name, and address, and once we have him, it will be routine to find the others. And be assured, Captain, that if anyone, including Colonel Baker, were to interfere in our duty, there is ample room in Fort Lafayette."

Butter glanced at Puffer, and then looked at Haggerty. Puffer's threat was so obviously overblown that it alerted Butter to the possibility that these two were pressing him with more bluff than authority. He decided to take a risk, and return some bluff of his own. He said, "Well, sir, you're going to do what you're going to do."

Puffer shouted, "Sergeant!"

Butter suddenly had two troopers at his back. Puffer came around to Butter's side of the desk and started opening the drawers. He stopped at finding Butter's logbook in the bottom drawer. But before he could collect it, Butter reached down and grabbed it away.

Puffer laughed and looked to Haggerty. "Major, I think we can quit the talk now."

Haggerty nodded in agreement. Puffer gestured to the four troopers to close in.

Nevers was quicker than all of them. He was immediately up holding the tin wastebasket. He jumped behind the desk, and spoke to Puffer, "Here, suh, I can he'p ya. Let me pick de Cap'n's garden fo' ya."

Puffer was as surprised as Butter. Nevers did not wait for a response. He bent down and started stuffing the papers in Butter's desk into the wastebasket. Once the drawers were empty, Nevers bumped Butter aside. Butter clutched the logbook to his breast. Nevers jumped, driving his fingers into Butter's side. Butter fell back into his chair—without the logbook.

Nevers stood apart from them all now, holding the logbook like a snatched purse. He dropped it into the wastebasket and bounded away for the trash on the other desks.

Puffer said, "That will be sufficient."

Nevers continued anyway, and was rifling through the wastebasket behind Lafayette Baker's desk when Puffer barked again.

"I order you to stop it! Sergeant, hold that man!"

Nevers was too fast. He spun away from the troopers, and placed the wastebasket on the floor near Puffer. Nevers had covered it with a dark cloth. Puffer reached down to strip off the cloth. There was a crackling sound as flames burst from the wastebasket.

The battle that followed was not sincerely violent. Nevers danced aside. Butter vainly tested his strength against the four troopers. The two aides and small lieutenant failed to keep the flames from consuming the papers. Lo' Josh sat with open delight in his niche and called encouragement to Butter's struggles. Puffer screamed threats. Haggerty retreated to the side and waited.

Soon, Butter and Nevers were seated on the floor back to back, surrounded by boots and angry breathing. Puffer began his threats again. Haggerty disappeared for a short while up into the Astor House, and when he returned, he was holding a telegram, and he called Puffer aside for a consultation. Butter presumed that Haggerty must have wired the Hoffman House for orders. Whatever the result, the interrogation that followed was as expert as Butter had ever witnessed. Haggerty maintained the reasonable line, "Just tell us what we want, Captain, and we'll let this pass." Puffer maintained the irrational one, "Disloyal officers disappear at Fort Lafayette! And your nigger here won't get a cell for what he's done—more like a rope!"

Butter answered them as meekly as possible. He was certainly intimidated. And he was equally worried that they might tire of this game and just go ahead and pursue John Oliphant as best they could. However, Butter's fears were mitigated by two odd distractions. First, he could feel his logbook pressing his ribs, for somehow in the melee Nevers had managed to slip the logbook that Butter had thought he had seen destroyed back into Butter's belt.

The second distraction was the clock. It showed nearly thirty minutes past seven when the front door opened and Lafayette Baker and four other detectives arrived to recapture New-York's Secret Service Headquarters.

More than an hour later, Butter and Nevers were completing yet another tour of the circumference of the graveyard behind St. Paul's Church just across from the Astor House and headquarters. The rain had eased to a dirty mist, and the dank night had settled in such a way that St. Paul's steeple loomed above like a finger thrust through a cloud. Across Vesey Street, the Astor House showed infrequent lights on all floors. It was the theater hour, and many of the guests were off to the political meetings that had replaced theatricals for this last night before the Election.

Butter was indifferent to all the lights but two. He studied Oliphant's suite on the third floor, lit up brightly for guests. He also went up on his toes to peer over the graveyard wall to the dim glow about the drawn shades at No. 12. Haggerty's and Puffer's carriage and mounted escort were still drawn up at the curb, expectant and military.

Butter rocked back on his heels and turned to Nevers. "Tell me again how I did right."

"You did right," said Nevers.

"You could put yourself more into it. And if I did right, how is it that they're still over there? How is it that I feel they might be dividing me up like Jesus's robe? How is it that I know that the easiest way for them to settle their argument is to blame it all on me?"

Nevers moved on a step and pointed to a large gravestone. "You like that piece shaped like a milestone? I'm more partial to the tablet shape myself. A good granite stone. It would say, 'Nevers,' with a nice line of scripture below. Like from the Epistles. 'From henceforth let no man trouble me; for I bear in my body the marks of the Lord Jesus.' And the date below that. Sometime in the twentieth century."

"If you're trying to soothe me, you aren't doing it." Butter continued to pace, and said, "Go back to your theory about Tom Hines."

"Like I was saying, that boy's a dodger. The reports mentioned that they raided the house of a Doctor Edwards while they were searching for Hines. The Doctor says his wife's sick in bed, and starts screaming about tyranny."

"How do you know this again?" Butter had only been half listening. Tom Hines seemed a fascination for Nevers, and Butter, belatedly, was trying to understand it.

Nevers was not willing to explain. He had sources of information that Butter had come to understand were both extraordinary and unchallengeable. Then again, Nevers did have access to General Dix's telegraph wire. Nevers continued, "I'm thinkin' that they didn't look under that lady's bed. Always, when chasing a man, look under the bed. And in the bed, and in the mattress. And in coffins, and—" Nevers pointed to a fresh-dug grave. "In graves. Men on the run go into holes at first chance. You got to go in after 'em."

"You've caught someone in a grave?"

Nevers laughed. "I've been in one. I've been in a coffin too, and a mattress. Dodgers like Hines can make themselves small."

Butter stared at the fresh grave. "Mr. Nevers, it's shooters who are after us. That Captain Puffer has me hanged up on a wall in Fort Lafayette, and you beside me. And it's shooters that we're supposed to be trailing. If Haggerty and Puffer would just leave, we could explain ourselves to Colonel Baker. And get back to work."

Nevers looked toward the Astor House. "Don't fret yourself about General Butler's twins. As long as we can see 'em or hear 'em coming or going away, they ain't troubling us. I told you, if you can see it or hear it, it ain't dangerous yet."

Butter moved along the path to the rear projection of St. Paul's. He used the brim of his hat as a windbreak to try to relight his cigar stub. He failed, and Nevers was suddenly there with a match like a torch. Butter puffed hard. Calmer, he considered asking Nevers how he had managed that trick with the burning wastepaper basket. But then, what about the sleight-of-hand that had put his logbook back inside his pants? Butter sighed and let his mind spin until—

"Morgan!" cried Butter. "John Morgan's a damned ghost. I mean, he's dead and in his grave two months! But he's everywhere now! A damned regiment of ghosts that no one sees or hears until they're on you. That's how dangerous those guerrillas are, Mr. Nevers. Those Rebs'd try robbing heaven of Stonewall Jackson if they was ordered to, and they'd fire the golden gates to cover their escape."

Butter waved his hand out over the graveyard, more than an acre of leaf-strewn grass with dark slabs of gravestones encircled by a low stone wall. He continued, "There could be a company of Mosby's men, or Morgan's, right there, their mounts down flat with them. And this is all you'd see till you saw muzzle flashes and little red dots like mosquitoes flyin' past the corner of your eye. And then they'd come at you with that Reb screaming— I just pray God that John Morgan stays dead, and that Tom Hines stays out west, and that John Oliphant don't turn those boys of his loose on this town. Because—Lordie."

Nevers bumped Butter, and pointed toward No. 12. The door was ajar. Several figures emerged to dive into the carriage. The escort spun around, and the whole caravan rumbled up to Broadway and turned north. Simultaneously, Butter and Nevers cleared the graveyard gate and strode toward the open door.

Secret Service Headquarters now smelled of the remains of a meal of pork and cabbage that were scattered on trays and plates throughout the room. At the top of the room, Lafayette Baker sat far back in his chair, his bootless feet up on his desk. Five other detectives, all in the distinctive black dusters that their colonel favored, lounged on the periphery. Lafayette Baker's diminutive brother, Milo, and his other, middle brother, Calvin, were seated together on the back steps, still eating their supper from plates propped on their knees. Edgar Quillermouth, the pasty-skinned ex-medical student, was at Butter's desk to the left, smoking a cigar and pouring himself successively smaller drinks from a bottle of port wine. Bob Dailey, who had arrived from the New Jersey ferry in the last hour, had made himself a roost on Butter's cot. The most fearsome of the group, to Butter's mind, was the stumpy, jug-eared John Odell, Baker's personal bodyguard. Odell was camped in a chair beneath the gunrack to the right, at the corner of Baker's desk; he was chewing tobacco with an artilleryman's rhythm—a half-dozen rotations of his jaw for every ejaculation into the cuspidor propped between his boots.

Lafayette Baker had spread his two Colts on his desk, and looked to have been cleaning them while he interviewed Haggerty and Puffer. Butter had noted such a routine before and knew that it was a way for Baker to contain his anger and remain dug in. Lafayette Baker's present mood seemed more ambiguous. He was picking his teeth and fanning the cigar smoke in the room from his face with a folder that bore the insignia of the Army of the James.

Butter stood at ease. Nevers was beside Butter, perhaps even a step in front. Butter waited as long as possible for Baker to begin, but as the moments passed, it became clear that he had best start as best he could. Butter cleared his throat, and said, "Colonel, I'd like a chance to tell my side of it. I didn't want to go to the Hoffman House yesterday. And then General Dix showed up and lectured me. And then General Butler lectured me. And right away they wanted to arrest the Rebs. And they tricked me into giving them John Oliphant's name. And I didn't tell them—"

"Amaziah," interrupted Lafayette Baker, "you're a cool one for chasing horse thieves and Johnny Mosby and border raiders. But you've got to learn. You don't please the general staff by trying to out-talk them. And you sure as Satan's waiting to welcome Bobby Lee don't please me by talking to them at all."

"Yes, sir. But General Butler said that you said that I was to work with them."

"Amaziah, there's working with and there's talking to."

Butter mumbled, "It was them who was talking mostly, sir."

"And you being impudent right back, eh?" Baker stopped fanning the folder. "I'm the one who talks and back-talks for this bureau, right? I leave you on Friday with a handful of farmboys to follow around so that they don't get lost. And Ben Butler sleeping on a sofa at the Hoffman House, and John Dix itching with his hemorrhoids at the St. Nicholas. And when I get back here, Ben Butler's arresting gold speculators and is looking to rustle the Copperheads, and John Dix is apoplectic and is spreading telegrams of doom like manure, and you're playing with two staff puppets who are so upset their eyes are buggish. And they're swearing they want you fed to the fish off Fort Lafayette!"

"Sir. Sir, I—" Butter was too flustered to know where to begin. "Sir, they ordered me to—"

Butter stopped, because Lafayette Baker was laughing. Baker pressed his lips together, puffed his cheeks, and rolled back farther on his chair. The others joined in, Edgar Quillermouth tapping his hand and giggling, the Baker brothers spraying food to keep from gagging, and Bob Dailey prone and guffawing. John Odell spat in rapid-fire pings.

Lafayette Baker capped their entertainment by flinging the Army of the James folder into the charred remains of the wastebasket. Baker said, "You did fine, Amaziah. Fine. Except for your talking loose to the general staff."

Butter shifted his feet. "Yes, sir."

Baker continued, "You address your Maker and me, and me first, here on. You've got the lawman's blood in you, I see that. And you're hard when you're pushed, and made those puppets flop around like their strings was cut. But you've got to learn to be close-lipped. The law's worst friend is a governor, and the next worst friend is a military governor. Still, fine, fine. Didn't he, boys?" The others murmured. "Didn't he, Guv'ner?"

Nevers slid closer to Butter, and said, "There's nothing burning in this town but trash. And the jails are mostly empty because the Copperheads want to get out the vote. It ain't Chicago, and it ain't about to be."

Lafayette Baker raised his chin to Butter. "That's high praise, Amaziah, high praise and hallelujah."

Butter was flattered, and also puzzled. What, after all, had he done but do nothing except what Nevers had told him—and then get into trouble by doing nothing at all? Butter wanted to unburden himself further, and perhaps to make his mark on this operation. He pulled out his logbook and began, "I would like to give my report, sir. They aren't voting yet. And these Rebs are more than farmboys. I imagine you've heard tell about Tom Hines in Chicago. It seems, sir, that we've got a fellow just like him here in New-York. This John Oliphant. I expect Major Haggerty mentioned him to you. Mr. Nevers' men found him Friday night. Right here. Upstairs in the bar. And I've got it all here—"

Butter hesitated, because Lafayette Baker did not seem to be listening. Baker had shut his eyes and made his face a mask—flat, dreamy, and faraway. Baker's only movement was to shift the toothpick back and forth in his mouth. John Odell spat again.

Edgar Quillermouth said, "Tom Hines is a dead man."

Butter thought their conduct eerie. He tried to regain their attention by continuing, "John Oliphant's the master agent here, I'm pretty sure. I figure he's out of Toronto, one of Jake Thompson's agents. He's rich, and very smart and cool. I've been watching him and—"

Butter stopped again. Lafayette Baker looked asleep. Butter glanced quickly around the room. They all seemed oddly distracted, or absent. Butter waited, and reminded himself of a most important opinion. Butter understood very little about Lafayette Baker and his detectives, and trusted them even less. Also, he did not really belong among this lot. His presence was an accident of politics. Butter wore his uniform less neatly than he should, and he had complaints against the Army that would never be satisfied, and yet he was in blue and proud of it. For all his quarrel with Haggerty and Puffer, they were soldiers too. These men were not soldiers.

Butter held out his logbook. "My report on Oliphant and the guerrillas is in here, sir." Lafayette Baker was moving away. He coiled his legs back and brought his feet down neatly into his boots. He was then up and over to squat at his banker's safe. He spun the combination slowly, sprung the lock, and removed a cash box from the top shelf. He placed the box on his desk and used a key to open it. He then placed a thick envelope on his desk in front of Gouverneur Nevers.

Lafayette Baker said, "Two thousand dollars in greenbacks, Guv'ner, as agreed. Did I get my money's worth?"

Nevers did not touch the envelope. He said, "I expect you did, so far. I do believe the Cap'n is right that these Rebs are more than farmboys. They're guerrillas of some stripe, and they've been trafficking with the Copperheads. Also, the Copperheads are ripe for trouble. And the Sons of Liberty got plans, big plans, even if they've got no nerve."

Baker said, "But Ben Butler's scared them, right? And the guerrillas are cut off. And the city's going to the polls in buttons and bows?"

Nevers said, "That looks right. I'll agree tomorrow night."

Baker asked, "You figure, with Lincoln reelected, the Copperheads'll settle down?"

Nevers said, "New-York's more Copperhead than Union. They hate the Draft, the colored, and Lincoln. There'll be another recruiting call before Christmas and a Draft by spring. There'll be trouble long as there's this war. And me and President Lincoln ain't moving on."

Butter was watching closely. He had never seen Lafayette Baker more serious, nor had he seen Gouverneur Nevers more grave. Still, what was going on here?

Butter was even more puzzled when Lafayette Baker then produced another envelope from his cash box and laid it atop the first. Butter squinted: The first envelope was plain gray; the second envelope was larger, and white. There was a word written on the second envelope's face, "Weed."

Baker spoke to Nevers. "There's two thousand dollars more there. It's what the president's friends want to pay you and yours to keep New-York loyal. Acting loyal and looking loyal."

Nevers pulled off his scarlet gloves and took up one envelope at a time, counting the money slowly, his fingers twirling and his lips moving. When he finished, he put the envelopes in his morning coat and his gloves back on, and said, "All in order, and agreed."

Baker pointed at Nevers's chest. "All's in order for me if there's not fighting outside the saloons this time tomorrow night. I'm satisfied, so far."

Lafayette Baker shut the cash box, and continued, "After tomorrow, Guv'ner, if there is to be trouble here, I must hear about it first. I don't want to hear about it from Mr. Stanton or John Dix. I want to tell them that it's coming, eh? You expect that two thousand'll do it?"

Nevers said, "Unless it don't. I've a question. What about the Sons of Liberty and the Copperheads?"

Baker said, "Their day is coming. Like judgment. Not today. Not tomorrow. Soon. Mr. Stanton won't forget New-York, and neither will I. After the Election."

Nevers nodded. "Good. And also—Tom Hines coming my way?"

Lafayette Baker turned around to put the cash box away. He slammed the safe, spun the dial, and spoke firmly, "Not yet."

With that, Lafayette Baker waved his hand and the other detectives were up. Baker dropped his Colts into his holsters, pulled his rain cape over his duster, and launched himself toward the front door. John Odell was at Baker's hem like a hound, and the others trailed behind. Lo' Josh opened the door.

Butter was more confused than ever; he called, "What about me? What about my report?" The detectives plunged through the door. Butter was in pursuit. He got outside to find Baker and the others mounting up. Butter appealed to Baker. "Colonel, what am I supposed to do? Aren't you interested in my report? Aren't you taking charge of the surveillance?"

Baker eased his horse toward Broadway, and leaned away from Butter, saying, "I'm to my bed, and so are the boys." Baker was a skilled but impatient horseman, and he had to rein his mount sharply when Bob Dailey's horse blocked his path. Baker adjusted his seat, and added, "I'm due in Washington tomorrow. You've done the job well, Amaziah. Mr. Seward'll gloat when I tell him. So finish it."

Butter jumped away from Edgar Quillermouth's horse as it backed suddenly from the others. All the mounts were restless and irritable, and Butter retreated to the safety of the sidewalk. He spoke to Baker again. "But aren't we going to do something about the Rebs after the Election? Aren't we going to arrest them? They are guerrillas, and still dangerous. And what about John Oliphant? He's the most dangerous one. Shouldn't we grab him tomorrow night?"

Baker started his horse forward. He said, "What're your plans tomorrow, Amaziah?"

Butter was following in a fast walk. "About Oliphant or the guerrillas?" There was no response.

Butter continued, "Mr. Nevers' men are with the Rebs, so I'm free to watch Oliphant. Mr. Nevers tells me that he's meeting a European steamer."

Butter raised his voice over the clatter of the horse hooves. "There's a lady named Mrs. Winwood arriving! On the steamer *Australasian* from Liverpool, landing at Jersey City! He's got rooms for her and her party here at the Astor House!" Butter swallowed. He was directly under Oliphant's suite.

Baker did not look back. He raised his arm, and called, "Tomorrow'll be a great day for the Union!" And then Baker and the rest were off in a spirited trot across Broadway and into the mist at Ann Street.

Butter stood alone on the corner. Without the protection of the Astor House, the wind doused him with spray. He planted himself more securely and watched the night growl. A horsecar emerged from Ann Street and banked right to roll onto Park Row. An ad hoc convoy of carriages swayed with the gusts as they jerked up Broadway. A flood of wind like a large blow bent the treeline in City Hall Park and rippled the muddy pools in the road. Gradually, the mist was transforming back into a cold rain. And still Butter stood by, five minutes, ten, more—waiting and brooding.

Eventually, Nevers appeared from out of the mist, not from behind Butter, but from the direction of the main entrance of the Astor House. Nevers held onto his hat because of the wind, and asked, "Hot rolls and greens with chicken soup from the best kitchen I know, Cap'n?"

Butter sighed. "No." He looked up at the lights in Oliphant's suite. "I shouldn't leave, I guess."

"He's at his dinner, and we should get ours. There's a long night ahead. We ain't going far." Nevers pointed up Broadway. "All quiet for now."

Butter was not satisfied, with anything. He turned to Nevers. "Help me, if you can. Why was Colonel Baker congratulating me? What did I do? Stand up to Ben Butler and those two bullies? I didn't do anything but follow orders. All weekend, all I've done is follow orders, and follow you around, and do nothing."

Nevers said, "Maybe that's what you were supposed to do."

Butter said, "Nothing? Four thousand dollars is a lot for nothing, ain't it? That money he gave you. It was for helping me, wasn't it?

Nevers nodded. "Service promised. Service delivered. Service promised again."

"But what service? Following them around? All right. You're good at it, but still, four thousand? Is anybody that good?" Butter shrugged. "It beats Army pay. I guess there're folk in this town that can afford to pay that for security. I did see the name on that envelope. Weed. That's Thurlow Weed, isn't it? The party boss. My dad says Thurlow Weed's what's wrong with this country."

Nevers smiled. "Some men fight. Some men pay for the fight."

"So Weed and his friends pay? And we fight? Or do we? And men like John Oliphant pay, and the guerrillas fight, or do they? Lordie, there's a lot of money changing hands on both sides for not much happening but my fretting."

"It's good you fret," said Nevers. "You fret smart sometimes."

Butter was now truly flattered. He said, "Yes, I—I did do something, didn't I? I figured out John Oliphant, didn't I? You believe me, don't you? A little?"

Nevers said, "A little."

"Well, why didn't Colonel Baker? You listen to me. General Butler listened to me. So why didn't he? Did you notice? It was as if he didn't hear me. Or didn't want to."

"That man has his ways."

"You did notice?"

Nevers nodded back toward headquarters. "I saw that man get us out of a kettle of trouble. I saw him pick us up and fight our battle for us. I saw him laugh and tell us we done good. I saw him pay me for what's been done, and for what ain't been done yet. That's what I saw."

Butter said, "Every time I think you're going to tell me something I need to know, you tell me what I already know."

"How about me tellin' you that I'm hungry, and you should be?"

Butter laughed, and conceded the point. They splashed across Broadway carefully for the carriages and riders that could appear suddenly out of the gloom. They brushed the tip of the park and skipped over the seam in Park Row cut by the horsecar tracks. To the left, on Newspaper Row, the *Tribune* and *Times* buildings shone like catercorner towers of industry. Nevers took

Butter to the right, however, toward the also lit up *New-York World* building. They proceeded down Beekman Street to the corner of Nassau.

Here there was a small restaurant, which a swinging sign out front in the shape of the front page of a newspaper identified as the White-Coat Cafe. The large front bow-window revealed a bright, warm, crowded room, with a counter and several booths. The coming and going patrons looked to be from the colorful lower orders of journalism—gnomish pressmen, big-headed teamsters, tattered runners.

Butter was charmed in spite of his anxiety. He glanced back toward City Hall Park and shook the water from his greatcoat. Nevers opened the door. The cafe's cheer emanated like a potent new friend. Butter thought about all that trouble back there, behind him for the moment. He also thought how lucky he was tonight to be at the door of a dry room full of wonderful aromas rather than in a mud hole in Virginia.

Butter looked to Nevers, and quoted, " 'Fair is foul, and foul is fair, hover through the fog and filthy air.' "

Nevers said, "The food's better'n that here."

TUESDAY AFTERNOON, ELECTION DAY,
NOVEMBER 8

The weather deteriorated through the night. By the afternoon of Election Day, yet another violent and more ominous storm had settled upon New-York. The rain pummeled the long lines of voters at the polls, swept the streets with an icy spray, and churned the harbor with monumental gusts.

Out on the Hudson River, navigation was truly perilous. The main channels were ripped by foghorns as the pilots of the ferries, frigates, and steamships fought their way through the mist.

Butter looked out on the river from the New Jersey side, at the Cunard Company's pier in Jersey City. The rain crashed toward him in curtains. The wind sheered off the tops of the waves to make white water. And the fogbank made New-York seem a distant, ghostly heap against which the river traffic looked tiny and desperate.

Yet these wretched conditions did not abate the enthusiasm of the throng gathered near Butter at the Cunard pier. The crowd was eager to welcome their friends from their nearly two-week crossing from Liverpool. For just then gentlemen were raising their hats to point to, and ladies ducked out of the protection of the passenger shed to see, the sleek line of Cunard's transatlantic paddle-steamer, *Australasian,* as it emerged out of the fogbank at mid-river.

Australasian sounded her horns and released bursts of black smoke. There was a definite jerking of the portside waist paddle, as the pilot slowed the forward progress of the ship enough to let the southerly current of the river work for him.

Australasian, at about 360 feet and 48 abeam, was not as famous an oceangoing steamer as the swift *Scotia* or the behemoth *Great Eastern.* But she was still in the first ranks of passenger vessels, and could maintain her 3300 gross tons at an admirable ten to twelve knots on the arduous westerly route. She carried the British flag, because the war had flattened the American maritime trade. All passenger lines were now controlled by powerful consortiums in Liverpool, from the pioneering Samuel Cunard, whose fast ships and twenty-five-year experience reaped profits and prestige, to the fledgling and bookkeeperish National Steam Navigation Company, whose lumbering ships (seductively named *Louisiana, Pennsylvania,* and *Virginia*) catered to the immigrants.

Cunard's *Australasian* was happily in between the record-setting steamers and the turtle-slow and overladen ships from Ireland and Germany. She was wood-built, with iron bands and a double-bottomed hull, and was nominally rigged as a brig, with a mast fore and aft. She could carry several hundred first- and second-class passengers along with fourteen hundred tons of cargo and eighteen hundred tons of coal, and make the always dangerous long leg of the westerly run, Liverpool to Halifax, in about ten days, with another two days to Boston, and a final day to New-York. Her steam engines were of the older, oscillating type, which were slowly being obsolesced by the new dynamos for the screw propellers. But *Australasian*'s paddles could handle all but the heaviest sea (when the crew would switch to sail), and could get by on less than a hundred and thirty tons of coal a day. In all, *Australasian* was sound, steady, and, what was most important, had a record of safety in a trade that too often had seen similar ships vanish mid-ocean, or in a fog.

Given the storm, *Australasian* rocked more than slid toward the Cunard Company pier. Finally, she let go her anchors and gave a celebratory blast from her whistles as she nudged to a standstill at the southside berth. The

Cunard pier was constructed like a village that had been cantilevered out over the water. There were two barn-like warehouses at either end, an open square in the middle that included the passenger shed and the customs official's hut, and pathways on both edges for the longshoremen to service the steamers and the coal barges. *Australasian*'s sister ship, *Persia,* was already lying at the northside berth. Now, with the two of them tied up together, the pier's steam cranes, swinging chutes, and loading ramps were fully engaged, and the work was feverish.

When the wind came up in a battering gust, it cut free the "Welcome to America" banner that the Cunard clerks had strung along the passenger shed. The conditions were so bad that there were only a few bold passengers at *Australasian*'s hurricane deck rail, yet they performed for a multitude, calling and waving to the welcomers. Then, with a sharp squawk, the brass band provided by the Cunard Company struck up "Yankee Doodle Dandy." The oompah of the tuba established more than a beat. It announced: The wild sea was behind! The adventure was well done! Here was solid land! The music entertained everyone, and brought more ship's passengers to the rail. Soon, a covered gangway was swung up to attach at the ship's waist, and the disembarkation from *Australasian* began in earnest.

Butter remained back from the excitement. The passenger shed was open at both ends, like a big-top circus tent parted to admit the show. Butter was loitering near the northside portal, by *Persia*'s gangway. He would periodically stroll out into the rain to circumnavigate a pyramid of barrels, and then he would return along the same route. This gave him some exercise and permitted him to maintain his close watch of John Oliphant and Captain Kennedy.

Oliphant and Kennedy were standing clear of the rush at *Australasian*'s side. The welcoming crowd had pressed up to the cordon around the gangway, but Oliphant and Kennedy demonstrated only a cursory interest. They stood serene and still, smoking and talking. They were attended by a coachman from one of the two carriages that Oliphant had hired. Oliphant held his walking cane and a long thin box from a florist. Butter had gotten close enough to them during the ferry crossing from New-York to observe Oliphant opening and closing the box repeatedly—putting in and taking out and amending a card he had written. They were yellow roses.

It looked to Butter that this would be a long wait. Butter set out on another stroll around the pyramid of barrels. The wind sent a wave of rainwater across the pier, and Butter jumped clear of the splash. Butter ducked under a lean-to by *Persia* and looked back to *Australasian.*

Butter liked the big ships. In the fall of 1861, he had enjoyed a short leave from the First Maine encampment at Augusta to sail with some other officers up to Halifax to witness the astounding port call of *Great Eastern.* She had been bearing British troops to reinforce Canada's defenses for fear of an invasion by the United States during the so-called Trent Affair. Butter had ignored the politics of the event for the wonder of the iron-hulled and massive steamer, nearly 19,000 gross tons, and larger than *Persia* and *Australasian* together. Butter had listened to the gossip of the old salts, "Steel ships a-comin', sure!" and had carried back with him a print of *Great Eastern* at full steam at sea. At Christmastime, on leave again (the First Maine had not left for combat service until March 1862), Butter had shown the print to his family. His youngest brother, Tom, had made a shrine of it. His father had said, "Iron ships? Not till I'm in the ground!" And his 89-year-old Great-aunt Mercy (whose father, Amaziah Chisholm, had been with George Washington at the battle of Long Island) had laughed at the ship, "It's big —what ye want me to say? Ye think I'm old?"

It was another half-hour before Butter saw some activity from Oliphant and Kennedy. The stream of passengers was finished, and the steam crane was swooping again and again down into the ship's hold. Oliphant beckoned a Cunard clerk, and handed him the box of flowers. The clerk skipped up the gangway to pass the box onto one of *Australasian*'s stewards. When the steward reappeared, he came off the ship toward Oliphant and Kennedy, and he was carrying an envelope. Oliphant took and read the note, and then he and Kennedy went forward at last.

Butter aimed to see as much as possible, but because there were just shipping clerks and customs officers about now, he could not follow Oliphant and Kennedy directly. Butter hugged the wall of the passenger shed and pretended to be interested in the work of the steam crane. There was a pair of Army officers standing nearby, dressed in the ostentatious red pantaloons and tall, feathered helmets of a New York Zouave regiment. Butter placed himself so that the Zouave officers were between him and Oliphant and Kennedy. He idly listened while the Zouave officers debated how many cases of Madeira they expected to receive. One officer thought Butter was being friendly; he asked, "Are you waiting for a special consignment too?"

Butter said, "Yes, yes. Great day for it!"

The officer winked, and said, "Watch these boys, Captain. They keep things for themselves, and say they're lost."

Oliphant and Kennedy were now at the foot of the gangway, each tightly holding an umbrella that they pointed into the wind. The steward stood talking with them under the protection of the single piece of canvas that covered the gangway. Another wall of rain struck them, and ripped their umbrellas aside, pushing the steward against the handrail.

The Zouave officer asked Butter, "Whiskey?" Butter leaned closer to him. The officer continued, "Are you waiting for whiskey from Liverpool? We might have some wine to trade."

"No, no, I can't—" Butter backed away. And when he looked to the gangway again, there was a profound change.

Oliphant had mounted the gangway and moved halfway up the incline. He held his umbrella out toward two female figures making their way slowly down under their own umbrella. One female was a small Negro, dark-skinned, spindly, with white splashes in her hair where it poked from her bonnet; she held the umbrella with one hand and used the other to support her companion.

The second woman was slender, brunette, and white, in a full-length black traveling cape with the hood up. The Negro woman was supporting the white woman like a convalescent charge.

Behind these two was a parade of Negroes: two adolescent girls with arms full of boxes, including Oliphant's roses; two gangly adolescent boys weighed down with several valises each; a big-chested young man bent over with a trunk on his back; and finally a white-headed ancient in a black top hat and handsome livery who was carrying a large valise and a huge umbrella.

And farther up, at the rail, standing still, but attached to this procession, were two white men. The first was a tall, fair-complexioned and middle-aged man, who looked to be the confident European gentleman abroad in a floppy brimmed hat that did not conceal his shoulder-length and snowy white hair. The other man was a double-chinned bodyservant who was hefting luggage.

Oliphant adjusted his cane and umbrella to free his right hand. He reached out to the brunette. She continued a step without reacting. Oliphant gained her attention when, in a dance of bumping umbrellas, he took hold of her hand. She stopped and lifted her head.

Butter presumed that this was Mrs. V. H. (Narcissa) Winwood, for whom Oliphant had reserved two adjoining suites at the Astor House. Mrs. Winwood appeared to Butter, from forty feet, and in the rain, to be a convincingly beautiful woman who was much reduced by illness. Her eyes were swollen, her lips were off-color, her cheeks were concave, and her pallor was gray and deathy, as if fasting had become starvation. Nevertheless, her wasted face had the effect of emphasizing her vivid and perfectly symmetrical features. Then the sad balance of Mrs. Winwood's face was upset by a succession of contradictory emotions. It was as if there were a delay between what she saw, how she felt about it, and how she expressed her feelings. She opened her mouth and shut her eyes and launched herself into Oliphant's embrace.

The Negro woman was crying now, and Oliphant reached out to embrace her too. He got them both down the gangway and toward the protection of the passenger shed overhang. Kennedy helped with the umbrellas. Oliphant held tightly to Mrs. Winwood, and she clung to him. The other Negroes came off the gangway to surround them both, and soon they were all exchanging exuberant, heartfelt greetings.

Their remarks were mostly thanksgivings. "Mars Jan at las'!" and "Lord, Lord, Mars Jan!" Oliphant touched everyone's face and hands while keeping Mrs. Winwood at his breast. When the customs officer approached, the ancient Negro manservant took charge of the little company, and handed over a stack of documents in a case. There was a brief exchange with the customs officer, Oliphant speaking, Kennedy speaking, the customs officer pointing from person to person. The ancient Negro appeared to close the official business when he spoke to the customs officer, "We're househol', suh."

Butter felt the intruder. He had shifted his position to the side of the customs officer's shack, and was within easy earshot. But he held back. This seemed too private a moment for them. It was simply a family reunion. But then there was that mysterious gentleman with long white hair, who had come off *Australasian* with his servant to join the party at the periphery.

By now, Mrs. Winwood had recovered enough to speak. She stood slightly away from Oliphant and nodded toward the gentleman. She said, "Henry Blondel, John, you know."

Oliphant put out his hand, and he and Blondel shook formally and gracefully. Oliphant introduced Kennedy, "My good friend, Mr. Kennedy —Sir Henry Blondel."

So, thought Butter, he was an Englishman. There was more to the exchange, but Butter could not hear because of the storm, the hard bash of the waves against *Australasian,* and the screech of the steam crane.

The ancient Negro now organized the gathering. Butter assumed that they were about to depart for the carriages, and indeed the coachman raced up the pier toward the street. However, there was a delay. The company eased over to the edge of the shed, near the Zouave officers, and not twenty feet from Butter. They all seemed to be watching the steam crane lower its cargo net into *Australasian*'s hold. Presently, the steam crane dipped once more and emerged with a long wooden crate cradled in the cargo net.

At this, the Cunard clerk went from Oliphant out to the longshoremen. The ancient Negro and the big-chested Negro walked into the rain to help a crew with a hand wagon. The cargo net cleared the ship's side and swung back over the pier.

But then, a gust of wind struck the crane and its wires. The net shuddered and twisted back against the ropes of the aft mast.

"Please!" cried Mrs. Winwood. She broke from Oliphant and leaped out into the rain, her arms straight up toward the cargo net. The net swung back again and descended quickly toward the pier. She continued walking toward it, acting as if she wanted to catch the long crate. The steam crane operator saw her, and adjusted for her interference, but he could not control the play of the net.

Oliphant and Blondel caught up with her simultaneously. They took hold of opposite shoulders to pull her free of danger while shielding her with their backs. Kennedy was the quickest of all. He went right to the cargo net as it swung toward him at eye level. He shoved it back with both hands.

"Well done, Mr. Kennedy!" called Oliphant.

"Very well done, sir," added Blondel.

Oliphant and Blondel started Mrs. Winwood away. Kennedy waved to the operator, and the cargo net settled with a soft bounce. The longshoremen were at it immediately and loaded the crate onto the hand wagon.

The ancient Negro then took command of the procession; he was most solicitous of everyone's welfare as they set off in a line toward the pier's exit —the Negroes in front, the hand wagon in the middle, and Kennedy, Oliphant, Mrs. Winwood, Blondel, and the bodyservant behind.

Butter followed from a near distance. It was some time before the party reached the carriages. The crate was loaded on a flatbed wagon provided by Cunard. The carriages set out along Hudson Street for the ferry wharf less than two hundred yards away.

Butter stood impatiently at the facade of the pier, watching the caravan rock away from him through the mud. The rain had slackened some, but Butter could see new and darker clouds tumbling from the west over the dreary collection of warehouses and empty brown fields of Jersey City. Less than a quarter-mile south, there was activity at the Morrison Canal basin, and less than a quarter-mile north, a long freight rolled into the New Jersey Railroad yards. Butter sucked on his unlit cigar stub and waited as long as he could before the beginning of a new downpour forced him under an awning. Nearby, longshoremen were struggling with a train of hand wagons that brought up the trunks and crates from *Australasian* for the teamsters' wagons waiting at the loading ramp.

After a while, a shabbily dressed Negro, assisting a teamster, stepped away from his task, and drifted toward Butter.

Butter wiped his beard, and nodded in greeting. "I was wondering how long it was going to take, Mr. Nevers."

Nevers pulled out a bright linen handkerchief from underneath his greasy clothes and began to work at the dirt on his fingers. He said, "What do you want to know first?"

Butter gestured up Hudson Street. "Shouldn't we get on? They're likely to get the next ferry."

Nevers held out the rag to catch some rainwater, and went back to work on his hands; he said, "We know where they're going. They've been two weeks at sea. They're to the Astor House. The gentlemen'll buy drinks around and listen at the bar for Election rumors. She'll bathe and rest and dress for dinner."

Butter smiled. "You really don't like that ferry, do you?"

Nevers hissed, "Shallow draft boats on a day like this do loosen my teeth."

Butter grunted. "It's the only way back. Come on, let's get to it." They started out into the downpour. Butter pointed toward the ferry house. "Yellow roses, Mr. Nevers, he got her yellow roses. There's something mighty mysterious about that, and about her. Did you see the way he greeted her? Yellow roses. That means fidelity."

Nevers held the brim of his hat; he leaned into the wind and said, "I can do you better than that, Cap'n. Stewards are gossipy souls, and that Mrs. Winwood makes an impression."

"What is she to him? And what's the Englishman doing here? And what—" Butter sighed. "All right. Here's my first question. What's in that crate that's so important?"

"Easy," said Nevers. "Her father's coffin."

TUESDAY EVENING, ELECTION DAY, NOVEMBER 8

She was Mrs. Venable Hawkes Winwood, but her name was Narcissa Royall. Nevers agreed with Butter that she was a handsome woman who had likely been stricken with the melancholia of grief. Nevers did not agree that she was mysterious. Nevers opined, "Planter's lady."

Mrs. Winwood, about 40, was the daughter of J. Granby Royall, now deceased, of Beaufort, in the Sea Islands of South Carolina. Her husband, Confederate Brigadier-General V. H. "Hawk" Winwood, was missing in action in Virginia. Mrs. Winwood had been living in London for several years, at the St. John's Wood residence of her stepmother's sister, Lady Alice Blondel. According to *Australasian*'s assistant chief steward, the white-haired gentleman was Lady Blondel's brother-in-law, Sir Henry Blondel. Blondel was said to be the second son of a wealthy English lord from the north of England, and he was also said to be an invalided Royal Army brigadier.

What Butter wanted to know most crucially was what Mrs. Winwood was to Oliphant that he should have welcomed her so tenderly.

The simple answer, Nevers returned, was that she was his sister-in-law. The full answer, Nevers said, required more information.

Butter took special notice of Nevers's interest, and it pleased him greatly. Butter felt that at long last someone was agreeing with him that Oliphant was a serious threat who needed to be closely studied.

Back at No. 12 Vesey, during a pacifically auspicious Election night, Nevers also agreed with Butter that things were routine enough—the guerrillas at their hotels, Oliphant upstairs at dinner—to permit him to investigate Mrs. Winwood further.

Nevers's plan was to gain the familiarity of the Negro servants surrounding Mrs. Winwood. However, the ancient Noah, who had been Granby Royall's gentleman's gentleman, and the Negro woman Rosemary, who was Mrs. Winwood's personal maid, both proved totally unapproachable, no matter how Nevers and his people tried. The four adolescents were also unattainable, because they were all blood relations of Rosemary's, and were much under her eye in Mrs. Winwood's two suites.

This left the big-chested man, named Michael. Nevers enlisted one of his bokes, Roger Barnes, a glib and resourceful former slave from the Sea Islands. Roger Barnes was able to befriend Michael in the part of the Astor House basement that was reserved for storage, deliveries, and stableboys.

Soon, Roger Barnes persuaded Michael to sneak out from Noah's control in order to tour Broadway. Nevers joined them, and with Roger Barnes's help, slyly questioned the congenial but guarded Michael. Later, Nevers returned to No. 12 to report to Butter what he had learned of the Royalls.

The Royalls, according to Michael, were "big buckrah." In the Sea Island dialect known as Gullah, this meant that they were wealthy plantation owners. The Royalls, before the war, had owned several Sea Island cotton and rice plantations, the chief among which had been "The Acreage," where Michael had been born. The patriarch Granby Royall had lived in a so-called big house on Port Royal Island, in the grand planter's village of Beaufort.

"Miz Cissa," or Narcissa Royall (Mrs. Winwood), was the eldest of five children. She had become the mistress of the family at 14, after her mother's death. Narcissa Royall's supremacy had continued even after her father had remarried an English widow, Pamela Tempest of Liverpool. Narcissa Royall had married a Virginia planter's son and West Point-trained soldier, V. H. Winwood. They had produced two daughters before he, "Hawk" Winwood, had gone off.

"Mars Jan," or John Oliphant, was a Royall cousin from the North. Oliphant had arrived in Beaufort shortly after Hawk Winwood had departed, sometime in the mid 1850s. Within the same year, John Oliphant had married Narcissa Royall's younger sister, Camellia. Oliphant had then taken control of the Royalls' fortunes, despite the fact that Granby Royall had four sons, two by each marriage.

The Royalls had been forced to abandon their homes at the very beginning of the war. In November 1861, the Union fleet had attacked the Confederate defenses of Port Royal Sound and smashed all resistance, forcing every white person in Beaufort to flee. The Royalls had traveled to their relatives' home in Charleston. But then, with all their Sea Island property confiscated except "The Acreage," the Royalls' fate had darkened the more, when their Charleston house had been destroyed in the great fire that swept the city around Christmas 1861.

The Royalls had relocated again to their relatives in Savannah, Georgia. Soon after, Granby Royall had collapsed, and his wife, Pamela, had elected to take him and their young twin sons home to England, along with Noah, and Noah's great-grandson, Michael.

Mrs. Winwood had arrived in London with her entourage in the spring of 1862. Oliphant had visited them frequently at the St. John's Wood townhouse ever since.

The youngest of Mrs. Winwood's two brothers had been killed early in the war. One of Mrs. Pamela Royall's twins had died of fever in London. This past summer, the other twin had been killed at sea on a Confederate raider. And then the eldest Royall son had been killed in the Army in Virginia. Granby Royall had gone into his final decline not long after, and he had died in late September.

Mrs. Winwood had returned to America in the hopes of gaining the means to transport her father's corpse home to Beaufort, for burial at the St. Helena Episcopal Church. Mrs. Winwood planned to entrain for Washington immediately, in order to plead at the Navy Department for permission to enship through the blockade for Port Royal Island, which was now fortified by Union troops as part of the so-called Department of the South.

Butter stopped Nevers's discourse. It was a few minutes to midnight. Butter rose from his desk and pointed to the clock to announce the moment. He also commented, "What we've found, Mr. Nevers, is a family that's been completely smashed up by the war."

Nevers said, "That's what shows."

Roger Barnes was cracking and eating walnuts at Baker's desk. He had been listening and contributing to Nevers's account, and now added, "Dem Royalls. Big buckrah, dey gone where e'en Jesus ain' fetchin' dem back, no mo'."

Lo' Josh then surprised them. He rocked forward in his perch by the front door and began clapping in a musical beat. He sang, *"No mo' peck o' corn fo' me, no mo', no mo'. No mo' peck o' corn fo' me, many t'ousand go!"*

Lo' Josh halted to see if the others approved. Roger Barnes produced a mouth organ and sounded a chord. The two of them finished the song, *"No mo' driver's lash fo' me, no mo', no mo'. No more driver's lash fo' me, many t'ousand go!"*

Butter and Nevers applauded the spirit. These last moments of Election Day were weighty. Butter went to the door and beckoned Nevers. They walked out together onto Vesey and up to the corner of Broadway, trailed by Roger Barnes. The rain had ceased completely, though the night remained thick with moisture. It was also filled with the chaotic sounds of politics.

There were packs of men prowling Broadway and into City Hall Park. Their mood seemed volatile if subdued. Butter heard some bravura shouts from what must have been Copperheads.

"Where's Butler! Boooo!"

"Devil hang him!"

"Three groans for the New Orleans Jeweler!"

He also heard some corresponding baiting from what must have been Republican partisans.

"Little Mac's still shoutin', 'Reinforcements!' "

"Not enough votes live or dead to he'p him now!"

"Three cheers for Abraham Lincoln!"

The factions kept well clear of each other, however, and were content only to snarl while they awaited the results of the voting. There was little actual physical threat in their manner. Butter concluded that this was a credit to the War Department's shrewd decision not to post Butler's troops in the city but rather to keep them off island. The unseen was always more intimidating than the seen. More, bivouacked troopers would have invited the Copperheads to create ugly confrontations.

Butter could acknowledge that Stanton had been astute within the limits established for him. And he could now see that Dix's and Butler's anxieties over the defense of the city had had less to do with tactics than with their own jealousies and ambitions.

Butter could also see the true savvy of Secretary Seward's insistence that there be no arrests in New-York. If Stanton was wise, Seward was a genius! This belligerence tonight was a mere waltz of competitive gangs. Let them curse Ben Butler. Let them growl at the Union. There were no martyrs to celebrate, and there was no incident to revenge. These were definitely not mobs, and they did not look to becoming mobs. The city was safe! Election Day was nearly done!

Butter, Nevers, and Roger Barnes gained the apex of City Hall Park to enjoy the view in the round. There was a rowdy group on the steps of the Astor House singing patriotic songs that were sprinkled with vulgar references to Jeff Davis in petticoats. There was another drunken party marching south singing a crude ballad about Mary Lincoln and the "ape" president. In the park itself, there was a more disorganized crowd, especially about the cowshed-like recruiting station where posters promised bounties of $750 total for three-year volunteers.

The grandest assembly was the ebb and flow of men along Newspaper Row, from the *Tribune* and *Times* buildings at the triangle north of Spruce Street to the *World* building at Beekman Street. At all three newspaper buildings, figures leaned out of upper-story windows to call down Election bulletins from the telegraph rooms. Also, riders would appear out of the night like Paul Reveres to call out predictions or rumors to the crowd.

One fellow in a clown's costume trotted up to the park to cry, "Governor Seymour's got the city with a majority of thirty-five thousand! No more!"

Nevers turned to smile at Butter. "No mo', no mo'."

Another rider approached to cry, "Abe's beatin' Mac from here to Californee! But Seymour's got the city for the Copperheads!"

The next rider went too far with his message. "Jersey's gone Copperhead, and New York might follow. It's neck and neck with Lincoln fading!" For this, he was doused with beer and dragged from his mount.

Butter tried to look through the branches to the City Hall tower clock. "I can't make it out, Mr. Nevers. How long?"

Nevers held up his pocket watch, and said, "I'm a touch ahead."

St. Paul's sounded midnight first, and then the other church bells knelled up Broadway like rolling joy. For tonight, it was the sweetest music Butter had ever heard, and he offered his hand to Nevers. "Congratulations, partner."

Nevers took Butter's hand, and said, "And not a shot was heard in anger."

Butter laughed. "All along Broadway and all through the city! They're beaten! The damned Sons of Liberty are whipped! New-York's just wet, not on fire!"

Then they both laughed, and danced a little with Roger Barnes accompanying on mouth organ. Butter felt free, and more awake than at dawn on the Penobscot and making for the bay. Even New-York looked good to him now.

Nevers suggested that they retire to an intimate establishment of his experience for a celebration. Butter was tempted. His Puritanism prevailed. Also, Butter had a yearning for the roast chicken he had only admired last night. And so Nevers compromised and led the way to the White-Coat Cafe.

The little room was packed, but not impossible, since the pressmen were at their labor early in order to get out an especially vital Election edition. Also, Nevers knew the counterman, a bald and long-armed Negro named Summer Lee, who made certain that Nevers was able to secure his favorite booth by the window.

Republicans poured in with eager anticipation of happy Election results —for this was well known as Horace Greeley's men's den (Old White-Coat being the cafe's namesake). Soon, however, it was announced by a self-elected master of ceremonies that there would be a delay in the first returns. It seemed that many telegraph wires were still down because of the severe storms that had battered the North daylong from Chicago to Bangor.

Butter ordered a meal of chicken, new potatoes, and carrots. Nevers sampled the peaches, and Roger Barnes tried the house stew. Once the food had arrived, and Butter's appetite was slightly curbed, he made room among the plates for his logbook. He wanted to record the evening's events while he picked at the remains of his meal.

Butter added a fourth page to Oliphant's section, with the new information about the Royalls. Butter worked at a chicken wing, and said, "A rich, slaveholding family of Secessionists, Mr. Nevers, that's the Royalls for you." He wiped his fingers and wrote, saying, "They've got to be marked for that. Oliphant's another Yankee who married South. And lost his sense." Butter popped some stuffing in his mouth, and added, "Still—"

Butter could not hate the Royalls. Their fall was very American. He assumed that the Royalls had watched the war come as the Butters had, and perhaps had played an active part in the politics of the period, as the Butters had. There could not have been a prosperous American family who had not experienced the anger, fear, and calamitous stubbornness of the last decade. For Butter, the difference between the families was that the Abolitionist Butters had been right, and the slaveholding Royalls had been wrong.

Or, at least, that is what Butter would once have concluded absolutely. Since those certain days of 1861, Butter had seen Virginia, Maryland, and Pennsylvania fields littered with swollen corpses. Since those certain days, Butter had done murder. He was three years older in his politics now, and immeasurably more confused and mournful.

Tonight, Butter considered amending his opinion: The difference between the Butters and the Royalls might be that one hailed from secure and ever more wealthy Maine, and the other hailed from the Sea Islands—that portion of South Carolina that had been blasted by an invading fleet and destroyed by an occupying army. Beaufort's homes now were said to be Army hospitals; the estates were said to have been abandoned to the swamps; the yellow fever epidemics were said to keep everyone out but the Navy and the freed slaves.

Butter asked himself, what would he have done if his home had been Beaufort and not Bangor? The answer seemed simple. He would have fought until hell opened up. But this was exactly what he had done anyway. Butter did not feel smart enough to solve this problem. Fate was hard, and humbling. And there was also the unacceptable fact that the Royalls had owned slaves. Slavery was repulsive and sinful. It was wrong!

Butter pulled the skin off the chicken breast, and went at the meat. He spoke to Nevers, "I've been thinking. It's a high price the Royalls have paid. For being born South, and wrong." Butter could see that Nevers and Roger Barnes were not following his non sequitur, but he added, "A God-help-them, too-high price."

Butter drew question marks in his logbook. He wrote in capital letters, "ROYALL." He tried an anagram, as he had learned to do when examining captured Rebel messages (Mosby had liked word games). Butter had "LOYAL" with an "R" left over. He circled the "R." None of it showed anything new about Oliphant.

Butter looked at Nevers. What had Nevers said before? Something like, "That's what shows?" Butter said, "Hey! Shows? What do you mean? Is there something about the Royalls that doesn't show?"

Nevers was now eating apple slices in heavy cream. He licked his spoon and turned it over. "It was Michael. What he said and didn't quite say. I've been cogitating on it."

Butter sensed that he had discovered a rich vein; he said, "Go on. Tell me. I'm asking. Here I am. You said, ask."

Nevers told Roger Barnes to return to No. 12 to fetch any incoming messages. Once he was gone, Nevers seemed to relax. He also spoke more speculatively than Butter had ever heard him do. Nevers began, "Michael was testy when I asked him about his life in London. He said their house was busy with Southern gentlemen, regularly. He was bragging, like slaves do, about his masters and how fancy they are. These visiting gentlemen wore uniforms for the big parties. Michael said, 'Gemmen's fandangos.' He said, 'Virginie gemmen' and 'Carolina gemmen.' The English wore uniforms too. And they liked Michael for his talk. The Gullah, you know?"

Butter pictured great balls; he also tried to imagine the meaning of such celebrations attended by Southern and English officers. Butter said, "What else? Who were they? When? Do you think—?"

Nevers continued, "I say Michael got testy, and cuttin'. 'What'e for?' says he. Then Barnes and him went on in that Gullah jabber about how I'm a 'miss-siege-senator.' Do you understand, Cap'n? For my keeping company with white women? I don't mind that, as long as I get what I want when they say it. I kept at Michael about these trips he said he took with Mrs. Winwood and Oliphant. Michael swelled up and boasted how he rowed 'Miz Cissa' and 'Mars Jan' and some gentlemen in uniforms around a harbor.

They were inspecting ships. I asked him if it was at Liverpool. He started to answer, then closed up. Some fellows have been slaves too long. It gets inside them, like their momma's voice. See nothing, say nothing, be nothing."

Butter said, "There were no names? Like Mason, James Mason?"

"There were no names," said Nevers.

Butter was writing in his logbook again. James Mason, the brilliantly augustan former United States senator from Virginia, was the Confederate commissioner to Great Britain, the de facto Rebel ambassador to the Court of St. James. It was also a fact that for three years James Mason had been scheming to persuade the English government to recognize the Confederacy as an independent republic at war with the United States. In addition, it was well known that James Mason was a chief of the Rebel Secret Service in Europe, and that as such he had directed a network of secret agents for those same three years, raising money for the Confederacy and using that money to transship arms through the blockade and also to build or outfit Rebel warships in the so-called neutral port of Liverpool.

Butter scratched and scratched with his pencil; he pushed Nevers. "Mrs. Winwood's been abroad for years. Oliphant's been visiting her for years. There must be more."

Nevers said, "I'd tell. Michael's suspicious too. What're you writin'?"

Butter pointed at the logbook. "What I think. That she's an agent too. Or just as good as one. A Rebel hostess."

Nevers shook his head in disapproval. "Jes' what you see, Cap'n. I don't see other than that she's a sickly Sea Island belle."

"Whoa! You started," protested Butter. "You told me that it's what you don't see that's dangerous. You see a sick belle. But I think what's underneath is dangerous. Just like Oliphant, and all those guerrillas. And now she's said to be off to Washington City. And maybe Oliphant's going with her, a man who we know is capable of plotting the destruction of New-York. Whatever else, it can't be good to have him in the capital."

Nevers sank an apple slice, and said, "She's going with her daddy's corpse too."

Butter tapped his logbook. "You should listen to me! I was right about John Oliphant. He's one of their big ones. And look what he leads us to—some mission to Washington! He's seven times Tom Hines!"

Nevers pointed his spoon at Butter. "It ain't for me to say what he is, not with what I know. And I'm thinkin' that it ain't for you to say what he is neither."

"You mean because of Colonel Baker? Because Colonel Baker doesn't like me thinking independently? Or because I might be right, like I was about Tom Hines, and because I'm stubborn?"

Nevers said, "You are stubborn."

"But not wrong?" tried Butter.

Nevers smiled, but did not reply.

Butter grunted and continued to write. He was not going to bother himself just now trying to persuade Nevers to his opinion.

Presently, Nevers excused himself, saying he was going out for a while. Butter reviewed the puzzle. He had thought his questions about John Oliphant mooted by the failure of the conspiracy. Now Oliphant seemed transformed into an even deeper mystery.

After another half-hour, Butter was so far inside his imagination, and doubts, that he did not flinch at the first cries of celebration. But the hosannahs and hurrahs increased, and then Nevers was back.

"Look here, Cap'n! Ain't this worth it, worth it all?" Nevers held a large wet sheet like a prize—one of a number of similar sheets being passed around the room. They were proofs of the inked-up, cold-type front page of the *New-York Tribune,* dated November 9, 1864. Nevers flapped his sheet out, and let it unfurl before Butter.

"THE VICTORY—Lincoln Re-Elected—He Has Nearly All the States—All New-England for Him—New York Close but Pretty Sure—New Jersey for McClellan—Pennsylvania Union on Home Vote—Delaware and Maryland Union—The West All Right—Copperheads Nowhere."

There was also disturbing news, despite the overwhelming number of states for Lincoln. In New-York's twenty-two wards, McClellan had beaten Lincoln by a two-to-one majority, 73,734 to 36,737. And though New York's gubernatorial race was still too close to call, the Democratic incumbent governor Horatio Seymour had enjoyed a similar majority in New-York City over the Republican candidate Reuben Fenton.

Butter watched the Republicans in the cafe suffer the local election results. It was clearly a disgrace that the most powerful and populous city in the nation should have revealed itself to be anti-Lincoln and anti-Negro. There seemed little comfort for them in the narrow majorities for Lincoln in the neighboring Queens County, Kings County, and Westchester County.

The local election news was so grim that, at 3:30 A.M., there remained the dark possibility that New York State was not, as Greeley's *Tribune* had declared, "Pretty Sure," but that it actually might go for McClellan and Seymour. It remained too close but to hope—in a state with more boys in blue than any other—with results still not in from the distant counties reporting slowly because of the downed wires. Butter watched the Republicans worry, and was again reminded of Seward's correct caution against arrests. In a state where politics seemed a balancing act, counterforce might very well have given the election to the Copperheads.

Butter was accordingly delighted to read that in Maine, even though the Radical Republican Downeast towns, like Bangor, had not yet reported because of the storms, the electorate had already provided a heavier majority for Lincoln than it had in 1860. And New-England was a seamless display of Lincolnite triumph. Butter felt proud when he thought of Bangor voting in the rain. His father would have been at the church tonight, praying for Lincoln, and for his sons, and awaiting the news.

Butter's pleasure did not last. It was sometime not long after—when they had the first complete issues of the *Tribune*—that Lo' Josh and Roger Barnes arrived at the booth in a rush. Butter was reading an anecdote to Nevers about the New-York Democratic financier August Belmont, and he did not immediately look up.

"Cap'n," said Nevers, "there's something here for you."

Butter crushed the *Tribune* in his lap. Lo' Josh looked particularly somber. He had a telegram in his hand. Butter felt his panic. No man with three brothers in the Army and two young sons in Maine could avoid thinking the worst at every unexpected telegram. Butter said, "No. Tell me. What is it?"

Nevers said, "It ain't death."

Butter opened the envelope, but upside down. His apprehension made his first reading useless. It was from Lafayette Baker.

Nevers shoved a bowl of cut fruit at Butter, and said, "It's for the best for now, Cap'n."

Butter said, "He's ordered me back. Colonel Baker's ordered me to Washington. Immediately."

Nevers said, "It's done."

Butter said, "What? You knew about this, didn't you?"

"I'd a clue it was coming," said Nevers. "You did too. It's done here, for now."

"It's because of Oliphant, isn't it? It's because I'm right about Oliphant?

It's not done here, and you know it. Those guerrillas are still out there. And so's Tom Hines. And John Oliphant is capable of anything, anything! I'm right. I've been right since my trip to Calais! And what do I get for it? They treat me like a mule! And I'm right!"

"Being right ain't what it could be in this work," said Nevers.

Butter felt his anger building. "Oh, you're comfort, you're just comfort."

Nevers smiled like a man with secrets. He then lifted his right hand to reveal a small envelope. He said, "This is for you, Cap'n, knowing your funds are low and your bones are weary."

Nevers slipped out the contents of the envelope and stuck it in the cut fruit. It was a railroad ticket, for the New Jersey Railway—Jersey City via Philadelphia for Washington City. And it was not a soldier's fare at $5.00, but rather a rich man's at $8.50. Nevers tapped the ticket. "There's a connecting ferry at nine-thirty, for the express train at ten. You best get to bed. You'll need your sleep."

"Why?" barked Butter. He was now furious. He felt he was being paid off. "You tell me why we aren't arresting Oliphant! You believe me about him, I know you do! Arrest him now!"

"For what?" asked Nevers. "His bad company and good manners?"

"Don't try that on me! I've seen the Secret Service work. There ain't habeas corpus since— Hell, there ain't even badges! Colonel Baker and his boys just bash and grab!" Butter made a fist and shook it. "Oliphant's the damn center of whatever the Rebs're up to! And I've learned one thing from this war. If you get the damn center, you have a chance to win!"

"I don't disagree," said Nevers.

Butter startled. "You don't?"

Nevers continued, "I suppose what I think is that we don't know enough yet about John Oliphant to say who's the center, or who's winnin'."

Butter mumbled, "You don't?" Butter suddenly saw something shockingly new about Nevers. He guessed part of it, "Mr. Nevers, is Oliphant on that express train at ten? And Mrs. Winwood?"

Nevers said, "Most likely. And the coffin too." Nevers took off a scarlet glove to pick up an apple slice; he continued, "I've been thinkin' on that story you told me yesterday. About that king murderer and his lady. 'Macbeth'? About what Macbeth said when he was up against the fellow who was going to get him for his crimes, and lop off his head."

Butter was staring at Nevers. It was slowly coming upon him that Nevers was, and always had been, considerably more than his assistant or even partner in this operation. Butter helped Nevers's memory. "MacDuff. It was MacDuff that beheaded Macbeth."

Nevers continued, "That's it. MacDuff. That's what I want to say to you. 'Keep on, MacDuff—' "

"No," interrupted Butter. " 'Lay on, MacDuff—' "

Nevers beamed. "I got it. 'Lay on, MacDuff, and damned be he that first cries, hold enough!' "

Butter understood Nevers clearly now; he said, "You're saying that it isn't done here, or anywhere, aren't you? That you see the Rebs for what they are, and are ready to track Oliphant as long as it takes to get him?"

Nevers said, "None of it ain't done."

Butter tested his new opinion of Nevers's identity; he asked, "Mr. Nevers, do you know why Colonel Baker didn't want me to talk about Oliphant, or why he's trying to call me off the trail?"

Nevers was matter-of-fact. "No, I don't, Cap'n, and it surely is a puzzle for me same as it is for you. But like I said, that man has his ways, and you've got to work around 'em."

Butter nodded in agreement, but also with great satisfaction. He was right about Nevers too. Butter tried to seal their bargain with a restatement of his purpose. He said, "They shouldn't have tried against Maine. I mean, that's what really peeved me, and still does. It's where I live."

Nevers nodded. "New-York's where I live."

Butter smiled. "I just wish the folk on our side were all on our side."

"Amen," said Lo' Josh. Lo' Josh and Roger Barnes squeezed into the booth. Roger Barnes started a tune on his mouth organ, with Lo' Josh humming along.

Butter was soothed. He sat back to chew on his cigar stub, weighing his alternatives. He might have continued to speculate. He might have sworn he was going to confront Lafayette Baker about Oliphant as soon as he returned to Washington. He might even have declared that he was going to demand he be transferred back to Bangor immediately, or even to the First Maine, to escape the intrigues of the Secret Service.

Yet none of these choices seemed as compelling to Butter as what was suddenly at hand. For Butter felt possessed by a profound revelation. He had finally realized that he was no longer William Seward's man or Lafayette Baker's man. He was now, as he had been since he had set foot in New-York, in the care and control of Gouverneur Nevers. Butter had never been in charge of anything. Butter had worried for five days that he might be a scapegoat. He had actually all the while been a figurehead. Gouverneur Nevers was not only the chief detective of the Department of the East, he was also the Secret Service commander in New-York.

This fact did not upset Butter. Indeed, he found it wholly comforting. Nevers was bizarre, elliptical, tauntingly illicit, and deliberately disquieting. But he was also easily capable of that quality called leadership. Butter could only hope that Generals Grant, Sherman, Sheridan, and Thomas had as much confidence in themselves. At just this moment, Butter truly thought Nevers a prince among men.

And if Nevers did not want to say aloud what he believed about Oliphant, and what he planned for Oliphant and the guerrillas and the Copperheads, so be it. Butter had his assignment. He put the ticket to Washington in his logbook and shut it. This was to be a secret battle. He would fight it alongside Nevers, until he could not.

Lo' Josh began singing to Roger Barnes's tune, *"Pray on, pray on, pray on den light us over! Pray on, pray on, pray on de Union break of day. My bruder come to see baptize, in de Union break of day, in de Union break of day!"*

It was then that the counterman, Summer Lee, called to Lo' Josh, over the roar of the Republicans and pressmen. What he called was really a toast, except that Summer Lee held up only a glass of water, and Butter, Nevers, Lo' Josh, and Roger Barnes had only apple juice, or half-eaten apples. Summer Lee shouted, "Gentlemen! God bless you! Dat de Union shall live and slavery shall die! Abraham Lincoln!"

PART TWO

THE ORDEAL
OF JOHN OLIPHANT

April 1855 and November 9-19, 1864

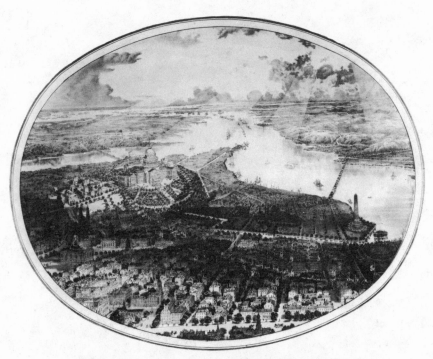

WASHINGTON CITY, DISTRICT OF COLUMBIA

CHAPTER 5

John Oliphant at the
Sea Islands, South Carolina

APRIL 1855

The second time John Oliphant ever saw Narcissa Royall, he was physically stunned, struck with awe as if by an unavoidable and sensuous force from the front. And if he did not fall on the spot, he was certainly spun around inside himself like a boy on a bursting day set loose in a wandering wood. She was his God-given discovery. Indeed, he was so possessed by her presence that it did not occur to him, in shock at this sudden fortune, that he could both take such extreme pleasure in the sight and smell of—her scent was jasmine and the night's sea air—and also humanly love so white-eyed and full-hearted a creature.

It was the spring of 1855. Oliphant had ventured into the South on a mission of mercy. His mother, Alice Cross Oliphant, was dying in Philadelphia, her throat eaten by cancerous embers that twisted her bedridden body with afternoons of silent pain. It was her desperate wish, and hoarse command, that something final be done with the property that she had inherited the year before in South Carolina—a house in Charleston, a cottage in Beaufort, and two Sea Island cotton plantations on the barrier islands of

Ladies and Hilton Head. This bounty had passed to her, with corresponding debts, through a Byzantine set of circumstances initiated by the death of an aged, childless relative, a Talbird of Charleston, who himself had inherited the Sea Island property from a family shadow, John Cross, Beaufort tavern-keeper and indigo entrepreneur during the Revolution. It was a tiresome tangle of allegiances, slights, and documents that nonetheless had resulted in Mrs. Oliphant's profit and burden. This latter obtained because it was a decided embarrassment for the Reverend John Darling Oliphant, master of a boy's seminary, self-absorbed philanthropist (American Tract Society, Presbyterian Board of Foreign Missions), and ostentatious Abolitionist (American Anti-Slavery Society, American Abolition Society), that his wife's estate, and soon his own, should contain Carolina soil and chattel slaves. And so, in order to settle this lingering parental dispute—which had become grotesque because of a husband's zeal and a wife's doom—the earnest eldest son, John Cross Oliphant (inadvertently bearing the name of he whom the Reverend Oliphant called "the impious bugbear"), embarked on a paddle-steamer from Philadelphia to Charleston for his first experience deep below the Mason-Dixon Line.

Oliphant disposed of the Charleston house straightforwardly within a week, and for what he considered a most fair price in a city he regarded as at once dazzling, vain, and hard-driving. He had spent his years since university in busy pursuit of wealth in sober Philadelphia and high-handed New-York, with annual trips to Great Britain to visit, invest, and explore; in all, he had been Europe-regarding as much as self-regarding. Now, by accident, he was plunged into the wholly extraordinary rhythm of Charleston, where he found American citizens like performers in some enormous romance: planters, traders, factors, shippers, idlers, and soldiers of fortune swirling about genuinely astral belles who themselves were en route to shop or to parade with platoons of fancy-dress Negro servants—and all this strange noise and lush fury of cotton and rice profit, of moist weather and courtly love-making, in a city that nature had blessed with ultramarine vistas and that wise patrons had constructed with eccentric verve. These Carolina people were excitable and exciting, at least for a dry Presbyterian soul like Oliphant. He thought their beautiful homes, cornucopic markets, ornamental clothes, and overwhelmingly polite manners incomparable—literally— for in comparison the North's cities were drab vaults, London was worm-worried, Paris was blasé and presumptive, and Rome—that hot, ancient haunt that had captured his imagination during a consuming, youthful love affair—was grimy and ill-winded. Charleston dealt, and sang, and danced, and teased, and desired. Oh yes, the passion was right out in front of him, and if he did not blush, he did puzzle at what happy geography and tropical air had done to the same sort of Anglican and Calvinist souls who had settled the Puritan North.

With their open-faced emotionalism there was also their endless, playful, prodigal talk of this and that, but always of their vain, earthly wants. Yet what talk! Of a lover's quarrel in White Point Garden that had ended in a stabbing, of a duel at dawn near the Mill Pond that was said to have disposed of a debt and a liar with one shot, of a fatal train wreck on the South Carolina Railroad that had factions threatening gunplay, of a mysterious Huger thoroughbred at the Washington Race Track that might be a bribe to leave a certain belle alone, of a Cuban escapade by boys runaway from the Citadel, of a suspicious fire on Accommodation Wharf that implicated a spurned adulterer, of skyrocketing cotton prices and stately rice profits and a shipment of impossible-to-find silk from Liverpool that was being held under guard for taxes (Charlestonians thought taxes to be pure deviltry), and most of all of marriage—the arch, coy, clever talk of engagements, estrangements, relations, and concubinage. Oliphant heard a flood of chatter, from a city in verbal competition with the virile confluence of the Ashley and Cooper rivers.

It was true that Oliphant did not understand most of what he heard. Was this serious anger or bravado? Brutal revenge or negotiation? And what he understood, he did not know how to measure, with the exception of one topic: the bright-edged gossip of the politics of slavery. First and last this spring, there was Kansas. And it was with the Kansas talk—a subject so intensely popular that one might have thought Kansas in the next county —that Charleston showed Oliphant the undercurrent of its persuasion. In Philadelphia, there was a pall for the results of the Kansas territorial election that had brutally delivered up a pro-slavery legislature and a warning to the Abolitionists that the slaveholding squirearchs of the South were willing to corrupt democracy to ensure the expansion of slavery into the West. It was hardly secret that Southerners had hired Missourians to cross into Kansas to help overwhelm the Free Soil homesteaders at the polls; indeed, it was part of the Southern provocateurs' strategy that everyone should know that they were willing to undo the fragile compromises of 1820, 1850, and 1854 that maintained the states half-slave and half-free if this was the only way to protect their interests. Oliphant's father was accordingly in double mourning

—for his Alice and for his hope in the infant Free Soil party. The ideologues in New-England were scarlet-faced and vengeful.

In Charleston, Oliphant found, there was anxious and cautious celebration: joy for the victory in Kansas and the affront to the imperious Yankee senators like Sumner of Massachusetts, Chase of Ohio, Seward of New York; worry that Kansas might be a Pyrrhic victory that, because of its obvious illicitness, would drive the Abolitionists into new and more devout conclaves, like the fledgling Republican party. In the streets, at the Planter's Hotel, at the market, at the wharves, in carriages, cafes, and offices, Oliphant overheard hollow-sounding boasts, "Pierce has promised . . . !" and "Bless Missouri!" and "Kansas slave and God Southern!" and he also witnessed grandiloquent men take any opportunity to declare their opinions in such a way that they cited political names as an astronomer might identify meteors falling from heaven: Andrew Butler and Barnwell Rhett of South Carolina! Charles Sumner and Edward Everett of Massachusetts! Stephen Douglas of Illinois! Judah Benjamin of Louisiana! Jefferson Davis of Mississippi! Not to forget the ever invoked chant, "Mrs. Stowe and Uncle Tom!"

Soon, the darker political elements in Charleston began to remind Oliphant of the mood in his father's study. He looked to find some relief, and was quick to agree to a short trip to look over his mother's Sea Island property. Yes, Charlestonians were ever polite, but they seemed to seek his attention at dinner in order to give a lesson on how he, gentle Yankee, did not really see the South and slavery for what they were: Destiny, they said. The astonishment of hearing, at a dinner party held by the Talbird agent on the eve of Oliphant's outing, an educated planter—a Princeton graduate like Oliphant—actually opine, "God's truth, you can't trust the Constitution, for Ol' Tom Jefferson was an Abolitionist in his secret heart!" convinced Oliphant that if he wanted to continue enjoying the South he had best avoid politics, at least until he had unloaded the Sea Island plantations and could plan his escape. Also, to be fair to the Talbird agent, Mr. Wigg, and the others who had hosted him, Oliphant's upset was not entirely due to the press of the South's prejudices and doubts. He was heavily grieved by his mother's illness. He could see that this Southern trip was in part in consequence of the way the politics of slavery cut into every family and heart.

The truth was that Oliphant had become as impatient of his father's piety and right-mindedness as he had become of the irascible preachiness of the Southerners in the papers, and now in person. His mother was dying. What did America's future matter? He wanted to be quiet, pensive, alone. He wanted to cry, and felt he had no extra pity for the ragged slaves he saw, for the beastliness he was sure these overdressed planters and checkered-pants traders practiced on their human property. Slavery was wrong and stupid. Death was wrong and stupid. Both might or might not be fated. Let others sermonize. Let others fight. The woman he loved more than any human being was struggling to live a day at a time because she did not know how to surrender to pain, because she loved life as she loved God, her Savior, and her family. Oliphant wrote her a long letter, full of cheer and exuberant descriptions of his journey so far, and then he embarked on a schooner for Beaufort on Port Royal Island, before dawn, Tuesday, April 10, 1855.

Oliphant realized he was in the hands of the Princes of Serendip as soon as the coastal schooner, *Chicora,* cleared the windward side of St. Helena Island and came about for the broad mouth of Port Royal Sound. Here was a wholly other and profound world. It had a biblical feel, and compelled him into metaphor as it drew him into its completeness, *Chicora* sliding south with the flow tide for a brief stop to offload supplies to exotic boats (long, open craft carved from cedar trunks and rowed by very dark-skinned Negroes) come out from shore. The Sea Islands appeared to Oliphant like living puzzle pieces that God, in his playful mood, had chosen not to close against the swampy face of the Carolina coastline. And here, at Port Royal Sound, was the entrance to the richest heart—the verdant marshlands, green river ribbons, and airy loam of the boundlessly profitable Sea Island cotton plantations. But that was money-talk, Oliphant thought, and he did not care, for now, to weigh credit and debit when there was such sun-blessed wonder to enjoy.

Hilton Head Island to the southwest wore its white dune beaches festooned with sea oats and wild flowers like a pearl necklace laced with seaweed. The mass of beach and marsh to the northeast seemed a juggernaut, but was actually—according to the other passenger on *Chicora,* a commercial traveler named Saulmann—several distinct islands fitted against the huge, triangular St. Helena upstream. This nearest beach, with its white tip, darting sandpipers, and laconic pelicans, was Bay Point of St. Phillips Island.

Saulmann, a middle-aged chipmunk sort of man, responded happily to Oliphant's curiosity, and showed himself the philosophical tour guide when he said, "Pretty is as pretty does!" and strode to the waist of the ship with Oliphant for better observation.

Chicora made full sail again and, with the tide, was hard across the two-mile-wide sound toward the spit, four miles due north, where the sound divided into two channels. The left was the Broad River that stretched upstream two dozen miles to the railroad town of Coosawhatchie and then several dozen more miles to its head in the upland cotton fields of the Barnwell District (South Carolina called its counties "districts"). The right channel was the Beaufort River that twisted a dozen miles upstream, between Parris and St. Helena islands, between Port Royal and Ladies islands, to the bend in the river that enclosed Beaufort itself.

Even these magical names of places and waterways, however, seemed pale to Oliphant before the sublime beauty of the landscape. Everywhere to see were the flapping fronds of the tropical palmetto trees that had permanently bent trunks because of the almost constant onshore wind, and also the oversized sycamores and pines in deep groves, and most especially the awesome, immortal-looking live oaks—that Olympian of trees—indomitably anchored by aboveground roots, squat at the waist, with spreading, gnarled limbs and foliage too thick to see sunlight through. And all of the noble live oaks, whether in motley clusters or singular stands, were decorated with the most exquisite natural phenomenon Oliphant had seen since purple Scottish heather—that is, this Spanish moss, its webs of gauzy strands tossing without gravity, eerie, gentle, otherworldly, like dust balls and yet not, like old clouds from heaven broken up, painted silver, and draped over the Sea Islands by angels.

Yet this place was most decidedly earthly and vividly alive, with bright water birds fishing at the shore, roosting in the trees, breaking out of the marsh in a start—like that flight of brown ducks, or that single osprey on the hunt, and particularly like the herons of all sorts: the snowy egrets poking along the marsh's edge, the Louisiana herons on one leg picking at insects in their feathers, and the army of great blue herons lifting from the creekbed to starboard. Oliphant fixed upon these hoarse-squawking great blues— impossibly wild constructions with a rich, gray body and orange beak—and flapped his arms once in mimicry. That is how a man would look if he flew, Oliphant thought, trailing long legs and pointing his beak toward the daylight moon above.

"It's vastly prettier than it does, sir," said Oliphant to Saulmann, and then he laughed, waving at the color of the flora beneath the hot green canopy of the trees. He meant the pure white of the dogwoods, the choice colors of the azaleas, and the bright whites and yellows of the lilies. This was the ripest moment of the Carolina spring, and the voluptuous gardens of St. Helena Island to starboard made Oliphant blink and blink again. For a moment he believed he could taste the air, for the fragrance here was thick with jasmine mixed with the heavy salty moisture of the sea, and a whiff of something familiar. What was it? Orange blossoms growing boldly in the tangle!

Oliphant was humming to himself by the time *Chicora* had maneuvered the last mid-river islet just off the marshy knoll of Ladies Island, opposite the village of Beaufort. Mozart seemed light-hearted enough, Oliphant thought, but perhaps too formal; he switched to the footloose and zesty Liszt. Oliphant felt like dancing. He was on his toes, as whimsically buoyant as he had been since his summer in Tuscany.

He could even laugh at the sleepy perfection of Beaufort itself. The village was behind more bushy palmettos and vast live oaks draped with the Spanish moss. The marsh grass appeared to grow right up to the very edge of a street of trim, two-story clapboard houses, painted bright white, but none too recently, with the settled-in look of cottages and the pride of rustic palaces. And—more wonderful—many of the houses were draped with wisteria, and surrounded by stunning red, white, and fuchsia azaleas.

The Beaufort dockside was also delightful in its lazy provincialism. There were a few fishing boats which had not gone out for the day, nets laid out and being worked upon by more very dark-skinned Negroes, and half a dozen horses tied up beneath a lean-to, feeding in oats bags. Beaufort was at easy peace in the afternoon sunshine, a huge bank of puffy white clouds on the horizon, and one dirty dust cloud on the shore. The dust-up was from a post chaise moving toward the dock behind an old Morgan; there was a Negro driver and a female passenger. She was dressed in rosy silk, with a large-brimmed white bonnet that flapped like wings. Oliphant made sure she was a pretty young woman—he wanted Beaufort exceptional in every way —before he went up to the quarterdeck to thank the captain and to inquire how often *Chicora* called here. He expected to remain no more than a week.

Saulmann gave last-moment advice on the hostelry and the local customs, "These darkies speak Gullah, and're a most to-themself people, like their masters."

Oliphant thanked him and took up his bag and made ready to disembark. There was a Negro workgang prepared to offload *Chicora,* and two white men were standing near a dock shack. Everyone was relaxed, calling out confirmations of the fine weather. Oliphant skipped over the gunwale with a laugh, and landed neatly on the wharf. His hat flew off, though, and bounced to the floating dock below the wharf. A little Negro boy fetched it quickly. Oliphant ducked down to reward him with a silver coin. The boy said, "T'ank you, suh, but fuh me, fuh me?"

"Spend it dearly," said Oliphant, recovering himself and turning back toward the town. He was aware that there were men on the wharf who seemed to be frowning at his exchange with the boy. He thought to address the issue with a smile all the way around. Up the wharf, he saw Saulmann directing an ancient Negro in blue livery toward him. Oliphant carried on right until the Negro coachman addressed him.

"Pa'don, suh, was yuh Mars Ol-fant?"

Oliphant, still anxious that he might have committed a faux pas by giving the boy silver, said, "Is that your son, or grandson? He helped me, so—" And then he realized the man had used his name, Oliphant.

The Negro coachman said, "Miz Cammie fo' you, suh."

Oliphant had not expected to be met. Mr. Wigg had written ahead for him, to the co-inheritor of the Ladies Island plantation, "Old Cross," a Mr. J. Granby Royall of King Street, whose deceased first wife was second or third cousin to Oliphant's mother. It was as much a confusion of relations as property. Mr. Wigg had said matter-of-factly, "The Royalls're local gentry—what they call big buckrah—and won't trouble you. Might chance buy the lot from you if they've straightened their money affairs."

Oliphant did not wish to be impolite, but he truly did not know what the Negro coachman was intending. He smiled again, and took a step away.

The coachman pointed to the post chaise. "Dere's little Miz here fuh yuh suh. Dere, 'pontops de rig."

Oliphant looked to the woman in the white hat. The coachman took his valise. The woman rearranged herself on the back seat. Oliphant crossed toward her. The rosy dress was creased, as if it had been put on and off and on again without pressing. Her smile overwhelmed her rumpledness, however, a pink burst around her prominent teeth. Her hair was very blond and curly under her hat, but her eyebrows and coloring were those of a brunette. There were good shoulders and a lovely long neck. At perhaps 20, she was, in all, a casual beauty, still more girlish than womanly.

There was a delay between them, until Oliphant realized he was expected to speak first. "I am John Oliphant, from Philadelphia. How can I be of service, miss?"

"Oh, Cousin John, I knew you'd be like this!" And she laughed.

Her name was Camellia Royall. She said that she and her family had expected him the day before, and that she had met three ships in two days. She said, "Not that Yankee kin come every day, and it is the rage to fuss over one's Yankee friends, but, sirrah, I don't mind your knowing that I am quite black and blue with meeting ships!"

Camellia Royall further said that she hoped he had enjoyed his journey, though she was sure, "Such a worldly gentleman, and so fine, could not be amused much by the life of his country kin."

Camellia Royall emphasized that she was very sorrowful for Mrs. Oliphant's illness, and that she hoped it was some comfort to him that Mrs. Oliphant was now included in the Royalls' evening prayers. She would have said much more of other matters, and with equal pluck, had not Oliphant, at some point, communicated that he was very moved by the Royalls' concern, and that he anticipated with pleasure meeting the Royalls—perhaps this evening, after he was settled at the Beaufort Hotel.

Camellia Royall exploded, half laughter and half arm-flinging upset, bouncing hard enough to disrupt her hat. "Oh that place! Our Beaufort Hotel?! Why, it's for factors and drummers and other sorts! What would Narcissa say? You, dear man, thought you'd stay at the Beaufort Hotel? What mad notions you must have of us. The Beaufort Hotel! Get up here. Jack, let's get on! Sit here, Cousin."

"I'm to go with you?" asked Oliphant.

"Cousin John, you are to go with me! We've already missed two suppers and two teas with them eye-popping at Chinaberry to fuss over you with their ways! And Narcissa says if I don't get you there for the next tea, the good 'n' foolish ladies of Beaufort'll have it told that we've eloped to Charleston!"

John Oliphant, suddenly a little in love, climbed up to take a seat beside the generous, keen-willed, and outspoken Camellia Royall. The coachman, Jack, brought the post chaise around and set off east on Bay Street, the main thoroughfare that displayed the shops, warehouses, offices, and commercial buildings, including the brick-built Beaufort Hotel, of a town that the North called the Newport of the South. There was a great deal of the oyster shell and lime mix called tabby, which dated the center of the town long before the Revolution, when, according to Camellia, "We had silk worms here, true! And indigo as juicy as melons!"

Camellia enjoyed her role as expert guide as much as Oliphant enjoyed his role as inquirer. There at the corner of Scott Street, she said, was the Verdier House, a two-story frame house on a raised foundation with a small centered double portico; the lower porch was the spot from where the aged Marquis de Lafayette had addressed the citizens of Beaufort in his frantic stopover in 1825. "The poor good folk expected him daylong, with him tidebound on Edisto," explained Camellia, "and they had to proceed with a great ball at Barnwell's Castle with no guest of honor. Then they went home to their beds like good Christians, and with the night black as tar got up again and marched down to meet Lafayette with torches, except I expect not in their nightshirts. As I was prepared to do for you, I promise!"

And here along New Street, as they turned north, were the close together and well-fixed summer houses of Beaufort's first families, the Barnwells, Heywards, Elliots, Rhetts, Talbirds, Verdiers, Bulls, Smiths, Stuarts, and so many more, all seemingly linked and crossed, the names spoken by Camellia with such respectful sarcasm, like a child reciting a history lesson of the regents of Great Britain, that Oliphant lost interest in everything but Camellia's melodious voice and effervescent manner. And she would occasionally pause in her discourse to point her fine jaw and raise her hand to greet acquaintances on porches, at windows, or riding by, and then call a high-pitched "Howwwwooooo!" that must have reached the addressed like a birdcall, but was nevertheless returned with equally vigorous salutations.

At Craven Street, Camellia tossed her head at one of the many two-story frame houses on tabby foundations—this one with a house-length double portico along its southern facade, and distinctive for its parapet and kitchen annex. "That's Granby House, where I was born," she said. "And where my brother, Talbird, and his wife, Sally Peniclair, live, when they're not off to Savannah with her sort, and never mind. Behind, that sweet little house that needs a board or two, can you see? That's yours now, the Cross House. We shall explore later, we're late—you must not think me rushing you—for tea!"

They turned east again, away from the grid of streets about Bay Street, and toward the tract of marshland and groves of live oaks that fitted into the Beaufort River like an elbow. To this point in the tour, Oliphant thought the clutter of summer houses and cottages both charming and precious, the seasonal showplaces of a planter squirearchy that favored its traditions more than its standoffish privacy. Those open-faced, lushly set cottages were definitely a neighborhood of friends and relations. But here, along King Street, was a wholly different and astonishing panorama: more than a dozen great houses that deserved the description of baronial. Some were older, and bore auspicious names, like "The Castle" and "Blythewood" and "Marshland"; others were newly built or still under construction, and were situated carefully among large gardens so as to reflect rather than compete with each other's elaborate designs—the strong columns, sweeping verandahs, broad piazzas, magnificent tall windows. The planters, enriched by the Sea Island cotton boom, were quiting their plantation "big houses" as well as shedding the simplicity of the summer homes in the town center. They were transforming Beaufort into a camp of absentee landlords who dwelt year-round in their cotton and rice palaces.

As the post chaise crossed Hamilton Street and approached Pinckney Street, Camellia sat straight to point to the corner property at King and Pinckney. "Chinaberry," she said. "That is Chinaberry, Cousin, and don't mind the mess."

The Royalls' was one of these great houses, then, called "Chinaberry." It was brick built on a stone and tabby foundation and large-scaled, with a breezy two-story double verandah on its southern facade that showed six windows and eight columns above and below. And it was made deliberately asymmetrical by the back rooms attached to the first story of the rectangle like afterthoughts. It looked the airy fortress of pride, wealth, and hospitality, and was named, according to Camellia, for the Tree of India in leafy pink and purple bloom in front of it.

Yet Oliphant could also see that there was, indeed, a mess. The house was oddly unfinished, and not as if work was still proceeding. The Means House across Pinckney Street was very new. The grand mansion behind was under construction. Chinaberry, however, looked tenuous, fragile, vulnerable, as if the wild garden that surrounded it might yet reclaim it. The shutters were unsecured, the roofing was patchy, the woodwork needed details, and everything needed paint or whitewash. The rear yard, enclosed by an incomplete brick wall, was a junkheap of lumber, bricks, sandpiles, and muddy pools that in all could not hold back the surging field grass.

Inside Chinaberry though—and they entered from the Pinckney Street side, beneath the lilac fragrance of the spreading Tree of India—the furnishings and decor were superbly done, and reminded Oliphant of an English manor house where he had passed an immaturely amorous holiday. The interior was Oliphant's confirmation that these Royalls were more of the same fussy anglophiles who seemed to dominate Carolina society. The

Charlestonians had always been gossiping of London, Liverpool, and the Queen. It had been Oliphant's English clothes that had persuaded them most, not his Northern manners.

Then again, to Oliphant's relief, tea-time at Chinaberry was anything but pompous or off-putting. Camellia introduced Oliphant to a regiment—literally company after company—of curious, cheery faces, mostly female and middle-aged to elderly, or female and infant to adolescent. The action centered upon the feast of oysters, biscuits, breads, butter, jellies, buttermilk, and China tea that the Negro servants produced in a march of trays. Oliphant ate happily, particularly of the exquisite oysters, and strolled beside Camellia through the two drawing rooms. He was not quite sure what the cause of the general excitement might be. It might have derived from the event itself. He was too overwhelmed by names and relationships, with only Camellia's whispered assistance, to measure accurately the size of the Royall family. He did wonder where the males might be. His cousins looked a self-satisfied matriarchy who talked of their menfolk as if they were entertaining, or whimsical, or inexplicable, or simply absent, heroes.

Certain individual introductions and conversations did begin to explain Chinaberry's ambience to Oliphant. For example, Mrs. Pamela Tempest Royall, J. Granby Royall's second wife, was a youngish English matron, perhaps 35, diminutive, glowing—a dainty woman whom European society might have regarded as perfect. Oliphant thought her passive in comparison to the exuberant Camellia. Mrs. Royall occupied Oliphant with questions about his education and travels in Europe; accordingly, Oliphant realized that the Royalls had somehow learned a deal about him, and wanted to know more. In return, Oliphant learned that Mrs. Royall was the younger daughter of a now-deceased member of the House of Lords, who had swelled his estate with profits from the Manchester cotton mills. Yet while Mrs. Royall's biography interpreted the house, it did not tell Oliphant much about the myriad of kin and what Camellia called "kin-in-law" who were assembled therein, these aunts, grannies, nieces, and friends of godmothers who brushed by to inquire of Mrs. Royall—with Oliphant in earshot—"How is it such a handsome man has not married?" or who approached Oliphant directly, "You must have immeasurable affairs to have been so much in London?" or "One prays you will visit us soon at Heron Hill—or Blue Creek—or Tidewater—now that you've declared yourself half-a-Southerner."

There was also Laura Royall, Camellia's younger sister by several years, who was shy among the women, and given to off-balanced glances at

Oliphant. She was Camellia's like—her hair golder still—but not yet as possessing and pretty. Oliphant tried to please her by complimenting her flounced dress, but it only made her retreat further. Later, he was able to remark upon the beautiful weather to her. She said flatly that she was home from the French School for Young Ladies in Charleston because of the funeral of her best friend the week before. Oliphant offered his sympathy. Laura smiled. "Narcissa says that tears for those with Jesus are more happy than sad—what do you think?"

The majority of the party seemed to arrive with or after Oliphant, as if an alarm had been sounded. One of the latecomers was the eldest Royall sibling, Narcissa, and here was a moment that Oliphant long after reconsidered. He was standing between Camellia and Mrs. Royall, overlooking the gathering that had seemed to draw back in order to observe a drama. Narcissa Royall arrived in a rush in her dusty blue riding clothes—a long plain skirt, tight-fitted jacket, and broad felt hat with a green plume. She was a rich brunette with what appeared to Oliphant to be a geometrically perfect oblong face.

Camellia explained that Narcissa was just in from Ladies Island. With Narcissa were her two half-brothers, Mrs. Royall's twin sons, Harry and Phillip. Camellia was careful to introduce the boys first, as if they were young gentlemen about town. And they returned a formality that exceeded their age, which was about 7.

"Pleased sir," said Harry, who was as dark as his brother was fair, "and most welcome to Chinaberry, I'm sure."

"Most happy you have arrived safe, sir," said Phillip, "and please excuse our tardiness at your welcome."

Both boys bowed deeply. Camellia and Mrs. Royall smiled at their show. Narcissa was equally satisfied, congratulating them with a nod. Then she offered Oliphant her ungloved hand, and curtsied as Oliphant held on.

Camellia said, "This is my dear sister, Narcissa—Mrs. Winwood! Narcissa, I've told Cousin John we'd provide him a full accounting of us, and I doubt he's had a free breath since I found him. And you should have seen! There he was off the ship, and I was glad, most glad, but in a start I looked again and he was gone! Like the Spectre Buck! I thought, what devil's work is this? A blessed man and then air! I looked again, and he was back. He'd lost his hat, you see, and gotten down below the wharf to fetch it. What a beginning! You can be sure I've not let him go from me, or taken my eyes away since!"

Narcissa said, "Welcome to the Low Country, Cousin." And when Oliphant finally released her hand—surprising himself for how long he had kept hold of her—she added, "You feel the man and not the spectre to me." She paused to laugh. "You must have Camellia tell you the legend of the Spectre Buck, to appreciate her adventure. And please appreciate our united feeling of good fortune that we have discovered our Northern cousins, the Oliphants."

Oliphant replied, "It has been an adventure of pure pleasure for me, Mrs. Winwood."

And to Oliphant's continuing amazement, that was all he said or did at his first meeting with Narcissa Royall. He would often, over the years, thrash about in his memory for another word, or perhaps a nuance, some indication that he had recognized her extraordinary presence. There was nothing more. He did remember flattering himself by thinking that Narcissa had studied him perspicaciously—so that it was as if he was watching her judge him, his clothes, his style and temperament. And he did remember her remark to him before she excused herself and blended into the swarm that long and luxurious afternoon that the Royalls commenced to seduce John Oliphant to their hearts. Narcissa said, waving her hands over the happy faces filling the room and slapping her riding gloves on her forearm to raise a puff, "My, yes, what a dust we do make."

Oliphant did not see Narcissa again for three days. Camellia presented Narcissa's excuses Tuesday night. Narcissa had returned to her plantation on St. Helena Island, Indigo Reach, because of sickness in the slave quarters. At the time Oliphant did not think more than that the managing of crops, land, and people must represent a ceaseless challenge to the planters quite apart from the odium of slavery. He would learn in the next few days that the planter's life was much more wearying, and much less opulent, than it appeared in the drawing rooms of its Beaufort mansions.

On Wednesday, Oliphant contacted the lawyer Mr. Wigg had recommended that he secure to mediate his affairs. He traveled with Mr. Odingspell, a chatty, sour, gray little snuff addict, out to inspect part of his mother's inheritance—Old Cross, the 152-acre Sea Island cotton plantation that adjoined the Royalls' 200-acre New Cross on Ladies Island, a cork-shaped mass that lay due east of Beaufort across the river.

On Thursday, Oliphant arose before dawn and met Mr. Odingspell in order to embark on a river sloop to travel down to Hilton Head Island. There they inspected the 304-acre Sea Island cotton plantation, Four Owls, that adjoined the estates of the Draytons and the Popes. Oliphant passed Thursday night on Hilton Head as a guest of the Drayton overseer, Mr. McClasweitz, who had administered Four Owls for the Talbirds in Charleston.

Oliphant was relieved to be able to return to Beaufort before noon on Friday. Yet he felt no corresponding relief with what he had heard and seen on his tours. He now understood that it would not be straightforward to sell off his estates, and that it would be a special struggle to execute his mother's wish to free the slaves she now owned—about thirty on Hilton Head (including a dozen children), and another dozen at Old Cross (mostly older field hands, since the Royalls' slaves did most of the work there). Very simply, Oliphant had learned that one did not tell slaves they were free without also having to make some preparations for how they were to live after they were put out of the only homes they had. And there seemed no place in the Sea Islands for freed slaves other than on the sandspits or in the worst swamps. Every other piece of land was owned, claimed, or under water half the time.

More, Oliphant was extremely disturbed by what Mr. Odingspell told him of the Royalls. They were in debt so deeply and pervasively that they had avoided bankruptcy from season to season only by miracles of luck. J. Granby Royall, whom Oliphant had yet to meet because he was away in Savannah, had inherited the best part of his estates through his first wife, Mary Cross Talbird (Mrs. Alice Cross Oliphant's second cousin). Mary Royall's death, at age 30 in 1838, had rocked the Royalls, who had then lived at their rich St. Helena plantation, Indigo Reach. Worse, the decline of cotton prices in the 1840s had plunged them, along with every Beaufort planter, into despair. They had sold off slaves to shore up, but because of the economics of slavery (one's major assests were one's human property), to sell off slaves meant to produce less cotton in the labor-intensive Sea Island cotton cycle, and thus to fall further into debt.

The Royalls had been saved by a number of shrewd marriages. The oldest son, J. Granby Royall II, called Johnny, had married an heiress, Elizabeth De Treville, with an estate on Edisto Island. The second son, Talbird Royall, had married a Savannah heiress, Sally Peniclair. And Granby Royall himself had remarried to a young English widow and heiress, Pamela Tempest, in 1847. The eldest child, Narcissa, had married about the same time as her father—to a spectacular Virginia gentleman soldier, Venable Hawkes

"Hawk" Winwood. Hawk Winwood had come from tobacco country and soldiered in the Mexican War, but had agreed to settle on St. Helena Island on his wife's dowry, the 350-acre Indigo Reach.

No sooner had the Royalls secured themselves with their marriages than the cotton prices had recovered, rising steadily into the 1850s, and bringing astounding wealth to Beaufort as well as to the whole of the Deep South. Nonetheless, Granby Royall had spent his money as wildly as he had needed it desperately before. One of the results of this extravagance was Chinaberry. And the sad incompleteness of Chinaberry, supposedly a vanity for the new Mrs. Royall, was a bald demonstration that all was not well with the Royalls.

The Beaufort opinion, according to Mr. Odingspell, was that the Royalls had overreached themselves in their aggrandizing celebration. This was a constant possibility in cotton growing. Every planter was dependent upon the credit that was extended to him from harvest to harvest by his factor —the broker who actually shipped and sold the cotton to the mills in the North or Europe. The factors—in Beaufort, Charleston, Savannah—were controlled themselves by bank credits in the North and Europe. The balance between credit and annual profit or deficit was a risk-filled and argumenta- tive arrangement. It required careful, balanced management of the land, the crop, and the bondsmen who worked the land and the crop. And because Sea Island cotton (a prized long silky fiber, with a two-and-a-half-inch boll as compared to the half-inch boll of upland cotton) required year-round care —manuring, bedding, hoeing, thinning, picking, cleaning, packing—a planter's attention to his estate had to be rigorous and ceaseless. Even a successful planter was usually extended in credit to a point where any unusual financial or personal burden could upset his equilibrium.

After Mr. Odingspell had explained the agronomy and economy of the Sea Islands to Oliphant, he joked, "The North holds the money. The South spends it."

Oliphant said, "In Charleston, they say the South earns money for the North, and the Abolitionists profit even as they vilify."

Mr. Odingspell gasped. "You wouldn't be one of them—Abolitionists— would you, sir?"

Oliphant laughed. "Not Free Soil either. I'm a Whig, such as the poor party is, here and there, and missing Mr. Webster and Mr. Clay."

Mr. Odingspell declared, "Good, then, good. And contrary, sir, contrary —cotton earns! For North and South. Abolitionists and Fire-eaters be damned!"

Oliphant asked, "And you—a Fire-eater? No?"

"God rest John C. Calhoun I am no such creature, no, sir! I wouldn't sit with them Rhetts, no sir! But Mr. Oliphant, this is Fire-eater country. My wife says there's more talk of secession than seduction. You've heard of the Secessionist Oak, ain't you? It's not a day's ride from Beaufort, at Bluffton, and like my brother-in-law used to say, it's spreadin' its acorns far afield."

Oliphant asked, "Are the Royalls—are they Fire-eaters?"

Mr. Odingspell laughed. "No, they're just debtors."

The Royalls were in eclipse then, even as the cotton trade shone in gold. Mr. Odingspell said that the rumors as to what had precipitated their most recent decline were inexact. Some said Granby Royall was a blockhead. Some said that the daughter-in-law on Edisto Island, Elizabeth, had objected that her slaves should be sold to balance the accounts, and that her husband, Johnny Royall, had heeded her despite the fact that a field hand could bring over a thousand dollars at auction. Others said that Mrs. Royall's estate in England was based upon mill property, which had declined in value for unknown reasons. There were also the usual possibilities that the slaves had been badly handled, the overseers were indolent, or the factors were dishonest and the debts were long-term obligations that had come due. And the building of the Beaufort mansion had been a reckless decision that might have undone any of the cash-poor planters, even the powerful Barnwells, Draytons, or Heywards.

Mr. Odingspell mentioned one more piece of hearsay, and gave it emphasis regardless of the lack of evidence. He said that Hawk Winwood had taken to heavy gambling and carrying on with disreputable people in Charleston before he had departed suddenly with his manservant the year before. Mr. Odingspell concluded, "He's off, and too hard a one not to be off a long while. He ain't expected back by half the district, and ain't wanted back by the other. She'd pay his debts in gold. He's hard, but that girl's harder. Granby Royall'd help her with what he had. You met her? She's in the saddle of that family. Since she's a girl. You did meet her? Hawk Winwood was a headlong man on a warpath. Narcissa Royall'd pay his debts, certain she would."

News of the Royalls' crisis darkened Oliphant, and his moodiness confounded him. What were the Royalls to him? Distant cousins and slaveholders. No, they were more. They were a mystery, and something else he could not yet describe, though he felt it. He accepted that his emotions were raw because of his mother's plight. Still, Oliphant was most uncomfortable feeling so topsy-turvy. It was not his nature.

He was therefore most unprepared for what greeted him upon his return to Chinaberry Friday afternoon. The whole household was upside down. An overnight expedition to Narcissa's plantation was imminent. Camellia grabbed him up, teased his glumness, and rushed him to dress. Departure followed within the hour. Oliphant and Camellia rode in a large green barouche with Laura, Mrs. Royall, and the returned J. Granby Royall. The smaller carriage behind contained the twins and two Negro servants, the gentleman's gentleman, Noah, and a perky young woman who was the nannie, Maum Nancy.

Oliphant was amused that the Royall household conducted itself so independently of its men, the proof of which was that he was finally able to greet and converse with the patriarch only when he was across from him, knee to knee, en route for the Ladies Island ferry. Granby Royall was not large, was thin-waisted, clean-shaven, fleshy faced, with the fairest of complexions, fine white hair, and a reddish bald spot. He was clearly a gentleman who had enjoyed his fifty-odd years. He was distinguished by a hearty laugh, several gold teeth, and dark blue veins that stood out on his neck and temples. Oliphant thought him pleasant company, though taciturn for a family that talked so exuberantly and constantly.

Granby Royall did apologize for not being present to welcome Oliphant until now. "Sure, sir, that my girls have made you the apple that shines. I am their inevitable Papa, and proud, aye, proud. Don't you find them sweet as cane?" Oliphant returned a compliment. Granby Royall puffed himself in his light gray morning coat—his tailor a fair equal to Oliphant's—and just when Oliphant thought he might make a paternal pronouncement, or at least satisfy himself by asking after Oliphant's business concerns, he spoke sentimentally, glancing around the carriage and then at Oliphant. "When I was young, like you, I was on the rampage, on the rampage, no time for cultivating bouquets. Yet the garden is work too, and it rewards, sir. There's too much fooling around in men's lives for the *things* of cool sense, when life is warm and fragrant."

Camellia blushed and cooed. Mrs. Royall kissed her husband's hand, and ducked to bump her head on his shoulder. Oliphant accepted Granby Royall's punnical suggestion to enjoy the garden of life, and he relaxed. The little party continued to exchange small talk that meant little and entertained much: the ferry ride happy with Laura's recitation of the birdlife; the road across Ladies Island quick for Laura's and Camellia's descriptions of the estates they passed. Their patter was poetry to Oliphant, for every grove had a musical-sounding name, and every property boundary had an eccentric family tale attached.

At the first crossroads, they were joined by the second son, Talbird Royall. He was amount a dappled gray and trailed by a post chaise bearing his wife, Sally, and their infant daughter in the arms of their Maum Millie. Talbird Royall, whom Oliphant had met on Wednesday at Old Cross, rode along-side for a while in order to chat with his father and Oliphant. He was a jaunty, soft-spoken, compact man, about 25, with a red beard that matched the coat of the hunting dog that ran beside. His long nose, like Camellia's and Laura's, was not his father's. Oliphant had liked him on Wednesday, and waved a cheery hello. Talbird Royall called back a cheerier salute, and then he and his dog raced along the road to take the forward position in the caravan as it rolled through a swampy lowland and over a bridge and onto St. Helena Island.

Their destination was Indigo Reach, the Royall plantation managed by the Winwoods, at least, by Narcissa. It was seated off the St. Helenville Road, several miles northeast at the main crossroads at the centerpoint of the lateral bulk of St. Helena. They passed cotton fields either being hoed by or, if already planted and hoed, then being manured by clutches of Negroes working near lone wagons. Oliphant saw neither slave indolence nor overseer brutality, simply endless hard labor on small cleared fields that would yield very high prices per pound of cotton come the fall harvest. Everywhere there were Fripp and Pope lands, and, in the distance, there were glimpses of the so-called big houses, which were really old or rough-built plantation cottages—Mulberry Hill, Orange Grove, Captain John Fripp's, or Captain Oliver Fripp's. By early evening, under a silken blue sky with light so soft it seemed like gilding, with snowy egrets lifting in pairs from the creek to the right and trios of buzzards hovering above the swamp, they arrived at a wash where there was a turnoff from the St. Helenville Road. They crossed a causeway toward a semicircle stand of live oaks and pines.

Tucked inside the grove was a collection of structures, from huts to barns, but the primary building was a pale tabby house. It was modest sized—a rectangular first floor of perhaps four rooms, a second dormer floor with two front gables. At the front there was a low wooden porch supported by slender cedar pillars; at the back there was an extension of several kitchen rooms both open and enclosed with porches. Two huge chimneys flanked the main structure. The house was established on a small rise, and was surrounded by flowering bushes and climbing vines.

Oliphant thought it a pastoral dream. It was less imposing than the Beaufort cottages, but seemed to him more of-the-earth and substantial. The breeze shook the Spanish moss hanging from the backdrop of live oaks, making the house appear especially well anchored and still in a swimming landscape. A school of people animated the scene then, alerted by the approach of Talbird Royall's trotter. They burst off the front porch and from the out-buildings, black and white faces, adults and children, hollering and gasping with grand expectancy.

Narcissa descended the sloping walkway to the carriage drive turn below the house. She wore a long blue smock over a pale green muslin dress— fancied up for company, but practical too, her dark hair pinned up with mother of pearl combs. A large loop of keys flapped at her hip, and she carried a straw basket of cut herbs under her right arm. She had a tired, kind smile. The mud on her hem showed that she had been at work in and out of doors. She waved hello with her left arm, extending her body forward. Thus distracted, she tripped on a plantation dog that was yapping at the invasion of Talbird's dog. She saved her balance by reaching out her right hand to catch Talbird's leg above her, but this action scattered the herbs to the ground. She recovered with a take-life-easy shrug, laughed at herself, and stooped to collect the herbs.

It was then, at this his second encounter of Narcissa Royall, that Oliphant felt himself captured as if magically—spellbound!—by this handsome, graceful, diligent, independent, and splendiferous woman. Indigo Reach was hers, and hers entirely, to feed, repair, plant, harvest, doctor, and enrich. Oliphant saw a woman, just past 30, whose force of will held all that she was and had in cultivation and civilization in a wetland that could take back her treasure in a season. Oliphant saw a woman to honor, to venerate, to come home to, to be buried by. It was not love that he felt for her then; it was more an adoration of the feminine in this one beautiful woman. There was desire too. Narcissa had a fuller shape than Camellia's, and was less fashionably pretty, but her body was as commanding as the fertility of the earth, with nearly a decade behind her of managing babies, soil, crops, people and their fates. That day, as soon as Oliphant climbed down from the barouche to help Narcissa pick up the herbs, he felt his need to be near her and to remain near her. It overcame him and captured him and propelled him to kneel on one knee beside her and scramble for cloves among the excited hounds. He was happy. The Royalls gave him the greatest pleasure he had ever known.

Oliphant spoke, "Mrs. Winwood, this is lovely, lovely."

"You like my home, Cousin?" she said. "I'm glad you do, thank you."

Oliphant stood, and held out the herbs he had gathered. Narcissa moved toward him, but then Camellia was in her arms. The two of them spun around in glee, halloing and kissing. In their dance, they bumped against Oliphant. He could feel their heat and passion. These were two dazzling females from some vision he had read of, perhaps in the Bible, perhaps in verse. He felt transformed for being part of such an occasion. He felt possessed by their bountiful hearts.

The whole family surrounded them then, Narcissa hugging her father and embracing Talbird, Sally, and the baby; Mrs. Royall and her twins intertwining themselves in the group in order to greet Narcissa's two daughters; Camellia moving from niece to nephew to kiss them wetly and laugh. Oliphant had no opportunity to escape this circle of parents, siblings, and offspring. Still, his Puritan heart could not directly participate. He stood by, hands at his sides, feeling his need to touch them, but disobeying his want. Eventually, the squealing settled to a general chatter, and Narcissa grabbed Oliphant by one arm while Camellia took him by the other.

Narcissa said, "Surprise upon surprise for you, Cousin. You do like my home? I spy it in you, phosphorescent man!"

Camellia said, "He'll glow less when we cool him with drink!"

Oliphant started, "Lovely, lovely—" but was unable to continue, because Narcissa and Camellia were hurrying him up the slope toward the house. They actually seemed to lift him a little, even as the breeze lifted the smell of jasmine and the salty air and parted the Spanish moss like a veil. Oliphant tried again to speak, and laughed instead.

Camellia teased Oliphant for his sudden inarticulate giddiness. "He does sweet-talk without end, for a Yankee, doesn't he, Sister?"

Narcissa said, "Dear man, he acts kidnapped. And perhaps he is. We shall be true to the pirate rage. Hold him tight, Sister. We shall show our prisoner where some of us brigands were born. And what surprises we have to turn the head of this handsomest of captives."

Narcissa's surprises were several, and arranged to follow head upon tail of each other. They were to be a large demonstration of a homey dictum that she offered Oliphant as he surveyed her domain: "Proper place, Cousin, and proper time, and proper use, that is how one finds errors in their infancy and routine in chaos."

Oliphant jested that he had not heard a ship captain or a bank teller put it better. Narcissa jangled her keys in reflection, and slowly came to understand that he meant to compliment her. Her mind was already in motion toward the first surprise—the welcoming meal that night, of turtle soup, oysters, pies of ham and shrimp, cabbage, boiled mutton, roast turkey, pots of buttered rice, fruit, and cakes, which was followed with a general removal to a table set on the back verandah to watch the beginning of a great plantation event.

While the dinner party sipped from Granby Royall's traveling case of Madeira and sherry, the Negro menfolk gathered by torchlight with their dogs and set off into the pine hollows on a possum hunt. The dogs howled in the distant chase. The children screeched nearby in anticipation. One Negro child especially came to Oliphant's attention—Jimmie, the 5-year-old grandson of Narcissa's chief house servant, Maum Rosemary. Jimmie was fascinated with Oliphant's clothes and manner, and was soon imitating the way he stood, sat, and gestured. Jimmie even found a cedar stick to match Oliphant's walking cane, and made a paper hat that resembled Oliphant's French floppy-brimmed one. Oliphant was charmed by the attention and presented Jimmie with a clay pipe from the set he had bought in Charleston.

It was Jimmie who awakened Oliphant early Saturday morning. He had come into the room to watch Oliphant sleep, and made a noise inadvertently while inspecting Oliphant's boots. After breakfast, Oliphant set out with Jimmie—with Maum Rosemary's permission (Jimmie's parents were both dead of fever)—to explore the plantation grounds. Oliphant found the barns well stocked, the ginhouse orderly, the livestock neatly divided into hog, chicken, goat, and horse pens. Narcissa's February-planted gardens were already rich. Oliphant also found that Jimmie did not care to go down to the slave quarters. Jimmie lived in the big house with his two sisters and Narcissa's two daughters, Sophy and Martha. He was obviously wary of approaching the other Negro children without his grandmother's approval. He did take Oliphant to a good vantage, however, so that from a distance Oliphant could see the slave quarters spread out in a dell of pine and chinaberry trees. There were several approximately twenty-foot-square tabby and cedar cabins, rude and whitewashed, all smoke-draped with the morning cooking fires. Oliphant wanted to see more, yet, uninvited and unescorted, he did not dare to trespass.

Jimmie then pulled Oliphant in another direction entirely, in order to show him the live oak that was his favorite part of Indigo Reach. He said, "Me lub be up dat tree. Den me free like de buzzut and de great blues!"

Oliphant could not observe the daily routine of the Royalls' slaves—about two dozen adults here and an equal number of children—because they were too excited by Narcissa's second surprise. There was to be a wedding at noon of two Negro couples. The brides, Phoebe and Coffee, were from Indigo Reach and they were marrying two brothers from the nearby Elliot plantation of Town's End.

The service was held on the front porch of the big house. The parson, a tiny Anglican from St. Helenville, the Reverend Dillion, arrived with the Elliots—an older couple who fussed over Oliphant. There were as many white faces as black at the ceremony—Fripps, Stuarts, Smiths—for the neighborhood seemed delighted to gather at Narcissa's beckoning. And Narcissa was very much in control. She provided yet another feast: of turtle steaks, venison, wild ducks, cured hams, rice pots, pound cakes, custards, and pies for the white masters and the wedding party; and of enormous pots of venison and oysters in rice with fruit pies for the general Negro population who collected on the back porch. She also gave the two couples wedding presents: a pile of blankets, bedding, cotton mattresses, and bolts of muslin. The loudest praise from the Negroes was for the two spinning wheels that Granby Royall gave Phoebe and Coffee as their dowries, though Oliphant could see that the spinning wheels were actually from Narcissa. She had arranged this extravagance so that her father would garner praise for his generosity.

Narcissa even provided two new broomsticks, which the couples hopped over again and again to uproarious cheering. Narcissa's Negro overseer, a black-skinned nub of a man named Joseph, explained the custom to Oliphant. "Fer who de driber and who de mule in de house. He dat trip, he 'fore de plow. 'N it best dat de man do de fallin'." Oliphant thought Joseph was jesting, but was unable to learn more of the folk custom as the Negro assembly exploded in singing and dancing to music from a fiddler and a man who played "de bones."

Once the celebration had quieted, and the dancing had moved with the Negroes to the rear of the house, Oliphant was able to separate himself from the planters and to find a spot on the lawn where he could be alone with his thoughts.

He was trying to judge the Royalls, and along with them, this planter society. And it seemed impossible to him to reach a conclusion about the Royalls without looking carefully at slavery. He was certain of the fact that the Royalls and their neighbors regarded the Negroes as human property—like mules before plows! His temperament could not ignore his father's Abolitionist opinions; nor would he ignore the fact that slavery was shocking when viewed for the first time.

Yet he was also struck by how thoughtfully the Royalls treated their slaves—like dependents, as if they were children, to be housed, nurtured, pleased, even indulged like the darling Jimmie. Then again, Oliphant could not overlook the obvious obligatory bargain here, that in exchange for these parental services the Negroes had to submit themselves to daily toil for their masters, or to absolute judgment by them.

Oliphant thought it all so strange! After nearly a fortnight in the South, and four days studying slaveholding near at hand, Oliphant was still unable to state to himself his feelings about the nature of slavery. He could only approximate to himself that slavery seemed an intimate tradition, one that enjoyed the assumptions and power of any correspondingly deeply fixed institution, like marriage. Indeed, Oliphant knew that the slaveholders called slavery "our peculiar Southern institution."

There was nevertheless the monumental question of the morality of slavery. For the Negro, Oliphant understood, *to be free* was an apotheosis. "Freedom" was in the slave's everyday language; it was held up as the ultimate goal and virtue. It was no less a desired thing than *beauty* and *to be beautiful* was to the planters. And Oliphant asked himself, What human being would voluntarily choose to be ugly, or would accept that he or she had to be ugly? And what sort of human being would choose to keep another person ugly if it was in his or her power to grant beauty?

On the lawn before Indigo Reach, Oliphant ate venison from his plate and drank wine from his cup and pondered the Royalls and slavery. It was while he was in this mood that Narcissa chanced to approach him. She and Camellia sashayed over to ask after his comfort. Oliphant, forgetting himself, spoke out loud thoughts that he was unsure of inside himself; he said, meaning to be gay, "I am very happy, Mrs. Winwood. Who wouldn't be? On such a day, even Uncle Tom could find peace."

Narcissa flared at him. "Oh, Mrs. Stowe and Uncle Tom. Mrs. Stowe and

Uncle Tom! Mrs. Stowe and Uncle Tom!! Ding, dong, ding, dong! Spineless cant and false piety, and not a flick of common sense or decent intelligence. This is my life!"

Camellia gripped her sister's arm. Narcissa softened. Still, Oliphant had seen the fire in her, and she did not conceal it in her conclusion. She said, "You shall see of us what you shall see, Cousin. As for those who defame us—rope is never ready for the Pharisees. And, I suppose, a cross is never far from pharisaical hands."

Oliphant was prevented from exploring Narcissa's political philosophy further by her third surprise—a continuation of the expedition. And Narcissa and her two daughters, a black-haired and a red-haired child, 7 and 5, were joining the party. Soon enough, leaving Maum Rosemary and Joseph to manage the ongoing wedding party, the Royalls were off in the carriages by the short route to St. Helenville, a hamlet of a dozen summer cottages and two church spires at the mouth of a broad creek and at the shore of the vast St. Helena Sound.

Their new destination was Edisto Island across the sound, and The Acreage, the 650-acre Sea Island cotton and rice plantation owned and managed by the Royalls. They were met at the St. Helenville wharf by the oldest son, J. Granby "Johnny" Royall II, at the helm of a thirty-two-foot single-masted sloop, and they hurriedly loaded their baggage and a cold supper for the crossing due east to Edisto. It was a glorious fifteen-mile sail with the ebb tide across a seascape first green with splashes of white wavelets and then made purple and orange by the sunset. They came about into the shadows of the evening and raced darkness to landfall at Clark's Inlet on the windward side of Edisto. The broad rolling white beach was laced with twists of seaweed and speckled with hopping gulls.

Here there was a ramshackle wharf and another small settlement, Eddingsville, that was mostly factors' warehouses and rugged log cabins, with a periphery of slave quarters glowing in firelight. Oliphant had no time to inspect the village—the swampiest and crudest place he had yet seen—for they were off immediately in two carriages and a flatbed wagon. They rolled and weaved five miles north into the wooded interior of Edisto to The Acreage. Although it was too dark, and Oliphant was too tired, to gain a good view of the plantation, he could determine that it was larger and busier than either New Cross, Old Cross, or Indigo Reach.

The big house was the now-familiar pale tabby rectangle, with several cedar-built extensions that indicated a long and many-handed history. Johnny Royall was a dark, lordly figure, larger than his brother Talbird, with a thick torso and heavy brown beard. He was said by Camellia to be a first-rate horseman who had raced his own horses in Charleston and won a goodly amount of money. Johnny and his wife, Elizabeth, had four children under 5 years of age, and presided over a large household staff and more than ninety slaves including children.

A curious feature of The Acreage was the wood-built praise house, a form of church for the slaves, that stood like an A-shaped chapel not far from the big house. Oliphant went outside to observe a late-night celebration in the praise house. Mrs. Elizabeth Royall followed Oliphant out, and explained, "They're devout people, Mr. Oliphant, very devout. And tomorrow is Palm Sunday."

She was a shapely, olive-complexioned woman of 24, whose family's wealth, she said, had originated in Barbados sugar plantations. Oliphant escorted her back into the house, and they were served excellent French brandy in delicate snifters. Elizabeth took Oliphant over to an oil painting, a landscape of a cataract on the Nile River. Oliphant admired it, and said that he had visited Egypt in his student days.

Elizabeth then made what Oliphant thought to be an unusual speech. "My sisters-in-law have written that you are a man of the world. I do hope this means we two shall agree in the face of their stubborn dismissal of my religion. I am Presbyterian, like you. And we must do sentry duty against their priestly Anglicanism and cold suspicions. We must also guard our hearts from deceit and wickedness. It is the eve of Easter Week, and a special time for us, isn't it?"

Oliphant was taken aback. He tried to respond with a trivial observation about Easter falling so late in April.

Elizabeth did not seem to understand him, and pressed her odd point. "I knew you would understand! The Lord must save us, each and every one, and it is happy, oh so happy, to have a kindred spirit under my roof at this sad and triumphant time with whom to seek our Savior's love and to celebrate his entry into Jerusalem!"

Oliphant was puzzled by Elizabeth's confession of faith, and by her intimation of an understanding between them regarding Presbyterianism. He assumed her piety had long since established the obvious standoffishness he saw between her and Narcissa, two strong minds at the spiritual poles of the Royalls.

And Oliphant's observation was confirmed when Narcissa, before retiring Saturday night, caught Oliphant at the bottom of the stairs; she said, "I've learned my sister-in-law has already apprised you of the untrustworthiness of the local Anglican clergy? No. It isn't a serious parting between us. She has her mind, and I mine. Nonetheless, we 'cold' Royalls—yes, I know it is her opinion—we chilly Royalls shall deliver you to the warmth of Calvinism on the morrow. Did I say warmth?"

Oliphant appreciated the humor, but wondered about the mystery of this promised delivery. It all became clear Sunday morning with Narcissa's fourth surprise. The whole houseful of Royalls and guests was awakened early, fed a heavy breakfast, and poured into the carriages. The road was alive with planters and slaves en route to worship God. The majority of the planters and their families drove to the Episcopal church at the mid-island crossroads. The majority of the Negroes walked to the Baptist churches (and a Methodist one they passed) that were distributed in the groves, either on the plantations or on common, unplanted ground.

The Royalls, however, ten children and more than a dozen adults including the servants, drove on past the Anglican crowd for the Edisto Presbyterian Church up the road half a mile. Narcissa, Camellia, and Laura giggled when Oliphant finally saw their destination. Elizabeth glanced sternly at the trio and nodded her head sympathetically to Oliphant. Oliphant was amused by both demonstrations, and also by the sight, a white clapboard structure that seemed a marriage of the church architecture of the North and the South. It had a two-story box shape with arched windows, a stout white steeple, and a courtly facade of four, heavy grooved columns that supported a plain entablature. Behind the church was a low-fenced graveyard set in a deep piney wood that was drenched with blooming azaleas and dogwoods. The gathering of carriages and people before the church was modest-sized and comely. These Carolina Calvinists looked to Oliphant to avoid the monotones of their Yankee kindred for pastel dresses, white and buff morning coats, and high top hats.

All the worshippers knew Elizabeth Royall and her brood, and were eager to welcome the extended Royall clan. Narcissa appeared familiar with the neighbors and introduced Oliphant to the Hext family. In a pause, Narcissa asked Oliphant, "How does this compare to your father's parish?"

Oliphant wanted to compliment with a witticism. "My father, when he was in a parish, would have said, 'Carpentered by disciples, though to be occupied by ingrates!' I say, no comparison, Mrs. Winwood, none."

Elizabeth Royall overheard, misunderstood, and commented, "We cannot hope to match the grandeur of Philadelphia, Mr. Oliphant. We do hope that we worship with like zeal, and keep our house of God an inviting home for all ages and sorts."

Oliphant returned, "You must believe me—this is sublime, everything here, sublime, Mrs. Royall. When I say, incomparable, the contest is unequal, in your magnificent favor."

This settled Elizabeth Royall's opinion of Oliphant as the Treaty of Paris ended the Revolution. She beamed. She took Oliphant from Narcissa and Camellia and escorted him into the Royall pew. The Royalls overflowed into an adjoining De Treville–Langdon pew. Oliphant was seated at the junction of both boxes, catercorner from the benevolent-looking Granby Royall. Oliphant shared a hymnal with Elizabeth, and, during the service, exchanged more than a few glances with her in order to communicate his pleasure. The pastor, a dutiful sexagenarian, only mentioned hell once, and otherwise preached lucidly from the Gospels concerning the disorderliness in the streets of Jerusalem before the Savior's arrival. The best part of the service for Oliphant was the singing, since the Negro servants who filled the galleries of the church gave of their voices fully and with a spirit that sounded transcendent. Oliphant had never heard such resonance, and was amazed. After one especially vibrant chorus, he looked to Narcissa and smiled. Narcissa waited for an opportunity, then leaned across the wall of the pew to whisper, "My maumer, Aunt Rosemary, she taught me, 'You buckrah have books and such, but the black folk have the Lord's ear.' "

Elizabeth again overheard, misunderstood, and interjected, "The Lord has ears enough, and eyes enough, for all his children, and their repentant cares."

At this remark, Oliphant and Narcissa shared their earliest intimate glance —the two eldest children of two proud families revealing to each other their understanding and tolerance of rivalrous siblings.

Oliphant saw an additional quality in Narcissa's gaze. He stared overlong at those symmetrical features and those judgmental eyes. His intelligence came to him like a gift. He saw in her the delight of a designer, as God was the Great Designer of heaven and earth. He asked himself what his discovery meant. Why should she be so obviously and exceedingly satisfied at his pleasure in this robust company on this sunny Carolina day on this fragrant island in this garden archipelago?

Oliphant's curiosity about Narcissa's motives increased throughout the day until the great gathering at sundown of Royalls, De Trevilles, and Langdons for a feast at The Acreage. At last, after dining, Oliphant was moved to try out his newfound theory that Narcissa had some design behind all her surprises.

He spontaneously followed her from the table and caught her at the base of the stairs before she went up to say goodnight to her daughters. It was not a good time to linger in conversation, what with the other adults distributed throughout both drawing rooms and servants sliding all about with trays, so Oliphant decided that he must speak forthrightly. He hoped his bluntness might penetrate Narcissa's presence of mind and get to her candor, and beneath that, to her heart.

"Mrs. Winwood," he began, "I've had a day—day after day—of serene delight. I am wondering, though—"

"How so, Cousin?" She ducked her head to arrange her pale gown; she took the first step and turned, so that she was at eye level with Oliphant with her shawl tucked up like a mantle.

"We could easily have attended Palm Sunday services in Beaufort, without this extraordinary procession," continued Oliphant. "That is, I—I am under the impression that you are not usually a voyaging family."

"That may be. Papa has enjoyed this. We should do it more. We see little of Johnny, and Elizabeth does need attention."

"It was for me, isn't that true?" Oliphant exhaled. "To come this long way in this fashion? For Presbyterian services on Edisto for Presbyterian John Oliphant?"

"Why, what is it that you'd suppose?"

"I'd suggest that you are quite the most extravagant maker-of-gestures I have ever imagined. I'm knocked."

She replied, "And not happy?"

"It is crucial to you that I am, isn't it? Please, yes. I am happy, and happy again, and happy over and over. What man wouldn't be? Your family is a memory of unspeakable joy."

"My family?" She lowered her voice. "Yours too. We must always be together in this splendid memory you propose. Really, you're the most pleasing reader of books and thinker of thoughts we Royalls have ever found among us."

They both laughed, Narcissa somewhat more fully than Oliphant, to Oliphant's embarrassment. He was anxious that she not think him prosaic or pompous. He wanted to impress her. Oliphant said, "I must, I must say, I want you to know, this—that you are extraordinary. That you are a rare find for me. It is true, the Oliphants are bookish. I am dull and bookish. And I am too much contained by unlivable and unlived ideals, and too much defined by commercial and banal pursuits."

"No, no!" she said. "Ideals and ambitions, books and economies, they are necessary, and much missed here. No, Cousin,"—Narcissa nodded—"I am struck by your learning, and wish that I had had more of it, and wish and wish. I can't imagine further along." She made a traveling motion with her right hand, and pulled it back. "I would assume, from your speech, that you do understand how very much it is my wish and my hope and my prayer that we remain together in your remembered joy, spoken and not spoken yet?"

Oliphant smiled. "My father would say, 'This is a prayer that rings of proposal.' "

"Why, John!" And she blushed. Oliphant stepped back, then forward again. Narcissa recovered first, and said, "I am flattered supremely. A married woman should hear such things! And let the jays scatter their seeds where they will."

It was Oliphant's turn to blush. "I didn't mean—"

"I *am* a married woman," Narcissa interrupted. "My sister—"

Oliphant heard himself talking; he was headlong. "Camellia is a beautiful young woman whose heart is as honest and full as your own."

Narcissa closed the bargain before Oliphant realized there was a document to sign, or a peace to gain, nourish, and protect. She said, "We're agreed on this, you and I, and have much to discuss, true? And time to do it in, not forgetting your mama's illness. We'll have the time, won't we, John? Your departure is exaggerated, isn't it? You shall remain among us as long as you can, short of Our Lord's Kingdom actually coming on?"

"Yes, yes, Narcissa. Yes, short of that, yes."

Narcissa reached out with her right hand to touch Oliphant on the mouth with her fingers. She ran her fingertips across his lips. Her message for secrecy was a ticklish and silent one. Oliphant stood still when she turned to disappear up the stairs. Now he was truly dumbfounded. She had overwhelmed him with her final surprise of this expedition; that is, even when he thought himself her equal in the conversation, she had outmaneuvered him. How powerful was she? Narcissa had persuaded him to an arrangement between them—profoundly concerning the Royalls—the terms of which he did not know! She had asked for and taken a carte blanche! And like the rest of the Royalls, Oliphant felt himself now at Narcissa's call, and happy for it!

This was not his only intuition standing there, finding his hands, pulling out his pipe and tobacco pouch. At last he understood in a gust of good feeling what had eluded him this past week of serial discovery in the Sea Islands. He talked to himself, "Paradise, John, snake and apple and all, you've found Paradise."

Then he laughed, and searched his pockets. He needed a light. He looked up the stairway. He decided to go to Camellia. She liked to light his pipe. He would sit with her, and chat of Palestine, and await Narcissa's return.

CHAPTER 6

John Oliphant at
Washington City, District of Columbia

WEDNESDAY AFTERNOON, NOVEMBER 16, 1864

Narcissa lay lightly on her left side, one leg behind her to intertwine with Oliphant's legs. Her buttocks were fitted against his hip, her shoulder blades nestled under his shoulder, her arms tucked like wings against her own breasts, and her hands folded beneath her chin to provide a neat cushion. She was arranged so gracefully because she was not deeply asleep, only relaxing in a hazy nap.

It was a seasonal afternoon, muggy and misty, and they had thrown the bedcovers back during their love-making. Oliphant relaxed half upright beside Narcissa, his whole body rotated slightly to provide her a fleshy rest. He was smoothing his cheek and lips with a crooked finger. He glanced at the moist and shiny hairs about his penis, and then up across the room to the embers in the fireplace at the far wall, and then he let his eyes wander over the chairs and settee draped with their clothes to the satinwood vanity table at the left wall that was stacked with Narcissa's jewelry box, brushes, and things in the midst of several vases of cut flowers. Beyond, he looked to the double door that was ajar and to the balcony behind. Out there, the ivy on the iron banister was a slick, green band against the brownish orange and yellow of the upper reaches of a gigantic chestnut tree that spread its aged limbs like a friend across the breadth of the second floor rear of the Georgetown home of Narcissa's great-aunt, Mrs. George (Louisa Granby) Turning.

Oliphant felt a chill; he hooked the comforter with his foot to bring it up on his knees and gently over Narcissa's legs. She kicked it off and rolled farther into her hands and pillows. She also made a humming sound, and flipped her hair out of her face.

Oliphant said, "Fine," and fixed the cover on his legs only. Narcissa became overheated in her passion, sometimes to the point of fainting. Her body still showed pools of pinkish skin on her back and splotches of red at her neck. It made her look healthier. Oliphant traced his left hand down along the valley created where her rib cage joined her pelvis. Her skin was too white. She was too thin. He gripped her hip point like a saddle horn and pulled her buttocks closer.

Narcissa's body was a precious atlas to Oliphant. Here was the geography of a frantic forty-year life that he could read with sympathy and caution for what it told of the interior life of a woman. She thought her feet too small and inadequate for the demands of hiking and riding that she had endured in her ceaseless business in the Low Country, and afterward. They were squarish, with close-together toes and a minor arch, not what they should have been for the running of a family and the running from her starkly imagined fears: from the fear of emptiness when she had lost her mother to the lingering complications of too many and too near births and miscarriages when Narcissa was 14; from the fear of abandonment when her father had placed her in a Washington City school between her fourteenth and sixteenth years, 1839–41; from the fear of heartbreak when her star-crossed suitor, Hawk Winwood, had gone off to the Mexican War after their betrothal in 1846; from the fear of a wasting death like her mother's after Narcissa's second consecutive miscarriage in 1854.

Narcissa's legs were lean and long, to Oliphant's delight. She thought them "stickish, and most scarified." There were indeed scars, like mementos of her velocity. The burn mark on her left ankle, copper-penny-sized, was from when a pan of boiling soup had upset in this very house, when she was 15, an accident Narcissa explained had been the result of a tantrum she had launched upon her two guardians, Aunt Louisa and Maum Rosemary, when they had kept Narcissa from attending a Marine dance at the President's

House. The jagged line on her right kneecap was from that horrible night when she had tumbled down the stairs with her father in December 1861 as they were trying to save the family and their Charleston house in the great fire. And the white lines on her hips and the backs of her thighs were from childbirth, the commonplace expanding and shrinking of flesh, and Narcissa was alternately annoyed by and proud of them—what she had to show in flesh for her daughters Sophy and Martha, who were now 17 and 15 and living in Savannah with Camellia.

Her back was straight and very downy above her buttocks, with prominent shoulder blades that were a product of a posture that Oliphant had once thought overstiff. As he had come to know her, he had understood that she walked so carefully and upright because of her mother's advice. One of Narcissa's shoulders was higher than another, and her mother had told her she must compensate with a stern gait. It was silly of Narcissa, and another sort of person would have let herself become more natural. Yet Narcissa idolized her mother's memory, and often talked to herself, "Up girl, up!"

This controlled posture naturally pushed her breasts forward. They were Oliphant's pleasure—not large, and not matched, the left nipple formed with a notch. Oliphant teased her that she was God-given with an extra half teat. She did not always enjoy the joke, because it spoke to her doubts about her sense of nurture. She could weep in her frustration when a loved one did not obey her decisions for them.

She had wept in the fall of 1855 when Oliphant had insisted upon taking his new bride, Camellia, on an extended European honeymoon; for he and Narcissa had already been lovers then, and she had thought Oliphant only deferring the test they must suffer—to solve the triangle—a test they had failed again and again over the years. She had wept when Granby Royall had ordered the whole family to flee Beaufort for Charleston—and not for Indigo Reach or The Acreage—during the Federal invasion of Port Royal Sound in November 1861. She had wept when her stepmother Pamela Royall had ignored Narcissa's pleas and had taken the very ill Granby Royall home to London—because a severe case of erysipelas had supervened from the bruise he had suffered in his fall with Narcissa in Charleston and his foot had had to be amputated in Savannah. And she had wept in her bleakest manner when her surviving half-brother Harry had volunteered into the Confederate Navy at 16 without telling any of his family, and had left England for blockade running on the doomed C.S.S. *Alabama*.

Importantly, for all her tears of frustration, Narcissa was not given to displays of anger. She was a cool thinker and a dispassionate strategist. This diplomatic temperament was what had made her—a profoundly patriotic Southern partisan—such a remarkable agent in London. None among the Confederate emissaries in London and Liverpool could surpass her sense of intrigue or her ability to coax aid from the English. Oliphant had once overheard the stridently anti-Confederate Lord John Russell himself, foreign minister of Palmerston's so-called neutral government, describe Narcissa: "A damned rock of an island! Not seamed or occupied. A damned appealing monolith in petticoats!"

Oliphant had repeated the image soon after to Narcissa, and she had said, "The old flirt *wants* what he won't buy!"

In London, Narcissa was indeed wanted, a much sought guest and much attended hostess. She had entertained at her stepmother's townhouse in St. John's Wood. Oliphant had admired her social and political power, while he had admitted to her that he was often jealous of the warren of English game that surrounded her at the fetes.

For Narcissa in full feather was a striking human being. An English admirer had said, and Oliphant had playfully agreed, that her face was a meeting on high ground of alabaster radiance and self-possessed purpose. Those quick hazel eyes did seem to aim that mighty jaw like a cannoneer sighting a target, and then she pronounced, eruditely and musically. She was a grand talker. She liked homey stories and liked to retell them with colloquially accurate dialogue. She particularly favored stories that "dripped yolk on long-beards"—her way of saying how she deflated the pompous. Narcissa was such a renowned raconteur that Oliphant had long thought there was a question as to her effectiveness as a partisan. The English admired her as if she were a famous stage actress, and did not uniformly hear her illustrations of Southern indomitability as accurate. They thought her spinning yarns, and loved her for it, and did not seem able to understand that her pleas for sympathy, money, and help for the Confederacy were not part of an anecdote but real, and desperate.

There were opinions other than Oliphant's of Narcissa's worth as a Confederate partisan, and they were more sanguine. Oliphant had once questioned Judah Benjamin as to what he wanted of Narcissa in England. Judah Benjamin had recruited both Oliphant and Narcissa as agents in the winter of 1862; he was then Confederate secretary of state at Richmond, having left the United States Senate with his friend, Jefferson Davis, and having first served as Confederate secretary of war before moving to the

Confederate State Department in a corner of the former Virginia Statehouse. But Judah Benjamin was more tellingly a longtime Beaufort neighbor of the Royalls, on King Street, just down from Chinaberry, where he had passed his summers—an inelegant fox of a man, crescent-bearded, long-haired, round-waisted, with a weakness for sweets that he claimed could exhaust his Louisiana sugar plantations. Oliphant had known from the first meeting in Richmond, in March 1862, what Judah Benjamin wanted of him, for Oliphant was tailor-made as a courier and confidential agent in Europe. But what was Narcissa for? Oliphant had waited for an opportunity to meet with Judah Benjamin alone at his home in Richmond—while Narcissa was resting at the hotel—and had asked him straight out. "Why risk Mrs. Winwood, sir? This will be exhausting and perhaps dangerous business. What can she be for?"

Judah Benjamin had twinkled. "To put the head on the great John C. Calhoun statue the English make of us! To show, Mr. Oliphant. To show that will of hers, to show what is fighting here, and what is worth fighting for here. Mr. Oliphant, if she is not, who is, the South? To show, God, to show!"

Oliphant rolled to his left to enclose Narcissa with the length of his body. He ran his left hand over her hip and past the fleshy pocket at her belly into the dark hairs at the curve of her sex. She brought her right leg up and clutched him there and then squeezed her thigh muscles.

He said, "I love you."

She spoke into her hands, a muffled "Don't."

He said, "I know," not truly knowing why she had spurned his sentiment.

After a moment, she said, "I do love you, I do." She groped back her hand for his face. He kissed her palm, and then shifted his weight to get up on top of her by rolling her onto her back. She let her hair spill over her face, her arms fall like swinging spars, and her legs sink flat and open. Oliphant took hold of her right hand again and kissed the four knuckles and then the fingers. Her hand, like the rest of her, was battered—a fingernail split, the thumb scraped badly from when she had helped manhandle Granby Royall's coffin into the conservatory downstairs. Oliphant took her hand to his throat. He arched up to use his arms and legs to cover her torso like a blanket. Her flesh felt loose, and was sallow across her chest and belly, from the precipitous weight loss this past summer. She was only a little stronger than she had been the week before upon disembarking *Australasian.*

Death gouged at Narcissa Royall. In nine months, she had suffered the loss of her last brother Johnny, her last half-brother Harry, her husband Hawk Winwood (long estranged but never divorced), her brother-in-law Lucas Rogers who had been Laura Royall's groom (and who was missing in the battle for Atlanta), as well as her father Granby Royall. And all this had come after three years of funerals and defeats. Oliphant thought it a miracle that she was able to sleep through the night, or mostly, and that she still had an appetite, however inconstant or mercurial, for food and sex.

Oliphant raised his head. "We should talk. We must make plans."

"Not now. I don't want to think. If I do, you'll leave me."

"Narcissa, don't do that. I am not leaving."

"You'll go. They all have. The order will come and you shall appear at the door and then you shall go."

Oliphant jarred her. "Look at me. Look. Open your eyes. I am not leaving. You are talking like this because you're discouraged. That's all. And you must remember we have made a fair beginning. We are here, aren't we? And the Navy Department is not the last recourse. This is a bribe city."

"What is there? They don't want him buried! They don't care for decency! They are afraid of an old man's corpse! They aren't Christians!"

"We care. We're right." Oliphant calmed himself; his abruptness had upset her. He must avoid dissidence, for it seemed to make her feel hopeless. He continued, "Your father wasn't a Rebel, and they can't prove that he was. He was a kind old planter, and they know it, and they know he lost everything and his life by bad luck. They do believe that. It is part of war to suspect and resist the innocent. We shall prevail upon them, for we are telling truth. It will take more time. Mr. Fox did agree to see us, Narcissa. In this business, that is a concession. We now have to move on to other officials—to use the interview with Fox in our favor."

That morning, Narcissa and Oliphant had finally won an audience with the assistant secretary of the navy, Captain Gustavus V. Fox, a placid man with a reputation of having Lincoln's ear. (Lincoln was said to have observed, "Fox is the Navy Department.") Fox was therefore the man who held the power they needed to get themselves and the coffin on board a Federal ship bound for the headquarters of the Department of the South on the beach at Hilton Head Island, and from there up to Beaufort. They had sat in the Navy Department corridor all Friday, Saturday, Monday, and Tuesday, not daring to give up their place in line for luncheon, given the chaos around them of other favor seekers and bereaved relatives searching for missing sailors. Then, Tuesday evening, Oliphant had pressed a sum of money into the correct hands, and this morning they had secured an interview with Fox that had lasted five minutes. It had closed with Captain Fox grinning. "It can't be done. Not now. Not any way." Oliphant had protested politely. Fox had said, "Good day, sir, good day, madam, and please—what you ask is impossible now."

Oliphant had explained to a stony Narcissa en route back to Georgetown what the obstacle might be to their extraordinary but not impossible request: in a word, Sherman. Major-General William T. Sherman, hero of Atlanta in September, and savior of Lincoln's presidential campaign, was widely rumored to have prepared his army at Atlanta, following Election Day, for a new campaign in the South. The *Washington Morning Chronicle* had announced, November 9, that Sherman had burned Atlanta and was marching on Charleston; but the next day the *Chronicle* had withdrawn the rumor, and had hinted that Sherman had withdrawn to Chattanooga, and was still preparing his seven corps for a campaign. It was all a deliberate confusion of military gossip. Nevertheless, the certain result was that all Navy activities into Port Royal Sound, the Federal occupied coast closest to Sherman's army, were restricted. By accident, then, Narcissa's suit to bury Granby Royall had run head on into the biggest wall of secrecy in the war.

Narcissa had listened to Oliphant's explanation, and burst, "Damn Sherman! Damn him and his inhuman murderers! Damn him for eternity!"

She had followed this with a morbid frown. It had frightened Oliphant when, after their return, she had pulled him upstairs to her room, and pulled at his clothes and her own. Her love-making had been very needful and finally sad-making.

It was now hours later, and Oliphant could see that the woman in his embrace was not ready to debate tactics. It was her nature to pout after a disappointment. She was first a charger, and only long after a plotter. For now, she must accept that a bold move was futile. He lay quietly atop her until he was sure she was not going to weep. He decided to change the topic, for pouty reasons of his own. He said, "I have a dinner engagement with your friend, Henry Blondel."

She cleared her hair from her face. "You didn't tell me."

"I am now. He sent his card this morning, before you came down. He hints that he might have found an opening for us at the State Department. You didn't tell me that you had asked his aid in this."

"When? On Sunday? No, we only talked. He's always known that we would have to struggle to get to Beaufort. We just chatted pleasantly." After services on Sunday, the 13th, at Georgetown's Presbyterian Church down the road, Narcissa had gone off with Blondel for a drive. They had asked Oliphant to accompany them, but he had thought their invitation half-hearted, and had begged off.

Oliphant asked, "What did you talk about?"

"Henry's a good friend, John. He was most good to me when Papa died. You know this. I couldn't have— You agreed he should help me. It was your idea."

Oliphant had been in Paris when Granby Royall had suffered his final decline in September, and had been en route to London when he had died, September 30. He had arrived at the townhouse with only a day until his sailing date from Liverpool, but had delayed it a full week to help Narcissa make her plans. Then he had been obliged to sail for Canada, because of Beverley Tucker's cotton deal. Blondel had come forward then, and had promised Oliphant he would help get Narcissa and the coffin onto a steamer to follow. It had been very generous of him, because Pamela Royall had been too stunned to assist by the death of her last son and then her husband. Oliphant had been acquainted with Blondel for over a year—since the man's return from India—but had only met him twice before October, because of Oliphant's travels. Oliphant regarded him as a congenial and melancholic fellow, most attentive to his older brother, who was Pamela Royall's brother-in-law. Then again, Oliphant did not deceive himself about Blondel. He was jealous of him. And he felt threatened by Narcissa's affection for him —a striking, sad-eyed, invalided widower, with a privileged position in the peckish henhouse of English society.

Consequently, Oliphant spoke cautiously. "Is there anything you might want to tell me? About Blondel? No delicate secrets now, not after— It's too late for that."

Narcissa spoke as if in normal conversation, and not lying naked beneath him. "What is it you want me to say?"

"The truth. What we have. The truth."

"This is me, John, not one of your agents. If Henry says he can help, I am sure he means it. He has a childhood friend in the embassy here. He told me. A confidant of Lord Lyons. A Jew with influence over Lord Lyons."

"I suppose. His note didn't say what he had in mind specifically."

"John, there is no need for this suspicion. He's a good friend, that is the extent of it. He came over with me to help me. But also to see the country, and the war close on. He is a soldier. It is what he knows. But India nearly killed him. You can see it in him. Do you know about his laudanum? He's not what he appears. That malaria killed his wife, and might kill him too. His hair is white, and he's only forty-two." Narcissa turned her head in profile. "Don't do this. We have enough trouble without distrusting each other."

"Amen," said Oliphant. He lowered his head onto her upper chest. He was too off-center to hear her heartbeat. The moments passed, marked by the popping embers in the fire and then the churchbell outside chiming 4 P.M. Narcissa had told Oliphant of the wakeful nights she had passed in this room as a schoolgirl, longing for Beaufort at the same time she fancied the military suitors in Washington whom she was too young to attract. It still had the ambience of a girl's room—pure colors and virginal clutter, with dolls set atop the wainscoting. There was a big red-haired doll in Oliphant's field of vision. It reminded him of his daughters.

Narcissa shifted beneath him. "You do agree, and believe me? It is crucial that you do. I need your faith. I can't lose you too. I understand about Papa. I feel we can find a way. I lose confidence sometimes. You hold me up. I need you. I have always needed you. We're a match! Neither of us can carry on alone. Oh, please, I do love you for what you have always done for me. I always shall. John?"

"Yes, I'm here, I'm listening."

Narcissa took hold of his chin and pushed his head up. "And?"

"I was thinking of things. Your red doll. Things in general."

Narcissa whispered, "Cammie?"

"No. Well, some. About you and her being alone. What it would be like for you both without me. For you. I worry about you. I make a fool of myself over a troubled Englishman. And yes, I was thinking of Camellia. She's there with all the children and has nothing but our letters, if they get through. I think about how much better it would be if you could get to her, or I could. What can we do for her here? Write her of death, and worse."

"She said we must do what we must." Narcissa referred to the last letter from Camellia that had gotten through the blockade, via Mexico, dated June 29; it had contained news of Laura's bereavement, and also the fact that Narcissa's eldest daughter Sophy was engaged to a Georgia officer serving with General Hood.

Oliphant leaned on his elbow away from Narcissa's face. "I was thinking of Camellia a lot last night. She sounded strong in her letter, she did. She made it sound as if we shouldn't worry. And yet she doesn't know the worst."

"She's known Papa was very ill."

"Yes." Oliphant sighed. "God knows about the mail. My September letters got to Richmond, I'm reasonably sure, but from there— I know Camellia can stand up. I know you can. It's me who's weak. What sort of help am I? I doubt, and defer, and shrink. Oh, the things I worry about, Narcissa, the small, intangible things. And Camellia has never questioned us, all these years. I worry about that too. I don't understand how she can be so—how you sisters can be so—stout-hearted."

"We are what is left, John, with Laura and Sally and Elizabeth and the children. We must trust each other. Always."

"I hear the lesson."

"Don't pull away from me." Narcissa closed her arms about Oliphant's neck and used her right leg to urge his weight down onto her pelvis. She extended her whole body to make it level beneath him, and then opened her legs and brought them up to grip him with her thighs at his hip. She pulled his face down to hers as she sank into her pillow. She kissed him on the lips, very heatedly and needfully.

Oliphant returned the kiss. But at the same time he felt far away and lost. He was beckoned back to Narcissa by the feel and smell of the tangy wetness of her sex that pressed up against his abdomen. He broke the kiss and ducked his head, so that he spoke to her neck. "Narcissa, Narcissa, what is wrong with me? Why am I so afraid? As I've never felt before. Is it just me? In New-York, I felt as if everything I've done for three years has been for nothing. As if it was all hopeless. As if I can't help you, or myself, or anyone. I feel so incompetent, and useless."

"Is there something you're not telling me about Canada, about what they wanted you to do?"

"No, no, it was a waste, and is done with. Their schemes and their plots. A waste. I told them so before I left. I wired Canada, and I passed on a note to Richmond, and I told them that I thought them all foolish. I wanted to tell them that I quit, but I didn't. They won't listen to me, but so what? I can't make them understand that all that's left is to make a deal. I can't instruct the world, and if I could, what would I tell it? That there is no victory? That there is only hope? And do I believe that? Can I make myself believe that again?"

"Oh, my dear, dear friend, oh John." She kissed him lightly on the face and stroked his hair. She added, "You are very brave, John, and very honest. You can do anything."

Oliphant smiled. He needed her so. He loved her so. He said, "You can make me feel that I can do anything."

She kissed him harder on the face, but when she relaxed into her pillow, she spoke tentatively. "I can't make you stay when you have to go."

Now it was Oliphant's turn to reassure her; he said, "Yes you can— anything, anything at all."

"Then make love to me again, and make us happy."

"Narcissa, I can't, I just can't." She moved, and he moved, and they laughed like fools. Oliphant said, "Can I?"

Narcissa's great-aunt's home, the Mason-Coxe-Turning House, stood amid older townhouses, neat shops, and homes converted to rooms-to-let on Georgetown's sedate Washington Street, just north of the village's main thoroughfare, Bridge Street. The house was set right up on the sidewalk. It was brick-built, with a cut-stone facade—a double house, really, that had never been divided, box-like and crowned by a corniced roof and double chimneys, with a single mahogany door off-center to the north up a small stoop. Otherwise, it was anonymously gray, with walls on three sides to enclose sugar maples, black oaks, and dogwoods at its flanks in addition to the great chestnut tree in the rear garden.

Since the beginning of the war, and especially since the Second Battle of Bull Run in July 1862, the house had usually been close-shuttered and unlit. As daylight faded in the low stone-gray sky on Wednesday afternoon, however, the windows on the first floor of the house showed a warm, yellow light.

At a quarter to five—the grandfather clock at the base of the stairs chiming once—Oliphant stepped up to the small window in the mahogany front door to peek out into the weather. The mist had eased. The overcast did look to be lifting in parts, but the wind was strengthening, threatening either more rain or a cold snap.

Oliphant turned to the side table to brush the sleeves of his dress coat. He had chosen his newest and most fashionable evening clothes and a bright, undyed Sea Island cotton shirt. He thought that he looked the very sober and refined diplomat who was intending either to deliver a war note or to attend a charity ball. He had also decided on his best silk top hat and black chesterfield-sac overcoat, which heightened the effect of a latter-day Puritan off to stroll the corridors of state power, and piously. He reached into the stand for a large English cane umbrella with an ivory handle.

He waved that umbrella's handle at the north-side parlor door, but did not tap because he heard a voice from inside. He stepped quietly through the door to find Maum Rosemary seated before the fire. She was reading to her three grandchildren and one grandnephew, Jimmie, Jinna, Nell, and Cato. Jimmie waved to Oliphant and smiled. The reading sounded familiar to Oliphant, and he listened while Maum Rosemary concluded a scene.

It was indeed something of Walter Scott's, Maum Rosemary's favorite author. In her dowdy green wool and skull cap, she was a pedagogical and energetic old woman, over 60 now, and self-confident in her special station as senior female in the family. It had once been a shock to Oliphant to learn from Narcissa that Maum Rosemary, through the bizarre nature of slavery, was Narcissa's aunt—the bastard daughter of Granby Royall's Charleston uncle. And thus Maum Rosemary was Granby Royall's cousin (and Louisa Granby Turning's niece). It was not a talked-about fact—nor was it unheard of in other slaveholding families. The surprise of it had long left Oliphant. Maum Rosemary was a profoundly integral member of the Royalls. Oliphant had come to depend upon her, as did Narcissa, as the steady and central hearthkeeper. Maum Rosemary closed the volume on a bookmark.

Oliphant said, "Maumer, I shall be out the evening. She's asleep."

Maum Rosemary replied, as he knew she would, "I'll take up a tray."

"You goin' to de President's?" asked Jimmie.

"Mind yer own, boy, and keep de peace," said Maum Rosemary.

Oliphant said, "No, Jim, I'm not. Near there though. What is it?"

"I do set, sir, on seein' President Lincoln for myself." His sisters and cousin agreed. Jimmie added, "We all make it a shine-eye-ting!" And they giggled.

Maum Rosemary said, "Mars Jan, ye carry on and don't mind dese and don't get wet feet."

"Yes'm," said Oliphant, slipping out of the room with a wave. He knew Maum Rosemary's fear of pneumonia. He also knew the genesis of Jimmie's inquiry. Narcissa had had the four adolescents tutored during the two and a half years in London, and their corresponding raised expectations of life —Hyde Park in comparison to St. Helena Island—were revealed in the size of their dreams. More pertinently, the Sunday before, Oliphant had told Jimmie, now 14 years old and as wide-eyed and eager as ever, that a "new world" would follow the war. Somehow, in the discussion that followed,

Jimmie had secured a promise that Oliphant would take him into Washington City to visit the Capitol building and possibly the President's House. Oliphant, as a father, knew that it was foolhardy to promise children unless one intended to deliver a prize immediately.

Yet there was a dark reason why Jimmie and the others had remained in Georgetown, and in this cluttered, drafty house, in the week since their arrival. The District of Columbia was not safe for Negroes. Tens of thousands of former slaves, called "contraband" since 1861, had fled into the District to squat in hovels and open fields right up to the White House grounds. Their numbers and indigence, and uncertain status as emancipated slaves but not enfranchised citizens, had so far overwhelmed the ability and the willingness of the United States government to care for these so-called wards of the state. Not only had it proved impossible to house or doctor them adequately, but also there had not been enough food for them—simple soup and bread were beyond the talents of the officiating Treasury Department. In desperation, some freed Negroes had fallen to theft and worse, and even those just stunned into passivity by their wrenching transformation still represented a beggarly threat to the community's sense of security. And there was always that awful fear of disease, for the epidemic rate in the "contraband" camps was withering. The result of so much failed planning and ignorance by 1864 was that Federal soldiers, lawmen, and vigilantes routinely patrolled the District of Columbia against the not infrequent acts of crime. There were regular and ghastly tales of brutality against the camps, including murder and burnings-out.

Mrs. Louisa Turning's house was a necessary refuge for Maum Rosemary and her charges. The only other occupants of the house were the two aged Turning house servants (emancipated in 1861), Bessie and Daniel; they cared for the brittle nonagenarian Mrs. Mason Turning, who lived as a recluse on the third floor, an aunt of the long deceased Mr. George Turning. The Turnings themselves were scattered throughout America by the fury and paradoxes of the war—sons, grandsons, and nephews in both the Union and Confederate armies; daughters, granddaughters, and nieces in Virginia, Maryland, Pennsylvania, New Jersey, Massachusetts, and Alabama, either awaiting news of their loved ones or mourning a death.

Mrs. Louisa Granby Turning, the stocky, white-haired matron, now over 80, whose stern portrait hung over the parlor fire, had expected to be present to receive her favored grandniece, Narcissa, and the corpse of her nephew,

Granby Royall. However, she had been called away in October by sickening news; she was now off in Virginia not only to help fetch the body of one of her grandsons-in-law, a Union soldier killed in the Shenandoah Valley, but also to help yet another granddaughter through the shock of the loss of first her Confederate husband at Petersburg and second her farm, which had been burned by General Sheridan's campaign to scorch the earth of the Shenandoah Valley.

It was the saddest sort of coincidence that Narcissa's husband, General Winwood, was missing and presumed dead in the massive cavalry raid in July that had brought Sheridan's wrath down upon the Shenandoah Valley. Confederate General Jubal Early's ten thousand cavalrymen had dared reason and Grant to attack to within sight of Washington City. It had been a desperate assault that Oliphant presumed might have been part of the original Confederate effort to discredit Lincoln's bid for reelection.

The result of all that now, in mid-November, was numbing grief. Narcissa had read Mrs. Turning's letter of explanation for her absence, and said, "The country is united on one certain thing, John. The national anthem has become the Death March."

Oliphant regarded this remark to be cynical of her, and knew it was not characteristic. Still, it was accurate as to the Turnings. They were a true District of Columbia family in that their loyalties and sacrifices were so split by the rebellion that after the war it might require a battle of family ghosts to sort out all the enmities in a crowded haunting of this forlorn house.

The house already had the aura of spirits. Mrs. Turning had arranged the portraits and photographs of her posterity on the tables in her parlors, and had tied black ribbons about the dead ones. To walk from the north side of the house to the south side was to stroll a field of the unforgotten.

Oliphant winced at this morbidness as he crossed the hall and passed into the south-side parlor. Here, the air was thick with the funeral smell of old roses. For off the parlor was the conservatory, which Oliphant had to pass through to get outside. And in the conservatory was Granby Royall's coffin, set up on blocks and covered with wilted garlands of roses.

Narcissa had fixed a trio of candlesticks at the base of the bier, and she had set a small photographic portrait of Granby Royall between them. Her Bible was there too, for she sat out here each evening reading from the Gospels. Oliphant had been with her in 1859 when she had arranged to have photographs made of the whole family during the Christmas holiday in

Charleston. Or had it been Easter? There had been a comet that year. It had been after John Brown's Raid. Narcissa had remarked upon the comet, "An omen, sure, but not for a new grandson." And then she had insisted upon the portraits. And within a month Camellia had delivered Granby Royall another granddaughter.

Oliphant was not comfortable with the suggestion of the supernatural. This was a dead man's photograph. Here was the box of his embalmed remains. His immortal soul was in heaven, with his Savior and his Creator. This was Oliphant's belief. His further conviction was that this coffin deserved a grave and a stone and a proper Christian burial in a place chosen by the deceased and sought by his family: St. Helena's Episcopal Church in Beaufort. All together, these opinions had presented Oliphant with a quest. He must get Narcissa through to Beaufort.

After his ambition in October, this was not much of a hope to hold on to. The cotton scheme that had brought him across the Atlantic had been there to grasp. Oliphant had applied his talent to the parley in New-York. Had he actually believed in it? It did not signify. He had done his work and passed on his best advice that the deal was a failure. Oliphant was soon vindicated when the scheme was abandoned. A telegram on Election eve had told Oliphant that Montreal no more trusted Lafayette Baker—who had actually presented himself to Beverley Tucker in Montreal—than had Oliphant. The telegram had also said that Beverley Tucker would not be traveling to New-York, and that Oliphant was released from his service as a go-between.

Oliphant had greeted this news with disgust, and a turning inward. To blazes with Beverley Tucker, George Sanders, Jake Thompson, and their fantasies! Let Judah Benjamin sort it out!

Oliphant felt no less distaste for the fate of Captain Longuemare's scheming. Oliphant had telegraphed to Judah Benjamin via the relay operator in Baltimore (who converted Oliphant's cipher into his own cipher for a secret courier through the lines to Richmond) his extremely negative opinion of the Election Day conspiracy.

Fortunately, nothing more had come of Longuemare's plan. The Sons of Liberty had backed down; Martin and Headley and the rest had been left without a sensible mission. And Oliphant had been spared further exasperation by Longuemare—and the fiery Katie MacDonald—thanks to the fact that Richmond had chosen not to interfere. At least Judah Benjamin and War Secretary Seddon seemed to have some sense of proportion left.

Election Day in New-York had passed with no more risk than the flooding in the street, and with no more jeopardy to Kennedy than too much of Oliphant's wine—and that swinging cargo net off *Australasian.*

Oliphant had parted affectionately with Kennedy at the ferry in New-York the morning after the Election. He had also given Kennedy the strong advice that he should quit New-York and sail for New Orleans as soon as possible to visit his parents. Oliphant had said, "The war might be done for us, Mr. Kennedy. Take the chance. Declare a ceasefire and get home for Christmas."

Oliphant had also communicated to Richmond, via Baltimore, that he was leaving New-York for Washington City on personal business. That had been a week ago. Richmond had Oliphant's Georgetown address. But Richmond remained silent in return.

And why? Because the war really was done, thought Oliphant, and because the Confederacy was a ruin. How could anyone go on? To Oliphant's mind, not only the war but also the meaning of the war was lost, or simply abandoned, for North and South, for white and black. He could see this in every grim face. It was late, very late, for Oliphant, for the Confederacy, for the Union too. There was only time to heed one's heart, and to save what one could of life. Let Richmond, let Washington look to its own as well. Oliphant wanted to cleave to his family, and to Narcissa.

Oliphant left the house in a rush. He was talking to himself, and quoting Narcissa's favorite epigram, "What a dust we make!"

He felt momentarily pleased by the evening coming on and the possibility of actually finding a way to give Narcissa what she desired. He crossed the rear garden in large steps. He did not look up to Narcissa's room.

Noah and Michael were smoking at the potbelly stove in the carriage house. They prepared the landau quickly for Oliphant, hitching up the fat bay. Michael was unhappy when Oliphant told him that he would prefer that he and not Noah drive.

Oliphant explained, "It's liable to storm again."

Michael protested, "I was gwine out later."

Noah was annoyed. "You here, bubbah, and you gwine's now!"

"It isn't necessary to stay, I shall get home on my own," said Oliphant. Michael cursed. When Noah stared him down, Michael bent to his task. Michael routinely slipped away at night now; he also speculated openly to Maum Rosemary about enlisting in the Army and boasted of his freedom to come and go to the adolescents. Oliphant was not unsympathetic to the man's dilemma—a bondsman in the North. While Noah walked out the landau, Oliphant handed Michael a dollar bill that he took without remark.

In the landau, Oliphant chose to ignore Michael's moodiness. They used the carriage track between the townhouses and gained Bridge Street so hurriedly that Michael had to fight with the bay to prevent a collision in the traffic. Oliphant tucked his scarf close and watched the night settle over the cozy brick farming village of Georgetown.

At last light, they were stopped on the stone bridge that was the single link from busy Georgetown to the vacant-lot-like periphery of Washington City. Below them was Rocky Creek, a narrow, muddy stream that meandered south to intersect with the Chesapeake and Ohio Canal and then flowed onto a swampy basin that opened into the Potomac River. Oliphant was attracted by the campfires below in the deep ravine. He could see a "contraband" camp in the mud, on both sides of the creek. There might have been hundreds of people down there; all that showed were clutches of children standing about the fires. Farther along the ravine, in silhouette against the blue glow of the horizon, there were more children climbing the wooden superstructure of the watchtower that Georgetown had built in the early days of the war to signal the approach of the enemy from Virginia. They had called it Mosby's Steeple. Now, the tower stood abandoned, many of its crosspieces stripped off in order to help hold up the shacks below.

The watchtower shook as the wind gusted up from the river. Oliphant protected his face and then his hat. The next he looked, they were out of the traffic and across the bridge. Michael cursed the bay, and she accelerated toward Pennsylvania Avenue. Soon, they were caught up in the outermost spokes of the circular and geometrical pattern of the capital's streets, like being dragged into a vast machine by giant gears that turned clockwise and counterclockwise, in secular time, and drove the screeching crankshafts of the war.

WEDNESDAY EVENING, NOVEMBER 16

By seven o'clock, the chandelier-lit dining room at Willard's Hotel was a rolling battlefield of words and impotent demonstrations. The gentlemen were dressed grandiosely for minor gains as they hunched in close counsel at the round and square tables, blew tobacco smoke through the candelabras, and wagged fingers at the darting servants for more wine, sweets, and attention to fortify the debates. It was another ordinary evening in the hotel of choice for Republicans, Union partisans, general staff officers, and field-grade commanders on leave with permission to enter the capital, along with the ever anxious and sharp-eared newspapermen, the fashionable nabobs, and the aides-de-camp pausing in their self-congratulatory pursuits to feed upon the gossip and intrigue.

Willard's Hotel stood six stories tall above the mire of Pennsylvania Avenue at the northwest corner of West Fourteenth Street. It was only a few hundred yards from the White House and the surrounding prickly maze of Cabinet palaces, and was thus a stopping place so convenient to the powerful that it hummed like a dynamo of government, especially after dark, when it was invested with a brilliant vanity. What men wanted or might want was discussed and wept about in daylight up the street at a secretary's or assistant secretary's office; however, what men meant or might mean was the singular topic each boisterous evening at Willard's. The suites were caves of favor-seekers. The hallways were avenues of doubt. The public bar was a font of pride. The drawing rooms were lavish nests of ladies and their gigolos. The ballroom was less an auditorium than a circus big top. The barbershop was the stage to display one's four-day-old, front-line beard. And the main dining room, with false vaulting arches, ostentatious plaster-of-paris designs, and as much drapery as at Balmoral Castle, was the voluble and absolute arena. Since the war, it was said that Willard's was the refuge of more scheming and plotting heads, more aching and joyful hearts, than any comparably sized building in the world; and here, in the dining room, was the aristocracy of cunning.

The dining room's high court this evening tossed up gossip of a menu of names. There was the flat soup of George B. McClellan, now resigned (November 14) from the Army in the disgrace of yet another mixed defeat, though his fate was not unhappy given the influence of his supporters (an offer of an enormous salary as president of the Illinois Central Railroad) and the opinion that Lincoln had prevailed less in the polling places than in Mobile, Atlanta, and the Shenandoah Valley. The idle wisdom tonight was that a political victory that had depended upon combat could just as easily become a political defeat come the next battle.

And there was also news of satellite figures, like appetizers, that sated palates for a time: Stanton was out of his sickbed and back breathing fire at the War Department; Senator Sumner was still eyeing Seward's job at

State; Seward was rumored to oppose, or perhaps merely not to support, his old adversary James Gordon Bennett of the *New-York Herald* as the new minister to France; cranky Salmon P. Chase, the resigned secretary of the treasury, was said to have reconsidered his peevish disapproval of Lincoln and to be yearning for the chief justiceship of the Supreme Court; and the ancient attorney general, Edward Bates, exhausted from years of fighting Seward and Stanton over the suspension of habeas corpus and civil rights in general, was certain to resign in disgust at any hour.

And then, these hot side dishes of the roasting and boiling Cabinet dispensed with, there was the ever popular game of U. S. Grant, the blue-eyed, stoop-shouldered, and openly worshipped lieutenant-general of the mightiest army ever assembled, who still insisted upon reigning from that canvas tent with carpeted floors at City Point, near Petersburg, lest he be accused of being a parlor-room commander like the reviled Henry Halleck, and lest he be caught in the merciless, chatty ambushes in this very room.

A scrutinous diner, and eavesdropper, would have reached past all these tidbits soon enough, for he would have sensed when he entered the arena that there was only one desired dish the assembled hungered after—the special of the day, the week, the month, and perhaps the war. The topic was Major-General William T. Sherman and his seventy-thousand-man army at Atlanta. One could smell it thick and tart; one could taste it like saddle of venison; one could hear it sizzle in the hirsute or beardless mouths.

"Well, what of him, then?" said a baffled imp from State, stuttering, "Wh-wh-where?"

"I don't make as much of Sherman's silence," started a slick-headed major in the sky blue of the Invalid Corps, "as I do of the Richmond papers' silence of Sherman's silence."

"Sir, I insist, it's a week since the *Indianapolis Journal* said he was leaving Atlanta burned!" said a gambler in the company of his card players for the evening, including three western congressmen.

"But they retracted it, depend on it," said a big-eared youth.

A Navy officer, just back from the tedium of the blockade off Fort Fisher, said, "Fortress Monroe has confirmed Sherman's on the warpath."

His captain shot, "But how, which way, what kind of warpath?"

"Boston is most certain when it says Sherman wears gauntlets and not kid gloves," protested a Yankee trader, and when his partners guffawed, he added, "They say he must not fail to level behind what he can't protect!"

"Hot words, I'll grant, hot words," laughed a financier.

A Treasury official said, "Atlanta's burned, or it's not burned, or it's seceded to sit with Jesus—what do we care?"

"Chicago guarantees that Sherman's left Atlanta in three grand columns," declared a man with a bloated face of whiskers, who saw that his speech had attracted many turned heads, so he pounded, "He shall sweep the Southern states like an angel of death!"

"Nonsense, nonsense, laddies, no one knows," admonished a retired admiral, who looked old enough to have run from the British once upon a time. "No one and not especially the Army don't know."

"So where is he going, if he is going—? I don't wonder it is confusing," said a foreign-looking man, who whispered to his lady companion in Italian, "They are hens about roosters."

"He shall charge and blast them to hell, that's his aim," allowed a tall, strange fellow. "He and his four horsemen, to hell."

"Yes, Major, what does Sherman intend?" asked a lady like a pin in this barn full of haystacks, and trying to please she added, "Victory, I'm sure."

"Tell us first," said one side of the room, quoting Greeley and common sense, "where he could be, and then we shall know where he might be tomorrow."

"Yes, yes, first, where is he?" said the other side of the room, citing the *National Intelligencer* and the obvious, "and then we can figure how long he will be there."

And eventually, the murmur was united in overfed unison, "Where is Sherman?" and again dyspeptic, "Where is *Sherman?*" and again gaseous, "Where is *Sherman?*"

One table at least was exempt from this gluttony of talk. Sir Henry Blondel was bent forward, and he was sweeping the tablecloth with his bare hand. His very long white hair fell from his shoulders to skim the lip of his brandy snifter. The ash from his cannon of a cigar scattered and settled behind where his hand had already swept. Oliphant was seated at an angle toward Blondel, one leg crossed over the other, and was sucking on his briar pipe so deeply that his exhale bathed the table in a broad cloud. Oliphant's tea was tepid; indeed he had eaten his duck so slowly that it too had cooled before the waiter had cleared it away. Oliphant now studied Blondel's bowl of chocolate ice cream as it melted.

"I do hope, I do, what I've said has helped," continued Blondel. He looked up to see if Oliphant was following his presentation after his small interruption for housekeeping. Blondel had recounted most of his biography up to the Christmas before. He had only hinted at his relationship with Narcissa, however, and therefore Oliphant thought Blondel's next remark disingenuous. Blondel said, "About myself, about the sincerity of my affection for Mrs. Winwood."

Oliphant leaned forward and removed his pipe. Blondel might have continued talking if not for an odd disturbance at a nearby table. Four gentlemen were arranged there in relaxed camaraderie, sharing a decanter of cognac and smoking luxurious cigars. Two of them were in dinner dress like Oliphant and Blondel; the other two were undeniably splendid in Confederate uniforms—gold braid, gold buttons, red sashes, striped pantaloons, and dress sabers as beautiful as sunbursts. This pair represented a Washington phenomenon, the result of Lincoln's General Order 126, posted omnipresently, that permitted "Secessionist soldiers" free access in the District of Columbia, and also free food if desired, in exchange for their taking of the loyalty oath to the United States. The capital was thick with Confederate deserters and parolees. And there could have been no two finer specimens of Rebeldom than these diners. They were not young, however, and close inspection showed their bitterness. As such, they were spectacles that aroused Union officers to sputtering disgust. Also, for their own alcoholized reasons, the Secessionist quartet had taken to presenting overloud toasts to Confederate commanders, dead and still fighting. With each new name, angry white eyes uncovered across the room, in particular from a long table of soldiers in the sky-blue dress of the Invalid Corps. Blondel and Oliphant had to pause when the Confederates declared, "I give you the memories of James Ewell Brown Stuart and John Hunt Morgan, who could ride with the wind, but couldn't dodge a back-shooting coward!"

The Confederates cheered and rattled their table. A tremor passed through the room. And then the vacuum of breathing was filled again with dry, droning voices. The Invalid Corps soldiers turned aside and huddled.

Oliphant took charge of his thoughts. "Please continue, Sir Henry—that's a bad business, and not going to improve."

"I've not seen worse," said Blondel, nodding toward the Confederates, "on three continents—never. The hatred of men who know each other intimately—never." Blondel tucked his hair behind his ears and furled his eyebrows. The white hair did mislead about his general vigor; he had a pink, round-cheeked face, and looked a man accustomed to being welcomed and listened to. There was also a friendly laugh and a weighty tone of steadfast compassion. Oliphant had yet to see any of the ornamental eccentricity that served as fashion among Blondel's class of Englishmen these days. Blondel collected himself, and continued, "I was speaking of my affection for Mrs. Winwood. My desire to see her comforted in this terrible moment. I feel I'm not getting this right. I'm too roundabout for this. I could profit from some of the American to-the-pointness."

"One's heart is a roundabout thing," said Oliphant.

Blondel smiled. "You are very kind. Mrs. Winwood has been equally kind to me. When I think of her, I see her caring like a crown."

Oliphant said, "She is a ceaselessly generous woman."

"Yes, yes! And now she has lost so many, and needs so much!" Blondel held his hands as if they were a bowl. "I have asked myself, what can I do? Oh, this accompanying her abroad which she makes much of, was little, the least of it. I want to do more. And need to do more. I look to you for guidance. I've hoped we could be friends—after we come to know each other better. That is why I have gone on about myself, so tiresomely. I wanted you to know that I am prepared to do whatever is asked." Blondel tapped the table above Oliphant's knee. "You are the last man—it sounds dreadful—the last man in the family. Dear God, forgive me."

"It is true. There it is."

"Unless, of course, this wretched news about General Winwood is incorrect, and he's prisoner or—"

Oliphant interrupted. "There are casualty lists and prisoner lists. I have corresponded with Richmond. It's a done thing, Sir Henry. The Shenandoah Valley was reduced end to end. And General Winwood was lost somewhere near the Potomac, or Harper's Ferry. The unburied dead—the mass graves —a done thing."

Blondel said, "It does take time, and is cruel either way, to announce prematurely, or to allow hope. I know. I have—had—a close friend who is still not found in India, and it is seven years!"

"That was the Sepoy Rebellion?" asked Oliphant.

"The massacre, Mr. Oliphant, like all rebellions." Blondel sucked on his cigar. "Tell me, please, I am curious. Mrs. Winwood and the general were living apart? Since the war?"

Oliphant said, "Before that. For a long time. Their situation was irreconcilable. Or so I was told. It was never anything I understood either. I never met the general, and I arrived in Beaufort nine years back."

The Secessionists at the near table broadcasted, "I say, God bless Jubal Anderson Early, and make the waters open before him as before the Israelites, and crash on his enemies like on the godless Egyptians!"

There was a screech of chairs on the hardwood floor. Because of his July cavalry raid, Jubal Early was a hero to the legion of Southern sympathizers in the District, and was anathema to the Union supporters. In children's prayers, it was said, they either said goodnight to Old Jubal, or asked God to protect them from him. A grandfatherly diner stood in the dining room and flung his dinner napkin at the Secessionists. "For pity's sake, show some decency here."

Blondel shifted again. "You haven't asked me any questions really. About what I've said. I couldn't have done all that well."

Oliphant said, "You speak well for yourself, sir, and humbly. You're a soldier of the Queen, as you say. India sounds to me like a dream. I have never seen a battle. I have notions of them, and dreams, but—not yet, thank God. It hasn't happened. As to your hopes. I appreciate your sincere concern for Mrs. Winwood's welfare."

"And yours! And your whole family's! I am offering what I can marshall to help you and yours caught in this war. I've seen the war differently this last week than I had understood it reading the papers in London. What matter these John Bright debates of liberty and slavery? What matter the rams, or the blockade? Your country is destroying people like woodchips! The rational thing—the only thing—is to escape!"

Oliphant said, "To save what I can, yes, sometimes I believe that."

Blondel continued, "It is right. Mrs. Winwood has told me of your family, and of Mrs. Oliphant's heroic protection of your children, and Mrs. Winwood's. Mrs. Oliphant needs our help too. I'm making a botch of this. I want to help. I need your help to do so."

Oliphant started to reply, yet restrained himself to fiddle with his pipe. He relit with his dull-gold lighter decorated with the Spectre Buck. Oliphant had the measure of this man now. Blondel was in love with Narcissa. It was not a surprise. Still, the fact of it pressed him. Oliphant thought, fate proposes, and fate disposes. And there was always more, and more confusing, to follow. Oliphant now understood that the purpose of this dinner was so that Blondel could bargain with Oliphant, and with his own fate, in order to win Narcissa. There were tangible and imaginary obstacles in the way of his suit, yet to Blondel they must seem inconsequential in comparison to his desire. His wife's death had dropped him into a pit of defeat, and the opium dependency that he alluded to, and Narcissa had confirmed, remained a curse of his wild self-pity. But Blondel was trying boldly and honestly to climb out of his trouble. By chance, in London to mend after leaving India and retiring from the Army, Blondel had found someone spectacular, Narcissa, to grab hold of. And she seemed as needful as he. Oliphant recognized the symmetry; he had grabbed hold of Narcissa, and she of him, in their own time and way. Oliphant saw the worth, risk, and compulsion for Blondel. He also saw the truth. Oliphant decided to confess himself, if obliquely; he said, "Narcissa and Camellia are the touchstones of my life."

Blondel brought his chair closer, and bent his head to Oliphant's. "Dear God, yes. I want to help you all get away safe, out of Washington, out of Savannah, out of America. I know this sounds presumptuous. It is. I am sharing my heart. You are an accomplished man. Mrs. Winwood—Narcissa —has told me of your successes, and what her family owes you for your commercial and financial prowess. I know you have lost much in South Carolina, and yet are far from being without resources. There are many avenues, now, and after the war, again— The cotton trade will return with brass bands. I want to help repair all the damage that you have suffered. I've said I have three young children at home with my mother. I am free, for now, to make my own way. You must hear me. I am your servant. Oh, please, sir, if you want my help! If you can say so!"

"You could really get them out of Savannah?"

"I have ideas," said Blondel. "And friends in government, mine and yours. My father and brother have no small influence. I think I could muster more. We can get Narcissa to Beaufort, and bury that poor man, and then we can give it a try. We aren't old men yet, you and I. We can give it a try, John."

"We can do that, Sir Henry," began Oliphant. Blondel threw out his hand to dismiss the formality, and mumbled "Henry." Oliphant smiled. Blondel was offering profound fraternity. Nevertheless, Oliphant thought this conversation proceeding too quickly in one direction. His instinct was that it was too soon to seal a bargain for Narcissa, or for himself and his family. Oliphant equivocated. "You— Have you told Narcissa about Savannah?"

"I didn't—couldn't—promise. It seemed boastful, and cheap."

"Very sensible, yes, yet we have gone far in our discussion about our future, about hers, for her not to have been consulted."

Blondel said, "I have worried about this. I have hope, I have reason to hope, that she would hear my appeal as fairly as you have. And with the addition of your approval, I have special hope."

"So you have spoken to Narcissa about your affections?"

Blondel laughed. "I've done my best. Yet, as you say, the heart is a roundabout mechanism, and she is an intimidating woman."

Oliphant smiled in return. But it was pretense. He was touched by fears as if by invisible hands. To lose Narcissa! To gain Camellia! To lose America! To gain peace! And the threat and the promise and the reward and the sentence were all consequent upon shaking the hand of this man, Blondel, who did not know the whole truth, who could not guess the most shameful and yet most crucial part of the truth! What did honor require? What did decency demand? What did love command? Oliphant felt spontaneously pulled backward and pushed forward by his intelligence. He also felt that his own heart was suddenly a secret to him.

Oliphant steadied himself, and tried to plunge; he began, "I don't know, I don't—" He sighed. How could he do this? How could he not? He said, "Henry, I am a prisoner of my circumstances."

"Please, John, I have guessed. I know some, about your service, about Richmond."

"No, no," said Oliphant, and then he stopped. "You do?"

The Secessionist quartet and their adversaries interrupted again with another unhappy and this time stunning distraction. The youngest companion of the paroled Confederates stood with his glass held high like a torch, and tried to outdo the gods of war. "Brave soldiers of the Confederacy, I propose a toast to the greatest warrior and most honorable American and the undyingest champion of our cause that walks the earth like a giant—a giant of irreproachable might, a giant to sweep the devils aside with his left arm while with his steely and unbent right he punishes the tyrants who make war on women and children and burn out the homes of the innocent and steal the food from the destitute, in brief! In brief! I give you! I give you! Robert E. Lee, the heart of the brave, the soul of the free! God Almighty keep him safe!"

A thick wine glass flew from across the room and just missed the speaker to bounce on the floor and crack against the back wall. The dining room was half empty now for the theater hour. The remaining pontificators and heavy drinkers were gathered mostly in the inner circle of tables. The crash of the glass stilled them like the first sky burst of a barrage. The Secessionist speaker took two drunken steps backward without turning his gaze from the direction of his adversary, and in slow motion he raised his leg to smash his boot down on the glass shards. He cried, "Smote the damn Yankees!" His other civilian companion cheered, "Hooray for Dixie!" The two parolees watched the charade in anxious anticipation.

They were unprepared for the new attack. A man of indeterminate age, shrunken inside his baggy sky-blue uniform, crossed the floor to the Secessionist table with the speed of a charger at a rampart. He had a cane. He hobbled twice more as he raised it. He crashed the cane down on the table, and then down again on the back of one of the Confederate parolees. The victim toppled onto the table, dragging glasses and dishes atop himself as he fell to the floor. The Invalid trooper set himself again—to kill. Murder was clearly in his face, his teeth bared and eyes squinting shut. The other parolee intervened, grappling with the attacker. The Invalid trooper screamed, "Goddamn ye, Rebs, goddamn ye to hell!"

The bystanders were in a frenzy. There were cries of "Stop! Stop!" There was the rush of the other Invalid Corps men to protect their comrade. There was the fright and then the anger of the civilian diners. The undamaged Confederate acted badly, because ambiguously—he restrained the attacker, but he also shook him in a belligerent fashion, shouting, "No, no, what've you done? You've killed him!" The Confederate then saw his peril, but was unable to save himself as he was clubbed down by another cane-wielding trooper. The aged admiral got across the room to insert himself between the contestants. "Enough! Help that man there, and belay that!"

This might have stopped the fight. But when the first victim was rolled over, his face was smeared in gore. The original speaker knelt down to clean his dinner companion's face, and then looked up at the two assailants. "In the back, that's your mettle, cowards, back-stabbers!"

Vile screaming followed, and another surge. By this time, Blondel had escorted Oliphant toward the exit, and was forcing a path for the two of them through the clerks, waiters, and lobby patrons cascading into the room to watch. Oliphant bounced off a large captain of cavalry who then fell down heavily because he had been on canes. But Oliphant was unable to help the cavalryman up because of the crush. Oliphant hid behind a pillar and looked back at the riot.

There were men drawn up at smashed tables. Some were staring at each other's clothes to try to establish friend or foe; others were breaking up chairs for weapons. It would not be a quick battle, because one could assume there were more than enough Southern sympathizers in the room to test the Union soldiers. Oliphant saw one little nugget of a man sneak up to draw out the saber of the wounded Confederate parolee. Many screamed and gasped, because for a moment it appeared that this was an assassin who intended to hack like a John Brown manqué. Instead, the sneak only tried to break the blade over his knee, and failed, dropping it with a howl of pain. The original adversaries were now so surrounded by bobbing heads that Oliphant could not see the central contest. He could only hear the whine of peacemaking and the barks of provocation, "Traitors!" "Blackguards!" "Shame! Shame!"

Oliphant reached the lobby and found Blondel again. They walked around each other for a few moments, starting sentences and then glancing away to calm themselves, and always keeping their attention on the dining room. Finally the hubbub did subside, and without shots or further injuries. Diners began coming out in groups, some with food smeared on their coats. Their expressions were neither angry nor resigned, more as if they were close to weeping. Oliphant saw one coatless fellow who proceeded to rip off his own shirt.

Blondel took Oliphant's arm and ushered him toward the public bar. Blondel made a fluttery motion with his fingers, and said, "Savage, bloody savage. I have seen nastier, when these savages came down on us with spears, and us with our Napoleons. It was God-awful— But that was India!"

Oliphant lifted his right fist to his mouth, and mumbled into it, "Soon we shall be down to teeth and nails."

LATER WEDNESDAY EVENING, NOVEMBER 16

The riot at Willard's darkened Oliphant, and soon after he excused himself from Blondel's gentle company. He left not only an unfinished cognac but also an unfinished confession. Blondel bade farewell at the bar. "I shall wait upon you, John, and your direction."

Outside, the night sky had grown big with the breakup of the overcast. The moon was so bright, four days short of full, that the Milky Way was overwhelmed with moonbeams. Oliphant found the North Star as he pulled on his top hat. Its certainty purchased him some comfort. It was colder now, and a determined wind ruled Pennsylvania Avenue, bending the long line of ailanthus trees, scattering the leaves in small cyclones, whooshing so strongly that it often drowned out the muck-sucking trot of the passing horses.

Oliphant climbed into a two-wheeled hack that presented itself suddenly. He gave the Georgetown address and settled back. He was distracted by the upcoming lights of the Treasury building at the West Fifteenth interruption of Pennsylvania Avenue. The gas illumination gave a blue patina to the beige facade. Oliphant knew the bright windows behind the columns—this was a neo-classical temple of money—were for the Counting Room, where they would be as usual working all night to tally the greenbacks. There would be companies of Treasury women there, bent over the long tables, with green eyeshades and inky fingers.

This image produced another. He pictured Narcissa, Camellia, Laura, and his own daughters, Alice, Mary, and Faith, and Narcissa's daughters, Sophy and Martha. And then he saw Narcissa again: how she would be when he arrived home, downstairs in the conservatory, before the bier. Maum Rosemary would be after her to come in from the damp. Narcissa would say, "After a while, Maumer," and return to her reading. And when he came in, he would sit beside her, and she would ask, "What shall we try tomorrow?"

Oliphant rocked forward and shouted through the speaking window in the sedan top. "Driver! Listen here! We must go back!" He had been selfish and irrational. His primary goal must be to bury Granby Royall. He shouted, "Back to Willard's, now!"

It was some time, however, caught in the traffic at Lafayette Square, before Oliphant's hack arrived back at Willard's and waded into the tangle of hacks at the curb. By then, Oliphant was resolved to bargain as openly as necessary with Blondel. And if the price were the truth about his feelings for Narcissa, he would pay what he could of it—he could try!

Oliphant was so committed to his course that he did not instantly recognize the tall, white-haired figure in top hat and cape emerging from the bright entrance of Willard's. The hack slid the last few feet to the sidewalk. Oliphant had a dollar in his hand. The driver—a huge, long-armed Negro in a slouch hat and voluminous overcoat—reached around to open the cabin door. Oliphant put the money in the man's paw and pushed one leg forward to step out. It was then that he realized that here was Blondel again, less than ten yards away.

Blondel was not alone. His companion was a portly, bow-legged gentleman in evening dress, who had a moustache shaped into twirled points in the Continental style. The stranger moved up behind Blondel and got his attention. The bustling crowd momentarily closed around them. They reappeared, this time laughing at something behind them. They stopped to look back at a most attractive woman in pale blue silk and a long red cape who was just then leaving Willard's with an elderly gentleman.

Oliphant did not announce himself. He watched Blondel and the stranger walk over to a four-wheeled coach that occupied the corner of West Fourteenth and Pennsylvania like a gun frigate. The stranger gestured to the driver, then opened the cab door to remove his walking cane. There was some sort of gold seal on the cabin door. Blondel and the stranger set off on foot, north on West Fourteenth. The private coach swung around to follow them.

Oliphant got down carefully, and said, "Driver, I am going to walk for a while—"

"How's that, sir?" said a small figure atop the hack.

Oliphant looked up to the driver's assistant—a dwarfish Negro in a top hat whom Oliphant had not seen before. He started again, "I would like, if you would follow me, while I walk."

"Yes, sir, happy to, sir," said the driver's assistant.

Oliphant marched to the corner; he waited for his hack to clear the jam-up and reach him. Forty yards on, Blondel and the stranger were walking arm in arm from one pool of gaslight to another. Oliphant tapped his cane umbrella and proceeded. Blondel and the stranger weaved through a flock of pedestrians coming out from one of the high-priced bawdyhouses, then crossed the intersection east, and then crossed again to the north side of F Street. F Street was a stately thoroughfare of older and grander houses that was defined in this section from the Treasury building at West Fifteenth to the Patent Office at West Ninth as Embassy Row.

Blondel and his companion strolled another half block, then veered into the carriage drive of a majestic brick mansion set back from the street amid half-naked trees. The house was lit for a ball. Luxurious coaches and carriages lined the drive and the street. There was a stream of guests into both the main entrance and the door of the wing to the left. Oliphant remained on the south side of F Street to study the affair, and also to inspect the stranger's private coach more closely. Even in bad light, the seal was a piercing icon close up: the imperial lion of Her Majesty's government of the United Kingdom of Great Britain and Ireland.

Oliphant returned to his hack, and asked up to the driver, "What is that house there—one of the embassies?"

The driver's assistant leaned across the giant knees of the driver, and replied, "Why, yes, sir—let's figure. It's been a few years since—yes, sir. That back there's English. There's Russia. Yes, sir, it's the Frenchers. Unless it's Austria, I never did know."

Oliphant handed up a five dollar greenback. "I would like you to wait for me, and there will be more." The driver's assistant's cheerful assurance of obedience followed Oliphant across the street. He pushed through the coachmen and into the flock of guests crowding up to the main entrance of what was indeed the Legation of the Second Empire of France.

The house itself was a three-and-a-half-story English-looking construction, with a slate roof, six gables, and three chimney banks; the two-story west-side wing reproduced the details. Oliphant expected the interior would be the opposite of this understated facade, and was not disappointed, for this was a mission established under the Bourbons that was now the showplace of Bonapartism reawakened. There were the usual feathered sentinels at the doorway, and then there was a swarm of bewigged servants receiving hats and wraps. Oliphant mixed up behind a handsome group of American couples, and inched forward.

He assumed that his excellent French would help him bluff through his lack of an invitation. However, there was no opportunity for masquerade. The crush of gowns in the vestibule, the general growl of excitement in the central hall at arriving beauties, the rainbow display of uniforms from every sort of army and navy, all revealed to Oliphant that this was international pandemonium rather than Washington elitism. More important, given the number and urgent pomposity of the American merchantmen present, it was clear that the wealthy and powerful were welcome without need of explanation. And why? Once inside, Oliphant was able to reconnoiter the packed drawing rooms and, with his polylingual talents, to ascertain the vocabulary of tonight's sycophancy, for over and over he heard the name and its synonyms spoken in facile reverence:

"Maximillian!" "The Archduke Maximillian!" "The fated younger brother of Francis Joseph I of Austria!" "The heralded Emperor of Mexico!" "The new wearer of the Crown of Montezuma!" "The Savior of the Mexican Empire!" "To his Excellency, Maximillian, and his beautiful Empress, Carlotta!" "Long live the Emperor of Mexico, the Catholic Champion of North America!"

Oliphant took a glass of champagne and continued his tour. The specific ambition of the assembled, once revealed, did not amuse him. The French ambassador Monsieur Mercier was entertaining in order to introduce his two special guests, a pair of Mexican aristocrats. Until recently, it was said, the two barons had been resident in Spain, in exile from revolution-torn Mexico. Now, they were in Washington City on behalf of Mexico in order to collect the proposals and contracts of American investors for the so-called renaissance of their country. Bluntly, this meant that Maximillian's new imperial government in Mexico City was shopping for weapons, and railroads. The French embassy was illuminated like a covered bazaar, and the moment was right for buying and selling the tools of empire.

Oliphant was able to correct his first assumption that all of the capital's society was represented. The United States government was absent in the extreme. Over there, by the painted screens, there were British Navy swords and Prussian Hussar boots and the beards of Spanish chevaliers, but there was no blue dress uniform of the United States Army; over there, by the porcelain display of memorial plates, there were diamond-studded Brazilian and Austrian and Italian popinjays, but there were no emissaries from the State Department. And over there, quaffing wine as if it were air, there was a squadron of Continental fortune hunters like starlings encircling the bejeweled and garlanded American wives and their ripe daughters, but there was no senator—Republican, Democrat, or Copperhead—and perhaps even no congressman, though perhaps there were, given the House of Representatives' reputation for contrariness.

And why was France's sponsorship of Mexican agents anathema to Lincoln, Seward, and the Congress? The answer was a mountain range of intrigue: Lincoln and Seward despised Europe's adventurism in Mexico, but they would and must obey, for the moment, Lincoln's dictum, "One war at a time!" Meanwhile, France's emperor, Napoleon III, had maneuvered to place Maximillian, the younger brother of Emperor Francis Joseph I of Austria, on the so-called throne of Mexico. This had been the capstone of three cynical years of international opportunism, and it looked to reestablish Catholic imperialism and reactionaryism in North America.

The more he walked among them, the more this gathering disgusted Oliphant. Worse, the more it all shamed him, because for most of his last three years he had done the bidding of a Confederate government that had conspired with Napoleon III in his crude Mexican endeavor in the hope that Richmond's collaboration would win diplomatic recognition from France. Oliphant's duties for Judah Benjamin had taken him again and again into Paris, to John Slidell, the Confederate commissioner whose job was to stroke Napoleon III and his inner circle of greedy, backboneless aristocrats. The details were immense and dark. The simplest explanation of Slidell's work was that Napoleon III's libertine clique and the Confederacy shared the same banker in Paris, the French Jew, Baron D'Erlanger (whose son had married one of Slidell's daughters). The further sad fact, for Oliphant, was that Jefferson Davis and Judah Benjamin were willing to concede to Napoleon III fully half of North America, from Honduras to Oregon, if such a fantastic concession would win French support. Oliphant knew there had even been talk of the so-called gradual emancipation of the South's slaves if that political stroke could overcome Europe's distaste for the Confederate cause. Oliphant had watched and participated in a series of questionable plays in the last year, as Davis and Benjamin struggled to offset the losses on the battlefields with theoretical giveaways in diplomacy in the future. How it appalled Oliphant to consider what must have been the contents of the notes he carried to Paris. How it tormented him that these people tonight, these European aristocrats, were supposedly more his allies than not, and that they were all together supposedly scheming in opposition to the so-called tyranny of the United States.

Oliphant raised his glass in the direction of Capitol Hill. God save America! God bless Lincoln and Seward for standing up to Paris, Vienna, London, Madrid, and Berlin! Europe's ruling class was mightily intimidated by the potential strength of America, and the actual potency of its warfleet, even an America fractured by civil war and teetering on the edge of bankruptcy because of the size of its debt to European money-lenders like Prussia. Napoleon III was a whining, whoring, lying thief! Francis Joseph was a bloated, fratricidal coward! And Oliphant thought no better of sly Palmerston of England and brutal Prince Bismarck of Prussia for standing by like buzzards, waiting to pick off what they could should Napoleon III and Francis Joseph I, arrogant and distrustful allies, either succeed or fail in Mexico.

And Oliphant the American knew that nothing would more please the most dangerous of the lot, England, than to have America split apart permanently, first by the Confederate rebellion and then by the vivisection of the North American continent by imperial flunkies like Maximillian. Palmerston had pontificated, "Britain has no permanent friends or enemies, but only permanent interests!" And again, when liberally disposed and Protestant England was faced with the possibility of Europe's Catholic and reactionary regimes actually constructing a reactionary tyranny in the world, Palmerston had said, "England does not go to war for an idea!"

And so while the buzzards of Europe circled, Mexico writhed. In 1861, a joint military expedition of Britain, France, and Spain had toppled the liberal and reform-minded republican administration of Benito "The Indian" Juarez by landing troops on the Mexican coast under the pretense of only wishing to collect on outstanding debts. In 1862, Britain and Spain had withdrawn from the debt scheme, yet France had remained and reinforced in order to make deliberately humiliating demands upon Mexico City. In 1863, France had ordered its lancers to attack, and they had easily captured Mexico City and driven out the last of the republicans in order to welcome back the exiled aristocrats. Then in 1864, on June 12th, Archduke Ferdinand Maximillian of Austria, the kind-faced, well-intentioned, but imperially ambitious younger brother of Francis Joseph I, had arrived at the old, vermin-ridden Spanish palace in Mexico City in order to be crowned emperor of Mexico. Maximillian had immediately begun writing letters: to Emperor Dom Pedro of Brazil to propose an alliance of Catholic empires; to President Jefferson Davis of the Confederate States of America to propose an alliance of neighbors with the buffer state of Texas between them; and to President Lincoln of the United States of America to propose an alliance of a fledgling power with a beleaguered one.

It was a matter of quiet pride to Oliphant that while Dom Pedro returned Maximillian love notes, and Jefferson Davis returned Maximillian duplicitous felicitations, Abraham Lincoln, the republican stalwart whom Europe decried as a backwoods ape, and as the missing link, refused to open Maximillian's letters. Instead, Lincoln sent private word to Benito Juarez in hiding in north Mexico that truth and democracy would always prevail, and that he should hold out.

Yet tonight Oliphant was forced to consider that Maximillian's plotting was beginning to take hold, for here were his French allies conspiring to woo America to this new and ersatz Empire of Mexico. Juarez was said to be desperately pressed in the Sierra Madre Oriental mountains with fewer than two thousand diehards. No less than Horace Greeley was writing editorials hopeful that Maximillian would first renovate Mexico and then proceed to annex the remainder of Central America to reform the corrupt governments —the mad dream of the Knights of the Golden Circle come round once more! And here, several hundred yards from the White House and the State Department, America's financiers, merchants, and railroaders were flirting with the minions of France and Mexico.

Would the United States be seduced by such naked conduct? Narcissa would have said, "If there's profit in it, the Yankees would sell buttons to hold up the devil's britches!" Worse to contemplate, would even irascible but pragmatic Seward himself lay down with Napoleon III in order to keep him from the Confederacy's skirts? Would even principled but supremely cagey Lincoln read Maximillian's love letters?

Oliphant sighed, and thought, What do I care any longer? Let these warmongers strut their phalluses! Let these gold tarts lift their petticoats! Let them coo of Lincoln I, Emperor of Africa, and Jefferson Davis, King of Cotton Mouths, and Maximillian, the Archdupe! Oliphant the American had soiled himself in their bedcovers long enough, and was done with them! He was furloughed or retired or deserted or forgotten from the Secret Service, or any other kind of bidding! What matter their intrigues? I quit! *"Sauve qui peut,"* the French would have said—Save what you can! Tonight, Oliphant agreed. He was here for other game—to protect his heart and to search out secrets.

Oliphant found Blondel on the second floor by a gilded mirror outside the ballroom. He was standing with his companion, the dapper, portly gentleman whom Oliphant could now reasonably suppose was an English diplomat, perhaps the Jew whom Narcissa had mentioned.

The receiving line wended up the stairs two by two and into the ballroom. Oliphant squeezed through the line and then hung back, to watch Blondel and the Englishman watch the reception. Inside the ballroom, a string quartet played unobtrusively beneath the chatter of the audience that lined the walls while the French ambassador and his chargés d'affaires, two silvery characters with the ease of fathers carving roasts at Sunday dinner, and the Mexicans, two matched conquistadores dressed like peacocks, conducted the music of diplomacy—an operetta, certainly, a whirling overture followed by a grinning first act. And here were the American voices straining in their toneless French salutations, the Yankees as usual both eager and awkward at courtliness. Blondel and the Englishman laughed at the spectacle when yet another pear-shaped American introduced himself by imitating a Continental bow, his legs twitching, and then turned to urge his female companion and two daughters to perform the curtsies that predictably made them wobble and fall two short steps backward.

Oliphant thought, Oh citizens! But then he bricked up his censure. He tried to remain hidden in the crush of the crinolines and tailcoats spilling out of the ballroom, and yet to slide as close to Blondel as possible. He meant to eavesdrop. The roar of the general flattery was too much. He was just puzzling what to do when Blondel and the Englishman jumped across Oliphant's field, within ten feet, to approach the very same beauty in the pale blue gown whom they had admired at Willard's. Oliphant retreated down the narrow hall that connected to the front of the house. Blondel and the Englishman spoke to the beauty with such animation that Oliphant suspected romantic intrigue. She was slanty eyed and tallish, with a thin neck and large bosom, and with curlicued light brown hair. In order to show off a vivid diamond necklace, she wore a low-cut ball gown that incompletely covered her breasts and hid even less when she pushed up against the Englishman to laugh easily.

"Monsieur Oliphant, yes?" Oliphant pivoted in surprise to a diminutive man in the light blue uniform of the French Navy. He was ruddy faced, gray-bearded, round-shouldered, and beaming. He continued, "Max Mille-rand? London, last year? Captain Cook?"

Oliphant relaxed—the Cook enthusiast! "Of course, Max, I'm sorry—Captain?"

"I was not so encumbered then. The buttons should not annoy you. I hope not. I said I was more than I wanted to be."

Oliphant spoke in French. "We parted friends, and meet again the same, Max."

Millerand replied in French. "Excellent, John, excellent." Millerand was ignited in his own language. "We must do for the shortage of wine here-about. To annoint our reunion! Come with me, we have a little private party out of the way. If you are alone?"

Oliphant glanced back at Blondel, shrugged in his most Gallic imitation, and permitted Millerand to escort him to the front of the house.

There was a lengthy corridor hung with oversized oils of heroes and guarded by inconspicuous three-legged tables, each supporting Oriental statues or painted porcelain clocks—more clocks than anyone could want except to hoard, all meticulously showing 9:40 P.M. Millerand opened a door at the end of the corridor that led to a small stairway up to a servant's landing, where he knocked once on another smaller door and then stepped into a quiet, warm, tobacco-rich chamber. Of several men on sofas, one young one popped up, and Millerand waved him at ease. They were all comfortable in their unbuttoned coats and loosened ties, arranged about a low cherry-wood table that was covered with towering green magnum bottles of champagne like a magical glass city. They were also well along a tourist's journey of woozy speculations about the American women in the house. Millerand introduced Oliphant as "my fellow Cook scholar," and the welcome by the others was genuine. Oliphant sat while Millerand identified each of the drinking companions: a shiny nosed junior naval officer; a brooding gentleman with a bald spot and cavalier's boots who looked about Millerand's age; and two young gentlemen appearing to be military men dressed this evening as innocent raconteurs.

"How fantastic to find you in this way," continued Millerand, pouring Oliphant a full glass; he also offered the cigars he had procured just before discovering Oliphant—"First class, rolled by monks!"

The others laughed, and returned to discussing their bashful plots to find romance soon enough.

Millerand spoke to Oliphant. "You are the only American I know in America, I think. We are just arrived in Baltimore, and everything is fantastic, fantastic! Is the magnificent Mrs. Winwood in Washington with you? And the dashing Mr. Royall? What parties they could give, not like this fortune-hunting folly."

Oliphant replied with enough of the facts about Narcissa to provide continuity. Millerand was sincerely grieved at the news of Granby Royall, and roamed at length with his thoughts about the death of a beloved parent. It was the same sort of exaggerated philosophizing that had first attracted Oliphant to Millerand in London and afterward, when they had revealed their mutual fascination with the great navigator, Captain James Cook, R.N., F.R.S. They had pursued their friendship with visits to Cook's birthplace, to the British Museum, and to the Admiralty's record offices. Oliphant had suspected that Millerand the French hobbyist was also a French secret agent, though seemingly not one dealing directly with Confederate matters. Oliphant had also assumed that Millerand knew him as a Confederate agent. Their comaraderie was a happy accident in the sea of spying that flowed from London to Paris, Vienna, Berlin, and St. Petersburg. They had never spoken of their official duties; they had been too busy debating Cook's second voyage to the edge of the Antarctica ice pack, or speculating about Cook's third voyage and why he had defied the Hawaiians who had killed him, or dreaming aloud of the day in the future when they could escape their lives and run away to the South Seas to explore paradise for themselves.

This meeting tonight was the obvious result of their inability, as of yet, to flee their responsibilities. Oliphant did not think this sad. To have such a dream was a joy, and to share it was a pleasure of life. Now Millerand was revealed for what he wanted to quit, a French naval officer on unattached and mysterious service in America; and Oliphant was equally uncovered, as a most inexplicable Southern agent wandering his enemy's camp in evening clothes, and alone.

Millerand poured Oliphant another brimming glass, and the two drank silently for a time, avoiding further talk of death. Oliphant puffed on his pipe, and Millerand twirled his cigar, both listening to the young Frenchmen's stories. One of the naifs, Charles, declared he was ready to meet the enemy and would Bertrand come along? Millerand leaned over to Oliphant. "I hope these seadogs don't worry you with their fantasies of conquest? They have been told that the Puritan woman is tough. I should remind them that like the finest of grapes, what is tough on the outside, so, when peeled, the inside—" Millerand rolled his whole face. The young naval officer, Jongleur, guffawed so hard that he rolled half off the sofa.

Oliphant returned, "I shall say, that the American vineyard is not as various as the French, but from what I know to be true, it is as ready for harvesting in its season as any, and brave, and smooth, and ages well enough to make drunkards of us all."

This gained unanimous applause, even the moody chevalier joining in heartily, and the room of strangers became a clique of celebrants. *"L'amour! La femme! La vie! Le guerre!"* The bliss required more toasts to the young gentlemen, Charles and Bertrand, as they departed for the front.

Soon after, Jongleur went in search of more wine, and Millerand discarded the vocabulary of double entendre to broach the topic of the real war, and Oliphant's jeopardy. He began delicately, less curious than hopeful. "You have not spoken, John, of your family. They are safely out of the South?" Oliphant winced. Millerand added, "Safe, nevertheless, safe?"

"The blockade is impenetrable, Max, and to have them travel overland is also dangerous. They are with good friends, and well stocked." Oliphant decided not to pretend. "I do worry though. I've not seen them since Easter last year."

Millerand said, "How wretched for you—and them."

Ensign Jongleur came in the door. The music outside was raucous; there was male singing from up the stairwell as well. They poured themselves more wine. Oliphant was surprised when the melancholy chevalier, Monsieur Paul Fresque (whom Jongleur inadvertently called "Captain") spoke up, "My sympathies, Monsieur Oliphant. Might I ask where your family resides?"

"They are in Savannah, Georgia, do you know it?"

"Savannah!" burst Jongleur, but then he pulled back and mumbled, "Excuse me, excuse me."

"No, go on, what is it?" said Oliphant. The three Frenchmen stiffened. Oliphant strengthened his voice. "Do you know something about Savannah? Is it yellow fever?"

Millerand said, "Nothing like that. The Ensign is not well informed." Jongleur continued to apologize. Millerand held up his hand, and said, "We have many wild reports. But then, this is politics. I am sure you could hear delirious talk about Mexico City tonight."

Oliphant said, "War is not politics. I don't believe that."

Fresque said, "It is, sir. Life is politics, and so is death. We are each helpless when opinion changes. We must do the bidding of the mob, or at least the mob of the powerful."

Oliphant said, "That might be true in Paris, or Mexico. In my country —in this country—war is murder, and endless killing, and meaningless death, and destruction that will degrade for a hundred years. War is the devil. Civil war is hell on earth."

Millerand said, "My friend is a religious man—a Protestant idealist."

Ensign Jongleur tried timidly, "America is said to be the New Jerusalem."

Oliphant smiled. "That makes me an apostate, and a fool."

Fresque blew out his cheeks. "You are in good company with us. It interests me, though, that you search for meaning in politics. It is like looking, eh?—for a theme in wine." He drank from his glass and kissed the air. "Wine is happiness. Politics is unhappiness. Why not? War is the lusty face of the misery of politics. Exciting ruin! Erotic carnage! There is a symmetry for the age. And we do not need to invite in the priests to tell us when to do which. We march from city to city—drinking and cursing and dying."

Millerand gestured with his cigar. "If John is a pious dreamer, you, Paul, are a sentimentalist. And a soft-headed cynic." Fresque nodded in agreement. Millerand added, "I shall remind you of your neat equation, however, when you are next too gloomy to come out of doors, or we are in Berlin."

Oliphant started, "I'm sorry, I understand your delicacy on my behalf, and—" Oliphant took hold of the table. "If you do know about Savannah, anything at all, it is profoundly important to me that I learn what I can just now. There is an Englishman, a retired brigadier, who has offered to help me get my family out of Savannah in return for my support in his suit to marry my sister-in-law, Mrs. Winwood—" Fresque and Jongleur leaned closer; Millerand sighed. Oliphant continued, "He has also said that he could help get me to Beaufort, in South Carolina, through the blockade, to bury my father-in-law. Now, Beaufort is in Union control, but Savannah—can he do this? I need your counsel, gentlemen."

"This English brigadier?" asked Millerand.

Oliphant named Blondel, and told what he knew of him, including the fact that he was related by marriage to Granby Royall's widow. Perhaps Millerand had met him at the London townhouse? Oliphant admitted that he had followed Blondel here tonight, and also spoke of Blondel's companion, the English diplomat who might be a schoolmate of Blondel's and a Jew in the Foreign Office.

Millerand said, "The white-haired man, then. I saw him, yes, how could I not? You were staring. And they were wooing the comtesse. Oh yes, she's married to one of these old reactionaries we call Bourbonists—though she's an heiress from Boston, Franny Jones or Brown or somesuch. I think I know the Jew too."

Oliphant asserted, "What I need to know, Max, is about Savannah."

Fresque began, "Monsieur Oliphant, Savannah—"

"We don't know, John," interrupted Millerand.

"I was saying," Fresque continued somewhat crankily, "that Savannah is one of any number of cities that the American Army and Navy could destroy as a political gesture. I don't make sense of it. I don't. But I am only a sentimentalist. My emperor says America is mad, and my empress says Lincoln is the missing link. But they are titled republicans, eh? I do wonder."

Ensign Jongleur moved over to whisper to Millerand, the aide to his mentor. Oliphant was rattled now, as well as dizzy with the wine. He could not properly light his pipe, fumbling with the flint piece on his lighter. He waved the lighter at Fresque, and said, "My wife gave me this as a wedding present. That is the head of the Spectre Buck. From a hunting tale in the Carolina Sea Islands. About the ten-point stag that you see the day that you are not hunting for it—and when you return prepared to bag it, it has vanished. I don't know why I am telling you this."

Millerand took Oliphant's arm at the elbow. "John, please, we have—I have—upset you. I shall repair what I can. We shall find General Blondel, and try the American way." He added in English, "Ask him what he intends straight-out."

The international reception had advanced well past the simple receiving of financial propositions. The second story was littered with the clues of peccadilloes that would invite crimes of marriage come the morrow. For tonight, unhappy couples had parted in their separate quests for the grasp of love, and they had separately found devotion with strangers whose accents intimated exotic nakedness. No one believed. But pretense was an exciting altar. In the hallway, there were American redheads on footstools or French blonds on divans, their faces bent to knock against the wet noses of suitors kneeling at their feet; there were also wagging female fingers in the whiskers of chevaliers trying to place their boots in such a way that her thigh would have to press through the crinolines and rub his knee when she attempted flight; and there was shattered glass enough, and shed gloves and fans enough, to suppose that the scratching behind the half-closed doors was not a house cat.

Millerand towed Oliphant through the statuary of seduction. A marble embrace! An alabaster kiss! A stony pout! And the illusion of larger-than-life artwork, and not drunker-than-sense humanity, was helped by the fact that the gaslight had been snuffed. Shadows reigned. Some couples carried their own candles; others found the dark and used it.

"We were more subtle in my day," said Millerand; he started down the stairs and then turned to observe, "But I think to myself, Max, this is your day. And scandal obtains only to sell novels."

The first floor was better lit. The little fathers of several nations were bumping up against each other in another kind of taunting. The older little mothers were petting the buffet tables, where the miscellaneous guests sounded the bottom of their longing with food tossed down like pennies. Millerand sampled a pound cake as they searched. The front vestibule was still jammed with arriving guests. Oliphant squeezed against the doorjamb to follow Millerand outside. Millerand wrapped his arms about himself because of the chill air, and tried, "They might've gone, John?"

Oliphant saw that his hired hack was still on station across F Street, and twenty yards away stood the Englishman's coach; he replied, "No, I'm sure not."

"There is one good possibility, then; come now." Millerand charged back inside, and Oliphant pursued closely. They pushed past the haughtiness of the first floor, and the naughtiness of the second, up the main staircase to the darkened third floor. Here, Oliphant was reminded of a very tired bawdyhouse weathering a gale that blew from within. Doors slammed. Voices demanded. Passions screamed. No gentleman could ignore that husky female noise. Oliphant said, "Good God, Max, is this safe?" Millerand seemed to know his way, yet he shocked Oliphant and himself when he opened the first door. Hot pink air struck them just before they stopped to stare. Several gentlemen were arranged about a lit fireplace. There was a gown on the floor. And before the fire a voluptuous, fair woman, half-naked in her chemise, pirouetted around and around like a figurine in a music box. She had her arms behind her head and her mouth open. One could see right through the cotton, and that was an undeniably shapely dark patch at her loins. Millerand closed the door again. "We can get around the other way."

Their destination was the Ambassador's private library—two cozy, book-lined asymmetrical rooms joined by a cutout archway, with a suit of French armor on guard at midpoint. Millerand and Oliphant entered through a panel that, once closed behind them, concealed the door as part of a mural. The air was orangish yellow from the well-fed fires in both rooms. The height of the two chambers was considerably lowered by the bank of tobacco smoke that hung at eye level, and stung.

Oliphant anticipated more burlesque perversions. He was a moment realizing that these voyeurs were another sort. For the larger of the two rooms was filled with straight-backed men standing or lounging about, the firelight reflecting off their hair or moustaches. Oliphant thought of a casino, especially since the center of attention was a circle of chairs drawn up to a hexagonal table near the Ambassador's dainty desk. There, like gamblers, well-groomed military men hunched forward while tall seconds peered over their shoulders. Because of the dimness, and the single oil lamp on the table, the blue, green, white, red, and gold uniforms in the chairs seemed to be headless and to move as if without bodies in them. Regardless, an excited argument proceeded indifferent to the coming and going of observers.

"Don't instruct me, General, how Grant envies Sherman's talent to flank march!" boomed a voice. "This would be Sherman's last folly! To divide a successful army and to wade into enemy territory without hope of resupply until the sea? It is not a bold risk, it is insane!" The speaker at the table was Germanic, using rudely bent French, and he punctuated his assertion by hitting the table and adding in German, "If such a commander returned to

me, I would march him to the hangman!" This caused deep laughter from
the onlookers. Encouraged, the speaker began an anecdote about Napoleon
at Leipzig in 1813, and thereby betrayed his Prussian identity.

Millerand and Oliphant pushed forward to the suit of armor. There were
several women in the recesses of the room or draped on military shoulders,
and Oliphant thought he saw the slant-eyed comtesse. He did not investigate
further, because he was too attracted by the soldiers' game. Stacks of half
unrolled maps and empty leather mapcases were spread out on the floor or
heaped on the table. At a glance, Oliphant recognized maps of Virginia,
Maryland, Pennsylvania, Kentucky, Tennessee, Alabama, Mississippi,
Georgia, and the Carolinas.

Oliphant whispered a question to Millerand. "A war collegium?"

Millerand replied, "Reviewing the battlefields through the bottom of
their decanters."

Oliphant agreed. He could also see that the war college was well along
into the chronology of the war. The hexagonal table was covered with a
large-scale map of the Eastern seaboard to the Mississippi River. Oliphant
did not know if it was their sense of humor or lack of it that had provided
a box of painted metal soldiers—children's toys—that were spilled around
the oil lamp. There were tiny Hussars with sabers raised, tiny Lancers at the
charge, tiny bear-hatted Imperial Guardsmen on the march.

"General, let us keep to the issue," began a Frenchman across from the
Prussian; he placed two toy Hussars at north-central Georgia, and continued,
"Here is Sherman at Atlanta. Jefferson Davis has two effective armies in the
field. General Hood's here, one hundred miles west of Atlanta"—he placed
a toy Imperial Guardsman at the juncture of Tennessee, Alabama, and
Georgia—"and General Lee's here at Richmond and Petersburg."—he
placed another two Guardsmen in Virginia—"We can discount Lee, because
Grant has him immobile in the trenches."—he placed eight assorted soldiers
in an arc like a crescent moon around southeast Virginia—"So, as my
esteemed English colleague has said, the whole of the Deep South is uncovered before Sherman. If Sherman were to split his army like this"—he took
one Hussar—"and send a corps into Tennessee to protect Nashville and
Chattanooga and the railroads from Hood, then there is nothing to prevent
him from marching the rest of his army south, or east."

The Prussian protested, "Nothing except that his men can't eat when
Hood cuts the supply line behind him." Oliphant saw a flash of jowly white
whiskers; the Prussian was old enough to have been at Waterloo, and indeed

began another anecdote about Napoleon's retreat from Moscow.

The Frenchman waited for the Prussian to finish, and then said, "The question before us, General, is which way will Sherman go, not if!" He was thin-faced with gray hair like feathers about his bald plate, and he showed small white teeth.

Another Germanic voice said, "Why shouldn't Sherman winter in Atlanta? He is fortified, and well provisioned. Why go anywhere?" His French was good; and when he leaned into the light, Oliphant saw what he presumed was the uniform of an Austrian cavalryman, a genuine Hussar, with very striking scars and heavy eyes. He added, "Sherman can send out a corps to block Hood, I agree, that could be reinforced from Nashville. And in the spring—"

An unseen figure contributed, "Sherman cannot wait because Lincoln must win this war before his inauguration in March or suffer bankruptcy. If not, there won't be a nation worth ruling. Only debtors, beggars, possibly anarchists."

The aged Prussian barked in French, "Diplomacy and politics, *wunderbar!* I am to believe that Grant would risk his best fighting force because Lincoln is afraid of his own people? This isn't Mont St. Jean—there won't be futile charges here! They have been fighting for three and a half years. Sloppy soldiers but magnificent fighters, like Sherman's. They lust to fight!"

Oliphant was not surprised to see Blondel's white hair dangle into the light. He had been standing with the comtesse, and now he sat on the arm of a chair to lean to the Prussian; he said, "I must disagree, General. The Americans are sick of the war, and hate it so much they will do the unthinkable and risk the impossible to end it. That is why Sherman shall leave Atlanta—now, immediately, if he hasn't already as the rumors say he has. He has wasted weeks chasing General Hood. Now he will apply himself in force and risk his army for one wild opportunity to destroy the South this coming winter, so that the South cannot fight again in the spring."

"Yes, exactly," said the Frenchman, "the unthinkable, Sir Henry."

"I suggest Mobile." The Austrian picked up the toy Hussars. The junior officers pressed closer to learn what they could of the Habsburg talent for grand marches. The Austrian instructed, "Sherman will block Hood. And abandon Atlanta. And make a long sweep southwest into Alabama, through Montgomery, down the Alabama River to besiege Mobile overland, and link up with Admiral Farragut's fleet. The advantage is that it would draw Hood to battle. And if not, if Hood were able to outfight Sherman's blocking corps, Sherman's main army could still get back to protect Tennessee. The disadvantage for Sherman is that it will be necessary to march over 300 miles in enemy territory. But we have seen Sherman cut free from his supply lines before, for the overland march at Vicksburg last year, and for the march on Atlanta last summer. He knows how to forage. He will eat Alabama."

The Frenchman said, "I applaud the method, General, but not the cuisine." The laughter was raucous.

A junior officer asked, "How do you mean abandon Atlanta?"

The Austrian replied, "He would have to destroy it—the railroads, the warehouses, the defenses, so it is useless to Hood if he were to reinvest it. That is the rumor, yes?"

"Let me suggest another route," began a civilian, silver-maned and long-fingered, looking to be a diplomat, or perhaps a military attaché for the ribbons on his lapel; also, his French was too perfect. Oliphant suspected Danish or Russian. The diplomat moved the toy soldiers from Atlanta to Andersonville, in south-central Georgia, where, he said, Sherman could march to free the starving thousands of prisoners of war in a camp there, a most popular victory for Lincoln. Then, he said, Sherman could march to the coast, either due south to Pensacola, Florida, or east to Fernandina, Florida, both seaports under Union control. He added, "The commandants on the coast could send out wagon trains to meet Sherman's army."

The diplomat's discourse was generally approved by the other diplomats present and generally disliked by the old soldiers. Men challenged each other's common sense in several languages, including Russian. The crowd circulated, refilling glasses, congratulating spokesmen as if they were jousting champions.

Oliphant was sure that Blondel had yet to recognize him. Blondel abruptly turned away from the war collegium and back to the comtesse. Oliphant could now see the portly Englishman standing beside the comtesse at the ambassador's desk. Oliphant alerted Millerand.

Millerand studied the Englishman, and whispered, "Yes, John, I know him. That is Isaac Keats, of the Foreign Office, in a fashion. Your General Blondel has powerful friends."

"He's an agent, then," said Oliphant, "of major influence?"

"We are agents, my friend. Isaac Keats is a spy, and notorious for a winter in St. Petersburg during the Crimean War."

The Prussian was hammering again at the folly of Sherman dividing his army. Sherman must winter at Atlanta, he said, and then destroy Hood in the spring, while Grant reduced Lee. Winning wars, he said, meant killing soldiers, and not roaming from village to village like post riders.

The Frenchman countered that the Union had wasted three years trading the Confederacy man for man on the battlefield. Since the spring, he said, Grant and Lee had slaughtered each other's armies like stockyard butchers, and to what end?—exhaustion in the works, ruinous morale in the ranks.

The Austrian insisted that the capture and holding of cities like Montgomery, Alabama, was crucial, because it demoralized the enemy population.

The diplomats repeatedly stressed that Lincoln did not have the leisure to march his armies over great amounts of territory in the hope the enemy would lose heart, nor did he have time to wait for a spring resolution to the Richmond and Petersburg stalemate: Lincoln must win the war soon, somehow, miraculously.

There was shouting at the suggestion of a so-called miracle. "This is military science!" "This isn't a crusade!" "Why not sue the pope to intervene then?"

"Excuse me, gentlemen," spoke up a new voice in a broad, twangy French, "from what you say, there is only one route for General Sherman." He was a medium-sized, fair man, lightly bearded with a large head, and in dinner dress. Oliphant had thought himself the single American present; however, the man's inflections and manner indicated a polished Yankee. When the Yankee took an empty seat and picked up a toy Imperial Guardsman, Oliphant saw that the man's left cuff was pinned up for a missing hand. The Yankee continued, "General Sherman must march east. That is what you have overlooked. For Charleston, and damn the cost! And at Charleston"—he placed the toy soldier on the Carolina coast—"he must besiege the city and reduce it. He must shatter the foundations of the rebellion. He must feed the Fire-eaters their own fire. And salt the fields, and poison the wells. Charleston, gentlemen, must be sent to hell."

The Frenchman drank from his glass, and said, "I think you are serious."

The Yankee flicked over the two Guardsmen representing Lee. "If Lincoln'd done it three years ago, after we took Port Royal, the devil'd have fine company tonight."

The Prussian roared, the Austrian nodded, the junior officers guffawed while waiting a witty reply. The Yankee tapped the toy soldier he had placed on Charleston the way a man might call attention to a bold bet; he looked around for general approval to his proposal for a coup de main. Instead,

Blondel emerged from the epaulets and braid again and sat on the arm of the Yankee's chair.

"I appreciate your zeal, sir," began Blondel. "We have been debating military strategy, past and future. What you recommend is vengeance."

The Yankee responded, "The meaner and sooner the better for me and millions more."

Blondel said, "Very well, I shall take into account that your temperament could be the Union War Department's as well, and shall amend our guess-work with a compromise of all the proposals." Blondel used his cigar to push the toy Guardsman at Charleston along the coastline and over the Sea Islands to Savannah. Then he took up the Hussars and Lancers at Atlanta. "Sherman has upward of seventy thousand men. He could block Hood with ten thousand, knowing that they would be reinforced from Nashville. Then Sherman could cut free from his supply lines, as he did in Mississippi last year. He could burn Atlanta to deny the enemy a staging area at his rear. He could then march to the sea at Savannah. He could feint to Augusta, but he would most certainly intend to go on to Savannah for resupply from the Department of the South at Hilton Head. En route, he could destroy everything of military use, especially Macon, and the state capital at Mil-ledgeville, and the railroad. His army could live off the stores of the popula-tion, with the summer crop in now. It could be done. It would be terrible, and dangerous for discipline and morale, but yes. His chief obstacles would be the rivers around Savannah. And once at Savannah, he could offer the city sharp terms, either surrender or oblivion, because he wouldn't be able to enjoin a long siege. And once resupplied, he could turn for Charleston, indeed, for the whole of South Carolina, and north, to march up behind Lee at Richmond."

The Prussian said, "The most reckless, most risk-filled plan ever pro-posed."

The Austrian said, "And the most inspired. A masterstroke."

The Frenchman said, "Into the belly of the enemy."

A junior officer asked, "But sir, the demand on Sherman's troops?"

Blondel said, "They are what they call Western men, from their North-west, and very rugged. It is much the same army that Grant had at Shiloh and Vicksburg. Look at the facts. Grant fought at Shiloh with Sherman, Thomas, and Sheridan, and gunboats up from Farragut's fleet at New Or-leans. Now, two and a half years later, the same men are on hand. Grant and Sheridan at Virginia. Sherman and Thomas at Atlanta. Farragut ruling the

Gulf. And while Grant struggles to make the Army of the Potomac and Army of the James fight, Sherman has men who are as hard and— They fight like the Southerners."

Another junior officer said, "I've seen it, at Atlanta. It was not human." Another officer said, "I was at the Wilderness, and Spotsylvania Courthouse, and I couldn't believe—I couldn't—"

Blondel continued to the Yankee, "You would have your revenge, sir. Sherman would have his victory for all time. And Lincoln would have his Union restored at a great cost. And the devil, I suppose, would have his usual due. I do not overlook the fact that Georgia and South Carolina are undefended civilian populations. This is not the kind of war we in this company have been trained to fight. It is awful to contemplate what Sherman's men might do. And if you do mean what you say about Charleston, I suppose you mean the same for Savannah."

"I mean it, damn right!" said the Yankee in English. "The Rebs started this war. Now we're to finish it!" He corrected his posture, and spoke jocularly, "Of course, they could avoid it if they'd surrender while they still have something to eat."

Oliphant leaped forward and was speaking all of a sudden, too loudly and with too much anguish for this debate. "What kind of a man are you?" Oliphant reached the table. "Those are mothers and babies! Those are pensioners and invalided cripples and helpless Negroes and boys under 14 because the rest are at the front! Sherman has tens of thousands of veterans who only know killing and plundering! That isn't a battle! It's the devil's work! You cruel, cruel man—shame on you!"

Blondel was the first to recover from Oliphant's assault; his surprise showed on his face, but he spoke evenly. "I only—please, Sherman could be sleeping fitfully at Atlanta tonight. This was only a re-creation for old campaigners. Please, I'm sorry."

Oliphant studied Blondel for any condescension in his attitude; he found only embarrassment. It was a moment of nakedness between them, and Oliphant felt his embarrassment too.

The Yankee addressed Oliphant. "I didn't get to tell you what kind of man I am, there, cousin. I'm a loyal man. I left part of me at Rappahannock Station to prove it. So what's your stake in this? You look like one of these foreign strutters, but you sound the damned Reb."

"Mr. Oliphant's family is in Savannah," explained Blondel in French; then he spoke to Oliphant in English, "And I beg your forgiveness, John, for myself and for all of us, for speaking so loosely at your expense. I didn't know you were here, but that isn't an excuse. I have been an idiot, John, and I'm sorry."

The Prussian arose and spoke to Oliphant. *"Mein Herr, vergeben Sie mich, bitte."* The Frenchman and the Austrian added their apologies gently and earnestly.

Oliphant felt Millerand's hand on his shoulder; Millerand said, "I apologize too, John, that you should have had to learn about Savannah like this."

Oliphant felt the tears of his upset. He had experienced a momentary rage, and he pushed it back down. He swallowed before beginning again to Blondel. "Are you sure it's to be Savannah?

Blondel hesitated, sagging a little, and then he replied, "It's just a theory, John."

Oliphant nodded, and spoke to them all. "Thank you, gentlemen, I forget myself. I shouldn't have— Thank you for your sympathy."

Blondel returned, "It is the least we can do. The least I can do. And we must do more, much more."

THURSDAY, NOVEMBER 17, FRIDAY, NOVEMBER 18, AND SATURDAY AFTERNOON, NOVEMBER 19

The secrecy of Major-General Sherman's whereabouts and intentions deepened, like a spell cast over Washington City that promised renaissance even as it afflicted. And no one was more spellbound than John Oliphant.

Oliphant quit sleep Wednesday night for lying next to Narcissa and listening to her breathing. He had chosen to withhold from her the episode at the French embassy, and had even offered her a made-up version of his dinner conversation with Blondel. It was not like him to deny Narcissa intelligence, and it felt absurd to deceive her when there was so much trouble, but then, he reasoned, what good would it have done to frighten her too? Yet he also knew that he could not keep the bad news from her for long.

He must find a solution! Here he had assumed that Camellia was safe and Narcissa was in jeopardy. And now! Was Atlanta destroyed? What might

Sherman do to Savannah? There must be a solution! And so, after passing Thursday morning staring into the flames in the parlor fire, he launched himself in search of a patchwork remedy. For he determined that he would use whatever was at hand, including his newfound European allies, both English and French.

On Thursday afternoon, Oliphant returned to the French embassy with Captains Millerand and Fresque. The plan was for Millerand and Fresque to interview the French ambassador in order to promote a scheme to list Oliphant's family in Savannah as French national dependents. The hope was that the Oliphants and their relatives would then be eligible for the lists of French citizens in the South who were slated for evacuation by French warships permitted through the blockade. Such an arrangement had suited the United States and France in October at Charleston, and there was reason to believe that a mass panic in Georgia or South Carolina could move Seward to oblige Napoleon III's ambassador again.

For it was not true, as Oliphant learned, that Lincoln and Seward were uniformly hostile to Napoleon III. They were playing a difficult game expertly—hinting that they might recognize Maximillian's crown in Mexico if and only if Napoleon III continued to refuse to recognize the Confederacy. Millerand explained to Oliphant, "Lincoln sends congratulations to the Emperor on the birth of a nephew one day, and Seward recognizes a Juarezistan consul at Philadelphia the next day. Believe me, John, it is the economy of whores—promising a gift that is long since given away, and then mentioning a fee."

Oliphant replied somberly, "Mr. Benjamin does no less in Richmond, and without the fee."

Fresque joked, "Ah, then he misunderstands the French—we like to pay for our pleasure. A priceless treasure is too much to herself, and she resents ownership."

Millerand continued with the jest. "In comparison, your Puritan women, John, bargain with what they would never sell. And they bargain for power."

Oliphant played along. "You would have me believe that America is some grand Mrs. Stowe, or Mary Lincoln."

And their laughter helped Oliphant through the long wait at the embassy, which concluded with the chargé d'affaires coming down to the reception room and announcing to Oliphant with convivial Gallic ambiguity, "We shall definitely look into your application when it becomes appropriate."

Thursday evening, Oliphant's English allies were less amusing than Millerand and Fresque, yet they advanced much more in terms of information and
action, and genially. Oliphant again dined with the wholeheartedly fraternal
Blondel, but this time they were joined by the British Secret Service agent
Isaac Keats. They withdrew from Willard's to the privacy of the club dining
room at the British embassy, also on F Street, a house not unlike the French
legation's with the exception of the massive furniture and a silence rivaling
the tombs of Egypt at twilight—heat-popping fireplaces and the low buzz
of distant, noncorporeal whispers.

At the table, while finishing a bottle of wine and sampling the soup, Keats
listened to Blondel's explanation of Oliphant's problem with a kind, blank
face. Keats was a cannily attractive man, wide-girthed and wiry-haired, with
almost furry eyebrows and deep, heavily lidded eyes—in all, features that
were overdrawn and potent. He smiled carefully, and spoke delicately at first
in such a way that one understood he was used to being closely attended.
The twirled moustache was not his only vanity. He had a luxurious, baritone
voice.

"I do understand, Mr. Oliphant, that Sir Henry has the highest regard for
you and your family," said Keats, "and my friendship with Sir Henry is such
that I offer you my services without reservation. If, Mr. Oliphant. If you
are frank with me just now, at the birth of our acquaintance, with regard
to your work."

Oliphant smiled, and replied with the part of the truth he had known he
would have to exchange. He recounted matter-of-factly his service for Judah
Benjamin, and also Narcissa's service. Blondel did not comment. Keats then
asked a few question of clarification, chiefly about the Confederate purchase
and secret fitting-out of warships at the Laird Brothers' shipyards at Birken-
head, opposite Liverpool on the Mersey River. Oliphant was not coy,
because most of the intelligence about the blockade runners was out-of-date
and now the stuff of legend, especially the high drama surrounding the escape
of the C.S.S. *Alabama* from the Laird yards before the Royal Navy could
impound her. Keats did probe pointedly for the exact names involved in the
debacle of the Laird rams, the two sophisticated steam-driven ironclad
warships fitted with seven-foot-long underwater spikes to ram wooden ships
that the Confederate agents had tried to sneak out of England late the year
before. Still, Oliphant had the impression that he was not telling Keats
anything he did not already know. The dialogue seemed more Keats's way
of testing Oliphant's sincerity to deal.

Finally, Keats said, "Then, we have an understanding. And I thank you. I also say that this matter is even more urgent than Sir Henry, last night in his dramatic cloth, presented it. Depend on it, Mr. Oliphant, your family is in profound danger."

Oliphant said, "I do understand that, Mr. Keats. Since last night—I have been thinking about what is most important to me. I have always tried to help others. Now—this might sound foolish—I am prepared to help myself, regardless of the risk and—" Oliphant tried a smile. "I should say that I am ready to be reckless."

Keats spoke gently, "We really should dine first. One needs one's supper. And then we can talk of our triangular persuasion. The soldier without his sword, and adventurous. The gentleman without his country, and rash. And the Jew without his hunger, and curious." They laughed, and Keats added, "Shall we sample the rack of lamb?"

Keats did not pause in his discourse even through dinner, however. He possessed a vast working knowledge of Washington, and the sort of specifics of Union war plans that indicated that his sources could make every Cabinet member's desk an open drawer. He did avoid speculations about Sherman, though he permitted a slip that Oliphant recognized was intentional—he named General George Thomas as Hood's adversary in Tennessee. This implied that Sherman had indeed dispatched a corps to block Hood and that Sherman was elsewhere with the main body of his army.

Keats cared little for military matters, though; he spoke of battlefields as a man might speak of a modern and unusual performance of a classical play —diverting, but nothing more. Keats instead concentrated on tales of the executive and congressional branches of the United States government, and their chaotic, paradoxical war aims. He had a quick opinion of every important personage: Welles at Navy was a weakling; Stanton at War was "consumed by crusading"; Fessenden, the new secretary of the treasury, had inherited "a nation in receivership" and was incoherent. Keats regarded Seward as "a genius with dirty fingernails—the product of a political system that exceeds its parts!" and as "the slyest international statesman after Prince Metternich of Austria—Seward is a contemplative cock, who fights best beak to beak." Keats thought Charles Sumner, the Massachusetts Radical Republican senator and intimate of the Lincolns, "a dangerous saint."

All this elevated quipping had a direction, and Keats came to it in his time. He compared America and its government to a feuding family. And, like a family, it had circles within circles, swirling around the surrounded paterfamilias, whose strength or lack of it affected all the cousins and in-laws as well as the immediate mate and offspring. Also, the behavior of even the most distant relative, say a great-niece's husband, could influence the head of the family. Abraham Lincoln was the father of fathers then, whom Keats said was a "rude-born Westerner, a man suited to shopkeeping and meticulously honest change-making." Nevertheless, while Lincoln did dictate, he could also be moved by the most weak-voiced entreaties. One did not have to shout, or threaten, or show gold. Lincoln really did think of himself as a neighborhood storyteller and available ear; and so Lincoln really did hear dearest the sobbing of the meekest. Keats said, "He is a man who believes in his own parables, and who prefers children to anything—just does."

Importantly, Keats said, Lincoln was not an elevated king. He was stronger than a monarch on one hand, because his tenure was on the common people's level, was poetically fleeting, and was generally confirmed by popular ballot as extraordinary, deserving, and virtuous at some point in near time. More, Lincoln the president was so mortal as to engage the patriotic support of even his adversaries: today he ruled and tomorrow he could be gone. Lincoln was weaker than a monarch on the other hand, because he had to attend to every dark thought: each success was the people's or the government's; each failure was Lincoln's.

Oliphant interrupted, "I have heard that he is very troubled."

"You underestimate by several tens of degrees," said Keats. They had their coffee now, and had gone into the clubroom to smoke by the fire. "I should say that President Lincoln is withering. He is isolated beyond my sense of human endurance. It is grave, and concerns my government daily, and in the extreme."

Keats then stunned Oliphant by describing in detail a Cabinet meeting at the White House the week before, November 11. It had been attended by Lincoln, Seward, Stanton, Fessenden, Usher, Dennison, and the President's private secretary, John Hay. Keats meant to illustrate Lincoln's long-standing loneliness and defeatism, yet he did more—Oliphant heard in the anecdote a chief executive become desperate, and deathy. At the meeting, Lincoln asked John Hay to open a sealed presidential memorandum that he had ordered each of the Cabinet officers to sign on August 23, 1864, without benefit of being able to read what they were endorsing. The memorandum read, "This morning, as for some days past, it seems exceedingly probable that this Administration will not be reelected. Then it will be my duty to so cooperate with the President-Elect, as to save the Union between the

Election and the Inauguration; as he will have secured his election on such ground that he cannot possibly save it afterwards."

Keats recited from memory; he added, "Seward was furious with Lincoln for having tricked him into signing such a document. He told Lincoln that McClellan, if he'd been elected, would have responded, 'Yes, yes,' and then would have stalled and done nothing. And the Cabinet would have compromised itself for nothing, for all time. Lincoln was sympathetic, but blunt. He told Seward, 'At least I should have done my duty and have stood clear before my own conscience . . .' Seward later told Stanton, 'His conscience and my country!' Stanton dug at Seward in return, 'Your country, my oath!' "

Oliphant excitedly interrupted Keats. "I had no notion. August 23rd? That was before the Democratic Convention! That means Lincoln was conceding before he had an opponent! I thought the Election was a pantomime! McClellan was two-faced and cloddish. But this means Lincoln was ruined in August! He meant to quit!"

Keats said, "At least, dealing with McClellan, he would have compromised his ambition to emancipate the slaves and restore the Union. The effect would have been the same as quitting. If McClellan had won, there would have been a ceasefire November 9th. By tonight—there would have been chaos."

Oliphant sprang to the mantelpiece. "The war would have been over!"

"We do not have to suppose, Mr. Oliphant," said Keats. "That memorandum has great significance even with the present result. First, Lincoln was so unsure of his own Cabinet that he felt it necessary to trick them to endorse what they surely would have rejected if informed of. Second, Lincoln was willing to negotiate with the Confederacy in distress, *as president.* He believes himself bound to find peace regardless. He is reelected now, but is still of a peaceful temperament. He isn't the tyrant or blood avenger the papers, and your Mr. Davis, make him. He is the beleaguered, tormented father. Ready to help. Eager to repair. Quick for peace, and to show mercy. If Mr. Davis were to ask genuinely—let that thought go."

Oliphant said, "Stanton would never! Sumner would lead a revolt!"

"There is that possibility," said Keats. "The fool's gold fortunes of war did save Lincoln's Administration. Farragut, Sherman, and Sheridan were the Republican platform in the end. And yet for all that, Mr. Oliphant, and for all the ludicrous factionalism in the Democratic party, the Republicans could only persuade just over half the electorate. It was a sweeping victory in your

Electoral College—by states—but then, only the Northern states participated. It was no popular triumph. And the people were heard. And they cried for peace. Now, Lincoln must preside. And he must do so beholden to the manner he retained his authority, and yet attendant to those cries."

Oliphant whispered, "Sherman, it's always Sherman now, isn't it?"

"Excuse me?" said Keats. "No, no, don't mistake the military for the government. To win a battle, or even a war, is not to rule a nation. Do you agree, Henry?"

Blondel smiled. "From what I know, the beaten soldier is the better man."

Keats said, "Yes, my friend, yes." The three of them paused, each in his own reflection. Keats stood up at the mantel with Oliphant. "I have another irony for you, Mr. Oliphant, and one that must guide you. In the United States government, two factions obtain tonight. You have only identified one—the vengeance clique. The other faction is pacific, and sickened by the slaughter and depredation. Lincoln leads it. Yes, Abraham Lincoln leads a faction that also has included McClellan, the two wicked Seymours, and the bitter Vallandigham. It is so strange a fact that it must be true. Lincoln is president because he is the premier peace-seeker of the war party. And tonight, Lincoln might be the only member of the peace-seekers. He cannot rely upon anyone, perhaps not even his own wife, since she entertains Sumner routinely. And Sumner uses her to influence Lincoln with his peculiar and self-righteous appetite—Sumner's *caneized* plans for revenge."

Blondel commented, "Now I see why we're fretful for Lincoln."

Keats nodded. "Lincoln is alone, truly alone, and the lone man for peace, tonight. His health, his mental faculties, his sleeplessness, his hallucinations —I pity him. We all should. Yet paramount, he is the answer to many problems. To yours, Mr. Oliphant."

"How can that be?" asked Oliphant. "You don't pretend he isn't responsible for Sherman, wherever Sherman is. And I can guess. I know!"

Keats held up his hands, palms out. "I have told you. Lincoln must accommodate his tenure to the forces that reelected him. It can be worse yet. Without Lincoln, God knows what Seward, Stanton, Sumner, and Washburne, all of them and their bone-rattling fury, might try. The Radical Republicans want the South made into a desert. I am sincere. Lincoln—weak and weaker each day—is holding this weary nation together. Such as it is. Crude as he is. Buffoon in their eyes. Lincoln stands up. The commonest commoner who, destiny's wit, has become the father almighty. Until he isn't."

Oliphant turned to stare at Keats, and spoke firmly. "I must ask, what is England's ambition then?"

"I wouldn't acknowledge that question tomorrow," said Keats. "Here, tonight, in this little piece of England, I shall paraphrase my prime minister. England has neither fast friends nor foes, only fast interests. My government would not be helped by an America become destitute."

Oliphant also paraphrased. "God save America, and let it muddle through."

Blondel nodded in sympathy and looked to Keats.

Keats looked to Oliphant. "Do you hear my recommendation?"

"Lincoln," said Oliphant. "Narcissa and I must go to Lincoln, and plead for mercy."

With Oliphant's goal established—an audience with Lincoln—the next step was to convene all his allies in order to formulate a plan of approach. But first Oliphant knew that he had to catch Narcissa up on the affair, and he had to do so as calmly and candidly as possible.

He returned to Georgetown Thursday evening to find Narcissa awaiting him at the door. He could see that she had intuited that there was something brewing, and with a very few sentences he communicated the facts and gravity of the situation. She only blanched once; she said, "Sherman marching on Savannah?"

Oliphant replied, "That is Henry Blondel's thinking, and it seems well informed."

Narcissa closed her eyes a moment and stopped breathing; she regained herself when she said, "I shall never forgive them. And I do not want to argue about it further."

Oliphant took her cold hands with his cold hands, and said, "Narcissa, Narcissa, we must look to our own now."

Narcissa pulled away and busied herself putting Oliphant's formal cape-coat in the closet. When she turned back, she said, "We shall have them all here tomorrow night for dinner, because we need to plan."

Oliphant tried, "I was thinking we could secure a room at Willard's. A neutral site might be—"

Narcissa closed the discussion. "Don't be foolish, John."

Oliphant winced, but did not comment.

And so, Friday morning before breakfast, Noah and Michael were dispatched to deliver invitations to dinner at Louisa Granby Turning's home in Georgetown that evening.

Past dark, Blondel was the first to arrive, on horseback. He was followed closely by the British embassy coach bearing Isaac Keats and his lady companion, the comtesse, who, as simply Franny Wooster of Boston, was soon revealed as not only the eldest child of a prominent Boston foundry owner, but also the goddaughter of Senator Charles Sumner of Massachusetts himself, the reigning silver-maned Elijah of the Senate, Radical Republicanism, and Lincoln's inner circle. Franny Wooster was quick to disarm any apprehension about herself, however, when she joked about Sumner, "Oh, he likes pretty things just like any other man."

Soon after, Ensign Jongleur arrived at the door to convey the regrets of Captains Millerand and Fresque. They had been called to duty that afternoon, and were even then en route to Mexico. Jongleur had delayed behind with the express obligation to deliver to Oliphant Max Millerand's farewell note. It read: "I shall pray for you, my dear friend. And we shall all meet again in the Sandwich Islands, to ascend the volcanoes at Hawaii. And if you reach Mauna Loa first, remember me there. MM."

Narcissa and Maum Rosemary supervised the fete with an overwhelming warmth and vivacity. And yet Oliphant experienced a disturbing downturning. Narcissa's mood, and indeed the gay spirit of the party itself, was in such contrast to the mortuary atmosphere of the day, the facts, and the Mason-Coxe-Turning house that Oliphant found himself withdrawing emotionally from Narcissa and the others.

Oliphant's mysterious retreat was not of a sudden. He had felt it begin the night before the moment Narcissa had seemed to dismiss his counsel and concern with, "Don't be foolish, John." As a result, while Narcissa had raced away to confer with Maum Rosemary on her choice of chicken gumbo for the meal, Oliphant had sat silent at the parlor fire; and while Maum Rosemary had stayed up half the night rehabilitating the Turning silverware, Oliphant had lain in bed and had been so wrenched by the clinking sounds from downstairs that he had covered his ears; and while Narcissa had been up early Friday morning to shop, Oliphant had left the house altogether for a walk down by the Potomac; and, when it had come time to dress for dinner, while Narcissa had dashed through the house checking the smallest preparations, so that she had to rush her own toilet and to cry out for Maum Rosemary's assistance with her gown and hair, Oliphant had stood beneath the great chestnut in the rear garden and watched the leaves fall and the darkness descend.

And now, as the guests assembled, Oliphant was aware that there was further deterioration of his mood. He sat in the north-side parlor and watched Narcissa entertain her guests as a man might stare at a surprise reminder of his youth. He puffed on his pipe, and kept covering his mouth for no sensible reason. Why was he so lethargic? What could be the cause of this dizzying sense of frustration?

Then, at a moment of loud laughter in the room, Oliphant solved his puzzle. This was a simple child's pout. All the night before and all day, he had been pouting. But why? He thought a moment, and guessed. He had assumed that it would be Narcissa who would resent this makeshift solution to their problems, that it would be Narcissa who would sink in frustration for their bad luck. Instead, she seemed willing to embrace every possible action, no matter how improbable, as if she were awakening from a long drugged sleep to find herself able to fly. Where only days before Narcissa had been grief-stricken and ready to quit, tonight she seemed transformed into an exuberant voyager.

Now it was Oliphant—the polite, even-tempered, all-knowing Oliphant —who was acting the defeatist, and who heard himself snorting at kind remarks, and who saw himself being curt to the fraternal Blondel and cool to the solicitous Franny Wooster. And worse than being impolite, Oliphant knew that he was being indifferent to his own supposed best interests. For how could his gloominess help anything? How could his poor behavior help Camellia and three daughters he had never been much of a father to? And yet, the more Narcissa swooped and cooed at her party, the more Oliphant sank back and sighed. And why?

Narcissa's excitement continued through the meal and filled Mrs. Turning's long, candle-lit dining room. The mirrors that flanked the looming sideboard threw the diners' faces about the room in such a way so that Narcissa, at the table's head, could study her guests from several sides: Keats and Franny Wooster at her left hand, Blondel and Oliphant at her right hand. Narcissa used her intelligence, reigning over the conversation, holding the guests together with questions and glances. Keats, once again, did much of the speechifying. But there was as much humor as sober detail, and Blondel and the comtesse would on occasion applaud some quip of Keats's or Narcissa's.

For Narcissa was equal to Keats's wit and perspicacity, and almost did as much speculating as he. She possessed a knowledge of Washington and the

United States government that was twenty-five years out of date but rich. She grasped the military situation in Georgia and Virginia completely, so that she was able to outline a schedule that would place Sherman at Savannah before the New Year, while Grant thrashed uselessly at Richmond and Petersburg. She understood Keats's characterization of Lincoln intuitively; and she welcomed the proposal that Lincoln would more be influenced by honesty and charm than he would be by connivance or resistance.

What did Narcissa propose? How did she think she could approach Lincoln to ask to bury her father in Beaufort and to save her family in Savannah? Narcissa the secret agent now presented herself as Mrs. Winwood the Peace Commissioner. She drafted in the air her speech to Lincoln, and her suits to Sumner and Seward, if it came to that. She explained in detail how she would accomplish with ad hoc diplomacy what all the armies and all the intrigue had failed to achieve. For all to see, Narcissa was magnificently animated in her midnight-blue gown, a woman reborn from bereaved supplicant to buoyant emissary. For she was not only prepared to secure her own family, she was also ambitious to plead the case for an armistice in order to protect her beloved South from complete destruction. Mrs. Winwood the peace commissioner intended to approach Lincoln, and then, having won Lincoln's support, she intended to continue. There was mention of Richmond. There was talk of the persuasion of Jefferson Davis.

Blondel sat at Narcissa's arm in rapture at her performance. He leaped to her chair whenever she rose during the meal, lavished compliments on her ideas despite her redundancies and excesses, and glowed when she asked him for his arm to lead the guests to the parlor for coffee and sweets. It was the conduct of a man so dizzy with love that he was past caring how he appeared. If Narcissa had asked him to leave that night for Savannah, he would have tried, certainly he would have done. His heart was open, and it made him young. His heart was presented, and it made Narcissa bold.

Narcissa's boldness frightened Oliphant. He feared that her optimism was contrived—that she was not ascending to these schemes but declining to these fantasies. It was not her nature to promise and not to deliver, or to hope for the impossible. Oliphant had known her as practical, straightforward, cautious, hard-working, and very realistic. Now, she seemed otherwise—perhaps disoriented by the miasma that was spreading throughout the country as the war moved into increasingly deranged violence. Was she being true to her heart? Was she being false to her history?

And yet, how could he hope to know such things when he could not even be sure that it was Narcissa's illusions that frightened him the most. Might there not be another, darker cause of his gloom—the fundamental reason he was pouting?

Jealousy was certainly available, because of Blondel. And guilt was always available, because of his adultery. Oliphant asked himself, What do I feel hardest and deepest of all just now? Oliphant thought, I am angry. Oliphant realized, I am nearly in a rage.

Narcissa must have seen this or something similar, because afterward, the guests gone before 11 P.M. in order to rest for the contest planned the next day at the President's House, she surprised Oliphant by suddenly appearing in the north-side parlor, and sitting next to him on the sofa before the fire.

"It went well, don't you think?" she began. "Issac Keats is what you said, oh my! A genuine English spy! And the comtesse! They must be lovers. I don't believe that story about the Adamses asking him to look after her. And Max, what a lovely man to have sent his ensign with the note. He is your dear friend, I think, and we shall pray for him too. Volcanoes! How I would like to go to the Sandwich Islands with you! And Henry thinks so much of you too, John. He told me so in the gentlest way. He envies you, he said, and he worries for you, and your health. I told him you're as fit as ever. You are, aren't you, John? You are all right?"

"I don't know what is bothering me," Oliphant tried. "Yes, I'm fit. And Max is first-rate."

"What is it, darling? No, tell me. Is it Henry?"

Oliphant shrugged. "Nothing like that. It's tomorrow, I suppose."

"John, I am aware of Henry's behavior, and if you ask me, which you haven't, I think he's assuming, no, presuming much more than he has any right to. I've told him so. I have."

"Sir Henry—Henry—I like him, Narcissa, I do. It might be easier for me if I didn't. He's a good man, and a true man. I haven't said, about the other night—what it was that he wanted to discuss at dinner."

Narcissa leaned closer. "You said it was about Papa."

"Partly. It was about you, too. He was asking me about you, as the man of the family. The last man. About you."

"And what did you tell him?"

"What could I tell him? He wants—"

Narcissa interrupted abruptly. "Stop this. You should have told me. So that's why you were watching us. You should have told me. Why have you started keeping things from me? Really, you should have said that's why he wanted to dine with you."

"Well, now you know. What do you make of it? Of his offer?"

"And what would you have me say? That he's ambitious? That he's a troubled man, and wants much? To me, what we want is much more important. Really, John, we have the lives of our family to worry about. What would it serve to fret for Henry's notions—good-hearted or selfish?"

"You think he hasn't understood that? He has offered to help without conditions. He wants more than simply marriage. He wants to help us. He has arranged this all, you know—Keats and the comtesse and I can't guess what else tomorrow. He's the most competent sort of man. Like I used to be. I've seen him—at Willard's the other night. And at the French embassy. The way they all listened to him. He's commanding, and, well, true."

"And are you pressing his suit?"

"Narcissa, it's more serious than that. He has offered to help the whole family, to relocate us, to sponsor us, to rescue us—"

"Let him put all England at my feet! What I want is Papa at rest, and Cammie and Laura and our babies, and Sally and Lizzie and their babies— are you hearing me now? Our family, yours and mine, I want them safe. That is what is before us, to try and to do. Henry's world is as far away as London, farther. Are you there, John? John?"

"Yes, Narcissa, I am here, I'm listening."

Narcissa leaned to kiss Oliphant on the bridge of his nose. "I also want you to come up with me. You can't sit here and fret alone, and it is so damp down here, and I don't want to sit with you when we can get into bed and fret together warm and close. Do come up with me. We have much to review. And please don't say that you're off for another dreary walk. I need you to talk with me. I'm stirred up, and—John?"

Oliphant looked at her, but he truly was not listening. He was thinking how he might tell her that he was afraid and angry and beaten and in despair. He was thinking how he could tell her all at once that the war had been a catastrophe, just as he had known it would be, and that the South of her youth was gone forever, and that whatever their future might be it could never be happy, and that he did not want to be the person that he was, and that he was so frustrated he felt like bursting because he could not help her, or Camellia, or anyone, most especially himself. Oh, what did he want to tell her most?! That they were finished! That she must go on without him!

That he was useless, and a failure! That he felt closed in upon by that invisible hand, and that at any moment it might flick him into nothingness!

And what did he say? He said the most difficult thing of all; he said, "Narcissa, it's that I don't believe anymore."

"What do you mean? Believe what?" She took his hands, and pressed them together, and took them up to her mouth and kissed them, again and again, and said, "I love you, John Oliphant."

"I love you, Narcissa."

"You won't leave me? You will stay with me tonight, and tomorrow, and forever? I need you. I don't know what is ahead for us. But I do know what has happened, and that without you, dear, wonderful, sweet, kind, true, true man, I can't think. Tomorrow is for us. You must believe that. Tomorrow, oh my dear, what a dust we shall make!"

She folded herself against his breast, and held on. "Say yes, John, say yes."

The telegram from Baltimore was delivered about noon, Saturday. Everyone was dressing for the adventure, and so Oliphant was able to get down to the front door first. When he saw the telegram was addressed to him, he did not move to open it. Whatever was inside, it could wait an hour or two. Also, Maum Rosemary was upon him immediately to ask after the bell, and then Narcissa called down. Oliphant slipped the wire into his inside breast pocket, and then he went back up to Narcissa. He did not tell her the truth.

Saturday afternoon, November 19, was cool and bright, with vast cloud banks in a single plane that seemed to heap upon themselves to form a gray and purple marble-like sky—slabs here or shattered pieces there, all with creamy edges. Oliphant had hired a large barouche because Maum Rosemary and the adolescents were coming along. Oliphant sat up on the driver's seat with Noah. Michael had asked to be excused; in fact, Michael had communicated that he was not attending in such a way as to have upset Noah and Maum Rosemary—"Divil's got him," Maum Rosemary had said. Fortunately, Jimmie's full-bodied jubilation carried the party's spirits down Pennsylvania Avenue. Despite the cool weather, they put the carriage top halfway down so that Oliphant and Noah could help with the children's curiosity. For Jimmie was a continual series of questions during the drive: "How big's President Lincoln?" "He can split rails like dey say, one swing?" "Like me, he's born in a log cabin like me?"

Narcissa answered yes to everything, while Oliphant provided the details.

Noah whispered to Oliphant, "Dere weren't no sleep fer dat boy las' night, an' won' be dis'un."

When Jimmie chanced upon asking after the meaning of "emancipation," Narcissa addressed this more difficult subject delicately. "Being free is for grown-ups, Jimmie. You don't want to leave your grandma, do you?"

Jimmie said, "If we're free, we can all go home together, can't we?"

Narcissa replied, "Yes, dear."

At West Seventeenth Street, where Pennsylvania Avenue was interrupted by the carefully wooded rectangle of the executive branch, Oliphant expanded his introductions for the adolescents. He pointed out the drab Navy Department and the auxiliary old War Department as well as the new-built and monolithic brick War Department along West Seventeenth. He was about to identify the ranks of the Army and Navy officers on the walkways when he stopped himself. Narcissa was frowning, and kept her eyes fixed on the White House in the near distance. Oliphant recognized that this was the same superstitious conduct of their five days of calling at the Navy Department: She had refused to look, and had gone inside blindly—her eyes actually shut—on Oliphant's arm. Now, at least, her eyes were open, but Oliphant was forced to wonder about her resolve. This was such a delicate plot, and if she could not face the innocuous— He had argued with her about this point. She had declared that the President's House was different. She had claimed she knew it better than Mrs. Lincoln did—a result of all of her frolicking there at dances when she was 15. Still, Oliphant thought, she should look at Stanton's fortress, just once. When Jimmie asked Narcissa about ironclad ships, Narcissa cut him off. Oliphant turned back around to criticize her. And she cut him off too. "Never you mind that, just go on ahead, and Noah, don't heed the jam-up."

Noah slowed the barouche as they neared the White House's iron gateway. The traffic in and out was constant, and the semicircular drive was filled with expensive-looking landaus, barouches, and coaches. The president's Saturday afternoon levee looked well under way at past 2 P.M. It also appeared that half of official Washington had decided to attend what was, after all, a second-class affair in comparison to the formal Tuesday evening levees.

Oliphant passed the time while Noah negotiated the drive by talking to the children. Jinna wanted to know about the statue that stood in the small grassy oval before the White House. Oliphant explained, "That's Tom Jefferson, the author of the Declaration of Independence and a co-author of—

You see that thing in his hand? That's meant to be the Constitution." Jinna and Nell both said they thought Jefferson's statue looked moldy. Oliphant allowed that bronze still wore better than flesh, and that the real Mr. Jefferson would now be over a hundred and ten or twenty years old. Jimmie and Cato pointed to the impressive and sparkling bronze statue behind them, across the road in Lafayette Park. Oliphant explained that that was Andrew Jackson, a famous president of the United States who was born a poor boy in South Carolina like Jimmie and Cato, and who rose to fight Indians and John C. Calhoun, and to win. Oliphant laughed at their amazement. "See how he waves his hat? That's because he's happy to be in heaven." The girls squealed when Oliphant began the tale of why Jackson had been called "Old Hickory."

"He was whupped?" burst Jimmie.

The plan they had worked out the night before called for Narcissa to arrive late, well after Keats and Blondel were to have approached Mrs. Lincoln and to have proffered a gift—a peace offering. The comtesse was also to have long since taken position with her godfather, Senator Sumner, and to have sown the rumor that an extraordinary peace commissioner was expected today at the levee. Beyond this, the plan relied upon so many variables that Oliphant thought it best to concentrate merely on getting his party inside and hoping for luck.

They left Noah to attend to the carriage and walked the last yards to the enormous columned portico of the President's House. This was the unimpressive side of the house, and the damage done to the grounds and facade by the army of pilgrims that daily tramped here had made what was at best a backdoor appearance into a meager one. Also, a beautiful, gold inlaid coach and four stood just at the portico, its team outfitted with silver harnesses, its footman resplendent in furs and gold-trimmed pantaloons, and the coach's presence so overwhelmed the plain, chipped, weather-worn President's House with the trappings of aristocratic privilege that Oliphant wanted to laugh—more, wanted to make a speech on the juxtaposition. But his audience was too distracted, and when he saw Jimmie, Cato, Nell, and Jinna hop with awe and collectively gasp as they stepped to the White House door, his heart raced with theirs. Jefferson and Jackson really had lived here! This was America's first home! He caught up with the adolescents. The small vestibule bustled with visitors, and off to the side there were attendants taking coats; there were also huge, fur-coated servants in riding boots. Narcissa turned to Oliphant and smiled. Then she began an introduction to the house she knew so well and that Oliphant, despite many years of opportunity in the 1850s, had never visited.

The President's House was divided into three parts off a wide, carpeted, lengthwise hall. The right-hand, west wing was for the president's family, and was partitioned off by bronze and ground-glass screens across the hall. The center body of the house contained the state parlors, the Blue, Green, and Crimson rooms, so-called for their distinctively colored furnishings. And the left-hand, east wing contained, on the first floor, the grand East Room, and on the second floor, the president's offices and Cabinet Room. Narcissa also assured the children that Mrs. Lincoln had a very large kitchen in the basement.

Narcissa stepped over to Oliphant. "And there's where I was first kissed, a tall boy, like a carrot, from Virginia." She pointed to a closed door to the right, to the Crimson Room. "And he was named Lee, I swear!"

Oliphant looked about for an official welcomer or card-taker. There was no one in authority, not even a guard. The public was truly welcome, and also in a hurry. The hallway was so busy that Oliphant and Maum Rosemary had to corral the adolescents. Maum Rosemary said, "You hold Jim, and I can handle these'un." Soon, though, Oliphant was being dragged forward by the hand as Jimmie surged with the crowd, and Oliphant could only beckon Narcissa to follow as closely as possible.

The crush and rudeness of the assembly at the archway to the East Room stopped even Jimmie. It was a plain-dressed mob, dusty frock coats worn at the sleeves, simple dresses in flat colors—none of the finery of a gaslight reception. Yet it made up for its ordinariness by acting feverishly. And there were crude hellos from strangers directed at Narcissa, who stood out like a gem in her rose gown and white point lace shawl with her headdress of white velvet and lace. Oliphant closed up with her to offer protection. He was now most irritated with the crowd. Keats had promised that Saturday's levee would be dull and ill-attended. What could this be?

They worked their way into the East Room. All Oliphant could see were the heads of the people and above—the ceiling frescoed with cupids and flowers, three chandeliers hanging like upside-down wedding cakes. There were holes cut in the damask drapery and the lace curtains, and there were huge swatches hacked out of the carpet, as if a short souvenir hunter had wandered free with a knife. Jimmie complained he could see nothing but backsides. Narcissa asked if Oliphant had yet spied Blondel. Maum Rosemary grumbled that she could smell liquor on the breath of the ruffians. Nell and Jinna were frightened by the crowding, and Cato wanted to be lifted up to see Lincoln first. Finally, Narcissa said, "Can you see if they extend around to the right rear?" Oliphant said he thought so. She said, "Good! We've rocks to jump over, but good. Come on, they've opened the Blue Room."

Back they went hand-in-hand down the hall. Narcissa was in command and confident. She found an alcove and then a door; she smiled to Oliphant, *"Coûte quecoûte!"* ("Come what will!"), and opened the door. They tumbled inside to find, when she closed the door again, that they were alone like a family of refugees inside what Narcissa said was the president's favorite parlor, the Crimson Room. Oliphant wondered which president she meant. He also felt giddy with the anxiety of an intruder. The parlor room was sumptuous, with crimson satin and gold damask furniture, a grand piano, and walls covered with gilded and colored hangings. The bank of southern windows was trimmed with gilded cornices; and there were ormolu and porcelain vases holding cut flowers on the windowsills. It was both grand and homey, and the view of the Potomac and Virginia hillsides was spectacular, if one excepted the tent encampment of the president's Pennsylvania cavalry bodyguard in the foreground, and if one overlooked the appalling heap of the contraband camp at the river's edge.

Narcissa waved her hand at the view, and then pointed to the partition to the left. "The parlors connect, you see? The Blue Room, the Green Room, and then this one. When there is too large a crowd, they open them one at a time." To demonstrate, she reached over and popped a small door in the partition. She commanded. They poured into the breach.

"Here there!" called a military man, jumping at them. "Hello!" Oliphant startled at the man's suddenness and red uniform. He was also surprised by the size of the crowd pressing at them, for the White House staff had opened both the Blue and Green rooms by now. Oliphant looked again at the officer and relaxed. It was Blondel, in his brilliant red dress tunic and striped pants, a chest of medals, a blue sash, and a heavy sword, with his ornate hat in hand. He was acting the happiest of men, spinning to greet each of them. "So glad! I worried about you for the confusion! So glad!"

The crowd roared again, and edged still more into the Green Room. Blondel began to explain the fuss, but Oliphant could see for himself. Here, with their backs to him, were handsome celebrities facing eager admirers. Lincoln was not among them. Instead, Mary Todd Lincoln stood midpoint in a group of five; she was tiny and fussily dressed, with a heavy black-corded silk, a black velvet and lace headdress, and a white point lace shawl that could have been the fraternal twin of Narcissa's. To Mrs. Lincoln's right side was a blocky, silver-haired potentate leaning hard on a gold-headed cane, whom Oliphant presumed was Senator Sumner, because the comtesse, Franny Wooster, stood to his side holding his arm. And on Mrs. Lincoln's left side was the solution to the success of this levee: a stiff-backed and diminutive couple dressed in satin and sable with small jeweled crowns on the backs of their heads. And behind them stood four giant Cossacks in animal skins like a wall of flesh and beards. Blondel laughed. "Russians, wouldn't you know? A prince of the blood and his bride, come to call on the czar's favorite ally. Lincoln ran when he saw them, I wager."

Oliphant started, "This is impossible, Sir Henry."

"No, no, quite a chance, actually," said Blondel. "Isaac says it should make them game for anything."

Narcissa leaned against Oliphant and whispered, nodding toward Mrs. Lincoln, "What a silly thing she is. What happens when you marry North and leave the South, I suppose, but really!"

Keats joined them from the side and gave a summary of what had happened so far. Mrs. Lincoln had indeed welcomed their approach and their gift, and was eager to meet Narcissa. Senator Sumner had been intrigued by Franny Wooster's story, and said he would be pleased to sit in on the parley. It was hoped that Mr. Lincoln would join them later. Should all go smoothly, Narcissa could expect to speak with the president before supper —perhaps at supper. Also, Senator Sumner, Keats had explained the night before, was a slave to Franny Wooster's wants, and Mrs. Lincoln was girlishly dependent upon Sumner's counsel. The key to the plan was Sumner then, until Lincoln arrived, and, as Keats had said, luck-was-the-weather. Keats now added, "Mrs. Winwood, it is time to meet your potential benefactress. Let us try our luck."

Oliphant wanted Narcissa to turn away from the others for a moment to confer with him in private. He assumed she would, in fact, and was left leaning awkwardly away when Narcissa turned toward Blondel and giggled. Blondel crooked out his arm. Narcissa reached out, and had ahold of Blondel when she stopped herself and turned back to Oliphant. "You're coming too, aren't you? What do you think?"

Oliphant said, "Someone should stay with Maumer and the children. I shall be right here. You're for it, and the best." He did not mean what he said, and he hoped that she would protest and insist that he stay by her side.

She returned to Blondel, however, and Oliphant stood with his hands on Jimmie's shoulders watching Narcissa parade off with Blondel and Keats. Oliphant recovered quickly, and led Maum Rosemary and the adolescents to the Green Room's windows. They wedged down the hem of the velvet carpet, to the accordion-like outcropping of the opened partition to the Blue Room. Oliphant was off to the side of the celebrities now, with a good view of Narcissa, and also with a vantage on the front of the crowd as the press of people banged against the Oriental objets d'art and the huge gilded mirrors.

"Where's de president?" asked Cato. "I wanna see too."

Jimmie answered, "He's a comin'. Dat's his Missus."

Mrs. Lincoln looked to be enjoying herself as the reception line passed along. The Russian prince flirted with Mrs. Lincoln and his bride, a dainty blonde woman who did not seem to move. Senator Sumner was also attentive to Mrs. Lincoln, leaning over to her to pat her arm like a husband giving encouragement. Sumner concerned himself with his goddaughter, too. Franny Wooster, without any real claim to special blood or office, appeared the ruling hostess here. Oliphant had thought her sheepish at dinner, and vaguely libertine at the embassy reception. Today, she shone with a cheerful beauty. And when Keats gave her a prearranged signal, she dismissed the functionary who was bringing forth the next admirer. The path was open for Narcissa and Blondel.

Oliphant could not hear their conversations because of the hum of the assembly. He could presume from what he saw and anticipated. Franny Wooster sang to Senator Sumner. Blondel carried Narcissa forward. Keats stepped in behind Franny Wooster. Sumner acknowledged Keats with a glance and smile. Narcissa gave her hand to Sumner and curtsied playfully. Sumner kissed her knuckles and spoke. Keats, Franny Wooster, and Sumner turned inward. Sumner introduced Blondel to Mrs. Lincoln. Blondel bowed and stepped back. Narcissa curtsied again, and Mrs. Lincoln returned the gesture. Narcissa spoke and held up a flap of her white point lace shawl. Mrs. Lincoln blinked, then smiled and held up her shawl as well. Oliphant had puzzled as to who had provided a modest Illinois lawyer's wife with what he knew to be two thousand dollars' worth of dry goods. These two belles seemed to think, or were willing to pretend, that their mutual taste in shawls was good reason to regard each other warmly. Mrs. Lincoln introduced Narcissa to the Russians.

The exchange that followed was not short, and required many of Narcissa's butterfly hand gestures that she used for her overrich French. Mrs. Lincoln turned away momentarily to take up a jewel box from a lady behind her, and then she held the jewel box between Narcissa and the Prince and opened it. The Prince's delighted reaction made Mrs. Lincoln beam. Sumner reached over to tap the box. Narcissa took another bow. Oliphant knew the cause of all this orchestration was the gift that Keats and Blondel had given Mrs. Lincoln, saying it was from Narcissa. It was more candidly a bribe. It was one of a set of three diamond and pearl bracelets; the other two were with Camellia and Laura in Savannah. Narcissa had entrusted hers to Keats the night before. Keats had ordered the inscription altered that morning, having "JGR LOVES NR Christmas 1840" changed to "PEACE November 1864."

Narcissa was now beckoning her family to come forward. Maum Rosemary shyly pushed Nell, Jinna, and Cato before her. Oliphant urged Jimmie along, but he resisted. "I'm stayin' with you, Mars Jan."

The levee was thinning, as 3 P.M. and the ringing-out neared. Even the most prominent persons—congressmen, socialites, merchants—were drawing back from the Green Room, presuming that Mrs. Lincoln would not overstay her reception. Also, it was finally clear that the president would not attend.

Jimmie would not accept that his hero was not going to appear to shake his hand. He studied the room; he wandered a few steps toward a burly and authoritive looking Union officer to ask after Mr. Lincoln. When Jimmie returned to Oliphant he was very unhappy. He pressed himself against the window glass to survey the White House grounds; he moaned something about his luck. And then, to Oliphant's consternation, and by what Oliphant believed was a secret magic that children possess so completely that when it is gone and they are adults the world becomes either insipid or tragic, Jimmie was able to broadcast a gleeful, "Golly!" He pulled Oliphant to the sill. "Ain't he? Ain't he?"

Out on the grounds, there was a tall, bony, bearded man, hatless with a black frock coat flapping behind him as he made his way heavily to the west. A small young clerk followed him, carrying a large portfolio, an umbrella, and a voluminous overcoat. It was too far a distance to make out the faces. Oliphant knew that Lincoln was anti-social, and that fleeing Russian royalty was understandable even in a raconteur. Nevertheless, it was too far. The pair proceeded against the wind toward the treeline that screened off the Navy and old War Department buildings. Lincoln was said to spend more time in the War Department's telegraph room than in his bed. Still, Oliphant could not be sure it was Lincoln. And he wanted to interpret the world correctly for Jimmie. Jimmie was as close to a son as Oliphant might ever have, and he deserved the bottom truth. Oliphant said, "We shall see him later, Jim, we shall."

Jimmie was not appeased. He redoubled his claims as the figures receded and were lost. "I know'd it was, sir, I know'd I seen him! These possum-huntin' eyes did it, yes sir!"

"Excuse me, I hope I'm not interfering, but I overheard and—" It was a young woman, standing suddenly beside them. She paused to make certain Oliphant was not offended, and then she continued to Jimmie, "That was the president. You're right. I would know those elbows from any distance. That was President Abraham Lincoln."

Jimmie grinned. "Thank you, ma'am, I knew it was him!"

Oliphant also thanked her—a pretty, dark-haired, understated young lady, wearing very neat clothes—and he apologized for the fuss. She laughed, and explained that her young cousin had been as insistent when he had visited once. Oliphant was charmed; he introduced Jimmie and himself, adding that this was their first call at the White House.

She said, "Oh, if you could only see it in the spring!" Then she curtsied, and said her name was Bridey Lamont. Something seemed to frighten her then, because she pulled back abruptly, curtsied again, and walked away. She returned to the side of the burly Union officer, whom Oliphant noticed was standing with the help of two walking canes.

By now, Mrs. Lincoln was withdrawing to the Crimson Room via the same door that Narcissa had found to bring them all in here. The Russian prince and princess and Cossacks followed. Then all Narcissa's party, Sumner in the lead, started in that direction. Narcissa beckoned Oliphant. Oliphant hesitated.

"Jimmie," Oliphant said, "they're going to meet Mr. Lincoln now."

Jimmie, his loyalty divided, said, "Aren't you comin'?"

Oliphant looked up to see Narcissa stepping toward him. He shook her off and grimaced. He felt it best if he remained a supernumerary. At least, this idea suited his present sense of discomfort. Narcissa kept coming, and Oliphant said no, but quietly, so that she was able to see his lips move but perhaps not to hear him. It did stop her, and she twisted her face in disbelief. Oliphant smiled to calm her. He spoke to Jimmie. "You tell Miss Narcissa that I have gone outside for a smoke, and shall be along presently."

Oliphant strode off through the East Room without looking back. He did need a smoke. He also needed to collect himself. He wanted to rid himself of his oppressive doubt that Narcissa's peace commission was just more futility and vanity and— No, let that go, John. Yes, it's true that Mary Lincoln is gem-hungry, and would agree to almost anything for such a bracelet. And yes, I won't ever have a hope as innocent as Jimmie's again. But still, I could try! But then, what could I say to Lincoln? What was the use of any talk?

Oliphant knew he needed so much, then, and so urgently, that he bypassed the confusion in the vestibule and went outside without his hat, coat, or walking cane. It was more bother to avoid the rush of the carriages, for the crowd was as turbulent in retreat as it had been in attack.

Oliphant got onto the White House lawn in self-defense. He drifted hands-in-pocket toward the center of the oval park. The sky was quilted purple and gray now, and the light was indirect. A gust of wind came up, and Oliphant went over to find shelter behind the statue of Thomas Jefferson. Oliphant glanced at the Constitution in Jefferson's hand, and thought, It was not ever meant to be cast in bronze. The South had regarded it a tissue like a marriage contract, to be dissolved when either party offended the other. Now, the North regarded it as a document like a death warrant, to be shown at the gates of Richmond, Atlanta, and soon enough Savannah. Should Narcissa petition Lincoln for peace? Better she pay the executioner to strike the blow cleanly.

Oliphant patted his morning coat for his pipe and tobacco and lighter. It was difficult in the wind, but once he got the pipe lit, his nerves did seem to improve. As he returned the Spectre Buck lighter to his coat, his hand struck the telegram from Baltimore.

He could no longer pretend that it was not there. He pulled it out and opened it with the stem of his pipe, pushing again and again along the envelope's seam.

It was orders from Richmond, via the relay operator in Baltimore. It was signed by a code word that represented the collective authority of the Confederate Cabinet. It was in cipher, of course, so he could not read its particulars without his cipher book to translate. But Oliphant saw in the text the *nom de guerre* used by W. A. Longuemare, and he certainly recognized the configuration for New-York.

His intuition told him more of what it said. He heard a noise behind him, but ignored it. He was staring at the telegram the way a man might consider the prophecy of his future laid out in entrails.

He thought, I haven't quit. I cannot resist my duty. This is the way of the world. It will be an eye for an eye, a wrong for a wrong, a city for a city. It will be New-York for Atlanta and perhaps Savannah, too. And I will go along, because I have nowhere else to go. Because Narcissa is lost to me, and I am lost to myself. Because I want to.

And what does that make me? A fool.

Someone was talking behind Oliphant. He thought he heard his name, but no. He was numb. He was barely able to talk to himself. He whispered, "A damned fool."

CHAPTER 7

Amaziah Butter at
Washington City, District of Columbia

WEDNESDAY, NOVEMBER 9, TO
WEDNESDAY, NOVEMBER 16

Upon Captain Butter's return from New-York on Wednesday, November 9, he anticipated either a cool reception or a high-handed maneuver by Colonel Baker. Accordingly, Butter rehearsed a story to himself that would not be a lie—Baker could smell falsehood—and yet would omit any hint that he had followed Oliphant from the New-York ferry to Georgetown before he reported to Secret Service Headquarters. The major problem was that he could not explain an eighteen-hour delay between the reception of Baker's telegram in New-York and the presentation of himself in Washington—not unless he made up a story.

Butter crossed Pennsylvania Avenue in a slow stride, climbed the steps of 217, and pushed through to the duty desk. It was past 9 P.M., and the sergeant at the desk directed Butter to the lone clerk in the back of the room. The clerk handed Butter an order signed for Baker by Usher Skelton. Butter was to report immediately to the detective Edgar Quillermouth in Alexandria, Virginia. Butter read the order again and barked in protest. The clerk shrugged and went into the telegraph room. Butter was so aggravated, however, that he then barked at the duty sergeant. The sergeant nodded sympathetically and pointed upstairs.

This was all so frustrating to Butter that he forgot his position. He would make a fuss before they sent him off on more of their dirty business! He charged up to the second floor intending to confront Lafayette Baker with the whole story about John Oliphant. Instead, he found a darkened hall and only a light from the clerk-copyists' office across from Baker's suite. And when Butter ducked in, planning to bark some more, he was dumbfounded by Mrs. Lamont's fresh smile. She sat at a desk covered with reports arranged into four stacks; she had obviously been at work through her dinner, with plates stacked neatly on a tray behind her. She rose and asked Butter how she could help him.

"I'm looking for Colonel Baker, ma'am."

"He's off at the War Department with Mr. Skelton, Captain," she said. "Won't you sit? You look very tired."

"I can't," said Butter, who then did sit. "I've been ordered to get across to Alexandria. To Edgar Quillermouth. Do you know what this is?"

"I copied the order, Captain—that is my handwriting, but I can't tell you more than what I overheard. They are short-handed just now, and Mr. Quillermouth asked for you. He left this afternoon—to arrest a Confederate courier, I think."

"What did he say about me? Did he mention a John Oliphant, or anything —you know, was Colonel Baker peeved?"

"The Colonel hasn't mentioned you at all. I said it was Mr. Quillermouth who asked Mr. Skelton for you." She put down her pen, and tapped a particular stack of reports. "We were under the impression that your work in New-York—I mean, I had heard you were a complete success. Weren't you? Is something wrong? Can I help?"

Butter looked overlong at her. She was like a friend, even if she was mostly a stranger. She did not seem as suspicious now as she had at the War Department. He started, "A success?" but then stood and excused himself, for his innards churned like a mad machine. He fled to the outhouse.

When Butter thought over his folly later—and he had much time to self-criticize while convalescing the following week in Bridey Lamont's bed —he realized that his first bad mistake was at the very beginning. He should have stayed with her and talked through his upset. But they had banished him! What injustice! Here, he had volunteered out of invalidhood in order to track the Rebs from Nova Scotia to Georgetown, and because he had met the challenge, and had gone beyond to inspired detective work, he was to be rewarded by being posted to Virginia as a thug. And they would not even confront him! There was to be no opportunity to scream, or to demand he be returned to Maine, or even to confess his zeal, if that was his crime. The only consolation was that it could have been worse—that they could have ordered him back to the First Maine at the Jerusalem Turnpike.

And so Butter, emerging from the outhouse, and ignoring his hunger and sleeplessness, flung himself into the first available quartermaster wagon in a fit of self-punishment. At the Long Bridge—the mile-long pontoon-bridge river crossing at Maryland Avenue—he had a long wait for a ride across. Finally, he climbed onto an ambulance carrying six wheezing boys over to the so-called Camp Displacement, the huge depot of the hardest and most shirking cases in the Army. The boys should have been going to hospital, but then, Butter thought, leave it to the Army to send invalids into disgrace.

He could not find a ride downriver until midnight, and then it was with a foul-mouthed teamster who made the six muddy miles to Alexandria a torment by singing of California whores with very large pudenda, "Big as a bear's paw, red and grizzly!" Butter lay awake, and suffered through the man's crudity by thinking of Maine at the first snowfall and of his family; again, he experienced the odd phenomenon that his wife's face could blend wholly into the softer features of Mrs. Lamont—or was it that he was forgetting Desire?

The streets of Alexandria were as gloomy as a battlefield. Butter stumbled about in the dark. He got useless directions at the riverbank from ferrymen complaining about having to transport quarantined soldiers. He lost his way in the oldest section of the town, where there were ancient burnt-out brick houses and ditches filled with horse skeletons. He had been this tired only a few times—the long ride across Maryland to Gettysburg, and that night before Fredericksburg—and he knew there was jeopardy in such wooziness. He was hallucinating by the time he found the hotel, and was too reduced to protest when Quillermouth would not open the door of his hotel room. He slept half sitting up in the hall. Quillermouth did get him up for breakfast, undercooked pork and stenchful eggs, and did show him consideration when he let Butter sleep in the room at midday. Still, Butter's mind was slipping, and he could not understand the details of the operation. He depended upon Quillermouth and the two assistants, Dupont and Colquitt (lanky, childish Virginians whom Butter suspected of being Rebel deserters), to tell him where to sit and what to watch for. Mostly, he was left to stare at the mist. Quillermouth did provide the general information that the suspect, George Patterson, residing in the same hotel in the rear room at the stairs, was a Rebel courier en route from Toronto to Richmond, and that his whereabouts had been sold to the Secret Service by his family for greenbacks. Yet Butter lost focus when he tried to speculate how Patterson might pertain to Jake Thompson, or to the Rebel conspiracy in New-York, or even to Oliphant.

Butter might have recovered with more sleep. However, a pouch arrived by rider Thursday evening with an order that they were to break off the watch and arrest Patterson for transport to Old Capitol, where he would be interrogated scrupulously. There was another order in the pouch, for Butter. It was again in Mrs. Lamont's handwriting and again signed by Usher Skelton. It dispatched Butter into Virginia upon completion of the Patterson affair, this time to fetch a captured Mosby guerrilla from Front Royal in the Shenandoah Valley and to transport him back to Old Capitol.

Butter became so angry at this new assignment that he fell over the line between depression and stupidity and made his second bad mistake. Patterson's arrest was the usual Secret Service kidnapping—"bash and snatch" they called it. At midnight, they broke down the man's hotel room door, whipped him with a blackjack when he awoke screaming, gagged him and tied a sack over his head, chained his hands to his ankles, and dragged him by his feet down the back steps to a waiting buckboard, where they heaved him into a trunk. Butter's disgust was such that he tried to provide Patterson some uncalled-for care. He reached into the trunk to straighten Patterson's bare legs before they sealed him up. Patterson was ignorant of Butter's mercy and kicked out when touched, striking Butter very hard in the forehead, pushing Butter's spectacles hard against his eye sockets.

Later, at the Orange & Alexandria railroad depot, Butter's eyes throbbed, and there was blood on the bridge of his nose. He whimpered for the pain while he waited for the first train to the Shenandoah Valley, which was about ninety miles east on the Manassas Gap line.

To keep going like this, without decent rest, was his third bad mistake. Yet Butter's whole body was betraying his judgment now. The last week in New-York had shifted him to the nighttime, so that while in daylight he felt slow-footed, at night he felt aggressive. Now, at night, he aggressively persuaded himself that if he brought in this Mosby guerrilla in good form, he might be permitted to remain in Washington. Baker did not know John

Oliphant's whereabouts. Butter hoped this might be the advantage he needed to catch Oliphant in some sort of treacherous intrigue and to prove to Baker that he was right about Oliphant. Failing that, he could throw a tantrum, presuming he could find Lafayette Baker to throw it in front of.

Butter boarded a troop train before dawn Friday morning, and found a spot on the floor in a car of officers of the Fifth New York Cavalry and several Michigan regiments who were all laid out like logs. Underneath the screeching, rhythmic clatter of the train as it rolled slowly into Virginia was the ceaseless gossip of several wide-awake junior officers whose agitated certainty revealed them to be fresh troops. Their talk was entirely of the Shenandoah Valley and the spectres of Jubal Early and John Mosby. A single mention of Sherman was hooted.

Virginia's sublime Shenandoah River gave the name to what had come to be called the Valley of Death. The Valley's geography was like a sack open at both ends that was rolled out between the Blue Ridge and Appalachian Mountain chains from Winchester northeast to Staunton southwest. Once, Lee had poured Stonewall Jackson and himself into the sack for its grain and foodstuffs to feed their army as they struck north in 1862 to Antietam, and Lee had returned again along the same route in 1863 to Gettysburg. Then, Lincoln had called upon Grant in 1864 to hammer Lee with a meat axe from the Wilderness to the siege of Richmond and Petersburg, and the Shenandoah Valley had become a sack for corpses. For after Jubal Early's raid against Washington in July, Grant had ordered Major-General Philip H. Sheridan into the Valley to exterminate Rebel resistance, no matter the cost. And from September to late October, no less than fifty thousand battle casualties on both sides had made the Valley a desecration —the burning out and murdering of civilians a blot on the Union command. Yet there was no neat military way to subdue an enemy in so open a field. So Sheridan had chased Early, slaughtered thousands while losing the same number, and then chased him again, up and down along a ninety-mile track of graves and cinders. Early was whipped in mid-September. Then Early had rallied his starving, barefooted troops for a superhuman blow at Sheridan's army at Cedar Creek, and Sheridan was whipped in mid-October. Then Sheridan had rallied his troops with a mythologized ride called "Whirling" by the newspapers ("I here took the affair in hand. . . ." Sheridan had telegraphed) for a counterattack against Early that carried supremely. Early's army died with its belly empty.

In the Valley, however, the Confederacy could fight past death. It was three weeks now since Sheridan's ride, and the Valley was haunted with screams against the Yankees. The trees were armed. The creeks could kill. Again and again, the Confederate ghosts stabbed at Federal concentrations and blocked Sheridan's ambition to lay a railroad through the Blue Ridge in order to close on Lee at Richmond from the west.

The grandest of these Confederate ghosts was Lieutenant-Colonel John Singleton Mosby and his notorious 43rd Battalion. Mosby's Raiders had long been a Union nemesis that had now been transformed by the Confederate collapse into an infamous scourge—six hundred irregular horse soldiers who, it was said, rode moonbeams and ate fearlessness as they paralyzed fifty times their number with the threat of night raids. It appeared that Mosby could operate at will from Cedar Creek to Winchester, and it was certain that he was a holy hero to Valley residents, who would hide his men in their children's beds if asked.

In desperation, Sheridan approved outrages, arguing, "Since I came into this Valley from Harper's Ferry, every train, every small party, every straggler, has been bushwhacked. . . ." The Federals began burning out whole villages in retaliation, torturing for information, and executing Confederate prisoners, especially Mosby's men, as outlaws. The worst incident had been at Front Royal, when Brigadier-General George A. Custer, a 25-year-old daredevil, had hanged six of Mosby's men. They had cursed him at the end of the rope, "Mosby'll kill ten for every one of us!" Mosby had retaliated in late October by executing four Union troopers. But there was nothing Mosby could do about the concomitant Federal extremes, such as the routine firing of flour mills, hay barns, silos, and stockyards, or such as the Union policy of herding chained civilians onto troop trains, so that when Mosby attacked, Virginians died first.

In his sleep, Butter thought he overheard that his train carried hostages. There was a voice above him explaining, "At Winchester, they say, when they hit 'em, this ol' cousin stands up to the window of the car, and he yells out, 'Shoot trew me, Johnny, shoot da damned Yankee!' "

But when Butter awoke, he wondered if it had been a nightmare. Friday afternoon was grim enough. It had taken ten hours to travel roughly a hundred miles of on-loadings, delays on sidings, and off-loadings. The last sixty miles had been on the difficult Manassas Gap line through the Bull Run mountains and twisting across the plain and foothills into the Manassas Gap itself, the gateway to the Valley. And here at the foot of the Blue Ridge range, just inside the Valley, was what remained of the farming and railroad village of Front Royal. Where there once must have been a depot, there were now decaying layers of captured stores piled like cords of wood; where there once must have been a main street, there were now herds of cavalry remounts and bony pack mules; and where there should have been a town center, there was the trembling bivouac of a badly beaten up infantry brigade —two Pennsylvania regiments and a New York one splayed in mud and a drenching dampness.

Butter had a difficult hour trudging among hostile noncommissioned officers trying to locate the brigade's acting-assistant-adjutant-general; and when he did find him he was presented with a porky, innocuous farmer's attorney named Kaiser, from Altoona, he said. Kaiser explained that his senior officers were either on leave or in the hospital with dysentery, pneumonia, or weak hearts. The brigade's general was dead from infection, and there were also sixty men quarantined with what might be measles.

Butter stopped the man's complaining and asked for the prisoner. Kaiser heaved phlegm and led the way to the sod-built cabin that served as the brigade's stockade. Most of it was given to captured deserters from both armies, who were either penned up out back like hogs or chained together out front. Kaiser boasted to Butter that this prisoner was the second Mosby guerrilla they had captured in a week. He added that the first one, Edmunston, had tried to bribe the guard, had then tried to escape off the train, and had also tried to bribe the guards in Alexandria. Kaiser opened the crude door. "These Mosbys are crazy, Captain, crazy with hate, and just crazy."

Kaiser's prologue was obviously meant to prepare Butter for discovering that this new Mosby guerrilla, Dingledine, had been bound hand and foot with rawhide and then had been sewn inside a stinking horseblanket. Butter cut the boy out, freed his hands and feet, and did not comment. But when Butter carried Dingledine outside, and Kaiser protested about security, Butter let go a shout at the man's birthright that sent Kaiser away huffily.

Dingledine was too weak at first to walk, and he had soiled himself. Butter ordered a guard to fetch clothes and shoes from the dead man's pile nearby. Butter could not get boots on Dingledine because of the swelling of his feet. He carried him again to a cooking fire at the brigade's tent-made chapel. Dingledine ate and vomitted, and it was a few hours before Butter had a fully alive prisoner. Butter got him back to the depot's crushed platform, and fixed them both a place out of the wind against an overturned caisson.

Butter then relaxed but kept his Army Colt in his lap, less because of Dingledine than because of the grumbling from passing troopers, "Save a long trip, soldier, with a long rope!"

Butter's fourth and final bad mistake was partially forced upon him—but then it was also a culmination of two days of his soreheadedness—when word got around about his prisoner. The railroad men thought Dingledine a mark of Cain. The first two troop trains to stop at Front Royal refused Butter permission to board. And the engineer of the next train (two baggage cars and three horsepen cars) shook off Butter's request belligerently. However, it was now past 10 P.M., and Butter was not going to be denied. The staff officers in the baggage cars barred Butter's entry too. Butter crossed to the opposite side of the horsepen cars, and pushed Dingledine up. He pitched dirty straw and manure out the open doors to make a roost for them with blankets and oats bags. It looked like it was going to be a frigid ride, but once they started to roll, Butter decided it was sufferable. True, his eyes still hurt him, and the cut on his nose kept filling with puss, and he had not slept lying down flat in three days, and whatever he ate passed through him like poison, and there was that lingering weakness in his knees from Petersburg. Yet he could push these ailments aside now as minor, because he was on his way out of the Valley.

Instead, he could more completely burden himself with brooding about Washington City ahead—about Oliphant, and Baker, and Wetherbee and Rufus at the War Wagon, and even about Mrs. Lamont. Butter paced and slumped and paced some more. He was willing to upset himself with his worst expectations. He was even willing to confess that his temper, pride, and stubbornness were life-threatening weaknesses. Butter welcomed any fantasy, then, in order to pretend that he was not in a reeking stockcar lurching through the Blue Ridge Mountains, the only light from the lantern he used to write by in his logbook, the only company a dozen officers' mounts and a sleeping farmboy who by some twist had become a devil of the state.

In sum, Butter mesmerized himself. Yet no matter how he excused himself afterward to Mrs. Lamont and Wetherbee, none of these distractions, fears, or tricks of the imagination could adequately explain how a man could be so foolish as to fall backward off of a moving train.

Butter's panic overcame the pain in his lower back as he rolled over and arose to see the train vanishing into the black night. He looked hard and saw three choices: He could quit; he could push into these woods and hope to find a farmhouse where they would not kill him outright as a Yankee; or he could catch that train.

Butter ran for his life. He cried out every few steps, "Stop! Stop!" But it was a futile plea, as wasted on the train as on the wicked pain in his hip. He ran on and on, first after the sound of the train, and then only after his hope. At some point, the train rounded a bend and Butter was left alone, a heaving, sweating, wild, wild man, his greatcoat soaring behind him, his arms swinging like chicken wings, his thoughts reduced to a single, succinct scream for God Almighty's attention, "Shit!" Nevertheless, he did continue to run under those thick clouds racing across a crescent moon; he did continue to run with so much pain that he knew if he stopped he would not be able to start again; he did continue to run because there was nothing else to do, and he did not want to die.

The miracle that stopped the train on a grade appeared at first to Butter as a way for fate to torture him further. At any moment, he knew, that train could rumble off. He closed on the last car, one hundred yards, fifty yards, twenty yards, and then he fell into the gravel. He had misjudged the distance. The stockcar was just above him. He could not speak. He rolled himself over, and might have lain there indefinitely, with the security of having the prize so near, if the train had not then vibrated with the engagement of gears. Butter was up and inside the car like a hound. Dingledine remained tucked up and asleep. No one on earth had known that Butter had gone missing, and now no one knew that he had returned from the doomed. Butter chanted, "Shit! Shit! Shit!" and fell forward into the straw.

Butter did not know where he was when daylight woke him. Then he felt the pain and was fully informed. They were stopped on a siding outside of Fairfax Station, about ten miles from Alexandria, while a supply train groaned past moving south. Butter had a momentary hope that they might be headed on the spur into the Long Bridge and Washington itself, but, for whatever reason, they were diverted northeast. By the time they slowed outside of the Alexandria yards, Butter had established his plan. He slid over to rouse Dingledine, and waved the Army Colt at him for emphasis. He ordered Dingledine to cut out and saddle two Army horses. And when the train stopped again on a bend, so that the men in the engine could not see the opposite rear side of the stockcar, Butter had Dingledine get the mounts down.

The hard part was to get Butter mounted, because he could no longer sit up. Dingledine eased the second mount up to the door and pulled when he was told. Butter screamed and screamed. Then they were off on stolen horses. Butter lay on his belly, dangling his pistol and repeatedly warning Dingledine that if he tried to run, Butter would not only shoot at him, he would also tell the eventual pursuers that worse than being a Mosby, Dingledine was a horse thief: He would be hanged without ever seeing a jail.

They achieved the ferry at Alexandria before noon. It was just a barge pulled by a steam tug from Alexandria to the Navy Yard, but Butter thought it wonderful in comparison to the jostling of the horse. He did not dismount, however, because the horse's warmth seemed to soothe the pain. They regained Pennsylvania Avenue at Fifth Street within the hour. Butter knew he should keep on to Old Capitol Prison. The temptation of Secret Service Headquarters won out. Now it was Private Dingledine, C.S.A., who carried Butter to aid. They did not stop at the challenge of the duty sergeant. Butter cocked his pistol and told Dingledine to keep on to the second floor. At Lafayette Baker's door, Butter slipped to the floor, and called, "God damn, I've come back!" Butter pounded on the wall. "I'm back, I'm back!"

Butter was gasping against Dingledine's knees when the door opened and Usher Skelton emerged waving a pistol. Then there were legs all around Butter, and he saw Mrs. Lamont's face above him. He realized slowly that the horror in her look must be because of what he looked like, unless it was because of Dingledine's black and blue bare feet. Butter said, "Thanks, Reb." Or at least he remembered saying that. Butter also thought he heard Dingledine say, "Damn Yankee!" before he heard nothing at all.

How Butter got into Mrs. Lamont's bed was that she put him there, with the assistance of Major Torrance Wetherbee, Job "White-Pine" Mills, and Mrs. Lamont's young sister-in-law Miss Vera Lamont. Why he got there was more revealing, and, once he had learned the particulars, profoundly persuaded Butter to Mrs. Lamont's part in all things.

It had been instantly fixed by Usher Skelton that Butter was unfit for service and was again invalided. It was also assumed that Butter had no room of his own in Washington, and that he would need medical attention regardless. An ambulance wagon was sent for. By this time, Mrs. Lamont had intervened authoritatively. She learned from White-Pine that Butter had a bosom friend nearby, and she asked White-Pine to fetch Major Wetherbee. Wetherbee arrived like a boulder off a mountain, a large, sandy-haired, angular, and once virile Marylander who had become as militant in his drunkenness as he had once been in his nature. Wetherbee took up Butter's body like a child's and announced that he would shoot the first son-of-a-Republican-bitch who tried to stop him. Mrs. Lamont caught up with Wetherbee at the front door, and learned for her trouble that Wetherbee would sooner let Butter float down the Potomac than be thrown into one of the pits called hospitals. Once Wetherbee, growling and spitting, had communicated that he aimed to transport Butter to the notorious saloon the War Wagon, since what he thought Butter needed was bourbon whiskey and rest, Mrs. Lamont not only forced a compromise but also took the solution upon herself.

And so the ambulance wagon made a detour from its usual rounds and descended down Pennsylvania Avenue to the corner of West Eleventh Street. Here on the ground floor was the popular bookshop of Blanchard and Mohun; above was the drygoods emporium of W. D. Lamont & Brother. Importantly, these two shops represented only the front half of a three-story double house. The rear half of the double house, opening onto the wooded interior of the block, contained the meticulously neat, cozy, and well-furnished rooms of the two Lamont women, war widow and war orphan, respectively.

Butter awoke Sunday afternoon to feel a long red tail flapping on his pillow and against his whiskers. He was not entirely ignorant. He knew he had been evacuated here and knew something of where he was, for he had discerned through his pain the voices of Wetherbee, White-Pine, and two angels. He also recalled conversing with his rescuers about Dingledine, and about how he had outrun a locomotive as only Natty Bumppo could have done. This latter reminiscence had been encouraged by Wetherbee the night before as he had doctored Butter with bourbon whiskey. And so, as soon as Butter touched the tail, he knew that it was attached to the ancient and massive Rufus, Wetherbee's red hunting dog.

Butter remained flat on his back and experimented with the trouble in his hips. The pain froze him, and made him wet himself a bit. He relaxed and examined the room by just moving his head. There were two dressers, a vanity, lounge chairs, two wardrobes, dark green and blue wallpaper in floral patterns, partially shuttered windows, and then a body in the bed on the other side of Rufus. It was Wetherbee, asleep so silently and deeply in his usual stupor that he looked cheerful and peaceful.

Butter wanted his spectacles to study details, but did not know where they could be. He sighed. "Hello, Rufus, remember me?" Rufus wagged harder and raised his head at the foot of the bed. Butter added, "Are we in heaven, old fellow?" Rufus's yawn made Butter yawn, and that put him back to sleep until the Lamonts, with two young children, arrived back from church, and there was a maternal gathering at Butter's bedside to exchange identities and motives.

The Pennsylvania Avenue shop of W. D. Lamont & Brother had once been the southernmost of a chain of similar shops established in the 1850s by William Drake Lamont simultaneously with, and because of, the advance of the railroad companies from New Jersey to the capital. All the shops had been based upon the original family store in Trenton, New Jersey, which had been operated successfully for forty years by the Drakes of Trenton: a father who had served in the Continental Army during the retreat from Philadelphia to the winter despair of Valley Forge, 1777–78; and a son who had served but had not fired a shot in battle during the War of 1812. The precocious grandson, W. D. Lamont, had been prevented from enlisting in the Army for the Mexican War, 1846–48, by the stubborn determination of his mother and his wife, both of whom had insisted that his sentimental patriotism did not exceed his familial responsibilities. Later, W. D. Lamont had altered the name of the family shop, and subsequent chain, to memorialize his brother, David, who had fought at Mexico City and died of dysentery in New Orleans on his way home. In 1861, the very middle aged W. D. Lamont had realized his life's dream to honor the war-like tradition of his mother's family, the Drakes, and had rushed to the capital in time to join the Army of the Potomac camp in Virginia near Bull Run River. W. D. Lamont had survived the first battle of Bull Run because he had remained in camp as an acting quartermaster, but he had not survived the summer— possibly because of a weak heart, bad kidneys, and the panic-stricken retreat of the Federals to the capital under that merciless July sun.

W. D. Lamont's eldest son, David Drake Lamont, was then a member of the New Jersey State Legislature; he was also a well-spoken Democrat who deeply distrusted the Abolitionists and the Republicans for having engineered Lincoln's election despite the certainty that it would fracture the Union. Nevertheless, David Lamont saw his duty, and followed his two brothers into the Army. David Lamont's second wife, Bridey (David was ten years older than she), and infant son soon followed him to the capital. David Lamont spent most of 1862 in the War Department, where he contributed his experience at the procurement and distribution of supplies to clothe and shelter the burgeoning Army of the Potomac. In late November 1862, David Lamont rode out with a wagon train to Major-General Ambrose E. Burnside's huge army in order to deliver long-delayed shipments of winter coats. He stayed on with General Joseph Hooker's staff to observe at what became the battle of Fredericksburg. Officially, David Lamont was missing in action since his failure to report for muster on the retreat across the Rappahannock River on the evening of December 15. A reasonable assumption was that he had fallen at the base of Marye's Heights in one of the half-dozen assaults against impregnable Confederate positions on December 13, and that he had been buried in the mass graves carved out during the truce between Lee and Burnside on the 14th.

As Butter lay next to Rufus and Wetherbee listening to Bridey and Vera Lamont recite their family history, however, and overcall and contradict each other as to the final events of David Lamont's life, he realized that these two women had not been willing to assume that there was anything reasonable about the war. For two years, they had remained in Washington in order to search for David Lamont in hospitals, on lists released from the Confederate hospitals and prisoner-of-war camps, on lists of prisoner exchanges, and by interviewing those men they could find who were near or with David Lamont the night before and the day of his disappearance. Meanwhile, the W. D. Lamont & Brother chain—always a pioneering effort in shopkeeping—had faded with their hope, so that now only this shop and the original in Trenton remained. And even these two were threatened by debts to European manufacturers that only the bluster of the patriarch himself could have solved. One remaining Lamont brother was home in New Jersey after being crippled by the kick of a horse; the other had died the previous spring at Cold Harbor. Vera Lamont ran the shop in Washington with the help of two other war widows, who lived on the third floor of the double house with their many children, and also with the help of a crippled trooper named Kindermann who lived in the stockroom. The primary merchandise had become mourning clothes, the sales of which had boomed in 1864 to the point that, along with Bridey Lamont's $100-a-month salary from the War Department (a position she had secured through her husband's comrades) and the money they received from the rental of David Lamont's Trenton home, the Lamont women were able to maintain themselves and their many charges by blood, marriage, and adoption.

"David wasn't a soldier like you, gentlemen," said Vera Lamont.

At another point, Bridey Lamont said, "He didn't want this war."

"He wanted to be governor of New Jersey," explained Vera.

Bridey Lamont also explained, "David should have been in the Congress working for peace, and not out there. He thought the war was insane."

Still later, Vera Lamont said, "The officers we have found from the Fredericksburg battle, they say it was murder to send those men against the cannons. Murder, they said, again and again, murder."

"We pray," said Bridey Lamont. "There are many who've come back after a year or longer. There was a boy from the Richmond prison, from Libby. He'd been missing since April of last year. And we have had fellows who didn't know themselves for months, and some who still don't. And they miscopy names on the prisoner lists."

"Prayer can't hurt," said Vera Lamont.

"Mr. Lincoln attends our church regularly," said Bridey Lamont. "The Second Presbyterian. No one prays harder than the president."

"We've done some good," said Vera Lamont. "It hasn't been a waste."

"I prayed for you last Wednesday," said Bridey to Butter.

Vera smiled. "We prayed for the three of you today at church. Billy wanted you to know that he prayed for the dog too."

These confessions were not conveyed of a piece and sedately. They were rather presented over several hours of talking and scrambling while Butter and Wetherbee were force-fed soup and tea, while Billy, Bridey Lamont's 4-year-old, wandered in and out of his nap or his 2-year-old sister, Maude, appealed for attention, and while Vera tried unsuccessfully to get Wetherbee to surrender his ruined uniform for cleaning. Vera was a diminutive brunette woman, under 25, not as pretty as Bridey, still pleasant-looking and very clean, with a fierce busyness that animated her features and made her agile and quick. She was capable of picking up a room, preparing the children's supper, and serving medicinal foods even as she tended the fire, corralled her nephew, and maneuvered Rufus and Wetherbee. Butter thought Vera either brave or wrathful; she threw her domestic talent at Wetherbee and was not bewildered by his misanthropy—it seemed to encourage her to ever more devious assaults at his self-contempt.

Finally, Bridey chased everyone out. Alone with Butter, she declared herself: He was free to go when he could walk on his own, and he was even free to go if he wanted to crawl onto Pennsylvania Avenue like a derelict. In the meantime, he would remain in this bed because it was the only one long enough for him to lay prone. Also, he was a simpleton for his modesty. She said she had grown up with a brother and two male cousins and had seen more naked men than women in her life. She closed saying that pride was the devil's germ and sleep was God's cure.

Butter awoke again in the humming darkness. He felt the helpless child to discover Bridey Lamont standing over him. She said he must eat more of the soup, and that she would feed him to spare the bedcovers. Butter conceded that he was more injured than he had wanted to admit. He apologized for his earlier, silent ingratitude. She seemed to appreciate his honesty and eased her reserve; the result was that she was both softer and more comfortable in command of the situation.

She also wanted to know more, and chatted excitedly while Butter accepted scoop after scoop of soup, "What is wrong with Major Wetherbee? He hates this and that, hates everything! He won't take more than a mouthful, and sits there with the door ajar and his hand on the bottle. We don't try to get that from him. Vera's father was much more difficult toward the end, and we know what to do."

Butter tried, "Don't push at him—"

Bridey Lamont continued, "I know, I know, he's most skittish. He looks at home by the fire, I have to say, and he's good with children. Billy adores the dog. And now Major Wetherbee's told Billy stories that make him rapturous. When I put Billy to bed tonight, he wanted to know when Major Wetherbee was coming back, and if he can come talk to you about black bears."

Butter managed a joke. "Anytime, anytime, I used to wrestle 'em—"

"That's the sort of thing he tells Billy," said Bridey Lamont. "Did you take an axe to this War Wagon? Is that so? And your bear-riding? The worst one was about John Brown. He said he had John Brown on the ground, and pointed a shot gun at him, and John Brown said, 'Shoot! You can't kill me! Shoot! I shall live forever!' "

Butter held her wrist to stop the spoon in order to talk. "Tory likes that story. And must like you to tell it." Bridey Lamont nodded. Butter added, "I've not known Tory to deceive about himself. He was with the Second Dragoons, under Colonel Robert E. Lee, before the war. He could have been at Harper's Ferry. The marines made the final assault. But it is possible."

"And about him setting fire to his father?" she asked.

"Tory's a Marylander. His family's fought with Lee since the war. Do you understand? That's not something a man can figure. Tory's also a West Pointer. He's made some hard choices not to have a division or corps of his own. He used to say that he's sworn to defend the Constitution but he's not sworn to take pleasure in it. About his dad, yes. Tory was with the part of the Second Dragoons that was given over to Colonel Baker two years back to chase Rebs like Mosby. They called them Baker's Rangers. That was before I came in with the First D.C. So what I know, I don't really know. They say they were chasing stragglers after Gettysburg, up on the Monocacy River, in Frederick County, Maryland. That's where Tory's from. And there were wrong things done on both sides. After Gettysburg, it was like the world had gone wrong for a while. The ambulance trains never stopped."

"He did burn out his family?"

"He takes responsibility for it. Yes. The answer's yes." Bridey Lamont shook her head. Butter continued, "You mustn't assume. This war goes on and on, and there aren't any delicate men left, or women, neither. Tory was with the regiment at Sycamore Church. You know. They were obliterated. He was captured, but got out of Libby Prison somehow."

"One boy told Mr. Skelton that they shot and shot with those special rifles of theirs. And shot and shot."

"I haven't asked Tory about it yet," said Butter. "He'll tell me someday. He's one of the hard cases now. He hasn't reported back to duty since he got back from Libby. And they haven't sent for him, I expect. He's let the Colonel know he aims to kill him if he's ever given cause, like meeting him. It's not sensible. Tory marks Colonel Baker for something. About Mosby, or chasing Mosby, or the rest. Colonel Baker's done a share of the wrong in this war, his share. You know some of it. It was worse before."

"Captain Wetherbee's resigned his commission then?"

"No, he's a soldier. If you asked him, he'd say he was garrisoning the War Wagon in case the Rebs try for it. He's a hard case. It means—he's made his own kind of peace."

"And what about you, Captain Butter?"

"Oh, I expect—you mean about making peace?" Bridey Lamont nodded. "I've looked at it. While I was running after that train, I thought about this being crazed behavior for a boy from the deep woods. I'm a curious fellow, though, and—stubborn. And when I get up the next time, I intend to keep myself on what I'm curious about and let the Colonel catch his own locomotive engines." Butter took another spoonful of soup and swallowed slowly. He added, "Something I know about hunting. The man that wanders from the track might make a dinner rather than having one."

Bridey laughed, spilling soup on Butter's beard. "And what is it that you are hunting? Or are you being charming?"

"Maybe," Butter began. "There's also this Rebel gentleman named John

Oliphant. The Colonel knows— Oliphant knows— I know something!"

Bridey wiped his whiskers. "A secret?"

And Butter laughed. "Glory hallelujah, maybe the secret of the war!"

The fever that overwhelmed Butter very early Monday morning pushed him deep into his fear of death. He had watched stronger men than himself survive a wound and make a brave beginning at convalescence only to collapse inexplicably and then succumb so suddenly it was like a sunset. Inside himself, he was terrified, and prayed simply and passionately whenever he could untangle his mind.

Bridey and Vera Lamont understood the peril as well and fought. They forced liquids into him, cooled down his body with ice, and resisted the recommendation of the first physician to administer morphine. They were of the opinion that Butter was so weakened by his cumulative exhaustion that any further dulling of his senses could only inhibit his natural recuperative power. The second and third physicians agreed with the Lamonts; they provided herbs that miraculously eased Butter's pains and lowered the fever intermittently.

The crisis passed Tuesday after dawn, when Butter awoke from a nightmare about falling into a pool of foam. He was actually floating in his own sweat. Bridey Lamont was sitting beside him, reading. He said, "Hello, I'm back, Butter's back."

She shushed him and wiped his face. Soon Vera came in to help her change the bedclothes. They made him eat more chicken soup and urinate in a bottle before they carefully laid him back to sleep. Butter came out of his drowsiness later to see Wetherbee also standing over him, with a silly smile and a head shrouded in cigar fumes. Wetherbee said, "They're good, they're very good, those two witches. I kept tellin' 'em to let you go with your pants and boots on. They hid 'em from me. Hell, Zee, I haven't been taken that serious by the ladies in years. Can you smell my cigar? It's all they'll let you have for now. Let me whiff it up good for you."

By Wednesday morning, November 16, Butter was recovered enough to be restless and fretful. He insisted he be permitted to prop himself up to watch the clock on the vanity. He calculated that it was forty-nine hours since Bridey Lamont had agreed to Butter's hallucinatory plea that she telegraph Gouverneur Nevers in New-York for help. And he knew that it was a full week since he had followed Oliphant to Georgetown; by now,

Oliphant could have escaped anywhere, including to Richmond. Butter's failure seemed complete. What he had to show for two months of hard work was a bruise from his thigh to his shoulder that Tory Wetherbee said made Butter look as if the blue uniform were becoming his new skin.

Butter also had a fair insight into the reports in the newspapers that they had brought him. Here was an item that General Benjamin F. Butler and his staff were expected in Washington today after their triumphal send-off yesterday at the Fifth Avenue Hotel by the grateful citizens of New-York. The Reverend Henry Ward Beecher had stood up on a chair to make a rousing speech, thanking Ben Butler for his steadfast defense of the Union and its first city in the crisis just past, heaping all the praise for the peacefulness of Election Day upon Butler and his staff (Haggerty and Puffer were named), and finally speculating that Ben Butler's fame would spread across the country in waves so that someday soon enough the echo would return, "Butler for President!"

Butter did not flinch at the Butler news. He was accustomed to the injustice of the so-called superior officer gathering the praise due his subordinates. And he was too taken by the other items that were like clues to a crime that had yet to be committed, or if it had, had yet to be revealed, or if it was, had yet to be understood.

In Montreal, for example, the Rebel agent and provocateur George Sanders had hired counsel for the St. Albans raiders being held in British custody, and he was successfully maneuvering the Canadian colonial government not only to refuse extradition to Vermont, but also to delay a trial in Canada. There was even mention that George Sanders might be able to have all charges dropped because Canada had no jurisdiction in the case. New-England was said to be enraged. And the political situation between the United States and Canada would not improve with the statements coming out of Montreal; the newspaper report read, "The leader of the raiders [Lt. Bennett Young of Morgan's Raiders] said that his raid was made to retaliate for the acts committed by Grant, Sheridan, and others not in accordance with civilized warfare. The St. Albans raiders are loud in boasting of their work, and threaten all sorts of retaliation in case any punishment is inflicted. Their friends are trying to delay the proceedings until instructions can be got from Richmond."

In Chicago, Butter read, six more members of the outlawed Sons of Liberty had been arrested. All the arrested claimed innocence of the charge of seditious conspiracy and also ignorance of the sabotage plot on Election

Day. There was no mention of the infamous Captain Tom Hines.

In the Shenandoah Valley, Butter read, the speculation was that Jubal Early's attack at Cedar Creek on October 19, which had almost carried the day until Sheridan's famous ride, had actually been planned as the first stage of an assault that was meant to have carried into Pennsylvania as a terror raid in order to influence the Election there. It was now speculated that Early's attack might have been the military aspect of a coordinated effort by Richmond to throw the Union into turmoil on Election Day.

Butter was not concerned with the voluminous speculations about Sherman. The scale of the failed Confederate conspiracy on Election Day was fantasy enough for him. What passionate desperation! To throw a starving army against superior numbers in the Valley, to rob banks in Vermont like outlaws, to connive with anarchists like the Sons of Liberty in New-York, to aim to release thousands of depraved prisoners upon Chicago, and to try God knew what else in Washington! Indeed, Butter could only pray that God Almighty was mindful of John Oliphant's conduct in the capital, because Butter on his blue rump was not going to stop him or anyone. Butter pushed the newspapers away. He tried to calm himself by taking up a gift from Bridey Lamont, a new volume called *The Maine Woods, A Week on the Concord and Merrimack Rivers* by Henry D. Thoreau. It did not work. He was envious of Sheridan. Oh, to make such a ride, and to do one's duty, and to help save the Union!

Butter's nap into the cool, muggy twilight of a misty day left him resigned. He was not an intellectual like Mr. Thoreau. This sickbed was the finish. He was beaten. It was time to quit. The trail was cold. The game had escaped. Another hour of such futile daydreaming and Butter abandoned even self-accusation. He cheered himself by getting out of bed to get to the w.c. by himself, with the support of two hickory canes that had belonged to W. D. Lamont. He felt more joyful still at the imminent homecoming of Bridey Lamont. Unlucky in war, he was inexactly aware that he was experiencing feelings that could only be appropriate to those who are lucky in love. For the present, he was alive and safe, and his home was several hundred miles to the north, and Bridey Lamont was his personal savior. He sighed: Whenever he thought how happy Bridey made him, he thought how unhappy this would make Desire; and whenever he thought how happy Desire would be to know that he was invalided and probably coming home again, he thought how unhappy this might make Bridey, or himself.

This soul-searching was abandoned too when Butter heard footfalls from the direction of the central stairs. They were adult steps. Butter arranged himself for Bridey, so that he would look the promising convalescent in pressed pants and clean flannel blouse. There was a knock on the door. Butter said, "Yes?"

"Excuse me, Captain, are you awake?" It was Vera Lamont; she peeked in. "Oh? Should you be up like this?"

"Fine, I'm fine, Miss Lamont."

"There are two men here for you."

Butter sensed her uneasiness, and asked, "Who are they?"

"They wouldn't give me their names," she said. "They asked for you."

Butter's panic got his feet on the floor; he asked, "Is one short and lean, and the other broad as a bulldog?" Vera nodded yes and frowned. Butter reached for his boots. He imagined two faces, Edgar Quillermouth and John Odell; he imagined Room 19, the interrogation chamber at Old Capitol Prison; he imagined Lafayette Baker's angry face. Butter pulled a boot on and felt his genitals contract, and when he pulled on the other boot, his bowels rumbled. Butter said, "Vera, I'm ready now."

She said, "I can ask them to leave. You're most unwell."

"No, no, I'm well enough for this." Bridey had reported that there had been nothing said of him at headquarters for two days. In the Secret Service, Butter knew, extreme silence could mean extreme jeopardy. Butter said, "Show them in. Give me a moment to get ready. Don't worry, there won't be trouble. Here, would you help me?"

Vera was reluctant, but she did help him pull on his uniform coat and button up. She smoothed out the bedcovers while Butter, on his hickory canes, took a turn in front of the mirror. He had never looked paler.

Vera said, "I don't want to interfere. Should I fetch Major Wetherbee? He said to, if there was need."

"I think not," said Butter. "Tory wouldn't understand."

"But I don't understand!" She was agitated now. "Can't I send them away? Bridey will be home soon. And Major Wetherbee said they weren't to take you. He—"

"Please, I know what I am doing. I have endangered you all by staying here. I know how this business works. Lordie, I have done it. Show them in." Vera tried one more time to protest. Butter smiled at her spirit, and said, "It isn't that they really need an invitation to come for me, Miss Lamont. It is just polite."

She left the door open, saying at the last, "What kind of a war is this?"

Butter mumbled, "A war kind of war." He was standing on his canes like a weeping willow tree. He breathed deeply, straightened as best he could, and watched the doorjamb fill with the two most unexpected human beings.

The pair of strangers—a dwarf and a giant, both Negroes—wandered in behind Vera Lamont. Butter looked blankly at Vera, and she shrugged. The dwarf roamed to the window, then back to the wardrobes, tapping the carpet with a blond wood walking cane. Butter tried to speak and only babbled. The dwarf turned and asked if he was Captain Amaziah Butter of the United States Volunteers. Butter coughed at the smell of the dwarf's pipe—a sharp, earthy odor. The dwarf continued in a conspiratorial tone to ask if they could confer in private. Butter nodded to Vera Lamont, who shut the door behind her.

The dwarf introduced himself as Virginia John Goodenough and offered his card. He also said that he was called Wild Jack. The card was a facsimile of the Jack of Spades, with a place for his name, and below that, "Free Gentleman of Color," and below that, "Hotel Henri IV, New Orleans," and below that, "Confidential Inquiries."

Butter sat down on the bed to study the card. Wild Jack Goodenough was small only in terms of his child's arms and tiny legs; his torso and head were those of a full-sized and vigorous man. He was dressed madly for a simple citizen, but elegantly for a New Orleans gambling man: a morning coat in red and white vertical stripes and pantaloons in dark gray, a gold and silver checkered vest, a gold tie and a dark blue cape, crowned with a light gray top hat. He also had a full black beard and moustache and steel-rimmed spectacles, which he adjusted as he closed his presentation by introducing his associate, Joshua Rue. Here was a man whom God had granted what had been left over when God made Wild Jack; Joshua Rue was a casual giant, not tall so much as massive, with a much darker color than Wild Jack's and with broad features that were established permanently in an exuberant smile. His long wiry hair was parted in the middle of his head and flopped over his ears like a helmet. Wild Jack commented that Joshua Rue was not the simpleton he looked. Wild Jack explained that the giant was hard of hearing. Joshua Rue also had hands so big they were like bear paws. He seemed shy about his hands, keeping them out of sight in the pockets of his tent-like frock coat.

After several false starts, Butter believed he had their measure, and said, "I'm correct in— You're from Mr. Nevers, in New-York, isn't that true?"

Wild Jack was now opening and searching drawers, showing found objects to Joshua Rue, and returning them to their place; he smiled at Butter and spoke to Joshua Rue. "He asks if we were sent by a Mr. Nevers of New-York!" Joshua Rue hummed. Wild Jack spoke to Butter. "Sir, please, our work requires profound confidence."

Butter tried, "I suppose I can guess. So why ask? Perhaps it's for me to tell you about John Oliphant, the Reb agent. Did Mr. Nevers explain?"

"He asks if he might explain about a Mr. Oliphant!" Joshua Rue hummed. Wild Jack had half climbed into Bridey Lamont's wardrobe; he looked over to add, "If it pleases you."

Butter said, "He's in Georgetown a week now, I hope. A house on Washington Street. With his sister-in-law and entourage. I shall write it down. No—" Butter began the story of Oliphant in New-York and after, while Wild Jack turned his attention to the blanket chest. Butter switched to his suspicion of Lafayette Baker, while Wild Jack switched to the empty wardrobe. Butter stopped talking to see if this might matter. Wild Jack continued his strange searching. Butter sighed. "Just what is it that Mr. Nevers has sent you for? Do you understand what I am saying? Oh, what's the use?"

Wild Jack looked up from running his hand under the rug's hem. "Mr. Rue, he wants to know why we are here, and what is the use?!" Joshua Rue hummed. Wild Jack said, "What we have been told is that we should involve you more directly in our assignment."

"How's that? I'm in charge here! Who are you? And what are you looking for?"

Wild Jack said, "He says, Mr. Rue, that he is in charge! And he asks what we are looking for!" Wild Jack ran his hand under the mattress on the far side of the bed. "Why do you ask?" he said to Butter. "Are you hiding something?"

"No, of course not," said Butter. "But why are you—?"

"Mr. Rue, we are telling Captain Butter he has our sympathy!" Wild Jack stepped in front of Butter. "Captain, you have our sympathy. Your wounds have curtailed crucial aspects of our assignment. This is why we have delayed until tonight in approaching you."

Butter started softly, "You delayed? How long have you been watching me? How much do you know? Do you know where Oliphant is?"

Wild Jack shut the last night-table drawer and flipped the Thoreau book open. "He wants to know, Mr. Rue, if we know everything!" Joshua Rue hummed, nodding vigorously in affirmation. Wild Jack closed the book.

"Are you well enough to accompany us, Captain Butter?"

Butter put his weight forward on his legs. "What?"

Wild Jack said, "I am telling him, Mr. Rue, we are henceforth consulting allies!"

And before Wild Jack could speak to Butter, Butter was up. "This is so like Nevers! I'm the fool! If you'd just said straight out! Yes, yes, where to? Where are we going? Georgetown?"

"Mr. Rue, Captain Butter has agreed!" Joshua Rue opened the door. Wild Jack twirled his cane. "We aren't going far, be assured, and we have a hack," said Wild Jack. "Three blocks. Willard's Hotel. The dining room. To observe Mr. Oliphant and an Englishman, Sir Henry Blondel. And yes, Captain, we do know everything—so far."

Saturday, November 19

What made Bridey Lamont cry with frustration was that Butter accused her of treating him like a prisoner of war, and when she protested, he further accused her of treating him "like your sacred husband, who you tried to hide in here from the war!" What made Butter repent was that Captain Wetherbee, dozing against Rufus on the bedroom's divan, awakened long enough to inform Butter that speaking to Mrs. Lamont like that was jackassedness. What made Vera Lamont burst into the bedroom, her robe incorrectly buttoned in her upset, and lecture Butter and Wetherbee on their bad manners and cruelty to Bridey was that earlier in the evening—it was now well past midnight, and so very early Saturday morning—she, Vera, had admitted in confidence to Butter and Wetherbee how delightful it was to have menfolk strutting around the house again, even if one was a brooder and the other one was a drinker; and Vera also declared that now, in consideration of this abuse of Bridey, she was furious and suspicious, and ready to turn Butter and Wetherbee out even if one was a cripple and the other one was a lout.

And what set this whole unhappy episode in motion, Bridey crying and Billy crying and Vera breaking an empty whiskey bottle in the fire, was that the household had been awakened by another unannounced visit from the two Negro detectives, Wild Jack and Joshua Rue, who had entered through the kitchen window and had sneaked up to Butter's room. They had stayed long enough to communicate to Butter the details of Oliphant's dinner party in Georgetown Friday night. They had fled when Bridey Lamont had interrupted to declare that the hour was very late. Butter had then slapped the bed. "This is important!" Bridey Lamont had reminded him that this was not an Army camp. Butter had said that he would be damned if he would waste another day in this bed. Bridey Lamont had reminded Butter of his collapse Wednesday night at Willard's Hotel, the last time he had charged out on his canes; she had further declared that the only thing worth risking his life against was his own bad judgment. Butter had then made his accusation about Bridey's marriage and motives. He had heard himself hurt her as badly as a man could damage a widow and a friend. Meanwhile, the result was the tears and the shouting and apologizing and pleading. In the end, Bridey recovered to say that there was nothing said or done by men and women that did not look better in morning sunlight.

Saturday morning, November 19, might have improved the relationships in the house if not for several more sudden blows to harmony. First, Butter got himself dressed and downstairs to the kitchen table on his canes in order to display his recovery and strength only to find, in the copy of Friday's *New-York Tribune* that Bridey had brought home for Butter and yet failed to remember to carry up to him the night before, that there was a small item that reported the sighting of a suspicious vessel, thought to be a Rebel privateer, off of Castine, Maine. Butter barked at Bridey that he was annoyed that this very significant news had been kept from him, and he demonstrated his ill-temper by grabbing at the fried eggs on Wetherbee's plate, and thus deliberately eating forbidden food in front of the caretakers who had put him on a restricted diet.

This childishness moved Wetherbee to cause more trouble; he said, "You were off your feed last night, Zee, it's plain. That said"—Wetherbee piled marmalade on a hot buttered biscuit—"I see your troubles." Wetherbee looked around to see if the Lamonts, busy at the stove and the water pump, were listening in; he proceeded to whisper to Butter, "We're not the first worn-out boys these've rescued."

Butter did not understand what Wetherbee meant by this confidence. They were interrupted by the children sweeping into the dining room for their breakfasts; also, Butter was distracted by trying to eat from Wetherbee's plate without being caught; also, Wetherbee was preoccupied trying to sneak whiskey into his coffee cup. Only after some calm had returned to the room was Wetherbee able to explain what he had learned from the stockman,

Kindermann, about a Massachusetts major named Henderson whom the Lamonts had rehabilitated in the summer of 1863, and about a handful of lieutenants whom they had billeted last Christmas, and about a pair of Pennsylvania artillerymen whom they had put up and nursed last spring, and about the parade of other officers that had stayed here off and on. Butter listened and darkened. Wetherbee closed, "There's good Christians in the world, Zee. There's loneliness in the world, too. I'm not choosing. I'm wanting you to know."

The major intrusion to the household, however, like a series of wild blows against Butter's conscience, and also against a chance for Butter to repair his disenchantment with Bridey Lamont, was the return of the Negro detectives. They quickly took places at the table. Joshua Rue ate each flapjack with a single bite. Billy Lamont struggled to imitate the feat. Wild Jack revealed his sweet tooth with the construction of marmalade mountains. Wetherbee amused himself by showing card tricks to Wild Jack. The Lamont women sat at opposite heads of the table and carefully observed the carrying on.

Butter tried to show his mastery of the situation by openly conducting an interview with Wild Jack about Oliphant. He expected Bridey Lamont to object, or Vera Lamont to clear the table and the room. In anticipation and out of mischievousness, Butter emphasized the potential risk in, and the necessity of his personal attention to, Oliphant's imminent attendance of a White House levee. Wild Jack's intelligence was as current as that morning, because his informant was the Royall household servant, Michael. Butter made Wild Jack repeat his report four times, twice for Joshua Rue and once for Butter, and once to annoy Bridey Lamont. Wetherbee yawned. Vera Lamont drank her coffee and watched the kitchen clock.

Finally, Bridey Lamont said, "If you are asking me, Captain Butter, in your peculiar way, if I would be free to accompany you to the president's levee this afternoon, I should say that it would be easy for me to get home early from the office, and it would be a welcome entertainment."

Wild Jack brightened. "She is saying, Mr. Rue, that she is coming along to help us!" Joshua Rue ate and hummed. Wild Jack spoke to Bridey Lamont. "We regard this as an excellent decision. Captain Butter still requires close escort, and it would avoid another accident like Wednesday's."

Butter began a gruff objection. Wetherbee guffawed. Wild Jack remarked that Mrs. Lamont was completely informed of the affair, so why not? Butter repeated himself about the potential peril. Wild Jack said that Oliphant would be accompanied by several females himself. Butter boomed that this

was Secret Service business. Wetherbee retreated from the table. Vera La-
mont took up the plates. Bridey Lamont smiled. Wild Jack exchanged with
Joshua Rue, and then reminded Butter that Mrs. Lamont was more officially
Secret Service just now than Captain Butter was.

Butter's sulking withdrawal for the remainder of the morning did little
to prepare him for the White House. He knew the problems were profound.
This could be a plot against the president! At the same time, he felt put upon.
So far from receiving the respect he deserved for his voluntary surveillance
of John Oliphant, Butter was certain that he was being mocked by those
around him. Wetherbee's attitude was tolerable, since Wetherbee's opinion
was that Butter was a fool to try to do more than survive the war with a
safe, warm seat. Wild Jack, Joshua Rue, and Gouverneur Nevers in absentia
were only occasionally upsetting for the assumption they seemed to hold that
Butter was central to this affair but not entirely competent. It was the
Lamonts whom Butter found unbearable, for their attitude that he was
fragile, thick-headed, and self-destructive. Wednesday night had been an
accident! The rioters at Willard's had knocked him down! It took practice
to learn how to wield two canes!

A most irritable and competitive Butter met Bridey Lamont at the door
at 12:30 P.M. She tried to soothe him, but he refused to speak. He also refused
her help out to the horsecar for the journey up Pennsylvania Avenue. His
temper was not eased by the consideration of the other passengers, who were
quick to give way to so handsome and needful a couple. More, the conductor
was elaborately careful to keep the standing passengers clear of Butter's legs,
and to force his assistance when Butter tangled the canes getting up to
disembark at Lafayette Square. And there were many kind farewell remarks
from the crowd, the general sentiment best expressed by the horsecar driver,
who leaned out as Butter and Bridey Lamont crossed to the White House
gate to call, "God bless you both!"

Butter grimaced and grumbled. But when the charity continued inside the
White House, servants offering chairs, gentlemen offering their arms to
escort him into the East Room, Butter started shouting, "Get away!"
"Damned busybodies!" "Leave me be!"

Bridey Lamont endured Butter's misbehavior and stayed at his side despite
his attempts to separate himself by swinging his canes wildly and backing
against the walls. As the crowd at the levee swelled, however, and Mrs.
Lincoln, Senator Sumner, and the Russian entourage made their spectacular
entrance, Butter and Bridey Lamont were forced together. Once, when a

phalanx of dignitaries shoved bystanders aside, Bridey Lamont was thrown against Butter. She hunched up and turned to lower her head against his breast to secure the protection of his bulk until the threat had passed and she could look up to say, "I'm sorry."

Butter stood unreconciled. He did not want to show weakness. He did want a cigar. The only way to smoke without asking Bridey Lamont's help was to work over to a bench at the rear of the East Room. He sat, and kept Mrs. Lincoln in sight as he lit up. He knew the interior of the White House fairly well from the visits he had made the previous winter with Lafayette Baker, Majors Conger and Wetherbee, and the other captains of the First D.C. to confer upstairs with the president and the Cabinet about chasing Mosby. Back then, War Secretary Stanton had been obsessed by Mosby's guerrilla raids, and had convinced Lincoln that any threat to Washington's security was a stab at the Union's fortitude. Butter could now only wonder what Stanton would do if he knew that a man like John Oliphant was calling on the White House today. Butter had differed with Stanton and Baker about chasing Mosby (he had thought burning out those suspected of aiding Mosby was stupidity), and Butter now differed with Baker about pursuing Oliphant. And Butter did not forget that Oliphant might represent no less a threat than Mosby. Wild Jack Goodenough was armed.

It was Joshua Rue who signaled that Oliphant had entered the mansion. It was Mrs. Lamont who saw the signal and passed it on to Butter with a whisper, though she did show her excitement when she grabbed his arm to help Butter stand up. Butter and Mrs. Lamont moved into the Blue Room and to the front of the crowd that was formed in a semicircle of adulation to observe the celebrities in the Green Room. There was a long delay, and several times Butter challenged Mrs. Lamont's certainty that she had seen the signal. She withstood his anxiety by trying to converse about the Russian prince and princess and the beautiful woman on Senator Sumner's arm. Butter harrumphed and rocked on his canes; at one point he stepped backward onto Mrs. Lamont's foot. She gasped. He apologized. She nodded. She also surprised Butter soon enough, asking, "Is that your Mr. Oliphant and Mrs. Winwood?"

Butter looked to see John Oliphant slip into the Green Room through a door in the partition behind Mrs. Lincoln. Wild Jack was suddenly in front of Butter with his right hand inside his morning coat where his revolver would be. Butter whispered loudly, "No!" Butter pushed forward along the windowsill into the Green Room. Oliphant did not look threatening, rather tentative and confused. Joshua Rue came up behind Butter, and Wild Jack was moving again stealthily through the seam of the crowd to Butter's front. Butter stood ten feet away from Oliphant. Bridey Lamont was at Butter's arm, asking, "What are you going to do to him?"

Mrs. Winwood was much improved from when Butter had last seen her ten days before. More intriguing to Butter, Mrs. Winwood seemed the center of attention of her coterie. The English brigadier and the English diplomat pressed up beside her; her Negro servants stood in her shadow; and Oliphant hung behind her like a protégé. Mrs. Winwood was striking, yet Butter assumed there was more to her power than beauty. Wild Jack had provided all the necessary information about Oliphant's visit here today except for the crucial motive. Why were Oliphant, Mrs. Winwood, and the rest here?

Butter studied them, and guessed wildly, and hoped that they had not come to assassinate. But what could it mean that Mrs. Lincoln was now receiving Mrs. Winwood? Was Senator Sumner part of their plot? Was the president going to appear and present a target? Why was Oliphant staying back from the receiving line? Was Oliphant armed? And what could Butter do about this situation if he had to? Could he attack Oliphant with his canes? But why was Oliphant here? Butter reminded himself of his firmest conviction about the Rebel Secret Service: *Because if I were them, I'd be dangerous too.*

"Pardon, suh, pardon?" It was the Negro boy who was with Oliphant; he was addressing Butter. He asked, "Is President Lincoln comin'? Can you tell me when? Please?"

Butter was unable to react. The boy wandered away to the window. The boy spoke to Oliphant, and Oliphant answered him. Oliphant seemed anxious but paternal, dividing his attention between watching the boy and watching Mrs. Winwood.

"Golly!" the boy burst suddenly. "Ain't he? Ain't he?"

Oliphant turned to the window; he spoke to the boy. "We shall see him later, Jim, we will."

And then Bridey Lamont was with Oliphant and the boy! Butter could not hear what she was saying, or what Oliphant replied. She laughed. Oliphant bowed. Bridey Lamont declared, "Oh, if you could only see it in the spring!" Then she was back at Butter's side, flushed and beaming.

Butter said, "What could you be thinking?"

Bridey Lamont said, "He's most charming, Amaziah, truly, and kind, very kind. I wanted to know. Don't be angry, please?"

Butter started, "No, no—" and saw all at once what had to be done. It was a sudden vision, acutely clear in conception, and yet just as quickly it transformed into a vagueness that was nonetheless compelling. Butter's conviction followed, and provided him a strength of purpose that felt God-sent. It also put words in his mouth. As Mrs. Lincoln retired with the Russians, as Oliphant shook off Mrs. Winwood's beckoning and drifted out of the East Room, Butter began moving and giving orders.

Outside again, on the White House's portico, Butter and Bridey Lamont faced each other with the familiarity of the long wed. He let her button up his greatcoat and wrap his scarf. She took hold of him to help him past the grand Russian coach and up onto the grass of the little oval park. Butter kept his eyes on Oliphant. Oliphant was standing with his back to them some yards ahead, near the statue of Thomas Jefferson. Bridey Lamont glanced toward Oliphant, then stepped in front of Butter. She said, "You won't hurt him, will you? Please don't."

Butter replied, "You know what he's part of. You can go home if you want."

"I'm not leaving. I think I should see what this is that I am part of."

Butter considered an impolitic and rude reply. Bridey Lamont had a forceful soul, though, and that meant she was probably more than he could hope to control or fend off just now. Butter leaned into his canes and set out across the lawn.

Oliphant was reading a piece of paper. It looked to Butter like a telegram. Butter glanced once more at Bridey Lamont beside him, and then he began speaking from five yards away. "Mr. John Oliphant?" Oliphant did not react. Butter spoke louder. "Mr. John Oliphant?!"

This time Oliphant did turn around. He put the telegram in his pocket and took his pipe out of his mouth. He said, "Yes?"

Butter continued, "Mr. John Oliphant?"—he was within a yard now, and stopped heavily—"I am Captain Butter, of the—of the provost-marshal-general's office at the War Department."

Butter hesitated; he had confused himself. Should he have said Secret Service? Did it matter? Butter thought, I don't want to be Secret Service. I like being Captain Butter of the United States Volunteers.

Oliphant also hesitated, but he did not look to be surprised. He started

speaking then, flatly and calmly. "Am I under arrest? I don't mean imperti-
nence. But— I don't want to argue. You see, I have some people that I
should let know. My family. Inside the President's House."

"Why are you here today, Mr. Oliphant?" asked Butter. "Do you intend
to harm the president?"

"What?" Now Oliphant looked surprised.

Butter pressed. "Answer me. Do you intend to harm Mr. Lincoln?"

"No, no," said Oliphant. "It's my family. They're inside. We've come
here today to seek the president's favor. It's about my father-in-law. We're
trying to get his coffin home, to bury him in South Carolina, and—"
Oliphant's voice thickened, and he breathed deeply as he continued. "And
to ask the president to stop the killing in Georgia. I know this sounds odd.
But my wife and children are in Savannah, and General Sherman— I'm
trying to answer you. The answer to your question"—Oliphant sighed once
more—"is that I am here today for mercy's sake. Also, for peace. It's true,
for peace."

Butter snapped, "You are a Rebel agent, Mr. Oliphant. I know what you
have been doing since you crossed the border on October thirty-first, and
it has not been peaceful. What part have you to play in the Rebel conspiracy?
Is there now to be an attack on the capital? Is Mosby part of your plot? You
must tell me."

"Mosby? God, no! I am here with my sister-in-law. She—"

"Once more, sir. What is your part in this conspiracy?"

"I have nothing to do with a plot against President Lincoln. Or with
Mosby. I am not a soldier. I am a man of business. My wife's family is
Southern. My father's family is Northern. I am an American citizen. I am
telling the truth."

Butter moved closer to Oliphant, placing the tips of his canes before each
of Oliphant's boot's toes. He stared down at him as best he could given the
angle of his own posture. "I know about New-York. I know the names and
whereabouts of each of your party—Kennedy, Martin, Headley, Ashbrook,
Harrington, Price, Chenault, Cook, Dennis. I know the shop on Washington
Place. I know the Sons of Liberty. I know your house in Georgetown, and
your association with the Englishmen, and your associations at the French
embassy. I know of the townhouse in London, and of Mrs. Winwood's work
in the Rebel Secret Service, for Mr. Mason. I know of the Royalls in
Beaufort, and of Brigadier-General Winwood. I know all, sir, all, except

what I have asked. And I do not accept your answers. What I must have is the truth. It is the only thing that might help you now. But I can't make promises about your future."

Oliphant was as still as Jefferson's statue. The wind ruffled his clothes. He remained dumb. Butter was satisfied for the moment. He had not expected to get what he wanted in one assault. He had meant to show his enemy the breadth of the battlefield, the weight of the opposing forces, and the improbability of escaping this day with anything like a victory. Like any experienced commander, Butter had used as much bluff as firepower. So far, however, he had only peppered from long range. It was time to flush with action across a wide front. Butter gestured toward Bridey Lamont.

"This is Mrs. Lamont," said Butter, "also of the War Department. And behind you are two more of my colleagues. I would like you to come along now."

Butter lifted his fingers in a signal. Joshua Rue came up with Oliphant's coat, hat, and walking cane. Oliphant took them slowly, and as he pulled them on he looked to the White House, then to the vaulting gray sky, then to Wild Jack standing apart from them a little, yet vigilantly, a tiny figure in a cold green field smoking his pipe with persuasive intensity. Oliphant finished his gloves and turned to Bridey Lamont.

"We have already met," Oliphant said, bowing. "I forget myself, Mrs. Lamont. I am sorry, for this."

She said, "So am I, Mr. Oliphant," and cupped her hands together.

"Would there be a chance," he continued, "that you could tell the boy, Jim, that I have been arrested? No, don't say that. That I am away? Yes, you could say I have been called away. Mrs. Lamont, it would be a great favor."

Butter pointed a cane toward the front gate. "Forget that, now. You aren't arrested until I say you are. We're going now."

Oliphant took a step and somehow misjudged the flower plot about the statue's pedestal. He smashed down a small new branch of a cut-back rose bush. He froze, and delicately pulled back his foot, so that he was looking down at the damage when he began, "There isn't someone else taking Mrs. Winwood, is there? Mrs. Winwood is most certainly not part of any conspiracy. She is a peace commissioner. She knows nothing of whatever you think me party to. Is she to be taken too?"

Bridey Lamont shook her head. Butter barked, "This is between you and me, Mr. Oliphant, and I'd appreciate your full attention!" Butter saw Bridey

Lamont wince, and he also saw Oliphant's pain. He relented enough to add, "I'm not making war on women and children, like some, if that's what you need to know."

Oliphant said, "It is, and thank you."

They left the White House grounds in a sedate procession. Joshua Rue strode next to Oliphant; Butter and Bridey Lamont strolled right behind. Up ahead, Wild Jack had crossed to the center of Lafayette Square, in front of Andrew Jackson's statue, and was awaiting the approaching horsecar—four tired horses hauling a shabby car that overflowed with shoppers and military men.

There was a rush of those getting on from the White House side. It was easier mounting from the Square, and Butter again found that his invalid-hood cleared a wide space. An elderly man offered Butter his seat. Butter urged Bridey Lamont to sit first. In the indecisiveness that followed, Butter ended up seated next to Bridey, with Oliphant standing at Butter's shoulder and Joshua Rue towering behind, while Wild Jack inserted himself beneath the parcels held by two matrons.

The car lurched onward. The conductor slipped through the jam to collect money for tickets. Butter was prepared to pay for all five in his party; however, the conductor sagged at Butter's dollar bill. Oliphant was quick to provide the correct coins. Butter twisted back to say, "Thanks," only to see that Oliphant's expression was far away.

Bridey Lamont whispered to Butter, "Where are we going? Can't you tell me? It doesn't help that you're sullen, and so curt to him."

"What?" Why was she angry with him? He replied, "The Capitol build-ing first."

"Can you arrest him? What about Colonel Baker?"

Butter did not have a good answer, and ignored the issue by pretending an interest in the view. The horsecar rolled right toward West Fifteenth Street in front of the cracked and chipped brick facade of the aged State Department building, where there were a few supplicants climbing the stone steps like worried insects. And then the car rumbled past the Treasury building only to halt again for the boarding of exhausted women just escaped from their shift at Treasury's Counting Room. From here, down the flat, straight mile and a quarter to Capitol Hill, Pennsylvania Avenue made wartime Washington as much a prosperous village as the so-called national one. Along here the military was briefly outnumbered by what served as Washington's society—as badly and plainly dressed as it was—who were out to see, to shop, and to be seen. The mood was inquisitive and not entirely sober. And the autumnal colors of the deciduous trees lining the avenue like sentinels blessed the idling and the rushing, and concealed some of the mud with gay pastels. Willard's Hotel on the left was the usual continual hubbub, and the matinee at the National Theater was just letting out a crowd at the intersection of West Thirteenth. On the right, through the openings in the hodge-podge of houses and shops off Ohio Avenue, backing on the open sewer of the Tiber Creek canal, one could spy the pinnacles of the gothic towers of the Smithsonian Institution above the treeline, like a lost sandcastle. And on the left, Bridey Lamont darted a look at her shop, but was blocked by the crush in the car and the looming breadth of Joshua Rue.

The conduct in the horsecar depended upon the district: It was pretentious for the hotel crowd, cheery for the theater crowd, and actually combative for those looking toward the excitement at the Centre Market between West Ninth and West Seventh. The car crawled through the chaos of wagons at the open-air stalls of the market. Passengers were now attacking and under attack as they tried to find a place. A young mother wrestled two children into her lap on the bench across from Butter; the baby was indifferent to all; the boy kicked playfully at Butter's knees.

Once past the bright facades of Brown's Hotel and the National Hotel, Butter became impatient with the progress. He stood up as the car started the creaking climb around to the northwest slope of Capitol Hill. And at the New Jersey Avenue stop halfway up the incline, Butter slid down from the car. This was also the closest stop to the Baltimore Railroad Depot, so Bridey Lamont had to struggle to get down with half the rest of the passengers. She laughed for her escape. And then they were off again, with Joshua Rue, Oliphant, and Wild Jack trailing.

The Capitol building sat white and commanding above them. Butter paused frequently to rest, spinning around to take heart from the panorama. It was twilight, and the grand smear of red sunlight highlighted the streaked gray clouds in the western sky above the gray Potomac and the orange and brown carpet of trees. The only man-made creation that caught the eye was a broken obelisk that was actually the unfinished monument to George Washington.

Bridey Lamont spoke to Butter. "You're not strong. This is too much."

Butter turned from her to look back at Oliphant, and frowned. He continued his slow ascent. They were before the north wing of the Capitol, the Senate chamber; it was largely darkened, the Thirty-eighth Congress still recessed for the Election. The whole Capitol building was in the last stages of a rejuvenation and transformation. The Senate wing was still wrapped with a wooden scaffolding, because they had not finished whitewashing the facade. And there were construction supplies and all manner of rubbish across the mall. A full paint bucket must have fallen from above to where Butter now stood, because he was on the edge of a cracked white pool.

Butter poked a cane at the paint chips and waited for Oliphant to get up close to him; Butter said, "You say you're a citizen, Mr. Oliphant. Does this place mean anything to you?"

"You mean the Capitol?" asked Oliphant. "It is the apex of the country."

Butter could see that Oliphant wanted to speak at length, and so he deliberately pulled away; he moved around the Senate steps and swung rhythmically on his canes across the mall to the foot of the central stairs. Butter looked up above to the year-old and still incomplete Capitol dome. And when Oliphant neared him, Butter turned. "If you mean it's the heart of our democracy, I'll hear you out."

"Yes, of course, the metaphor is unimportant," said Oliphant; he opened his arms. "I should say, the metaphor is profound. Head and heart, the head and heart of the country, where we think and where we feel. We are in agreement. The intellect and the emotions are not neighbors. They are the same, the same."

Butter said, "Like the North and the South."

"Yes, yes." Oliphant smiled. "I shall not underestimate you again. May I try again?" Butter grunted. Oliphant continued. "My father brought me here when I was ten years old. There wasn't this magnificent dome then— a lesser one, and these wings weren't even contemplated. You could see the brick face. There were more trees too, and the park out there was overgrown. I'm remembering from a child's mind. I thought it all magical. The biggest building, the most exciting place. Like the Parthenon for Alexander. I have seen the Versailles Palace now, as a grown man, and I know that my feelings once upon a time just here are incomparable. I remember huge men with hoary faces and godlike voices. And there was a pack of wild dogs out there in the woods that day, runaways mostly. I saw a man stand up there on the steps and shoot at them with a long rifle. My father was a pastor from Philadelphia, who had come down to lead a prayer before Congress. On the schooner *Mayflower,* my first sea voyage! After that man shot the dog, my father stood me right here and said that he wanted me to come back here someday as a member of Congress. When I did, he said, I was never to carry a weapon. I was to devote myself to ensuring that no man ever need come here armed. This is a place of peace and debate and fair-mindedness, he said, and when the guns come out, men cannot hear themselves talk. For years, I thought he meant it. Even now, if I touch a gun, I have trouble hearing. My ears ring."

Butter scraped a heel. "I've had that problem."

"Yes," said Oliphant, "yes, yes. I'm rambling. I apologize. You indulge me. To answer you succinctly, and from the heart, this is the first and last for me. It can make me weep. I'm sentimental. It's an inheritance."

Butter saw Oliphant had Bridey Lamont's attention. Butter turned away and began the ascent up the central stairs. He moved sideways at first, then back and forth like a mechanical man toward the colonnaded portico. There were carpenter's boxes stacked like hay bales outside the main door. Butter cantilevered himself up into the shelter of the columns and leaned hard against a crate, gasping and sweating, but triumphant. Bridey Lamont did not hesistate to come up to wipe Butter's face. Oliphant offered his handkerchief as well. Butter permitted their care until the throbbing in his hips abated, and then he got himself away from them and up to the main door. Wild Jack opened the way.

The rotunda was overgrown with trash. There were also heaps of drop cloths and stacks of boxes. The major presence, however, was a wood-built superstructure that rose up into the dome like a mockery of the Tower of Babel. The whole party stood beneath the catwalks, peeking upward two hundred feet to the pale silver glow of the dome's windows. The smell was of paint, turpentine, and the lingering odor of the workmen, for while the dome had been topped and dedicated, it was far from finished. The single sound was dripping water, probably from a pool of rainwater that had collected up in the dome in a storm.

Bridey Lamont pointed up, and said, "It should be beautiful, if they ever finish."

"I had thought it would be more like a cathedral than it is," said Oliphant. "Like the Duomo in Florence. I see now it is going to be less sublime, more open—a crossroads and not a place of worship."

"My husband, David, said that too." Bridey Lamont stepped away; she had her arm and finger up in the air a moment until she rotated and pointed down at the marble floor. "He brought me here when we first arrived. The dome was still open at the top then. After Christmas in 1861. There was the same mess here, though. David said that he wept, like you said, Mr. Oliphant, that he wept when he thought of his son, and his son's son coming here, just here, and crossing over the same steps we made that day. David said this building was a meeting place for all the men and women who had made America. Their spirits too. A crossroads, I suppose. David said, 'We made this what it is, Bridey. Our sacrifices and our dreams. It's ours.' He was so happy. And we both cried. I am going to bring Billy just here someday, and tell him, and have him stand where his father did. I shall bring Maude too."

Oliphant said, "Is your husband gone?"

"He's been missing for almost two years." Three Union officers appeared suddenly from the right-hand corridor, walking close together in conversation; they ignored Butter's party and easily maneuvered around the scaffolding and trash as they proceeded on to the left-hand corridor, toward the House of Representatives' wing, their voices rich with fraternal jubilation, their boots pounding in unison. Bridey Lamont watched them without moving her head. Then she said, "All right, then, David's gone." He was killed at Fredericksburg." She paused. There was the whooshing sound of the updraft to the dome. She added, "I suppose he's part of the building now."

Wild Jack choked, and covered his mouth, but could not conceal that he was laughing. He tried to speak to their bafflement. "Mr. Rue, she says her husband's dead and become a part of this here!" Joshua Rue hummed. Wild Jack continued, "We want that, Mrs. Lamont. When we're gone. Mr. Rue, we can be here too! I could be way up there!" He indicated the top of a column. "And you could be down here in that pedestal! Wouldn't that be a joke, Mr. Rue, that I should look down on you!"

Bridey Lamont and Oliphant also laughed. Butter bit off his own reaction, and turned to tap his cane at the door. Joshua Rue swung the door open, and Butter was outside again, at the top of the stairs with his back to them. He boomed, "Mr. Oliphant!" They were quiet behind him now. Presently, Oliphant was at his side. Butter said, "We've had our fun. I didn't bring you here to listen to you brag about your pilgrimages to the capitals of Europe, or your boyhood patriotism."

"I understand. Of course you didn't."

"We took out the guns about four years ago."

"I see your position, certainly, and I am sympathetic."

"And the reason we took out those guns was not because of wild dogs, no, sir. It was because your friends in Richmond forgot their place as equals and walked out of this building and refused to come back. They defamed what this is, and I'm not looking to debate with you its spirituality. It's a place for men to be as stupid and contrary as they want. But here! President Lincoln says if your friends would come back here we could put away those guns you're so sensitive about. Four years now we've been waiting. If what you and your friends want is so high and righteous, let them come back here and speak it out in front of everyone. That's liberty, Mr. Oliphant. And you don't need me preaching and I for certain don't want to cross words with you because I'm not up to it. I've been carrying guns that aren't good for sport and doing harm to men I never hated and having a hard time sleeping and praying and hearing too long now to control myself like I should. Hard of heart, sure I am, and sick at heart, and tired, very, very tired."

"Yes, I understand. Yes, yes," said Oliphant.

"And what I'm sickest about tonight, and having the hardest time hearing, is you, the truth from you! I'm wore out at your cool deceit."

"You have been patient to listen to me," said Oliphant.

"That's finished." Butter then commenced the final phase of his assault, but shakily, so that he was soon required to allow Joshua Rue on one arm and Oliphant on the other to help him rock gradually down the Capitol steps. The wind was driving straw and leaves across the mall in small waves. There was more carriage traffic now, and riders were pulling away from the House of Representatives' wing. Off the mall, there were huddles of clerkish pedestrians making their way over the symmetrical walkways that flanked the broad stretch of East Capitol Street. This avenue extended from the Capitol building eastward to the vanishing point, and was marked with pools of yellow gaslight and, in the far distance, crisscrossing shadows of wagons. Butter guided his party along the northeast pathway into the maple and evergreen wood. It was a two-hundred-yard ordeal for him to the barren intersection of East First Street with Maryland Avenue at a forty-five-degree angle and the thin mud flat of A Street North at a ninety-degree angle. Three-quarters of the crossroads was empty lots, mostly treeless with mud lakes, and in the near distance was a contraband camp called Swampoodle.

The fourth quarter of the intersection, at First and A, was covered with a barnlike, three-story building. It looked less old than decayed, many of the bricks worked free from the masonry to leave gaps in the walls. Its distinction was for its two large fan-shaped windows at midpoint of both the north and west faces. The bottom half of the building was poorly whitewashed and splashed with mud. There were sentries at the awning-covered entrance on First, and more guards at intervals east and south along green-painted fences. Also, the windows of the building were fixed with bars.

Butter said, "You know Old Capitol Prison, Mr. Oliphant?"

"Yes, everyone does." Oliphant stopped at the curb, then started walking again tentatively. Oliphant said, "It's foolish of me, really, but I've been thinking. How do you know when you're beaten? What is it that tells you?" They were halted beneath the awning. Oliphant looked down, and re-marked, "I saw this tiny old woman in New-York. She carried a skull. She was mad, probably. But ever since then, I've been wondering if— Well, I've been thinking about being finished."

Butter waited. Oliphant did not continue; he seemed to have withdrawn inside himself again, as if whatever he had to say was contained by his fear. Butter was encouraged. His plan to rock Oliphant into a confession was working, so far.

From here on in his plan, Butter knew, he would have to innovate and bluff. Butter told the sentry that they were going in for a tour. The sentry called the corporal of the guard, who admitted them to a vestibule, and to the stench of the prison—human waste in a clinging damp air. Butter introduced himself cursorily. This was going to be more difficult than he had supposed, because the garrisoning company had been changed since the winter before, and was unknown to him. The sergeant of the guard was sent for.

While they waited, Butter lit his cigar to fight the stink. Then he asked the corporal of the guard the crucial question, "Is Superintendent Wood on premises?"

The corporal of the guard said that Mr. Wood was away at the War Department for the evening.

Butter relaxed momentarily. He might just be able to get away with this. Presently, the sergeant of the guard arrived, a chunky, unhappy looking man with a mouthful of tobacco, named Whelan. Butter told Sergeant Whelan that he and his party were here to talk with the prisoners in Room Number 16. Whelan wanted to know Butter's authority. Butter said flatly that he was First D.C. Whelan showed his suspicion. Butter asked for an escort. Whelan stalled; he walked around Joshua Rue, sniffed at Wild Jack, and he crudely hung over Bridey Lamont.

Whelan said, "This ain't a good nest for a lady, sir."

Butter blew smoke at him. "How many robins here tonight, Sergeant? And give me that escort, now!"

Butter led them past the two guard rooms to the central hall; it was two stories high, and encircled by the stairway and the upper balcony. This part of the prison was eighty feet across. The main floor was kept dark, and echoed with distant slammings of doors and the hum of male voices. Butter turned at the main stairs. "The building was put up after your English friends burned the Capitol building in 1814, Mr. Oliphant. James Monroe and John Quincy Adams were inaugurated here. It was the Capitol for thirteen years. John C. Calhoun and Andy Jackson stalked this stairway. Down through there, where they feed them maggoty pork and week-old bread, by order of the War Department, General Lafayette shook everyone's hand twice, when he was here on his tour. Twice, because they just kept coming up to him to thank him. Up there, I want you to see what you and your friends have made this building."

Room 19, at the first landing, was the superintendent's office and also the interrogation room, where William P. Wood, a 44-year-old Virginian, routinely questioned the incoming prisoners. Butter pointed to the door; he said, "I've seen what they do in there, and I don't want to talk about it, Mr. Oliphant—this here, where they scare them. I'm a soldier, and I mark you that I've had to bring men here. I mark you."

They climbed to the first story, a filthy and cold corridor in the gloomiest gaslight. The Senate and House chambers had been subdivided over the years into schoolrooms, and then boardinghouse rooms; they were now partitioned into cells numbered 14, 15, 16, 17, and 18. Each door was marked by a single sentry. There were Negro attendants pushing two food carts from door to door and pulling out large bowls that they then filled from a pot. Butter told their escort guard, Private Mayer, to see how long it would take for Room 16 to be served. As Mayer went off, Butter took Oliphant to the windows at the rear wall of the corridor; he pulled a rag out of one broken pane. "You can see the sinks from here that make this sweet air. And the gallows. Look. Look at the courtyard, Mr. Oliphant!" Oliphant poked his head close. Butter continued, "That low barracks is for the Confederate officers before they ship them to Elmira, or Point Lookout, or Fort Delaware. It's said they actually prefer it here, since they get blankets, and their mail if they can pay for it."

The food carts had moved on. Private Mayer came over to say that Room 16 was ready for inspection. Butter looked to Bridey Lamont. "Do you want to see this? I can have the Private take you back downstairs—"

"You just attend to your own," said Bridey Lamont.

Butter shrugged. "Open up, Private!" Mayer helped the Room 16 sentry unlock the door. Butter commented, "This was the House of Representatives. Henry Clay ruled here."

Inside, the gaslight revealed a row of rough tables at which two lines of men were seated at their meal. The men became silent as Private Mayer walked in and stood at attention. The walls were covered with graffiti, including a full-sized drawing of a man on a horse that the epitaph identified as Stonewall Jackson. The bunks along the walls were piled with luggage, since the vermin infestation prohibited any use of them, and the prisoners preferred sleeping in the straw on the floor. The fan-shaped window showed the last purple light of the day. Butter squinted from one corner of the room to the other and estimated twenty-five prisoners in a chamber perhaps forty feet by twenty feet.

One fellow arose from the table like a host and spoke to Butter. "Good evening, sir, what is your pleasure?"

Another man, corpulent, aged, bright-eyed with a white crown of hair, spoke out. "There's a lady, Winn. Welcome ma'am, have you had your supper?"

The first speaker, who looked like a Sunday-dressed-up farmer, said, "Don't be afraid, you are among friends."

Butter pushed himself forward. They had mistaken him and his party for new prisoners. He waved them off, and announced, "Mr. Oliphant, I introduce you to the current celebrities of Old Capitol. These are Western men, and the most troublesome Virginians. Disgraced Federal officers are in Number 17, and your ordinary Virginia planters and merchants are in 14, 15, and 18. But here are the dangerous men—editors, preachers, town fathers, and the usual sort of American iconoclast. There aren't any spies here, just loudmouths. And a few queer sorts who might have written a book." Butter waited until Oliphant was well into the light. "Gentlemen, I introduce John Oliphant, a citizen who's unpersuaded about defeat."

The white-crowned ancient asked, "And who are you, Captain?"

Butter smiled. "I am Captain Butter, of Colonel Baker's First D.C." The assembly gagged as one. Butter pointed. "You, sir, what was your offense against the Union?"

The farmer said, "Don't answer, Dennis, he's one of Baker's."

A middle-aged man with a hawk face arose. "I said Lincoln's an ape and a tyrant, and his gang's a thievin' pack of bushwhackers, and I'll say it again!"

A dainty man, balding, and gentle as a church steward, laughed at Butter's question. "If I knew my offense, sir, I might begin to know how to get out, and how much it'll cost!"

"You were arrested in your bed at night," said Butter, "isn't that so? And humiliated in front of your terrified family? They said they were Secret Service, and you were a traitor or a Reb. Or they said nothing at all. They chained you and threw you in a sack or trunk and stomped you if you hollered. And then you were dropped in here, where they let your family bring your clothes and money for your upkeep, but not to visit you. Perhaps they've interrogated you. But they haven't charged you. You haven't seen a judge, and there isn't hope for an attorney or trial."

The church steward nodded. "Oh, I have hope. They searched me, but I hid it good."

This delighted the diners, who tapped their utensils in appreciation, one offering a toast with his cup, "Boldly said, sir!" Another adding, "Hid it, in his mouth, hid his hope, bravo!"

A most elderly gentleman, brittle and bent, in well-cut though shabby clothes, emerged from the shadows of the entertainment. "Captain Butter," he began, "I do not know what you seek from us. This is our supper hour. I ask you to respect our privacy." He put a foot up, and leaned over his knee, as would a man used to being listened to closely. "We were kidnapped, or condemned by strangers, or mistaken for our neighbor, or we were devilishly clever until we were not. Some're sympathetic to the government in Richmond, others're antipathetic to the so-called government—the so-called newly elected government—in this city. We've been here months, or weeks, and one of us since Easter, and we shall remain until they break us, or we disappear, or we pay the piper." He slapped his knee. "Sir! It don't give you the right, because we haven't our rights, to break in and display us like hogs! There are spies at this table, spies against us, and it's the lies your gang likes most!" He eased back, and took hold of his waistcoat, Henry Clay style. "I was born under a despotic king whom my papa helped throw out of this country like a broken chamber pot, and now I shall die under a despotic president who ain't fit for a chamber pot. I am saying that I'm too far along to fret for your lies. I did once. I don't no more. I am Chester Howell Lee, of Leesburg, Virginia. General Lee is no close relative of mine, though I wish he was, and I wish he was my son, that he would please his papa by treating Mr. Lincoln and his sorry Abolitionists with the hospitality we've had. And my offense? I have read the Constitution my kinfolk wrote and paid for, and read the part too about treason not proved unless by jury trial and two witnesses in open court. And God help me, I have believed it. I still do."

Butter waited on the small applause and bitter mumbling from the prisoners. Butter said, "Mr. Lee, thank you. I apologize for this disruption." Butter turned to Oliphant. "Did you have any words for your victims, Mr. Oliphant? For they are, they are." Oliphant drew back to Bridey Lamont's side. Butter pushed off on his canes for the door.

The white-crowned gentleman came forward, with a basket in his hand. "Noticing your interest in us, Captain, we have taken up a collection for the children of Mrs. Rose O'Neal Greenhow, the bravest woman in the Confederate cause, who was resident in these walls some seven months. She's gone to heaven and a kinder fate now, don't you know, leaving behind orphans. It would be a rare moment if you were to overcome your Colonel Baker's prejudices and help."

Butter looked into the basket and thought that he might have been in some clubroom, after the theatricals, the members now gathered with wine and cigars to do good works. Butter still had that dollar bill from the horse car, but he hesitated. Oliphant did not hesitate, and reached past Butter to slip in a fold of greenbacks. Oliphant also seemed ready to comment, but then only exhaled and followed Butter out.

The door was slammed shut. Butter tried to hide his uneasiness by chatting like an art connoisseur about the prison. "Up above are the solitary apartments, where they kept Rose Greenhow and Belle Boyd and other special guests—like you'd be, Mr. Oliphant." Butter stopped. Bridey Lamont was looking away. Oliphant stood patiently but absently. Even Wild Jack and Joshua Rue seemed distracted. Butter had meant to intimidate Oliphant, yet now he realized that he had also intimidated himself, and that he looked cruel. More, Butter recognized that his spontaneous battle of wits with Oliphant had disintegrated into yet another of the war's commonplace military stalemates. Butter tried, "Perhaps we've seen enough?"

Bridey Lamont said, "Yes, Amaziah, I don't know if this was right."

Oliphant stepped over to her. "You should get out into the air."

She had her hands at her face. "It isn't what you think."

What followed was an inarticulate exchange: Butter insisted that he would escort Bridey Lamont outside; Bridey Lamont protested that she did not want to be coddled; Oliphant stood close to her and spoke reassuringly. Finally, Butter started down the stairs, while Oliphant and Joshua Rue walked close behind with Bridey Lamont.

The sergeant of the guard, Whelan, was lurking in the guardroom, and came out to block their path. "You wait here, now, Captain. I want you to sign my book here, if you're what you say."

Butter waited until Private Mayer crossed in front of him; he said, "Don't try to stop me, Sergeant. Don't think it, don't look it, don't do it."

Whelan started, "Who are you to tell me, four legs?"

The sergeant was wrong. Butter was wrong. Nevertheless, Butter felt his fury, and shouted, "Get out of the way!"

Sergeant Whelan held his ground. "I'll arrest you all for this!"

Butter turned, and said, "Mr. Oliphant, take care of her now." Butter then moved inside the brief period of time he knew always existed between first alarm and first salvo. He grabbed Oliphant by the coat sleeve and propelled Oliphant and Bridey Lamont past him toward the front door. Sergeant Whelan, as expected, tried to stop them. Butter cried, "Wild Jack!"

The attack was instantaneous. Joshua Rue screened Butter's back. Butter used his canes to take down Private Mayer. Wild Jack came out of the shadows with his arm raised straight out at Sergeant Whelan's head. Whatever weapon was in Wild Jack's hand could not miss at this close range. Sergeant Whelan cursed and stopped. Joshua Rue quietly picked up the corporal of the guard and held him against the wall. Butter stood on Private Mayer's rifle.

Whelan threatened, "They'll get you for this! They will!"

Butter threatened, "Open the door, or your corporal will when you're past caring!"

The front door did then open, but from the outside. The sentry called out, "Prisoner coming, Corporal of the Guard!"

Two men eased inside the door. The first was in wrist chains. The second was the Secret Service detective Calvin Baker. Calvin Baker surveyed the scene and smiled. "Good evening, Captain Butter. Hello, Mrs. Lamont. Can I help?"

Sergeant Whelan started shouting. Butter could not risk a debate; he outshouted everyone. "Go! Go on with her, Mr. Oliphant! Wild Jack, go!"

They fled like goats down Capitol Hill until they regained Pennsylvania Avenue and the shelter of an oak and chestnut wood. Butter stood apart from Oliphant and Bridey Lamont, resting against a tree trunk, heaving for breath, and thinking. He felt absolutely determined. He had gone too far in his free-lance mission to turn back. Now Lafayette Baker would know about Butter's pursuit of John Oliphant. Now, whatever the truth of the mystery that had made Lafayette Baker overlook Oliphant's threat, the game was reduced to a simple end for Butter. Butter would be discarded. Into Virginia or into Old Capitol? Virginia, probably, but it did not matter. He was committed to his course, and he was also right. He knew he was right!

Oliphant was central to some kind of Rebel conspiracy! If they were going to punish him, they were going to have to banish the truth as well! Yes, I'm afraid of them, he thought, but I'm stubborn too. And I'm right! I'm right!

A hack approached from out of the swarm of traffic on Pennsylvania Avenue. Joshua Rue leapt out from the cabin of the hack. Butter looked back up the hill and signaled. Wild Jack in the rear guard closed in a trot; Wild Jack said, "They're not coming after us, not yet. And I don't think they're going to chase."

Butter took Bridey Lamont from Oliphant's guardianship; he said, "Bridey, I'm sorry, it's done. We're going home. There's nothing to worry about for now."

"I'm not so delicate, Amaziah." She pulled back from him and pointed up Capitol Hill. She said, "I've often wanted to know what happened to them, those prisoners. I've copied and recopied the orders that sent them there. That dear old man, Chester Howell Lee, I wrote out the order that took everything he owned. They burned him out, too."

Butter expected her to turn on him to show her temper again; he was surprised when she obeyed his urging and climbed into the hack.

Oliphant was suddenly beside the cabin door, talking to Bridey Lamont; he said, "We all feel fault, Mrs. Lamont."

Oliphant opened his stance so that he could address Butter too; he continued, "The education for me has been that even after this profound discovery—that blame is an illusion—even then, there isn't any release. You must continue to make choices, every day, choices. There was a young woman in New-York who helped me understand this. She told me a story about Ireland and the famine, how a man found members of his family dead at the door while waiting for him to get home from the mills. He had to pick them up and bury them properly. He had to make choices, you see, even when they were all dead. He had to choose."

Oliphant looked at Butter, and continued, "You know what I've discovered about this war? I've found that you cannot stop the momentum of ignorance. Ignorance has become like a flood, a raging unstoppable river in flood of men and women and mistakes and crimes and deaths. And it can't be stopped. You stand there and feel it washing over you. And it hurts. And the pain gets worse. And yet, you must continue to choose. You must!"

Oliphant paused, stepped back, and threw his hand at the sky above the Capitol building, where the moon hung brilliantly, one day short of full.

Oliphant sighed. "It's a beautiful land that God gave us, yet we are so far, so impossibly far from where we should be."

Butter could not think fast enough to figure out if Oliphant was telling him something he wanted to know. What did he mean, a flood of ignorance? And what choices? Oliphant sounded like Thoreau and those Massachusetts intellectuals. Always mistaking the wilderness for a metaphor, and making rivers and forests into some sort of bookish puzzle. Butter especially did not like the way Bridey Lamont seemed to like what Oliphant had said, and seemed to understand him. America was beautiful, so what? Oliphant was a Rebel agent and a fancy liar!

Butter pushed past Oliphant and climbed up into the cab next to Bridey Lamont. He looked back down to Oliphant. "If you're done with your speechifying now, we're away."

"I was trying to help you understand me," said Oliphant. "I was trying to understand myself, too. I don't know why. There I've done it again. I keep apologizing for my excesses."

"Well, that's just fine, but I don't understand you," replied Butter. Butter heard Bridey Lamont make a disapproving sound. Butter added, "As for help—I'm grateful for your help back there at Old Capitol, I won't deny it."

Oliphant said, "Yes, and I'm thankful for my freedom, if that's what I still have? Am I free?"

"Freedom's what you make of it, Mr. Oliphant, that's what my education has taught me." Butter liked the way he had said that, and continued, "I'm guessing we're not done on the subject of your freedom."

Butter stretched his legs, and the pleasure tingled up his spine. Butter thought of his own jeopardy because of what he had done today. Oliphant was obviously shaken and weakened, but he had not broken in any way that Butter understood. Butter decided to try a last shot at Oliphant. It was a long and late shot, but he felt it was in the right direction.

Butter said, "I expect Colonel Baker'll have more to say about your freedom too, won't he?"

Oliphant spoke quickly. "Yes, I suppose he will."

There were wagons and horseriders all around them. Oliphant looked around at the activity on Pennsylvania Avenue. He stepped closer to the hack, and asked, "Captain Butter, am I genuinely free to go?"

"All the way to blazes. Mr. Oliphant, all the way."

Butter nodded a farewell to Wild Jack and waved to Joshua Rue. Butter might not be able to arrest Oliphant, but he could keep him closely watched.

And Butter was fairly sure that he had put the fear of God and the secret police into Oliphant. If Oliphant had not blinked at Lafayette Baker's name, he had recognized it.

Butter glanced once more at Oliphant and saw a man as worn down as Butter felt. Then Butter told the hack driver to move.

Butter's delayed reaction to the physical ordeal of the afternoon settled upon him like bad weather even before Bridey Lamont got him out of the carriage and to her front door. She had to call Vera Lamont and Wetherbee for help. Butter permitted them to carry him upstairs and lay him out on his bed. But when Vera appeared with a basin of water to wash him, he misbehaved, and when that was not enough, he yelled.

Later, after a nap, Butter would only permit Wetherbee into his room to bring him his supper on a tray. Butter recounted the events of the day to Wetherbee in summary fashion, until Wetherbee, squatting by the fire with Rufus just as if they were at remount camp and these wallpapered walls were Virginia woods, grumbled that he had heard enough. Wetherbee said that Butter was a damned fool to tangle with Lafayette Banker over this damned fool of a Rebel agent.

"But Oliphant is a dangerous man, and there's no one that seems to care but me," protested Butter. "He's a bad one, Tory, I swear."

"Baker's the bad one, Zee," said Wetherbee. "He's the worst of the bad ones, because he thinks he's right all the time."

Butter said, "I'm the one who's right here. And Colonel Baker doesn't care. So why is Baker protecting Oliphant, if he is? Do you think he's protecting him? I've seen him track down men like Oliphant for weeks, without sleep, just like a hound on the trail. Yet Baker wouldn't listen to me in New-York. And he sent me into Virginia to get me out of the way. So why? What's Baker's business?"

Wetherbee said, "There's more gold in this war than lead. You said that Oliphant's a rich Reb. And you know rich Rebs, who're smart, can get what they want in Washington. If you need me to learn you that, then you must've forgot that I forgot. I forgot it all."

Butter continued, since Wetherbee was acting like his old self, savvy and argumentative. "You know what kind of man Colonel Baker is, Tory, and he isn't for sale. Baker's no traitor either. He's cruel, and he's done wrong, but he's loyal. My guess is that Baker is using Oliphant in some operation.

He's done that before. But Oliphant's not a turncoat. I've seen him up close now, and listened to him, and Oliphant is not going to play Judas for any kind of reward. The truth is, I don't have a good guess as to what's going on between Baker and Oliphant, if anything is."

Wetherbee spat in the embers of the fire. He began again, his tone weaker and sadder. "Oh, aye, Zee, I remember what I forgot. I remember now. Here it is. You either shoot the enemy, or you don't. Chewing about it beforehand just makes you a chatty target for them. It also makes you corpse-like, with your mouth open. You have to break the dead man's face to get him lookin' respectful to meet his Maker."

Butter watched Wetherbee and felt pity. Butter needed help, but Wetherbee needed more help, and of the sort that only patience and time could give. Butter said, "You don't mean that, Tory. It's all right to talk. There's more than dying to talk about."

"Hellfire, Zee, I forget," said Wetherbee, spitting again. "I forget. At Sycamore Church, it was, and I forget."

Butter sat forward. Whatever darkness had ahold of Wetherbee, it was not just Sycamore Church—massacre or not, Butter knew Wetherbee was too complete a soldier to have succumbed to one bad battle. Butter wanted to hear about what had happened to Wetherbee inside Libby Prison, a dungeon ten times worse than Old Capitol; he asked obliquely, "You have a notion to go on with your story, Tory?"

"What story's that?" said Wetherbee.

Butter decided to ease up on Wetherbee. It was not yet time to get at his demons. Butter tried to bring the subject back to his own troubles. "Oliphant was going on about defeat today. He talked about how defeat disguises itself, like some tiny old woman with a skull. He talks like that. An intellectual."

Wetherbee stood up to leave; he turned to say, "If he was talking about defeat, he ain't met it yet. A man that's beat, Zee, he forgets that too, he forgets that he's beat." With that, Wetherbee opened the door for Rufus and walked out, waving goodbye to Butter over his shoulder.

"Goodnight, Tory," said Butter.

Butter lay back to review the day one more time. He did not want to contemplate Wetherbee's deathiness, yet his talk with Tory had helped him. It had at least reminded him that he did not want to die and that there were more important things than Oliphant. Like friendship. Then again, Butter knew that he must have a plan for his future. He opened his logbook and wrote out a list of questions about Oliphant, Baker, himself, and even Bridey Lamont. Then he answered them with what were, in the end, more questions. This was not as frustrating as he had thought it would be. There were mysteries, and it was good to look at them written out. Butter began to feel like a half-cocked intellectual. It was not awful.

It was tiresome, however, and he did not realize that he had fallen asleep until he was awakened, very late in the evening, by Bridey Lamont.

She was in her lavender wool robe, and she was carrying a sterling silver tray with a bottle of Wetherbee's bourbon, two glasses, and a small pitcher of water. She began, "I know I'm out of place. I didn't want to waken you, but I had to. I have the feeling that you will go away tomorrow."

Butter spoke sleepily. "It might be right. It might be time to face Colonel Baker."

"Do you have to? I mean, why are you doing this? Why do you have to keep after John Oliphant? You're not one of the detectives. Why isn't Colonel Baker doing this, or helping you? I know it isn't my concern, but it seems to me that you've done your duty. And—why are you keeping what you've been doing from Colonel Baker? Do you truly think John Oliphant is after the president? Or that he's what you said, a master agent? He doesn't seem like that."

Butter was awake enough now to sense that her questions were less an interrogation than they were sympathy. Still, he did not want to argue. He said, "I can't answer you. I haven't got many answers."

"Then why do you have to go tomorrow? You're safe here, and you're not well yet."

"Bridey, I have to go. I just have to."

"That's what David said, Amaziah. In this room. He said, 'Bridey, I have to go.' Before Fredericksburg. That's what I have as his epitaph, 'Bridey, I have to go.' It isn't much."

"No, it isn't." Butter lowered his head. "But I do have to."

"David didn't have to go to Fredericksburg, and you don't have to go tomorrow. I wish someday one of you men would admit to your foolish pride and tell the truth."

Butter answered, "Yes, Bridey."

She set the tray on the nightstand, and poured them both a finger of whiskey with two fingers of water. She handed Butter his glass; then she sat on the bed at Butter's knees. The oil lamp made her neck look very white. She smelled of soap.

She began again. "I didn't come in here to badger you, so I'm sorry for that. It's that there probably won't be time for us to talk in the morning, with the children and church. And I want you to know that I wasn't honest with you today. I understand you better now. You did what you could with what you had, I suppose. You believe you have to go on with this, and I was pretending that you were being stubborn. You are a little stubborn. But that wasn't why I was so difficult. I was angry. I was angry with you."

Butter sat up, meaning to comfort her.

"No, let me talk," she continued. "I was angry because I wanted you to be someone you can't be. I wanted you to be a man who could make me feel safer, who could make safer and easier what no man can. I blamed you for my own troubles, and I wanted to belittle you. I wanted to show you up in front of everyone, including John Oliphant. I mean, he's not my enemy, Amaziah, is he? And I really don't think he's your enemy. I'm the one who gives myself the worst trouble. Is it so different for you? Oh, what I'm trying to say— I'm not sure of this. You should hear this anyway. You were kind to me today. Oh, kind, kind, in your way, kind. I was out of place going with you like that, and I apologize. I'm still out of place."

"Bridey, oh, Bridey." Butter sighed. What she said made too much sense for him to speak to all at once. He tried to solace her by joking. "How can you be out of place? This is your bedroom."

She laughed and drank a sip; she did not seem to like the whiskey, but she drank again, and said, "I think that you accidentally let me see, today —that you let me become aware of things that I did not want to know. I did. I didn't. I was unfair, assuredly, when I once said that you and Major Wetherbee were soldiers and David wasn't, as if there was evil in being a soldier. As if we weren't all, each of us, part of the ugliness in this war."

"You mean Old Capitol Prison? Bridey, you aren't responsible for that."

"Don't tell me I'm not! At least John Oliphant understands that! Blame is an illusion, he said. You can't blame others. We're all responsible. I'm an American citizen too, even if I can't vote! I have the right to be disgusted with what I have done!"

Butter was unfastened by her anger. He did not have a response. His education and experience deserted him. She had a fire in her that frightened him and unhorsed the very ideas that he depended upon. He drank his whiskey and waited, dumb.

"I am speaking of responsibility, Amaziah. That's what John Oliphant was talking about at the end. He spoke of the choices we all must make, regardless of the circumstances. That even after we accept responsibility for our sinfulness, we must still make more choices. You know what sort of choices those are. You men always speak of your choices, as if we women didn't make the only choices that signify."

She drank again. She was not looking at Butter, rather toward the bureau and the picture frames of her family. She continued, "John Oliphant spoke of the most difficult choice in life. Between the right thing to do, and the right thing to do. At times, you must choose between them, and there's no telling which is more right because they're both right. Between faith and faith."

Butter felt threatened by her talk of Oliphant. He said, "I can't figure why you treat him as if he were right! Oh, he's charming, and the cool gentleman. But he's not right! He is the enemy, Bridey. The enemy! My enemy! He's as conceited and two-faced as he can be! And if you don't see that, then I can't say you understand me!"

"Perhaps I don't understand you," she replied evenly, not showing any upset at Butter's temper. "Perhaps none of us understand each other, and we pass our lives alone and perplexed, and our prayers to God are misheard too, and it's no use to try."

She returned the glass to the tray, pulling herself into a guarded pose, her legs folded beneath her, her hands locked together into a pillar of support. She listened to her house knock and whisper in the night as she collected herself, and then she continued. "Perhaps, Amaziah. Yet I do not believe it. I shall never believe it. And perhaps it is sufficient for us to believe that we want to know each other. I wanted to know you. From that first time, when we helped that poor old woman looking for her son. I could see that you were kind, and homesick, and, well, kind. And I wanted to know John Oliphant today too. That's why I went up to him. He's as kind a man as you. And David, as kind a man as David was. I was curious. I still am."

Butter leaned toward her, and said, "There's a lot of kind men in this war, Bridey."

She looked up. "Yes, there are, and I've met more than a few. I've liked more than a few."

Butter whispered, "Bridey?" In an easy motion he brought both his hands together and then down like a lid upon her clasped hands. He did think to conceal his wedding band with the fingers on his right hand. He said, "You're smarter than I am, Bridey, and braver, much braver. Men are kind, true, but they frighten me sometimes. Women too, I suppose. When I was a boy, alone in the woods, or with my dad and brothers, it was easy, it was so easy. It isn't that way anymore. I don't know why I'm doing what I'm doing. I do think I should see this business with Oliphant through to the finish. I listened to Oliphant today too. He did say something that struck me hard, and I've been thinking on it. He talked about the momentum of ignorance in life. The flood of ignorance, he said, something like that. That frightens me too, that maybe I'm being swept along. That maybe I shouldn't want to know more than I do about things. But I do. And I think you're brave for wanting to know things too. Brave. Lordie."

"I'm not, Amaziah. I'm not what I want to be. I'm a coward for the way I've acted since David went away."

"I'm the coward, Bridey. And what I'm most afraid of just now is my feelings for you. They're not right, and it all sits on me."

Bridey Lamont laughed, and whispered, "I understand," and got a kiss on the lips for her sense of humor.

Butter proposed a wood cord of foolishness then, and kept talking and moving in a familiar and athletic way, because to hesitate would have been to risk examining what he was doing. She was a beautiful woman, and she was considerably more urgent than even beauty without clothing and in her own bed. Butter liked her long, high breasts with their small, dark nipples, and he liked her fleshy belly with her pubic hair trailing up toward her navel, and he liked the animal smell of her when she reached for what she had lost through no fault of her own and did not know how to get back without fault. They used the words of love as colloquially and sensuously as they can be used, and they relied upon their bodies to unearth the release that the Bible holds out the possibility of without erotic details. Butter felt very good, and very purposeful, and then he felt happy and irresponsible. There was a moment first inside her when the idea of power seemed irrelevant, because this was where all the stories began again. And there was the rhythmic search for bliss, all the world remaining outside and what was inside becoming a splendid and warm memory. Some men babble. Butter held his breath. Some women groan. Bridey Lamont pronounced.

PART THREE

THE ATTACK ON NEW-YORK

November 19-30, 1864

NEW-YORK, NEW YORK

CHAPTER 8

Amaziah Butter
at New-York, New York

EARLY TUESDAY MORNING, NOVEMBER 22

At first light, War Secretary Stanton, in a voluminous gray frock coat with the collar turned up over a heavy scarf, was standing lopsided and belligerent in his office at the War Department. He had regained some of his health, and there was the color of anger in his cheeks. He was glaring over the stacks of reports on his desk. They concerned the Copperheads, especially the secret society called the Sons of Liberty, and they also concerned the Confederate Secret Service in Canada.

The reports were in the handwriting of dozens of clerk-copyists from provost-marshals' offices as farflung as Colonel Alexander's at St. Louis, Colonel Oakes's at Springfield, Brigadier-General Hays's at New-York, and onward—Leavenworth, Saint Paul, Columbus, Wheeling, Harrisburg, Philadelphia, Trenton, Hartford, Providence, Boston, Brattleborough, Concord, Augusta. Also, there were large brown folders stamped "Secret" from the State Department's listening posts outside of the country, at Halifax, St. John's, Muncton, Quebec, Bermuda. Captain Butter's written report from Bangor in mid-October was on Stanton's desk, and so was Mrs. Lamont's hand copy of the report that Captain Butter had made in this room on November 1.

Stanton was not alone in his deliberation. William Wood, the squirrelish superintendent of Old Capitol Prison, was seated hunched up and expectant by Stanton's desk. Colonel Lafayette Baker was bouncing on his toes by a bookcase, his hands clasped behind him like a man waiting for a train. Judge-Advocate-General Joseph P. Holt, his unhappy face like a bust of Vengeance, was pacing the carpet runner that extended from Stanton's desk into the clerks' vestibule. Major Levi Turner, General Holt's assistant, was seated at the long credenza next to Provost-Marshal-General James B. Fry; they were sharing a pile of biscuits, but both were eating as a man might chew tobacco, for distraction and not sustenance. And all about these potentates were their various clerk assistants, like Usher Skelton, who were seated on the hardwood benches as unobtrusively as possible, their copybooks open and their pens ready for communications to the telegraph offices and the staffs in the catacomb of the War Department.

This precise moment was at the end of yet another urgent pre-dawn debate on the same burdensome subjects: What to do about the Copperheads? What to do about the Sons of Liberty? What to do about the Rebel Secret Service?

For weeks now, since before the Election, each of the commanders in the room had agreed that action was necessary. Yet because of the opposition from other members of the Administration, particularly Secretary of State Seward, these men had been forced to amend their ambition in parts. Colonel Baker had suggested arrests in Canada and quick transportation of the prisoners across the border. General Holt had urged arrests in the East, and in the big cities like Boston and New-York. Major Turner had recommended beginning with selected arrests in the border states of Kentucky and Maryland, and particularly in Baltimore, the well-known Rebel enclave. General Fry had wanted reinforcement of his provost-marshals' offices before any arrests were made.

In all, they had chewed the fat of this argument for so long that they each showed the upset of indigestion. It was too late, one said. It was not yet time, another said. It was never going to be time to give these traitors what they deserved, said a third. And what had they really meant to say at every one of these cranky debates? There was actually a moat surrounding the Federal prison of Fort Jefferson on the Dry Tortugas off Florida; and there was actually a shark kept in that moat that the inmates called "The Provost-Marshal." That moat was where these commanders would have liked to have thrown the Copperheads, the Sons of Liberty, and the Rebel agents. All of the names in those reports were guilty of treason. That had never been at issue, and had not been the question at this debate just concluding. The profound question had always been, and remained this morning, When to arrest them?

Stanton threw his hands at the reports in wordless frustration. Major Turner started talking, repeating his earlier argument that there must be caution and restraint. Even without the legal inhibition of habeas corpus, he said, there was good reason to strike piecemeal and judiciously, or the arrests were likely to be thrown out of court.

Nonsense, commented General Holt; he continued that the excuse of restraint was gone with the obstreperous, old-fashioned, and now resigned attorney general, Edward Bates of Missouri.

Superintendent Wood agreed, and gleefully, because his Old Capitol Prison had always been a target of Attorney General Bates and his carping about civil rights.

The excuse of the Election was gone too, continued General Holt, who had let his anger over this issue show for weeks since he had been overruled by Seward.

General Fry spoke up that one more excuse was gone as well; he said that it was no longer necessary to hesitate because of their worry for the far greater risk in releasing General Sherman's army from Atlanta. He declared that the public would now welcome aggression in all quarters, to match Sherman's in Georgia.

It was Colonel Baker's time to speak. He reintroduced an idea that they had, earlier in the debate, resisted as too audacious. Baker said that they should consider Thanksgiving Day more completely. In October, President Lincoln had declared that Thanksgiving Day, Thursday, November 24, was to be set aside as a national day of celebration, when everyone should try to be at home with their families or loved ones, to "humble themselves in the dust" and to pray to the "Great Disposer for a return of the inestimable blessings of Peace, Union, and Harmony throughout the land."

Whatever Thanksgiving meant, continued Lafayette Baker, it would have the effect of making citizens pacific for twenty-four hours. Also, they would be at home, and they would be so bloated by food and drink that they would react sluggishly to an intrusion. What was true for patriots was also true for Copperheads. Bluntly, said Lafayette Baker, Thanksgiving Day would unlock hearts, and would make it easy to unlock doors.

General Holt pointed at Baker. "Say it, Colonel, say it. You mean a mass arrest on Thanksgiving, don't you?"

Lafayette Baker replied, "Beginning in the morning for the worst of them, and continuing all day for the rest."

General Fry asked, "Where? The East? The Northwest?"

Colonel Baker said, "Everywhere. Your men. Mine. Everywhere. And quietly. The newspapers won't catch hold till Friday, if they do."

Superintendent Wood said, "We haven't got room in the jails."

Lafayette Baker said, "There's always room in Old Capitol or Fort Lafayette, and we'll use Willard's too." They laughed, all except Stanton.

Major Turner asked, "What about Canada?"

Lafayette Baker nodded. "That will have to wait. First the foxes in the coop, then them outside." They laughed again, all except Stanton.

Stanton began his customary foot-tapping and the fluttering of his fingers. He showed his four gold teeth when he stretched open his mouth. But he did not speak yet. Through the window behind him, there was enough light so that the tops of the trees looked an ashen green. The birds were noisy and hungry.

General Fry relaxed with his coffee. Major Turner broke another roll and buttered it absently. Superintendent Wood picked at his coat sleeve. Lafayette Baker eased back on his heels and looked toward the exit. General Holt cleaned his pipe bowl while watching Stanton's face. They all understood that this was Stanton's decision to make, and that he would either dismiss the matter until another day or issue a final pronouncement. Stanton cleared his throat tentatively. His voice was still raw from his illness, so he spoke slowly. He said, "All of them. That you can. All of them. Thursday. All."

Stanton leaned down to write on a piece of paper, and it was done and finished. His command had become the will of the American people. He wrote, "Arrest them all."

EARLY THURSDAY MORNING,
THANKSGIVING DAY, NOVEMBER 24

On New-York's East Side, the contiguous Fourth and Sixth Wards rested upon the remnant of a drained lake and the gaseous residue of old swampland that had been reclaimed from the East River by silt, detritus, and time.

"Bloody Ould Sixth" was the home of the city's most sophisticated and muscular gangs, like the Roach Guards, the Plug Uglies, the Shirt Tails, the Chichesters, and the now supreme Dead Rabbits. All of these gangs were able to feed on government graft in exchange for delivering the vote to the Democrats and their party machine at Tammany Hall while at the same time the gangs fed upon the rewards of hooliganism and extortion in exchange for delivering the inhabitants of the tenements a peculiar security.

The hearthfire of the Sixth Ward was called Five Points, a crossroads not three stones' throw northeast of City Hall at the junction of narrow streets named Cross, Little, Water, Orange, and Mulberry with the broad avenue of Worth. The heat of Five Points was the most intense on the so-called hallowed ground of Paradise Square, a triangular park at the exact center where, it was said, the strong walked with brickbats until the stronger walked upon them.

The Sixth Ward was Irish and it was cruel; these were immigrants and children of immigrants who had been cast out of one island by persecution and so were holding onto Manhattan Island with a well-learned intolerance for strangers. During the Draft Riots of July 1863, the phalanxes of the mob had risen from Five Points like the fingers of a spreading flame, crying, "Kill the rich!" and "Down with the Black Republican nigger-loving sons-of-bitches!" Always in the forefront of the rioters had been the elements of the gangs, especially the Dead Rabbits, who had advanced into battle in their blue-striped pantaloons and undershirts behind their standard of a hare skewered on a pole. Also in the vanguard had been the Bowery B'Hoys, the arch enemies of the Dead Rabbits, who were from the north of the Sixth Ward in the bawdyhouse and show palace district along Bowery Street, and who had plunged into the fight wearing their distinctive battered stovepipe hats, and also with tactics slightly superior to those of the Federal troops. For that mad week, July 12–18, New-York had experienced the awful miracle of competitively cutthroat gangs who had united to stab at the jugular of the Union. Then the War Department had sent in field artillery, and grape shot had torn off the face of the uprising.

The Fourth Ward, south of the Sixth and due east of City Hall Park, was not as well organized or ethnologically defined as "Bloody Ould Sixth." It was an older district in most ways, because it was the outgrowth of early New-York's burgeoning seaport that had crept up South Street for more deep water anchorages. By 1864, the occupants of the Fourth Ward were not a blend of types but rather a depository of cast-offs—the most desperate Irish mixed with the half-breed, quarter-breed, and most mongrel of the city. The skin color there was neither black nor white but gray. It was a riverfront, not a neighborhood, and it was wholly dependent upon South Street's shipping firms and Front Street's warehouses.

Yet the busy shipping commerce in the Fourth Ward should not have misled the observer. In comparison, Five Points was civilization. The Fourth Ward had become the worst possible place in America, a sinkhole of self-hatred. Politics there was either kill or be killed, and had nothing to do with votes, graft, or the Draft Riots. There was no Draft in the Fourth Ward, unless, it was said, it was Satan's Draft and to hell. The clergy were not the only unwelcome group. It was true that New-York's Metropolitan Police Force was extremely wary to venture into the Sixth Ward, and usually let the Dead Rabbits enforce the law of strength there. In the Fourth Ward, however, the police did not even consider poking into the tenements, saloons, and hotels. They battled the thugs only when they came outside, and then only in rear-guard, retreat actions.

The gangs in the Fourth Ward were shadowy. They had names, like the Buckoos, the Swamp Angels, the Slaughter Housers, the Hookers; yet there was no certain way to know at any one time if a gang existed or was a legend, because no one would admit to membership unless at his death and in order to demand revenge. Also, in the Fourth Ward, because preying upon the squalid tenements was unprofitable, the spectral gangs and the major criminals had to depend less upon group tactics than upon random income from pilfering the warehouses, shanghaiing sailors, and maintaining the gambling and whoring dens. Capital, not muscle, was god here, and in a way Adam Smith had not intended in his famous treatise. In the absence of any godly institution in the Fourth Ward, the invisible hand of commerce had stripped America naked, so that a man in extreme reflection would admit to preferring to be rich and dead rather than poor and alive. It would also have been fair to say, if unfair to Adam Smith, that the invisible hand moved the most efficiently in the Fourth Ward when it reached not to determine supply and demand but rather to flick the blade or twist the garrote that settled some fortunes and began new ones.

Gouverneur Nevers explicated the political philosophy of the East Side of New-York to Captain Butter as they pressed through the riff of Beekman Street that sloped from the front door of the White-Coat Cafe down into the sinister putrescence of the Fourth Ward.

It was near 2 A.M., Thursday morning, November 24—the first hours of Thanksgiving Day—and the carousers and parasites were out in force. Some were bundled in rags with their hands upturned toward Butter. Others stood bold and square-shouldered, studying Butter for a weakness or an inclination to barter. Up ahead, there was a crowd gathered below a tenement window to witness a howling brawl inside that sounded like the murder of girls by chickens. Butter glanced up to see a bare-chested, tuberculoid female smeared with green paint who was screaming curses down upon the bystanders. When she saw she had Butter's eye, she yelled at him, "Bastard! Bastard!"

Butter jumped, and closed up quickly to Gouverneur Nevers, making sure that he had Wild Jack and Joshua Rue on his flanks. Nevers had warned Butter that an officer's tunic down here, even under a greatcoat, was like wings at the gates of hell. Yet Butter's imagination did not allow for the possibility of disguise. His blue coat was all the armor left to him now, and he would wear it until the War Department changed its mind once again. The significant fact for Butter was not the magical effect of the clothing, however; it was rather that he still wore the uniform as a free man. Butter was in New-York and in wobbly motion on a single cane instead of being in Virginia and in the works, or in Old Capitol and in chains.

Not that Butter understood why he had not been punished for his pursuit of Oliphant. He could assume that Colonel Baker must have known of his unauthorized mission by the previous Sunday morning. Butter had chosen to stay at Bridey Lamont's house Sunday and to await either word to report in or arrest. Nothing had happened, other than Butter's further confusion in his affections for Bridey Lamont.

By Monday afternoon, Butter had decided that it was best he go voluntarily into Secret Service Headquarters and again try to tell Lafayette Baker the whole truth about Oliphant. Butter had expected to be reprimanded and reassigned immediately, but facing Baker had seemed a better course than waiting for Baker to react. To his consternation, Butter had found that he was to be ignored. Lafayette Baker had not appeared at headquarters all day. Usher Skelton had refused to interview Butter, and had sent word through White-Pine that Butter was still rated on invalid leave. Butter had gone home with Bridey Lamont more puzzled than ever before and feeling left out.

Then, very late Monday night, something momentous had happened, and Butter had felt returned to the bull's-eye. Wild Jack and Joshua Rue had appeared to tell Butter that John Oliphant had slipped their surveillance sometime that evening from the room he had taken at the National Hotel after parting from Butter on Saturday evening. Butter had panicked, and had wired Gouverneur Nevers of Oliphant's disappearance; Butter had added in the telegram, "John Oliphant may be coming your way, and he truly is seven times Tom Hines."

Butter had arisen groggily and unusually late Tuesday morning. He had nevertheless been determined that he must locate Lafayette Baker, or some-one in even higher authority at the War Department, and warn that he was convinced that there was an imminent Confederate Secret Service attack somewhere, by someone, and that Oliphant was the mastermind behind it and in charge.

Butter had not gotten far with his plan. For while he had been eating a hurried breakfast with Bridey Lamont, and speculating as to how it would be his fault if anything horrible were to happen to the president, Wild Jack and Joshua Rue had arrived with amazing news: Gouverneur Nevers was beckoning Butter to return to New-York. Why? Because Lafayette Baker earlier that morning had telegraphed an order to Nevers to prepare for a mass arrest of the Sons of Liberty in New-York beginning Thursday morning, Thanksgiving Day; because the arrest lists had not included either Oliphant's name or the names of the Rebel guerrillas; and because the Rebel guerrillas —Martin, Headley, Kennedy, and the rest—had disappeared from their hotel rooms in New-York the night before, at approximately the same time Oliphant had disappeared from his hotel in Washington.

It was now thirty hours since Butter had arrived in New-York to help Nevers find Oliphant. Not only had they failed to do so, but also they had not yet been able to locate any trace of the guerrillas. Nevers and Butter had not wasted time debating what might be about to happen. They knew there was trouble coming. They also knew that the advantage was momentarily with the enemy. For Nevers had been obliged to deploy his detective force throughout New-York, Brooklyn, and the New Jersey waterfront in prepa-ration for the mass arrest. Nevers's men were therefore unavailable to con-tinue the search for Oliphant and the guerrillas at least until Friday.

The summary result of so much bad luck, bad planning, bad judgment and plain mysterious cunning was that Nevers, Butter, Wild Jack, and Joshua Rue were charging into the breach lacking either a good plan or reinforcements. And from what Nevers had told Butter of where they were going in the Fourth Ward, Butter understood that this was a very risk-filled and perhaps reckless venture. Yet there was a rumor about Oliphant that had to be tracked down. And to do so, Nevers had told Butter that they had to go "underground."

Nevers, Butter, Wild Jack, and Joshua Rue turned north onto Water Street, the Broadway of these pariahs—narrow, rutted with slime, and badly lit. A gang of sailors approached them head on, singing a bawdy tale in ruinous French. Nevers laughed, and translated the chorus, *"Up Monique! Up Clare! Up Jacqueline! Up there!"*

Water Street was an open sewer that looked comfortable with itself. There were bodies that might have been corpses under overturned carts, and children hanging out of tenements to drop rocks on pedestrians, and a dead horse blocking a doorway; and everywhere along the walls there were people sleeping, or perhaps too subdued to do more than lie there. Butter observed that there was no sloth here. All were working or being worked upon. And if they were not happy, they were busily diverted. The numbers were also striking. Whereas Broadway at this hour was deserted, Water Street was as crowded as a market at midday. Charity looked very dear here, and souls very cheap. At the same time, Butter felt what he recognized was a thrill. This was sin. It was fascinating. A man grinned to show Butter three black teeth and a black tongue. A youngish woman opened her bodice to show Butter her scars. And when another woman started to raise her hem, Butter tripped on his cane.

Nevers must have seen Butter's amazement, because he slowed the pace to explain the sights. Butter's Puritanism was disoriented by Nevers's respectful tone of wonder. After Butter grunted once too often, Nevers thickened his slang, and played a first-rate tour guide in the Inferno.

"That palace over there is One-Armed Charley Monell's Hole-in-the-Wall," continued Nevers. "The gins's bad, the dangler's fast, and the mab's whaleized. They sell boys to first mates, and just anyone. The temple up there is Patty Conroy's Lonesome Crib. It's said to have the best gooh west of China and East of Araby. You know what gooh is, don't you, Cap'n? The prices are cheap, but for what these emperors can pay for Venus's curse, there ain't too cheap. And up ahead, at 304, that's Reverend John Allen's mission. It ain't what you think. The best bingo and the highest price cats. Bleak, that's what they call it, bleak, that's John Allen's. Reverend Allen quit Union Seminary when his flesh strengthened and spirits lifted. He prays over his card dealers once a week while the girls sleep."

Butter was not relaxed, but he was growing accustomed to the noise, the smell of bad meat and the swamp, and the dizzying suddenness with which people approached him as a mark. He was almost ready to ask questions, and started to point, when Nevers suddenly jerked his thumb to Wild Jack and Joshua Rue. They took the point. Nevers took Butter's arm tightly. The four of them turned abruptly into a crowd that was assembled at the door of a three-story brick house that the gilded sign identified as No. 273 Water Street, the infamous Kit Burns's Sportsmen's Hall.

Nevers whispered to Butter, "Forgive 'em for what you're going to see, Cap'n, since they don't know why God made them, and the devil's a dreamer, and Kit Burns is one of the devil's best." Nevers was laughing.

Two gnarled thugs stood with their arms crossed at the swinging gate just inside the door. There was no fee, just the rope-made gate, with a sign in several languages that said, "No Gunplay." Butter absorbed the gin in the air. The floor was covered with sawdust; the walls and ceiling were painted a moldy green; the bar was made of crude boards; the stairs to the right led up to the prostitutes, or whatever else they were called, cats, gooh, mabs, gooseberry puddings. Butter tried to question Nevers again. Nevers was concentrating on his task; he signaled Wild Jack, then got Joshua Rue in front of him and Butter to serve as a ram through the crowd.

A roar exploded from the rear of the house. Butter could not see the cause of the excitement, but eventually they struggled to a vantage over the heads of shorter patrons. Butter looked down on a large arena; it was ringed by sandbags and a wooden retaining wall, with poles at various intervals. Two men were dragging burlap across the dirt floor of the arena to smooth the ground. Other men sat on the sandbags, holding sacks and boxes.

A clattering and angry argument erupted across the arena. The arguing was actually wagering. Paper money flew hands to fists, and men cried out numbers and names. Clapping began in fits and spread across the assembly. The noise became a taunting beat, whap! whap! whap! Butter could hear a name being called out beneath the pounding: "Sherman! Sherman! Sherman!"

A small Negro stood up on the sandbags with a burlap sack in his hands. A cheer cut the applause. Another Negro stood opposite him, perhaps fifteen feet across, with a wooden box that he set down on the floor of the arena.

A bell sounded three times, and the wagering speeded up until the bell sounded three more times. The crowd pressed up against the retaining wall. Butter was transfixed. What were they going to do? What was in those sacks? The crowd was now screaming in unison: "Sherman! Sherman! Sherman!"

The bell sounded again. The Negro opened the box, and three black creatures charged out in three directions. Butter gaped. Rats! They were rats, black and preposterous, not only long but also stout, with naked red tails. The gallery was mad with expectation. Then the small Negro upturned the burlap sack, and out fell a small, stringy-legged dog, brown and white, with a huge jaw and a bobbed tail.

The dog, perhaps part dachsund and part terrier, was spinning as it hit the ground. It was off instantly to the cover of the retaining wall. This was just a feint, though, for the dog stomped one rat down and bounced across the arena. The other two rats closed quickly on the dog and pulled it down. But the dog had a trick of rolling over and over on its side. The rats tried to keep behind the dog's shoulder, because of that snapping jaw. The dog rolled into the retaining wall and came up snapping. There was a crunch. There were squeals. The dog screamed.

Butter did not turn away; he did speak pleadingly. "Mr. Nevers?"

"There's new heroes every night," explained Nevers, "in Kit Burns's rat pit. It used to be they named them Grant or Lee."

All four creatures lay in the arena. The gallery implored one of them to get up to resolve the wagering: dog or rat? The far-side rat made a try, and collapsed, twitching. Then the dog did stand, and got halfway across to its keepers before it slumped again. It used its front legs to crawl back to the retaining wall. The keeper closed the sack over the dog and raised his prize to cheers. The crowd responded: "Sherman! Sherman! Sherman!"

It was several minutes, while another cycle of wagering began, before Wild Jack brought the victorious dog handler to Nevers. He was a short, dark-skinned Negro, skinny and big-nosed, wearing an overcoat and a skull cap. Nevers introduced him to Butter as Mr. Snow.

Butter knew there were to be negotiations to do with their destination, so he hung back behind Nevers. Butter wished that Nevers would stop acting so cheery; after all, it had been Nevers who had said that going "underground" would be "chancy."

What had not occurred to Butter until just now, examining the Sportsmen's Hall, was that when Nevers had said "underground," he had meant it. Kit Burns's rat pit was as far down as Butter had ever imagined. Yet from what Nevers had hinted earlier when he had proposed this enterprise, it was not the end of their journey.

Nevers closed his deal. Nevers signaled Butter, and they followed Mr. Snow back to his cluster of dog handlers. Mr. Snow seemed to be giving instructions to his assistants. Then Mr. Snow was off again, Nevers, Butter, Wild Jack, and Joshua Rue close behind him, through the back door of the house. The last Butter saw of the rat pit, there was a fat man in the arena entertaining the wagerers by offering to bite off the head of a rat for a quarter. When the quarters rained down upon him, he did bite, and there was blood over his face, and the crowd screamed, "Jack the Rat! Jack the Rat!"

The alley was black. Butter could hear running water. They turned and turned into closes strung with ropes and tarpaulins and down a passageway that was so narrow that Joshua Rue had to ease himself through sideways. Finally, Mr. Snow kicked on a door that was below street level, and it opened. The gaslight was low, and the ceiling was lower, so that Butter had to walk in a crouch in order to favor his bad hip, and was unable to study the tunnel openings that seemed to line the passageway. It was downhill to a broad door that opened only after Mr. Snow had banged repeatedly. A brace was lifted, and the latches sprung noisily. The passage was wider now, with large chambers off to each side that emanated human sounds. They halted in an antechamber that smelled like bad air and old dung.

There was a huge Negro man wearing an animal skin coat who was seated by stone steps. He had an axe handle across his lap. Mr. Snow addressed him, "Dese gemmen askin' fer de Prezdent. Dey say dey from Master Linkum."

The guard stood, waved his axe handle at Nevers, and laughed.

"Dat's what dey say, Master Linkum," continued Mr. Snow.

The guard walked behind Butter. The guard was actually larger than Joshua Rue, and Butter thought he could see Nevers grimace. The guard turned and started up the stone steps. They followed, climbing into darkness. Butter could hear dogs barking. A trapdoor opened above them, and when Butter emerged in his turn he saw they were in a long chamber with a wooden floor. The odor of dung was stronger here. The barking grew louder. Butter could see empty wire cages along the wall. The guard pointed at them to wait, then he went ahead.

Butter asked Nevers, "Are we still underground?"

Nevers said, "I don't know where we are. This could be City Hall."

Butter said, "Are you serious?"

Nevers said, "We ain't supposed to know, Cap'n. What you have got to know now, and remember, is that the man we're about to meet is named George Washington. It doesn't matter how crazy you think he is, he's George Washington. And sometimes, he thinks he actually is George Washington. You address him as 'Mr. President.'"

"Who's George Washington?" asked Butter.

Mr. Snow said, "He's de Prezdent."

Butter did not like this. He could also see that Wild Jack looked somber, and that Joshua Rue held himself like a frightened child. Butter wanted to ask more questions of Nevers, but Nevers was not acting conversational, nor was he any longer acting sure of himself.

The guard returned halfway down the chamber and beckoned them. They ducked through a small door and into a dim, windowless chamber. There was the smell of incense in the air, heavy enough to subdue the odor of the dung. There were also more wire cages along the wall, and some of them held dogs that growled but no longer barked. Butter looked up to rafters. It was like a barn here, and he sensed that there were human beings above in the lofts.

The only two-legged animal to see in the room, however, besides Mr. Snow and the guard, was an ancient, gray-headed, gray-bearded Negro in slopclothes. The old man was seated at a workbench, his hands folded before him, like a craftsman interrupted in his task. At the old man's feet was a very large dog, which yawned to display a mouth like a bear trap.

The old man spoke excitedly. "Here now, boys, what's dis?"

Nevers began, "Good evening, Mr. President. These are my associates, Mr. Goodenough and Mr. Rue of New Orleans. And this is Captain Butter of the Secret Service. I am Nevers of the Department of the East. Mr. Lincoln has sent us to you to ask a favor, for the Union cause."

The old man, George Washington, said, "Mr. Linkum done outta ratdogs, and he wants some o' mine?"

There was laughter from above, and the dogs barked with a high, exuberant pitch.

When there was calm, Nevers continued. "Mr. Lincoln does not need ratdogs, Mr. President. He does need your help. It has to do with the Five Points gangs. I have heard word that a large sum of Rebel gold has been paid to the gangs, recently, yesterday. Twenty-five thousand in Rebel gold, or more."

George Washington said, "You got my ears now, boys."

Nevers said, "The Rebs are planning to set the city on fire, Mr. President. Sometime today, we think. When the fires start, the Rebs want the Five

Points gangs to rise up like last July. The Rebs want the gangs to shoot up Broadway and to raise hell."

"Dem Micks got all dat red jes' to be Micks and raise hell?"

Nevers nodded. "The Rebs want to destroy the city, and they need the gangs to cause so much trouble the fire department can't stop the fires."

"And you don't want dat?" said George Washington. "But seems to me, yer in de wrong place, boy. Dem Micks got dis deal, whyn't ya fuss at dem? Or go tell de Frogs? You ain't de Frogs, is ya?"

"No, we aren't the police," said Nevers quickly. "We are from Mr. Lincoln, and Mr. Lincoln does not want New-York set on fire. And I can't go into Five Points." Nevers paused; he was presenting himself very carefully and patiently. Nevers repeated himself. "I can't go into Five Points, because of what they'd do to me. You know what the Dead Rabbits would do. I have come to you, because the Dead Rabbits will listen to you."

George Washington hummed, acknowledging the compliment; he said, "Dem Micks don't mind nothin' 'cept red, lots o' red."

Nevers said, "They will listen to you, Mr. President. Because they need to do business on the riverfront, and they can't without your approval."

"Dat's true, but dat don't mean dey gonna listen hard."

"They will when you tell them that Mr. Lincoln knows everything," said Nevers. "And when you tell them they can keep the gold—the red—and luck to them. They are to do nothing, however—nothing. Tell them too that if they make trouble today, or tomorrow, or at any time help the Rebs, then Mr. Lincoln knows who they are and is coming for them. There won't be Frogs coming either. Just soldiers. And there won't be arrests or talk when Mr. Lincoln's soldiers come. It will make last July look like a governor's pardon."

George Washington replied, "I could do dat. I could tell dem dat. But why? Ya askin' a lot dere, boy, but you ain't payin' nothin'."

"We have no money for you, Mr. President," said Nevers.

"How ya figure we ain't been paid by de Rebs too, and won't give you to de Micks now?"

Nevers nodded. "I don't."

Butter finally understood the anxiety he had seen in Nevers, Wild Jack, and Joshua Rue.

George Washington said, "Jes' niggers do dis fer Mr. Linkum fer dirt, eh boy?"

Nevers said, "The Five Points gangs will give you dirt. What would there be left for you if they ruled Broadway?"

"Dey do, and dey do," said George Washington.

Nevers said, "There's worse, Mr. President, there's always worse."

"What's de Ben say?" asked George Washington; he flicked his hands in two directions at once. Butter noticed what he had missed before. George Washington was blind. No, he was more than blind. Those dark patches that Butter had taken for deep-set eyes were actually eyeless sockets.

Nevers turned to Butter and poked him. George Washington spoke again. "You speak up, Ben boy. You figger dere's call fer de niggers to he'p Mr. Linkum, Ben boy?"

Butter finally understood; he was "Ben boy." Butter had been thinking over what Nevers had said, and spoke his mind. "Yes, sir, there is a reason. We think the Rebs are going to destroy New-York, and you live here."

George Washington laughed, and the unseen audience above laughed too, making the dogs yelp along. George Washington continued, "Is dat where you figger dis is, Ben boy? Dis ain't New-York."

Butter rocked forward on his cane. George Washington did not seem angry. Butter said, "I understand. I suppose it isn't New-York. Then there's another reason." Butter saw Nevers shake his head, but he spoke anyway. "You should help because it'll help win the war."

George Washington asked, "What war, Bennie? Ya got notions, Bennie. From de Secret Service, eh? So tell me, what's dis secret? What's dis war?"

Butter was irked. "The war! The war between the states. There's a hundred thousand Negro men in this war. That war! I saw them die at Petersburg just like everyone else. That war! To restore the Union and free the slaves. That war!"

"Slaves, huh!" said George Washington. "What we care 'bout slaves? We fight rats. We hates rats. Dat's de war. De war dat made me like dis. De rat war! Dat's de war we fightin'."

Nevers tried to block Butter off, but Butter skipped awkwardly forward a step, and boomed, "The war! You should help us because you want to be free, damn it! Because you don't want to live down here with the rats! Because you won't have to live down here if there's no Negro anywhere who's not free! That's why you should help us! That's what I say, and that's what Mr. Lincoln says! Free together or the rats for all of us, Mr. President!"

George Washington was clapping his hands slowly, once, twice, thrice. His applause was joined by those above in the rafters, all of them clapping in unison, irritating the dogs into a howling pandemonium. It was some time before George Washington stopped his applause, and it was longer still before the chamber was quiet again. George Washington petted the head of his guard dog and spoke calmly. "Ya make a speech, Bennie, ya make a good speech.

"I shouldn't blame you," said Butter, feeling misunderstood but also something of a scold. "We've all got troubles."

"No, Bennie, my ratdogs favor what'cha say. If it were jes' mine to say, I'd give ya to de Micks fer a piece o' de red. But I got to mind my ratdogs, I do, I got responsibilities, I do, so I won't give you to de Micks."

Nevers interrupted, "And will you warn the Dead Rabbits and the other Five Points gangs to stay out of it?"

"Now, boy, I ain't heard nothin' dat make me want to do dat."

Nevers pointed at George Washington; he said, "The Cap'n here, I know him to be a good man, and he's told you what's in his heart. To ask him to say more would be to mock him. So you listen to me now." Nevers strode forward, leaned toward George Washington, and opened his arms beseechingly. "Freedom, Mr. President. That's why you should help. Freedom. And if freedom ain't enough of a reason for you, then we've come to the wrong place and the wrong man."

George Washington asked, "Who ain't free, boy?"

Nevers dropped his arms. "I'm not, and my children aren't."

"And I ain't," spoke up Wild Jack; he stepped toward the workbench, in defiance of the bear-trap-mouthed dog. He continued, over his shoulder, "I'm telling him we ain't free yet, Mr. Rue!" Joshua Rue nodded. Wild Jack said to George Washington, "And if you'd eyes in your head instead of meanness, President Ratdogman, you could see that what kicked Mr. Rue and made him deaf, and what starved my momma so that I'm half a man, it wasn't no rat!" Wild Jack stepped back. "Mr. Rue, I told him he can't see freedom down here! All he sees is rats!"

Butter waited. George Washington looked to be brooding. The chamber was silent. Butter sensed that a judgment was coming and straightened himself.

George Washington shifted in his seat. His guard dog rolled over on its back. George Washington reached down to stroke the dog's chest. He also laughed, threw his head skyward, and said, "Well, boys, I frees ya. Ya free to go. Git!"

Thursday Afternoon,
Thanksgiving Day, November 24

The shop door of MacDonald's Fine Instruments stood halfway open. There were glass shards on the doorjamb and more of the same inside. A Negro detective was stooped over with a dustpan and broom to clean up what he could. The gaslight in the shop was turned up to reveal the display cases shoved aside, the violins, cellos, and horns taken from the wall and piled together like weapons, and the two upright pianos opened for inspection. The search had been very thorough and yet not destructive. The rear store-room showed more disarray, as piano crates had been pulled apart and the packing straw spilled out. Upstairs, the parlor was generally undisturbed, with the exception of the fireplace, where several bricks had been removed. The front hall was stacked with luggage, including steamer trunks and hatboxes. There was another Negro detective making a list of the pile of luggage. The clock on the side table showed 4:55 P.M.

Wild Jack appeared at the top landing of the stairs and waved to Gouverneur Nevers, who was standing still in the front hall. Behind Wild Jack, Joshua Rue stood with three portmanteaus under each arm. Behind Nevers, Butter peeked into the adjoining dining room. The table was set for a family dinner of at least eight people. Nothing had been damaged here in the search. It was also clear that no one had ever sat at that table. Butter paused to study the details of the room. It was so lovingly arranged that it made him homesick. And everywhere was the wonderful aroma of roasted turkey.

There were men's voices from the rear of the house. Butter followed Nevers into the kitchen. Two of Nevers's best men, Walter Daggett and Louie Delta, were standing together next to the central table. A red-haired woman sat with her back to Butter. The profile of her face was cut stone. Before her, on the table, two large turkeys lay untouched on a serving platter, surrounded by covered dishes that had been positioned like satellites.

"Mr. Daggett," began Nevers, "that will do. The young lady is not going to cooperate, and you can go now."

Daggett said, "Uh, yes, suh," and moved like a released spring, followed by Louie Delta. As they left the kitchen, Butter thought they could have played their roles more convincingly.

Nevers's original plan had been that while he and Butter remained outside the house, Wild Jack and Joshua Rue would conduct a search, and Walter Daggett and Louie Delta would make a bullying pretense of interrogating Katie MacDonald about the Sons of Liberty in the most general terms. They were not to mention the Rebel guerrillas. It was approximately twelve hours since Katie MacDonald's father, Augustus, and her brother, Barney, had been arrested in the general raid by General Dix's acting-assistant-provost-marshals, under the command of Brigadier-General Hays, and had been removed in chains to Fort Lafayette, where they were to be charged with treason. The remaining occupants of the MacDonald house, women and children, had departed soon after the raid for the refuge of relatives' homes.

Katie MacDonald had stayed behind, however, a mysterious resister. Nevers had posted one of his own men outside the house with intructions to watch her closely, and to follow her if she departed. She had remained indoors all day in order to perform a bizarre drama. She had packed all the family's clothes and brought the luggage down to the front hall. Then she had worked in the kitchen as if nothing had happened and her family was expected for Thanksgiving dinner. At what should have been the appointed hour for the family gathering, she had placed all the food in serving dishes on the kitchen table. Then she had waited, reading a book, at the kitchen table. She had shown no fear when Nevers had sent in Wild Jack and the others just after 4 P.M.

"I want to apologize for the zeal of my men, Miss MacDonald," continued Nevers; he walked around the table to the kitchen door, which had been torn from its hinges and then leaned back into place, though incompletely. "And you should know that I'm of the opinion that you have little to tell us. Even if you did, you wouldn't.

"I don't know who you are," she said. "I know what you are—more of them that came this morning. So I'll tell you what I told them. I'd sooner to hell than leave this house. And I'd sooner betray the Christ child than my family and friends."

Nevers looked over Katie MacDonald's head, and shrugged to Butter. Nevers softened his voice. "I apologize again for not introducing myself. This is my colleague, Captain Butter of the Secret Service. I am Gouverneur Nevers of the Department of the East. Those were not my people who broke in this morning, but—I'm not going to ask you to distinguish between us. I'm also not going to bait you. We haven't come to ask you about the Sons of Liberty. That's all done now."

Katie MacDonald said, "It isn't even begun."

Butter nodded to Nevers, in order to show his approval of this new tactic. Nevers's ruse—to flatter her stalwartness—had failed. It was time for a direct assault.

Nevers said, "Miss MacDonald, the Cap'n and I know of the Rebel guerrillas, and of Captain Kennedy and your close friendship with him."

"You know nothing," she said.

Nevers said, "We also know that they plan to attack the city tonight, using Greek Fire, like the St. Albans raiders." He lowered his voice. "I won't labor with what we know. Miss MacDonald? They must be stopped. If they do this thing, there's no hope for them ever in this country. They'll be hunted down and executed. We're not here to make threats. We need your help. Miss MacDonald? We need to get word to them to break off the attack. If they do, they can leave the city like they came, and that will be the end of it." Nevers almost whispered, "I can promise that."

Katie MacDonald looked across to Butter, who was leaning by the stove for warmth and to ease the strain on his legs. She said, "When my nephew, Tommy, my brother's boy, when he left this morning, he asked where his dad was. I lied to him. He was crying, because your men broke the children's door, looking for what? I took Tommy up and— I lied!" She was looking through Butter. "What else can you do to me? I lied to a baby. If it's my help you want, then here it is. Be sure, brave men, that I'll help put the rope round my neck."

Nevers spoke even more seductively. "Tell me where they are, Miss MacDonald. Or tell me how to get word to them. Or go tell them what I've said yourself. And there won't be any rope for anyone, and the only lies'll be those we all take to the grave."

She said, "There's none to tell, and naught to tell. And if it's a liar you call me"—she gestured at the turkeys—"I know I am, for making this meal that will never be eaten."

Nevers moved to the doorway and signaled. Wild Jack and Joshua Rue came in and deposited the portmanteaus on the floor. Wild Jack began, "Men's clothes. Nine different men. No names inside. Gun oil. Set of spurs. Red buttons. Much of it's freshly laundered. There's also this." He placed a small Bible on the table. "I'm telling about the Bible, Mr. Rue!" Wild Jack opened the cover. "The inscription is to R. C. K., and reads, 'Even the youths shall faint and be weary, and the young men shall utterly fall: But they that wait upon the Lord shall renew their strength'—"

Butter joined in from memory to make a duet. " 'They shall mount up with wings as eagles; they shall run and not be weary; and they shall walk, and not faint.' "

Wild Jack added, "It's signed, 'Your loving Mother,' and dated December 25, 1850."

Butter said, "It's Captain Kennedy's."

Katie MacDonald reached out, and Wild Jack handed her the Bible.

Butter said, "His mother's a good Presbyterian soul."

Katie MacDonald said, "She's a Methodist woman."

Butter said, "I take blame for this, Miss MacDonald. I could have stopped John Oliphant in Washington. I could have tried. He spoke of you to me, I think, a story about the Irish famine. And about choosing. We need you to choose. Oliphant's the ringleader. He's the one who's ordered this attack. He has paid a bounty to the gangs of this city to rise up with the attack. And he has probably purchased the guerrillas an escape plan. He'll destroy the city and run, and leave you all to pay with your lives. He's a man torn up inside himself with defeat. He's the one we want most. I can't figure that he's a friend of yours. I should have taken him any way I could. I botched it. Help us find him, or help us get him, just him, and it will be sufficient. He's beaten. You're beaten. Choose, for mercy's sake—I'm asking, please, choose decency."

She appeared to Butter to be half smiling; she said, "If you know the good book so well, you Protestant hypocrite, then cast your stones, cast and cast and cast, and be damned with you." She looked toward Nevers. "As for your crushers, let 'em call in the troops again to stick mothers and babies with bayonets. What's holdin' you then? Not your decency, is it? Decency? Begod, I should hope that you've learned how to break that bond."

Nevers showed his frustration. "It's the innocent who will suffer the most! If they fire this city, and the gangs rise up, you don't imagine it'll be the Black Republicans that get scorched? No, no, no more than they did in the riots. When he was here to protect this city, do you know what Ben Butler's battle plan called for? To secure the landing berths to get the rich out and the troops in! Not a company was deployed to protect the common people! I promise you, it'll be you and your kind who'll suffer. And my kind, sure, sure! Those rioters were mad! They strung up a 4-year-old girl and tortured her with ice hooks! Did you see? Are you blind? If not for yourself, then for them, all of them. Don't you know, woman, don't you know what will happen if you don't help us?"

Butter stood next to Nevers. "Miss MacDonald, you are all we have! We must get word to them! The arrests today were secret! We can't hope for the newspapers to scare them off! You must help us! You're beaten! We're desperate!"

Katie MacDonald had her arms crossed. Nevers and Butter were right behind her. She was shaking and rocking. Butter could feel her heat. He did pity her, and he also felt cruel-minded. This was making war on a woman, and he would be a fool to deny it, as he had been a fool to think he was exempt from such a shame. But it was to save women and children!

Butter grasped the head of his cane, and cried, "Please! Please!"

Nevers said, "Miss MacDonald, you must help us."

Katie MacDonald was at the turkeys with both hands before Butter could understand, and she was tearing apart the birds and flinging meat in all directions before he could move to aid a human being in a rage of distress. He was astounded by her fury, and frightened too. She screamed, "No! No! No!" and flung and ripped. "No! Never! You monsters! Never!"

She had a wing of the bird now, and turned to swing out at Butter back-handed, then came around to strike Nevers. She threw her hips to shove the table back, so that the serving dishes crashed on the floor. Her face was purple, and the muscles in her neck were throbbing. She kept screaming, "No! No!" She had Kennedy's Bible in one hand and a turkey leg in the other. She swiped wildly at Wild Jack and turned on Butter. She was too quick, and he was too clumsy. She raised on her toes and smashed the leg down on him like a club. Butter could not defend himself. She struck at his chest, and then his eyes. Nevers grabbed her from behind, but he could not control her power. She kicked through the broken crockery and backed away from them to her stove. She was screaming only sounds of hatred now—gagging, spitting, screeching, with guttural sobs.

Nevers was in a crouch and holding his arms out. "Enough now, lady, enough."

She found her voice. "Get out of my house! Get out! Get out!" She pointed the turkey leg at the broken door.

"We're going," said Nevers; he gestured to Wild Jack and Butter. Butter was backing away while wiping grease from his face. Nevers continued soothingly, "If you want to reach us, there will be a man outside. Just one. And nothing else. No more questions."

Katie MacDonald turned away from them for the closet. She took out a mop and bucket. She was not crying.

Butter and Nevers did not talk again until they had regained Washington Square Park on foot. It was a cool, bright evening, the last-quarter moon above and a heaving breeze from all points—exactly the sort of evening that would whip a fire into a conflagration.

Butter watched several boys playing a game by the gaslight on the park lawn; one boy threw a rag ball and another hit it with a short stick and then raced to tag a tree, while the other boys chased the rag ball. Butter slowed to watch the boys. The game's rules seemed arbitrary. He envied the boys their enthusiasm. He started, "I'm in need of my supper, Mr. Nevers, and a rest for my hip and back." Nevers watched the boys and sagged. Butter had never seen Nevers so disturbed, and he tried, "You think it's tonight?"

"Maybe, Cap'n. They could have hit us on Election Day too, acting on their own, and didn't." One of the boys threw the rag ball at the runner as he loped toward another tree. Nevers added, "Anybody's guess why they waited till now."

"I can guess," said Butter. "Because Oliphant wanted to get Mrs. Winwood to safety. So he delayed the attack."

"I don't put as much on him as you do," said Nevers. The boy with the stick was back where he started when they finally hit him with the ball. All the boys were shouting. Nevers said, "There have been too many accidents along the way for Oliphant to have thought it all out."

"You think I made this up? That I'm crazy? That Colonel Baker's not been protecting Oliphant? That Oliphant's gone to Richmond instead?"

"No—you're mostly right about Oliphant," said Nevers. "Or you are now. Any man who can get away from Goody and Rue, he's up to mischief, and bad trouble."

"It was that telegram! At the White House! It must have been! That telegram ordered him to New-York! It was right there in front of me! All I had to do was take it from him! Instead of trying to impress him! He was so cool, and I was so stupid!"

"That telegram could have been anything. And it still wouldn't have told us what we need." Nevers held his hand out before him and counted off his fingers one at a time. "They've got the men, and they've got the method. What they need is the moment and the magic. So when? If it was me, I wouldn't hit tonight. The city's all stirred up for the feasting." He pointed at the boys as they began the cycle of their game again. "There are too many people where they wouldn't be except for the holiday. I'd wait until things were quiet and routine again."

Butter said, "That ain't much of a defense."

"Timing, Cap'n, it's timing they've got for an ally tonight. But the longer they wait, the better our chances to find them. My bokes are back in force tomorrow. And then I can search this city like a melon for seeds."

"If we survive tonight," Butter asked, "we're not beaten?"

Nevers did not reply. They were at the base of the park, off Thompson Street. Nevers waved to stop a hack, and said to Butter, "Are you ripe for a supper of the national bird, Cap'n?" Butter wanted more reassurance, but decided to go along. Wild Jack and Joshua Rue climbed first into the cabin. Nevers offered Butter his hand up, and, when Butter hesitated, gave Butter some comfort; he said, "It is fair to figure they're going to hit tonight. They don't know it, but we're defenseless. Tomorrow, it's a new battle."

Nevers gave an address on Bleecker Street, and the hack moved off west. Butter wanted Nevers to start his speculating again; Nevers only sat back and tapped his mouth. After a ride so brief that Butter realized it had only been out of consideration for his legs, they were just a few short blocks south of where they had begun at Washington Place. However, this was Bleecker at Carmine Street, a four-block-square area that was predominantly settled by Negro families. It was a street not different from the others of surrounding small frame houses, shirt and button factories, horse stables, and warehouses, with the special distinction that everyone knew that a row of the tenements on Carmine near Varick had been burnt out in the Draft Riots.

The hack halted in front of a narrow, beige house tucked between two brick-faced buildings. The windows were brightly lit. Wild Jack and Joshua Rue raced up the stoop. Butter was slower, and Nevers took him by the arm. Butter could now see that Nevers had been silent because he was still arguing with himself. Butter asked, "Is this your home?"

Nevers did not hear; he said, "We're going to get hit. We can't stop it. That's what we must accept. We can't stop it. No use. You agree?"

Butter sighed. "Too well, Mr. Nevers. It feels like Fredericksburg."

The vestibule of the house was lined with umbrellas. Butter heard children's voices as the inner door opened. A beaming Negro woman said, "Oh,

Gubbie! At last! Where've you been? They're starving! I can't hold them!"

Nevers introduced Butter to his sister, Mrs. Charlotte Daggett. Her laughter puzzled Butter until he realized it was because of Wild Jack and Joshua Rue. Once the coats were taken, Nevers guided Butter out of the way because of the approaching stampede of small children who surrounded Wild Jack and climbed on Joshua Rue like a tree.

Mrs. Daggett led Nevers and Butter into the parlor. Butter said, "It smells delicious, ma'am. We've not eaten since breakfast."

She said, "With Gubbie, you're good to get that much. Was it at least hot food?"

Two more women entered, and Nevers introduced them as Miss Valentine, a freckled young woman of about 20, and Mrs. Henry, rotund and gleeful for the way Wild Jack was then producing playing cards from the children's ears. Butter counted eleven children in the hall, all of them young enough to be shorter than Wild Jack, and all of them representing a rainbow of skin colors—red-tinged, all shades of brown, sallow-skinned, one chubby and black as coal and hanging on the frock coattails of the similarly black Joshua Rue. The adults stood back to watch the children squeal and dance. At one point, Butter said to Nevers, "This is your family?"

Nevers laughed. "Part of it. The Northern part. The Northern, New-York part. On Bleecker part."

Mrs. Daggett brought them each a glass of wine; she left them to talk while she began the engineering of dinner. Butter and Nevers sat before the fire, listening to the celebration throughout the house. Butter gazed about the room—a cozy home, not wealthy, neatly kept, a worn carpet, one small crack in a wall, a huge Bible on a stand at the front windows. There was also a photograph on the mantelpiece that was arranged like a shrine; it was of three Negro men linked arm in arm, all wearing the uniform tunics of Union volunteers.

Butter pointed at the photograph. "They're all still living, yes?"

"Praise God, as of today, yes, sir, Cap'n."

"Your brothers?"

"One half-brother," said Nevers. "One uncle, and one brother-in-law— my sister Charlotte's husband, Joe. In Virginia tonight, with Ben Butler, the colored division of the Twenty-fifth Corps."

"So are mine—my kin, my brothers, near Petersburg."

"Yes, sir," said Nevers. "Maybe they're sharing some bird too."

"Maybe," smiled Butter.

They toasted each other's families. Nevers seemed embarrassed by this display of sentimentality, and squatted up to the fire to poke at the logs. "Tell me about Fredericksburg," he said. "How was it? I don't mean the killing. I mean—you attack, they counterattack, you counter-counterattack?"

"The waiting is the hard part," said Butter. "It's mostly waiting." Butter stretched his legs and remembered how much he did not know about Fredericksburg—or the fights before at Middletown, Winchester, Cedar Mountains, Second Bull Run, Antietam, or even the fights after at Rappahannock Station, Brandy Station, Aldie, Middleburg, Upperville, and then Gettysburg. What did Butter know about battle other than the fear and the waiting? He decided he could make it up, and he could fret another day about his ignorance of the battles he had fought; he said, "The tactics are simple. You scout with cavalry. You establish your perimeter, and your front lines across from theirs. The barrage begins. You attack in strength by walking into clouds of smoke. There's this zinging sound. You load and fire, but it feels like nothing. There's smoke and noise, and your innards are queasy. When you can't keep on, you sit down, or lie down, or fall down, and wait. They counterattack. You know they're coming. You try to contain them by reinforcing what they think are your weak points. There's never enough men. It's a guess. You wait, and they come on. If you last it out, it begins again—"

"Hold it," said Nevers; he overturned a log, and the flames came up from underneath. "It's containment. You know you're going to get hit. So you contain."

Mrs. Daggett was at the archway. "Gentlemen, dinner is served. Gubbie, I want to see you stand up. These kids cannot wait. Gubbie!"

Nevers obeyed her, and helped Butter up. "This fire," he pointed at the logs, "takes time to catch. It needs to be stoked and fed. This Greek Fire the Rebs got, it ain't different. It explodes at first, but it needs time to build after. They'll have to set fire to places that are hidden from quick discovery, until the flames build and the fire is out of control. And if I were them, I'd plan to fire as many places as possible, all over the city, to start a panic, to bedevil the fire department, to give lots of fires a chance to get going." Nevers took the shovel and scooped ash back into the fire. "If we can't figure when they'll hit us, and if we can't stop them, we can prepare to contain. Do you follow me? And if we contain their first hit, we can beat their magic. Maybe. To beat magic, you've got to survive the first hit. Contain, Cap'n, contain. And survive, and get them when they've wasted their magic."

Butter made two fists. "So the challenge for us isn't when they'll hit, it's where they'll hit?"

Nevers spoke into the fireplace. "Some place secret, some place small like this, some place available to strangers like them. A lot of some places."

"Like a closet, maybe," said Butter. "Lordie, where? Where not?"

Mrs. Daggett was back at the archway. "Gouverneur Nevers! Right now! Right now!"

CHAPTER 9

John Oliphant
at New-York, New York

LATE THURSDAY EVENING,
THANKSGIVING DAY, NOVEMBER 24

Central Park was an 843-acre reach of scrub trees and rock outcrop-
pings and pastorage so poor that the squatters as well as their pigs and goats
lived in quiet despair. Following the financial panic of 1857, the city government had poured public monies as fast as possible into transforming the park
into a pastoral retreat; yet it had done so not out of any devotion to
aesthetics, or even out of the utopianism of the two designers, Messers
Olmstead and Vaux, but rather as a way to provide employment to the
destitute day laborers in the poor wards, and most especially to provide large
graft rewards to pinched city fathers. What emerged, despite the motive,
were the rudiments of some ethereal possibility, stretching along the serpentine Grand Drive from the Merchant's Gate at Fifty-ninth Street and Broadway over the storybook subdivisions of the park that were characterized for
daydreaming with names such as The Playground, The Green, The Mall, The
Ramble, The Lake, and, north of the vast, bisected Croton Reservoir, The
Meadows, The Great Hill, The Cliffs, and Harlem Lake at One Hundred
Tenth Street. Wild dogs and kept hogs still foraged the granite ledges, and

the squatters' shanties still filled every nook at the southern edge, but the future was there for anyone who would see it: a city so grand that this park would truly become central and the stuff of temperate serenity.

In one of those shanties—just inside the park at Fifty-ninth off Fifth Avenue—John Oliphant stood, hands in pockets, pipe in mouth, peeking through a gap in the canvas curtain down upon The Pond. The Pond's surface was absolutely black in contrast to the moonlit shore, and looked to be in the shape of a sleeping dragon here at the outer limit of the city. Beyond, Oliphant could see a line of illuminations from the west side of the park that were probably street lamps that, in the intense clearness of the night, resembled a string of campfires like an army encampment. That western part of Manhattan Island was still farmlands, however, with a few houses of recluses and visionaries. Oliphant was trying to picture what the park, and the north of the island, might look like in fifty years or perhaps a century. Yes, he thought, a century or more, when he would be safely gone, and what he was doing would be forgiven, or perhaps at least forgotten.

Behind Oliphant, in the shanty's single room, seven young men were gathered about a splintered board they had propped upon two crates. They were occupied with a most present and this-worldly concern.

"Play on, play on," said Lieutenant John Ashbrook, clicking his tongue.

Lieutenant James Harrington said, "He's countin' his winnings and has run out of fingers."

Lieutenant John Price said, a little harshly, "If'n he'd deal the cards, we might relieve him of the burden."

Lieutenant Leslie Dennis snorted, "Relieve!"

Lieutenant Tim Cook spoke to Price. "If how you say that's how you mean that, sir, I hope Captain Kennedy's a sport."

Captain Robert Cobb Kennedy smiled. "I have come late to this splendid vice, and I am disposed to permit you Kentuckians to instruct me as to how to lose as well as how to win. Nonetheless, I am grateful, and in a sporting humor, and the game, as I understand, is poker." Kennedy began to deal the cards, left to right, carefully, left-handed. "You call out if I err, Lieutenant Price."

Price replied, "I surely will, and I'll thank you to mind that I am of the great state of Maryland, meaning no harm to Kentucky."

"I do apologize," said Kennedy, laughing. "Five of a kind, these Kentuckians, and then you and me."

"Gad, Jamie," said Ashbrook to Harrington, "the man's a natural."

Dennis snorted again. "Natural."

Cook said, "Five of any kind on this table, and I'll show six of a kind in lead."

Harrington hissed mockingly, "Now, Tim lad, this ain't the way. I've seen it before. The first time with cards in their hands, and these New Orleans gentlemen sprout wings, and soar."

James Chenault picked up a turkey wing and waved it at the pile of paper money on the table; his voice cracked in his eagerness. "We'll keep Captain Kennedy aloft till dawn, and let the sun at his wax!"

There was a moment of group bafflement. Ashbrook said, "Oh, Jim, what does that possibly mean?"

Chenault shrugged and bit the wing. "I guess I ain't sure. I heard it."

"It's that Greek story," said Kennedy; he scrupulously placed the undealt cards on the table, and picked up his own hand of cards as if they were five butterflies. "Isn't that right, Mr. Oliphant, that Greek tale?"

Oliphant left the window and walked up behind Kennedy distractedly; he cleared his throat. "Icarus and Daedalus, Mr. Kennedy, you know."

They were wagering a round now, flinging greenbacks down like rags, flipping coins in the air that clunked on the paper money. Oliphant suspected that as a group and as individuals, Kennedy excepted, these young men had never before played with so much money. After almost four weeks in New-York, the pecunious farmboy in them was fading. They had seen enough war in their time to be ancients; but this past month had been their virgin introduction to wide-open American luxury. It now showed in their personal contradictions: Money was still what you squeezed, rolled in a ball, and hid away; but then again, wealth was what you threw around and prided yourself upon. More confusingly for them, this money had been given them not as earnings but as a weapon. They could use it like pistols and sabers, and indeed there was much swashbuckling at the poker table. This made their spirits as high as the apogee of the tossed coins. Here were seven taut, gregarious, competitive young men in long overcoats and slouch hats slapping shoulders and laughing heartily and having fun. There was also room on their makeshift table for good cigars nestled in seashells and several pairs of gentlemen's kidskin gloves. New-York had not only altered their opinions of cash, but it had also transformed their sense of fashion. Their linen was white and clean; their coats were good wool; their vests were silk; and their boots, cigar cases, and billfolds were fine leather. And yet, they had held on to their appetite for frontier cuisine and table manners. They were eating with their fingers from two flat baskets of cold roasted turkey cut in strips, another basket with loaves of hard bread, and a bowl of cooked potatoes balanced on a hillock of salt. There were also mugs of beer at their elbows, a pint of whiskey between Ashbrook and Harrington, and a pewter flask between Cook and Dennis.

These were the two pairs of young men who evidenced the strongest bonds in the room: Ashbrook the jocular conversationalist and dexterous card player, and Harrington the cynic; Cook the suspicious, libertine debater, and Dennis the quiet man. These four also gave hints of a newfound pleasure with the ladies. It was Harrington and Cook who wore the best silk vests, Dennis who boasted of a certain scratch on his throat from a night with a prostitute, and Ashbrook who could whistle the popular tunes of the bordello. Ashbrook also made a clicking sound while he played his cards that annoyed the youngest of the group, James Chenault. But Chenault was either unable or unwilling to protest aloud. The Marylander, John Price, kept his own counsel, and displayed the manners of a first-rate horseman—haughty and opinionated.

The wagers went down again with vigorous banter. There was a pause while the bluffing—they called it "bragging"—absorbed their attention. Kennedy tucked his cards to his chest and turned to Oliphant. "Oh, Mr. Oliphant, how does that story go again?"

Price said, "Keep in the game or get out, Captain."

Kennedy said, "I shall play, sir, I shall. Mr. Oliphant?"

"You remember, Mr. Kennedy," said Oliphant. "You all do." Seven happy faces glanced up at Oliphant, their eyes very bright in the oil lamp light—moustaches, light beards, long noses, black locks, bony contours, and Kennedy's golden aura. Oliphant smiled. "About the father and son who flew too close to the sun."

Kennedy said, "Tell me the story again, please?"

Ashbrook said, "Yes, do, sir, the wax and the wings, right?"

"It's about love, isn't it?" said Chenault. "I remember something about love."

Cook said, "That's all you know about love, now, Jim, ain't it?"

Oliphant said, "A certain brand of love, Mr. Chenault." The men approved in unison. Oliphant could see they knew the heart of the tale, but wanted, like children, to be spellbound anew with the same old drama. He began, "A father's love for his son. Daedalus and his son Icarus were marooned on an island. Daedalus knew the secret of flight. He made wings out of seagull feathers, for he and Icarus to use to fly back home. They attached them to their bodies with wax they made from the fat of a slaughtered lamb." Oliphant relit his pipe.

Ashbrook burst, "Blast, where's my luck!"

Harrington said, "There's no luck in this game."

"Poker is life," said Price. "The skillful player is he who asks the least of the cards."

"No puzzles, now, Lieutenant," said Ashbrook.

"And then what, Mr. Oliphant?" said Kennedy. "They flew?"

"Like my luck, out the window," said Ashbrook.

Oliphant nodded. "They learned how to fly, yes. Daedalus was wise and slow. Icarus was strong and brave. Daedalus told Icarus that he was to observe him closely, and follow even closer. He warned that there was danger only if they flew too near the sun. If they did, the wax would melt, the wings would fall off, and they would die. The lesson was that strength and daring are not entirely what is needed to fly. One must obey nature's laws even while defying them."

Chenault said, "I don't remember that part of the story."

Ashbrook cried out and slammed his cards. Kennedy was displaying his cards to the others, and said, "I understand this three of a kind is superior to your two two-of-a-kind, Lieutenant Price, though two of yours are queenly, and very attractive."

Ashbrook groaned. "He must be a gambler."

Cook said, "We know he's an eye for the ladies, specially in passing."

Kennedy waited out the laughter. "I swear to you, sirs, that if my mother knew—I've never gambled—not—"

Ashbrook asked of Harrington, "This ain't luck?"

Price said, "It ain't skill."

Kennedy was again required to count his winnings, but was relieved of the next deal. The men snacked, smoked, drank, and worked their hands and arms of tension. Kennedy stacked his coins and smoothed out his paper money, asking, "Excuse me, Mr. Oliphant, then—your tale—it was because Icarus disobeyed his father, or nature, or what? That was why he fell?"

Oliphant said, "No, no, Mr. Kennedy, you are incompletely informed. There are several possible ends. It is a true story. The conclusion has suffered with the retelling over the centuries. Perhaps you have not heard that Icarus obeyed his father. They flew close to the waves and escaped the island." Oliphant walked to the door, struggling to open it. Chenault called out another question. Oliphant responded, "They lived happily ever after."

Oliphant went outside. He was thinking of obedience. The spinning of the yarn had upset him again. There would always be so many possible ends of a story, it was vanity to believe that he could figure out just the right conclusion to any story, particularly his own. Yet he could try! He had made the myth of Icarus and Daedalus into a homily on obedience. And obedience did explain so much of his present mood, place, and purpose.

The Saturday evening before, he had obeyed his instincts and taken a room at the National Hotel, across Pennsylvania Avenue from where Captain Butter had left him.

He had been profoundly shaken by Butter's peculiar interrogation and by Old Capitol Prison. But what had upset him the most was his fear for Narcissa. He had known that he could not return to Georgetown. He had had to assume that he was being closely watched. It would have been reckless to have attempted to get back to Narcissa, for it would only further have implicated her in whatever the War Department had against him, or whatever they might subsequently invent against him. That wild, treacherous man, Lafayette Baker, of the "Death To Traitors" badge, had warned him in New-York that he was the law in Washington. Old Capitol was clearly justice in Washington.

In his hotel room, how humbled Oliphant had felt by the word "law" and the word "justice." They had pressed upon him like terror. Captain Butter had been very convincing of his authority and information and had made his points effectively, invoking Lafayette Baker's name, showing Oliphant the dungeon. It was true that Captain Butter had everything about Oliphant's activities in New-York and Washington upside down and distorted, but then again, it was also true that in order to sidestep Captain Butter's questions, Oliphant had been obliged to deceive about his activities in New-York and Washington.

And so Oliphant, all Saturday night in Room 222 of the National Hotel, had stared into his future and had realized that, having lied to escape Captain Butter, the truth would no longer protect him from Captain Butter. He had realized that anything was possible now. Then his imagination had exploded: He had seen himself in Room 16 of Old Capitol; he had seen Narcissa in the same cell in Old Capitol where they had kept Rose O'Neal Greenhow; he had seen Rose Greenhow drowning in the North Carolina surf when she had tried to escape a foundered blockade runner; he had seen Narcissa drowning off Savannah; he had seen Savannah in flames.

Then Sunday morning had arrived, and he had not been arrested, and the shock had eased enough for him to dare countermeasures. He had sent a messenger to Willard's for Blondel. Oliphant had spent the rest of the morning in a nearby church in order to pray and to prepare himself. At the appointed hour Sunday afternoon, Blondel had appeared in Willard's lobby, bringing with him not only Oliphant's requested lettercase, but also the surprise of Isaac Keats. Oliphant had sat in the public bar with them and listened to worse upon worse: Narcissa's audience with Mrs. Lincoln had ended without the president appearing; the best Narcissa had been able to achieve was an invitation to meet the president at the Tuesday evening reception; since then, Narcissa had been bleak, not for herself but for Oliphant, whom she was sure was arrested.

Oliphant had paused after Blondel's summary, and then he had obeyed his wisdom. He had said that Blondel must get Narcissa out of Washington immediately. Blondel had balked. Oliphant had said, "No delay, none, no objections, no contingencies, none. It must be done now!"

Isaac Keats had then looked at Oliphant's torment, and had helped by speaking to Blondel. "Henry, this is our business, John's and mine, and we know it as we know battlefields."

Blondel had tried to resist again; he had addressed Oliphant, "John, she's threatening to go to President Lincoln to get you out of prison."

Oliphant had asked for a few moments to consider. He had opened the lettercase, pulled out his cipher book, and, sitting at Willard's bar with more gold-buttoned bluecoats in the room than gentlemen, had deciphered the telegram from Baltimore. It had been rash of him, but he had felt driven to solve a logical contradiction—his need to hold on to Narcissa and his need to protect Narcissa. And when he had known for certain that the telegram was a fool's solution to his dilemma, Oliphant had obeyed his heart. He had spoken to Blondel. "God bless you, Henry, you must do as I say. If you love her, you must. She must be saved, and she won't save herself, and I can't help her any longer. London, Henry, take her to London. Savannah is either lost or it isn't, and there's little she can do. It's for others now. As for Granby Royall, the man is dead. Bury him in Georgetown and get on to England. It must be done. You must do it."

Blondel had said, "She'll never go without you."

Oliphant had said, "You must make her. And tell her, remind her, that no one—remember now—no one ever catches the Spectre Buck. It's a nonsense story. My wife's story. Narcissa will understand."

"The Spectre Buck," Blondel had said. "That is all?"

Keats had smiled. "You are off to Richmond, is that it, John, Richmond?"

Oliphant had smiled too. "Richmond? Something like that."

Now it was four days later, and John Oliphant, in obedience to Richmond, stood on a carpet of brown pine needles before a shanty in New-York's Central Park, and he was thinking of obedience and what a cold excuse it was for fate. The shanties across Fifty-ninth showed cooking fires and a rudimentary homeyness. New-York lay open tonight like a self-satisfied manse, its burghers sated with the national bird and dreaming of better days ahead. The newspapers tomorrow would carry columns of Thanksgiving's sermons that had only the most offhanded connection with the front-page reports of Grant's, Sheridan's, and Sherman's armies, for they would all speak most thankfully of a shining utopian image of this city rising out of the doom of the war and the bedrock of the island. Oliphant could look across Fifth Avenue to see such a prospect—the stacks of white granite blocks that each day were used to fill in the skeleton of the New St. Patrick's Cathedral there as its twin gothic towers rose luminescent and hopeful. Another year, and certainly another decade, and the gaps in the lots to the east would be filled, and those shanties would be cleared for stone-built homes, and what was now an outlying tenement neighborhood would begin developing into a new roost for the well-to-do. Oliphant could just see it! New-York was splendid, potent, and limitless. Nothing could stop its inevitable ascension to a world capital, nothing whatsoever, not even fire.

"Mr. Oliphant, am I disturbing?" It was Kennedy with a briar pipe in his mouth. "They've asked me to sit out some hands, for pity's sake."

"You seem to have mastered the game," said Oliphant.

"My mastery is my lack of expectations, sir. That isn't my opinion of myself, sir. Miss—a good friend of mine told me so."

"You are more discreet than the cards permit, Mr. Kennedy."

"Yes, sir. Well, no, sir. I shall think on this, sir." Kennedy lifted his top hat and flagged the night sky. "About ten o'clock, I figure." Kennedy fidgeted with his pipe. Oliphant sensed that Kennedy wanted something, and he waited attentively. Kennedy began slowly, "About the story, sir—those Greeks."

"I thought you liked that story."

"I did. It's not me complaining. It does come to me that there was another end to it. An unhappy one. Sir, I'm sure that Icarus fell into the ocean. Not that I don't like your version."

"Up there, Mr. Kennedy, if it weren't for the brightness of the night, up there, you could see Icarus tonight." Oliphant smiled at his inspiration. "Icarus has a constellation of his own. The Greeks so hallowed his daring and courage that they put him in the sky for all of us through the ages to appreciate, to learn from, and to remember. That isn't unhappy."

"No, I agree." Kennedy searched the sky, bending so far back that he momentarily lost his balance and spun around to Oliphant. "I do like a good story. Was there another end too? You said—"

"Men cannot fly," said Oliphant.

"I've dreamed that I flew, or can," said Kennedy. "Have you?"

"Men cannot fly, Mr. Kennedy, and Daedalus was wrong-headed. There is no secret of flight. They never had a chance to succeed. It was Daedalus's love for his son Icarus that made him propose the project and try to live it out. But it failed on the beach. They played out their lives on that island, envious of the birds, and also prayerful for what God had given them. Alone or not, this is a fine world."

"Amen," said Kennedy; he stepped back and laughed, and flapped his arms in slow motion, then faster. Soon, he was working his head, shoulders, arms, and hands with balletic grace, hopping in place and squawking for verisimilitude. He cried, "Oh, to fly, to fly!"

Ashbrook, Harrington, and Chenault were at the doorway, cheering Kennedy. "Higher! Leap for it! Higher!"

Chenault ran out and tried to imitate a bird lifting off; he went straight at a bush, and over it, calling, "Caw! Caw!"

Kennedy got up on a boulder. "Watch me, gentlemen, watch close, it won't be a long flight, but watch!" He leaped up holding his coat out behind him and landed neatly in the pine needles.

They stopped their games abruptly as two figures then emerged from the direction of the street. The shanty was set on a small rise, in a stand of evergreens, and so they had a good vantage on whoever should approach. The intruders looked bent over with heavy parcels, and were in great haste as they negotiated the wood planks fixed over a drainage ditch. Once on the incline, it was clear that the lead man was Lieutenant-Colonel James Martin, who was swinging two black bags and breathing hard for the load and climb, and also because of the minie ball that had never been removed from near his lungs. Behind him was the muscular Lieutenant John Headley, who was struggling with a two-and-a-half-foot-long black valise, so that he had to halt every dozen paces to switch it from hand to hand. All the men had come outside now, and were gathered tightly together to welcome their commander. Martin got up to Oliphant and nodded a greeting. Headley heaved the valise up to the doorway and groaned.

Ashbrook said, "That the Greek Fire, John?"

Headley said, "It carries as heavy as gold."

Chenault said, "And it does give off a gruesome odor."

Harrington said, "Pigshit, I'd say, smells like pigshit in July."

"On the horsecar coming up," said Headley, "they moved away from me. Fellow said I had something dead in there. It was humorous."

Price said, "Heavy as gold and smelly as pigs? Most impolite, I'd say."

"This ain't a ball," said Ashbrook.

"A good thing it ain't," said Headley, turning toward Oliphant, "as some of the ladies look to've reconsidered our company."

Oliphant reacted by turning to Martin.

Martin said, "Captain Longuemare's disappeared." The banter stopped. Martin waved the others into the shanty. They went reluctantly, aware of the trouble.

Headley remained outside, as second-in-command, and walked up close enough to Oliphant to display his scowl; he said, "I called on the address Captain Longuemare gave us. A chemist's shop. A gray-bearded citizen took me downstairs to a storehouse. I said that Captain Longuemare had sent me. He just handed over this valise. A big man. Didn't speak a word."

"But what about Longuemare?" said Oliphant.

"I was coming to it," said Headley.

Martin spoke softly, "We called upon Captain Longuemare early in the day, like we planned. No one to home. We didn't think hard on it. Later, I went back, while John was off fetching the goods. No one to home again, neither mister nor missus. And not likely to return was the testimony of the hotel clerk. Seems they ran off with their bags and cats, sometime this morning."

Oliphant tried, "There must be an explanation. Why Longuemare said last night—"

"A weakening of the backbone," interrupted Headley, "for an explanation."

"That does not follow," said Oliphant. "This is his plan. He's in charge."

Martin said, "He wasn't able to deliver the Sons of Liberty, so-called, like he boasted. He gave us money, but never enough, not till you came back. He made promises that soon all would be ready, but then postponed and postponed."

Headley spat tobacco juice. "Maybe he was never ready. And now that we are, he skeedaddles. With your gold, sir."

Martin shrugged. "We've got what we wanted from him, Mr. Oliphant. We're out of the barn. What should we care who closes up the door—or if?" Martin paused while Headley sniggered in appreciation of the jest. Oliphant knew Martin and Headley a little better now, and understood that their vulgarity, taciturnity, and easy hostility were actually a frontier form of diplomacy. It was a way for a man who had never had much except common sense and horsemanship, and perhaps dirt-farming, to measure himself up against all comers. Their homely rhetoric was always meaningful, however—when they said less, they meant more; when they joked, they were serious. It all reminded Oliphant of what the newspapers wrote of another Kentucky-born fighter, Abraham Lincoln. Martin repeated his barn-door metaphor one more time; then he finished his thought, "Course, sir, we could try for word of Captain Longuemare from Mr. McMaster at the *Freemen's Journal,* or maybe the MacDonalds."

"No, Mr. Martin, we must remain independent, as we agreed," said Oliphant. He tested Martin, asking, "Do you want to call this off? This isn't good, whatever has happened to Captain Longuemare."

"I don't, sir," said Martin. "At home, it's well known that it's more dangerous tryin' to dismount a runaway than to ride it out."

"Not to say stupid too," said Headley.

Oliphant spoke to the ground. "My orders were to help Captain Longuemare prepare and carry out the attack as soon as practicable. There has been no contravention of my orders. Now, with Longuemare missing, there can't be. Richmond does not know where we are. And I have no direct contact, like Captain Longuemare does. Did. You do understand me? This wasn't my making any more than yours. But now we are the remnant. And cut off. And on our own cognizance. This is between us."

Martin said, "What is it between us, then, sir?"

"Give me some moments, gentlemen," said Oliphant. He set out to tour the yard, clockwise. Oliphant did not feel the ground, though, because his mind was lifted above Central Park to look down upon New-York like a flying man. He had withheld so much from Martin and Headley, there seemed nowhere to begin to take them into his confidence. He had kept from them his run-in with Lafayette Baker—who was a double agent or triple agent or emissary of the devil, it did not matter. Lafayette Baker was the enemy out there tonight. And Captain Butter! Oliphant had kept from Martin and Headley the intelligence that they and their party had been trailed by Federal detectives since crossing the border on October 31, which probably meant that they had been betrayed by an informer in Toronto at the start.

Oliphant had not kept his knowledge of Lafayette Baker and Captain Butter from Longuemare. Yet Longuemare had convinced Oliphant on Tuesday that this business was always a near thing, and that Baker and Butter did not signify because they had done nothing. If they had been as truly informed as Captain Butter had claimed, Longuemare had argued, they would have arrested Oliphant in Washington. Consequently, they could be ignored as obstacles. Longuemare had also instructed Oliphant that he should not tell Martin and Headley about the close pursuit of the Federal Secret Service, because, he had said, "Rude boys don't understand gentlemanly heart." And then, Tuesday evening, Longuemare had led Oliphant, Martin, and Headley into Five Points to deliver the gold bribe to the gangs. Because of the press of time, Oliphant had only been able to procure half the necessary amount from Edmund Homes on Tuesday. On Wednesday, Oliphant had delivered the second half to Longuemare, who had said that he would deliver it to the gangs last night, Wednesday. But now, Longuemare was gone! He had become either a rich coward or a prudent traitor—unless he had been arrested.

What was left of the grandiose Election Day conspiracy were nine volunteers and Oliphant. Martin had rented this shanty on Monday, at Longuemare's direction, and on Monday night had redeployed his men in third-rate boardinghouses uptown near Central Park. Martin had not once challenged Longuemare's or Oliphant's recommendations, an indication to Oliphant of either good soldiering or a wild frustration for the past month. Martin was now so ripe for the attack that he seemed willing to elect Oliphant his controlling agent. Before tonight, Oliphant had represented to them a reluctant and untrustworthy ally, without a stomach for their work. Now, Oliphant had come to represent Richmond and command.

Oliphant turned the last quarter of the yard's clock face toward Martin and Headley. They were still watching him with open-faced patience, two long-nosed and not unattractive boys who had many times before waited in dark woods for their commander to tell them they were cut off behind the lines and without hope of getting home, and yet they were going to attack. And here was John Oliphant, who by accident, by default, by a mean twist, had become to them a voice of authority like John Hunt Morgan or Jefferson Davis. Oliphant wanted to be angry at this turn. It did not come. It felt so easy as to be nothing. Or perhaps it was so much that he was numbed by it even as he pretended to be in control. Oliphant bared his teeth as he passed an imaginary point of no return and took one more step toward Martin. Oliphant thought, How those valiant fools in uniforms said it for the newspaper reporters did actually seem to pertain, given their poetic vanity: The hour commands! Enough. It was time. Enough.

Oliphant stopped before Martin and Headley. "Mr. Martin, Mr. Headley —continue."

Martin said, "Yes, sir, and I'm glad, sir."

Headley said, "You are a very cool gentleman, sir."

Oliphant exhaled. They were not moving. Oliphant said softly, "Carry on, please," and breathed.

Martin pulled Headley sideways into the shanty. Martin called, "Gather round now, boys."

Oliphant waited for his heartbeat to slow, and then followed them inside. Martin stood behind the table, his hand on the black satchels. The black valise was on the ground behind him. The men were gathered right and left. Price parted from Chenault to provide Oliphant a view from the door. Kennedy changed his position in order to be closer to Oliphant. Martin began with the obvious—they looked well, he was pleased with their morale—and then provided a very brief dismissal of the meaning of Captain Longuemare's disappearance. Martin gestured to Oliphant. "Mr. Oliphant assures me that President Davis needs us who're left to do our best. That's what's asked, and what we can give, and our cause can take care fine, right, sir?"

Oliphant said, "I agree with that, Mr. Martin."

Martin said, "Jes' you boys mind that it is our fight to fight now. We never won a battle waiting for a secret army to join up. General Morgan took us across Kentucky with less support than we got. We can do this, because we got to and we've gone too far to go back. Our best advantage is we're free to keep on." He put his foot on a stool and leaned toward them. "I'm not asking anyone to go back. But like General Morgan said, ain't nobody wants you here if'n you don't want to be here."

"We're with you, Colonel," said Ashbrook.

"On your tail," said Cook.

The others counted off with, "Aye, Kentucky!" "For it, Kentucky!" "Sure all!" and from Kennedy a smile and, "We'll make a spoon or spoil a horn."

Martin straightened again. "Good. Here it is. This Greek Fire is tricky." He took a small vial from Headley; the vial was opaque, about four ounces worth, and corked shut. He set it on the table, and said, "It's a liquid, this phosphorus, that explodes in flames when it hits air. It burns right hot, and maybe hotter than any fire a match can start. What you do is either pour it out slow or smash the bottle. If you pour it out, it will steam up, and catch slow. If you smash, it will explode. Either way, don't get it on your cuffs now, or you'll be the barbecue and not New-York."

"Like to try her, Colonel," said Ashbrook.

"We'll get there," said Martin; he, like everyone else, had his eyes on the vial as if it were a crystal ball. Martin added, "We got twelve dozen of these, now, boys. More'n enough for mistakes. But careful, careful, when you handle it."

"Like handling the ladies, eh, Captain Kennedy?" said Harrington.

Kennedy accepted the laughter, and said, "It's a commonly held opinion."

Martin regained their attention by flipping the vial to Headley, who caught it like an apple, and flipped it back to Martin. Martin placed the vial on the table, and said, "First, I want to set the attack. Listen close here. What we're going to do is to set fire to the big hotels on Broadway and near about."

Oliphant tamped and lit his pipe in the pause. He had heard this Tuesday night, with Longuemare, Martin, and Headley in this shanty. It was Longuemare's plan and brilliantly sinister.

Martin repeated himself. "The Broadway hotels and the like. The best and the biggest. Where the Yankee lives and eats and celebrates his profit." They were silent. Martin pointed from one to another. "What I want you to do tomorrow is to prepare for the attack. We don't strike till tomorrow night. Tomorrow afternoon, you go to the hotels I assign, and register for a room on the third or fourth floor. High enough to keep it from being spotted right off. Not so high the fire'll get through to the roof before it builds very big. What we want is leaping fires."

"A good room, or what, sir?" asked Cook.

"Not top dollar," said Martin. "Wouldn't be correct with our looks and lack of luggage. I do want you to get yourselves a black bag like these here." Martin flipped open the satchels—inside there were carbines. "It costs a dollar. Put your overcoat in it to fill it up. Tell the clerk you're stopping for the weekend. When you get inside the room, muss it, like you've been resting. Then put your overcoat on, fold the bag up, and carry it out underneath. On to the next hotel."

"What time for all this, sir?" asked Chenault.

"I'm almost there, Jim," said Martin. "When you register, use as many different names as you can think up. I want you back here at six o'clock tomorrow evening. If you finish early, take a walk. Stay clear of Broadway and keep moving. I don't think they're looking for us. Still, it's safest to assume the enemy's on your butt. And no saloons or girls, right Timmy, right Les?" Cook and Dennis grinned and assented. Martin turned to Kennedy. "And no lady friends neither, Captain Kennedy?"

Kennedy said, "I understand you, Colonel."

"A guerrilla's keenest when he keeps moving," said Martin. "At six, we meet back here for final instructions and to get our Greek Fire. We'll use the black bags to carry the vials around, due to the aroma."

Harrington made them laugh when he said, "It is a powerful insult to the nose."

Martin spoke over their brief amusement. "Now, we're all to attack at the same time. The success of our work depends on setting so many fires in so many places that the fire companies can't get 'em out. It's like an attack along the line, first wave, second wave, third, and on. The first is eight o'clock. Eight. Here's how. What you do is go to the room and lock the door behind you. Pile the bedding and furniture together to make a bonfire. Close the drapes. Leave the gaslight on. Then pour out the vial on the pile. Pour out two. It will cook. The last thing you do is lock the door behind you. Leave the key with the clerk like you're supposed to. Be as cool as you can. Say, 'How do?' Go on to the next hotel. Now—"

"Gaaa—" started Chenault. They turned on him. He blushed.

Martin said, "What's 'at, Jim? Speak out."

Chenault said, "Sorry, sir, no account, sir."

Headley said, "Maybe he's thinkin' about givin' an alarm."

Chenault had his hand on his mouth. "No, sir, no, sir."

Martin studied Chenault. "It won't do, Jim. You can't. The fires are like a fuse. They need time to catch hold in the room and get big before they find 'em."

Chenault dropped his head. "Yes, sir."

Headley came up behind Martin, and said, "Remember our Atlanta, Jim.

They've fired it sure as that rain of fire's comin' on the sinners. Yankees don't care what they burn up. Homes, barns, stock, children. They like it."

Ashbrook approached the table too. "Not just maybe Atlanta. I'm thinkin' what I know Grant and Sherman did in Mississippi last year, at Jackson and Vicksburg. They burned the railroad, yes, sir, and anything else that folk could live in—then stole what they could carry and slaughtered the stock. I testify, I saw."

Price squatted down nearby and spat. "Since we're testifying, I can speak for the Valley and my kin. Because a man defends his home and crop, they shoot him like a squirrel, and burn his babies out. And launch these reprisals —ree-prize-alls!—on his neighbors. They hang a man for swearin' by General Lee, and shoot Mosby's boys like they was mangy dogs. They burn out and brag on it." He stood erect. "I swear, they brag, Grant and Sheridan brag!"

"God bless you, Jim Chenault," said Martin. "You got shame, and that's righteous. We each got it. This ain't no good way to fight a war. There ain't no good way. We volunteered to do this, and we are ordered to do this. We've got to show the Yankee that he can't fire our towns without reprisals of our own. We got to hit the Yankee where he sits." Martin slapped his hands together. "It's fire the Yankee preaches, and we can show him a sermon of flame!"

Chenault gestured pleadingly. "It ain't—sir—"

"It's good you spoke out," said Martin; he was pacing. "I should've spoke to it. I want us to heed the God-fearing Jim Chenault, who I've known to ride harder to guns than supper." Chenault grinned and relaxed. Martin continued, "I want us to look to ourselves now, like the preachers say, to our souls. We wouldn't be worth dirt as Christians or Confederate officers if we didn't think on what we're doin'. I know you're with me. I still want you to reflect. It's what sets us right over the Yankee. He started this war with hate in him, and it's damned him." Martin kicked the floor. "No speechifying. What's talk got us? Our people are starved out. Our General's back-shot. Our cause's denied justice."

Oliphant peered hard to see what Martin was doing as he reached under his overcoat. Martin's words were for revenge, and his heart was fury; however, his manner was increasingly exhausted and defeated.

Martin turned around with his Navy Colt in one hand, and picked up the vial from the table with the other. "I've had my say, boys, and don't want to hear myself no more. You boys jes' look. Their Reverend Sherman is in Georgia tonight, with iron in one hand, and a torch in the other."

Headley added easily, "He's pure devil, marchin' on innocence."

"Yankees don't justify," contributed Price, "and we don't have to, Colonel."

Martin said, "Anyone else want to make his peace?"

Kennedy unfolded his arms in the economical style of an orator and had their attention before he began. "Excuse me, Colonel. I want to address these gentlemen." Martin nodded. Kennedy continued, "We have not shared each other's company as much as I would have liked, since I joined up late due to my residence at a kind of Yankee hotel on a lake. So it's understandable you might have questions about me. So I want to speak for myself, by way of speaking for Georgia. I was born there, on the Oconee River, near Milledgeville. My mother's kin live there. I know you Kentuckians have fought hard. There was a Kentucky regiment at Shiloh Church that wouldn't quit after the powder was gone. I know you'll hear me correctly when I say that the only thing that surrenders in Georgia is night to day. My kin are the Cobbs, and I'm proud to say Howell Cobb's blood is in me too. I guess you know what Sherman intends for the Cobbs—since he's already done it in Cobb County—and for everyone else who resists him. Which'll be every living thing in Georgia above a bug. Maybe the mosquitoes too."

Kennedy rearranged his stance; he looked directly at the black valise on the floor. "So I want to speak for Georgia. The men are off with General Lee at Richmond and Petersburg, or with General Hood in Tennessee, or in the prisons like I was. Sherman's aiming to kill and burn his way through women and children, and he's doing it with the blessings of Grant and Halleck and Sheridan. Now I want you to know that I was at West Point, like them, and Sherman. And that makes me feel special shame for regular soldiers who fall to piracy and murder. Our West Point generals have been scratching in dirt for three years, and remain as clean as your sweetheart's hands in comparison. I can't say what Grant, Halleck, Sheridan, and Sherman are, Lieutenant Headley, but I am sure that they are not gentlemen. And that nothing I learned at West Point mentioned making war on women, and farms, and chickens.

"I beg your pardon, Colonel Martin," Kennedy continued, "but I have to say that I have abiding reservations about what I'm going to do tomorrow. I do know, though, that it won't be me alone who'll have to meet his Maker after this war to account for myself. I imagine I'll be somewhat back on line, with all those bluecoats ahead of me chewing St. Peter's ear."

Kennedy turned toward Oliphant. "Excuse me too, Mr. Oliphant. I think these gentlemen should know that your family is in Savannah, with all your menfolk dead and gone. I guess we know what Sherman's advancing on, Macon and Milledgeville and Augusta and Savannah. And we know that if General Lee or General Hardee or God Almighty can't stop him, he'll make sure he keeps his cigars lit. When we set off tomorrow, we should mind that we might be the only thing that can scare the Yankees from firing another Atlanta." Kennedy bowed to Oliphant.

Martin said, "You have words, Mr. Oliphant?"

"No, I do not," said Oliphant.

Cook and Dennis danced forward simultaneously; Cook said, "What's our hotels, Colonel?"

Martin gave way to Headley. Headley flattened a piece of paper on the table and used a pencil to guide his presentation. "Lieutenant Cook, you got the St. James Hotel, at Twenty-sixth and Broadway, the Hoffman House at Twenty-fourth and Broadway, the St. Nicholas at Spring and Broadway."

Cook patted his coat. "I need your pencil."

"No, Timmy," said Martin. "No writing. If you're caught, it'd hang you."

"Lieutenant Dennis," continued Headley. "You got the Fifth Avenue Hotel at Twenty-third and Broadway, and the Hoffman House and St. Nick too. We're doubling and tripling up on the big ones. Go in separate. If it's already on fire by the time you get to it, pass by."

Headley continued to read from his list, as if walking down Broadway with giant steps from Madison Square to Union Square, onto Canal Street, a flare out to Hanford's Hotel among the lumberyards on the East River at Grand Street, and then onto City Hall Park, then Fulton Street—the southernmost target being Howard's Hotel at Maiden Lane and Broadway. All together, there were twenty targets for nine men. Kennedy had a busy assignment; he was assigned to the City Hall area—the United States Hotel on Fulton Street, the Tammany Hotel and Lovejoy's Hotel on Newspaper Row at Beekman and Park Row Street, and finally the Astor House. Headley was assuming responsibility for the Astor and United States hotels as well, along with the Howard Hotel down Broadway, the Tammany Hotel on Newspaper Row, and the Everett House up at Union Square. The St. Nicholas on Broadway, between Broome and Spring streets, a one-thousand-room palace of marble floors and satin damask drapery, was to receive special attention—four strikes—because it contained the headquarters of General Dix and his Department of the East.

When they had satisfied themselves as to the logic of their individual assignments—no one being asked to travel too far afield—Martin lined them up for a recital. It was tedious of him, like a schoolmaster rehearsing his students for an examination, but the men soon learned to enjoy it; they transformed it into a songfest as they found the rhythm in the names and counted off.

Cook boomed, "St. Denis her Hoffman and Nickers, sir!"

Dennis mumbled, "Hoffman the Fifth St. Nick, sir!"

Ashbrook tried, "Lafarge St. Nick and Metropolitan, all aboard!"

Harrington cried, "The City's Metropolitan and it's International, sir!"

Price clapped, "International! Metropolitan! New York! Astounding!"

Chenault contributed, "Broadway's International, and Bowery's New-England, tho' Hanford's by the river, sir!"

And Kennedy declared, "The United States of Tammany, making for Lovejoy's Astor, sir."

Martin took on the most ambitious mission, to permit him to oversee all sectors; he was going to start at the Hoffman House and Fifth Avenue Hotel, get down to the St. Denis at Eleventh and Broadway, and then go onto the Tammany, the Belmont on Fulton, and Brandreth's, and finally the Howard at Maiden Lane. He failed to find a nonsense beat for his targets and dismissed the exercise. "They're all to rhyme with ash for trash, anyway."

The men clapped and danced as they repeated their lessons to themselves. Soon though, Cook stepped up to sound a protest. "I don't figure it, sir. Not entirely, Colonel. I've been trying."

"Speak up, Timmy," said Martin.

"Well, well." Cook removed his hat and shook out his hair. "How's a string of bonfires about to light up a city this big? That is what we're trying for, ain't it, sir? But we ain't firing the arsenals, not even near, and without black powder— How, sir?"

Martin said, "I promised you a demonstration. I can answer you best that way." He took up the vial of Greek Fire and went to the door. "Outside, boys, we'll have some fun."

Oliphant waited until they had passed out, and then walked over to the black valise of Greek Fire. He was curious to touch it. There did seem a heat rising from the seam. Oliphant bent over to sniff.

"Mr. Oliphant," Kennedy spoke out, "are you all right?" Kennedy was at the doorway, and looked worried.

Oliphant startled and recovered. "Yes, fine, Mr. Kennedy. It's the pastor's son in me, I suppose. Daring to get up against the fumes of hell and so forth."

Kennedy smiled in reply. Oliphant joined him at the door. Outside, the men were arranged around the yard in order to watch Martin and Headley. There was enough moonlight to reveal the dark, wide gash that Martin had scraped in the pine needle carpet. It ran straight up from the doorway until it hooked to the left. Headley was building small piles of leaves and pine needles at cross-marked intervals. Martin squatted at the top of the gash, and, uncorking the vial, poured a few drops on the first pile. A vapor rose from the leaves, increasing until it was like steam.

Martin said, "Now here's Broadway, from Madison Square to Fulton Street. You correct me if I get it wrong, Mr. Oliphant." Oliphant did not respond. Martin continued, "What we're intending is to fire along this line. Here's the St. Nicholas, the Hoffman, the Fifth Avenue Hotel." Martin moved in a squat toward them, pouring a few drops from the vial on each pile of debris, which then began to steam. Martin remarked, "Here's your New-England, Jim, off here on Broadway."

A breeze swept through the trees and across the yard; the first of the leaves burst into flames, followed by the ignition of the second and third piles down the line where Martin had poured the Greek Fire.

Chenault walked over to the pile identified as his target, the New-England House on Bowery. It made a whomp! as it lit up. He took up a handful of pine needles and fed the flames.

Martin was now squatting at the big pile of leaves before the shanty's doorway; he said, "We'll get the whole bunch here, around City Hall Park, from the United States Hotel to the Astor House." Martin stood. "Now do you understand, Timmy?"

By this time, the fire in the first pile, representing Madison Square's hotels, had ceased. Cook pointed. "Lookee there, Colonel. See? What's the good, when they burn out?"

Martin watched the model of the City Hall area spew vapor and then ignite. He stepped back. "You're cautious, Tim, and that's right. Here is what I know. First all, these are leaves and whatnot. And there's this. If you set fires all over at once, there's a panic. We've made arrangements to keep that panic running like the Ohio in April."

Martin used his boot to ease a pine cone into the fire, and continued,

"More'n a few of these fires are going to get gruesome. We're firing the big hotels, the tallest. Like towers of fire. The flames will jump to the buildings below, roof to roof. This'll make the fires link up, like regiments forming a brigade, and brigades a division, and on. One grand gruesome fire. When that happens, and I saw it once back home, it can't be stopped. It takes the earth and wind with it. Captain Longuemare said it's happened before in New-York. This big fancy city is just tall kindling. Am I right, Mr. Oliphant?"

Oliphant said, "New-York is terrified of such an event."

Headley contributed, "Captain Longuemare said that once they had to use black powder to blow up a whole block to stop a fire. They had to sit back and drink their beer and watch the city burn on the other side of the hole. Right, Mr. Oliphant?"

Oliphant said, "Yes, yes, terrified." The smoke from the piles before the door whipped around and swept against them. Oliphant blinked and turned away. Still, the aroma was not unpleasant—the bitter, warm air of leaf-burning in the fall.

Cook said, "I don't know, Colonel, I just can't see how it's going to work."

Martin grunted. "Get back, there, Jim." Martin waved them all back toward the shanty. He backed away himself, and raised the half-empty vial over his head. He aimed at an exposed rock. He threw. The vial shattered. There was a whoosh! The center of the yard instantly became a sea of yellow flame. Chenault began what would have become a Rebel yell, but choked it off when Martin scowled at him. The ten of them gathered together to stare at the miniature conflagration as it crackled and whined. Ashbrook edged close to the flames and casually scattered his deck of playing cards from the palm of his hand, using his thumb to make them go click, click, click into the fire.

When Ashbrook turned back to see their surprise, he said, "They weren't bringing me luck."

Cook laughed loudly. "Say, 'How do?' to the clerks, is that so, Colonel? 'How do?' "

Martin said, "That's what I want. Be as polite and thank-you-kindly as churchgoers at Easter. More so."

Headley flipped and caught the short stick that he had used to draw Broadway, and then flipped it again into the air; as it fell into the fire, he said, "There goes the Astor House!"

FRIDAY, NOVEMBER 25

Oliphant and Kennedy shared a room and bed on the top floor of a very old inn called the Captain's House, at the west side of Broad Street just off Exchange Place. The primary recommendation for the house was that the view from the top windows included both the copper roof and stout columns of the Old Custom House on Wall Street, and also the copper-faced dome of the New Custom House across the rooftops to the east. A secondary attraction to Oliphant was that the house was quiet and out of the way, since this was the oldest section of New-York and had become, over the decades, less residential than commercial and therefore absent of idle, prying eyes. There was one more reason why Oliphant had chosen the run-down Captain's House: He had stopped here on his first visit to New-York in 1846, at twenty years of age. It had been called the Dry Dock Inn then, and had been most respectable. From here, Oliphant had gone out into a world that had seemed vibrant, and possible, and most permanent.

Oliphant slept well; he awakened to find Kennedy standing fully dressed at the cracked glass panes of the bow window. It was after 8 A.M., and bright. Kennedy said, "No rain in sight."

Oliphant put his bare feet on the cold floor, and replied, "So I see, Mr. Kennedy. A good morning."

"A good omen, I call it, don't you agree, sir?"

Oliphant smiled. "The weather has been mild recently, for November."

"I used to think that it snowed in the North from October to April."

Oliphant laughed. "It does, in the north."

"I used to think that snow was magical. I was at West Point when I saw my first snow. We Southerners ran out in our drawers. It was before sunup. That was a day! I swam in it till I was blue. You might think the officers would've disciplined us, except they mostly were Southern too, and understood us. We made snowballs, and chose up sides for a fight. The boys from the South versus the boys from the North. We made out fine with our new weapon. I ate a snowball too. When I was in prison, we ate the snow because we were hungry. It snowed fiercely on Johnson's Island. It nearly made me hate the snow."

Oliphant waited until he was sure that Kennedy had finished his reminiscence, and then excusing himself, he attended to his toilet as carefully as the conditions permitted. He did not like having to wear the same linen and suit of clothes again; however, he had abandoned his wardrobe in Washington, and to have purchased new clothes to carry around was impractical. He also did not like the general dirtiness of the Captain's House. The luxury had long since gone from these rooms due to the traffic of the schemers and charlatans who were maneuvering the nation's finances in wartime. Speculation had made Broad and Wall streets into a crossroads of Babylon. Men gouged here. A battlefield report was occasion for profit and swagger, and— Oliphant stopped himself. He shut the privy door, lowered his pants, and squatted. He was beginning to think like his father. Perhaps he was even becoming his father. Oliphant spoke aloud to the privy door, "When murder is the work, the right hand must never know what the left hand does."

When Oliphant returned to the room, Kennedy announced that he was famished. They went down immediately to find themselves a barber, but Kennedy could not wait for Oliphant's shave to finish. Kennedy darted outside, and was back as suddenly to sit on a barber's stool and eat pastry filled with fruit preserves while he read the *Herald.* Oliphant had the *Tribune, Times,* and *World* on his lap, yet did not more than glance at the headlines, because he did not like bad news before his coffee. They sought out a good restaurant on Beaver Street, avoiding Delmonico's because of Oliphant's worry that he might chance upon Edmund Homes, who would want to know why he looked so strained and rumpled. Once at the breakfast table at a restaurant called Cape Horn, and sitting among splendid bankers and pretentious clerks, Oliphant was more irritated than ever by his stale clothing, and he decided to send a boy out for a new shirt.

They ate slowly, a large meal of eggs, fish, toast, waffles, strong green coffee, and stronger black tea, with more pastry yet for Kennedy. Oliphant was puzzled at how vigorous he was feeling. While he changed his linen in the washroom, he examined himself closely: He did feel strong, but his eyes were swollen like those of a mourner. He returned to the table with a quick step. His hunger and energy did not correspond to the previous episodes in his life when he had faced unknown perils—like voyages and stock ventures. He finally dismissed the mystery for the haddock, and turned his attention to the newly known perils in the newspapers. The rumors about Sherman were gone now, replaced by brutal fact.

"SHERMAN'S MARCH," announced the *Times:* "Rebel Accounts of His Progress—The Rapid Approach upon Macon—Nervous Comments of the

Richmond Press—Sherman's Marching Orders—The Army Moving upon Four Parallel Roads—The Regulations for Foraging and Subsisting on the Country."

Kennedy was reading Sherman's so-called marching orders, Special Field Order No. 120, in the *Tribune*. "Look at the fourth part, sir," he said, "where it says, 'The army will forage liberally on the country during the march.' Then it goes on to say that soldiers can't trespass or enter the houses. They're either ignoramuses, or they're lying ignoramuses. Four corps of hungry soldiers'll do anything—anything."

Oliphant was studying the *Herald*. "What do you make of this talk that Governor Brown might be trying to return Georgia to the Union to halt Sherman, or this that Alexander Stephens might be in Canada to receive a peace commission from Lincoln?"

"I said my say last night, Mr. Oliphant. I don't make anything of it but Yankee lies. I'm sorry."

"I still can't believe it," said Oliphant. "How could Lincoln allow this? You know I voted for Douglas—" He sighed. "How could anyone calling himself the president of—turn loose an army to devastate a defenseless population? Doesn't he know?"

"They've been doing it since the first, sir. They're just doing it out in the open now."

"It's unforgivable, it's barbaric, it's criminal."

Kennedy said, "Nobody's forgiving them, sir. Not now, not ever."

Oliphant offered, "My father told me that each man can experience the best of life and the worst of life, because he is the best of it, and the worst."

"That's a colossal epigram, sir." Kennedy drank his coffee. "And I don't think I understand it."

Oliphant smiled. "Neither do I, Mr. Kennedy."

Near 10 A.M., Kennedy asked Oliphant if he might guide him through the financial district hereabout, as Kennedy's own work for the day was best left until afternoon. Oliphant accepted the opportunity in order to forget his doubts and caution with the gay mood of the host. They strolled Wall Street from Trinity Church east, visiting the Old Custom House, now the United States Subtreasury and the depository for hundreds of millions in gold, and stopping at the old Stock Exchange at 40 Wall Street, where Oliphant provided Kennedy with a quick lesson in how government bonds and railroad, mining, and bank stocks worked. They also stopped in at the Bank of America and the New York Insurance Company, where Kennedy bombarded Oliphant with questions. Kennedy possessed a quick intelligence and a talent for numbers, and by the time they reached the New Custom House, Kennedy was willing to speculate how he would make his fortune —after the war.

Oliphant was amused; and yet as he looked about at the jammed floor in the New Custom House, at the mouse-like men and the eagle-like men and the plain rude men, he wondered if Kennedy was seeing them for what they were—brawling, duplicitous, greedy—or was already too far inside his dream of success among them for sobriety. It did seem to Oliphant that Kennedy delighted in the adventure of wealth more than good sense warranted. But then, illusion and great promises and fabulous ambition were part of capitalism, too, so who was he to censure another man for his taste? Kennedy was enraptured by Oliphant's explanations, and showed his envy of Oliphant, and flattered Oliphant to such an extreme that it made Oliphant laugh. It also made Oliphant consider Robert Cobb Kennedy once again. He was the gentleman-soldier first, certainly, and the Southern cavalier to the curl of his smile. Yet he was also shrewd, insightful, and calculating, like a Yankee trader. Kennedy's Louisiana had not prospered in the last twenty years because of the land alone; it was the home of driving men—like Judah Benjamin—whose eccentric code required them to playact the leisurely nobleman while they struggled to succeed. There was the contradiction of the gambler and the hoarder and the knight-errant in Kennedy, then, and to Oliphant's mind that might make Kennedy the essential capitalist: save yesterday, wager today, go out to fight again tomorrow regardless.

Oliphant was more charmed than ever by Kennedy. Kennedy would make the perfect protégé, the sort of loyal man one could install abroad as a representative and trader. Oliphant indulged himself such a dream—to make Kennedy his overseas agent. This made him feel hope. He escorted Kennedy to the East River and the Old Coffee Slip at the foot of Wall Street. He pointed to Pier No. 34, just downriver, now occupied by a single-stack side-wheeler. Oliphant said, "Just there is where the steamer once sailed for Charleston, Mr. Kennedy. I left here in September of 1855, for my marriage. My friends dined me merrily beforehand. I was quite seasick *before* I stepped on, and we steamed into a real storm. Not my wedding, a hurricane. Given your affection for omen-seeking, I mention that my first trip South that year was in beautiful weather."

Kennedy sheltered his pipe, to light up like Oliphant. "Sir, it's a fine memory. As for omens— I didn't get to this last night. She will be all right, your lady. Mrs. Oliphant will be. I feel that's right."

"Thank you, truly. She's a brave lady. The Royalls of Beaufort, all brave ladies." Oliphant pointed south. "It is Savannah they really want?"

"Sir, they want vengeance."

"It is what is left, isn't it?" Oliphant watched the flight of some gulls. "No, that isn't a question."

Kennedy faced the sun that was then hanging to the south over the harbor in a clear blue sky; he said, "I'd like to comfort you, sir. There's a verse, a Scotch verse, I learned in the prison. Intending no insult to good religion —if you please?" Kennedy caressed his moustache, and recited, " Trust to luck, trust to luck. Stare fate in the face. Sure your heart will be airy, if it's in the right place.' "

"Amen, Mr. Kennedy, say amen and, 'Hosanna!' "

They dined after 1 P.M. on Fulton Street, at one of the better cafes serving the ferry slip. Oliphant again ordered heavily—veal, rice, stewed tomatoes —and ate heartily, permitting himself several glasses of ale. After Kennedy reached the bottom of his second flask, he excused himself from his calf-liver meat pie and scooped up the black satchel he had purchased. Oliphant did not comment other than to agree that he would wait for Kennedy here. The United States Hotel was across the street, and City Hall Park was a short jaunt to the west.

Oliphant ordered tea and sweets, and had the morning's Washington newspapers to occupy his time. He was searching for any small item about arrests, or rumors of impending arrests. There was nothing like that. The front pages were dominated by the same grisly reports about Sherman as in New-York. The Washington editors called it "Sherman's Progress." There was also an account of Sheridan's continuing victories in the Shenandoah Valley. The pet phrase of the war correspondents was, "All quiet along the Potomac." Grant remained dug in and stalemated at Richmond and Petersburg. The rains in Virginia were early and heavy, and the two opposing armies were said to be sinking into the mud of their works, overwhelmed by what one journalist called "an impenetrable cloud of mist." The featured tragedy of the day was the death of Colonel John Marshall, United States Volunteers, in the Valley; he was a grandson of the celebrated patriot Chief Justice Marshall, and the papers presented lengthy biographies of the Marshalls in a smooth and effective attempt to give sympathy to all mourning families with the example of one prestigious family's ordeal. Thanksgiving Day was passed, and the grim wailing had begun again. And behind every paragraph about John Marshall was the unspoken beseechment, "How long? How long, Lord?"

After almost two hours, Oliphant had read every word three times about Sherman and his Special Field Order No. 120—that death sentence for Georgia and the South. The blood sacrifices on the battlefield were no longer sufficient. Now, there were to be national outrages against the most innocent. The glee in the reports told Oliphant that there was a madness loose. Men were not using language to describe; they were using it to celebrate death and destruction. Sherman was a man, and yet he was becoming a cry of rage and shamelessness. Oliphant knew from the Bible that such a cry cannot be ignored or silenced. It emanated from the past and afflicted the future. Nothing he nor anyone could do today could reach out to stop the disembodied cry, or shut it out. So why fire New-York? Richmond had not bothered to justify its order to Oliphant. Longuemare had been too caught up in the logistics to explain himself. Martin and his men had said, for revenge. Kennedy had said, to match blow for blow. But these were not reasons. They were more of the same cry. Was it an adequate explanation for Oliphant to confess that he was a mortal sinner, and so he heard the cry in himself? That he was no better and no worse than every other man and woman, and was fallen, and could fall again, and needed the miracle of grace to save him? Oh, theology! It was direction, not solution. Why then? Where were the reason and decency that had deserted America? Where were his own? What good was learning and faith for America's eighty-eight years, and for his own thirty-eight, if the nation and he could come to this, and oblige, and obey, and go on? Why? Oliphant thought, Is it an explanation that I am afraid? that I am angry?

Kennedy returned in an overheated mood, drank a glass of ale standing and then seated, and stuffed cakes in his mouth with his fingers, laughing and gasping. "As cane, sir, it was as sweet as cane!"

Oliphant said, "The Astor?"

"I've secured a suite on the fourth floor in the rear, and yours on the third floor as you asked, your favorite."

Oliphant was surprised that his suite had been available; it had felt so odd to be in New-York and not staying there. He paid the restaurant bill, and commented, "Fate, Mr. Kennedy, there's fate staring me in the face—my room waiting for me at the Astor."

They continued their tour west, to the Hudson River in order to remain well clear of Broadway. Kennedy was singing when they reached West Street. The day remained fair and gusty, and the activity at the piers was accordingly feverish—several California steamers having docked at once, and a large crowd at the New Orleans pier waiting to send off a double-stack behemoth. Oliphant saw how closely Kennedy watched the New Orleans-bound passengers, as if he were searching for a comrade or his own face. Oliphant did not tease, and they passed on.

They soon found a new game for themselves—reciting verse—and they practiced dramatic flourishes for the smallest happenstance, and especially at the sight of a beautiful woman. Oliphant ranged over Robbie Burns, knew his Psalms well enough, and seized upon Shakespeare's sonnets when he realized Kennedy's appreciation for them. Kennedy was Byron first and Byron last; he did know some Tennyson, and tried to do the "Charge of the Light Brigade" that he had learned in prison. They usually drifted back to old favorites, however, and spoke of love. Kennedy repeatedly demanded and rejoiced in one particular sonnet, No. 129.

" 'The expense of spirit in a waste of shame is lust in action,' " recited Oliphant one more time.

"Oh, sir!" said Kennedy.

" 'And till action, lust is perjured, murd'rous, bloody, full of blame, savage, extreme, rude, cruel, not to trust, enjoy'd no sooner but despised straight, past reason hunted, and no sooner had past reason hated, as a swallow'd bait on purpose laid to make the taker mad.' "

"What truth!" cried Kennedy.

" 'Mad in pursuit and in possession so; had, having, and in quest to have, extreme; a bliss in proof, and proved, a very woe; before, a joy proposed; behind, a dream.' "

"Here it cuts me," said Kennedy.

Oliphant finished, " 'All this the world well knows; yet none knows well to shun the heaven that leads men to this hell.' "

"I can't breathe for it," said Kennedy.

"Four centuries of men hard-breathing," observed Oliphant, "at least four."

"It won't ever end, you think, could men and women change?"

"Never," said Oliphant, "and if they did, the world ends."

"If only the ladies understood."

"They do, Mr. Kennedy; it is their secret, they do."

"I have in mind two ladies who keep the secret close and tight."

Oliphant laughed. "Only two?"

"In New-York. And no Southern lady would—" Kennedy turned. "Say it again, Mr. Oliphant. Maybe I've missed something."

Their afternoon idyll faded into the cool of the twilight and the approach of six o'clock. They arrived early at the Central Park rendezvous. Martin and Headley were waiting at the shanty, and were busy wrapping the vials of Greek Fire in newspaper with a twist at the top of the package, like a gift. The greeting was subdued, and the mood continued sober while others checked in—Ashbrook and Harrington, Price and Chenault. They occupied themselves smoking heavily and sharing a dozen ears of hot corn that Price had brought, with a slab of butter. Meanwhile, Martin and Headley separated the vials into nine groups, and kept back perhaps an additional two dozen for themselves. The seven had stored the vials in their satchels, and it was nearly half past six when Martin first spoke aloud what they were all thinking.

"We can't wait for Cook and Dennis," he said.

Ashbrook said, "You think they've been arrested?"

"I don't," said Martin. "I don't not. Mr. Oliphant, do you agree we should get on with it?"

"This is out of my experience," said Oliphant. "An extra amount of precaution does seem appropriate." When this did not move Martin, Oliphant risked the very sort of interference he was aware could confuse them and endanger them. They were like wild animals on the hunt now, and it was best to let them obey their instincts. Still, they had asked for his help; Oliphant tried, "We should have another rendezvous time, in case of exigency."

"Does that mean in case of trouble?" asked Chenault.

Martin said, "I didn't want to come back here again, Mr. Oliphant."

"Mr. Oliphant's right, Colonel," said Price.

Harrington said, "We might have to shoot our way out."

Headley said, "We told those boys to keep away from the girls."

"Let's not condemn, John," said Martin; he prowled the room, checking his watch. "We can't come back here tonight. That'd be stupid. One of us'd lead detectives back to all."

"Where are Timmy and Les?!" cried Headley at the door.

"Fort Lafayette is a likely address," said Harrington.

"That ain't neighborly talk, Jamie," said Martin. "It might be we're all

meeting again in Fort Lafayette. Here's what I say. Reassemble here tomorrow night, at six o'clock, here, right here. If you don't appear, we'll assume
you're taken, and we're going on without you. If there's trouble tonight,
keep moving, don't stop for pissing or even your mama's voice. Move!
Strike, and move! John Headley and I can take up the slack for Timmy's
and Les's hotels."

"And if we're taken, Colonel," said Price, "they'll make us talk. They'll
make Tim and Les talk."

"Sure they will," said Headley; he laughed and continued, "and they'll
tell 'em Kentucky's got bluegrass and godly folk. And if they take any of
us, they won't get more'n spit till after six tomorrow night. Cinch your belt,
and hold on. Sing 'em 'Dixie.' After six, we'll be gone."

"And remember this," said Martin. "You are Southern officers, acting
under the orders of your president."

Harrington said, "They'll hang us for outlaws anyhow, Colonel."

"Nobody's hangin' me so long as I can swing iron and ride," said Headley,
who repeated himself, and laughed again. Oliphant had not liked Headley
from the first, yet now he seemed necessary to the men's spirits. Making war
was foolish and defeatist, and now Oliphant could see that it required the
rash fool to lead the charge. Lieutenant Headley played the necessary part
with his exuberance; he boasted, "No matter what, Jamie, we die Kentucky,
and that's something no Yankee can ever have, ninety years on this earth and
fat!"

Martin's last pronouncement was a battle-cry. He said, "Georgia, the
Valley, General Morgan murdered at Greenville, and our homes. We've had
to read it in their papers. Now it's time they read about us." He breathed
in, and said softly, "It's right. Let's at 'em, boys. General Morgan, God bless
him, rides tonight."

Oliphant took hold of Kennedy's arm as they left the shanty with the
others. Ashbrook, Harrington, Price, and Chenault went west for the horse-
cars on Sixth Avenue to Washington Square. Martin, Headley, Kennedy, and
Oliphant went east, for the omnibus on Fifth Avenue to Madison Square.
Kennedy was able to keep pace with the loping Martin despite Oliphant's
dragging. Oliphant felt blessed for Kennedy. Kennedy carried himself and
anyone close to him with a whirling passion. Oliphant understood that his
affection for Kennedy was part moral and part aesthetic—the very handsome

younger brother whom Oliphant might have had if his baby brother had survived that fever at 3. But it was the physical Kennedy that Oliphant was thankful for, and cleaved to, as they mounted the omnibus, rode in silence, then changed to a hack north of Madison Square, leaving Martin and Headley without a wave.

They reached the Astor House at half past seven. In the atrium, besides the usual elegant scramble, there was a tumult for a bachelor's party being celebrated in a private dining room. Young men in preposterous hats were already openly drunk in the hall. Oliphant and Kennedy sidestepped several youths and called at the main desk for their keys. The evening clerk recognized Oliphant by face, but not by name, and bowed politely. Kennedy asked after the celebration. The clerk said, "They've got a Trojan horse—you didn't hear this from me—to wheel out later. I can guess what's inside."

Oliphant then asked Kennedy if they might toast their day. Kennedy looked quizzical. Oliphant told him that if this was to be his last evening at the Astor House, he wanted it pleasantly traditional. Oliphant almost said, Damn the risk. In any event, Oliphant looked like he had said it, and they linked arms to parade into the Rotunda Bar. It was awash in a Friday evening crowd that surged suddenly and swept Oliphant and Kennedy up the left side, near the taps. Oliphant ordered champagne. They raised their glasses over the black satchel that Kennedy had propped on the bar between them.

Oliphant said, "You are my beloved friend, Mr. Kennedy."

"Thank you, sir, and the same is true for me, sir. My Southern brother-in-arms, and forever."

"You will take care, Mr. Kennedy? None of this dying Kentucky?"

"I shall live forever, Mr. Oliphant."

"Simply outlive me, and I shall be happy on my deathbed."

"My grandfather died in his bed, my mother's father. Did yours?"

"Yes, and my father," replied Oliphant. "It is what comes to the good and the lucky." Oliphant gestured over the top hats toward the proscenium arch at the exit. "Shall we go upstairs? I've seen what I came to see."

Kennedy took up the satchel and the unfinished wine bottle while Oliphant paid. In the hall, they bowed to a pair of dazzling ladies with teeth like pearls and lustrous eyes. They got up to Oliphant's suite by taking giant steps. Inside, Oliphant said, "I have a request—a favor. Could you visit your room here last? I mean, could you visit the other hotels first? I shall wait here for your return."

"Certainly. Yes, sir. I understand."

"And another favor. May I have a vial?"

Kennedy searched one out quickly, and set it on a side table with the bottle of wine. He said, "I shall return—perhaps ninety minutes. Please, remember that Lieutenant Headley may visit here in the meantime."

"Yes." And then Oliphant was alone with his regrets. He kept the room dim, poured himself a glass of wine, and sat at the corner window overlooking St. Paul's. He waited upon the church bell to toll the attack hour of eight o'clock, and when it did, he held his breath until he could not. Broadway was serenely busy; the night was blue velvet and infinite; the wine was cool and tasted odd. What was it? Neither sweet nor bitter, and the bubbles did not tickle. His senses must be misbehaving. He listened more closely for fire bells, but heard only ship's whistles and the rattle of horses and wheels. He moved across the room to the secretary, took up a fine Astor House sheet, and tried to start a letter to Narcissa. He recorded the date, her address in London, and a shaky salutation, and then broke off. What could he be thinking? He must prepare for Kennedy's return! He must share in the doing of what he had helped to pay for!

The right and the left hand, he thought, the right and the left! He used his hands to push the furniture together in the middle of the parlor room; he kicked up the rugs; and he struggled with the secretary as it shed its books and papers like a runaway haywagon. He went into the bedroom and overturned the mattress. He hesitated. He had shared this bed with Narcissa three weeks before; he had shared it with Dorothea Longuemare too; and it was the same bedroom, if perhaps not the same bed, that he had shared with Camellia in the fall of 1860 when they had embarked on a second honeymoon after his father's funeral. This bed, he thought, this bedroom. He was not feeling sentimenal. He braced himself and yanked at the bedstead. He attacked the dressers, and pulled the extra blankets from the wardrobes. He even fetched the letter opener to cut open the pillows, scattering goose down from the bedroom back into the parlor.

At half past eight, Oliphant was at the windows again in order to study Lovejoy's Hotel directly across City Hall Park. Its windows were alight, as usual, and the same for the Tammany Hotel up Park Row in the distance. There looked to be something unusual along Newspaper Row, a man flapping his arms, but then Oliphant could see figures in a window above in the *Times* building, and they were signaling down to him. Barnum's American Museum was magnificently garish, as usual, lit like a dozen palaces and showing crowds at every level. Oliphant squinted, and found his eyes were tired; he closed them for a moment, discovering that it was a long moment until there was a knock at the door.

Oliphant called, "Mr. Kennedy?"

"The devil's little helper!" Oliphant opened the door. Kennedy was laughing with his hands on his hips, and he hopped inside. "I see your household's in fine disorder."

"Have you done it?" asked Oliphant. "Foolish question. You're safe? No, no, never mind. Let me say this. Where's the black bag?"

"Upstairs in my room here."

"Then the Astor's afire too?"

"No, sir. I have left the privilege to you, if you will?"

Oliphant stood by while Kennedy roamed the room. Kennedy picked up three oil lamps, dismantled them, and doused the pile of furniture with spirits of kerosene, continuing into the bedroom. When Kennedy emerged again, Oliphant said, "I am about to disappoint you, Mr. Kennedy. I can't do this. I hoped I could. I cannot."

Kennedy looked to the single vial on the table near Oliphant, and asked, "Do you wish me to?"

"No, I do not. How can I explain?"

Kennedy said, "There's no need." He set down the oil lamp, and walked over to snap up the vial and slip it into his pocket.

Oliphant began, "I want to explain, Mr. Kennedy. This is a home to me. This room, that room, here, this suite. A home, to come home to. I have lived here as happily as anywhere since the war. My home in Beaufort is now a contraband hospital. My childhood home was sold to strangers. London is an address, not a home. This suite is what is left me. My wife and I have lived here. And—I love this place."

"A clean thing, sir," said Kennedy. "A man shouldn't set fire to his own home. A cause cannot ask it."

"Oh, but they do, they do, and it leaves me empty—and unclean."

Kennedy took up the unfinished champagne bottle. At the center of the room, he poured the wine into the trail of goose down, and spoke out, "Mr. Oliphant's home, I annoint you! God bless and God keep!"

Oliphant relaxed, and if he did not laugh, he felt released. "Mr. Kennedy, a few more like you, and we might carry Jerusalem and that Promised Land."

It was time to go. Oliphant experienced no particular revelation in closing up and locking up and walking away from all that. He turned the key like any other, and saw a door in his face that he must turn from in order to continue. When they reached the top of the stairs, Oliphant was prepared to descend to await Kennedy's business on the fourth floor. He was perplexed to have Kennedy remain at his side down the stairs.

Kennedy waited until they were a few steps from the ground floor; he explained, "I couldn't do it any more than you, now, knowing it's your home. We shall leave the Astor to fate."

The atrium was in the midst of a very fashionable adolescent riot by the celebrants from the bachelor's party, who were harassing the patrons with inspired mischief. The hotelkeepers at the main desk looked to be under siege and showed strained courtesy as Oliphant and Kennedy dropped off their keys. The worst of the high-jinks was five sets of the boys who, in pairs, were pretending to be horses and riders, using wet mops and brooms like lances and truncheons in a jousting contest that aroused the cheers of their companions and their lady friends (much older and painted women). Soon enough, the boys had misdirected their fun, brushing against the sour lady friend of a military man. The officer insulted the boys' pedigrees. The boys returned loud disrespect. The officer boomed, "In my command, you'd learn the whip!" A large dandy called, "Whips are for mules, sir, and I see you've your complement of pack animals for the night!" The sour lady cried; the officer attacked; the clerks intervened; the assembly hooted. Oliphant and Kennedy strolled past.

"If the Yankees had a few more like that captain," said Kennedy, "we'd've carried Grant's divisions at Shiloh Church. I see why the Yankees let their rich boys buy out of service, and their farmboys crush the mud."

Oliphant said, "I couldn't agree more, and wish that it were so, or had been so for you. I think I mean that. All our lost Shilohs."

"I had Sherman under my guns, Mr. Oliphant. I know I did that day! He was right there. I couldn't walk, but I could still ride and talk, ride and talk. We were ready for it! One more assault—" They swept out the door and down the six steps to Broadway. Kennedy added, "We shall leave those rich boys to their fate too, and their Astor House to Lieutenant Headley."

They pivoted south toward the vanishing point in Broadway's canyon, and ambled along the curb listening for alarms and studying for signs of panic. Oliphant wondered why all should remain so ordinary. He also wondered what would be remembered about tonight once this great secret was revealed. This was the night New-York burned! But it all seemed so peaceful.

Kennedy halted them before St. Paul's. The chapel was open usually late;

the church board advertised a prayer service for "Our Armies." There was organ music and singing. "We could go in to pray for our people?" said Kennedy; he then pointed across to Barnum's. "Or we could take in the sights? Barnum's is open another hour, and you said that you had never been inside."

"Camellia so wanted to go in. I should have taken her."

"And Ned! You must see Ned!" Kennedy flipped a coin. "Tails it is!" He took Oliphant's arm to lead a weaving dash through the traffic across to Barnum's. They paid thirty cents each at the door. They marveled at the posters on the facade. "Three Fat Girls—One Ton—2,000 lbs.——Three Giants—24 Feet Tall——Two Dwarfs—17 lbs. each——Evening at 8— Linda of Chamoix & Waiting for the Verdict." They slipped into the flow of couples, oglers, and not a few children. Kennedy bought a glass of beer at the counter. They stood behind an iron pillar for refuge to calm Oliphant's intrinsic fear of the mob. And they were studying the faces of the patrons —the most spectacular aspect of Barnum's—when Oliphant heard fire bells outside. Kennedy pirouetted. Oliphant cocked his head—yes, definitely, fire bells, many of them, from two directions. Oliphant wanted to return outside. Kennedy pulled. "I've got you here! You must see it! And Ned! Oh, at least Ned!"

Oliphant agreed as he always did with Kennedy; it was impossible to escape the man's enthusiasm. And here, at Barnum's, Kennedy was even that much more compelling. Barnum's was a vast, jammed, noisy village. Oliphant thought of London's National Gallery combined with a cotton mill combined with a July Fourth fair. He thought of the gates of an earthbound heaven of wonders. He thought of fun.

In their haste, they could not admire the panoramas of famous battle scenes, famous deaths, and infamous executions that filled the first floor, though Oliphant did grasp the essential theme when he glanced at the re-creation of the murder of Captain Cook on Hawaii. Among the mannequins there was featured the so-called genuine war club that the natives had used to slay Captain Cook. Barnum's was the stuff of wink-eyed make-believe then—the way it should have been, the way we want it to be. Oliphant laughed at the painted backdrop—two smoking mountains meant to represent the volcanoes of Mauna Loa and Kilauea.

Kennedy knew the museum like a veteran. They used the side stairs to avoid the masses of people wandering in and out of the play in the Lecture Hall. Bypassing the second floor because of a crowd, they gained the third floor, where there was a truly ingenious collection of junk displayed in glass cases as if it were gems. The prize exhibit, by the excitement of the viewers, was a cabinet of powder balls that were said to have slain the great and the grotesque.

They halted at the landing again to listen at the window. The sound of fire bells was everywhere now, and there was a bewildered crowd pouring out of the Astor House. They watched a galloper emerge from down Broadway and turn toward Newspaper Row.

"We should go, Mr. Kennedy."

Kennedy reluctantly conceded. At the second landing, however, Kennedy jumped at Oliphant, and pleaded for just one more moment. Oliphant was immediately pulled inside, off the main corridor, to the Aquarium Room, where glass tanks held odd-sized fish that were advertised as either fearsome, extinct, or never-before-seen. There was also a pedestal supporting what was said to be the jawbone of the largest white whale ever killed.

"Here's my Ned, my darling Ned," said Kennedy; he pointed to a cage in the first tier of an assortment of cages containing penguins, snowbirds, egrets, and albatrosses—many of them stuffed and mounted.

Oliphant smelled human vomit and animal waste. There was not proper ventilation, and some of the birds looked sick. He observed, "They could keep them better."

"But Ned, sir, brave Ned! The Learned Seal!" said Kennedy. "He can count, and swim upside down, and balance a ball on his nose, and I've seen him read the Bible!"

Oliphant stepped up to consider a black and gray spotted seal, who was lying on broken rocks at the edge of a tiny, cold pool. At least it was alive, if insensate. The backdrop was painted with icebergs and a pennant, "North Pole." Oliphant could not manage a happy reaction; he tried, "I'm sure he's a noble fellow in his element. Another day, perhaps. I'm sorry. We should go."

Kennedy bent close to the cage. "It is sad, I suppose." He crossed his arms tightly. "What's Ned's learning got him? He's a noble animal. Look at him now. Be as good as a man and get caged. Be better and get caged. Be a man, be better, and get caged. That's what happens when you try. They cage all of us who try."

"Mr. Kennedy, we must go, we must." Oliphant could see that Kennedy's high spirits were vanishing as Kennedy tried to find magic in this poor seal. It occurred to Oliphant that Kennedy's affection for Ned might have something dark and confused in it with reference to Kennedy's year on Johnson's Island. Kennedy was straining to see some kind of a brother in Ned and that could not be healthy. Oliphant took hold of Kennedy. He had no plan other than to keep Kennedy moving and to get outside—as far as possible from whatever sorrow had captured Kennedy.

Yet as they reached the landing, Kennedy jerked free of Oliphant. He produced the single vial, stripped off the wrapping paper, and smashed it on the steps behind them. The flames were instantaneous.

"What have you done!" cried Oliphant.

Kennedy fell back into Oliphant's arms. The flames lunged at them. There were screams from people above them on the stairs. Kennedy stiffened. Oliphant gaped. Kennedy's face was empty, the beauty gone completely. Oliphant heard himself shouting, but was not in control of his words. Then Kennedy came to life, and cried, "I must save Ned! Ned!" Kennedy turned and lifted Oliphant, carrying him down to the first floor to deposit him inside the door. Kennedy screamed out to the crowd, "Fire! Fire! Save yourself! Save the animals! Fire!" Then Kennedy was gone back up the stairs.

The panic that followed was of a piece and yet so overwhelming that Oliphant lost his ability to discriminate. He was against a wall. He was on his knees. He was in the corridor. He was crushed into wax figures. He was pulled up. He was knocked down again. He threw himself into the waves of people and was dragged toward the exit. He was pushed through an already broken out window. He was in glass shards. He was on Broadway. He stumbled across the street to City Hall Park. Oliphant bent over and closed his eyes. "Thank you, Lord."

The crowd from Barnum's merged with the crowd out of the Astor House. Horses were felled, and carriages overturned. Fire bells sounded above the cries. Oliphant grabbed hold of a tree trunk and tried to make sense of the riot. Men screamed out. Oliphant thought, How did they know? A fire wagon team churned through the people on Park Row. The firemen screamed out. Oliphant could see the fire in Barnum's at the second-floor windows—and heavy smoke pouring from the upper floors. He could not see any smoke from the Astor House, but then the crowd was pointing to the Vesey Street side. Lovejoy's Hotel was curiously calm, but that did not matter now. Where was Kennedy? How could he find him? What was he to do now? And how did they know? For the people had found their voice and proclaimed:

"The Rebs've set the city on fire!"

"City Hall's afire!"

"South Street's in flames!"

"Rebs did it! New-York's under attack!"

"Where's rope? We need rope!"

"Where's the militia? Where's the mayor?"

"Reb gunboats, I swear! Shelling! Gunboats on the Hudson!"

"Broadway's afire! The St. Nicholas!"

"Hang 'em! Hang 'em all! Tonight!"

SATURDAY, NOVEMBER 26

Oliphant dreamed of a funeral. The mourners were formed up in front of him and very still. He knew the corpse in the bier was Kennedy. Yet why was Kennedy standing beside him? It was a dream. He went forward to pay his respects. He feared that the corpse would not be Kennedy, but rather that it would be a woman. It was like his mother's funeral, but then, it was different—a great black tent, a grass floor. Outside, they had dug the grave in a flower garden. There were azaleas and a live oak with Spanish moss. Oliphant could not speak. He was outside of the dream, watching himself in the dream. There was no one in the bier. There was a coffin already in the grave. He could not find his handkerchief, and he wanted to cry. He was unclothed. He asked Camellia for his pants. She wanted to stay in bed. He said he had to go. The funeral director stopped him and asked for his money. Oliphant was unable to convince him that this was a dream. There was no money in his billfold. Where were his clothes? Where was Narcissa? Captain Butter was waiting for him. Judah Benjamin was there, and said, "As a Jew, I understand what they want." Where was Kennedy? Oliphant confronted Captain Butter's lady, Bridey Lamont. She was crying. Oliphant told her that it was a dream. He was talking. What was he saying? "I'm sorry. I'm so sorry. I am to fault. I'm sorry. I was wrong."

The morning's light broke Oliphant's resistance, and he was awake. There was a scuffling noise. He flopped on his side. This was the old inn, the Captain's House. He had slept in his clothes. There was more noise. The door opened.

"Mr. Kennedy!"

"I'm sorry. I didn't want to awaken you." Kennedy's hands were filthy, his trouser knees were soiled, his coat sleeve was torn. He sat on the bed. "I might sleep now."

"Where were you? I lost you. Are you hurt?"

"I expected to die," said Kennedy. "All night, I wandered the streets, expecting to die. There were soldiers and detectives everywhere. They're arresting anyone alone, or young. I'm sorry."

"Fine, fine, no more questions." Oliphant got off the bed and went to the window. It was a cool, gray day, damp and threatening. He could not contain himself. "Oh, thank God you're alive, man! Thank the Lord! I was certain I had lost you!" Kennedy collapsed on a pillow. Oliphant continued, "You must sleep. I've had a few hours. We have time."

"We failed, Mr. Oliphant. We failed completely."

"I know. It doesn't matter. We're alive."

"It does, sir. We failed. I failed."

"Sleep, Mr. Kennedy. We shall talk later." Oliphant fended off Kennedy's protests another few minutes, and then was grateful for the peace. Kennedy fell asleep as fast as an infant.

Oliphant looked down upon Broad Street. Past 8 A.M., it was very calm, a few carts and people, and ship horns in the distance sounding the ordinary. Oliphant quietly picked up the rolled-up copy of the *Tribune* that Kennedy had brought in. He went out of the room to the privy. He needed tea and food. He also needed information. Horace Greeley's editors were equivocal in their estimation: "REMARKABLE INCENDIARISM—Several Hotels Set on Fire."

The account was tucked in the last column on the back page, along with all the other very latest news just before the presses rolled. Oliphant's mood was such, however, that he could not make himself read the story directly. He avoided his gaze to the left, the column of the late news from Washington City. The attorney general, Edward Bates, was rumored to have resigned. Judge-Advocate-General Joseph P. Holt of Kentucky was mentioned as the possible new attorney general. In the extreme West, the Sioux Indians were said to be gathering in large numbers to exterminate the white settlers. The Negro hero Frederick Douglass had addressed a huge audience at the Bethel Church on Capitol Hill.

Finally, Oliphant read the account of the fires. "A concentrated and skillful attempt was made last night by Secessionist thieves, conspirators, and incendiaries to set on fire our principal hotels, though, fortunately—at the time of this writing, 12:15 A.M.—without success in any instance, the efforts of the conspirators being in each case foiled by the early discovery of the fire before the flames had gathered any dangerous strength. . . ." Oliphant skipped down the column and read, "That the community has been saved from the terrible loss of property and life which might have been expected to attend such a plot, by its fortunate and early discovery, is a matter for profound thankfulness. . . ."

Oliphant studied the paragraphs that cited the particular hotels that had been fired, and the times the flames had been discovered: St. James Hotel at 8:43; Barnum's Museum at 8:45; St. Nicholas Hotel at 8:55; Lafarge House at 9:20; Metropolitan Hotel at 10:13; and Lovejoy's Hotel at 10:30, and Lovejoy's Hotel again at midnight.

Oliphant sighed. That was where Kennedy had gone, and why he was so depleted—back into Lovejoy's to finish what he had failed to do the first time, only to fail again, and to fail again at midnight.

Oliphant winced at the report of the arrest of an anonymous woman at the Metropolitan Hotel, and the mention of two more arrests of anonymous men later by the police. And here perhaps was Kennedy again, at 12:30, trying to fire the Belmont Hotel on Fulton Street. Kennedy must have gone back into the Astor to fetch his satchel of vials, or he might have met one of the others. Kennedy must have been utterly reckless, for the *Tribune* reported, "Strict watch was kept at all the hotels during last night, the doors of most of them being kept locked and guarded as to prevent the admission of any persons not belonging to the house, while many of the guests preferred to sit up all night in preference to taking the chance of being caught asleep should an alarm be given during the night."

Oliphant went downstairs to look for other newspapers. The night clerk demanded Oliphant's key. Oliphant silenced the man's complaints by paying for another night. He found the *Times* and *Herald* in a store on the corner of Exchange Place, and then went on to the pastry shop for some tea and food, and to buy Kennedy's favorite pies.

Henry Raymond's *Times*'s editors and James Gordon Bennett's *Herald*'s were more strident and accusatory than Greeley's had been. The *Times* was the most threatening: "THE REBEL PLOT—Attempt to Burn the City—All the Principal Hotels Simultaneously Set on Fire—The Fires Promptly Extinguished—Prompt Arrests of Rebel Emissaries—The Police on the Track of Others."

In addition to the targets already cited in the *Tribune,* there was mention of the Fifth Avenue Hotel, the Howard Hotel, the New-England House,

Brandreth's Hotel, French's Hotel. But here was terrible news! There was said to have been an attack on Walleck's Theater, and on the Winter Garden Theater. Who could have done such a thing? According to the *Times,* the crowd at the Winter Garden was saved from a catastrophic panic by the cool reaction of the Booth brothers on stage, performing *Julius Ceasar,* who had stopped the play to assure the audience that all was secure, and that they were going to continue the drama. And what was this report of an attack on East River shipping?

Oliphant studied closest the hints of imminent arrests. The Metropolitan Police were credited frequently as both instrumental in smothering the plot and close on the trail of the conspirators. There was no mention of the provost-marshal-general's office, or the War Department's Secret Service. And there were no good details of the arrests, other than repeated mention of this poor woman from Baltimore who had been taken outside of the Metropolitan Hotel. The police had bagged a demimondaine. Oliphant could assume then that the police were not completely informed. But there remained the possibility that the authorities had struck deep. The *Herald* said, "Several prisoners were detained during last night at Police Headquarters, preparatory to examination this morning."

Oliphant turned through the papers for other clues. The editorial page of the *Times*—Seward's reputed mouthpiece on national affairs—revealed by inference more than the news pages had in fact. "On the eve of the presidential election, the Government announced that information had been received in Washington of a conspiracy on the part of Rebel refugees in Canada and elsewhere to set fire to the major Northern cities. . . . At the time that Mr. Seward made this announcement, many persons affected to regard it as having a party object in it. Now. . . ."

Oliphant returned to the Captain's House in despair. What Captain Butter had told him was the heart of it: The War Department had known everything. The Election Day conspiracy was doomed from the first. Oliphant had ignored his correct intuition. Richmond had been wrong-headed—their grim plot had become a criminal catastrophe. And, Oliphant thought, it is now my crime.

Kennedy was still asleep, curled on his side. His Colt lay under his breast. Oliphant covered him with the blanket. Kennedy's hands were not just dirty; those were burns on his fingers and wrists. And there was a scorched odor from his hair. Oliphant pulled a chair over, sat with the other blanket, and propped his feet at the base of the bed. He watched Kennedy sleep. Oliphant thought, So Lee, so Early, so Grant, Sheridan, Sherman, now I know what it is you do. I have sent a beautiful young man to war, and here he lies, burned and beaten. Now I know what all those headlines of battles signify. And I revile it! To order such a boy in blue or gray to his death is obscene. Only God can forgive such a sin. And I have done it!

Sleep kept Oliphant from darker conclusions. When he awoke this time, his back pain was worse than his soul's. Kennedy was already alert, sitting up in bed, eating the pastries Oliphant had brought him and reading the newspapers. Oliphant got up to groan as he staggered about the room, trying to mend his bones. Kennedy was sympathetic and talkative.

"Have you seen this fuss they make of the Andersonville prison?" asked Kennedy. He held up the front page of the *Times:* "OUR PRISONERS—Their Release from Captivity—Thrilling Account of Their Sufferings—Horrible Barbarities of the Rebels." Kennedy continued, "They claim the death rate was one hundred a day. That they starved in the midst of plenty. I know some of these matters. It's the cold and disease that kill. The Yankees should look to their Johnson's Island, and Rock Island, and Elmira. They told us every morning we could live if we took their damned oath. We froze and starved because we wouldn't lie! And now—listen to this here!"

"Mr. Kennedy, we should dine. It is past noon."

Kennedy asked, "What's to happen?"

Oliphant was separating the papers in his lettercase. He made a pile of what would have to be destroyed, and a pile of what he would take along. For destroying was the cipher book. For keeping was his letterbook for Camellia, and his letterbook for Narcissa.

Kennedy seemed to misunderstand Oliphant's silence; he started, "Mr. Oliphant, I want to explain about last night. About Barnum's. Nothing much happened but smoke—I mean, the animals are safe, and Ned too. I don't know why I—"

"You did what you did," snapped Oliphant, "and if there's explanations to make, I should wear your ears off." Oliphant took out his billfold and counted; he had nearly two hundred dollars in greenbacks, and fifty English pounds. In his money belt, there was another five hundred dollars in greenbacks, and ten one-hundred-pound English notes. If escape could be purchased, he had the down payment. Oliphant continued, "Let us keep to the immediate future now. We need food, clean clothes, a shave, and bandages for your hands."

Kennedy tried to press his confession. Oliphant shook him off, and clapped his hands to encourage Kennedy to get up. Kennedy harumphed as he stood. "Well, sir, we also need a regiment to shoot our way out of this town."

"That is not how I see it," said Oliphant. "We walked in. We can walk out. I know some of this work. I have been doing it for years without understanding until now what an expert spectre I have become. I shall apply my talents. I have examined the newspapers carefully. The authorities always claim arrests in these cases. But I am skeptical. I shall put it to you another way. I am hopeful of our chances. We have a rendezvous at six o'clock."

Kennedy said, "Yes, sir. I still do wish that I had a fast horse and a half-day start."

Oliphant found that he could laugh. "A half-day head start? I thought you cavaliers only needed a half-hour."

Kennedy laughed too, and looked wonderful for it. "No one's that good, Mr. Oliphant. Not in the North. Too many roads, too few river crossings, and—huh!—the Yankees live here!"

The shanty's tin chimney showed gray smoke twirling into the cyclone of leaves that lifted from the treeline and danced over the street. It was not yet 5 P.M., and the deep blue of the twilight provided the sweep of Central Park with an ominous ceiling of clouds. Kennedy had insisted that they approach early, with enough of the day left to reveal trouble, but with the cover of the night to flee into. Oliphant thought this theatrical. There was no artifice in Kennedy as he gripped his Colt inside his overcoat and knocked on the door.

Martin opened up. "Yes, sir. You're the last to arrive, 'cept of course Timmy and Les."

"Is anyone hurt?" asked Oliphant. Martin shook his head, no. Oliphant stepped aside. Headley held pistols in both hands. Ashbrook and Harrington sat by the front window with repeating carbines. Price and Chenault were at the back window with more carbines. Oliphant swung his basket of food up onto the table, right atop an arsenal of pistols, shotguns, and ammunition. Oliphant had guessed that they would think more of gunplay than food. Harrington stripped off the basket's cloth to pull at the bread. The potatoes and corn were still hot, and Chenault whimpered at the touch. Oliphant looked back to Martin. "Have you taken their reports?"

"No, sir, that is, what, sir?" said Martin. "We made a botch of it."

"This mission is not a success, Mr. Martin," said Oliphant. "It is also true that the mission is not complete. Not until we successfully withdraw. You were at Chickamauga, I understand?" Martin's face puffed up. Oliphant continued, "Then you know that a major aspect of every battle is withdrawal. We are being pursued after failing to carry the point of attack. We shall retire in good order. Do I speak clearly?"

"Yes, sir, I understand, sir, exactly sir."

"Now then, are any of your men injured?" Martin shuffled to the table for food, and looked around at the others. Oliphant had achieved his aim. Martin, the tactical commander, was no longer necessary. Oliphant would direct the retreat. He had used the reference to Chickamauga on Martin, because he knew that Martin had commanded a remnant of Morgan's Raiders there, and that the Confederates' failure to properly follow up their victory that day, thus allowing the Federals under Rosecrans to escape to fight again another day, had set the stage for the Confederate catastrophe at Chattanooga two months later—exactly one year ago today—when Grant had used Sherman, Sheridan, and Thomas to break Braxton Bragg and scatter the Army of Tennessee to the wind, and these men to Canada.

Oliphant had also used rhetoric, which he knew none of these men could stand up to. Their guns were impotent now. The enemy was not only the police but also dispirited morale and lost momentum. The way out of New-York could only be found and secured with words. Oliphant knew he must tell them what to do, and he must also tell them that they could do it. He paused while the fact of his command penetrated their fear. Then he began what might prove the test of his life—to suppress his own sense of defeat in order to lift these boys free of theirs. He had got them into this, and he would be damned if he could not get them out. Damned! Oliphant pointed at Ashbrook. "You're limping, Mr. Ashbrook."

"Nothing, sir. I banged it. Got knocked down at the Winter Garden." Ashbrook smirked. "By two mean ladies, sir."

Oliphant said, "Is it true that you fired the Winter Garden Theater?"

Ashbrook looked to Martin. Martin said, "The papers're lying sir."

Oliphant said, "And Walleck's Theater and the Niblo Garden? Who gave the order to fire theaters?"

"None of us did, sir," said Martin. "Them papers're lying."

Oliphant said, "You must understand that they can say and prove whatever they wish, Mr. Martin. There is nothing to be gained now by defending your honor. And I want you to give it up. Are you being honest with me? There was no attempt to fire public theaters?"

"No, sir," said Martin. The others agreed passively.

Satisfied, Oliphant continued, "Now then, each of you, report your movements in summary fashion."

Ashbrook and Harrington listed the hotels they had fired. Ashbrook's injury had forced him to bypass the Metropolitan Hotel. Harrington had been chased out of the International Hotel by Negro porters, and had quit Broadway after 2 A.M. because every corner had seemed to hold detectives. Price and Chenault said there had been armed Negroes defending the Metropolitan Hotel. Chenault added that he had had the least trouble at Hanford's Hotel on the East River, but he had not reached it until after midnight, and then had had to avoid the Bowery because of the police.

Martin and Headley gave the most complex accounting. Martin had fired the St. Denis Hotel, the Fifth Avenue Hotel, and the Hoffman House without difficulty, but he had been chased by Negroes in a hack from Madison Square to Union Square, where he had met up with Headley. Headley had by then already fired the City Hotel, the United States Hotel, the Belmont Hotel, and the Astor House. Headley said that he had encountered Kennedy outside Barnum's by accident, where they had compared their progress, and concluded that either something was wrong with the Greek Fire, or the plot had been betrayed. Headley had then gone over to the Fulton Street piers in order to test the Greek Fire by firing hay barges. He had then rendezvoused with Martin at Union Square, and they had retired after 3 A.M.

"It was today we ran into the worst, sir," continued Headley. "Colonel Martin and I got up after ten, and after we read the papers, we figured we best get our luggage and get up here. We went on to the MacDonalds', and, phew!"

Kennedy jerked to the alert. "What! Did they get Katie? What!"

Martin touched Kennedy's shoulder. "We don't know. I got off the hack in front, and saw her through the window of the shop. There were several men in there too, and broken glass at the door. She saw me, and held up her hand like this." Martin put his palm out, and rocked his fingers. He added, "I ran for it. Detectives."

Kennedy burst, "How could you have left her? We must get her out!"

Martin said, "I'm miserable about it, Captain, but I couldn't help her."

Headley said, "It could explain how they knew about us."

Kennedy turned on Headley. "Never! Katie would never have talked! It was more likely your boys, Dennis and Cook! Damn you! You shall retract that accusation this instant!"

Headley came back at him hard. "I'll have my say, sir! We were betrayed! There is a culprit, or many of them! And your favorites are just as easily the darlings of the Yankees."

Kennedy lunged. "You crude bastard! You—" Martin blocked Kennedy off.

Oliphant said, "Mr. Kennedy!"

Headley, standing behind Martin, spun the pistols in his hands, so that he gestured at Kennedy with the butts; he remarked hesitantly, "I may not have enjoyed your fine education and privileges, sir, but my birthright is secure in Kentucky, where men own up to their shenanigans, and don't make altars of them."

Oliphant interrupted, "Gentlemen, I shall have a finish to this."

Headley appealed to Oliphant. "It's that you shouldn't protect Captain Kennedy, sir. He fired Barnum's. And that ain't no better'n what John did at the Winter Garden—" Headley stopped, and looked at Ashbrook. Ashbrook lowered his head. Headley said, "I've done it now."

Oliphant turned on Martin. "You have lied to me, Mr. Martin, about the firing of the theaters. You lied."

Martin lowered his head too. Oliphant turned his back on all of them. His plan was in danger of collapse. They were frightened, confused, and disgusted men, and perhaps it was wrong to treat them otherwise. Oliphant decided to amend his approach. He turned around and began again. "Gentlemen, we have all committed wrongs. No one of us is holier, or better, than another. I have misrepresented myself no differently than you have. It was mine to stop this mission, and I permitted you to try what was impossible. When I knew it was impossible! Hear me now. Let us make a bargain among ourselves that we shall henceforth be candid with each other. Mr. Martin?"

"Yes, sir." Martin waved to his men. They nodded. Martin said, "I apologize, sir. No more lies, sir."

"Save your contrition for Canada," said Oliphant. "As to Barnum's, Mr. Headley, it was wrong. Mr. Kennedy knows this, and must live with it. Mr. Ashbrook, I should not have held you up to ridicule alone when it rightly attaches to all of us. As to who betrayed us, or how—" Oliphant paused to get their complete attention. "I know, I have proof, I am certain that you were betrayed in Canada. That you have gotten this far is a miracle. And is also a demonstration of the possibility that you may get away. Do you understand me? It was not our Mr. Longuemare. It was not Miss MacDonald. It was not Mr. Cook or Mr. Dennis. And it was not the inadequacy of the Greek Fire."

"Maybe it was those Micks in Five Points, sir? The Dead Rabbits?" tried Headley.

"No! As far as we know, they complied with the terms of the contract," countered Oliphant. "There was no general firing of Broadway, and so they were not obliged to fulfill their obligation." Oliphant scowled at Headley. He must not lose their fragile unity with speculations about blame and fault. Let the future flatter itself with the vanity of history writing. He was here! It was a ruin! There was no certain goodness! There were only shadows, and half-truths, and horrors! Others might judge. Oliphant plunged onward. "Canada, gentlemen. Canada sent you and Canada betrayed you and Canada is where you must go. Now, stop this bickering, and put away those guns!"

Price started, "But there are detectives everywhere! They're hanging mad!"

"You'll have me do worse to you if you don't obey me," said Oliphant. "Now, the guns. In those cases." Martin took the lead by laying the shotguns in the long black satchel. The others followed with the carbines. Oliphant let them keep their pistols. As long as they were without offensive weapons, he could control them. Oliphant continued, "Mr. Martin, Mr. Headley, there are excellent descriptions of you in the afternoon papers, so you will keep your hats on and chins down. Mr. Price, Mr. Chenault, you are designated as the ordnance officers, and you will carry those cases of guns and ammunition. Mr. Ashbrook, Mr. Harrington, you are mess officers, and will purchase food for our journey once we are under way. We shall need a dinner and breakfast for ten men for now, no spirits, and plenty of sweets. You have money?"

"Some, sir," said Ashbrook. Oliphant handed him several bills.

Martin said, "Where are we going, sir? Canada?"

Headley contributed, "We'd figured we'd get horses, sir, and try for New Jersey first."

Oliphant said, "We are going out the same way we came in, by train from the Chambers Street Station. It will be watched of course. But once we get past the choke point, they won't have been so careful along the way. And we know the route, so there will be no surprises for us. We won't mistake commonplaces for hostility."

Headley was compliant. "Tonight, sir?"

Oliphant checked his timepiece. "There is a 10:20 P.M. sleeper on the Hudson line for Albany. We shall travel in a group. Like soldiers going home. They are looking for lone figures, so stay close up and brotherly. At the station, we shall purchase sleeper car tickets, first class. The cars open at nine o'clock. We will use local tickets that we shall also purchase to pass through the gate, and then use the sleeper tickets to board the cars." The men were gathered close to Oliphant now, their heads down. Oliphant continued, "We shall arrive in Albany tomorrow morning, and take hotel rooms near the station. There are no trains to the border until the evening. We will spend the morning in a church. In the afternoon, we will reprovision and purchase sleeper tickets again for the 6 P.M. train to the Suspension Bridge. We shall arrive at the Suspension Bridge Monday morning, and shall detrain to change for the day train to Toronto. I shall represent us to all inquirers, especially the trainmen. I shall also purchase all the tickets, and pay for all the rooms."

Chenault dropped some cheese on the floor near a crack in the boards, and brushed it with his foot into a hole. When he realized that Oliphant was watching, he shrugged and smiled.

Martin said, "It is a grand plan, sir. Tom Hines couldn't improve on it."

Oliphant did not know the name; but he assumed that the reference was happy, and that it provided the men some intrinsic comfort.

"Excuse me, sir," said Ashbrook; he exposed his pistol in his belt. "I agree with the Colonel—still, sir, what if there's trouble before we get out of New-York?"

"There won't be," declared Oliphant. "But I agree with your caution, Mr. Ashbrook. You should tell them, if you're taken, that you are Rebel deserters. There must be no shooting. They can hang you far easier for murder than for conspiracy. Surrender easily. Tell them you have deserted. Relate everything about this past month but that you set the fires. You can never admit that. Never." Oliphant spoke to remove their frowns. "Not in this century, anyway."

They laughed. Headley balked one more time; he said, "I'm not ashamed of what I've done, sir. I think you should know that."

Oliphant sighed. "Are there other concerns?"

"Is there—" began Kennedy; he mumbled, "Katie?"

"Mr. Kennedy," responded Oliphant, addressing Kennedy as well as all the rest, "if the War Department were to arrest and prosecute all of those with knowledge of or who were party to last night's events, they would require a division of troops in New-York to keep order. Whatever Miss MacDonald's situation, it will be that much happier if we do not approach her again."

"Just abandon her to them?" said Kennedy.

"We must leave her to defend herself," said Oliphant. "She is quite capable. Believe me, believe me, I know your problem. I have experienced it myself. It is best to go."

Kennedy brushed his cheek. Oliphant turned away from him; he was convinced enough of his strength now, and theirs, to add one more critical detail. Yet he realized he could not do it while facing them. Oliphant addressed the stove and coffee pot. "There is also this, gentlemen. You have not known me. You have not heard my name. There was not a John Oliphant in your lives. Never. This is an order, of course, and you must obey. I speak with the authority of the secretary of state and the president." Oliphant heard their ignorant obedience and smiled without pleasure. It was going to work. Oliphant turned back to them. "Each of you, say it."

Their assent was as uniform as their ensuing conduct. Oliphant led seven heavily armed men through the streets of New-York as a schoolmaster might have taken his class up a mountain for an evening communal with the heavens. They were alternately suspicious and playful, yet as they found their stride, they turned silly. They made bleating sounds, and called each other by the additional name "Lamb" so that James Chenault-Lamb passed apples to John Ashbrook-Lamb and John Headley-Lamb. Oliphant encouraged their amusement. It produced a mystical air of hopefulness that Oliphant thought might keep the authorities, and the wolves, at bay. When they arrived at the Chambers Street Station—a hideous brick and masonry structure that opened onto long tin-roofed sheds—and fell silent at the tangible risk of their adventure, Oliphant tried to reignite their folly by having Kennedy join him in more of their versifying. Oliphant gave them sonnets of love, helping Kennedy get through Shakespeare's No. 129. The others were captured by the learning and, because they could not match the poetry, provided balladeering.

It was a jocular and teasing group that Oliphant left in a circle while he bought the tickets. And it was a harmony of baritones, with Harrington's bass and Chenault's tenor, that Oliphant led to the gate. The gate attendant was impressed by Chenault's raw singing talent, and did not hesitate to pass them. They found the detached sleeper car, and boarded with the kind attention of a porter, who said he could fetch them liquor or women for their wait. Their laughter was raucous at the idea, Ashbrook offering, "We ain't seminarians!" Harrington offering, "Bibles! All we've got is Bibles to sleep on!" Oliphant declined the porter's offer with a greenback, explaining that they all needed their sleep, as they were bound for their families, for whom they must appear healthy, wealthy, and virtuous. The porter, winking, promised that they would not be disturbed.

Martin and Headley occupied the compartment immediately next to Oliphant's and Kennedy's. They were quick to present themselves to Oliphant. Headley attempted an apology for his troublesomeness: "You are the coolest gentleman I have ever known, sir." Martin added, "It is an amazement, sir, how you did this—easy as opening preserves."

Oliphant asked them to rest quietly. There was an hour of peace before all seven were gathered in Oliphant's compartment in extremely close quarters. They chatted furiously, smoked like a wet wood fire, and maintained a watch through the curtains of the crowd now gathered outside, from the gate to the cars. They gulped in unison as the locomotive backed into the sleeper cars with a shuddering bang! It was not too much to conclude that the several figures they could see posted at the gate were detectives, though they could as easily have been drummers or thieves. Oliphant stretched out his legs as best he could, and put his feet on the two bags of weapons that Price and Chenault had brought in. Oliphant closed his eyes and listened. He held his breath when the others stopped talking. There were male voices right outside the window. The worst was when other passengers struggled to get onto the car with their baggage, banging and cursing as they searched for their compartments. A woman's voice preceded a loud whack at their door. Ashbrook started his tongue-clicking sound. The noise on the platform outside was whining, crying out, grumbling. Chenault would peek under the curtain, and everyone would demand a report, which always was best summarized as "Nothing."

Finally, after lighting another smoke, Martin shifted in his seat, took off his hat, twirled it, and said, "If it comes, we go out the back, boys, and scatter in the city."

Oliphant said, "None of that. We're fine."

Headley said, "I won't surrender."

"Then don't," said Oliphant. "This is the fight. Here."

"I can't," said Ashbrook. Harrington and Chenault, seated on the floor, coughed and fidgeted. Ashbrook added, "I just can't."

"You can walk into guns," said Oliphant. "This is how you walk out of them."

"Chickamauga was easier," said Martin. "Bein' shot is easier."

Headley said, "Hell, that night we rode out with General Forrest from Fort Donelson was easier. And there were more Yankees than grass."

"Agreed, John," said Harrington. "Least we had a horse, and was movin'."

"That's good," said Oliphant, "think of what was easier. Mr. Price?"

"Sharpsburg," said Price. "It sounds crazy. One minute I had a regiment around me, and the next I didn't, but it was easier. The Yankees at least stayed in front of me. My neck didn't crawl."

The others stirred, blew smoke rings, settled. Oliphant, trying to distract them further, altered the terms. "What was harder, then? Harder than this? Was Shiloh harder?" They collectively groaned. Oliphant continued, "Yes, what was your worst time, Mr. Ashbrook?"

"Vicksburg," replied Ashbrook. "Sitting there and taking it for two months. You know 'Quaker guns,' sir? The logs we made masquerade as cannon barrels to scare the Yankee gunboats? We had this other fun we called 'Quaker courage.' After a bombardment, we'd try to piss, and that's mighty hard with your innards scrambled. The first to pass water in the direction of Useless Grant got the medal. 'Quaker courage.' "

"I never had trouble pissing my pants," said Chenault. "That day at Missionary Ridge. I was shamed till I smelled worse about. Those guns make you a baby."

Kennedy slapped Chenault on the back. "There's something harder ahead, mister. It has to do with the ladies. You'll be fortunate to keep infant status up against that pounding. Battle's easy in comparison. All there is to do in a fight is just keep shooting and walking. At least you have your pants on, and get to keep them on."

Martin said, "You are a caution."

Ashbrook applauded. "Pants!"

Harrington began, "There once was a girl in Chattanooga—"

The knock at the door made them all move as one fourteen-arm and seventy-digit creature, pistol butts and triggers and hammers and the hook on the bags and the clink of the carbines. Oliphant experienced the bizarre sensation of what it was to direct a machine that could kill without hesitation, and then he regained his common sense, and said, "Relax, gentlemen, the beastie does not knock." They did calm a little. Oliphant spoke to the door. "What's that?"

"Barney the porter here, sir; you happy and all?"

"Oh, fine, fine, Barney." Oliphant pointed. Harrington slipped the lock and opened the door. Barney's head came in, and he showed a cunning grin of missing teeth and a squash nose; he let the smoke clear from his blinking eyes. "Ten more minutes, sirs. A tad delay. Sure you don't want a bottle? Sleep better?"

"This is most considerate of you," said Oliphant. "We're content with our stories. What delay was that?"

Barney said, "Carrying on at the gate, ladies and luggage, is all."

Oliphant said, "Well then, we'll be sure to call you to turn down our beds."

"Lots of good-lookin' ladies on this train," said Barney. He winked, because he must have seen one approaching. Her face appeared just behind and above him then, an ethereal beauty, hooded eyes, broad forehead, round mouth, hair up with wisps of blond. Her pout was more fetching than any possible smile. With the instinct of a heroine, she paused overlong in the passageway in order to absorb the rapture of this gallery of young men. And then she was gone. Barney waited a moment and then snickered. "You boys been a long time away?"

Oliphant smiled. "Ten minutes is too long, Barney."

Ashbrook dared, "This prayer meetin' could break up at a moment's notice." He moved his hand under his coat, and brought forth his flask. "Have some scripture, Barney?"

"I'm 'bliged to dee-cline, thank'ee," said Barney. "The conductor, he's a Methodist visitor as to my affairs." Barney looked behind him at a woman's call, and grinned while closing the door. "Maybe I can come back and read your good book?"

"Mighty neighborly," said Ashbrook.

Harrington said, "Might be he can introduce us to that angel that passed."

Price observed, "An introduction like that, man might forget farewells."

Kennedy produced a single juicy sound that made them guffaw.

The hollow of time that followed enclosed them in a vacuum of terror. Oliphant would no longer insult their intelligence. He permitted each man to fight his own doubts by himself. Oliphant endured his battle by fussing with his pipe and taking out his watch. He studied the timepiece like a looking glass. His ceaseless journey was there, rendered in Roman numerals and stick figures. In his years of traveling trains, coaches, ships, and his one balloon ascension at Firenze, he had never missed a departure. It was an astonishing record—a man for whom the arbitrary had been an absolute—

the master of his fate who had never disobeyed something that did not actually exist. He thought, Earth I have owned and air I have drunk and water I have sailed upon and fire I have caused, but time is my better. Oliphant brought the watch face close to his own and saw himself captured by the minutes, even while he was en route to one more departure he could not miss. Oliphant saw himself complete and completely and completed. No, not completed. This moment needed a poet. What was available was a poem, for as the whistles sounded, and the car throbbed, and the wheels rotated, and the lurch of forward progress bent Oliphant and the rest into their fondest prayers, Kennedy began humming, then mumbled the verses, then spoke out clearly, " 'Before, a joy proposed; behind, a dream. All this the world well knows; yet none knows well to shun the heaven that leads men to this hell.' "

"Too much, Captain," said Martin.

"Never enough. Truth," said Kennedy.

The train was moving. Martin leaned over Price and lifted the curtain to look, bumping Oliphant when the train jerked. Martin turned his head to address Oliphant. "I have a question, sir, that I didn't think to ask before?" Oliphant nodded. Martin asked, "Why're we going to spend tomorrow morning in church?"

Oliphant closed his timepiece in his fist and did not answer.

CHAPTER 10

John Oliphant
at Niagara Falls, New York

SUNDAY, NOVEMBER 27, AND MONDAY,
NOVEMBER 28

The Sunday morning papers from New-York caught up with them at
Albany, and were readily available to all as they boarded the New York
Central Railroad sleeper for the Suspension Bridge and rolled out into
nightfall in the damp, cold, ghostly Mohawk River Valley. New-York's
citizenry was said to be enraged. James Gordon Bennett's *Herald* provided
the most elaborate account, and also indulged in the most speculation.

"ATTEMPT TO BURN THE CITY—Discovery of a Vast Rebel Conspiracy—
Twelve Hotels Fired by Turpentine and Phosphorus—Similar Attempts on
the Shipping—Prompt Frustration of the Scheme—Great Panic at Barnum's
Museum—Excitement at Niblo's and the Winter Garden—Full Develop-
ment of the Plot—Arrest of Four of the Principals—One of Morgan's
Guerrillas Implicated—His Arrest and Imprisonment—Vigorous Orders of
Major-General Dix—The Perpetrators to Be Tried by Court-Martial and
Hanged Immediately—Rewards Offered for Arrest of the Guilty—The
Latest Particulars."

The information was less substantial and threatening than promised, to
both the relief and perplexity of Martin and the others. There were still no

names of the arrested. The man identified as one of "Morgan's Guerrillas" was also unnamed, but the details did indicate that he was neither Cook nor Dennis, instead was the victim of bad luck, bad timing, and probably the need for the Metropolitan Police to demonstrate progress in the case. All told, the Sunday newspaper editors had done a credible job of re-creating the conspiracy from what they knew to have happened, yet it did read somewhat as a child might imagine his conception from the fact of his existence. The story lacked a sense of the ridiculous, and was overflowing with intimations of an omniscient, omnipresent intelligence.

There was nothing ambiguous about the prominently displayed copy of Major-General Dix's General Order No. 92, dated November 26; it read with the passion with which it had been composed: "A nefarious attempt was made last night to set fire to the principal hotels and other places of public resort in this city. If this attempt had succeeded, it would have resulted in a frightful sacrifice of life. The evidences of extensive combination, and other facts disclosed today, show it to have been the work of rebel emissaries and agents. All such persons engaged in secret acts of hostility here can only be regarded as spies, subject to martial law, and to the penalty of death. If they are detected, they will be immediately brought before a court-martial or military commission, and, if convicted, they will be executed without the delay of a single day."

For his bluster in the newspapers, General Dix suffered the most from the boyish mockery that rocked certain New York Central sleeper compartments past Schenectady and Amsterdam, Harrington opining in summary, "There's many a raccoon that'd be out of business, and many a fox that'd need to take up root digging, if Ol' Dix's curse was posted in the woods, and they could read. I say, shake a fist, Ol' Dix, and sweep up the feathers!"

Because the *Tribune* did not publish a Sunday paper, they were cheated of reading Greeley's wrath. Nevertheless, Henry Raymond's *Times* contained two items that, in addition to the mention of Morgan's guerrillas in the *Herald,* convinced Oliphant that there had been an organizing authority behind the defense of New-York. First, it was said that Police Superintendent John Kennedy (of Draft Riot fame, for the beating he had taken when he had tried to stop the mobs single-handedly) and City Council President Acton "were constantly in attendance at Police Headquarters and had their plans and forces so arranged that in case any disturbance had occurred it would have been immediately suppressed." This would explain the absence of the Five Points gangs; the authorities had known beforehand of the hiring of the mercenaries, and had moved to intimidate them.

More significantly for Oliphant, the lead paragraph in the *Times* seemed to reveal how completely Captain Butter had been in control: "The diabolical plot to burn the City of New-York, published yesterday morning, proves to be far more extensive than was at first supposed. It is already proved to the entire satisfaction of the authorities that the affair was planned by the rebels and had been in preparation for a long time past, the men selected to perform the work were sent to this city at various times and under various pretexts, and arriving here they formed themselves into a regularly organized band, had their various officers, including a treasurer, whom they could always find, and who was ready to supply them with money necessary to carry out their infernal work, and proceeded deliberately to mature their plans for one of the most fiendish and inhuman acts known in modern times."

Oliphant continued to study the reports as the train churned west, past Amsterdam now, on to Rome and Utica; however, he was unable to challenge his original assumption, or to locate any warrant for a change in his plans. He had seen Captain Butter's makeup at a close distance; he had walked and talked with the man, and knew something of his limitations. Butter was not a vain fanatic like Lafayette Baker, nor was Butter a simple-minded member of the avengers in New-England and Washington. Butter was a very tired individual doing a job he had been ordered to do. If Oliphant had been Butter, he would have tried to stop the conspiracy with any means at hand. If kindness might have worked, he would have consoled; if threats or arrests, he would have pounded and raided. Oliphant could not answer as to why Butter had released him on Capitol Hill. Perhaps it had something to do with Lafayette Baker, whom Butter had seemed ambivalent about; perhaps it had been a mistake, a momentary blindness or weakness or act of mercy. Butter had been wrong in the specifics about Oliphant's complicity then, but the telegram in Oliphant's pocket that day had proved Butter completely right, as if he had known prophetically—the soldier looking at war and seeing worse upon worse, and everyone's fall from grace. And now, after the facts of Friday night, Oliphant could too easily put himself in Butter's place. What must be done was to hunt down the men responsible and to bring them to justice.

In the middle of night, Oliphant got out of his compartment bed. He parted the curtain. He wondered if those were the lights of Syracuse approaching. He thought, How does it stop? Who stops it? When I tried to tell Captain Butter about the old woman with the skull, he scorned me. When I tried to ask him for help, he told me to go to hell. No, that was not fair. Oliphant flicked the flint to light his pipe, and also to find the word "treasurer" in the *Times*'s story. He looked outside again, and wondered where the Erie Canal might have gone, or if those lantern lights were from a barge making its way east. He closed his eyes and thought, Dear Captain Butter, I could have helped you as you could have helped me. We both could have been better men in this our common wilderness.

Oliphant did not dream unhappily; though it was too brief a sleep to produce vivid images, it did produce a fleeting vision of Chinaberry among Spanish moss. The car porter, a disappointment after Barney, woke Oliphant gruffly at Buffalo. He was dressed and comfortable in quick time. This was a through train to Toronto, which Oliphant presumed would mark it for special scrutiny at the border. Accordingly, Oliphant had his party prepared to slip off at the Suspension Bridge in good order. Also, Oliphant agreed with Martin that they should once again proceed in pairs and not as a group.

Oddly, Oliphant's expectation of frontier security was not confirmed. There was a line of soldiers at the depot, but there was no collection of detectives, or even senior officers, and the troopers stood their posts sleepily in the eerie predawn dark of gaslight reflected off steam and coal smoke. There was another lengthy freight train rolling on the main track toward Canada, rattling the pillars of the platform shed and tossing cinders to ping off the passenger cars. Oliphant and Kennedy detrained with a casual pokiness at what was the front of the train. Oliphant looked for but could not locate any Federal officer. The soldiers seemed more of the colored regiment from before, yet Oliphant was also unable to find the Negro first sergeant of the profound voice. The most official representative, besides a wheezy corporal, was the stout, hairy stationmaster who was in deep conversation with three of the trainmen, all bent over their watches and hardly glancing at the departing passengers. Oliphant did not return Martin's signal from up ahead. He did hold Kennedy back until the others had passed through the line of soldiers and into the depot building. A baggage attendant dragged his cart up to Oliphant and inquired after trunks from the baggage car. Oliphant gave the man a coin. "A mix-up on the road with our luggage, but thank you." The attendant grinned with mock sympathy. For a moment, Oliphant stared at the man's obliging passivity, and regretted his overcau-

tiousness about changing trains at the border. Yet it was too late to call
Martin and the others back. He would follow his original schedule. He
stopped inside the depot at the stationmaster's window, to ask after the next
morning train to Toronto. Oliphant knew the time already; he wanted to
show his face and make an impression that he was anxious, so that he would
be remembered, and remembered as being alone. Oliphant asked, "What
time was that again, sir?" The assistant stationmaster was greasy and sleepy;
he wrote it down sloppily on a paper. Oliphant gave him a dollar for his
effort, and the man beamed.

Oliphant fetched Kennedy. Outside of the northbound depot, they waved
off a hack driver and walked down the steps. The twin towers of the
Suspension Bridge loomed ahead of them, marked by gaslight fixtures. They
were headed for breakfast at the Centre House next to the southbound depot,
and had to pass under the bridge. The freight train was rolling heavily above
them and raining dust. They did not conceal their curiosity, studying the
guard detail at the entrance to the pedestrian roadway of the bridge—two
soldiers walking their posts, several more gathered near the left of the two
gazebos at a blazing fire in a tin drum. Kennedy asked if they might detour
to the railing at the precipice to take in the sights.

Oliphant answered, "You'll have light in half an hour for that, and I'm
hungry now."

Kennedy was frisky; he skipped over a rock that had splintered from the
bridge supports. "Is this where that Blondin fellow flew across the river?"

"I think that was over the gorge, down below, and he didn't fly. He
walked a tightrope." Oliphant sounded too stern. He halted once they had
gotten clear of the oppressive rumbling of the freight train. He could now
hear the ceaseless roaring sound of wind through the canyon. He considered
the cool, clear night. There was no real light in the eastern sky over the
southbound depot ahead of them, but the darkness was definitely thinning.
Oliphant corrected himself. "If you'd like to try your wings, why not wait
until daylight, so we can all applaud you?"

"Then I had best eat heartily, and no bird food—I want bacon!" Kennedy
turned once more from Oliphant and waved at the sky. "Sir, can you see
that Icarus now?"

Oliphant said, "I have a confession for you, and if you'll promise to come
along"—he waited for Kennedy's assent—"there is no constellation of
Icarus. I invented it, for your sake."

"Oh? Why's that, sir? Invented?"

"I wanted to warn you to be cautious. It was presumptuous of me, I know. But then— I was fighting a premonition that you have proved false." Oliphant softened. "You knew, didn't you?"

"I suppose. I did want it to be true. There should be a constellation of Icarus. There's the North Star! And the two bears! Are you certain there's no Icarus? There should be."

"No one can rewrite the heavens, Mr. Kennedy."

"You could; you could do it, sir."

"Could I get you to breakfast?"

They ascended to the square of shops, stables, boarding-room houses, and odd lodgements that served the southbound depot at the head of the road from Niagara Falls. Oliphant and Kennedy both looked to the chestnut tree by the depot building that had been the sight of Kennedy's upset that first day together. Kennedy pointed across to the stable, Raven's Tours, and wondered aloud if he could recover the money he had paid for the team and wagon to rescue those four prisoners of war. Oliphant said that that was behind them now, and there should be no going back. They finally reached the well-heated dining room of the Centre House adjoining the depot. They sat separately from the others, but were far from alone at their long table, with the chattering confusion of other travelers awaiting the first Buffalo-bound train. Oliphant studied the room and the elevated counter area for detectives, and concluded that his own party presented the most martial-looking presences. He watched Martin and his men consume heavy meals as greedily as schoolboys. Oliphant could not compete with Kennedy's appetite, but the food did lift his spirits, so much so that, with Monday morning bright and new outside the bow windows, he permitted Martin and Headley to join him and Kennedy at their long table. Soon, the other men followed to arrange themselves like operagoers, chairs behind chairs, elbows on the table. The room had cleared of the Buffalo-bound passengers now; however, new travelers were always arriving. Martin and his men drank green coffee and worked through hills of pastries, their mood exultant again, joking about comely ladies or the prospect of a night's sleep in a bed that did not vibrate. Oliphant approved of their antics—nothing made a man appear more innocent than silliness—and waited until fifteen minutes before their train time to speak; he began, "I've not purchased tickets for this part of the journey, gentlemen. You will get your own at the northbound depot. Do you each have sufficient funds? Good. Very well, you have a train to catch, and your midday meal at the Queen's Hotel." They groaned for their full stomachs.

Oliphant teased them. "I should imagine you will be popular enough not to have to pay for meals for a few days, with your stories of your adventure."

Martin looked hard at Oliphant. "You're not coming, sir?"

"I have business on this side of the border," explained Oliphant.

They shifted their chairs and turned to Oliphant with suspicious faces. Headley leaned forward to ask, "Anything you might need a hand with, sir? I know of where I can find these boys disposed to your style."

"It is very kind of you, Mr. Headley, and I appreciate your sentiment. This is a job for one man."

Chenault tried, "My papa told me there's nothing worth doing that ain't done better in company."

Oliphant smiled. "Your father is not incorrect."

Martin said, "Well, sir, are you set on this then? We don't have to go. We've been in worse trouble than that, and are likely to be again."

"Amen to that," said Ashbrook.

Headley said, "Sometimes you don't get it right the first time, and it's right to try again."

"I'm for that," said Ashbrook, making Harrington laugh, and Price clap.

Martin said, "They won't be expecting it."

Chenault added, "One more swing at 'em, 'at's what General Morgan used to say."

"Gentlemen, gentlemen," said Oliphant. They were more than half-serious. Here was the reason Grant could not crack Lee at Richmond and Petersburg despite six-to-one odds, and why Sheridan had to ride again and again into the Valley, and why Sherman marched cautiously against no known opposition. If Oliphant was going to get them moving, he must speak bluntly but tactfully. He could not mention defeat this morning, because they were feeling victorious; he said, "I am asking you to board the train. If necessary, I shall order it. We have been extraordinarily lucky. The wheel of fortune turns. It is a law of nature. I am thankful for your loyalty, and shall not forget it. It was once ours to go ahead. Now it is ours to go home. Please, obey me." Oliphant paused because his voice was strained. "You have only a few minutes, and tickets to purchase. You are visitors at the Falls, now en route home. You have enjoyed yourselves. Your faces must show idle pleasure. There must be no display of camaraderie at our parting. I shall see you off from a distance. Now, please?" Oliphant began to stand.

Martin arose more quickly. "Well, boys—"

They obeyed. Oliphant paid the bill and joined Kennedy outside.

Kennedy walked silently down the hill. Canada was now visible across the canyon as a monolithic wall of gray and brown cliffsides capped by a line of naked trees and sturdy evergreens beneath a cloudy and cold blue sky. This time passing under the bridge, Oliphant thought the wind in the canyon and the gushing sound of the rapids below, a sublime accompaniment. The morning traffic at the pedestrian roadway was routinely heavy. Oliphant expected Kennedy to request his look down into the canyon, and was puzzled when Kennedy did not.

At the now crowded northbound depot building, Kennedy got on line for his ticket, and Oliphant continued on to the platform. Oliphant was tapping his cane in a too quick beat, and stopped himself. He took comfort in finding a figure at the far end of the platform whom he believed to be the first sergeant called "Papa Pinkey." The military presence had become more conspicuous, particularly so across the tracks at the southbound depot. Oliphant thought of Harrington's chicken coop analogy. General Dix did seem more concerned with maintaining the fence wire than with chasing the foxes. But how pathetic the defense—the Invalid Corps officers were shrunken inside their sky blue tunics, and the Volunteer officers in navy blue looked even worse. The United States Army might be robust in Georgia; on the frontier, it was scratch.

The train chugged up from the vanishing point, exciting the platform in the usual ways—last moment checks on baggage, grabs at vendors for food, the rush of mail carts rolled out. Martin and Headley stood off smoking; Ashbrook and Harrington were beyond them; Price and Chenault relaxed on a bench. There was nothing to say, and Oliphant backed off still farther toward the stairs to discourage any exchanges. Then the train was upon them, and the scene was imminent.

Kennedy's approach did not surprise Oliphant; nonetheless, Oliphant lowered his head. "Please, no." He wanted to turn away, to run away, but could not. "Mr. Kennedy, please—"

"Your pardon, sir, I feel I must—"

"I beg you, I have ordered you—"

"About what you said, sir, about the task you have on this side—"

"Get on the train," said Oliphant. The others were already up.

"Yes, sir—I want you to hear me out. I've been thinking—about what you said about me and Katie. You said you had a similar problem. You weren't speaking of Mrs. Oliphant, were you? It's Mrs. Winwood, isn't it? Something that happened in Washington City?"

"My sister-in-law is very, very dear to me."

"I know, sir. She is a very great lady. What I have to say is that I wouldn't want to think that you were going back alone for her. I want you to know that I'm ready to help, if I can. Those Morgan boys aren't right for such city work, but I am, and you know it."

Oliphant could not speak. He raised his cane tip toward the train.

"I'm going on without you," Kennedy bargained, "only if you promise me that you're not going back for her alone. Or at all. I don't know what it was that you had to do in Washington, but it was likely more perilous than our little show."

"I'm not going back, Mr. Kennedy. I would like to. God bless you for your concern. I pray she's in safe hands by now. I left her with two most capable men, and she is not without her own genius."

"She's a very, very great lady, sir, and great ladies are a treasure not even the Yankees can get at—or rob us of."

"Please, Mr. Kennedy, it's not that."

"Don't be cross. You aren't, that I presumed to guess your affairs?"

"Dear man, I'm not cross. Not with you. Never."

"Your hand on it?" asked Kennedy.

Oliphant took the man's strength in his grip, and weakened paradoxically; holding on, Oliphant said, "We shall meet again, Mr. Kennedy. If we don't, and chance is the arbiter always, you will seek out Narcissa, won't you? And tell her that we wanted to go back for her. That we almost did, you and I. Promise me that?"

"With all my heart, Mr. Oliphant."

Oliphant withdrew his hand, and flipped it, two fingers out, as a man might urge another to take a bow to the audience; he spoke, "Up with you now."

Kennedy performed a dazzling smile, and hopped three steps backward up onto the coach steps. He did swing on the passenger hand bar. He did tip his hat.

Oliphant was persuaded enough to return a small acknowledgment of the farewell, by smiling, but then controlled himself and gave Kennedy and the train his back. He was inside the depot when the stationmaster's whistle sounded. He was at the telegraph window when the engine brought up its steam and the wheels began to screech forward. And he was second on line before the telegraph clerk when the train cleared the platform for the switching track onto the Suspension Bridge.

The clerk was smallish, under 15, and vaguely simple; he said, "Good morning, sir, pleasure, sir?"

"I want this wire sent to two addresses, you see?"

"Yes, sir," said the clerk, taking Oliphant's sheet and reading, " 'Captain Butter, Provost-Marshall-General's Office, Department of the East, St. Nicholas Hotel, New-York, New York, and Captain Butter, Provost-Marshal-General's Office, War Department, Washington City, District of Columbia. I have surrendered here at 8 A.M. Stop. I await your attention. Stop. Jn. C. Oliphant.' "

Oliphant requested a receipt, and paid with a large bonus in order to assure immediate transmission. He took the walk around to the southbound depot. Once on the platform, he went directly toward the two officers who looked most in charge, a round, gray-bearded, bespectacled Invalid Corps captain, and a lanky, heavily wrapped up Volunteer lieutenant, and introduced himself. Oliphant carefully explained who he was and what he wanted. In the course of the exchange, the captain said his name was Leonard. Leonard watched Oliphant with the look of a very competent man whose long illness had removed him a little from the world of affairs; he then asked Oliphant several incisive questions that indicated that he was not a man who would be mocked or fooled. Captain Leonard's lieutenant, Pennypacker, was excitable, and repeated much of what both Oliphant and Leonard were saying as Pennypacker conducted his own peculiar interrogation. Finally, Leonard told Pennypacker to call over the guard.

In the slight delay—Pennypacker waving to the other two officers as well as whistling for the first sergeant—Leonard spoke evenly and sternly to Oliphant, "If you are whom you say you are, sir, and I trust this Captain Butter can confirm your story, then it is difficult for me to believe that you would give yourself up for hanging. I have a law practice in Buffalo—had one, in any event. I have met repentant law-breakers. I have never met one quite like you."

"I respectfully disagree," said Oliphant. "They are all like me."

"No, they aren't. And this will go badly for you. You know that."

"I am not suicidal, if that is why you are skeptical," replied Oliphant. "Nor am I aiming to sit quietly in a cell. I intend to defend myself. I shall speak against all the barbarities."

Leonard said, "I don't know how it has been with you." He tucked up his muffler. "But in my experience, what you want is impossible."

Oliphant said, "I am surrendering, sir. I cannot leave my country again. I will fight my battle here, and openly."

Pennypacker, the other two junior officers, and the soldiers surrounded Oliphant. Manacles were produced and slipped on him with his arms behind his back. No one was talking, but the men were noisy with apprehension. The wind made Leonard shift his stance. Pennypacker asked what should be done. Leonard said this arrest must be kept confidential. A junior officer suggested the town jail. Leonard shook this off, gripped himself with his arms, and coughed deeply, making his chest rattle and himself double forward. When he recovered, his cheeks were much paler. Leonard told the big Negro first sergeant, whom he called "Pinckney," to hold Oliphant out of sight in the company stable. Leonard told Pennypacker to accompany him to the telegraph office. He detailed the other two officers to meet the incoming trains. Leonard spoke once more to Oliphant. "This might be a necessary course for you, Mr. Oliphant, but it is the beginning of a grave time for all of us."

In increasingly heated reflection that cold Monday morning and afternoon of his imprisonment—and First Sergeant Pinckney fixed him as comfortably as possible in a hay-filled stable—Oliphant began to see that his essential miscalculation in giving himself up to the authorities was that he had assumed that America was the same country it had been before the war. He had assumed that the people wanted peace, and not more war, and that the United States' citizens would accept the surrender of a repentant rebel in a spirit of both conquest and reconciliation. He had further assumed that personal honor and decency in America still meant that one must stand responsible for one's conduct. He had sought with his surrender to atone for his crimes, and more: He wanted his day in court in order to speak out a warning for what he knew the nation—his America—was doing to itself in the rage and agony of civil war.

His surrender was not meant as martyrdom. The excesses of General Dix's General Order No. 92 would not survive the forces that Oliphant could assemble. He had wealth, learning, more than a few well-placed friends in New-York, and a story to tell that could compromise dozens of powerful Union and Confederate personages. He would need only to tell the truth of his travels for three years, and he could make them shrivel in Washington, Richmond, New-York, London, Paris, Montreal, and Toronto. He knew the dates, places, and sums of their double-dealings. He could show that none of them on either side—on all possible sides of a polygonal conflict—was without stain. After all, in just his associations of the past month, he could denounce the governor of New York, the chief of the United States Secret Service, the Republican party boss in New York, and the leading Radical Republican in the U.S. Senate—not to leave out the British Foreign Office, the provincial government in Canada, France's Second Empire, and the Confederate Cabinet.

And it would not be treachery! No, to argue that would be to continue the pernicious and duplicitous game that had brought them all to this stalemate. One cannot betray the betrayers. One can only accuse them and reveal them and confess one's complicity. Oliphant no longer felt delicate about his sense of loyalty. Friday night had fired more than a few New-York hotel rooms. He was furious for his cowardly ambivalence, and was determined to rise above it. He must!

When Oliphant searched inside himself for his motive to surrender, he did not look farther than his deepest birthright. When he asked himself what profoundly mattered to him, he discovered that America was there, the idea of America was there, the dream and hope of America was there, and if not exclusively, then certainly passionately. He must make the rending choice between his responsibilities as son and husband and lover and father and agent and citizen. Enough of the abstractions of Southern liberty and Northern Unionism and Southern republicanism and Northern tyranny. He must get above those pleading voices and choose his country, and in so doing he must commit himself to its survival!

Why now? Oliphant pressed himself in self-examination. Why had he waited so long, and what was new? He had delayed because he was weak, selfish, and afraid, and he had arrogantly thought he could walk through the war. But at last the war had touched him. America was destroying itself and was being destroyed. The crisis that shook the earth beneath him was now a final peril. He must be scrupulous and prompt. He must think of the threat not only to his own family but also to every family, alive now and to be born tomorrow. America was the world's hope, and it was slipping into a pit, from Savannah to Niagara Falls. And what proof, John Oliphant? How did he know that the last catastrophe was imminent and that anarchy loomed? The answer was simply this: That he, the most fortunate and blessed of men, could have been so personally reduced to have attempted to set fire to the city he cared for and dreamed for more than any other was a certain revelation that there was a madness upon this country like a fever, and it was as real and deadly as a fever, and it must be stopped!

It was what he wanted, to stop it. He had concluded that the way to stop it was for each person to stop himself or herself. Say, No more. Confess, repent, hope, continue. This was what he looked to say before his accusers and judges, and to the newspapers. This was why he had surrendered. It was not meant as a final act, but rather a new direction, a change in strategy.

But this was where Oliphant had miscalculated. The war had changed everything like a forge. Oliphant might have changed for the better and the future. America had changed for the worse and the past. Reason was in eclipse. A people with so much blood spilled cannot be expected to govern sanely. There were half a million dead combatants. Their kin cried, Someone must pay! Vengeance ruled, the irrational whispered, and hatred replied— in the government, the Army, the homes, churches, and graveyards. No one man's humility, or bravery, or act of confession could speak to the outcry. How could Oliphant answer the depredations of thirty million people, even with an Appalachian range of truth? Everyone was sickened by the madness of the war, was deaf and dumb to sense. Everyone had lost sight of the face of peace. All had eyes for, and were the eyes of, a murderous mob.

It was the same in Niagara Falls, as Oliphant learned throughout Monday afternoon. The word of Oliphant's capture had spread like a half-truth. Captain Leonard was visited by the town fathers from the courthouse. The town sheriff and county sheriff separately demanded custody. The telegraph wire from Buffalo was blunt and insistent. Captain Leonard and his three officers were overtaxed and besieged. Leonard was not a timid man, just a sickly one. He visited Oliphant several times to keep him informed, and perhaps also for some sympathy. At noontime, over bread, soup, meat, and tea, and at midafternoon, and again at twilight, Leonard put his position baldly:

"I've been told that I can expect no reinforcements from Buffalo. I've been told that there're detectives en route from New-York. I've been warned that your friends in Toronto aim to rescue you. I've been warned that your life should be forfeit immediately to protect the town and the county. I've been personally threatened by the mayor, the stationmaster, and the engineer of a train. I've been reprimanded by men, telegrams, generals, and adolescents."

At some point, and the afternoon's events tended to blend together for Oliphant, so that one consultation melted into another, Leonard called upon Oliphant, and slumped in exhaustion. "I'm going to hold on to you,"

Leonard declared. "I'm ordering my men to repel any attempt to take you. I would thank you if you'd extend yourself and cooperate, so I won't have to keep you chained."

Oliphant thanked him for his concern. Leonard flared, "Damn you, I'm not going to let you martyr yourself. I'll not have it!" Oliphant bent his head. Leonard was seated on a nail keg, with a horse blanket for a shawl over his greatcoat. The heat from the stable's stove was rudimentary. Leonard shivered as he added, "I know these aren't your responsibilities. I apologize. And I apologize for the accommodations. Are you well here?"

Oliphant thanked him again, and the confrontation eased. Leonard left him alone. Oliphant lit his pipe and drank his tea. First Sergeant Pinckney and his men were military as well as solicitous. They provided plenty of blankets, kept his tea hot, and served his meals generously. Pinckney compensated for his company's lack of numbers and isolation in a hostile neighborhood with innovation and savvy. The company stable, a flat-roofed one-and-a-half-story barn at the end of a muddy trail a quarter-mile from the southbound depot, was transformed into a tumbledown fort. Because it was set off in the woods, backing on a mossy stream, it enjoyed a good field of fire back toward the Centre House. Pinckney augmented his security by having the wood for three bonfires prepared in a triangular pattern out front. He visited Oliphant often, not to talk but rather to study the stable. He assigned a Sergeant Newell and others to clean out the hayloft, both for fear of fire and to construct a haystack blockhouse on the dirt road. He also had a section of the back wall of the stable broken out in order to provide a route of retreat. By nightfall, and the first of a drizzling windstorm, Pinckney endured a regular tour of duty that might have overburdened four men: a quarter of an hour at the depot and the bridge, a quarter of an hour at the shacks and tents that housed his men, and a quarter of an hour touring the stable, and then all again.

Alone, Oliphant brooded more intensely. He began to see why he had miscalculated when he had surrendered. It was because he had been viewing his life with the eyes of a free man. Now that he was not free, he saw himself and history darkly. Free, he had been concerned for intellectualisms like destiny, justice, and peace. Not free, he was concerned for food, warmth, safety, and one awesome subject—his freedom. What he had abandoned was now his most precious desire. The irony was that it was only as a prisoner that he could see how futile his plan to give himself up to repentance had been. And only as a prisoner was he able to gain a deeper, more intimate perception of America's history. Here was only a touch of what it was like to be a slave, and it was crippling! Here was why the slaves seemed childlike —because when one is deprived of freedom, one is ever tenuous, clumsy, backward-regarding, slow-witted. And here was why it was true that America could not have proceeded another moment half-slave and half-free: because the fear of an imprisoned human being is palpable and corrosive. It assaults all enlightenment as it darkens and dooms. Oliphant experienced and conveyed the fear of the unfree in everything he did—deferring to Leonard, blinking silently at Pinckney, huddling and flinching at every strange sound. The gentleman submerged as the victim emerged. How acute to him now was Kennedy's loathing for his imprisonment on Johnson's Island, and the revulsion of that ancient, Lee, at Old Capitol Prison. And Oliphant realized that his intellect suffered his imprisonment as well. He caught himself thinking of excuses for his conduct, and blaming others, and whining about his plight. He also found that he was trying to reduce his problems to stark, simplistic conditional propositions: if only this, if only that, if only so much!

The most bizarre twist was that he did slowly come to see himself as a martyr. What foolishness, and yet it was there like the stormy night. It was not just that Leonard had suggested it, or that Oliphant had considered it in order to refute it, it seemed to grow out of the events themselves, as if the war could distort anyone who resisted or who tried to stand for hope into a martyr. From Bloody Kansas to Dred Scott to John Brown to Stephen Douglas, the clash and ruthlessness of the extremists in the North and the South, the Abolitionists versus the Fire-eaters, had seemed to demand that each new event be reduced to the clichéd drama of the martyr, and then had seemed to know exactly how to feed this contrivance to the confused citizenry. Soon enough, America had become little more than the melodrama of the martyr and the mob. It was a dark discovery to Oliphant that statesmen and citizens should crave to make decisions as if part of an Elizabethan play. It was a more desperate discovery to Oliphant that he could bundle himself up in the straw and understand how the people of Niagara County, terrified by lurid newspaper accounts and wasted by battle deaths, were long prepared and educated for what they intended that night.

Lieutenant Pennypacker brought the news. It was past nine, and the drizzle had become an icy rain that sprayed between the cracks in the walls. Sergeant Newell was back on guard duty, with a Corporal Tobie and eight privates who were rotating their posts inside and out. First Sergeant Pinckney was a half-hour overdue on his rounds. Oliphant heard the door open, and Pennypacker's voice, and then a shout and many men coming in hard.

"Over there, over there, Sergeant!" cried Pennypacker. Oliphant was up from his cot. The soldiers had a boy in manacles, whom they dragged into the stall opposite Oliphant's and chained to a post. The boy was crying. Pennypacker shook out his poncho and spoke to Oliphant. "Captain Leonard's been stabbed."

Oliphant said, "How is he?"

"It was because of you!" shouted Pennypacker. "Now, we've a mess! I've a mind to give you over! Do you know who this is who stabbed him? The sheriff's nephew!"

"He looks wounded too," said Oliphant.

"That's the captain's blood, and what do you care! Damn Reb spy! You caused this!" Pennypacker kicked an oats bag and barked at Pinckney to chain Oliphant also. Pennypacker started away; he tripped and fell over a harness collar. He did not get up easily, and Oliphant could see the man's fear in his awkwardness. Pennypacker stopped at the door to order Pinckney to rouse the whole company and assemble them before the Centre House; then he left hurriedly.

After a moment instructing Corporal Tobie about the boy's condition, Pinckney conferred privately with Sergeant Newell. Newell carried the manacles to Oliphant as a man might carry a rotting animal. Oliphant put his hands out, and asked, "Did you learn more about Captain Leonard?"

"Captain ain't dead, sir," said Newell, an older, red-eyed, easy-mannered man, "but de sergeant, he's powerful fretful, sir."

"Your first sergeant is a shrewd man," said Oliphant. "I watched him face down a gang of rock throwers a month ago. Do you know about that— those prisoners of war?"

"I heard of it," said Newell. "Pinkey's like dat. Contrary."

Oliphant said, "Yes. He handled himself expertly. And there was a Captain Ferry, who might have interfered from the platform, but trusted Sergeant Pinckney. I hope this Pennypacker has as much sense."

"Captain Ferry, he died, sir," said Newell. "Dis here's rough on captains. Rough on lieutenants and sergeants too. Rough." Newell closed the stall door. "Course it could be bad here." He smiled. "Could be Petersburg."

Oliphant was pushed back down by the news of Captain Ferry's death. With the manacles, it was cumbersome cleaning, packing, and lighting his pipe, and less enjoyable. He lay down in the hay and felt himself fleeing inward. He felt the nothingness of death. It was merely the sensation of sleep without rest. The night howled over the stable, and his mind bobbed along the line between memory and make-believe. He pictured the face of Narcissa, and then of Camellia. He undressed both sisters in the heat of a Beaufort summer, and after a rainy winter ball in Charleston, and on a spring weekend visiting Savannah. He saw them as they had been that last week at China-berry, in November 1861. On Sunday, November 3, the Reverend Walker, fifty years in the pulpit of St. Helena's Episcopal Church, had looked down upon his congregation and spoken of the fact that the Union fleet was rumored to be bound for Port Royal Sound: "My children," he had said, "this threatened evil will pass away like the snow before the sun." Then on Monday, word had come that the Union fleet was near; and the defenses of Hilton Head and Phillips islands were prepared; and Talbird Royall had ridden off with General Drayton to fight the Yankees to the death. On Tuesday, the guns of the battle had shaken the windows in Beaufort and at Chinaberry, and Narcissa and Camellia had directed the family to pack the carriages. On Wednesday, November 6, 1861, the Royalls had left their home for the last time, the Union fleet victorious and the Confederate forces in panicky retreat through the marsh. In his dream, Oliphant heard Narcissa declare to Camellia, "Never! Not my home! Never! I shall burn it before they can have it!" and he heard Camellia console Narcissa, "Oh, 'Cissa, we shall be back with our boys in the springtime, and wouldn't you be the rascal then?" Oliphant heard those booming guns again and again as he and the Royalls had fled up the tabby road, away from Beaufort and toward Charles-ton in a caravan of stunned planters, furious belles, hysterical children, and disoriented servants. He heard one gun thunder and the shell fly over his head, that strange *ouiz!* as the shell sailed by and exploded. Bang! He heard more, bang! bang! bang! Then he was awake. The banging was only a loose board in the rear stable wall. It was because of the cross-draft, with the stable door open, and First Sergeant Pinckney booming, "Look alive wid'cha!"

Newell called, "What's dat, Sergeant? You hurt, or what?"

Pinckney said, "Get dat boy up!"

Oliphant lay for a moment longer than his instincts wanted him to. He closed his eyes again to see Johnny, Talbird, the twins, Harry and Phillip, and Granby Royall all alive, and to see Chinaberry dark with sleep and the light at the gazebo where he and Narcissa and Camellia sat reading to each other—*As You Like It* Camellia's favorite, and *King Lear* Narcissa's special choice, if not entirely winning her approval. Oliphant opened his eyes again. Newell and Tobie were moving around in the opposite stall. The boy was crying again. Oliphant's stall door swung open.

Pinckney said, " 'Scuse me, sir. I got word from my captain."

Oliphant got up. Pinckney stood unevenly; he had one arm tucked inside his oilskin. "Are you hurt, Sergeant?"

"Banged a might, yessir," said Pinckney. "Captain Leonard's laid up at de hotel worse. He says you should know dere's a Captain Butter comin' for you from New-York. Says too, he don't figure we can hold you much longer tonight."

"What happened? Is it Lieutenant Pennypacker?"

"He had my men use bayonets on townsfolk! Weren't no one killed. But dey're madder'n sin. Rightly. De lieutenant got a beatin' too and's bashed in. Lieutenant Severance's in command now, and he's gonna give 'em dat boy back, but it ain't gonna stop 'em."

"And Captain Leonard?"

"He's no use to us, sir."

"Any of your boys hurt?"

"A few. More'n a few. Dey won't give us a doctor neither. It ain't good, anyhow I put it, it ain't good." Pinckney walked away to tell Newell to take the boy outside, and to wait for him at the company shack. He also asked Newell for the key to Oliphant's manacles. He waited until they had closed the door behind them, and then he returned to Oliphant's stall.

Oliphant held out his hands, and Pinckney unchained him. Oliphant said, "Would you have some tea with me?"

"I ain't got—yessir, I would." Pinckney sat on the nail keg, and took off his forage cap to shake water from his head. Oliphant used a rag to reach over the stall side to pick up the hot water kettle from the stove; he poured through the strainer, not hurrying, letting the domestic ordinariness calm him. Pinckney took the teacup with a wince. "Hot, nice'n hot," he said as he sipped. He did not look up as he began. "Didn't want dem boys to hear. It's badder'n I said. Dey got Pennypacker and two of my boys, and want to trade for 'em."

"I thought as much. That is, I didn't think you would've sat with me if it weren't very difficult."

"Dey got 'em at da hotel, and I can't get to my captain. Lieutenant Severance's jes' a boy—he ain't helpin'. He's holed up at da depot house. I guess what it is, is it's down to me. To us."

"Lieutenant Severance wants to turn me over to the townspeople, is that right?"

Pinckney grunted, drank the tea, leaned back against the boards. Oliphant lit his pipe. Then he got up and pulled his clothing together. He put on his top hat, picked up his cane and lettercase, and puffed hard enough to raise a white cloud of smoke. "You know, Sergeant, I thought I might stop the violence by surrendering. Not much of it. Some. I suppose it was vain of me. I don't imagine they're thinking about making me a guest of Niagara Falls."

Pinckney studied Oliphant. "We've met before, ain't we, sir?"

"I wondered if you remembered me." Oliphant pulled out his handkerchief. It was soiled from wiping his hands. He flopped it over his sleeve. "On the platform? About a month ago. You were magnificent. You told me, 'No surrender for Pinkey this day.' "

Pinckney set down his cup, rocked forward, and stood up. "I did, yessir, I did say dat." He fitted on his cap, fluffed out his poncho, and stepped outside the stall quickly.

Oliphant said, "Are we going now?"

"No, sir, we ain't." Pinckney was walking away, one side of his torso lower than the other.

"What do you want me to do, Sergeant?"

Pinckney was at the stable door. He put his hand on the latch and made the door squeak open. The rain cascaded inside. Pinckney did not turn, but spoke out, "Dere ain't no surrender, I promise you. I ain't sure dere should be. Dere jes' ain't." First Sergeant Pinckney was gone into the storm. The door blew shut.

Oliphant was left alone with three mules and a sleeping sorrel mare covered in blankets. He flared out his capecoat and gripped his cane and lettercase. He saw the puzzle, and that it was a small one. The solution was that he had become a fugitive again, and that he did not want to die. Canada and freedom lay across the wild Niagara River.

CHAPTER 11

Amaziah Butter
at Niagara Falls, New York

TUESDAY, NOVEMBER 29, AND
WEDNESDAY, NOVEMBER 30

Butter fixed his better thigh and swung down onto the northbound
depot platform. The rain had stopped, yet the powder gray sky threatened
anything from a torrent to a blizzard, and the wind was coming in swirling
rushes that transformed the dampness into a weapon. It was after 8 A. M. The
train was more than two hours late because of flooding along the roadbed.
Still, the Invalid Corps officer had his troops assembled in proper order
between the pillars of the depot building. Butter acknowledged the lieutenant—a tiny man in a poncho that touched the ground—and then he turned
away to work on his joints. His lower back was a slip knot that he could
not solve. Gouverneur Nevers stepped down from the car and joined Butter
in sympathy, helping him by placing his palm on Butter's back above the
kidneys, hooking Butter's shoulders, and pushing hard. Butter groaned and
sighed. Wild Jack Goodenough and Joshua Rue strolled past them without
a sign, headed from the depot building and their reconnoitering assignment.

Once Butter had found his balance, he presented himself and Nevers to
the Invalid Corps officer with a salute and a frown; Butter began, "You're
Lieutenant Severance? Did you get my wire from Syracuse? I worried it

485

didn't get through because of the ice storm." Butter waited as Severance displayed a sleepless night with a dull nod. Severance had an old purple burn scar that started at his fingertips and shot up his arm to emerge again at his throat, where it had eaten away half an ear. Butter pressed him. "I didn't get your reply at Buffalo, Lieutenant, if there was one. Is Oliphant still missing?"

Severance nodded again, and spoke timidly. "Yes, sir. It's me to fault about the missing reply, sir. Lieutenant Anderson and I have had the company by ourselves, sir. We've been hard put what with the Suspension Bridge to watch, and the trains, and the trouble, sir. I should've telegraphed you, sir; I meant to."

Butter and Severance had corresponded by the telegraph wire through the previous day and night, but with difficulty from Utica onward, and not at all after the ice storm had taken down the wires in the early morning hours. About midnight, Severance had wired Butter on the train that he had taken over command at the Suspension Bridge; about 2 A.M., Severance had communicated that Oliphant had escaped. Severance's last telegram had mentioned the possibility that local vigilantes had abducted Oliphant.

Severance was now struggling to explain both himself and the mystery of Oliphant's disappearance. He started and stopped, sputtered a little, and then tried, "The truth is that I haven't got a good idea about it, sir. Mr. Oliphant ain't found nowhere, not by us or the town sheriff."

"You must know something," said Butter. "What went on here last night?"

Severance replied, "I don't know, sir. I was so busy caring for the men, and for Captain Leonard and Lieutenant Pennypacker, who are badly wounded."

"How can you not know?" said Butter. "Did the vigilantes hang Oliphant? Have they taken him? Did he get across the bridge? Have you searched the town?"

Severance was shaking. "I know he's not found, sir. The town sheriff says he don't have him. I haven't got the men to search, and the town sheriff and the county sheriff have said that they're going to form up posses. General Green at Buffalo won't be sending reinforcements till this afternoon. And we've got to worry about the Suspension Bridge, sir. The Rebs in Toronto are said to be riding down here on a raid."

Butter let up. Severance was withholding something, and he was doing it because of his fear of the consequences. Butter said, "I'm not here to find fault, Lieutenant. Oliphant himself wired me in New-York yesterday that he had surrendered here, and was waiting for me to come get him. I've come to find Oliphant. That's all I want. Oliphant. I'll need to interview everyone who had contact with him."

"Captain Leonard's been asking for you, sir. He asked me to bring you to him as soon as you got here."

"Good." Butter saw Nevers roll his head, indicating it was time to move. Butter asked Severance, "What's coming from Buffalo?"

"Another company of coloreds, sir, and a pack of hounds."

"Then you do think Oliphant's still in the neighborhood?"

"Hounds can flush a body as easy as a man on the run, sir."

Because of Butter's legs, they made their way slowly down to the underpass. Butter had quit his last cane prematurely, and was far from healed. Sixteen of the last twenty-four hours on trains or waiting for trains had not helped. The stiffness deprived Butter of any serious curiosity for the sights. The Suspension Bridge did impress him—so much iron and ingenuity without need of wood beams. He did not ask after the Falls. Severance wanted to direct a tour anyway, and quickly mentioned the rapids below in the canyon, the whirlpool downriver, and the twin cataracts upriver, which they could not see from this vantage because of the escarpment.

Butter sensed that Severance was trying to win his approval. Butter asked if Severance was kin to the Severances of Oldtown and Bangor, Maine, several of whom had served in the First Maine and First D.C. Severance could not agree to the blood relation. He did say that he had been with the Eighth New York Heavy Artillery until they had gone on picket duty at Petersburg near the First Maine's Camp. Butter replied that his three brothers were in Virginia now, one in a Maine battery.

This was a slight connection between them; however, it pleased Severance enough so that he relaxed. He spontaneously offered an apology for his inexactitude about the events of the night before. He said that he had been required to take command of the company after Captain Leonard had been stabbed by a boy of the town and after Lieutenant Pennypacker had been clubbed while facing down the town sheriff. After that, Severance explained, the town sheriff had demanded custody of both Captain Leonard's attacker and Oliphant. Severance admitted that he had agreed to comply with the sheriff's request about midnight, but had only been able to supply the boy, because Oliphant had escaped from the company stable.

Severance continued, "First Sergeant Pinckney was the last to talk to the

prisoner. He's a most able first sergeant, sir, from near Schenectady originally. He was wounded in the Wilderness and at Petersburg. His men trust
him. I couldn't have gotten through last night without him. His side's caved
in a little from the fight when they clubbed Lieutenant Pennypacker. The
townspeople went crazy a little, and I guess we all got turned around. The
first sergeant tells me he don't know what became of the prisoner, and I
believe him."

When Butter asked if Severance had interviewed any of the men who had
guarded Oliphant, Severance replied, "That's not the way you do it, sir. The
colored keep to their own. They do their duty, and keep shut."

At the square about the southbound depot, Severance pointed to the
distant wood and the stable where they had kept Oliphant. He said that the
rest of the company was camped down that same road, and he also said that
Pinckney and a half-dozen wounded men were without doctoring until an
Army surgeon arrived from Buffalo. Severance added, "It was a bad night,
sir. An ugly night. Anything could've happened. It was black out there."

The Centre House's two large front windows were broken out and
boarded up. The front doors were cracked at the base. The lone sentry stood
before a shattered porch bench. Inside, the lobby furniture was in disarray.
The adjoining dining room was crowded, and noisy with talk. Those patrons
coming and going stared overlong at Butter and Severance. The desk clerk
moaned when Severance asked for a new room key and presented it to
Butter, inquiring, "There're two in your party?" Butter said that there were
four, but that this would do. Butter told the clerk that he would need a
voucher, for which the hotel would be paid by the War Department
eventually. The clerk replied angrily that he did not want anymore trouble,
that this was a commercial establishment and not a fortress. The clerk started
to list the damage done overnight. Nevers silenced him by paying for the
room with greenbacks.

Captain Leonard's room was as bleak as a hospital—the drape drawn, the
smell of sweat and dried blood, a single gas lamp, two beds, and two
wounded men. As they entered, Captain Leonard pulled himself up in bed,
put on his spectacles, and drew his tunic over his shoulders. Lieutenant
Pennypacker was prone on the other bed, with his face heavily bandaged.

The orderly busied himself setting two chairs by the wardrobe for Butter
and Nevers, and then rushed out to fetch coffee at Severance's suggestion.
Butter turned about slowly in the middle of the room, and felt his revulsion
as he relived his two terms in rooms like this one. The memory frightened

him, but also made him feel lucky. Severance introduced everyone except
Nevers. Severance was very tender with Captain Leonard, helping to arrange
the bedcovers. Captain Leonard's color was worrisome.

"I'm most glad you're here, Captain Butter," said Leonard. "Last night
—I lost most of it. This boy—I thought he was going to kick me. It didn't
occur to me that he had a knife." Butter inquired about his wounds. Leonard
ignored the question, and continued, "I saw there was trouble coming. I live
just twenty miles from here. I know these people. They're good people, and
loyal. They've given their husbands and sons to the Union cause. But I saw
that this was just too much to ask. I appealed to General Green, and he didn't
listen. Stupidity."

Butter said, "Lieutenant Severance mentioned some sort of riot."

"They're frightened, Captain," said Leonard. "They've had threats of
invasion from Canada since last Christmas. Half their menfolk are away in
the Army, and most of the rest are beat-up veterans like us. Damn it, Captain,
Toronto's a Reb city! The Rebs taunt us about it! There're letters in the
paper about raids, and rumors about robberies. Now this attack on New-
York, and one of the saboteurs here. It was too much for them. The sheriff
lost his head. He's not a bad man, not really."

Butter nodded and asked, "Is it your opinion that Oliphant was taken by
the sheriff, or these vigilantes the Lieutenant spoke of, or do you think he's
out there?"

Leonard coughed, "I don't have an opinion," and kept coughing.

Severance gave Leonard a glass of water, and said, "I told Captain Butter
about the dogs, sir."

Leonard drank, and it seemed to help him; he asked, "Was Oliphant
important? Is he important, Captain?"

"John Oliphant is one of the most dangerous Rebel spies in America,"
replied Butter. "He directed the attack on New-York, and is involved in
some sort of conspiracy against—in Washington City. He is Jeff Davis's
golden dagger."

Leonard coughed again, and there was pain in his eyes; he spoke hesitantly,
"I—know—about knives now, Captain. And—he's well disguised."

Butter waved away the direction of the speculations; he said, "Yes, yes,
he's clever. The truth is that Oliphant is a mystery. We need to capture him
alive. He knows a great deal about the Reb Secret Service, and about all their
plots with the Copperheads. I can't guess how much he really knows. I can
tell you that I once tracked him into the East Room of the White House."

Butter saw that he had Leonard's full attention now, and he moved to the foot of the bed, and continued, "You aren't the first to lose him, Captain. I lost him too, in Washington. We've all made our mistakes, a river of 'em."

Leonard bent forward. "He was a very earnest man, Captain. I told him that he was giving himself up to the hangman, and he tossed me off. He said you could vouch for him. I don't figure it. I've seen the criminal element. I'm an attorney. I've never seen one like him. He surrendered to me. He walked up. He could just as easily have walked across the bridge. No one would have stopped him. But he surrendered, and said you were coming for him."

Butter asked, "Was he alone?" Leonard and Severance nodded. Butter tried, "He just surrendered? And said what?"

Leonard swept out his good left hand like a public speaker. "The barbarities, he told me. He said he wanted to speak to all the barbarities. He said he couldn't leave his country again. That he wanted to fight it out in open court. It was very odd, Captain, very, very odd for a spy. He's either a lunatic or—what? Religious? I know that men do give themselves up to confess their crimes."

"He telegraphed me, you know?" said Butter, patting his coat where the telegram was tucked. "He told me he had surrendered, and that he was waiting for me." Butter glanced at Nevers and shrugged. "I don't understand it either. Sometimes, I suppose, a man does give up. I wouldn't have thought that he would. But, that doesn't mean he's not still dangerous. He's very rich, and has powerful friends everywhere, including in our government and in the British and French governments. Men like him don't have just one reason for doing things. He's arrogant, brilliant, and a grand liar. He fooled me, fooled us all, and came close to burning down New-York."

Severance interrupted, "Why'd he surrender then? I mean—"

Butter looked hard at Severance, not in accusation but in frustration. Severance misunderstood, and apologized for his question. Butter said, "It's all right, I understand you're puzzled. Maybe it's as simple as this. They're beat. The Rebs are beat. And they want to quit."

Pennypacker groaned inside his bandages; it might have been a sound of derision. Severance shook his head in disbelief.

Butter spoke to the floor. "We win, you see? You surrender to the winners, don't you?"

The orderly brought in a tray of coffee and breads. Butter asked for tea and fruit, and the orderly scampered. Meanwhile, Severance was repeating to Leonard what he had told Butter of the night before. At several points, Pennypacker raised his hand and tried to involve himself in the retelling of the night's events, but it was unclear if he meant to clarify or challenge something. When Severance mentioned the part First Sergeant Pinckney had played, Pennypacker slapped the bed. Severance leaned close, and tried to understand what Pennypacker was saying, but the man's jaw had been crushed. Severance finally calmed Pennypacker down by assuring him that everyone was to be interviewed, including Pinckney and the town sheriff, and even the telegraph clerk.

At the mention of the telegraph, Captain Leonard startled, and reached for his pile of clothes. Severance helped him. What Leonard wanted was something in his greatcoat. He produced two telegrams and offered them to Butter, saying, "For you, Captain. And one for a Mr. Nevers. Is that your assistant? They came for you care of me about nine last night. I'm sorry I didn't think of them till now."

Butter handed Nevers his telegram, and opened his own while breaking a roll and putting half into his mouth. Butter chewed and read.

It was from Lafayette Baker. Butter was on notice that he had been transferred out of the provost-marshal-general's office and the Secret Service, and that he was reassigned to the First Maine Cavalry on bivouac at Hancock Station near Petersburg. It said "Immediate."

Butter had expected this for so long that he did not even grunt. It did not matter that Oliphant was now revealed as everything Butter had said he was—a master agent and saboteur. Butter had challenged Lafayette Baker's unspoken but obvious wish that Oliphant be left alone, and now Butter was going to be punished for it.

What struck Butter as especially peculiar was that it had taken John Oliphant's telegram of surrender to force Lafayette Baker's hand. Butter knew from the telegram he had received at the St. Nicholas in New-York that Oliphant had sent an identical telegram to Butter at the War Department, where Baker must have gotten ahold of it. Lafayette Baker's reaction had been swift, and yet Baker, as an expert in bureaucratic intrigue, was using a minimum of force—not a court-martial, just a transfer.

Butter realized he should feel fortunate that he was not ordered to report to Fort Lafayette. However, it was impossible to feel good about anything just now, for his wife, Desire, had been proved completely correct, like a seer. Five and a half months later, Butter was going back to the Jerusalem Turnpike.

And why? Because of John Oliphant. But why had it been wrong to chase John Oliphant? There was an answer. Butter might never know it. The chief of the United States Secret Service did not need to explain himself to anyone but Stanton, and maybe not even to him.

Butter put the other half of the roll in his mouth. The orderly came in with tea and apples. Butter took an apple, and held out the telegram to Nevers; he said, "Colonel Baker's got me. I'm ordered to report to the First Maine immediately. I'm a trooper in transit, and out of the Secret Service."

Nevers took Butter's telegram, read it, and returned it.

Butter said, "I'm out of the Secret Service, Mr. Nevers. I want to say, 'Hallelelujah,' but it doesn't come. Not with Oliphant still on the loose."

Nevers chose a very red New York apple, and bit into it hard. While chewing, he said, "My boss—one of 'em—sees this road from another tree, Cap'n. I'm empowered to deputize. General Dix wants John Oliphant dead or alive. A little dead. And General Dix says that I'm not to let the Secret Service take Oliphant away from me. I suppose he means either Secret Service. He wants him in New-York."

Butter said, "What's it all mean?"

"For start," said Nevers, "it means there are a lot of roosters in New-York and Washington that are going to peck each other to capons over this John Oliphant." Nevers swallowed his bite of the apple. "For finish, it means that you're going back into the saddle in Virginia."

Butter moved closer to Nevers. The two of them were indifferent to the fact that there were three very surprised officers eavesdropping upon them like flies on the wall.

Butter said, "And in between the start and the finish, what do we do? Do you think Oliphant is out there?"

"As of right now, you're my deputy," said Nevers, laughing. "My Deputy Bobalishunist. So I'll tell you what I think. John Oliphant is a man on the run who's out of room to run. He's city folk, and he's trapped up against a river in open country. Yes, trapped, and scared, and smart."

"Can they get him?" asked Butter. "Can we?"

"Not with dogs," replied Nevers. "Dogs! What good are they? This is a gentleman hunt. No dog is going to find a gentleman. Only gentlemen find gentlemen, and they find them at the bar, or with the ladies."

Butter said, "His ladies are in the South and in the capital."

"Then he's thinking on them, and waiting for night before he moves. These country people won't catch him. They won't even recognize him. He's a gentleman. They're looking for a devil. We want a prince or—like that Scotch fellow Macbeth."

Butter shook Nevers off, mumbling, "Macbeth was different. He was crazy at the end, and thought he couldn't be killed by a normal man."

"Oliphant sure ain't crazy," said Nevers. "And we aren't looking to kill him, Cap'n, just take him back to New-York." Nevers scoffed, "Dogs! Do they think they're hunting some slave?"

Butter teased, "A gentleman hunt."

Nevers teased, "Jeff Davis's golden dagger."

Severance opened the drape, and Butter was reminded of the others in the room. Leonard sat utterly attentive, but baffled. Pennypacker had forced himself up on one elbow to listen.

Butter waved his telegram to begin his explanation; he tried, "Gentlemen, we believe that John Oliphant is still in the neighborhood, and that he will try to escape across the border tonight. This telegram relieves me of responsibility for the search. But you shouldn't worry. Mr. Nevers is now in charge here, by order of General Dix."

Captain Leonard said, "Who?"

Butter realized his oversight, and corrected the situation. "I should have introduced you. This is Mr. Nevers, the chief detective of the Department of the East, and the commander of the Secret Service in New-York City."

Leonard said, "He is?"

Severance looked at Leonard in open amazement, and said, "I don't get it, Captain. How're they going to find John Oliphant?"

Leonard nodded, and spoke to Butter. "Captain, why aren't you in charge? Do you think the sheriff is going to cooperate with—Mr. Nevers here?"

Butter saw Nevers smile. Butter explained, "We won't be needing the sheriff's help. We will need yours. This is to be a secret operation. There's no reason to upset the local people further."

"But Captain," said Leonard, "surely you see that—"

Butter interrupted him. "The War Department's usual way of fighting this war is to camp the Army on the safe side of a river and wait for the Rebs to attack. Well, this time, the War Department's made a wise choice of commanders, and we won't be waiting on the Rebs."

"It's not that, Captain," said Leonard. "It's that he's a Negro, and this is Niagara County."

Butter continued, "This time, the authority rests with the completely informed." Leonard was coughing. Severance stared at Nevers. Butter finished his thought. "Mr. Nevers is the man who saved New-York."

Nevers and Butter worked through the rest of the day preparing their plan to capture Oliphant. Their initial move was to enlist the aid of First Sergeant Pinckney. This proved more difficult than Butter thought it would be, because Nevers and Pinckney did not like each other at first glance, and a tension remained throughout the interview—Pinckney scoffing at Nevers's clothes and manners, Nevers revealing his short temper with Pinckney's sense of race loyalty. Fortunately, Wild Jack was able to serve as the mediator, and soon the conference in the company shack was productive if not happy. Pinckney said his only concern was for the welfare of his men. Nevers offered to hire a doctor to come across from Canada to care for the wounded troops, if Pinckney would explain how Oliphant had escaped, and would then agree to lend a hand in recapturing him. Pinckney agreed.

Butter listened respectfully to Pinckney's revelation that he had allowed Oliphant to escape rather than risk further confrontation between his men and the townspeople. When Butter asked Pinckney what Oliphant's mood had been, or what Oliphant had said to him at the last, Pinckney replied, "He said he was tryin' to stop de fightin' by quittin' hisself."

"And what else?" asked Butter.

Pinckney laughed. "Dat's all. I told him dere wasn't a soul to surrender to. Dat dere's no surrenderin'. No, sir."

"He meant to surrender then?" said Butter. "This is all an accident? He still might want to surrender to us?"

Pinckney shrugged, and said, "If it's an accident, lot o' folk gettin' hurt for no cause."

Butter had one more question, and he risked annoying Pinckney and losing his support. "First Sergeant, why did you let Oliphant go if Lieutenant Severance had already decided to turn him over to the sheriff?"

Pinckney looked hard at Butter.

Butter retreated, and apologized in a roundabout way. "I suppose I would've done the same thing. I suppose I once let him go myself rather than turn him over to a hangman."

The second crucial preparation for Nevers and Butter was to study the neighborhood. This was not straightforward either. Both the town sheriff and the county sheriff were out on the roads with posses, and had let it be known that the Army was to stay out of their way or else be treated harshly. Worse, the town of Niagara Falls was hysterical with rumors of escaped Rebel saboteurs, and of Rebel guerrillas riding from Toronto, and was not welcome to Army officers or mysterious Negro detectives asking questions about strangers recently arrived. Then too, Niagara Falls's very willingness to tolerate outsiders—as tourists and guests—also worked against Nevers and Butter. It was nosiness that people did not like here, because it was not good for business.

Wild Jack and Joshua Rue had done their reconnoitering work well, however, and had located a Niagara Falls blacksmith, a free man of color named Redman Briggs, who was kin to one of Nevers's detectives in New-York. Nevers and Butter spent the afternoon at the blacksmith's shop at the end of the Whirlpool Road, near the Suspension Bridge. They questioned Redman Briggs at length about the local citizenry and the terrain.

Redman Briggs explained that a fugitive trying to hide in the area really was trapped by geography. The village of Niagara Falls, one mile south of the depots, sat upon bedrock at a sharp bend in the Niagara River. South of the village was the broadest expanse of the river, the twin channels that emerged from about Grand Island to form a mile-wide sea that narrowed again into two channels racing toward the Falls.

North of the village was the railroad and the Army. East of the village was open country and knotty forestland, all of it either under cultivation or carefully posted and watched by farmers and horsemen. And west of the village were the twin cataracts, divided by the wooded Goat Island; below the Falls was the vast Niagara Gorge.

"You've seen the gorge in the pictures," said Redman Briggs, a not uneducated man whom Butter also thought the smallest and roundest blacksmith ever, not five feet tall and almost that around the waist, "and it's the same up close, 'cept colder. In the summer, there's a steam sloop, the *Maid of the Mist,* that you can ride around the gorge on. But there's nothing down there now. Only crazy couples try to go down the stairs from the Ferry House. It's cold down there!"

Nevers pointed at the tourist map that Redman Briggs had brought out to illustrate his lecture; Nevers asked, "Then there's no way out of the village south or west? There's not a way a man could get across the river?"

"Not by hisself," said Redman Briggs. "The crossing's at the Suspension Bridge."

"How about by boat?" asked Butter. "Could he hire a boat?"

"He could," answered Redman Briggs, "but it'd be a drunken riverman who'd take a boat out at night. This is a river! It moves!"

Nevers contributed, "I'd like to get word to the rivermen, and to the hack drivers. Can we do that?"

Redman Briggs nodded. "What sort of word?"

Nevers said, "That there's somebody willing to pay for them staying home tonight."

Redman Briggs smiled, and said he had a son-in-law for a riverman who would be very happy to hear such news, and another son-in-law for a hack driver who had not earned a dollar all month and who would be equally pleased. Redman Briggs added, "The tourists stopped coming last year, y'see. Business is misery. The sort o' guests the big hotels get is some fancy couples here for hanky-panky, y'know. But they used to come here from France! Not n'more."

Nevers said, "I'm also willing to pay for the hire of three carriages, and the service of your two sons-in-law tonight, and yourself."

"Union business?" asked Redman Briggs, leaning back on the bag of grain he used as a business chair.

Nevers did not reply. Butter began an explanation. "It's very important that we keep this as quiet as possible."

Redman Briggs shook his head. "It ain't that. If it's Union business, my family volunteers."

The final preparation was cautionary. Butter asked Captain Leonard and Lieutenant Severance to try to keep the new commanding officer arrived from Buffalo, Captain Portbellow, out of the way. Nevertheless, Portbellow, a slow-witted dairy farmer, quickly established himself as an independent thinker: He fortified the Suspension Bridge with his new company; he arbitrarily pulled certain passengers off the trains and interrogated them; and he sent a patrol out with a pack of bloodhounds to search the woods about the depot. Butter's suppertime meeting with Portbellow at the Centre House was unhappy. Portbellow yelled at Butter that he was in command of this post now, and no "skulking nigger detective" was going to tell him how to do his duty. Portbellow threatened Butter that he was going to begin a house-to-house search for Oliphant in the morning, and that he would just as soon arrest detectives as spies.

Butter's only possible diplomatic reply was, "You hold the Suspension Bridge tonight, and we'll be out of this county by first light."

Portbellow winced at the inference that there might be an attempt to storm the Suspension Bridge. He knew the rumors of the Rebel guerrillas riding from Toronto. It would be far worse for him to lose the bridge than it would be to lose a fugitive. Portbellow tried to soften his position; he asked, "How do you know this fellow ain't already gone across, Captain? Or ain't dead in the woods somewhere?"

Butter stood to leave; he concluded, "I don't. But I do know that if he's on this side of the river, we'll have him tonight, if you and the sheriff stay clear."

By Tuesday nightfall, Nevers and Butter had exhausted themselves, and yet were unable to rest as they discussed the plan of attack for the night. It was a very simple plan, based upon Nevers's opinion that Oliphant had taken a room in one of the major hotels in Niagara Falls, and was planning to hire a hack after supper and then just to ride across the Suspension Bridge. This was why Nevers had paid to have all the hack drivers stay indoors. Nevers had also paid to have the rivermen stay at home because of the small chance that Oliphant would try to hire a boat.

What Nevers proposed they do was to go from hotel to hotel, presenting Wild Jack and Joshua Rue as hack drivers, and, when Oliphant announced himself in need of a driver, they would arrest him and drive him back to the depot.

Butter did not have a serious challenge to all this. It was heavily presumptive that Oliphant was the coolest spy imaginable. But it did seem in keeping with Oliphant's bold and arrogant style. After all, this was a man who had spent one Saturday afternoon with Butter denying sincerely and convincingly that he had any connection to a Rebel conspiracy, and who had spent the next Friday evening trying to burn New-York. This was also a man who very probably had just strolled onto a train to escape from a city where every policeman and detective had been on the watch for him.

Butter's worst thought about the plan was that their luck was against them. For while the weather had remained indecisive all day long, switching from rain to sleet, it was now, for the first time in a long, warmish November, beginning to snow.

Butter looked out into the snow from the door of Redman Briggs's blacksmith's shop; he observed to Nevers, "Only soldiers and thieves go out on such a night, and maybe not even thieves."

Nevers said, "He'll come out, Cap'n."

"You think perhaps he's waiting for us? You think he wants to surrender, and is just waiting for us to find him?"

"That was before. He's on the run now. Just ask yourself, what would you do?"

"Tory," said Butter. "My friend Tory Wetherbee, he used to say that to me. 'Remember, Zee,' he'd say, 'they are us, so think what you'd do with us chasing you.'"

"And what would you do, Cap'n?"

Butter said, "I'd pray a lot."

The conditions on the road slowed everyone, and it was not until after 11 P.M. that the players were assembled in the blacksmith's shop. Nevers stood by the anvil and spoke to First Sergeant Pinckney and his half-dozen troops, behind whom were Redman Briggs and his two sons-in-law; Nevers said, "You're all deputized acting-assistant-provost-marshals, by order of General Dix, but that doesn't mean we can ride into town and knock on doors. So I'm asking you to exchange your Army coats and caps for these here." Nevers waited while Redman Briggs pushed out a wheelbarrow full of civilian clothes. Nevers continued, "If we're stopped, we are a party of laborers, looking for lodging."

"I don't like dat," said Pinckney. "You didn't say about dat before. We're Army, and we stay Army."

Wild Jack tried to help. "First Sergeant, it is for our own protection. The sheriff is likely to come down on soldiers more'n he is on civilians."

Pinckney stepped back, and said firmly, "No, sir. President Lincoln's mud-crushers we be, and proud of it."

Nevers saw that he was not going to be obeyed; he continued, "This Reb spy is staying at one of the big hotels. "We're going to ride from hotel to hotel until we find him, and then we're going to arrest him."

Pinckney objected again. "How d'you know dat? And how're we going to arrest him widout bringing trouble again, like last night?"

Nevers was curt. "I know that because I know it, and there won't be trouble if you do what I say."

"I don't like it," said Pinckney. "De Army don't sneak."

Redman Briggs contributed in a soothing tone, "The Army is here to protect the good folk of this town, and I know they'll be thankful when this spy is caught. They ain't bad people here, Sergeant. They're just people like everywhere else, scared and more scared."

"All right," said Pinckney. "But at first holler, we goin' back to camp, and put more logs on de fire, and let dese good people sleep on scared."

Within a few minutes, the blacksmith shop's doors swung open, and the expedition moved out into huge snowflakes that fell from the sky like white ash. The snow was wet enough, and the ground temperature still warm enough, so that the snow instantly turned into a frigid, opaque soup that collected in the rut marks in the Whirlpool Road.

Butter rode in the second carriage with Nevers, Pinckney, Redman Briggs, and his young son-in-law, the riverman Eleazer Jordan. The third carriage was driven by Redman Briggs's other son-in-law, Otis Maple, and carried Sergeant Newell, Corporal Tobie, and four privates. The first carriage in the caravan, rocking far ahead with two mares, and marked by its two covered lanterns, contained Wild Jack and Joshua Rue.

Niagara Falls boasted five first-rate hotels, despite the fact that there were not that many good roads. After a quarter-hour drive, the caravan crossed one of the best avenues, First Street, in the direction of the wood at Prospect Point. Butter found their position on the tourist map; they were a quarter-mile east from the Ferry House and the precipice above the Niagara Gorge. Then the caravan swung south into the business district and toward their first stop, the tall, wood-built St. Lawrence Hotel. Up ahead, Wild Jack and Joshua Rue had already eased their carriage into the turnabout drive.

Butter relit his cigar as his carriage halted fifty yards from the hotel entrance. Wild Jack and Joshua Rue were down from their hack and slopping their way to the door. Their assignment was to go right to the night clerk. If the clerk answered that there was a guest calling for a hack, they were to offer their services and signal Nevers. If the clerk said there was no one asking for a hack, they were to manage a look at the registry for the name and room number of any lone gentleman arrived in the last twenty-four hours. If there was any difficulty, they were to back off and signal for Nevers.

There was no reason for conversation, so Butter and Nevers sat silently side by side, shielding their faces from the storm, as Wild Jack and Joshua Rue reappeared and took to their carriage. The St. Lawrence Hotel was crossed off the list.

The caravan was off again to the next corner, and the second of the major hotels, The Falls. It was a tall structure, the grandest looking in town, with a tower observatory that overlooked the American Falls just to the west. There was a twenty-minute wait, followed by Joshua Rue running back to fetch Nevers. Nevers asked Redman Briggs to accompany him, and they were gone for another ten minutes; when they returned, Nevers waved to Sergeant Newell's carriage behind that all was well.

Nevers reported differently to Butter, however; he climbed in, and said, "The owner's on the warpath. He figured right away who we were and what we wanted. This town's been listening at keyholes and talking freely. We best be quick about our business."

Butter said, "No sign of Oliphant though?"

Nevers replied, "There'll be the sheriff soon, sure as daylight."

First Sergeant Pinckney, in the seat behind, leaned forward and grumbled, "I don't want to tangle wid dat sheriff again. He knows me, and he ain't stoppin' at no blue coat tonight."

Butter offered, "We'll find Oliphant before the sheriff gets here. It'll take some time for them to get word to the sheriff, even if they can find him in this weather. And if we don't get Oliphant before the sheriff arrives, we'll reconsider our plan."

Pinckney pointed at Nevers. "I want dis gemmen to say dat, sir."

Nevers did not acknowledge Pinckney's concern, and gestured for Eleazer Jordan to start up. The caravan turned left, past low-built shops and large brick houses, toward the squat, dark hotel called The Churches, off an old railroad bed.

The result here was immediate. Joshua Rue waved from the door, and the second and third carriages rolled up to the awning at the entrance. Nevers told them to stay seated, asking Butter to come along. Inside, the lobby was dimly lit and partially blocked off, the grand piano and the furniture covered with drop cloths. There were signs of construction on the overhead balcony. The clerk was in his nightshirt and sat hunched over on a small bench, guarded by Joshua Rue. Nevers exchanged a few words with Wild Jack by the main desk, and then had Butter show the clerk his officer's tunic under the greatcoat.

Nevers began, "We're from General Dix, and we're here for John Oliphant, a Rebel spy escaped from Army custody."

The clerk replied, "He ain't here, I told the little nigger. All I said, he might've been here. He ain't here now. Don't make trouble, please? We're closed up, and the proprietor Mr. Grogberg's away."

Butter said, "What exactly did you see?"

The clerk looked at Joshua Rue beside him, and then glanced at Wild Jack as he was dismantling the main desk for the registry. The clerk turned to Butter, and spoke haltingly. "A gentleman came in this morning. A stranger.

I sent him away. He wanted good rooms. With a writing desk, he said, and a window facing south. We ain't got such a room. We're closed. I told him. I'm tellin' you."

Wild Jack brought over the registry. Nevers stepped away to examine it. Butter and Wild Jack joined him. It was cool enough in the lobby for Butter to see his breath.

Butter asked, "Is he lying, Mr. Nevers?"

"Not that," said Nevers. "He was paid. Oliphant paid him to keep shut."

Wild Jack explained, "He sent Oliphant off. He don't want to say, 'cause he thinks it'll go bad for him."

Butter asked, "Why did Oliphant want a writing desk and a south window?"

Nevers said, "For letters and whatnot. He's thinking on the ladies and his kin. The window? Anybody's guess."

Butter said, "Do we search the place?"

Nevers reached for his billfold. "No, Cap'n, we buy the bought. This boy sent Oliphant somewhere."

The clerk named the Eagle Hotel, at river's edge. The Eagle Hotel faced south onto the International Hotel, the two of them situated like clapboard temples overlooking the bend in the Niagara River as it fell toward the Falls. They also fitted together symmetrically on opposite sides of the carriageway that ran down to the riverside and then up onto the small suspension bridge out to Goat Island. The difference between the two hotels was that the International was new-built, with several wings off the main manse, while the Eagle Hotel was older and more elegant, a single rectangular structure with many gables opening to the river view.

Nevers deployed Sergeant Newell, Corporal Tobie, and the four privates at the kitchen exit of the Eagle Hotel. Pinckney elected to remain in the carriage with Redman Briggs and Eleazer Jordan. Nevers and Butter followed Wild Jack and Joshua Rue. The front door was locked, so Joshua Rue pounded while Wild Jack, Nevers, and Butter checked their revolvers.

The clerk was huffy for being awakened. When he saw three Negroes and a soldier, he immediately threatened to call the sheriff. But he had to open the door past the chain latch to shout. Joshua Rue simply tore the door open. Nevers ignored the man's upset, and explained their intention. The clerk was dumb. Wild Jack raced inside, and had the registry on display when they reached the main desk.

There was a Mr. J. Johns of New-York registered in Room No. 12. The clerk responded that this meant the southeastern corner of the second floor. Nevers told the clerk to fetch the master key, and when the man showed no willingness to oblige, Joshua Rue persuaded him.

The hotel was empty of human sounds at this hour, but the wind outside made the windows rattle, and their footsteps on the main stairs sounded to Butter like cavalry over a pontoon bridge. Wild Jack led the way with an oil lamp. Joshua Rue took a mail sack out of the folds of his overcoat. The clerk was sluggish in his fright; he kept glancing back at Butter for help. Butter was stern-faced. And then, just as they turned the hall into the shadows made by the overhead gaslight, there was a pounding from behind them. Nevers waved them to a halt, and he and Butter took the clerk back to the head of the stairs.

It was Eleazer Jordan. "Papa Briggs sent me, mistah. We jes' seen men on horseback, on First Street, headin' dis way. Sheriff likely, sure."

The clerk mumbled, "Thank God."

Butter said, "They don't know we're here."

Nevers said, "They do if they went to The Churches."

"How many?" asked Butter.

"Can't see for countin' 'em, mistah."

The clerk exclaimed, "You're hangin' now!"

Butter said, "We can bluff it, Mr. Nevers."

Nevers snorted, and stopped the clerk's whining with a jab at his middle. Nevers told Eleazer Jordan to get back outside and around to warn Sergeant Newell that he would be bringing Oliphant out through the kitchen exit.

Eleazer Jordan said, "Dat Sergeant Pinckney, he's cursin' you bad, mistah," and then he hurried away.

They reached Room No. 12 in a single rush. The clerk fumbled the master key to the floor, and it was lost in the darkness.

Nevers showed his apprehension, shouting, "Mr. Rue!"

Joshua Rue took down the door as if it were a lace curtain. They dove into the room. A woman screamed. Wild Jack yanked at the bedcovers. The woman howled with terror, and a man screamed, "Help!" The clerk escaped Joshua Rue's grasp and fled. Nevers turned up the gas lamp. Joshua Rue jammed the mail sack over the man's head. Butter saw an open clothes trunk. The woman was young, naked, and hysterical; she grabbed at the bedcovers as she tumbled to the floor. Wild Jack emptied the water pitcher on her. She gagged and gasped, but was silent. Joshua Rue had the man on the floor. The man was working his naked white legs like scissors, and he was trying to cover his testicles with his hands. Butter could see that the legs were wrong, the scene was wrong, the woman was ludicrous. Butter kicked the clothes trunk, shouting, "No! Damn! No!"

Nevers had Joshua Rue uncover the man's head. Here was the middle-aged Mr. J. Johns of New-York captured with his lover. Wild Jack pulled the woman up and shoved her backward into the wardrobe. Joshua Rue added Mr. J. Johns soon enough, and sealed their cries with his bulk against the wardrobe door. Butter and Nevers went to the corner window to look down on the hotel's entrance. They could see many figures on horseback, carrying lanterns and covered torches on pikes.

Butter said, "The sheriff's found us! And there's the clerk! He's telling him where we are!"

Nevers said, "I count fourteen men."

Butter said, "What are you thinking? We can't fight them! And we don't have Oliphant, and don't even know where—" Butter broke off, unlocked the nightlatch, and threw open the window. The snow poured inside. He poked his head out the window into the wind. He cried, "Damn! Mr. Nevers! What direction is that?"

Nevers asked, "Why?"

"South!" said Butter. "That there is south! There aren't any south windows in this hotel that don't look on that big hotel over there! You can't see anything from here but another hotel! You can't see south from here!"

Wild Jack said, "That clerk lied to us! Mr. Rue, he lied! He didn't send Oliphant here!"

Butter turned back to Wild Jack. "He did send him here! But Oliphant wanted southern windows! He wanted to look south! He's writing his kin and looking south! He chose the International Hotel!"

"Yes, Cap'n, yes, you're right," said Nevers. Nevers decided quickly, telling Joshua Rue to put the man J. Johns back into the mail sack. They left the woman in the wardrobe and raced back downstairs to the hotel entrance with their load.

Outside, at the awning, the sheriff was waiting with men on and off horseback. Redman Briggs and Eleazer Jordan were appealing to the sheriff. First Sergeant Pickney sat in the carriage with his arms crossed. A member of the posse leveled a rifle at Butter.

The sheriff demanded custody of the Rebel spy. Butter looked back at Joshua Rue with the sack on his back and motioned for him to come forward. Butter also watched Nevers peel off from the awning and swing out into the darkness in the direction of the International Hotel.

Pinckney climbed down from the carriage and charged at Butter; he was clearly peeved, and told Butter, "Give dat man what he wants, sir."

The villager with the rifle directed at Butter shouted, "Now! Now!"

Butter ignored the posse and spoke to Pinckney. "I aim to, First Sergeant. What I'd like you to do is to go around to Sergeant Newell and assemble your men"—Butter pointed into the snowfall, in the direction of the river —"out there. For an orderly retirement." Pinckney grunted. Butter continued, "One more thing. Would you send Corporal Tobie running for Lieutenant Severance and reinforcements, and have him take the driver Otis Maple as his guide."

Pinckney frowned in suspicion. "Sir?"

"I believe you told Mr. Oliphant you don't like surrendering?" Butter looked up at the posse, and added, "I don't like it either."

Pinckney marched off. Butter turned to the sheriff. There followed a predictable exchange. Nevers's ruse worked to a degree. The sheriff was an inarticulate, grizzly man named Faulkner, who was actually the deputy sheriff of Niagara County. Faulkner bellowed to establish his authority. He ordered the sack emptied, and soon was in custody of a naked and grievously frightened J. Johns, who, once he was wrapped in a blanket, manacled by the hands, and slammed down into the slush by the carriage, protested his innocence meekly. He wept and pleaded. The Eagle Hotel's clerk tried to tell Faulkner everything that had happened in his hotel, including the inconsequential, with much shouting of "Nigger thieves!" and "Nigger abductors!"

The snow was heavier now, beginning to coat the ground, so the conditions were impractical for an open-air debate. Lights had come on in both the Eagle and International hotels. Men with overcoats atop their nightclothes were drifting out to congregate at the facing hotel entrances. It was well past 1 A.M., and the rest of the posse dismounted to mill around like the exhausted shopkeepers and adolescents they were.

Butter refused to answer all questions put to him. Faulkner appealed to Butter. "You can't have nigra boys breakin' doors, Captain, and expect cool heads." The Eagle Hotel clerk wanted everyone arrested. A rider suggested they should send for the town sheriff. Faulkner lost control as other voices made weary suggestions. The wind was bringing stinging flakes from all directions when Faulkner finally acceded to the clerk's demand that they continue the investigation in the Eagle Hotel.

The sudden shouting from the International Hotel overruled them all. "Murder! Murder!"

Butter, Wild Jack, and Joshua Rue launched themselves across the carriageway and the thirty yards to the International Hotel. The several onlookers at the door cowered out of Butter's stumbling path. Butter lurched into the lobby with his Army Colt drawn, scattering the gathered patrons. The hysteria had originated with a single half-clothed man who responded to Butter's uniform by falling to his knees and crying, "Save us! Murder! Up there!"

Butter spun around, and the patrons fell away. Butter was amazed at the number of women in the crowd. Niagara Falls truly was a convenient boudoir. Yet Butter was more persuaded by the sight of Deputy Sheriff Faulkner in close pursuit.

Wild Jack acted fast; he and Joshua Rue threw two men out the double doors and slammed them shut. Wild Jack drew his revolver on the hotel patrons, and cried to Butter, "Go! We'll hold! Go!"

Butter waded through the screaming crowd and pulled himself up the main stairway to the first landing, calling, "Mr. Nevers! Answer me! Mr. Nevers! Where are you?"

Doors slammed shut left and right along the hall. Butter moved by instinct toward the right rear of the hotel, where the southernmost windows must be. At the turn that bridged the main manse to the southwest wing, Butter confronted a knot of men and women holding each other out of fear. Two young women pointed Butter toward the far right. Butter kept on into the shadows, shouting Nevers's name and cursing. He found a stream of guests in an exodus down from the next floor, and followed an opposite course. At the top of the landing, there was a wide-open door, and bright lights. Inside the room, Gouverneur Nevers sat heavily in a chair, his head hanging between his knees.

Butter saw the revolver in Nevers's hand, and asked, "Are you shot?"

Nevers snorted. Butter kicked the door shut behind him, but it bounced back open. The double doors onto the balcony were open, and snow was blowing in. There were sheets of paper scattered at the desk. There was a pipe propped in the pewter ashtray on the desk. Butter said, "Answer me! Are you hurt? Did Oliphant do it?"

"I ain't shot," said Nevers, "and it wasn't Oliphant. Some good citizen hit me from the back."

It was a modest-sized room. The bed was untouched. There were a top hat, a capecoat, and a walking cane on the bench at the foot of the bed. Butter asked, "Where is he?"

Nevers twisted his neck and shook his head; he was gruff. "He ain't here. He was gone when I got here. I was just looking in when a mountain fell on me."

Butter walked to the desk. It had been shoved askew so that one could sit at the chair and write while looking out into the night. The cross-draft then swept up the sheets of paper and scattered them to the floor. Butter noticed a large gray envelope on the desk's leaf, weighted down with a letter opener.

He picked it up. It was addressed in sizable block letters, "Captain Butter/Provost-Marshal-General's Office/War Department."

Another gust of wind tipped the pipe. It smoked a little, and Butter felt the ashes. They were still warm. Butter spoke to Nevers. "He couldn't have been gone more than a few minutes. This pipe— And he left his coat and hat."

Nevers worked his shoulders, and nodded. "What's that you've got?"

Butter said, "He's left me a packet," and then he turned the gray envelope over. There was a terse message, which Butter read aloud. "Please post these letters in the event of my death, or if you do not hear from me within one month of the end of the war. Thank you. We shall meet again. My apologies for all of it, and for not telling you the truth. Jn. C. Oliphant."

Butter opened the envelope. Inside were two letters, one addressed to Mrs. Camellia Royall Oliphant, one addressed to Mrs. Narcissa Royall Winwood, both care of Mrs. Pamela Tempest Royall, St. John's Wood, London. Butter read the note on the back again, and looked out into the night as it spit snow at him. Butter said, "He's made me his postman. To his wife and to his sister-in-law. That Mrs. Winwood."

Nevers stood up, and asked, "Is his lettercase there?"

Butter looked around. "No, it's gone. Why?"

Nevers said, "Just asking."

"Why'd he run, Mr. Nevers?" asked Butter. "I really thought he wanted us to find him. So why'd he run?"

Nevers said, "We're death to him, Cap'n."

Butter went over to the bed. He picked up the walking cane, and felt its balance. It had a gold head, and was too short for Butter. Butter said, "He did send for us, Mr. Nevers. He did wire me to come get him. It must have meant something."

Nevers was inspecting the room slowly, still stretching his neck; he said, "It meant that he wanted to give up, and then he changed his mind. We are death, Cap'n. You can get tired enough to send for death, and then you can get untired, and run."

Wild Jack appeared at the doorway, and said, "They're all comin' lickety-split now. Are you gentlemen ready to go?"

Butter explained, "Oliphant slipped us. He must've heard the commotion downstairs and hid somewhere in the house."

"Maybe," said Nevers.

Joshua Rue then appeared behind Wild Jack; he was holding a dazed, bald-headed fat man.

Wild Jack explained, "This is Mr. McDowell, the hotelkeeper. We've drafted him to show us the way out, and I suggest a back way out, for that sheriff's got mean on his mouth. I said, we're runnin', Mr. Rue!"

"Not yet, Mr. Goodenough," said Nevers.

Butter threw the cane on the bed, and started toward the door. "We have to break off, Mr. Nevers."

Nevers fixed his top hat on his head, and protested, "Not yet, Cap'n. Oliphant's here, he's here! If we can just figure what—"

Butter said, "U. S. Grant himself doesn't win a battle on the first or second or third try. We're quit for now. We have it three-quarters done. We found him. He can't get away. The sheriff will hold everybody. What good are we in jail? We'll get back to the depot, and come back with the company. That Captain Portbellow will do what we tell him. It's time to go. We must contain—containment, remember?"

Nevers wandered to the writing desk; he looked out into the storm. When he turned back to Butter, his face was unreadable, but he was no longer protesting.

Butter asked the tremulous Mr. McDowell for a rear exit. McDowell pointed, and said there was a door to the gardens down that way. Joshua Rue pushed, and McDowell led the way. They descended from the racket of the sheriff's pursuit as fast as their various disabilities permitted.

At the bottom of the staircase, McDowell led a trail through stacks of lawn furniture, and he turned up the gaslamp at the door. McDowell then grinned mischievously, saying that he did not have a key and that the door was locked. Butter jerked McDowell aside and yelled at him. But then Wild Jack reached up to pop the door open easily.

Butter shoved McDowell away, saying, "Well, here's good luck for once!" Butter eased through the door into the storm, only to confront a peculiar version of his fortunes.

There was a stone-built landing and four stairs down to the pathway. Five more minutes—sixty more seconds!—and the wind would have drifted the snow up onto the stairway to make it as smooth as McDowell's head. But for now, there were tracks in the snow, those of a single human being. The tracks lead out into the storm.

Nevers saw the footprints and grabbed McDowell, dragging him out the door and shouting, "What's out there?"

McDowell replied, "The garden! The river! Please, don't hurt me!"

Nevers threw McDowell back and waved into the dark. "What else? Tell me!"

McDowell covered his head and balled himself up against Butter; he whimpered to Butter, "God help me, the river, that's all, the river and the bridge. The bridge to Goat Island."

Nevers growled and cursed. "Damn, Cap'n, damn!"

Butter wanted to advise or give comfort to Nevers, but what could he say? Oliphant had escaped them again, and Butter had told Nevers to quit too soon.

In frustration, Butter could only contribute that Pinckney and his men should be assembled by now up the way, and that Lieutenant Severance had been sent for, and that if they could reach Pinckney, they could escape the sheriff.

Butter added, "He can't get far, Mr. Nevers, not in this storm, without his coat. We'll get him in the morning."

Nevers grinned at Butter, but it was not a look of agreement. Nevers told Wild Jack, "You and Mr. Rue fetch the blacksmith and the soldiers to this bridge to Goat Island, and quickly!"

With that, Nevers pulled down his top hat, wrapped his scarf twice around his neck, tugged his scarlet gloves securely, and threw himself into the chase.

Butter did not hesitate; he abandoned McDowell and plunged after Nevers.

The two hotels were now lit up like birthday cakes. Their lights cast Nevers's and Butter's shadows over the garden path that led from the International Hotel to wind around a belvedere. Nevers and Butter found their way out of the garden and past a small bathhouse. The tracks vanished hereabout with the last of the good light. Nevers and Butter continued only to emerge suddenly in the sandbars that covered the shore like soggy sponges. It was too dark to see the river, but they could sense its closeness for the chorus of the current. They splashed through the marshy grass and were then up onto the carriageway. A few more steps, and they were at the foot of the small suspension bridge to Goat Island.

There was a gale off the river. They bent down to search for tracks on the carriageway, but in the wind, there was nothing. The night was a black snowing cavern except back the seventy-five yards to the hotels. Butter was gasping; he asked, "Where could he go? Do you think he's gone out there?"

Nevers did not have an opportunity to answer, for coming directly at them was a carriage bearing Wild Jack, Joshua Rue, Redman Briggs, Eleazer Jordan, and the soldiers.

Pinckney leaped down. He was furious, and screamed at Nevers. "Yer gonna get my men shot!"

Nevers pointed at the horsemen visible in silhouette between the hotels. Nevers ordered Pinckney, "Deploy your men, and hold this bridge!"

Pinckney boomed, "Da devil you say!"

Butter was still heaving; he started, "First—Sergeant! You know the company's comin'! Set—your defense!"

Pinckney turned to Butter. "I ain't gonna have my boys shot for no spat! No, sir! You tol' me we'd go if de sheriff came!"

Butter used the fingertips of his gloves to wipe his spectacles of sweat. He turned slightly to let the wind clear the moisture from his lenses. He spoke again when he thought he was in control of his temper. "We are the United States Army, and the sheriff and his men are brigands!" Butter realized he was not in control, but he continued, pointing at the hotels, "Ready to repel horsemen, First Sergeant!"

Pinckney uttered one gargantuan growl and then did his duty. He ordered Sergeant Newell and the troops down. They released the horses and rolled the carriage over on its side. It was a Barnum's show more than a defensive perimeter, with their backs up against the edge of America. Still, Faulkner and his men did not show an urgency to advance. They had gathered again between the Eagle and International. The lights started to go out as the posse must have slowly come to the awareness that they were easy targets for marksmen.

Butter moved from man to man in the line. Pinckney grabbed Butter's sleeve as they instinctively crouched together at the spokes of a wheel. Pinckney said, "Y'know what dat lawman called you, Cap'n?"

Butter looked toward the hotels. "They ain't coming at us—they're just talk."

Pinckney continued, "He said you a nigger-lovin' Black Republican son of a bitch."

Butter squinted. Pinckney was not smiling. Butter nodded, got back to the foot of the bridge, and found Nevers. Butter said, "It'll be about another quarter-hour at most, and then Severance should be here with reinforcements. We'll hear the drumbeat."

Nevers ignored Butter; he was questioning Redman Briggs and Eleazer Jordan about Goat Island. They said it was about seventy acres large in the shape of a peanut. The channel of the river on the far side of the island, rushing to the Horseshoe Falls, was about three times as wide as this near channel to the American Falls. The island was cut by pedestrian paths and by one serpentine carriageway. There were no settlements or living quarters.

Nevers asked, "Is there a way off the island?"

Eleazer Jordan replied, "No way offa dat island, no, sir, 'ceptin' to fly!"

Redman Briggs added, "Out there tonight, a man that lays down is going to die. We won't find him till spring!"

Butter interjected, "We don't know he's out there, Mr. Nevers. He could be hiding somewhere on the hotel grounds, or he could've headed back into the town."

Nevers was firm. "No! A man like Oliphant doesn't go into a storm unless he has a destination! That door was unlocked! There were tracks down this way! And before, when I got to his room, he was gone! Like he knew you were coming! Like he expected you!"

Butter thought Nevers was possessed—all he cared about was Oliphant, and not a bit for these men. Butter argued, "He ran, I agree. But he's scared. He left his coat and cane, and his pipe! You surprised him!"

Nevers snapped, "You're soldiering and not thinking!"

Butter hesitated. Nevers was more stubborn than he was. Butter tried, "Suppose I grant he's out there. On the island. Without his coat. We'll dig him out in daylight with reinforcements."

Nevers said, "You figured it—if he wanted you to find him, he would've stayed in his room! That's not a man who breaks and runs. He planned this somehow. He's smart! He knew you were coming. Smart men don't go into holes 'less they know that there's a way out! I know! I've been in holes! Help me, don't fight me. Think!"

Butter shook his head, and glanced back at the Eagle Hotel. "All right, the room was empty. The pipe was still hot. The letters were for me. He left his cane, coat, and hat on the bench. The garden door was unlocked. There were tracks. He was maybe five minutes ahead of us." Butter rubbed his gloved hands together for warmth, and added, "But you think he was waiting for me, that he knew I was coming. That means, he must have waited until he knew we were in the house, or at least until he heard the noise from the sheriff and all. He waited until we were almost on top of him. Then— what else is there?"

Nevers said, "Two things! Us being chased by the sheriff. And the snowstorm. He didn't figure that we'd be forced to run out the back way like he did. And he didn't figure that there'd be this snow to leave tracks. Without both of those things, us going out the garden door, and us finding the tracks, he's gone. We were supposed to think that he's still hiding in the house, because he left his coat. But he's gone!"

Butter said, "But gone where? Out onto an island in a river? Why?"

Nevers turned to Eleazer Jordan. "Say you were out there. How would you get off?"

Eleazer Jordan said, "Fly, I said, fly, mistah! Ain't no boat can ride dat current. De Falls're jes' dere!"

Nevers said, "Can you get below the Falls? Is there a way down?"

Eleazer Jordan asked, "Into de gorge?

"Goat Island ends at a cliff," said Redman Briggs. "At the edge, there's nothin' but the Falls and the cliff and the gorge."

Nevers asked, "Can you get down the cliff? Is there a way down to the gorge?"

Eleazer Jordan replied, "Mistah, dere's Biddle's Staircase."

Nevers asked, "With a boat, how far is it from the bottom of the cliffs to Canada?"

"Dere's de gorge, mistah!" shouted Eleazer Jordan. "No man can row de gorge in dis storm! No crazy man'd try!"

"Forget the storm!" yelled Nevers. "How far across?"

Eleazer Jordan jumped about. "Crazy! A boat from Canada tonight! Crazy!"

Redman Briggs touched his son-in-law to calm him, and replied, "It's a quarter-mile across the gorge, less."

"That's it! That's it, Cap'n!" cried Nevers. "He's hired a boat! They're coming from Canada to get him!"

Nevers grabbed Eleazer Jordan and screamed orders to Wild Jack and

Joshua Rue. Then Nevers and the others were gone onto the suspension bridge to Goat Island.

Butter took Redman Briggs over to Pinckney and Newell, and explained the situation. "We think Oliphant's trying to get across to Canada from that island, and we have to go get him." Butter looked once more at the field of fire, and the now darkened village of Niagara Falls. He did not want to leave these men until he heard those drumbeats.

Pinckney must have understood this, because he made it possible for Butter to go when he said, "It's de battle of Niagara Falls, Cap'n. We're due a citation on our regimental colors."

Butter said, "Yes, you are, First Sergeant." Then Butter was away, up onto the suspension bridge. He was following the two lanterns held by Joshua Rue and Eleazer Jordan some forty yards ahead. The bridge was iron-built, more than a hundred yards foot to foot, divided into four spans, with a double-track carriageway and a five-foot-wide pedestrian walkway on either side. Butter dragged along using the railing as a guideline and helpmate. The river showed itself where the lantern light reflected off of the white water. The sensation was that of walking over something impossibly swift and terrifying, like a stampede of express locomotives. The rush of the current was also intimidating, like spirits in a rage. Worse, Butter could not tell if it was the bridge that was swaying with the river and the wind or if that shuddering was because of his shaky legs.

Fear drove Butter forward in graceless leaps. He caught up to Nevers and the others as they gained the dip of the bridge at Bath Island, a rocky and woody islet at mid-channel that contained the remnant of a paper mill and the closed-up works of bathhouses. They pushed through the toll gate and mounted the last span that lifted them over a surging subchannel and put them onto Goat Island.

Eleazer Jordan explained that it was just a quarter-mile to Biddle's Staircase at the midpoint of the cliffs. It was not to be a quick journey, however, as they had to walk bent over to locate the path in the drifting snow. Once they were inside the groves of evergreens, the wind decreased. They crunched along in a freshly white world of snapping branches and the sweet, rank smell of persimmon fruit crushed beneath their boots. The terrain rolled up to the left and then down to the right into the bushes. Whenever the footpath disappeared, Eleazer Jordan halted them to listen for the river to make sure they were moving with the current. The American Falls soon served as their mark, for there was truly an incomparable roar from up ahead like a monster that beckoned even as it warned away.

Eleazer Jordan was guiding them by instinct now. He would turn from a bush, or tree trunk, to locate the path again simply by finding where there was no obstacle. The path took them along a landslide, and Butter could sense that there was nothing but a drop and then white water over rocks. Wild Jack toppled over an exposed root system on a hillock. Butter slipped repeatedly on the slick ground. Even Joshua Rue was troubled, for as he fanned the lantern back and forth to provide Eleazer Jordan as wide an arc of light as possible, he walked straight into a dead tree and went down.

While they struggled, Nevers and Butter called back and forth to each other, reviewing the events of the day in order to reinforce their intuition that this chase was not futile.

"He fooled us!" shouted Butter.

"You were the only one he was worried about, Cap'n," called Nevers, "and he figured you'd come for him after midnight—Secret Service style!"

"But why did he wait?" called Butter. "Why?"

"That way he knew that he'd be moving away from you, and not into you!" shouted Nevers, who then went down hard in the snow, and cursed. He arighted himself slowly, and added, "The pipe and coat and cane. They were props! He knew you'd relax at the letters too!"

"He must've wired across to Canada for a boat!" cried Butter.

"Or sent a runner! Half a treasure on deposit, half a treasure on delivery! A quick row across the gorge!" Nevers stopped, and said, "And then the storm."

"It was perfect until the storm!" returned Butter. "He must've known the longer he waited, the worse it would be! But he waited! Writing and listening and planning!"

"Smart, very smart!" called Nevers. "But not foolproof! There will have to be a signal! He'll have to show himself to signal!"

Butter said, "What! What kind of—signal?" And then he went down into a hole, howling when he hit on his knees.

"For the boatmen!" shouted Nevers; he jumped over to help Butter out of the hole. "Okay? Here we go. Listen now, there'll have to be a light. He'll have to show a light for the boatmen to row to, across the gorge."

"Lordie, Mr. Nevers, are we right?"

"We're right," said Nevers. "There's one problem, though."

Butter could hear the American Falls below them to the right, out over the blackness of the slope, and he recoiled; he shouted at Nevers, "What, what problem?"

"Tom Hines, that Reb dodger Tom Hines you told me about. If Tom Hines is comin' for Oliphant, then we're beat." Nevers laughed. "We'll never catch a dodger tonight. Only a gentleman."

Butter knew that it took them too long to reach the cliffs. And he knew that it took them much too long to work along the precipice to find Biddle's Staircase, located at a clearing midway between the American Falls and the Horseshoe Falls. Butter announced a rest break by tumbling to his knees and begging for mercy. Nevers clapped his hands to give encouragement, and danced across the clearing to a keeper's hut that served as the entrance to the staircase. Butter heaved for his breath, pulled himself up on Joshua Rue's arm, and stumbled forward.

Out over the cliff, there were varying tones of darkness. Canada to the northwest was invisible but for the lights on the far hillside that might have been the elegant Clifton House. America to the northeast was invisible but for the lights on the far hillside that might have been the Ferry House. The gorge was distinctive for being blacker than everything else around it. The storm flew at Butter's face, icy snowflakes like Maine ocean spray, and a tremendous wind that made him hold tight to his hat as he stepped forward cautiously to Nevers.

Butter started, "We're too late. He's gone."

Nevers was immediately wild. "No! He had minutes on us! We made it up! We caught up! He's here! We're on top of him!"

Butter said, "Be reasonable. He's won. We're finished. I am!"

Nevers grabbed the lantern from Joshua Rue and mounted the wooden platform that began the staircase. Nevers swung the lantern right to left, left to right, and again. He was signaling someone, and he was screaming, "Be there! Come on! Be there! I know you're there! Look at here! Be there!"

Butter peered over the edge of the staircase. He did not want to make that descent, not only because of his exhaustion, but also because of his natural fear of heights. Nevers kept waving the lantern. Butter appealed, "Mr. Nevers, let it go! We don't know he's down there! He could be behind us! Mr. Nevers?"

And then, as if in response to Nevers's obsessed certainty, and Butter's well-founded doubts, they were startled by the appearance of a light out in the gorge, toward Canada. The light flashed three times. Nevers switched the lantern in his hands and continued to signal. The light in the gorge flashed three more times.

Nevers gave the lantern back to Joshua Rue and jumped to the railing. He teetered over the edge, and cried, "Yes! Yes!"

The light in the gorge was definitely moving now, and it flashed three more times. The light was coming from Canada, and toward Goat Island.

Nevers called, "There! Down there!" He was not pointing to the gorge, but rather below at the cliffside. Nevers shouted back to Butter, "Oliphant's down there! I can see his light! He's signaling, below! Mr. Goodenough, follow me!"

Wild Jack replied, "Yes, Mr. Nevers! Wait on me, Mr. Rue!"

Butter was shoved back as Wild Jack fought past him to follow Nevers and Joshua Rue down the stairs. By the time Butter had recovered, they were well below him. Butter went to the railing where Nevers had stood. He looked at the moving light in the gorge, and followed a line of sight back down to his right. He cleared his lenses, stared and squinted, and then—dim flashes. There was a very faint signal light on the shore below, toward the American Falls.

Butter groaned, asking Eleazer Jordan, "How far down is it?"

Eleazer Jordan came up with the lantern. " 'Bout eighty feet straight down, mistah."

Butter groaned again. This was his fight too. He had to be there at the finish. Most reluctantly, he began the descent of Biddle's Staircase. He held the railing with one hand and Eleazer Jordan with the other. They rocked and slid on the slush. Butter's fear made it a struggle to breathe, and his genitals felt as if they had contracted back inside him. Butter gripped the railing so tightly that he picked up splinters through his gloves. He had to halt repeatedly to let the nausea pass. While he rested, he could watch the action below. He could see Joshua Rue's lantern. Along farther, he could see what must be Oliphant's light, and it was flashing continuously now. Was he hurt? Did he know he was being chased? Butter could also see that the moving light in the gorge was closing on Oliphant's position. Butter gave himself up to the race. He bounced down the steps. He did not realize he had reached the bottom until he stepped again and fell on the ice.

There was a steep beach of rocks and gravel here that fitted against the juggernaut of Goat Island like a flared skirt. There was also a boardwalk that shot out over the rocks to the right. But there was no handrail, and the footing was very poor. Butter got up with the help of Eleazer Jordan. They staggered forward together.

The roar from the American Falls, less than sixty yards ahead, crushed every other sound. Butter thought he could hear a man crying out. Was it Nevers, saying, "Oliphant! Oliphant!"? Or was it Oliphant calling, "Hurry! Hurry!"?

The boardwalk ended at a pathway built with slabs of rock. It was too slick for Butter, and he had to go down on his hands and knees for part of the way. He slipped once more to the gravel below. He stood in the loose rocks. The water was right there, splashing on his boots as the wind drove genuine breakers against the shore.

Butter cried, "Mr. Nevers, where are you?"

There was an answer, "Here, Cap'n!"

Butter leaped over a finger of water, and was suddenly atop Joshua Rue and Nevers. Butter asked, "Where is he?"

Nevers did not turn; he said, "Gone!"

Butter said, "Where?" The spray from the American Falls washed over them. Butter wiped his spectacles and turned completely around to get his bearings.

Nevers told Joshua Rue to hold the lantern high and wave it. The cliff was a sheer black wall. The American Falls was a crashing white wall just ahead—first the narrow sheet of water that was called the Bridal Veil, and then the vast rush of the American Falls proper, an immense presence that loomed in the darkness like a side of the parted waters of the Red Sea.

Wild Jack was at Butter's feet, searching along the shoreline. Nevers told them to spread out from Joshua Rue's light. Butter fell once more trying to inspect a crevice. Eleazer Jordan pulled him out of the snow.

Nevers cried, "Gone! He was here! Gone!"

Wild Jack lifted an object toward them. "Here's a lantern! Here's the lantern he used!"

Butter turned to Eleazer Jordan. "Where could he have gone?"

Eleazer Jordan pointed above them. "Check dat cave! Cave o' de Winds!"

Nevers yelled, "What cave?"

Eleazer Jordan explained, "De cave, up dere!"

Nevers grabbed him and told him to lead. Eleazer Jordan jumped across to a wooden platform. There was a stairway here, up the side of the Bridal Veil at a very steep angle. Butter was the last to get to the stairs, and climbed slowly for the icy footing. Butter did not think he could make this, and he was on his knees again as he reached the landing. He was halfway up the cliff now, staring out at the American Falls. He pulled his hat brim down to shield his face from the spray. Eleazer Jordan was suddenly there, helping Butter onto a rocky ledge that veered to the left, and then urging him up onto another wooden platform.

They were going underneath the Falls! Butter felt his way along the cliff, and could not look. Then the sound changed. The rush of the Falls was replaced by the whining and whooshing of wind that hit Butter from the front. He held onto his hat, and looked up. He was at the entrance of a black hole of an enormous size.

Butter cried, "We're under the river!"

Eleazer Jordan called, "Inside, mistah, it's easier inside!"

Butter went forward because he could not go back. It was quieter now, and easier to stand. Butter leaned against a wall, and shouted, "Mr. Nevers, where are you?"

Butter could see the light from Joshua Rue's lantern as it flashed off the walls of the cave. The cavern was huge! And there were shadows on the walls, which Butter realized were the silhouettes of Nevers, Wild Jack, and Joshua Rue as they searched. Butter tried again. "Mr. Nevers! Have you found him!"

Wild Jack was calling, "Mr. Rue! Can you see? Mr. Rue!"

Nevers appeared out of the darkness, and asked, "Where does it go? Is this it?"

Eleazer Jordan pointed. "More'n a hundred feet up and wide!"

Butter was profoundly frightened. He could feel the river above him, and the pressure in the cave made his ears pop. He took one step from the stone wall, and sheltered his face. He did not like heights and he did not like holes and he did not like this place! He had to get out! He held onto Eleazer Jordan.

When a gust of wind blew out Eleazer Jordan's lantern, Butter panicked. He screamed for Joshua Rue. "We need light! Bring the other light! Here!"

Wild Jack approached. "A devil's cave! The devil's work!"

Butter felt crazy. They were going to leave him! The walls were going to collapse! He saw himself drowning! He saw Oliphant drowning! Then a revelation emerged like a spectre. Butter screamed, "He's in the water! He went out in the water!"

Nevers was the first to understand; he ran out of the cave. Once Joshua

Rue had helped to relight the second lamp with his, they all descended hurriedly. Butter and Eleazer Jordan were the last to reach the wooden platform at the base of the stairs. Butter dared to make his own way down to the shoreline.

Butter called, "Can you see him? Is he out there?"

Nevers and Wild Jack were scrambling along the shore; Nevers cupped his hands at his mouth, and called, "Oliphant! Come back!"

Eleazer Jordan spoke to Butter, "Current's gonna get him."

Butter imitated Nevers, "Oliphant! Oliphant!"

They moved along the bank, away from the American Falls and back toward the boardwalk. They went down to the gravel shore again, and swept their lanterns back and forth in the snowfall, calling Oliphant's name.

Nevers drew his pistol. Butter reached over to stop him. "Don't!"

But then Butter had to jump back, because a longboat shot at him right out of the night to crash against the rocks. Joshua Rue was immediately at the two oarsmen. He dragged them out, one thrown into the breakers, the other half over the gunwale. Butter took hold of the bow with Nevers. Oliphant was not in the boat.

Butter said, "He's still out there."

Wild Jack put his pistol barrel into one oarsman's mouth. The man gagged a plea. Joshua Rue picked the other one out of the water and tossed him at Nevers's feet.

Butter did not care about them. He stepped down into the water until the waves were washing over his boots. He screamed, "Oliphant! Oliphant!"

Nevers was beside him then, and Eleazer Jordan too, all three screaming and leaping. Butter tripped on the underwater rocks, and caught himself from falling by holding onto Eleazer Jordan. Butter asked, "Can he swim to Canada? Can he!"

"Current's gonna get him, mistah! Straight into de rapids. You gonna find him in de whirlpool!"

Butter turned to Nevers. "We have to go out after him!" Butter crawled up into the longboat. Nevers joined him while Wild Jack and Joshua Rue forced the oarsmen back into their places. Eleazer Jordan shoved them off and leaped in.

They drifted quickly out until the oarsmen got them turned about. Eleazer Jordan took up a third set of oars at the bow and directed their course. The turbulence told them that they were perilously close to the rockfalls below the American Falls. Still, they screamed for Oliphant. Still, they waved their lanterns through the snow. Nevers tried to stand for a wider vantage over the black water, but was knocked down when the boat struck a rock. Nevers had his pistol out again, and Butter, understanding now that Nevers did not mean harm, brought his Army Colt out as well. They fired their five loaded chambers simultaneously into the air, the gunpowder flashes illuminating their anguished faces with red and yellow fire as they called out.

Bang! "Oliphant!" Bang! "Here we are!" Bang! "Swim here!" Bang! "Oliphant!" Bang!

Nevers reloaded with an extra cylinder as the longboat smashed underwater rocks and bobbed wildly before the vastly greater voice of the American Falls above them that spoke incessantly and irrefutably, the roar of the beast, the force of the Lord.

Once more they tried, for mercy's sake, for the horror all beings have of drowning, for the awful image of a man being dragged under when his strength gave out and he felt his body being rushed along until he felt nothing but the cold, and then nothing at all, the corpse to be pulverized in the rapids and deposited like flotsam in the whirlpool. Butter would pray later. For now, he screamed as Nevers fired.

Bang! "John Oliphant!" Bang! "Call out!" Bang! Bang! Bang!

EPILOGUE

THE PEACE OF
AMAZIAH BUTTER

December 1864-June and July 1865

WASHINGTON CITY, DISTRICT OF COLUMBIA

CHAPTER 12

Amaziah Butter in
the United States of America

DECEMBER 1864

December 4, *New-York Times:* "SAVANNAH—Sherman Approaching the City—The Augusta and Savannah Railroad Cut—One Column Threatening Augusta—Secret Expedition from Port Royal—The Effect of Sherman's March—Immense Destruction of Rebel Property."

December 6, Washington City: President Lincoln, in his address to a joint session of Congress, reported, "In view of the insecurity of life in the region adjacent to the Canadian Border by recent assaults and depredations committed by inimical and desperate persons, who are harbored there, it has been thought proper to give notice that after six months . . . the United States must hold themselves at liberty to increase their naval armament upon the Lakes. . . . The condition of the border will necessarily come into consideration in connection with the question of continuing or modifying the rights of transit from Canada through the United States, as well as the regulation of imports, which were *temporarily* established by the Reciprocity Treaty of 5 June, 1854."

December 9, Near Petersburg, Virginia: Captain Amaziah Butter stopped over briefly in Washington City, and then left by steamer for City Point, Virginia, en route to rejoining his regiment, the badly undermanned First Maine Cavalry, U.S. Volunteers, now serving as part of Brigadier-General C. H. Smith's Brigade, in the Second Division of Major-General Philip H. Sheridan's Cavalry Corps, Army of the Potomac.

The weather continued wretchedly cold and wet, with snow showers battering both the Federal and Confederate armies in their works. Butter, senior in his regiment to all but three officers, was immediately given command of Company M, which consisted of men transferred into the First Maine from the dismantled First D.C.

The First Maine, with its seven-shot Spencer and sixteen-shot Henry repeating rifles, was now said by the Confederates across no-man's-land to be a unit that "loads up on Sunday and shoots all week." The regiment was regarded by its Union commanders as among the most distinguished in the Army.

The First Maine was commanded by Lieutenant-Colonel Jon P. Cilley, a long-nosed and good-natured attorney, who was admired by his men for having twice returned to duty after severe wounds. Cilley had proved expert at knitting together the bickering elements of the First Maine and the old First D.C.

The regiment participated in the successful Bellefield Raid, December 9–12, during which a major Confederate railroad line to Petersburg was torn up, thus sealing off Lee's army from resupply from the south. Afterward, the regiment retired to its winter headquarters, off the Jerusalem Turnpike near Hancock Station, a mile from the front lines about Petersburg. It was now understood by the troopers, woodsmen all, that the winter ahead would be brutally cold and wet. The only solace for the troopers was that they knew they would not be called upon again, except for picket duty, until Lieutenant-General Grant reopened his campaign on Richmond in the spring.

⌣ ⌣ ⌣

December 14, *New-York Times:* "THE ST. ALBANS RAID—Release of the Robbers—The Judge Decrees that He Has No Jurisdiction—Queer Conduct of the Canadian Authorities—Excitement in Canada."

December 15, *New-York Times:* "THE FRONTIER—Important Orders From Gen. Dix—Rebel Marauders to Be Pursued into Canada—If Captured, Not to Be Surrendered, but Sent to NY for Military Trial."

General Dix's order noted in part, "It is earnestly hoped that the inhabitants of our frontier districts will abstain from all acts of retribution on account of the outrages committed by Rebel marauders."

December 16, Suspension Bridge, Niagara Falls: Federal detectives under the direction of Major-General Dix captured a Confederate naval officer named John Yates Beall at the Centre House. Captain Beall, a handsome, educated, and extremely wealthy Virginian, was legendary for his pirate raids on the Potomac River in 1863; he was especially notorious for having led the failed raid to commandeer the Lake Erie warship U.S.S. *Michigan* in September 1864.

Beall was at the Suspension Bridge that night because he had come across the border as a member of a raiding party commanded by Lieutenant-Colonel James Martin (and including Lieutenant John Headley and Captain Robert Cobb Kennedy). Their mission was said to have been to rescue six Confederate generals who were being transferred by train from Johnson's Island to Fort Lafayette. It was the opinion of the Federal detectives that the raiders' mission had also been to search out and rescue a Rebel spy, John C. Oliphant, who had vanished at Niagara Falls on November 30.

The Confederate raiders failed in their mission and, less Beall, escaped across the border. They were pursued into Canada by Federal detectives, however, acting under General Dix's General Order No. 97, "Commanders are directed to pursue the desperadoes wherever they may take refuge . . . or if it is necessary, to cross the boundary between the United States and Canada."

President Lincoln ordered General Dix to rescind this order two days later. By then, Federal detectives had infiltrated the Confederate Secret Service ring at the Queen's Hotel in Toronto.

On Christmas night, in a severe blizzard, Federal detectives staying at the Centre House in the disguise of well-to-do Copperheads crossed the Suspension Bridge in order to rendezvous with a Sons of Liberty commander—a New-Yorker named W. Larry MacDonald. At the meeting, Larry MacDonald solicited funds by boasting to the disguised detectives of his part in the New-York incendiary raid of the previous month. MacDonald mentioned the recent visit to Toronto of his niece, Katie MacDonald, who was seeking money for the defense of her father and brother jailed in New-York. MacDonald explained that Horatio Seymour, recently defeated New York governor, was not going to be able to pardon his relatives before leaving office January 1.

Larry MacDonald also boasted of the exploits of one particular Confederate raider, a close friend of his niece named Captain Kennedy. MacDonald said that Kennedy had been released from his duty in Toronto by Jake Thompson, and was preparing to depart for his home in Louisiana.

December 26, *New-York Times:* "SAVANNAH OURS—Sherman's Christmas Present—Official Dispatches from Gen. Sherman and Foster—What Sherman Found—150 Cannon 2000 Cars and Locomotives and 3 Steamers—300 Prisoners 30,000 Bales of Cotton—Twenty Thousand People in the City Quiet and Well-Disposed—Escape of Hardee's Army—Three Rebel Ironclads Blown Up and the Navy Yard Burned—An Almost Bloodless Victory."

Major-General Sherman's dispatches included a telegram to the White House: "To His Excellency, President Lincoln, Savannah, December 22. I beg to present you as a Christmas gift, the city of Savannah, with one hundred and fifty heavy guns and plenty of ammunition, and also about 25,000 bales of cotton. W. T. Sherman, Maj.-Gen."

December 29, Detroit, Michigan: Acting on a report from an informer, three Federal detectives, who had been posted at the Detroit terminal in search of guerrillas crossing from Canada, boarded an Illinois Central train. As the train moved out, the detectives confronted Captain Robert Cobb Kennedy as he slept sitting up. While Kennedy struggled, Lieutenant John Ashbrook, in the same car, escaped by flinging himself out the window and onto a snowbank.

Kennedy was found to have on him a month's Confederate captain's pay in gold and a twenty-dollar Confederate bill. He also carried a document identifying him as R. C. Stanton.

During the return trip to New-York, Kennedy tried to escape by flinging himself from the train, but failed, and was put in chains. He pleaded with his captors to give him a pistol and a ten-pace start and he would find either liberty or death.

Kennedy was imprisoned in Fort Lafayette near John Yates Beall. Both were scheduled for trial by a military court in January.

January 1865

January 1, Canada: The border crisis deepened, and now threatened Canada's three million citizens with embargo, blockade, and invasion. Ominously, passports were now routinely demanded by U.S. officials at the border crossings.

In Toronto, General Napier of the British Army addressed a call-up of Provincial Volunteers, telling them that their immediate duty was to patrol the frontier, not in anticipation of an invasion, but rather to provide security to citizens on both sides of the frontier. Nonetheless, General Napier, sensitive to the fervent Confederate sympathy in Canada, was careful to emphasize his respect for both the Confederate and Federal armies.

In Montreal, the St. Albans raiders, after having been released by the court in December, and after having been rearrested on the charge of violating Canadian neutrality, were found not guilty. Also, the second-in-command to Captain John Yates Beall on the Lake Erie raid was tried and found not guilty of violating Canadian neutrality, because he was understood to have been acting under the orders of the Confederate government at war with the United States.

In Quebec, the governor-general of the United Province of Canada, Viscount Monck, was besieged by a furious colonial Parliament which demanded that the United States government be appeased in some outsized fashion. The governor-general thereupon deployed a detective force to supplement the troops along the frontier. The urgency of the border crisis increased the political pressure in Canada to create a Dominion capable of dealing uniformly with the United States.

In London, the *London Times* further contributed to Canadian fears by publishing editorials critical of the Canadian government's conduct in the St. Albans affair. It was also understood that the British government was pressing Canada to avoid any further provocation of the increasingly belligerent United States government.

January 12, Washington City: War Secretary Stanton announced that he had complied with General Grant's request that Major-General Benjamin F. Butler be relieved of command of the Army of the James due to Butler's failure at the recent aborted assault on Fort Fisher, near Wilmington, North Carolina, the last of the major Confederate ports open to blockade runners.

There was also a widespread rumor that General Butler was removed from command because of his involvement in cotton trading with the enemy on Albemarle Sound, and also because of his command's illegal and arbitrary arrests of citizens in Virginia.

In his farewell address to the Army of the James, General Butler declared, "I have refused to order useless sacrifice of the lives of [my] soldiers, and I am relieved of command. The wasted blood of my men does not stain my garments. For my action, I am responsible to God and my country." To the Negro troops in his command, General Butler declared, "With the bayonet you have unlocked the iron-barred gates of prejudice."

Butler soon after resigned from the United States Army and proceeded home to Massachusetts to reestablish his political career. It was well known that he had ambitions for the Senate and the presidency.

January 18, Washington City: The Military Committee of the House of Representatives, chaired by Representative Elihu Washburne of Illinois, a supremely powerful Republican close to President Lincoln, visited Old Capitol Prison in order to investigate charges of misconduct by Secret Service Chief Colonel Lafayette C. Baker and Superintendent William P. Wood. The Committee found generally acceptable treatment of the prisoners; however, the Committee was also disposed to continue its inquiry because of the apparent Secret Service abuse of authority in arresting citizens capriciously and confining them for long periods without charges.

January 22, *New-York Times:* "From Sandwich Islands & etc. Heavy rains at Honolulu, 38 inches in twelve days. The volcano at Kilauea in the island of Hawaii is very active."

FEBRUARY 1865

February 2, Washington City: The Military Committee of the House of Representatives, investigating illicit cotton trading between the insurgent states and the United States, called Colonel Lafayette C. Baker to testify.

In his testimony, Lafayette Baker revealed the details of his counterespionage activities the previous fall with regard to what he called the Cotton Ring. Baker reported that he had been approached in October 1864 by a member of the Cotton Ring; he had been asked to travel to Montreal in order to escort the Confederate agent, Beverley Tucker, into the United States for the purpose of completing a multi-million-dollar deal in which the Confederacy would sell its blockaded cotton to the Cotton Ring. Baker declared that he had been acting as a double agent all the while. He said that he had been offered a bribe by the Cotton Ring of a promotion to brigadier-general in the Federal Army.

Under questioning, Lafayette Baker stunned the committee by revealing that the Cotton Ring was able to offer him his advancement in grade because it counted among its members very highly placed persons in the Republican party. Baker then named names, including Thurlow Weed of New York (Secretary Seward's patron and President Lincoln's fund-raiser), Leonard Swett of Chicago (President Lincoln's longtime political liaison there), and Simeon Draper of New York (an intimate of President and Mrs. Lincoln, and also the Collector of Customs of the Port of New-York).

Assistant War Secretary Charles A. Dana was also called to testify. Dana, 45, an ambitious and able man, a Harvard graduate, one-time member of the Transcendentalists, and a former correspondent for Horace Greeley, assured the committee that he had worked closely with Baker during October and November 1864 in an attempt to entrap the Cotton Ring in its schemes, and also to capture Beverley Tucker and perhaps his cohorts, Confederate secret agents George N. Sanders, Clement C. Clay, and Jacob P. Thompson.

In further testimony, Lafayette Baker reported the failure of his counterespionage mission to Montreal just prior to Election Day. Baker re-created the events: He crossed the border at Rouse's Point, New York, and stopped at the so-called Rebel den of the St. Lawrence Hotel, Montreal. He met with Beverley Tucker and George Sanders, who informed Baker that they were disappointed that he did not bear a written guarantee from the Cotton Ring. Baker reported to the committee on the occasion, "He [Tucker] asked me a great many questions as to parties who were interested with Mr. Durant, a go-between for the Ring—and a great many other questions I do not recall. . . . He treated me very handsomely." Baker returned to Rouse's Point on Sunday night, November 6, where he planned to rendezvous with Beverley Tucker, and where he also planned to arrest him. Tucker did not appear, for reasons Baker said were unknown to him. Baker finally returned to Washington via New-York.

Lafayette Baker concluded his testimony by saying that he and Assistant War Secretary Dana had pursued their investigations since November, but had not been able to advance their case against the Cotton Ring.

Elihu Washburne, the chairman of the House Military Affairs Committee —gray, stout, energetic, taciturn—was U. S. Grant's major patron in the Congress because Grant's hometown of Galena, Illinois, was in Washburne's district. It was said that Washburne wanted Grant to be president right after he was. It was therefore understood that Washburne would move very carefully against Lincoln's confidants.

Subsequently, Washburne passed on the findings of his committee to President Lincoln, along with several questions. Lincoln returned that he had met with Leonard Swett the previous fall about a possible promotion for Colonel Baker. Lincoln also communicated that he had taken Swett's recommendation under advisement, and that he would now also take the committee's work under advisement.

February 2–10, *New-York Tribune:* "THE PEACE MOVEMENT—Arrivals of Three Rebel Commissioners—Mr. Seward Meets Them at Annapolis—

They Are Supposed to Be at Mr. Blair's House—Speculations in Washington—Rebel Statements of Their Powers."

"THE PEACE MOVEMENT—Arrival of Peace Commissioners at Fortress Monroe—President Lincoln Goes to Meet Them—A Thousand and One Rumors."

"THE PEACE CONFERENCE ENDED—Returns of the President and Secretary of State—Contradictory Report of the Results—The Conference Said to Be a Failure."

"THE PEACE FAILURE—Jeff Davis Thereon—Report of Rebel Commissioners—Lincoln Will Not Hear of Disunion—He Demands Submission to the Constitution and Laws—The Conference Effects Nothing—Ravings of the Rebel Press."

February 8, *New-York Tribune:* "GENERAL GRANT AT WORK—The Potomac Army in Motion—Army of the James Cooperating—The Fifth Corps beyond Ream's Station—A Decisive Battle Looked For."

February 15, *New-York Tribune:* "THE LAKE ERIE PIRACY—Conviction of Captain John Y. Beall—Findings of the Court-Martial—The Culprit to Be Executed."

John Yates Beall, despite documentation that he had been acting under orders by his superiors in Canada and Richmond, was convicted on two counts: violation of the law of war and spying.

The officers of the court-martial explained in their verdict: "War, under its mildest aspects, is the heaviest calamity that can befall our race; and he who in a spirit of revenge or with lawless violence transcends the limits to which it is restricted by the common behest of all Christian Communities, should receive the punishment which the common voice has declared to be due the crime. The Major-General [Dix] commanding feels that a want of firmness and inflexibility on his part in executing the sentence of death in such a case would be an offense against the outraged civilization and humanity of the age."

The court-martial of Captain R. C. Kennedy, by the same officers who had convicted Beall, was granted a temporary delay. The prosecution had closed its case, but the defense had requested time to secure evidence in Kennedy's favor.

February 20, *New-York Tribune:* "SHERMAN'S TRIUMPHANT MARCH—Capture of Columbia, the Capital of South Carolina—Beauregard Declines a Fight—The Rebels Destroy Their Stores and Go Away—Charleston Isolated and Probably Evacuated—Subdued Tone of Rebel Press."

On the evening of February 17, and into February 18, Columbia, South Carolina, was destroyed by fire, while at the same time its homes, commercial buildings, and citizens were routinely robbed by drunken Federal soldiers and Confederate deserters. Also, the Negro population suffered open depravity—Negro women were tortured, gang-raped, and murdered by soldiers, and Negro men who attempted to defend their families were executed. Blame for the catastrophe was impossible to fix definitively, but it was equally impossible to avoid the conclusion that Sherman's army had rioted out of control. A Union officer testified later to the feelings of revenge among Sherman's troops: "I'm sorry for the women and children, but South Carolina's got to suffer, got to be destroyed."

An aged Columbia lady, battered and then burnt out by soldiers supposedly assigned to protect her during the riot, later concluded, "I cannot live long. I shall meet General Sherman and his soldiers at the bar of God, and I [shall] give [my] testimony in full view of that dread tribunal."

February 21, Near Petersburg, Virginia: The First Maine Cavalry, 446 troopers and 18 officers, was back at its winter quarters after participating in Grant's surprise attack at Hatcher's Run, south of Petersburg, which tightened the grip on Richmond and Petersburg. During the demonstration, the regiment was overwhelmed by the weather—spending one night in the open without food and with little fire, and awakening the next morning with the tarpaulins frozen so fast over the huddled troopers that the men had to be freed by axe-work.

Captain Butter received two letters at mail call, each containing St. Valentine's Day greetings. Mrs. Desire Butter wrote from Bangor that she and their two sons were well, that it had been a hard winter, and that she regretted her spitefulness of the previous fall. She wrote that she especially regretted not having answered his letters, and was very thankful to have him as her husband. She told him to walk with God and to keep his head down.

In the second letter, Mrs. Bridey Lamont wrote from Washington City that she and her two children were well, that it had been a hard winter, and that she hoped to see Butter again as soon as possible. She wrote that the night and morning they had spent together in December was a joy to recall regardless of their future. She wrote that she was very thankful to have his letters. She added a great deal of information about Colonel Lafayette Baker's testimony to the Congress about the so-called Cotton Ring.

Bridey Lamont closed her letter by charging Butter to be cautious and to keep his greatcoat close about him. There was a postscript reporting that Major Wetherbee was in hospital after a bad fall causing head injuries.

February 22, *New-York Tribune:* "CHARLESTON EVACUATED—The Official Dispatches—Full Account by Our Special Correspondent—Capture of a Vast Amount of Artillery—The City on Fire—Two-Thirds of It Probably Destroyed—Terrific Explosions Killing and Wounding a Great Many Citizens—Our Flag Floats on Ft. Sumter!!—National Salute Ordered."

A New-York correspondent, writing at a desk in the shattered offices of the *Charleston Courier,* reported that the city had been largely destroyed by a fire that he believed had been started by retreating Confederate forces aiming to keep the cotton stores from capture; he also reported that it was the Union command's opinion that the explosions had been ignited when children playing near the ammunition depot had amused themselves by throwing handfuls of black powder onto burning cotton bales. The reported further stated that all of the city's "Temples of Iniquity" (he argued that they were not churches, because they had blessed slavery) had been annointed by Sherman's artillery. He communicated that graffiti on the wall of the *Courier* predicted a ticket for the Election of 1868: Edward Everett (the prominent Boston Abolitionist) for president, and Frederick Douglass (the famous Negro orator) for vice-president.

Charleston was first occupied by the 21st United States Colored Troops (a regiment raised on Port Royal Island, South Carolina), and the 54th and 55th Massachusetts Infantry (Colored) Volunteers. The troops sang "John Brown's Body," promising, *"We'll hang Jeff Davis on a sour apple tree, as we go marching on!"*

February 25, *New-York Tribune:* "THE EXECUTION OF CAPTAIN BEALL—The Rebel Spy—Preparations for the Execution—Scenes of the Scaffold—The Death of Beall."

On Saturday afternoon, the 24th, at Fort Columbia on Governor's Island in New-York Harbor, John Yates Beall was led to the scaffold. He paused to make a request of the commandant: "I am at your service. You will oblige me by making this as short as possible."

Besides the soldiers of the fort, there were 500 citizens in attendance, among whom were Beall's mother and sister. The Beall women were in a state of nervous exhaustion because of the failure of their repeated appeals to President Lincoln for a commutation of the sentence.

The Virginian Beall was a strong, handsome, fair man, educated at Charlottesville, and a millionaire. He was dressed in a gray civilian suit with a waist-length cape and black turban cap. His arms were pinioned behind him at the elbows. His features were pallid and emaciated. He stood beneath the noose and observed, "How beautiful that sunlight. I never knew what its splendor was until I look upon it for the last time."

The gallows were constructed with a pulley and counterweight, so that rather than falling through a trap, the victim would be yanked upward to have his neck broken. The executioner was a felon who had been promised his freedom for this service; the executioner was hidden from the noose behind a screen, where he was to cut a rope to release the counterweight.

Captain Beall stood while the charges, finding, and sentence of the court-martial were read aloud. Beall was asked if he had a reply. He said, "Yes. I protest against the execution of this sentence. It is absolute murder—brutal murder! I die in the defense and service of my country."

Before the black hood was pulled over, and the noose fixed, Beall was asked if he had last words. He said, "No. I beg you to make haste." His neck was broken at 1:14 P.M.; the body was made to swing for twenty minutes as prescribed by law. Beall's corpse was given over to his family for interment.

MARCH 1865

March 4, Washington City: Inauguration Day began stormy and wet. The sun came out, however, as President Lincoln and Vice-President-Elect Andrew Johnson mounted the platform that had been constructed on the steps of the Capitol building for the ceremony of the oaths of office. The audience was large and excited, and in a singing mood, serenaded by brass bands performing traditional and popular scores.

Lincoln looked grave and emaciated, his formal coat hanging badly on him. In his address, Lincoln generally reached for a conciliatory tone toward the insurgent states. Nevertheless, he also declaimed, "Fondly do we hope, fervently do we pray, that this mighty scourge of war may speedily pass away. Yet if God wills that it continues until all the wealth piled by the bondsmen's 250 years of unrequited toil shall be sunk, and until every drop of blood drawn with the lash shall be paid by another drawn with the sword, as was said 3000 years ago, so, still must be said, that the judgments of the Lord are true and righteous."

March 10, *New-York Times:* "IMPORTANT FROM MEXICO—Particulars of the Capture of Oajaca [From Juarezistas]—Seven Thousand Prisoners Taken —Two Reverses Sustained by Imperial Troops—Recognition of Maximillian by British Government—Autograph Letter from Queen Victoria to Emperor Maximillian."

March 12, *New-York Times:* "COL. BAKER'S OPERATIONS—An Immense Trap Sprung and Nearly a Regiment of Bounty Jumpers Caught—27 Brokers Sent to Ft. Lafayette—The Biters Bitten—Thieves, Murderers, Bounty Jumpers, and Felons Generally in the Gang—They Are to Be Put in the Front Rank in the Next Battle—Col. Baker's Trophies—Skeleton Keys, Watches, Jewelry, and Jimmies."

March 14, *New-York Times:* "REBEL REPORTS—Whistling to Keep Their Courage Up—General Lee Thinks the Situation Hopeful—Grant, Sherman, Sheridan, and Schofield Just Where He Wants Them."

March 16, *New-York Times:* "THE DRAFT BEGUN AGAIN—Drawings in the Fourth, Fifth, Sixth, and Eighth Wards—Much Surprise but No Excitement —The Wheel in Motion Today."

— — —

March 21, *New-York Times:* "THE GREAT CAVALRY RAID—The Heroes of the Shenandoah on Horseback—Successful and Triumphant March—The Defeat of Early and Dispersion of His Entire Army—Railway Trains Captured—Railroads Demolished, Bridges Burned—Millions Worth of Property Destroyed—Interesting Letters from Rebel Soldiers to Jeff. Davis—Cool Reply of the Rebel President—Sheridan at White House on His Way to Join Grant."

March 24, New-York: On Friday, at Fort Lafayette, the day before his scheduled execution, Captain Kennedy devoted himself to writing letters and making his peace. Because he had tried to escape several times the previous week, including once when he used a poker to burn the lock off his cell door, Kennedy now sat at his desk in two pairs of interconnected manacles and leg irons. His cell was large, airy, and rudimentarily furnished—an iron bed, campaign chairs, a desk-table appropriated by the Federal Army from the Maryland State Legislature House—with a good fire and windows that overlooked the Verrazano Narrows.

Friday afternoon, Kennedy was visited by the Protestant Episcopal chaplain of the fort, the Reverend Mr. Burke, and was informed that there was little hope for a presidential pardon, since President Lincoln had left Washington on a tour of the front lines at Petersburg. The Reverend Mr. Burke, a small, gray, cheery man, asked Kennedy if he would pray with him. Kennedy balked. "My father was a good straightforward man, Reverend, and my mother was a Methodist woman, and I always said my prayers and all that, but what does it amount to? I'm to die tomorrow, and I don't know where I will go, or what shall be done with me."

A *New-York Times* correspondent was present in the cell, and later reported that the Reverend Mr. Burke told Kennedy that he should submit to the teachings of the church.

Kennedy replied, "Yes, that's all so, I know all about the doctrine. I suppose I ought to be a good Christian about this. But damn it all, I can't! No, I can't! And I'll die uncertain that there's another world—but what the Lord only knows. I'm not a bad man, and I've no fears as to exactly what will happen. I haven't hurt anyone except in this war, and I think—I hope —my character will stand investigation—in heaven, or wherever."

Kennedy was also visited by Federal detectives seeking more intelligence for their continuing pursuit of the Confederate incendiaries. Kennedy implored them to release Augustus MacDonald—Katie MacDonald's father—

who was still being held on charges that he had collaborated in the incendiary attack with his brother, W. Larry MacDonald. Kennedy still refused to name any other participants in the raid. After the detectives left, Kennedy composed a note to them that was in effect a tribute; Kennedy wrote, "In answer to your desire to ascertain the present state of my feelings toward you, I can only say that I bear you no malice. You did your duties as detectives with, perhaps, as much kindness toward me as any others would under similar circumstances."

Kennedy passed the evening recording other acknowledgments. To the officers of the court-martial that had convicted him, he wrote, "General [Fitz-Henry] Warren, the judges of the court, and Judge-Advocate-Major [John A.] Bowles are all honorable men, and treated me very fairly with one or two exceptions, and perhaps—indeed, I know—they meant right— but they certainly did very wrong." Kennedy did not mention here, as he had in other notes, his bitterness that the court had refused to admit into evidence the documentation provided by Richmond via Canada that asserted that Kennedy had been acting under the orders of his government in his activities of the November and December before.

Kennedy wrote at length of his affection for Brigadier-General Stoughton, who had served as his defense counsel: "The conduct of General Stoughton has been most noble. He came to my assistance when I was utterly friendless. Although I know that I would have done the same under the reverse of circumstances, I cannot properly express my gratitude and appreciation of his services. His conduct has almost disarmed me of any malice toward the Yankees, although they have made the fairest portion of my country a desert. Stoughton knows that when we were at West Point together, I was not sectional—that gentlemen were always welcome at my room, whether from Maine or Louisiana."

And of Lieutenant-Colonel Burke, commandant of Fort Lafayette (and nephew of the Reverend Mr. Burke), he wrote, "This is the only place where I have been treated decently by Federal officers, and Colonel Burke is specially deserving of my thanks. I've been in half a dozen prisons now— fully half of the war behind bars—but have never been comfortable till now."

Colonel Burke, a small, agitated, bearded man, with large moles on his temples, continued his urgent concern for Kennedy's welfare. He visited Kennedy's cell every two hours throughout the night.

At 5 A.M., Saturday morning, March 25, Burke took pity on Kennedy and ordered the chains removed so that Kennedy was able to sleep prone. At 7

A.M., Kennedy was awakened by his guards. He dressed in a gray civilian suit, white cotton shirt, without a vest. Presently, Kennedy was joined by General Stoughton—a handsome, long-haired man with a difficult step because of wounds at the Wilderness—and by the *New-York Times* correspondent. The three shared a large breakfast and chatted pleasantly. Afterward, Kennedy said that he would like to make a complete confession of his conduct during the incendiary attack, which he would like published after his death. The *New-York Times* correspondent, George F. Wilson, took Kennedy's statement. At the finish, Kennedy told Wilson, "I hope this will show that I wasn't a fiend, and didn't war on women or children, like they say, unless it became a matter of necessity in retaliation—but sir, I was ordered to do it, and they've been doing the same!" Kennedy was comforted by George Wilson's open sympathy and General Stoughton's quiet comradeship; he wept for the first time in the day.

Soon after, a guard entered with a package of photographs of Kennedy that had been made the week before. Kennedy sat at his desk and arranged the photographs with locks of his hair. He enclosed the several allotments in envelopes he had already addressed to his family and friends. While he was writing a letter to his mother and weeping discreetly, Fort Lafayette's supervisor of executions entered. The man, Eisen, described later by George Wilson as "beadleistic and eager for his task," proceeded to ask Kennedy questions about his height and weight. Kennedy answered Eisen indifferently, and wrote more feverishly.

At noon, Colonel Burke, the Reverend Mr. Burke, and Confederate Brigadier-General Beale (senior Confederate prisoner in the fort) entered the cell to share a light lunch with Kennedy, Stoughton, and Wilson. Also present were correspondents from the *Tribune, Herald, Evening Post, World,* and *Daily News.*

For forty minutes, they spoke generally of the war, and of the present prospects of Lee breaking Grant's siege at Richmond and Petersburg. The news of the morning from the telegraph wires at the various newspaper offices was of a major attack by Lee's forces on the left wing of the Army of the Potomac just south of the Appomattox River. The report that interested Kennedy the most was the bizarre coincidence that President Lincoln and Generals Grant and Meade had been scheduled to review a division at the Weldon Railroad at approximately the same time Lee had launched his attack, so that even now, as the battle raged less than five miles away, Lincoln and his commanders could probably hear both the marching brass bands and the sound of heavy guns. The casualties on both sides of the assault were said to be enormous. It was the opinion of the correspondents in the room that the Confederates were making a suicide attack to break the Federal lines and to capture Grant's railroad.

Kennedy said, "Perhaps General Lee and I are going to get free on the same day." Colonel Burke asserted the impossibility of Lee's chances. Kennedy replied, "I'm to die at the same time as my comrades, and if you'd give me my pistol, I could show you how a soldier faces death—not this miserable business with my arms bound. What I wouldn't give to be with General Lee today, and die going forward!"

Kennedy was still arguing with Colonel Burke when Supervisor of Executions Eisen came in with the Officer of the Day, Captain Black. Kennedy said, "All right, I'm ready for this thing." But as Eisen moved to pinion Kennedy's arms, Kennedy exclaimed to Eisen, "I don't know you, nor who the hell you are!"

General Beale appealed to Kennedy to submit in good order. Kennedy shouted at Colonel Burke and Captain Black. "This is hard for you damned Yankees to treat me so! I'm a regular soldier in the Confederate Army, and have been since the war began!"

Kennedy did finally allow his arms to be bound behind at the elbows, but then recoiled at the black hood. General Beale again asked Kennedy to die like a soldier. Kennedy submitted, weeping openly. As Kennedy stepped to the cell door, he inadvertently bumped into the doorjamb; he turned to speak through the hood, "Are you there, Mr. Wilson? Where? Well, goodbye, old friend, and be kind to me in that paper of yours."

It was a cloudy, windy day, and the light was gray in the fort's courtyard. The scaffold, the same one that had been used to execute John Yates Beall, had been raised in the middle of the yard. Men of the 17th United States Infantry were drawn up around the scaffold in a hollow square. Above, on the balcony of the fort, imprisoned bounty jumpers and bounty brokers had been assembled three deep to witness the execution. There were also a few civilians present, who had paid $50 each to come over from New-York by ferry. The man who was to cut the rope was a Maine deserter who had been promised his freedom in exchange for this service.

Kennedy was marched to the platform and seated in the backless chair beneath the noose. He immediately stood. As the charges, finding, and sentence of the court-martial were read aloud for fully ten minutes, Kennedy worked off the black hood. Soon, Kennedy was gazing around the yard, denouncing everything. "It's a damned lie!" "What hypocrisy—not even clever!"

Kennedy had been convicted both as a violator of the law of war and as a spy. The part of the reading that particularly aroused Kennedy stated, "The Major-General [Dix] commanding considers his duty as clear in this case as in that of Beall. The lives, the property, the domestic security of noncombatant citizens, must be protected against all invasion not in strict accordance with the laws and usages of Civilized states in the conduct of war. Crimes which outrage and shake the moral sense by their atrocity, must not only be punished and the perpetrators be deprived of their power of repeating them, but the sternest condemnation of the law must be presented to others, to deter them from the commission of similar enormities."

At the close of the reading, Kennedy pronounced, "There'll be rope in hell aplenty for you Yankees condemned by your own hooey!"

The Reverend Mr. Burke came forward to lead his service. When he finished, the Reverend Mr. Burke went to his knees and prayed for Kennedy. Kennedy remained standing. The Reverend Mr. Burke arose, touched Kennedy's breast, and asked him to resign himself to his fate. Kennedy turned away and asked Colonel Burke if he might have a drink. Colonel Burke did not respond.

Eisen approached Kennedy to replace the black hood. Kennedy backed away against the railing, and announced, "Colonel, I wish to make a statement!" Kennedy looked around the courtyard. "Gentlemen, this is judicial murder! This is judicial, cowardly murder. There's no occasion for the United States to treat me in this way. I die a gentleman and officer in the Confederate Army, and do not regret the path I have taken—I say, Colonel, can't you give me a drink before I go up? My lips are mighty dry."

There was no response. Kennedy stepped up and steadied himself beneath the noose. He permitted Eisen to replace the black hood and to fix the noose. Kennedy refused to sit, however, and was permitted to remain standing. Kennedy turned his head to the sound of Captain Black drawing his sword in order to signal the moment. Kennedy said, "I'm going to fly." And then Kennedy stiffened to attention and sang forth:

"Trust to Luck, Trust to Luck!
"Stare your fate in the face!
"Sure if your heart is airy!
"It will be in the right place!"

The sword fell and the counterweight rope was cut and Kennedy was yanked upward, his neck broken instantaneously at 1:16 P.M. The corpse was made to swing for twenty minutes, and was then cut down and laid in a pine coffin for burial in Brooklyn in the anticipation of the remains being claimed by Kennedy's family after the war.

March 25, Near Petersburg: Captain Butter was awakened at dawn by artillery fire nearby at Hatcher's Run. Only half the regiment was in camp —the other half on picket duty—but the troopers mounted quickly and rode to the sound of guns. By the time they arrived, the Federal troops in the front works had rallied and set about crushing Lee's massed infantry assault on fixed positions. The First Maine was posted to a wood, in case of another Confederate attack, which did not come. On Sunday morning, the white flag was out for the ambulances to gather the wounded and dead. Butter walked to the edge of the wood with his comrade, First Lieutenant Thad Bell. They discovered several Confederate soldiers' bodies. They had crawled here to die during the night. Bell examined their rifles, and found them jammed. There was no powder in their horns or shot in their pouches. Their bayonets were fixed. Bell said, "To the end, Amaziah?" Butter said, "Oh, hell, oh hell."

March 26, *New-York Times:* "KENNEDY'S EXECUTION—Singular Conduct of the Prisoner—Confession of His Guilt—A Full and Voluntary Statement of the Great Incendiary Plot—He Set Fire to the Museum, to Lovejoy's and Tammany Hotels and New-England House—He Dies a Death of Bravado —Terrible Scenes at the Scaffold—Our Police Vindicated and Their Theory Sustained."

In his article, George Wilson, the *Times* correspondent, included Kennedy's confession: "After my escape from Johnson's Island, I went to Canada, where I met a number of Confederates. They asked me if I was willing to go on an expedition. I replied, 'Yes, if it is in the service of my country.' They said, 'It's all right,' but gave no intimation of its nature, nor did I ask any. I was then sent to New-York, where I stayed some time. There were eight men in our party, besides me, of whom two fled to Canada. After we had been in New-York some time, we were told that the object of the expedition was to retaliate on the North for the atrocities in the Shenandoah Valley and elsewhere. . . ."

Kennedy named no names in his confession, nor did he provide any clues to the organization of the plot. He did admit his participation in the firing of several hotels, and that he had set the fire at Barnum's American Museum. He also spoke to the fact that the evidence in the court-martial was only able to link him to the fire at Barnum's, where a witness had testified he had seen Kennedy smashing a vial on the steps. Kennedy said, "I know that I am to be hanged for setting fire to Barnum's Museum, but that was only a joke. I had no idea of doing it. I had been drinking, and went in there with a friend. And just to scare the people, I emptied a bottle of phosphorus on the floor. . . ."

Kennedy's confession closed with a reiteration of his defense. "I wish to say that killing women and children was the last thing thought of. We wanted to let the people of the North understand that there are two sides to this war, and they can't be rolling in wealth and comfort while we at the South are bearing all the hardships and privations."

March 31, Near Petersburg, Virginia: The First Maine Cavalry was on the move with the whole left wing of the Army of the Potomac for the final assault on Petersburg and Richmond.

Near Dinwiddie Courthouse, twenty miles south of Petersburg and the Appomattox River, the First Maine, as part of Brigadier-General C. H. Smith's Cavalry Brigade (Sixth Ohio, Second New York Mounted Rifles, First Maine), was ordered to hold the crossing of the Great Cat Tail Creek against the vanguard of Lee's army as Lee attempted to flee Grant and escape into North Carolina.

That morning, Captain Butter, in command of a scouting battalion of six companies, was ordered out to reconnoiter across the rain-swollen creek and to find the enemy. Before noon, Butter's battalion, dismounted and walking up toward a crossroad, ran into Confederate skirmishers supported by Fitz Hugh Lee's Cavalry. The fighting was immediately hand-to-hand. The Confederates pressed ahead ferociously. Butter ordered a retreat, and was slightly wounded while recrossing the creek; however, he got his battalion back inside his own lines.

After 1 P.M., Confederate Major-General George Pickett's battle-worn division came on against General Smith's outnumbered but well-situated brigade. The terrain was piney woods, slopes and cliffs, and open rye-grass fields. The First Maine, dismounted and in a skirmishing line, met the Confederate charge firing their Henry and Spencer repeating rifles. The First Maine was forced back, but soon counterattacked up and over a slope to fix their position at the edge of a field. For the next four hours the battle was withering and chaotic but astonishingly professional—neither side showing weaknesses or inclination to break off. The First Maine twice repelled massed infantry and cavalry assaults. The open field was littered with the obliterated Fifth North Carolina Cavalry, men crying out for water or the help of a chaplain as the battle continued about them.

During the several pauses between the major assaults, the marching bands of the opposing armies dueled between themselves, one side playing "Yankee Doodle Dandy," the other playing "Dixie," the Federals replying with "Red, White, and Blue," and the Confederates responding with "Bonnie Blue Flag." The First Maine suffered one-fifth casualties, and retired after nightfall, out of ammunition.

On picket duty the next day, April 1, Butter kept his wounded foot clean, and also kept himself busy by mending his greatcoat, which had been torn in the retreat through the piney woods. He also thought to sew his money and letters into the coat. The understanding that day was that a large battle between Grant and Lee was raging nearby, but that the First Maine would not be called upon. That evening, they learned that their delaying action the day before had permitted Grant to get his infantry in place to meet Pickett's Division at Five Forks and utterly defeat him. The word was passed that Lee had now lost his last chance to get free of Grant into North Carolina, and that Lee would run. The word was also passed that Sheridan's Cavalry Corps (First, Second, Third, and Reserve Divisions—Smith's Brigade now in the Third) would be responsible for harassing Lee's retreating army west along the Appomattox River until the Federal infantry could overtake Lee and deliver the coup de grace.

APRIL 1865

April 4, *New-York Times:* "GRANT—RICHMOND AND VICTORY!—The Union Army in the Rebel Capital—Rout and Flight of the Great Rebel Army from Richmond—Jeff Davis and His Crew Driven Out—Grant in Close Pursuit of Lee's Routed Forces—Enthusiasm in the Rebel Capital—The Citizens Welcome Our Army with Demonstrations of Joy—Richmond Fired by the Enemy—Our Troops Save the City from Destruction."

Washington received news of the capture of Richmond and Petersburg on the morning of April 3. The celebration was spontaneous and hysterical. War Secretary Stanton ordered a ceremonial salute of 800 guns—500 for Richmond and 300 for Petersburg. Bands paraded along Pennsylvania Avenue playing every tune they could think of, including "Dixie," which Lincoln would later declare to be one of the spoils of war.

At the War Department, a cheering crowd gathered to demand an appearance and speech from the War Secretary. Stanton walked out onto the colonnaded entrance with 14-year-old Willie Kettles of Vermont, the operator in the telegraph room who had been on duty when Grant's telegram announcing the capture of Richmond and Petersburg had arrived, about 10 A.M. After a modest, humble speech, in which he offered thanksgiving to "Almighty God for his deliverance of the nation," Stanton brought forth Grant's telegram and waved it to the assembly. The crowd clamored for more, and Stanton read Grant's telegram describing the invasion of Richmond by the Federal troops and also communicating that Richmond was on fire in a general conflagration. The crowd roared, and Stanton asked what should be done with Richmond. The response was unanimous: "Let her burn!"

April 7, *New-York Times:* "THE REBEL ROUT—Lee's Retreat Cut Off by Sheridan—Burkesville in Our Possession—Lee's Army at Amelia Courthouse—A Junction Between Lee's Forces and Johnston's Now Impossible—Sheridan Hopes to Capture Whole Rebel Army—The Infantry Moving Rapidly to Support—General Grant at Sheridan's Headquarters."

"The Pursuit of Lee—Evidences of the Precipitous Flight of Enemy—The Roads Strewn with Arms, Caissons, and Wagons—The Rebels Fighting Without Spirit."

April 9, Near Appomattox Courthouse, Virginia: By one in the morning, Palm Sunday, what remained of General Smith's Brigade (about 1200 men) was deployed dismounted on Clover Hill, a gentle slope a half-mile from the village of Appomattox Courthouse that overlooked the main road to Lynchburg.

Smith's Brigade was now ahead of Lee's retreating caravan, and the men knew that what remained of the Army of Northern Virginia (fewer than

30,000 men) was coming down that road in a try for Lynchburg. It was here at Appomattox—rolling slopes and piney woods muddy from the rains— that Sheridan wanted Lee delayed long enough for the Fifth and Twenty- fourth Infantry Corps to overtake him.

At the First Maine's section of the line, centermost because of their repeating rifles, Lieutenant-Colonel Cilley directed the construction of makeshift works out of fence posts and dead wood. He also posted vedettes (mounted observers) down the front slope for fear of infiltration by skirm- ishers. The brigade was to spend the night in the open without fires. Every man knew that once the brigade's position was revealed at dawn, there would be an overwhelming assault.

Butter was unable to sleep, and walked down the hill with Thad Bell in order to visit with the vedettes and to listen to the Confederate supply wagons rolling in, the teamsters cursing in their exhaustion. At their large campfires, the Confederates sent up a great deal of music from mouth organs and flutes. Butter also heard psalm singing, although it was very weak and dispirited.

The First Maine was no less worn. The regiment had been riding and fighting for eight consecutive days along the Appomattox River, at Fame's Crossroads, at Sayler's Creek, at Briery Creek, at Farmville, including one ill-considered mounted assault on Lee's caravan that had resulted in heavy casualties. A third of the regiment was out of action, and those still in line numbered many walking wounded like Butter.

A vedette, Private Andersen of the old First D.C., asked Butter and Bell if Lee would attack in the morning. Bell grunted. Butter wished he could light a cigar. Private Andersen spat, and asked, "Don't Lee know he's licked, sir?" Butter laughed a little. Bell told the trooper not to talk, and to spit more quietly.

An hour before sunrise, the field artillery attached to Smith's Brigade (three-inch guns, Battery A, 2nd U.S. Artillery) opened fire on Lee's camp from Clover Hill. The Confederates reacted sluggishly and did not deploy for an assault until an hour after daybreak. By then, it was obvious that Clover Hill was being held by a single brigade. The butternut line of Confederate infantry stretched twice the length of the brigade. The butternut line came on in a walk. Confederate cavalry flanked Clover Hill to the right, and Smith's Brigade was forced back from the crest.

The First Maine, firing steadily, retreated in good order down the grade, into a wood, across a road, into a field, and toward another wood. Once, as the Confederate fire slackened, elements of the First Maine went forward again to fence posts along the road. The fighting was hand-to-hand.

By the road, Butter fired his Henry rifle deliberately, and he used his Army Colt before he reloaded his rifle. There was a moment when he thought he saw Thad Bell go down, and he jumped over to a grove. There was a Confederate officer sitting against a stump like a dead man, but he was not dead, only trying to reload his carbine with his one good arm. The Confederate officer, a captain in a filthy uniform tunic of Virginia cavalry, did not look up when Butter shouted at him. Butter knocked the carbine from the man's hand and asked him to surrender. The captain tried to get up; his beard was so caked with mud and blood that his lips seemed sealed. Butter grabbed hold of the man's tunic, yanked him halfway up, and then lost his strength and threw him back down. The captain fell on his bad arm and groaned. Butter screamed at him, "You're my prisoner, and you will please stop it!"

When Butter recovered his sense of the field, there were bluecoats running from the wood behind. The Federal infantry, despite having been forced-marched all night, advanced in a trot toward the breaking Confederate line. By chance, the colored division of the Twenty-fifth Corps had emerged from the wood right on top of the First Maine and Butter. The coats were blue, the faces were black, and the mouths were wide open howling a charge. The First Maine was ordered to retire from the field. The last Butter saw, the wounded Virginian captain was being carried back from the fire by two Negro soldiers.

That afternoon behind the lines, Butter was awakened by his first sergeant, and was told to listen. Butter immediately asked for Thad Bell and then remembered that the ambulance had taken him away. It was some minutes before Butter understood that the guns had fallen silent. There was a rumor that Lee had surrendered, or that at least there was a white flag on the field and terms were being sought. Chaplain Merrill, of the old First D.C., gathered the First Maine's remnants in prayer. The only sound to be heard above the swirling spring wind was that of men singing psalms of thanksgiving.

April 10, *New-York Times:* "HANG OUT YOUR BANNERS!—UNION—VICTORY—PEACE!—Surrender of General Lee and His Whole Army—The Work of Palm Sunday—Final Triumph of the Army of the Potomac—The

Strategy and Diplomacy of Luck—General Grant—Terms and Conditions of the Surrender—The Rebel Arms, Artillery, and Public Property Surrendered—Rebel Officers Retain Their Side-arms and Allowed to Retain Their Horses—The Stillness at Appomattox Courthouse."

April 15, Nottaway Courthouse, Virginia: At the First Maine's new bivouac at a shattered Virginia farming village midway between Appomattox and Petersburg, Butter was awakened from a nap with a surprise announcement. There was a visitor for him at brigade headquarters on the village green.

Butter thought it was one of his brothers and hurried down the road. It was Gouverneur Nevers, splendid in English clothes; he had come down from Richmond in a surrey that he had been told had once belonged to Jefferson Davis—but then, Nevers jested, Jeff Davis must have owned a herd of stallions and a fleet of carriages for all the souvenir selling of his property going on.

Nevers had been traveling for five days, searching the Federal army at rest throughout the countryside for his relatives, in order to calm the worries of his sister and in-laws in New-York. Nevers had also been searching for Butter. He had brought with him a case of champagne, a case of sweets, and a letter written by Kennedy and addressed to Oliphant care of "Mrs. Winwood, St. John's Wood, London," which Kennedy had left in Nevers's care before his execution.

Butter was delighted by the visit, and after presenting a bottle of the wine to General Smith and his staff, and distributing most of the sweets to the children loitering around the brigade kitchen, Butter and Nevers retired happily to Butter's tent. Along the way, they handed out bottles of wine to the officers of the First Maine. The general opinion in camp was that Nevers must be an agent from the Freedmen's Bureau come to start up schools, but that whatever the truth of his mysterious presence, the First Maine welcomed him, because it would never forget that Negro troops had saved the regiment at Appomattox Courthouse.

Butter was bursting with his need to argue his mind about November. However, he waited, gorging on sweets, while Nevers told of his adventures coming down from Washington. "They're still burying everywhere, and shootin' dogs to keep them from the dead."

Butter pushed aside the ghastliness of the last week of fighting, and heatedly recounted what Bridey Lamont had written him of Lafayette Baker's testimony to the Congress on the Cotton Ring. Butter reasoned that it must have been Oliphant who had been sent to New-York to negotiate for the Confederate agents in Canada, and that that was why Lafayette Baker had not permitted Butter to pursue or arrest Oliphant—so as not to compromise Baker's counterespionage.

Butter also argued that it just might be true that Oliphant had not been directly involved in the Confederate conspiracy until late in the month, and that this would explain how Oliphant could have spoken so sincerely of his affairs to Butter that day at the White House and the Capitol. Butter then confused his argument a little, conceding that perhaps Oliphant had known of everything about the conspiracy, but that he was not party to the incendiary attack until later. Or was he? Oliphant had told Captain Leonard in Niagara Falls that he had been the leader of the attack. Had he been telling the truth? And how much had Colonel Baker known about Oliphant's affairs?

Butter pounded his campaign chair and gestured north toward Washington. "Was Colonel Baker a double agent, or a triple agent? Was he working for Oliphant? Or was Oliphant working for the same men Colonel Baker was working for? And who was Colonel Baker working for? I saw Colonel Baker give you an envelope of money with Thurlow Weed's name on it, so why did Baker accuse Weed of collaborating with the agents in Canada? We were working for Colonel Baker, weren't we? Did we just stumble on Oliphant, and was that why Colonel Baker turned on me? But why did Oliphant try to surrender to us? Was he going to turn on Colonel Baker? But then why did he run from us? Do you see, Mr. Nevers? I can't figure this by myself. I mean, some of my answers make what I thought was an answer into a question again. Do you see?"

Nevers poured the wine. "It doesn't matter now. You've just won a war."

"It does matter, doesn't it? And we did, we won the war."

"We did," agreed Nevers. "So let go. You don't want to worry yourself until you ain't fit company for a stone. You're asking good questions. I can't answer them any better than you. I've got lots more myself—but I've had to learn to let things go that I'd like answered. Now you've got to. Let go. Drink up, and let go."

Butter relented after a while, and he and Nevers enjoyed their dinner watching a sublime pastel sunset. Each time Butter would try to talk about Lafayette Baker, Nevers would make him drink more wine. Nevers enter-

tained Butter by telling of Wild Jack Goodenough and Joshua Rue. The pair
were planning to sail for New Orleans; they hoped to go into either
hotelkeeping or politics—ambitions that Butter and Nevers toasted repeatedly. Butter asked after Nevers's family, and learned, as he had guessed, that
Nevers's half-brother and uncle were in that colored division at Appomattox
Courthouse. This made Butter weep a little. Butter told of his own brothers
—and how his youngest brother, Tom, had been at Appomattox that day
with the 20th Maine Infantry, and how he and Tom had enjoyed a joyful
reunion while watching Lee's army stack their weapons.

Soon enough, despite the wine, Butter drifted back to musing about
Oliphant. Butter wanted to know if Nevers thought Oliphant had escaped
from the American Falls. Nevers said that what he knew to be true was that
the body was never found in the whirlpool, not even after the spring
thaw.

Butter said, "I've worried about that. About the Cave of the Winds. We
didn't search it properly. I just had this notion that Oliphant was in the
water. You know what I mean?"

"Cap'n, he's gone, the man's gone, so let him go."

Butter complained, "But how can we know he's not at large?"

Nevers gave in to Butter's mood and sat up soberly, though he opened
another bottle of wine. After a moment, he said that a major reason for his
visit to Butter was to settle his own mind about Oliphant. And he hoped
it would settle Butter's mind as well. Nevers then related the details of
Kennedy's arrest, trial, and execution. He placed Kennedy's letter to Oliphant on the table.

Nevers said, "Kennedy gave me this. He wouldn't admit to anything,
even after I told him what I knew about Oliphant and the Falls. He just
said this was for Oliphant." Nevers broke off, and relaxed in his seat.
When he began again, he was speaking carefully. "Oliphant is gone, and
this letter proves it as much as it can be proved. Kennedy and Oliphant
were friends that die for one another. If Oliphant was alive, he would've
come forward to help Kennedy. There's a photograph, and some hair,
and a farewell note to Oliphant. Sure, I read it. Misery, pure misery.
They hanged that fellow out of meanness, while the rascals got scot
free. And big rascals. You read this, if you can, and you'll see. You
send it on to Oliphant's ladies. It's a eulogy for two sad men. Lord Almighty, Cap'n, there's enough sadness in this war for a new book of the
Bible."

Butter picked up the letter. "All right. Oliphant would have come forward—if he had known."

The next morning, Easter Sunday, Nevers was seated in Butter's tent on what should have been Thad Bell's bunk, and he was drinking coffee when Butter came in. There were tears in Butter's eyes.

Butter said, "They've killed Mr. Lincoln. I just heard. He's dead. A galloper just came in and told us. They shot him Friday night in Washington. My dear God, they've killed my president."

Nevers put down his cup and folded his hands.

Butter said, "Is it Oliphant, Mr. Nevers? I can't believe it's Oliphant. Please, God, it can't be Oliphant."

Nevers said, "No, rest yourself, it ain't Oliphant. It might be them in Canada, though. Them he was working for."

Butter said, "The galloper said it might be Wilkes Booth, the actor. He was there the night of the attack, do you remember? At the Winter Garden Theater with his brothers. The Booth brothers. They wrote them up in the papers for how they stopped the panic in the Winter Garden. Booth? Can it be Wilkes Booth?"

Nevers stood and reached for his coat. "I'll be going back now, Cap'n. It might be them in Canada too, and I've got work to do."

Later that morning, after Nevers had departed, Butter joined the First Maine at Easter Services in a glen. Chaplain Merrill started his sermon but could not continue for his weeping. The First Maine turned to psalm singing, and then tried, "Nearer My God to Thee."

April 25, *New-York Times:* "THE OBSEQUIES—President Lincoln's Murder Planned in Canada—One of the Seward Assassins a St. Albans Raider—Official Day of Mourning Appointed—Progress of the Funeral Cortege from Philadelphia—Demonstrations of the People of New Jersey—Reception of the Remains in the City—Arrival at the City Hall—Immense Turn-Out of the People—Appearance of the Corpse—Forty Thousand Persons Visit the Hall Up to 2 A.M.—Order by Secretary of War—The Murder of the President Planned in Canada."

Stanton's telegram on the progress of the investigation of the assassination was reproduced: "To General Dix, Commanding, Department of the East. This department has information that the President's murder was organized in Canada and approved in Richmond. One of the assassins, now in prison, is believed to be one of the St. Albans raiders. Edwin M. Stanton, Secretary of War."

April 28, *New-York Times:* "BOOTH KILLED—Full Account of the Particulars and Its Results—He Is Traced into St. Mary's County Maryland—Herold and Booth Discovered in a Barn—Booth Declared He Will Not Be Taken Alive—The Barn Set Fire to Force Them Out—Sergt. Boston Corbett Fires at Booth—He Is Shot Through the Neck and Dies in Three Hours—His Body Brought to Washington."

John Wilkes Booth died slowly over three hours, his body paralyzed below the shoulders. His last words were, "Tell mother I died for my country. I thought I did for the best." In Booth's possession were a diary, two six-shooters, a blood-stained dagger, and a bank draft for sixty English pounds drawn the previous October from the Bank of Ontario in Montreal.

War Secretary Stanton had turned over the pursuit of Booth to Colonel Lafayette Baker and the Secret Service. For the duty, Baker employed the single company of cavalry still attached to the Secret Service, commanded by two officers of the old First D.C., Lieutenant-Colonel E. J. Conger and Lafayette Baker's cousin, Lieutenant Byron Baker.

Booth's body was transported back to the Washington Navy Yard on the steam tug *John S. Ide;* it was transferred to the deck of the gunboat *Saugatuck.* Lafayette Baker was on hand in order to have the corpse identified by surgeons. Baker had the doctors cut out the section of Booth's spine that the fatal shot had severed (the opinion was that Booth had killed himself), and Baker kept it as evidence.

Lafayette Baker posted a guard over the body and returned to his headquarters to rest and to change his clothes for the first time in two weeks—since he had been called back from New-York after Lincoln's murder.

Later, Lafayette Baker visited Stanton at the War Department. Stanton congratulated Baker and presented him with a brigadier-general's star in reward. Stanton also said that it would be difficult getting Baker's promotion through Congress. (Indeed, Baker's promotion would never be approved, nor would he be granted more than a nominal share of the bounty money Congress voted for Booth's capture. And within a year, Lafayette Baker would be driven from his office by his enemies in the government, who included President Johnson. Lafayette Baker died of meningitis, ignominiously and in debt, in 1868, after self-publishing a memoir, *History of the*

United States Secret Service, that he hoped would vindicate him.)

Lafayette Baker returned to the Navy Yard that same night, April 27. On the *Saugatuck,* he discovered that thrill-seekers had gathered around Booth's corpse, and that a woman was cutting off locks of Booth's hair. Baker wrestled with the woman for the hair, and ordered the deck cleared.

At midnight, Lafayette Baker and his cousin Lieutenant Byron Baker lowered Booth's corpse into a rowboat and set out across the Potomac River. They were followed along the shore by a crowd of Southern partisans, and they had to pull hard into the mist to escape observation.

They crossed from the Navy Yard to the Maryland shore at Geesborough Point. There, they carried the corpse through a hole cut in the masonry of the wharf. They passed into a secret dungeon beneath the Cavalry Depot and buried Booth in a shallow grave inside a cell. When they were through, Lafayette Baker locked the door behind him, and he kept the key.

May 4, *New-York Times:* "THE ASSASSINS—Important Proclamation by President Johnson—Mr. Lincoln's Murder Planned by Leading Traitors— Most of the Traitors Are Harbored in Canada—Jefferson Davis Is Head of Assassins—He Is Aided by Jacob Thompson, Clement C. Clay, Beverley Tucker, and George N. Sanders—One Hundred Thousand Dollars Reward for Davis—Twenty-Five Thousand Each the Others—Ten Thousand for Wm. C. Cleary, Mr. Clay's Clerk—A Description of the Conspirators to Be Published."

At the trial against those who allegedly conspired in close concert with John Wilkes Booth, the Federal prosecutor, Judge-Advocate-General Joseph P. Holt, elicited voluminous testimony from witnesses in an attempt to establish that Booth had murdered Lincoln, and David Herold had stabbed Seward, under the command of the Confederate commissioners in Canada.

There was also testimony regarding other Confederate Secret Service schemes, such as an attempt in the summer of 1864 to transport into Washington a warehouseful of blankets supposedly infected with yellow fever.

The trial lasted through May and June, and ended with the execution of four conspirators and the imprisonment of four other conspirators. Also in late May, Jefferson Davis was captured in Georgia and placed in prison pending his prosecution for alleged crimes, including his role in the Lincoln assassination.

However, much of the testimony in the trial against the Confederate commissioners in Canada, and Jefferson Davis, would later be proved to have been either contrived or perjured.

Jefferson Davis would spend over a year in jail, but would never be brought to trial. Jacob P. Thompson, Beverley Tucker, and George Sanders fled to Europe, but later returned to America. They were never arrested.

The pardon issued in May by President Johnson to those who had participated in the rebellion excepted those men who had acted as spies or agents in Canada. Nevertheless, after the war, no member of the Confederate Secret Service would ever be brought to trial for his or her actions.

Moreover, there would never be presented or revealed or discovered any trustworthy or unambiguous or credible evidence that John Wilkes Booth, David Herold, and the seven others prosecuted in the conspiracy trial had acted at the behest of, or with the complicity of, or with the approval of the Confederate government, *or any other persons.*

May 8, *London Times:* "On the 28 April inst., at St. James' Church, Piccadilly, by the Rev. John Oakley, assisted by the Rev. Richard Blondel, nephew to the groom, Brig.-Gen. Sir Henry Blondel, K.C.B., Bengal Infantry (retired), to Narcissa, widow of the late Brig.-Gen. V. H. Winwood, C.S.A., and eldest daughter of the late J. Granby Royall, Esq., of Beaufort, South Carolina. No cards."

May 20, Washington City: Over the next week the victorious Federal armies were scheduled to parade down Pennsylvania Avenue from the Capitol building to the White House to pass in review before the president, General Grant, and other dignitaries in stands constructed in Lafayette Park.

On the weekend before the grand parade, Major Amaziah Butter (brevetted for his part in the battle at Appomattox Courthouse like other officers of Smith's Brigade) departed the new regimental bivouac at Ettrick, Virginia, and traveled on the cars to Washington. Because the First Maine Cavalry had not been designated to march in the review with the Army of the Potomac, Butter had volunteered to go to Washington to present the regards of both the First Maine and the old First D.C. to President Johnson.

Butter called at the White House, and then proceeded on to Bridey Lamont's apartment. The first hour of the reunion was subdued, but soon enough Butter found the sort of passion a soldier associated with the love of a woman. Bridey Lamont was heated, melancholy, capricious, resolute, talkative, and evasive—clothed or unclothed; and Butter, in his turn, matched her moods and desires.

By Sunday, after church, they were effortless companions again, and celebrated with a picnic by the burnt-out shell of the Smithsonian along with Vera Lamont and the two children. The weather was hot and lush. Washington was joyous and overflowing with officers on leave with their ladies, and with the encampment of several whole corps of troops awaiting the parade.

Monday evening, because Bridey Lamont was a close friend of the manager's niece, she and Butter were able to secure a table for supper at Willard's Hotel. The room was packed with dignitaries and diplomats, who were spouting fantastic toasts of devotion to "The United States *Again* of America." Butter and Bridey Lamont drank too much wine like everyone else. It was a time for heroes and heroines, and the balmy night was noisy with satisfaction. Butter and Bridey Lamont joined the impromptu waltzing throughout the lobby and parlors and out onto the sidewalk. Butter opined that he might be in heaven, and only once was pulled down, when, back in the dining room, a naval officer rose to toast absent friends. Butter wept, and Bridey Lamont held him, as the assembly sang "The Battle Hymn of the Republic."

The Grand Review of the armies began at nine o'clock sharp, Tuesday morning, May 23. Commanding the Army of the Potomac, Major-General George Meade, tall and arrogant in the saddle, led his staff in the vanguard from the assembly area at the foot of Capitol Hill. Because of the early hour, and the late night celebrating, neither the president and his entourage nor General Grant and his were in the reviewing stands when General Meade passed by.

However, everyone was prepared with their coffee and cakes by the time the Cavalry Corps trotted by. Major-General George A. Custer, leading the cavalry, provided unusual entertainment when his horse bolted in surprise when a young admirer tried to hand up flowers. Elements of General Capehart's Second Cavalry Division and General Devin's First followed. And then came the drumbeats and brass horns of the infantry.

Butter and the Lamonts had available to them excellent seats for the show from the window of W. D. Lamont & Brother. Yet Major Torrance Wetherbee insisted that they go outside. Wetherbee had joined them that morning from hospital (he claimed he had escaped), and was too excited to be controlled. Butter finally agreed with Wetherbee that it was wrong to make young David Lamont miss out on the feel of an armada of men and horses going by, perhaps for the last time; and so the whole party, and Rufus reluctantly, removed to the sidewalk at West Eleventh Street.

By noon, it was a roasting, band-playing day. Butter, Bridey, Vera, and Wetherbee took turns carrying out the children to present flowers to the marchers. The vendors on the sidewalk did a gold mine's worth of business selling beer and peanuts. And the Sanitary Commission ladies were pressed to provide enough water, tea, and cold salted potatoes to the overheated soldiers. No one complained, being too distracted by the singing and the cheering.

Butter was rewarded for hours of patience when, mid-afternoon, his younger brother Calvin rode by with his battery. Butter was not as discreet as he might have been about the Lamonts when he dragged Cal over to show him off to Wetherbee. Cal did not ask about Bridey, but as he rode off, Butter could see that he was frowning.

On Wednesday, May 24, the Grand Review continued, this time with Major-General Sherman's army, fresh from its victory over Joe Johnston and the Army of Tennessee in North Carolina, the last significant Confederate army in the East.

There was an obvious and severe contrast between Meade's gold-buttoned Army of the Potomac and the casually colorful Western men who marched behind Sherman. Also, the crowd along Pennsylvania Avenue was noticeably divided about the conquerors of Atlanta, Savannah, Charleston, Columbia, and Goldsboro. While the majority cheered for their heroes, there was an angry minority of Southern partisans who screamed along the curb, "Murderers!" "Blackguards!" "God will punish you!"

That evening, Butter was able to find not only his brother Cal but also his brother Augustus at a camp on the outskirts of the District. The three shared supper and wrote a joint letter to their brother Tom still stationed in Virginia. They talked of home eagerly. And it was not until Butter was on the ride back to the Lamonts that he realized that Gus and Cal had been trying to warn him from his infidelity in a fraternally roundabout way.

Butter delayed his departure back to Virginia through Thursday and the Grand Review of the Sixth Corps, and even through Friday and the renewed celebration for the news of the surrender in Texas of the last Confederate army. By Saturday, though, Butter knew it was time to go, particularly because he carried letters of tribute to the First Maine from the president and Congress for the fight at Appomattox Courthouse.

Butter left the Lamonts and Wetherbee after breakfast. Bridey Lamont accompanied him down Pennsylvania Avenue on his way to catch the ferry at the Navy Yard. They speculated about the future for W. D. Lamont & Brother, because business was vigorous in men's frock coats and lady's bonnets, so much so that Bridey said that she would be leaving government service soon to help with the shop. They touched upon Tory Wetherbee, and Vera Lamont's unreturned affection for him. They laughed about Bridey's children, and David's need for a companion like Rufus, and Maude's need for a tether.

They also talked of the beautiful morning, and of the much-needed cleanup of the city, and of how stunning and permanent the Capitol building looked with the sunlight reflecting off its whitewash. They talked about everything they could think of but what was right in front of them—that they did not know what to say or do about their love.

They climbed Capitol Hill and stopped very near to the same vantage where they had stood with Oliphant, Wild Jack, and Joshua Rue six months before. They turned to admire Washington City, baking and dust-making under a generous sky.

Butter was still trying to avoid the fact that he had to go; he started idly, "Gouverneur Nevers said that Oliphant is gone."

"It's terribly sad, Amaziah, that his wife will never know what happened to his body. I would have liked to have had David's body. It would have meant a great deal."

"I don't know, I don't. I sometimes think he got away. I dream about it even. It bothers me."

Bridey sounded perplexed. "Don't do this to yourself. Listen to Gouverneur Nevers."

"But what if he got away? What if he hid in that cave, and got clean away?"

Bridey shook her head. "Stop this. Have pity on him. He wasn't a bad man."

"How can you say he wasn't bad, after what he tried?"

"I know. But I also know that he wasn't bad. He tried to tell us that day that he was caught up in something awful, and he couldn't stop. He tried to tell us about the sort of choices we all have to make sometimes when we don't want to. I have to believe that he made the choices he could."

Butter raised his voice. "He chose wrong, Bridey, I do believe that!" Butter hesitated. Why was he shouting at her? He finished his thought flatly. "I've thought on it and thought on it."

"Oh, Amaziah, you can be so sure of things. It's your strength, but it's also overbearing at times. We aren't all like you—sure of things."

"But, Bridey, he was in with those who killed the president."

"You don't know that, and you can't prove it!" Bridey was suddenly angry. "And you will never heal from this war if you don't decide right now that you must forgive them just like they must forgive us. And it is not worthy of you to blame John Oliphant. I've let you joke about Macbeth and Oliphant. But that must stop. John Oliphant wasn't Macbeth, and Mrs. Winwood wasn't Lady Macbeth either. They lost everything, Amaziah, everything."

Butter nodded, and looked down. "I'm sorry, Bridey, I apologize. That was stupid of me, and cruel. I guess I feel guilty too. I killed Oliphant. I chased him into that river."

Bridey brushed Butter's arm in sympathy. "No, you didn't, and talking like that won't help you either."

Butter asked, "Why are we arguing?"

"Because I love you," she said.

"And I love you," he said. "So why?"

"We have to try and see as others do, Amaziah. We have to try. We have to."

Butter wanted to embrace her, but she was holding herself back. He asked, "What do you mean, Bridey? See as others do?"

"I mean that we are arguing because we have been selfish, and we know it. And now we have to stop and see us as others see us—Major Butter and Mrs. Lamont."

"We weren't really fighting about Oliphant?"

"No, not really," she said.

Butter sighed. "Do you think what we've done is wrong?"

"No, I don't." And now she moved closer to Butter, and said, "But I do think we now have to do what is right."

"What's right, Bridey? To stay with you and forget home? To leave and forget you? I'm not right no matter what I do. I feel like everything I've done is upside down. How can I choose?"

"You have to," said Bridey.

Butter laughed in frustration, and he felt miserable; he said, "I've done my duty, and I guess I'm going to do it again, but not because I want to. Because I have to."

Bridey leaned against Butter's chest and put her hands up to his shoulders; she was whispering, "My David talked like that, before he left me. Brave talk. And now it's no comfort, it's nothing at all."

JUNE AND JULY 1865

July 2, Bangor, Maine: In the last week of June, three hundred and fifty troopers and five officers of the First Maine Cavalry were mustered out of the Volunteer Army, Major Butter among them.

Butter had considered staying on in Ettrick as an officer in the Freedmen's Bureau, in order to remain close to Washington City. As June had passed hot and quiet in Virginia, however, Butter had reassessed his future. He had not heard from Bridey since leaving her in May. And when his appeal to her by telegram had gone unanswered, and when his second appeal to her via Wetherbee at the War Wagon had elicited from Wetherbee an enigmatic, "Go home. Or Mexico?", Butter had accepted the obvious. He had folded his tent.

He was the first of the Butter brothers to arrive home. He did enjoy the tumult he caused on Sunday, July 2, when, still ragged from five days of transit, he went directly from the depot into services at the First Congregational Church to take his place in the Butter family pew. The Butters sang together and squirmed. Butter did let his two sons sit on his knees. And Chip Butter did hand his son a hymnal, but then he must have been so flustered that he forgot that he had, because he passed his son another one soon after. Finally, the pastor took pity, and before he began the sermon, he stopped, leaned down from the pulpit, and said, "Go on now, you Butters, hug him!"

The reception that followed that afternoon was tearful and ebullient. The neighborhood boys gathered in the rose garden of Chip Butter's State Street house to glimpse the hero of Appomattox Courthouse. Bangor, a Puritan's boom town at the T-square of the slim Kenduskeag stream and the broad Penobscot River, was growing accustomed to welcoming its sons home with protracted celebrations. So that night, Butter stood with his father and uncles at the gazebo in the garden and listened to the reports of who had come home wholly safe, or disabled, or in a coffin, or not at all. Butter also heard what

Bangor wanted for its soldiers—the best, the very best, for the bravest of the brave. Soon, the whiskey and beer and bright starry night moved the assembled to demand from Butter what he realized would be the beginning of a lifetime of war stories. This night, however, Butter felt disoriented by the long day, and wanted to end it, and so he found that he had something very blunt to say: "The Rebs fought very well, and they never quit." There was protest from the gathering; one man said, "They surrendered, son, we whipped 'em." Butter tried again. "That's what they told me—but I'm telling you, I never saw Johnny Reb quit."

Throughout that first day, Desire was openly glad and attentive. She did not try to get Butter alone, though, and she shared him with all who approached. Also, she did not speak of their estrangement, even in passing, and later, after the party, as they walked to their home off State Street (the white salt-box Butter had been raised in), Desire had held her husband's hand and told stories about their sons. Desire was thinner than Butter remembered her, and somehow more content. That night, and the next, she lay next to Butter without touching him intimately. And Butter understood that it was best that he not turn to her. She fell asleep both nights while listening to his anecdotes heap upon each other, and agreeing with all his observations. Desire's newfound patience did not make her any less forthright; she did manage to communicate that she wanted Butter to take her on a fishing holiday soon, and also that she had been thinking of another child, maybe a daughter, because one woman was not enough to care for two sons and a hero.

All Bangor turned out in bliss and great expectation for the Independence Day celebration on July 4. Butter watched the fireworks and tried not to think of Petersburg. Afterward, Butter declined his father's invitation to come up to the house for another party. Butter had calmed down to the point that he wanted to go home early with his wife and children. They crowded into their carriage and rode home singing songs. While Desire put the boys to bed, Butter busied himself preparing his surprise. He took off his uniform and dressed in the new brown frock coat and black trousers that his mother had purchased for him. The clothes were a little baggy because of the weight he had lost, but he thought he looked as fashionable as he ever had, his beard trimmed and his linen shimmering in the gaslight.

When Desire came down, she startled at his display, and then she kissed him on the cheek and went into the kitchen. Butter called to her that he would like some tea. Desire came out quickly, pressed a letter into his hand,

and withdrew to the bedroom without explanation. She said, "Goodnight, my husband."

The letter was from Bridey. It was dated over two weeks before. Butter went outside to the stable to read it by lamplight with the horses and cats.

Bridey wrote of her children, and her store, and that Tory Wetherbee had left for Texas as part of Sheridan's command being posted along the Mexican border. She quoted Wetherbee, "We old soldiers aim to show those French-ers the flag, the line, and the door."

Bridey also wrote about their love affair. She said that she would always treasure their friendship as the only good part of the war for her. She also said that if she and Butter should ever meet again, it must only be as dear friends. She wrote that she would always be fond of him, and would always think of him in the fall, when the leaves turned and the earth was a many-colored and comforting blanket for the winter coming on.

There was an enclosure. It was a clipping from the *London Times,* dated May 8, that announced the marriage of Mrs. Narcissa Winwood to Henry Blondel in London. Bridey had written across the paragraph, "A new beginning."

Butter read the clipping again and again. Something had always nagged at him about Oliphant's relationship with his sister-in-law. After all, Butter had two sisters-in-law, and he was not moved to be as close to them as Oliphant had seemed to Mrs. Winwood. But then again, there had been the war. Butter decided that he could not make any more sense of it now than before. He wanted to be glad for Mrs. Winwood. It did not come. Instead, oddly, he felt sad for John Oliphant.

The next morning, Butter awoke with Desire's arms folded about his side. He stirred her awake gently, and without a word between them, but with urgency, they made love for the first time in nearly a year. After, Butter dressed and wandered to his desk in the front parlor. Desire was in the kitchen with the boys, and they were laughing. Butter wanted to join them, but could not. He also wanted to write Bridey, but could not, not this day.

When Desire called breakfast, Butter asked for a slight delay. He dug into his kit bag and got out his logbook. He did have letters to mail, if not one of his own. He pulled out Kennedy's letter to Oliphant and the two letters that Oliphant had left for him at Niagara Falls. He had not known what he should do with his charge as a postman until this morning, and suddenly it seemed as straightforward and simple a thing as life. The war was finished. He was home. There was peacefulness. There was also forgiveness. Butter thought, I can forgive you, John Oliphant, if you can forgive me.

After breakfast, Butter took Desire's mare and trotted down State Street to the post office. The postal clerk knew Butter, and asked in surprise whom Butter knew in St. John's Wood, London. Butter said, "The people of a man I knew—in the war."

On his return up State Street, Butter paused on the bridge over the Kenduskeag. He wanted to admire the busy beauty of a cloudless hot Thursday morning in Maine. The barges hereabout, the market below him on the floats, the masts of the schooners on the Penobscot just to the east, the already growling timber saws in the yards, and the feverish traffic on the riverfronts, all this combined to persuade Butter that Bangor was launched into its future with an incautious, unyielding momentum. He had teased himself, and Bridey, about entering politics, and about perhaps returning to Capitol Hill as a congressman. But now he could see that this vision was not credible. He could see that his destiny was here in a forest that was boundless and with a people who were tireless and alongside a wife who had loved him enough to have risked losing him three times, and had still held on, and was still willing to welcome him back, and to continue. He could also see that whatever was to come, he could thank God Almighty right now that there was a whole lot of trouble well behind.

Butter headed the mare up State Street, thinking of his brothers and their imminent arrivals, and of the news that Thad Bell was finally coming home from hospital, a little stiff, but whole. He was also thinking that it would be fun to plan a truly grand party for the veterans of what was already being called wistfully the Grand Army of the Republic.

Butter had not gone far up the road, though, when he turned back once more, in the direction of the Penobscot's current, south, toward New-York and Washington. He tied off the reins, relit his cigar, took out Bridey's letter from his frock coat, and read it again from the end to the front.

He could hear in her words the same voice, and the same passion, that had argued with him that last hot morning in May on Capitol Hill. Butter sighed, because he could also hear her last question to him.

Butter had said, "What? What is it, Bridey?"

And Bridey had said, "Oh, Amaziah, what is to become of us all?"

DRAMATIS PERSONAE

The United States of America

PRESIDENT: Abraham Lincoln of Illinois

FIRST LADY: Mary Todd Lincoln of Illinois

VICE-PRESIDENT: Hannibal Hamlin· of Maine; later Andrew Johnson of Tennessee

STATE DEPARTMENT: William H. Seward of New York, *Secretary;* Frederick W. Seward, *Assistant Secretary;* Charles Adams, *Ambassador to Great Britain;* J. Q. Howard, *Consul at St. John's, New Brunswick*

ATTORNEY GENERAL: Edward Bates of Missouri

NAVY DEPARTMENT: Gideon Welles of Connecticut, *Secretary;* Gustavus V. Fox, *Assistant Secretary*

WAR DEPARTMENT: Edwin M. Stanton of Pennsylvania, *Secretary;* Charles Dana, *Assistant Secretary;* Maj.-Gen. Joseph P. Holt, *Judge-Advocate-General;* Maj. Levi Turner, *Assistant-Judge-Advocate-General;* Maj.-Gen. James B. Fry, *Provost-Marshal-General*

ARMY: Lt.-Gen. Ulysses S. Grant, *General-in-Chief;* Maj.-Gen. Henry W. Halleck, *Chief-of-Staff;* Maj.-Gen. George Meade, *Army of the Potomac;* Maj.-Gen. Benjamin F. Butler, *Army of the James;* Maj.-Gen. William T. Sherman, *Military Division of the Mississippi;* Maj.-Gen. Philip Sheridan, *Cavalry Corps, Army of the Potomac;* Maj.-Gen. George B. McClellan, *formerly General-in-Chief and Army of the Potomac;* Maj.-Gen. Ambrose Burnside, *formerly Army of the Potomac;* Maj.-Gen. Joseph Hooker, *formerly Army of the Potomac;*

Maj.-Gen. Winfield Scott, *formerly General-in-Chief;* Maj.-Gen. John A. Dix, *Department of the East;* Maj.-Gen. John Pope, *Department of the Northwest*

SECRET SERVICE: Col. Lafayette C. Baker, *Chief;* William P. Wood, *Superintendent of Old Capitol Prison;* Usher Skelton, *Chief Clerk;* Mrs. Bridey Lamont, *Recording Clerk;* Milo Baker, Calvin Baker, Edgar Quillermouth, Bob Dailey, *Detectives;* Capt. Amaziah Butter, *First D.C. Cavalry and later First Maine Cavalry;* Job "White-Pine" Mills, Lo' Josh, *Attendants*

DEPARTMENT OF THE EAST: Maj.-Gen. John A. Dix, *Commanding;* Gouverneur Nevers, Virginia John "Wild Jack" Goodenough, Joshua Rue, Walter Daggett, Louie Delta, *Detectives;* Lt.-Col. Burke, *Commandant of Fort Lafayette;* Eisen, *Supervisor of Executions*

NEW YORK STATE: Horatio Seymour, *Governor;* later Reuben Fenton, *Governor;* Brig.-Gen. Green, *Militia Commander*

NEW-YORK CITY: George Opdyke, *Mayor;* W. Acton, *President of the City Council;* John Kennedy, *Superintendent of Police*

NEW-YORK PASTORS: Reverend Henry Ward Beecher, *Pilgrim Congregational Church;* Reverend J. P. Thompson, *Broadway Tabernacle;* Reverend Burke, *Chaplain of Fort Lafayette*

CONGRESS: Senator Charles Sumner, *Republican of Massachusetts;* Representative Elihu Washburne, *Republican of Illinois;* Representative Fernando Wood, *Democrat of New York*

ADVISERS TO PRESIDENT LINCOLN: Leonard Swett; Ward Lamon

OTHER GOVERNORS: Samuel Cony, *Republican of Maine;* J. Gregory Smith, *Republican of Vermont;* Thomas Seymour, *Democrat of Connecticut*

REPUBLICAN PARTY: President Abraham Lincoln, *Presidential Nominee;* Andrew Johnson, *Military Governor of Tennessee and Vice-Presidential Nominee;* Thurlow Weed, *Leader of New York Republican Party;* Simeon Draper, *Collector of Customs of the Port of New-York;* A. B. Durant

DEMOCRATIC PARTY: Maj.-Gen. George B. McClellan, *Presidential Nominee;* Representative George Pendleton, *Democrat of Ohio and Vice-Presidential Nominee*

FIRST DISTRICT OF COLUMBIA CAVALRY: Col. Lafayette C. Baker; Lt.-Col. E. J. Conger; Major Stannard Baker; Major Torrance Wetherbee; Capt. Amaziah Butter; Lt. Byron Baker

FIRST MAINE CAVALRY: Col. G. H. Smith, later Brig.-Gen.; Lt.-Col. J. P. Cilley; Lt. Thad Bell

MAJ.-GEN. BUTLER'S STAFF: Brig.-Gen. George Gordon, *Acting Chief-of-Staff;* Maj. Peter Haggerty, *Acting-Judge-Advocate-General and Senior A.D.C.;* Capt. Alfred Puffer, *Acting-Assistant-Judge-Advocate-General*

FEDERAL GARRISON AT NIAGARA FALLS, NEW YORK: Capt. Christian Ferry; Capt. Leonard; Capt. Portbellow; Lt. Pennypacker; Lt. Severance; First Sgt. Pinckney; Sgt. Newell; Cpl. Tobie

CITIZENS OF NIAGARA FALLS, NEW-YORK: Redman Briggs; Eleazer Jordan; Otis Maple; Deputy Sheriff Faulkner; Mr. McDowell

THE BUTTERS OF BANGOR, MAINE: Chisholm "Chip" Butter and Mrs. Louise Butter; Capt. Amaziah Butter, *First D.C./First Maine and Secret Service,* and Mrs. Desire Drummond Butter; Capt. Augustus Butter, *17th Maine Infantry;* Lt. Calvin Butter, *First Mounted Regiment, Sixth Maine Battery;* Lt. Thomas Butter, *20th Maine Infantry*

THE LAMONTS OF WASHINGTON, D.C.: W. D. Lamont (d. 1861); Maj. David Lamont (d. 1862); Mrs. Bridey Lamont; Miss Vera Lamont; David and Maude Lamont

The Confederate States of America

PRESIDENT: Jefferson Davis of Mississippi

VICE-PRESIDENT: Alexander H. Stephens of Georgia

STATE DEPARTMENT: Judah P. Benjamin of Louisiana, *Secretary*

WAR DEPARTMENT: James Seddon of Virginia, *Secretary*

NAVY DEPARTMENT: Stephen Mallory of Florida, *Secretary*

ARMY: Maj.-Gen. Robert E. Lee, *Army of Northern Virginia, later, General-in-Chief;* Maj.-Gen. T. J. "Stonewall" Jackson, *Army of the Shenandoah Valley* (d. 1863); Maj.-Gen. J. E. B. Stuart, *Cavalry, Army of Northern Virginia* (d. 1864); Maj.-Gen. Jubal A. Early, *Army of the Shenandoah Valley;* Maj.-Gen.

Albert S. Johnston, *Army of Tennessee* (d. 1862); Maj.-Gen. Joseph E. John-ston, *Army of Tennessee;* Maj.-Gen. John B. Hood, *Army of Tennessee;* Maj.-Gen. W. J. Hardee, *Army of Tennessee;* Maj.-Gen. John Hunt Morgan (d. 1864); Brig.-Gen. V.H. Winwood (d. 1864); Lt.-Col. John Singleton Mosby, *43rd Battalion*

SECRET SERVICE, IN EUROPE: James M. Mason, *Commissioner to Great Britain;* John Slidell, *Commissioner to France;* John Cross Oliphant, Mrs. Narcissa Royall Winwood, *Agents*

SECRET SERVICE, IN CANADA: Jacob P. Thompson, *Commissioner to Canada at Toronto;* Clement C. Clay, James Holcombe, *Commissioners to Canada at Montreal;* George N. Sanders, Beverley Tucker, Capt. Thomas B. Hines, *Agents;* Capt. John Yates Beall, Lt. Bennett Young, Capt. William Collins, Kevin Phillips, Francis Jones, Lt.-Col. Robert Martin, Lt. John Headley, Lt. John Ashbrook, Lt. James Harrington, Lt. James Chenault, Lt. John Price, Lt. Timothy Cook, Lt. Leslie Dennis, Capt. Robert Cobb Kennedy, *Special Service Agents*

SECRET SERVICE, IN NEW-YORK: Capt. W. A. Longuemare, *Agent,* and Mrs. Dorothea Longuemare

SONS OF LIBERTY: Clement Vallandigham, *Supreme Commander;* Representa-tive Fernando Wood, *Commander;* W. Larry MacDonald, Augustus Mac-Donald, Barney MacDonald, Katie MacDonald

THE ROYALLS OF BEAUFORT, SOUTH CAROLINA: J. Granby Royall (d. 1864) and Mrs. Mary Talbird Royall (d. 1840) and Mrs. Pamela Tempest Royall; Mrs. Narcissa Royall Winwood and Brig.-Gen. Venable Hawkes Winwood (d. 1864); Col. John Granby Royall (d. 1864) and Mrs. Elizabeth De Treville Royall; Capt. Talbird Royall (d. 1862) and Mrs. Sally Peniclair Royall; Mrs. Camellia Royall Oliphant and John Cross Oliphant; Mrs. Laura Royall Rogers and Capt. Lucas Rogers (d. 1864); Sophy and Mary Winwood; Ensign Harry Royall (d. 1864) and Phillip Royall (d. 1862); Alice, Mary, and Faith Oliphant; Rosemary, Noah, Michael, Jimmie, Jinna, Cato, Nell, *Slaves*

NONPARTISANS: Sir Henry Blondel; Isaac Keats, *British Secret Service;* Capt. Maximillian Millerand, Capt. Paul Fresque, Ensign Jongleur, *French Secret Service;* Edmund Homes; Franny Wooster

CALENDAR OF THE CIVIL WAR

1860

NOVEMBER. Abraham Lincoln was elected president of the United States of America.

DECEMBER. South Carolina seceded from the Union; it was later joined by Alabama, Arkansas, Florida, Georgia, Louisiana, Mississippi, Texas, Tennessee, North Carolina, and Virginia.

1861

FEBRUARY. Jefferson Davis, formerly U.S. Senator from Mississippi, was elected the provisional president of the Confederate States of America; Alexander H. Stephens, formerly U.S. Senator from Georgia, was elected provisional vice-president.

MARCH. Abraham Lincoln was inaugurated president of the United States of America.

APRIL. At Charleston, Confederate forces fired on and captured United States Fort Sumter in Charleston Harbor. In Washington City, Lincoln called for volunteers to suppress the insurrection; he also ordered the blockade of all Confederate ports and suspended habeas corpus from Philadelphia to Washington.

JULY. Confederate forces defeated Federal forces in Virginia at the First Battle of Bull Run. Maj.-Gen. George B. McClellan was given command of the Federal Army of the Potomac. Ulysses S. Grant was appointed a general of U.S. Volunteers.

NOVEMBER. Combined elements of the Federal Navy and Army invaded and captured Port Royal Sound and Beaufort, South Carolina. George B. McClellan was appointed general-in-chief of the U.S. Army. Confederate emissaries James Mason and John Slidell were forcibly taken from a Europe-bound English ship, *Trent,* by the U.S. Navy; they were eventually imprisoned at Boston.

DECEMBER. After a severe diplomatic crisis called the Trent Affair that bordered on war between Great Britain and the United States, Mason and Slidell were permitted to continue their journey to Europe.

1862

JANUARY. Edwin M. Stanton was appointed U.S. secretary of war. Soon after, Stanton appointed Lafayette C. Baker as chief of the United States Secret Service.

FEBRUARY. In the first significant Federal victory, forces under Grant captured Fort Donelson and Fort Henry in Tennessee.

MARCH. Judah P. Benjamin, formerly U.S. Senator from Louisiana, was appointed Confederate secretary of state.

APRIL. Federal forces under Grant defeated Confederate forces at the Battle of Shiloh in Tennessee.

JUNE. McClellan's Army of the Potomac failed to capture Richmond and withdrew after the Seven Days' Campaign in Virginia.

AUGUST. Confederate forces under Maj.-Gen. T. E. "Stonewall" Jackson defeated Federal forces at the Second Battle of Bull Run in Virginia.

SEPTEMBER. Maj.-Gen. Robert E. Lee's Army of Northern Virginia invaded the North through the Shenandoah Valley. McClellan's Army of the Potomac stopped Lee's advance at the Battle of Antietam (also called Sharpsburg) in Pennsylvania.

NOVEMBER. McClellan was relieved of the command of the Army of the Potomac.

DECEMBER. Lee's Army of Northern Virginia defeated Maj.-Gen. Ambrose Burnside's Army of the Potomac at the Battle of Fredericksburg in Virginia.

1863

JANUARY. Lincoln signed the Emancipation Proclamation. Burnside was relieved of command of the Army of the Potomac.

MARCH. Confederate cavalry under Maj.-Gen. John Hunt Morgan attacked Federal forces throughout Kentucky.

APRIL. Federal forces under Grant launched the campaign to capture Vicksburg, Mississippi.

MAY. Lee's Army of Northern Virginia defeated Maj.-Gen. Joseph Hooker's Army of the Potomac at the Battle of Chancellorsville in Virginia.

JUNE. Lee's Army of Northern Virginia again invaded the North through the Shenandoah Valley. Hooker was relieved of command of the Army of the Potomac.

JULY. Maj.-Gen. George Meade's Army of the Potomac defeated Lee's Army of Northern Virginia at the Battle of Gettysburg in Pennsylvania. Federal forces under Grant captured Vicksburg, Mississippi. New-York erupted in a week of civil disorder called the Draft Riots.

SEPTEMBER. The Confederate Army of Tennessee defeated Federal forces at the Battle of Chickamauga in Tennessee.

NOVEMBER. Federal forces defeated the Army of Tennessee at the Battles of Chattanooga and Missionary Ridge in Tennessee.

1864

MARCH. Ulysses S. Grant was appointed lieutenant-general and general-in-chief of the U.S. Army.

APRIL. Jefferson Davis dispatched Jacob P. Thompson, Clement Clay, and James Holcombe as commissioners to Canada.

MAY. In Virginia, Grant launched the Army of the Potomac and the Army of the James against Lee's Army of Northern Virginia in a campaign to capture Richmond; the major battles at the Wilderness and Spotsylvania Courthouse ended in tactical draws with huge losses on both sides: 63,000

Federal casualties; 20,000 Confederate casualties. In Tennessee, Maj.-Gen. William T. Sherman launched Federal forces (the Armies of Cumberland, Ohio, and Tennessee) against Maj.-Gen. Joseph Johnston's Army of Tennessee in a campaign to capture Atlanta.

JUNE. Lincoln was renominated the Republican party candidate for president. In Virginia, Grant pressed his attack on Lee; the major battles at Cold Harbor, Petersburg, and the Weldon Railroad ended in tactical draws with more huge Federal losses. In Georgia, Sherman pressed his attack on Joe Johnston.

JULY. In Virginia, Grant forced Lee to retreat his forces into Richmond and Petersburg, where Grant laid siege; the major fighting at Petersburg ended with more large Federal losses. In the Shenandoah Valley, Confederate forces under Maj.-Gen. Jubal Early launched a large cavalry raid that carried to the brink of Washington City. In Georgia, Sherman closed on Atlanta as Johnston was relieved of command of the Army of Tennessee and was replaced by Maj.-Gen. John B. Hood.

AUGUST. In the Shenandoah Valley, Federal forces under Maj.-Gen. Philip H. Sheridan launched a campaign to clear out the region of Confederate forces. At Mobile, Alabama, Federal naval forces under Admiral David Farragut captured the two Confederate forts protecting Mobile harbor, and thereby put Mobile out of the war as a Confederate port. In Virginia, Grant tightened the siege on Richmond and Petersburg, yet the Federal army suffered more large casualties for incremental tactical gain. In Georgia, Sherman pressed his siege of Atlanta; Federal casualties in the campaign to date exceeded 37,000. In Chicago, Maj.-Gen. George B. McClellan was nominated the Democratic party candidate for president.

SEPTEMBER. In Georgia, Sherman forced Hood's Army of Tennessee to flee to the west, and captured Atlanta. In the Shenandoah Valley, Sheridan routed Confederate forces under Early. In Virginia, Grant continued his siege of Lee at Richmond and Petersburg with no tactical gain.

OCTOBER. In the Shenandoah Valley, Sheridan again and definitively defeated Confederate forces under Early at the battle of Cedar Creek. In Georgia, Sherman rested his army at Atlanta. In Virginia, Grant demonstrated on Lee's flanks in preparation for a winter-long siege of Richmond and Petersburg.

NOVEMBER. Abraham Lincoln was reelected president of the United States; Lincoln received 2.2 million votes and 212 electoral college votes to McClellan's 1.8 million votes and 21 electoral college votes. In Georgia, Sherman burned Atlanta and marched toward the Atlantic through Milledgeville. In Virginia, Grant reinforced his works.

DECEMBER. In Virginia, Grant demonstrated against Lee at the Weldon Railroad, sealing up Richmond and Petersburg from resupply by railroad. In Georgia, Sherman captured Savannah.

1865

JANUARY. The United States House of Representatives passed the proposed Thirteenth Amendment that, when ratified by three-fourths of the states, would abolish slavery.

FEBRUARY. Lincoln and Secretary of State William H. Seward entered into peace talks with Confederate vice-president Alexander Stephens, but the parley proved a failure. In South Carolina, Sherman continued his march, capturing Charleston and Columbia. In Virginia, Grant again demonstrated against Petersburg.

MARCH. Lincoln was again inaugurated president of the United States. In Virginia, Grant defeated an attempt by Lee to break out of the siege, and soon after forced Lee to flee Richmond and Petersburg to the west.

APRIL. In Virginia, Grant captured Richmond and Petersburg, and soon after forced Lee to surrender the Army of Northern Virginia at Appomattox Courthouse on Palm Sunday. Lincoln was assassinated on Good Friday by John Wilkes Booth; Seward was badly wounded in a related attack. Andrew Johnson of Tennessee was sworn in as president. In North Carolina, Sherman accepted the surrender of the Army of Tennessee at Bennett Place, near Hillsboro.

MAY. In Georgia, Jefferson Davis was captured by Federal cavalry. In Washington, President Andrew Johnson proclaimed a general amnesty for those who had participated in the rebellion, excepting Confederate government officials, wealthy Southern property owners, and the Confederate agents in Canada.